MESMERIZED

MESMERIZED

Powers of Mind in Victorian Britain

A L I S O N   W I N T E R

THE UNIVERSITY OF CHICAGO PRESS ⚬ ⚬ CHICAGO & LONDON

ALISON WINTER is an assistant professor of history in the Division of the Humanities and Social Sciences of the California Institute of Technology.

The University of Chicago Press, Chicago 60637
The University of Chicago Press, Ltd., London
© 1998 by the University of Chicago
All rights reserved. Published 1998
07 06 05 04 03 02 01 00 99 98   5 4 3 2 1

ISBN (cloth): 0-226-90219-6

Library of Congress Cataloging-in-Publication Data
Winter, Alison, 1965–
     Mesmerized : powers of mind in Victorian Britain / Alison Winter.
        p.   cm.
     Includes bibliographical references and index.
     ISBN 0-226-90219-6 (hardcover : alk. paper)
      1. Mesmerism—Great Britain—History—19th century. 2. Great
Britain—Social life and customs—19th century. I. Title.
     BF1125.W56   1998
     154.7′0941′09034-dc21   98-21833
                                          CIP

CONTENTS

~ ILLUSTRATIONS ~

⤜ ACKNOWLEDGMENTS ⤛

DURING THE LONG passage of this book into print, I have incurred debts to more people than I can possibly name here, though I am grateful to them all. I am nevertheless glad to have the opportunity to acknowledge some of them individually.

The book has benefited greatly from conversations with, and critical suggestions by, many people working in Victorian studies, the history of science, and related fields. Among them I would like to record my particular gratitude to the following: Tim Alborne, Gillian Beer, Julia Borossa, Jim Chandler, Daniel Chua, Roger Cooter, Adrian Desmond, Patricia Fara, John Forrester, Alan Gauld, Jan Golinski, Anita Herle, Frank James, Daniel Karlin, Iwan Morus, Richard Noakes, Maggie Pelling, Mary Poovey, Robert Richards, Emma Spary, John Sutherland, Miles Taylor, Deborah Thom, Paul White, and Andy Warwick. More generally, I would like to acknowledge my debt to the cohort of students and faculty associated with the M.Phil. and Ph.D. programs in which I took part in the Department of History and Philosophy of Science at the University of Cambridge.

One of the most satisfying aspects of researching this topic has been the opportunity to work in ongoing collaboration with a smaller group of people who work in closely related areas. Katharine Anderson, Eileen Groth Lyon, Boyd Hilton, Jim Moore, Anne Secord, and Jim Secord have read my work at many stages in its development, and contributed much to it.

A number of individuals took the time to read the entire book manuscript; their many suggestions have vastly improved it. I thank Alan Gauld, Dan Kevles, Jim Secord, Helen Small, and the referees for the final version, Alex Owen and Bernard Lightman.

I would also like to thank my colleagues at Caltech, whose suggestions and conversations have made the work stronger; among them I should particularly mention Diana Barkan, Bill Deverell, Peter Fay, Kevin Gilmartin, Phil Hoffman, Cathy Jurca, Karen Rader, Robert Rosenstone, Jennifer Tucker, and Cindy Weinstein. Special thanks are due to Morgan Kousser and Mac Pigman. Dan Kevles has been particularly helpful—a continual source, not only of encouragement and constructive criticism, but also of that rare thing, tolerant skepticism. For help in preparing the final manuscript for publication, I would like to thank Maggie York and Marion Lawrence.

At the University of Chicago Press, Rodney Powell, Jill Shimabukuro, Russell Harper, Sue Ormuz, and Claudia Rex shepherded the book into print. I would especially like to thank Joann Hoy, who did most of the copyediting for the manuscript, for her hard work, her patience, and her intelligent and thoughtful suggestions, and Lys Ann Shore, who compiled the index. Above all, though, I owe thanks to Susan Abrams, executive editor in natural sciences, who has been extremely generous and supportive throughout the writing and publishing of the work.

I have benefited from the support of a number of grant-giving bodies and educational institutions during the period of research leading to the production of this manuscript. For support during my doctoral work, I am grateful to the National Science Foundation for the support of an NSF Graduate Fellowship. I would also like to thank the British Academy for a Small Personal Research grant (shared with Eileen Groth Lyon) to study the diaries of the Seventh Earl of Carlisle.

The pressures imposed on young academics both by the job market and by the sometimes intense academic environments in which they work often make it difficult to take the time to overhaul a doctoral dissertation thoroughly before sending it into print. I am extremely grateful to two institutions whose support gave me this opportunity. First, from 1991–1994 I was supported by a research fellowship at St. John's College, Cambridge. I would like to record my gratitude to the Master and Fellows of the College, as much for their encouragement and support during and after the period of my fellowship as for the financial and institutional resources that were made available to me as a junior research fellow. Special thanks are due to Howard Hughes, for giving me the benefit of his expertise in physics at a late stage in my research. Second, I would also like to record my gratitude to the California Institute of Technology, whose generous support made it possible to carry out substantial new research during the revision of my doctoral thesis.

I am very grateful to a large number of libraries and archives who have given me access to their material, fielded my many questions and, in some cases, introduced me to uncatalogued sources. There are too many to mention them all, but I would like to acknowledge some individually. First and foremost, I should like to thank the staff of Cambridge University Library, and especially the core staff of the Rare Books Room there. Among the library staff who have been particularly helpful are Brian Jenkins, Nicola Thwaite, Godfrey Waller, Anne Darvall, Gill Johns, and Adam Perkins. I am especially grateful to Nick Smith, who organized the collection of the Society for Psychical Research when it came to Cambridge University Library, and who, over the several years of my research, helped me find my way through its collection, giving me access to a great many unclassified works I would not otherwise have known about. I would also like to record very special thanks to Julie Anne Lambert, head of the John Johnson Collection of Printed Ephemera at the Bodleian Library, who was unusually generous with her help and her time during and after my visits to Oxford. Among the many other libraries and archives to which I am indebted, I would like to mention the Bakken Library; the Belfast Records Office; the Bodleian Library; the Bradford Records Office; the British Library and Museum; the archives of Castle Howard, North Yorkshire (and especially E. Hartley); Dr. Williams's Library; Edinburgh University Library; the Fitzwilliam Museum in Cambridge; the Flintshire Record Office; the Francis A. Countway Library at Boston Medical Library; the Guildhall Library, London; Hertfordshire Records Office; the Huntington Library; the archives of Imperial College, London; the archives of the Institute of Electrical Engineers, London; Kent Records Office; Kirklees Libraries and Museums; the archives at Knebworth House, Hertfordshire; Lambeth Palace Library; Lynn Archives, Liverpool; the National Library of Medicine (with special thanks to Elizabeth Tunis); the National Library of Scotland; the Pierpont Morgan Library; the Royal Institution of Great Britain (and especially Frank James); Somerset Records Office (and especially Tom Mayberry); Syracuse University Library; Newcastle City Library; Newcastle Public Library; the library of Trinity College, Cambridge (with special thanks to Diana Chardin and David McKitterick); the Department of Manuscripts at University College London, and the Museum associated with its Medical School; the libraries of the University of California, Los Angeles; the Wellcome Institute for the History of Medicine; the Whipple Library, Cambridge; the Whitby Museum (and especially Helen Walasek); and the Wisbech Museum. The staff of the Interlibrary Loan facility at Caltech's Millikan Library have provided an invaluable resource during my periods in Pasadena.

Some of the arguments presented in this book were tried out for the first time in conference and seminar papers, and they were made stronger by the discussions on those occasions. Subsections of various chapters were first published, in altered form, in journals and essay collections: *The Historical Journal* (part of chapter 9), *History of Science* (parts of chapters 4 and 5), *Social*

History of Medicine (part of chapter 7), *Victorian Studies* (part of chapter 10), and essays in the following two collections: *Victorian science in context,* ed. Bernard Lightman (University of Chicago Press, 1997), and *Science Incarnate: Historical embodiments of natural knowledge,* ed. Christopher Lawrence and Steven Shapin (University of Chicago Press, 1998).

I would also like to thank my family, for their encouragement and support, for their corrections to my grammar, and for years of arguments about the nature of scientific evidence. After more than 450 pages, I know that I still won't have the last word.

I owe a special debt to Simon Schaffer, whose generosity with his time and his intellect, and whose contagious fascination with all things historical, are impossible adequately to convey to people who do not already know him. I could not have hoped to find a better supervisor for my Ph.D. dissertation, and have continued to benefit from his inspiration and encouragement ever since.

Finally, my largest debt is to Adrian Johns, who has encouraged and supported me for more than a decade. Conversations with him have been a constant inspiration, from the earliest stages of research to the final revisions of each chapter. This book, for what it is worth, is dedicated to him.

An Invitation to the Séance

ARRIVING LATE AT A TEA PARTY in November 1844, a guest found a young acquaintance—a woman of intelligence and good breeding—laid out on a sofa, cold and senseless, her white face the visage of a corpse. Her guests were attending, with a mixture of fascination, fear, and skepticism, to the words of the man—a "distinguished Magnetizer"—who had placed their hostess in this eerie state. He had "dark, animal-eyes," could not "sound his h's," and claimed to be an expert in the practice of mesmerism. The power to create these effects, he declared, proved his "moral and intellectual superiority" over his subjects. The late-arriving guest, a lady of renowned intelligence and wit and wife of one of the greatest sages of her generation, could not let this pass uncontested. She challenged him to a mesmeric duel: could he prove his power over her? He took her hand in his and darted the other toward it as if flicking water from his fingers. A few uneventful moments passed. Suddenly she felt a current move from her hand into her body, an electric feeling such as she had once experienced when she touched a galvanic ball at a popular science demonstration. But even as the shock ran through her, she gave no outward sign of it. After a few more moments, the mesmerist relinquished her hand in disgust, unaware of the effect he had had. For her, the power of self-control she had exercised was the decisive phenomenon in the mesmeric experiment. In a letter to her uncle, she concluded that her power over herself proved *her* "moral and intellectual superiority" over her ill-spoken, bestial, and impudent rival.[1]

In Victorian Britain almost any member of society—from factory worker to aristocrat to priest—might succumb to the powerful attractions of the mesmeric séance. Anyone attending such an event would be familiar with its origins. It was the creation of the eighteenth-century physician Franz Anton

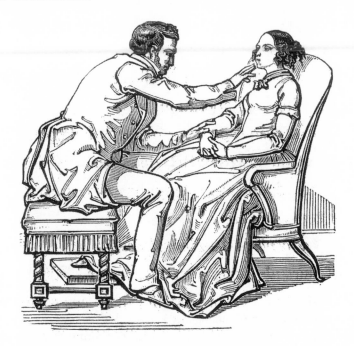

FIGURE 1 A common mesmeric posture, the magnetizer moving closely over his patient. The sketch evokes the intensity of the magnetizer's attention. Charles Dupotet, *L'Art du Magné-tiseur* (Paris, 1862).

Mesmer, who claimed that "animal magnetism" was an application of New-tonian philosophy to bodily health; skeptics gave his therapy the (initially pe-jorative) name of "mesmerism" to deny that physical forces were involved. As the practice spread rapidly through Europe, both terms came to refer to a wide range of different techniques, each claiming to give one person the power to affect another's mind or body.

By the 1840s most Victorians would have had some idea of what went on in a mesmeric séance. A group of witnesses would assemble, in numbers ranging from a few people in a parlor to thousands in a crowded hall. The mesmerist would seat the subject before him (or her, though most mesmerists were men). Everyone would fall silent and watch. Mesmerist and subject would stare into each others' eyes as he made "magnetic passes" over her (or him, though sub-jects were more commonly women; see fig. 1). These "passes" were long, sweeping movements of the hands skimming the surface of the skin without actually touching it, so close that each felt the heat of the other's body. Most experiments would begin this way; alternatively, the subject might gaze at a coin or button, or perhaps at the flame of a candle. After a period ranging from a few minutes to over an hour, the subject would sink into a state known as the mesmeric "trance" or "coma." She appeared to sleep, though her eyes might stay open for a short time. Mesmerists liked to paraphrase *Macbeth* at this point, declaring that "her eyes are open but their sense is shut." Her senses of smell and touch disappeared, as did all awareness of her surroundings. She also lost her speech and hearing, unless the mesmerist addressed her. A strange communion would develop between them: she would speak his thoughts, taste the food in his mouth, move her limbs in a physical echo of his. If mesmerism could transform a conscious individual into a living marionette, still more extraordinary were the active powers it gave to the mesmeric subject, once she slipped deeper into the mesmeric state. A new sense would open to her shut eyes. Subjects might claim to see events occurring in the future, inside the body, in distant lands, and even in the heavens. Often the mesmerist would loosen the experimental reins and follow his entranced guide through her mental voyages. Finally, after a spell of time lasting up to several hours, a different set of "passes" would rouse her from the magnetic sleep.

A twentieth-century observer transported to the scene might conclude that this was a trivial (if puzzling) parlor trick. Mesmeric séances were certainly frequent, even everyday, events. But the Victorians who attended them recorded a fascinating, disturbing, and sometimes even life-changing experience. Many saw in them the fulfillment of the mind's greatest potential. The mesmerist demonstrated the essence of influence; the subject displayed amazing new feats of perception and cognition.

After such a display, audiences would argue about the significance of the phenomena. What exactly was being tested remained one of the most ambiguous features of the experiment. Perhaps it was the person being mesmerized: was the subject faking? This was the first question people asked, and they went to extravagant and sometimes horrifying lengths to answer it. To prove that the ordinary senses had been suspended, the mesmerist and members of the audience fired pistols near the subject's ears, pricked her skin with needles, and waved smelling salts beneath her nostrils. There were crueler tests, too: acid poured on her skin, knives thrust under her fingernails, electric shocks run through her arms, and noxious substances placed in her mouth—vinegar, soap, or even ammonia. Experiments sometimes provoked physical skirmishes over her body. If the tortures produced a response, skeptics dismissed the experiment. If there were none, the trance was all the more plausible—or the fakery all the more skillful and reprehensible.

It was vital to determine whether someone were in an altered state of mind (and why), because issues of much greater significance hung in the balance. In the case of the h-less mesmerist, the reality of the effects was not in question, but their significance was quite another matter, because whatever conclusions one drew would involve ascriptions of relative social and moral standing. As experimenters asked each other how a particular trial was to be conducted and evaluated, they confronted the larger question of who could pronounce upon *any* scientific and medical controversy. And because there were often pronounced class and gender differences between mesmerist and subject, the volatile relations that developed in the experiments seemed to offer testimony about relative status. In the case above, the mesmerist was a potent class challenger; elsewhere, the trance would inspire one frail young maidservant to tell her prestigious physician (and an audience numbering in the hundreds) that he was a pathetic fool.[2] Alternatively, displays of new cognitive abilities became showcases of the kind of progress that could (one fancied) be achieved in the most utopian of educational schemes. The question of whether the effects were natural or supernatural made experiments a testing ground of faith and doctrine. In making their way through a mesmeric trial, people found themselves exploring the major problems of the age. Writ large, Victorians were not merely testing the reality of a particular phenomenon or the veracity of a particular person; they were carrying out experiments on their own society.

No wonder, then, that a large proportion of Victorians knew of mesmerism and its claimed effects, and that a great many people had witnessed it at first hand. Experiments and debates took place across Britain, in Ireland, and throughout the empire. Mesmerism was practiced in universities and mechanics' institutes, country houses and cottages, vicarages and town halls, pubs and hospitals. It could be found in bedrooms and on city streets, from London to the Highlands of Scotland and from Dublin to Calcutta. To comprehend its scope and significance, we have to examine the views of a very broad range of people: the aristocracy and their servants, the industrial middle classes and the "operatives" who worked in their factories, the preachers and their congregations, the doctors and their patients. In effect, we need to explore mid-nineteenth-century society itself—because that is what mesmeric experimenters were doing.

Mesmerism's relative obscurity in the late twentieth century has encouraged the idea that it has always been a "fringe" or "pseudo-" science, eking out a precarious existence on the margins of science or altogether beyond its borders. The relegation is anachronistic and question-begging. In fact, mesmerism became the occasion for contests over authority in science, medicine, and intellectual life alike, and these contests revealed the location and character of such authority to have been more insecure than historians appreciate. This book retrieves mesmerism from a historiography that places it at the fringes of society, and restores it to its central place among the preoccupations of Victorian culture. Rather than merely offering a new vein of information about a particular practice, however, it suggests, by example, that our map of the Victorian scientific and intellectual landscape should be redrawn to represent a greater spectrum of society and a more diverse range of issues.

The Potential of Victorian Mesmerism

This book provides a social history that reveals mesmerism to have been practiced widely and continuously from the 1830s through the 1860s and beyond. It furthermore demonstrates mesmerism's pivotal role in transformations of medical and scientific authority during this time. Finally, it describes how mesmerism and its associated practices could become tools for modeling the nature of human interaction and social power.

Mesmerism was pervasive in Victorian society. It influenced and was eventually assimilated into several major intellectual enterprises. Taking hold in Britain so much later than elsewhere in Europe, it appealed to the early Victorians as a very new and exciting science of life and mind.[3] Although mesmerists had made sporadic visits to Britain before the 1830s, it was in that decade that mesmerism's British career began in earnest, with a series of experiments that consumed the attention of London in the spring of 1838, only to end some months later in spectacular discreditation. But instead of retreating from the mainstream of intellectual life, mesmerism soon became even more significant to elite scientific figures, along with a large section of the wider reading public. During the 1840s itinerant lecturers fanned out across the country. They dramatized their power in public shows and jockeyed with skeptics and competitors for the audience's trust. These rivalries spawned many varieties of practice; hypnotism and its inventor, the surgeon James Braid, have become the best known. Rather than occupying a different world from orthodox or legitimate intellectual work,[4] animal magnetism called into question the very definition of legitimacy itself. The impact of the traveling mesmerists provides one indicator, showing how little consensus there was about the difference between legitimate practices and those beyond the pale. The itinerants taught and fought doctors in both Britain and, through the colonial press, Anglo-India. Mesmerism then entered sickrooms, country houses, and even church and chapel—and from there found its way into the pages of poets and novelists.

Mesmerism was not only ubiquitous but challenging within Victorian intellectual culture, as experiments became catalysts for competing assertions about the nature and seat of intellectual authority. For historians these experiments can show just how malleable scientific, medical, and intellectual cultures were during this time. Mesmerism is usually portrayed as alien to science and medicine, and even the most satisfying studies, which recapture practitioners' confidence during these years, aim to describe the "other side" of Victorian medicine.[5] If one does not preassign the centers and margins of the intellectual world, however, many representations of that world look even more contentious. Wherever the "center" and "margin" of intellectual life were ambiguous, mesmerism became particularly important. Definitions of science were malleable during these years. Individual luminaries were readily identifiable, but other aspects of scientific culture were less defined. Society could not agree about what could be said about natural law, nor was it obvious when, where, and how one could say it.[6] There were many attempts to structure the sciences in the 1830s and 1840s, with the founding of new scientific organizations and the publication of works on the relations between different fields of study. But these did not, in practice, consolidate the sciences or define an authoritative community of practitioners. What counted as a proper science, or as a "scientific" practice, remained open to dispute. Similar ambiguities surrounded the human body. There were no definitive medical orthodoxies to police the profession and to define a medical "heterodoxy," much less to expunge heterodox practitioners. So we must not presuppose the existence of a scientific or medical orthodoxy to explain why mesmerism did not become established; the very constitution of this orthodoxy was at issue. Whenever people carried out an experiment, this fundamental question emerged in a wide range of contexts, from the status of the medical profession to the intellectual might of the "common people." Far from being assigned a position on the sidelines of intellectual life, then, mesmerism became a means—or "medium"—for Victorians to explore and even to forge definitions of authority wherever they were open to question.

In the later phase of mesmerism's Victorian history, important changes took place in the authoritative status of the sciences and medicine. By 1870 new disciplinary divisions in science and medicine, brought on by reforms in university education and the new laboratories, left less space for the lines of inquiry that mesmerism required. Medicine became increasingly (though by no means definitively) regulated, partly in consequence of the Medical Registration Act of 1858. These reforms affected science as well, producing a professional class of scientists much more clearly separated from a newly "lay" public than their predecessors, who could more easily derogate a particular practice as marginal or popular. Much of what would become recognizable as modern science—an activity broken up into demarcated disciplines such as physics, biology, and chemistry—was only now coming into existence. It depended on the development of separate spaces (the new laboratories) that were identified with these different disciplines. Within the laboratories those new beings called "scientists" could be trained on the job to ask similar questions and to pursue similar researches in answering them.

Physiology and physics, the disciplines most relevant to mesmerism's areas of inquiry, were now laboratory sciences. Earlier in the century the manifold, but ambiguous, relations between physical forces and the mind and will formed one of the most tantalizing areas of scientific study. In the latter decades of the century, neither of these new scientific disciplines invited the use of human experience in the study of life, mind, and physical force, in the manner that their predecessors had done. An important factor in this change was one of the thorniest problems facing Victorian scientists: the question of how the self could play an acknowledged role in the representation of reality.[7] Self-registering instruments, new diagnostic technologies, and even "thinking machines" seemed to offer a way of representing nature without the taint of human agency. This maneuver was problematic and polemical at best. How could one hope to accomplish it in an area of study where the recording device itself—the human brain, mind, and will—was identical to the engine of human creativity? One disgruntled scientific writer gave a pessimistic answer. The lineaments of science, he complained, were taking shape in ways that disqualified fields of study to which subjective experience was admitted to be central.[8] The security of the walls built around the laboratory was to be purchased by excluding agonizing questions about mind that required an acknowledgment of human experience. There were to be no subjects in these laboratories. Thomas Henry Huxley's crayfish and John Tyndall's resistance box became their emblematic objects.

Finally, mesmerism was used by people of very different backgrounds, social positions, and interests to make conflicting claims about the nature of psychological and physiological influence. The period of mesmerism's career in Britain coincides with the age of grand reform. Both span the period from the debates of around 1830 and the debates surrounding the Second Reform Act of 1867. In mesmeric and reform literature alike, the British "social body" was defined by reference to physiology and medicine.[9] During these decades mesmerism provided forums for studying the laws by which human society functioned, or should function ideally. Whenever mesmeric experiments took place, a little bit of Britain was transformed into a laboratory for studying social relations. This was true right from the start. Trying to make sense of the entranced behavior of a young domestic servant raised uncomfortably stark issues of class and gender. Mesmerism also became the occasion for self-conscious reflections about the basis of race inequalities and the natural laws that helped one people to bend another to its will. Throughout its British career, mesmerism brought to the surface issues of power and authority that, however potent, were rarely acknowledged publicly. Mesmerism was not merely a means of staging a tableau of prevailing assumptions; nor was it just a tool to subvert existing relations of authority. It involved a dialect in which hidden assumptions became explicit, were challenged and explored, and then were either reinforced or transformed. For historians, then, mesmerism provides a window onto how Victorians portrayed relations in their own society—to use their terms, relations of sympathy, power, authority, and inequality. In certain circumstances mesmeric experiments had a significant impact on how people formulated claims about the nature of influence.

Mesmerism did not decline later in the century because scientists were more knowledgeable than hitherto, or because the British public was less gullible. Rather than being exposed as fraudulent or explained away by progressive science, it was absorbed into other practices, particularly psychic research, physiology, and psychoanalysis. It has often been yoked with these later practices, and a similar portrait of ambiguous authority could also (with adjustments) be painted of them. I have chosen to focus mainly on mesmerism, partly because its history is less known, and partly because the context in which it developed was very different from the one that would sustain psychic research toward the end of the century.

The later Victorian period saw a pronounced change in the representation of what one might call the physiology of influence. Prominent scientific and medical figures had learned from mesmeric debates that relations of communication, trust, and deference were not well established between themselves and the general public. Some people thought the solution lay in developing an understanding of mental action that could explain mesmeric phenomena and provide a sort of diagnosis of the mass ailment that led people to invest their confidence in mesmerists. My final chapter traces the development of a psychology of public judgment that sought to explain something that was as difficult to understand as it was desirable to master, namely, the phenomenon of agreement. What were the psychological processes by which people came to think the same things? Such psychological models, ironically, were not only reactions to but assimilations of mesmerism. They relied on particular understandings of unconscious mental action, of influencing the will through the power of looking, and of trances. Only in retrospect would it be possible to portray the new mental physiologies, which to historians look more "orthodox" than mesmerism, as unambiguously different from and opposed to it.

The new mental physiologies also had a significance beyond the scope of individual experiments. They supplied models of the psychological relations that some thought should exist between the general public and the intellectual elite. At the same time as the new laboratory sciences were making strong distinctions between qualified practitioners and everyone else, a more inclusive, consensual psychology undergirded the emerging definitions of the scientist and of scientific education. An old notion of scientific ability as something one was born with (or without) was giving way to a definition of scientific thinking as a skill that could be learned. It was now to be understood as a disciplined form of "common sense." Mental physiologists advised both on the nature of common sense and on how thought could be trained into its more uncommon, scientific mode. An aristocracy of knowledge was to be replaced by a meritocracy, with the help of consensual psychology. The scientific polity was open, in principle, to everyone. Still more generally, these new psychological and physiological claims complemented a particular view of what constituted a harmonious society. They gave a foundation for the "consensual" relationship of its different parts, a fulcrum on which the "age of equipoise" could achieve its balance.[10]

So my argument will be threefold: to confirm and explain mesmerism's prominence, to trace its involvement in contests over scientific and medical authority, and to argue for its role in portrayals of human interaction more generally. These lines of argument form a braid running through the book as a whole. They are not treated discretely, because the issues and events they examine were closely intertwined in Victorian culture. Mesmeric lectures or experiments could begin with a purpose as narrowly construed as a particular therapeutic treatment and end with a conclusion as fundamental as the revelation of new theological truth or with a battle over relations between the classes. Following the course of such experiments makes it possible to reconstruct the varied, changeable, and interrelated significances that this practice—and this period—held for contemporaries.

A New Understanding of Mental Powers

Over the past fifteen years historians have developed the makings of a dramatically new account of how people in the past understood mental powers. Far from exhibiting the stifling conformity long associated with the period, Victorian England is now recognized as having been populated by phrenologists, plebeian spiritualists, mediums, and psychic researchers. They lived in a broth more exotic than the so-called Monster Soup of the Thames: a potent concoction of magnetic fluids, vital powers, and swarming spirits. So did many of the more familiar physiologists, physicists, social scientists, and writers: Thomas Carlyle looked around him to find his friends "sleeping magnetic sleep," George Eliot shaved her head for a phrenological reading, Herbert Spencer wrote articles for a mesmeric journal, Michael Faraday built an appara-

tus for experiments in table-turning, and spiritualism inspired the famous logician Augustus De Morgan to question the nature of scientific proof. Mediums subverted conventions of the "angel in the house"; plebeian spiritualists
developed a legitimizing "democratic epistemology"; and bourgeois Victorians mapped their values onto the surface of the skull.[11] Several studies have
shown how conventions of class, gender, or political orientation could be
adapted to the task of establishing people's legitimacy and that of their work.
This book draws on such studies, but avoids an emphasis on one theme (such
as gender) in particular, because mesmerism's reflexivity about the nature of
influence made for a wider range of characterizations of power itself than in
other sciences. An unusually flexible approach is necessary to reconstruct
them.

Previous approaches to mesmerism have been threefold. First it is sometimes treated as a body of doctrine, whose lineaments are drawn from modern
hypnotism and cognitive psychology. The object here is a history of progressive discovery or the construction of a modern research discipline (not mesmerism but, say, cognitive psychology or modern hypnotism). To this enterprise a cultural study is not essential, and indeed it can be impractical, since the
most successful studies follow their science through different countries and
periods.[12] The second approach treats mesmerism as a prior incarnation of
psychoanalysis. Its history charts a trajectory between those two "wizards
from Vienna," Mesmer and Freud. Mesmerists sometimes appear in these accounts as sleepwalkers, roaming, almost unawares, over terrain later to be
mapped by more self-conscious investigators.[13] The third approach assumes
mesmerism to be always marginal, if not self-evidently false. It then appears
to have been a sort of cultural excrescence. One would study it using models that were developed to understand features of Victorian culture more
generally—the most common of which is the relationship between fringe and
orthodox medicine.[14] And as an epiphenomenon, mesmerism is properly the
passive recipient of established modes of explanation rather than a contributor to the development of new historical perspectives.

None of these approaches will be adopted here, though this book is indebted to all of them. Mesmerism will be presented not as a body of doctrine
but as a diverse, fragile set of practices whose meaning was very much up for
grabs. As for the phenomena these practices produced, I prefer the notion of
an "altered state" of mind to that of a state of lucid "unconsciousness," because modern concepts of the unconscious, heavily influenced by Freud and
his followers, have charged this term in a way that makes it misleading when
applied to the early and mid-Victorians. The notion of the "unconscious" did
not exist in the relevant sense until fairly late in the century.[15] Instead, early

and mid-Victorian experimenters shared a sense that they were producing in their subjects an unusual state of mind.

When modern readers consider the nature of such states, some of the experiments will look like patent frauds, while others will seem to have displayed some real effect. The divergence between Victorian notions of plausibility and ours is one of the most interesting features of these practices. Adjudicating these trials by hindsight would render even more difficult the already challenging and rewarding task of reconstructing the plausibility they had at the time. I will not pass judgment on the reality of the phenomena, because what is relevant to this history is not whether they happened but whether they *could* happen in Victorian eyes. Some of the most ferocious critics of mesmerism are as historically interesting as the fondest advocates, because they regarded the phenomena as possible (but in fact false). One goal of this book, therefore, is to use mesmerism to explore where the boundaries of possibility lay in Victorian society. Instead of diagnosing mesmerism, we can use it as a diagnostic tool to study Victorian culture.

Using mesmerism as a guide in this manner can be surprising, because mesmerism changed the geography of its social environment, making margins into centers and centers into peripheries. Mesmerism meant different things in different places. Conversely, it also *made different places mean different things*. Its performances changed the meaning of the sites in which it was practiced. Such changes came about because, as a science of mental action, mesmerism questioned what it was proper or possible to do in a particular place. Mesmerism transformed sickrooms into public halls, dining rooms into laboratories, hospital wards into theaters. The mental voyages of experimental subjects could collapse the miles between civilized London and regions of exploration and conquest—the Northwest Passage, the African jungle, colonial India. Mesmerism questioned the nature and status of "private" and "public," and the presentation of oneself as trustworthy. Thus, in revising the geography of private and public spaces, and offering new conventions of proper conduct, mesmerism was a means of asserting what should be the new rules, appropriate to the new times, for making claims about the nature of authority, and about authority with respect to nature. If this science transformed the meaning of everyday events, interactions, and objects, understanding these meanings and how they came to be requires stretching the attention in ways that do not conform to expected categories. In this respect the historical study of mesmerism is akin to the enterprise of the mesmeric investigator: both involve an assumption that the mysterious and bizarre activities of certain individuals can be rendered meaningful, if only one is imaginative enough to discover the appropriate context and set of rules.

Altered States

The parallel between history and mesmeric experiment—two interpretative enterprises involving altered states of mind—is particularly appropriate to the Victorian period. Generations of commentators from Karl Marx to Stephen Jay Gould have penetrated through eccentricity, sentiment, and the aesthetic that built the Albert Memorial, to extract from the Victorians a moral for their own times.[16] The Victorians present a puzzle: an apparently self-confident people acting according to principles that no longer guide us, but that nevertheless remain close to the heart of modern culture. Scholars have consistently sought to bridge the gap by describing the baseline state of a different cultural psyche. They offer us accounts of Victorian "conscience," "temper," or most ambitiously, "mind" in sum. We are powerfully drawn to deciphering these people—tracing out a framework and a set of conventions that will make their behavior meaningful. Borrowing the vocabulary of Walter Houghton's classic *Victorian Frame of Mind*, we might say that we want to understand that foreign frame.

One factor in our tendency to phrase the question this way is that Victorians were preoccupied with their own mental frame. In fact, one of our inheritances is this very way of questioning. They monitored their own sensibilities, took the measure of the influence they felt from each other, and speculated about the sympathies that bound them. They were motivated, in part, by the notion that one person's mind, or the mental character of a group, supplied a key to the collective mental features buried within an apparently fragmented society. Victorians therefore placed themselves in a predicament similar to the dilemma we face in studying them. There is a further similarity, in that their knowledge of this "frame of mind" was built upon the study of (initially) mysterious human action. In the same years that saw the heyday of mesmerism, Victorians invented a host of new enterprises to examine and categorize the various modes of the human psyche. The sciences of anthropology and ethnology aimed at recording and comparing people of different mental types; phrenology, physiognomy, and craniology linked the structure of the face and skull to the structure of the mind; and the proponents of sociology claimed they could trace the aggregate psyche of a population.

Mesmerism was one of the most energetic—if ultimately one of the most ephemeral—of these inquiries. Victorians felt compelled to study it not only because it presented an intriguing cipher, but because many hoped that decoding it would transform its latent meaning into a key for better understanding themselves. The mesmeric mind, rendered comprehensible, would illuminate the Victorian mind. Whether they succeeded depends on how one defines success, but their efforts had lasting consequences in at least one indirect sense. Victorian debates and mesmeric experiments contributed to the development of some of the fundamental assumptions, concepts, and interpretative tools we now bring to our study of these very debates and experiments. Acknowledging a relation between acts of historical interpretation and nineteenth-century ways of making sense, this book aspires to realize an ambition that resembles that of the mesmerists themselves. By studying Victorians' attempts to understand their mental powers, it uses mesmerism to explore society in Victorian Britain and beyond.

Discovery of the Island of Mesmeria

IN THE SPRING OF 1845, the popular family serial, the *New Monthly Magazine*, satirically announced the discovery of a new land: the island of Mesmeria. The explorer, Madame La Reveuse, embarked upon her travels after being placed in an altered state of mind by a mesmerist, Signor Phantasio. She lay before him, deep in the mesmeric coma, as she described her mental journey. The land she surveyed was temperate and fertile, and populated by a prosperous, civilized people. Curiously, however, it seemed that none of them was entirely conscious. Everyone was sleepy, if not actually asleep, and most manifested one of a variety of nervous complaints. "Epileptics" ran the government (albeit erratically), preachers "snored" in their pulpits, and a dozy corps of police kept watch as best they could against signs of wakefulness or sobriety. The "amazing" geography unfolding before her revealed a nation of somnambulists. After passing through the village of Drowsyhead, one came to the "province of Dreamland." Beyond it, near an "immense" field of poppies and mandragora, lay the region of Slumberland, bounded to the north by Bolstershire, to the east by the land of Nod, to the south by Somnovia, and to the west by the country of Featherbeds, which was "famous for its breed of nightmares." Mesmeria's queen was "the first Mesmerist in the island." There was also a house of commons in the metropolis of Reverie, all of whose members were gifted with nervous disorders. Justice was "fast asleep," but while this would be a sign of dysfunction in Britain, Mesmerians took pride in their comatose courts. In Mesmeria, it seemed, "everything was managed on mesmeric principles." [1]

Mesmeria was a Britain transformed by powerful forces. Anyone reading the article would have known how Madame La Reveuse had been placed in her trance and would not have been surprised at her narrative. They would have understood that the account was comic (or at least, it was trying to be), but also that the humor lay in the similarity her vision bore to serious descriptions of the mesmeric state. There was no need for the author to preface his tale with an introduction to mesmerism. By the mid-1840s it had become ubiquitous.

Mesmerism could be seen almost everywhere and was practiced by individuals of virtually all professions and classes. Samuel Wilberforce, Augustus De Morgan, Richard Whately, Harriet Martineau, Wilkie Collins, Alfred Russel Wallace, and Charles Dickens, to name but a few, participated in mesmeric experiments, and some of them continued to practice the science intermittently for the rest of their lives. George Eliot, Robert Chambers, Elizabeth Gaskell, and William Gladstone were among the people of prominence who had brief but striking personal experiences of it. Victorian scientific and medical luminaries such as William Benjamin Carpenter, Michael Faraday, Thomas Wakley, Charles Wheatstone, and Charles Darwin witnessed experiments and participated in debates. Mesmeric "infirmaries" were established in London, Edinburgh, and Dublin, and dozens of societies were founded.

The notion of an enchanted island, or of a population brought under a powerful new influence, made a frequent appearance in Victorians' discussions of their changing society. This imagery was particularly apposite to reflections about changes in cultural authority. Mesmerism and phenomena associated with it supplied a language for describing cultural change, a technique for studying society and the mind, and phenomena that, because they became the focus of violent contests for authority, provided indications of where intellectual authority was uncertain in Victorian culture. From the tumultuous 1830s through the last decades of the century, British subjects used mesmeric phenomena to explore some of the most central issues facing their society. By examining the different ways they understood the most ubiquitous experimental science of mind, it is possible to make a rough sketch of how they polemically represented social relations to one another.

British Society in an Altered State

When early Victorians reflected on the state of their society, they commonly observed that new forces were dramatically changing the social and political environment, and doing so too quickly for people to anticipate their effects. The "March of Intellect," a phrase that had great resonance during these years, heralded a thoroughgoing reconstitution of British culture, particularly of authority and modes of communication. The Whig legislation of the 1830s was

FIGURE 2 Robert Seymour's "March of Intellect" (1828) brings together the heady optimism and the apocalypticism associated with progress and reform in the late 1820s. Caricature Collection, Guildhall Library. Corporation of London.

intended to change the lives, minds, and understandings of workers, and to open the doors of political power to every sect. Steam and, beginning in the 1840s, electricity were transforming communication. People were traveling faster and farther in a day, exchanging letters with each other more rapidly, and routinely encountering people from a broader spectrum of society, than their parents might have done in a lifetime. Soon communication would not even require this speedy movement of bodies or objects. The electric telegraph, invented in 1837, started the spread of metal nerves to transport thought electrically from one part of the country to another. Before the century's end, its wires would traverse the globe.

The satirical caricature of "The March of Intellect" (fig. 2) anticipated the changes these forces would bring to the land. The "March" sketched the inexorable progress of an immense steam engine, an incarnation of scientific and technological development. Its eyes were gaslights (introduced in London in 1810); from its pipe issued balloons—a powerful symbol of progress since the French Revolution. The monster wielded a sweeper "headed" by the Whig reformer Henry Brougham (a "*Broom,*" the caption explained helpfully) that swept bits of old Britain into an immense hill of rubbish. It piled up quack doctors, a devil representing superstition, a mound of bills waiting to pass through Parliament, and a still higher heap of cases delayed at the High Court of Chancery. To fill the void came a new rational sensibility. The engine's head was made of textbooks, and it was crowned by the newly founded and reformist institution of University College London, Brougham's brainchild. With each bend of the knee, printing presses shed cheap books to feed "the little people of the Earth."[2] As it marched, the automaton proclaimed, "I come I come!!"

Scenes like this shouted of the immense transformations under way, but there was no consensus on whether reform was making society rational and efficient, or unhealthy and unwise. If a steam-powered sleeper could replace Jacob's ladder in a metaphorical "Railway to Heaven," there were also mutterings that "the Devil, if he travelled, would go by the train."[3] The "March" could be an apocalyptic scene, casting reform as a destructive process encouraged by an irrational population. The caricature's caption describes the mechanical beast in terms reminiscent of the book of Revelation. To the narrator appeared "a Vision," a "Giant form." The beast's "eyes where [sic] burning lights even of Gas, and on its learned head it bore A Crown of many towers. Its Body was an Engine yea of steam"; it "rose" and swept "the rubish [sic] from the face of the land." It tossed aside the "Crowns of those kings that set themselves above the laws," the "Special pleaders & their wigs [i.e., Whigs]," and the "Quack Doctors." Not even "the ghosts & those that whear [sic] Horns" were spared. In biblical language it echoed apocalyptic doommongers who warned that reform was literally the end of the world. The apocalyptic monster of progress would return over the next few decades, as in the 1840s, when the "railway juggernaut" was linked with a "manic" scramble for railway shares.[4] In short, "The March of Intellect" was ambivalent, leaving it unclear whether reform was a force that could save Britain, or a sinister power threatening to destroy it.

Early Victorians may not have agreed on the consequences of change, but they used a common vocabulary to describe it: the language of nervous conditions, altered states of mind, and potent fluids or forces. John Stuart Mill wrote in 1831 that there had been a "change . . . in the human mind" as profound as it was slow and insensible. When people finally became aware of it— as they were now—they woke confused and uncertain "as from a dream," not knowing "what processes had been going on in the minds of others, or even in their own."[5] Mill had been speaking of political issues, but religious confusion was described in similar terms. The historian and essayist J. A. Froude wrote in retrospect that people of the early 1840s floated on an open spiritual sea, where the "lights" were "all drifting, the compasses all awry."[6] The magnetic currents were disordered, and the result was a profound insecurity. A. H. Clough said his generation felt an almost "animal irritability of consciences" or "sensibility"; an early classic history described it as a "supermorality of the nerves and senses."[7] Thomas Carlyle's solution to the unease and disorientation was a purifying process that felt like "a stream of fire [rushing] over my whole soul," followed by an "annihilation of self" and a "healing sleep." As unlikely as it may seem, the result was a purposeful life of duty.[8]

Elsewhere, Carlyle memorably likened the "condition of England" to a paralyzing spell. Unemployed workers were imprisoned, not only by their workhouses but by a "horrid enchantment" from which they could not awaken.[9] Three years after Carlyle's gloomy diagnosis, one workingman, Alexander Somerville, testified to his own enchanted state. He described, not Carlyle's grim "torpor," but a moment of epiphany, when he glimpsed a utopian future. He had been present when the first railway linked Liverpool and Manchester in September 1830. On that occasion, he said, "people thought I stood and slept; and, when they heard the dream, they said it was very dreamy." The Carlyles in the audience might have thought it a bad omen when the wheels of Britain's first train rolled over one of her leading statesmen that afternoon,[10] but there were no railway juggernauts in Somerville's "dreamy" future. Now, in 1847, when he gazed upon the transformations already wrought by steam and electricity, he dreamed again, of a time when "realities shall go beyond any dreams that have yet been told of these things." He saw "thoughts exchanging themselves for thoughts," making nothing of the "geographical space" they had to traverse, except for the need "to give the battery a little more of the electric spirit." He also saw "man holding free fellowship with man; without taking note of the social distance which used to separate them, except, perhaps, the lord, (landed lord or cotton lord,) shall use a little more of the moral electricity, when conveying a thought to a working man, at the opposite end of the social pole, who used to be very far distant; that lord may put on a little more of the moral electricity . . . to carry the instantaneous message of one feeling, one interest, one object."[11] However people chose to characterize and to value the "new and mighty power" drawing them into the "new state,"[12] the language of visions, mental forces, dreams, and somnambulism provided a medium to express it. It was not by chance that opium should have come to mind in 1843 when Marx was casting about for a powerful metaphor to depict the influence of religion on the people.[13]

The power of this language of trances and dreams was enhanced by the fact that it went beyond metaphor. Altered states offered an experimental means of testing how real people's bodies and minds could be transformed. In 1838 London read that mesmerism had enabled a sixteen-year-old domestic servant to diagnose diseases and tell the future; in 1845 reports circulated that Faraday's discovery of the polarization of light had been anticipated some months earlier when "sensitive" women claimed to see light issuing from the ends of magnets; in 1851, after several years of mesmeric experiments, the popular journalist Harriet Martineau published a materialist philosophical work based in part on physiological inspirations resembling those of Madame La Reveuse (who was in fact modeled on Martineau herself).[14] Wherever mesmeric claims were made, the atmosphere was suffused with anticipation. In 1852, when table-turning and table-rapping arrived in Britain, Mary Howitt told her husband of a "feeling" running through all of society—pervading "all classes" and "all sects"—that the "world stands upon the eve of some great spiritual revelation."[15] In this case, the revelation was the "Other World" disclosed by spiritualism, but a similar message was carried through Britain by the waves of mesmeric experimentation: the human mind and body were conduits through which social, spiritual, or natural knowledge of great import would flow.

The connections between mesmerism and the state of society relied on the fact that, as Madame La Reveuse made clear, the state was a social body. Mesmerism's potential was enhanced by the physiological way in which people portrayed social cohesion. As Mary Poovey has argued, the question of how the country should be governed was asked in ways that joined the management of the body politic with the management of the body, and linked decision making on matters of state to dynamics of social intercourse and public opinion. As the ruling classes took the temperature of political and social affairs, they fretted over sources of political infection. The "constitution" and the "condition" of England drew anxious reflection from the public health movement, which built social improvement on clean living, to responses to the cholera epidemic, which portrayed Irish immigrant workers as foreign threats to the British "social body." Disease itself could be portrayed as an anthropomorphized foreign interloper, as in the caricature "John Bull catching the cholera" (fig. 3), in which a stout, rosy-cheeked John Bull "catches" and drives back a bluish-gray, turbaned, yellow-eyed Cholera climbing through a hole in the "wooden walls of Old England."

The notion of Britain as a social body fighting off alien pestilence gave mesmerism an added social charge. It, too, arrived from abroad. But unlike the cholera, there was no need to invent a human form for this influence or to argue that it might affect the social body. Alien interlopers and potent social influences were already part of the package. In the 1830s and 1840s a number of exotic and, some claimed, dangerous scientific lecturers began to appear in London. One of them—a small, spare man inexplicably missing his right thumb—was said to draw mysterious powers from this distinguishing physi-

JOHN BULL CATCHING THE CHOLERA

FIGURE 3 In the original watercolor of this 1832 caricature, Bull is rosy-cheeked, Cholera blue and yellow-eyed. Cholera is trying to grab the Reform Bill, which is lying on the ground. He is stymied by Bull, whose robust constitution, his "heart of oak" (the stick he carries), and the Board of Health, drive Cholera back beyond England's "Wooden Walls." Iconographic Collection, Wellcome Institute.

cal feature.[16] Another with his "piercing eyes," flowing mustaches, and long beard, caused women on Regent Street to "cover their faces and cry out" when they saw him.[17] Their physical appearance drew comment not merely because they stood out in a crowd, but also because of the power they claimed for themselves: their bodies demonstrated how one person could "penetrate" another with his "vital principle."[18] Even before they arrived, they were portrayed as seductive "foreign scoundrels," as novels described "dark and foreign-looking" magnetizers supernaturally wooing vulnerable nervous girls, or even using their power to kill.[19] There was talk of magnetic "orgies" in the Paris hospitals, and of predatory magnetizers deflowering virginal patients. One outraged commentator claimed that voracious Continental mesmerists were driven across the Channel in the search for "fresh food" to feed their "libidinous propensities."[20] The first mesmerists, and the practices they carried with them, were regarded as powerful foreign stimuli to the British public and the social body, both by those who thought mesmerism was a revolutionary new technique for scientific research and by those who thought it a dangerous sham.

The ambivalent figure of the mesmerist took on some of its significance from the medical and therapeutic terms people used to depict leadership. If people could not identify the physiological processes underpinning a healthy polity, they could at least point to causes of political sickness, and castigate those who offered false cures. Representation of leadership—especially false leadership—focused on the corporeal, giving political and cultural power a medical tinge. Reform was a process of healing the country, and leaders were the "doctors" or "quacks" (depending on the valence of the account) diagnosing its "condition" and prescribing a treatment. When Carlyle condemned his peers for placing their confidence in "the 'sham-hero,'—whose name is Quack," he did not mean doctors specifically, but charismatic figures whose fitness to lead was a chimera.[21] Authors across the political spectrum described political influence in terms of bodily power when they wanted to convey either potent or false leadership.

In this context mesmerism became useful to political caricature, and even in the early 1840s caricaturists could expect their audiences to have much more than a vague idea of what mesmerism was. When, shortly after Robert Peel came to power in 1841, *Punch* wished to attack his policies, its first issue tarred him as a quack mesmeric therapist (fig. 4). He was a positive "*fountain* of quackery," *Punch* wrote, as it sketched him infusing into the British lion magnetic fluid and false hope. Peel's posture is not a vague, stylized mesmeric pose but a very specific position stipulated in mesmeric textbooks of the period. The artist carefully positioned Peel with one hand pinching the closest thing the lion had to a thumb (the side of his paw), while the other hand gestures commandingly at his sleepy head. Behind Peel sits his "grand electric politico battery," ready to administer yet another subtle fluid—electricity—should the magnetic efforts fail. The battery was made out of two crucial supporters, Stanley (then colonial secretary) and Lyndhurst (lord chancellor). New taxes and the pension list dangle from it like the leads used in the fashionable technique of electric therapy. The éminence grise of Wellington looks on from the shadows as each pass further subdues Peel's subject. Stupefying "poor Jerves," *Punch* declares with relish, is a preparation for "*sticking it into him.*"[22]

Peel's tax initiatives drew a similar satire in the lower-brow "Mesmerizing John Bull; or, Bleeding Him for £3000" (fig. 5). Here "Quack Peel" assures Victoria that he has "got John in a mesmeric sleep." She is standing by, holding a bloodletting bowl, as the duke of Cambridge comments, "Aye, aye, here comes the golden stream again." The yearly tax "phlebotomy" is possible, it seems, only when John Bull "has his eyes shut, and his senses inactive."

A third caricature depended on a still more extensive familiarity with the ins and outs of mesmeric experiments. In 1841, when Britain negotiated an un-

ANIMAL MAGNETISM;
OR, SIR RHUBARB PILL MESMERISING THE BRITISH LION.

FIGURE 4 One of *Punch*'s first caricatures casts Sir Robert Peel as a mesmerist. The British lion's susceptibility is all too evident: his eyes close and his crown tips backward. Should animal magnetism fail, he can always use his "Grand Electrico Politico Battery" (powered by Stanley and Lyndhurst, with Wellington looking on from the shadows), primed to dispense an invigorating jolt of "New Taxes" and the "Pension List." *Punch* 1 (1841), 66.

usually advantageous trade agreement with France, *Punch* celebrated with a mesmeric depiction of the moment of triumph in "Royal Mesmerism" (fig. 6). The joke relied on readers' knowledge of several features of mesmeric practice. One was the fact that the magnetic influence usually ran from the charismatic French to the susceptible English, and from men to women. The other ingredient was the instability of mesmeric experiments—the fact that the apparently passive subject of the experiment sometimes seemed to seize control. Here, Britain's act of turning the tables of international trade was evoked in the mesmeric power of the queen. One commanding gesture placed Louis-Philippe in the magnetic coma, slumped in his chair and unresponsive to the

MESMERISING JOHN BULL;
OR, BLEEDING HIM FOR £3000.

QUACK PEEL.—I've got John in a mesmeric sleep, y'r Royal Highness ; so now you can bleed him.

CAMBRIDGE.—Aye, aye, here comes the golden stream again, a little phlebotomy every year, like this, will not be missed by the old boy while he has his eyes shut, and his senses inactive.

FIGURE 5 In "Mesmerising John Bull" (c. 1841), the stalwart incarnation of middle-class Britain is mesmerized by a wig-bedecked Peel. The duke of Cambridge, attended by Victoria, performs a phlebotomy draining Bull of £3,000. Purland scrapbook, National Library of Medicine.

promptings of a worried adviser. As his hat slipped from lax fingers, Victoria secured her "Commercial Treaty in favor of Britain."

The Entranced Explorers of British Science

The uncertain state of the polity presents a contrast to the purpose and energy with which early Victorians explored, studied, and conquered other places. In the middle decades of the century, geographical and scientific projects were establishing the empire of British science over the face of the globe with the unqualified confidence that would be advertised at the Great Exhibition.

FIGURE 6 Victoria applies her own brand of "royal mesmerism." Under her magnetic spell, Louis-Philippe signs a treaty that no right-minded monarch could accept. *Punch* 5 (1843), opposite p. 118.

Explorations of new worlds like the Arctic and Africa gave Britain sovereignty over virtually the last great unexplored lands; the opium wars of 1840–42 asserted her technological supremacy in the Far East; and colonial rule in India moved into a phase of consolidating the annexed regions. Victorians were mastering other "realms" as well, in cosmologies and natural histories teaching of nature's progressive development over vast expanses of time and space.[23] The relationships between the various sciences were also being mapped out, in general accounts of the "connection" of the sciences, the mutual "conversion" of forces, and the "correlation" both of natural forces and of the natural philosophers who studied them.[24]

Historians have often accepted the view of science they inherited from the more propagandist Victorian writers: in this age of imperialism, the exotic was taken over and redefined by the sciences that discovered it. The history of the nineteenth-century sciences would then appear to see consolidation and control by the orthodoxies of science, medicine, and technology and by the prestigious leaders of these fields. Such a history might seem to be confirmed by the fact that many of the sciences, institutions, and organizations we now regard as "modern" first appeared during these years. Examples include the term "scientist," the disciplines of "physics" and "biology" (among others), the reformed Royal Society, and several of the most powerful journals that even now dominate their fields. Even the fact that Victorian culture was well marked with what we usually call pseudosciences, or "heterodox" and "alternative" sciences and therapies, might seem a testimony to the success of science's imperial progress, since one might think that it was becoming possible to make a clear distinction between the orthodox sciences and these others. But Victorians did not treat their discoveries in such a simple and straightforward manner. Despite all their ambition and apparent confidence, they regarded science as unsettled. The proliferation of scientific societies during this period has sometimes been taken as a sign that science was becoming professionalized and that broad areas of agreement had been mapped out, but this, too, is the product of hindsight. There could be no agreement over the meaning and attribution of words like "expert" and "amateur" because natural philosophers had not divvied up nature's territories among themselves, or even secured natural knowledge as their own property.[25]

A constant source of anxiety among people who considered themselves experts was the confidence of amateurs to pronounce on scientific matters themselves. If many a "fashionable" family, as George Eliot put it, got its "science done by Michael Faraday,"[26] others did it themselves or, while revering the luminaries, found the (often conflicting) claims of traveling lecturers and pamphleteers perfectly plausible. The confidence of the educated classes in their own scientific judgment provoked Faraday himself, exasperated by what he saw as a lack of mental discipline, to demand that they should cultivate a humility that could leave them *"open to correction upon good grounds in all things."*[27] Faraday's instruction was part of a plea that the public should be open to correction by him, specifically, when he declared that table-turning (the practice that brought spiritualism to Britain) was a sham. His instructions were ignored. By the 1880s he was dead; spiritualism had gone from strength to strength. But Faraday, always the meticulous experimentalist, had seized the new resources given him by his own death to continue his electrochemical researches beyond the grave. The final word on the controversy was to come from Faraday himself. In 1887 the "late electrician" telegraphed an apology through the body of a spiritualist, confirming the validity of the claims he had dismissed in life, and implicitly (through his choice of "medium"), the public's power to make them.[28]

Throughout the Victorian period, the "public," however one might choose to define this entity, did not disqualify themselves from judgment on scientific matters. Even science's cultural power was construed in ways that individuals like Faraday considered inappropriate. As G. C. Lewis wrote in 1849, the "garb of science" was "captivating" to Victorians, but they understood it very differently from scientific specialists.[29] When they wished to express the cultural power of science, they often spoke of exotic influences rather than of the sober authority of individuals or institutions. That is, mesmeric influences figured in depictions not only of political power but of the cultural force of science itself.

A striking example of how people described this cultural power is the language used to describe the Great Exhibition of 1851. When Charlotte Brontë recorded her visit there in a letter to her father, she marveled at the "mania" that drove people to attend, and then the apparent spell they came under when they gazed upon the displays. "Only magic," she said, could produce the profound effects of its scientific and technological products: "none but superhuman hands could have arranged it thus, with such a blaze and contrast of colours and marvellous power of effect. The multitude filling the great aisles seems ruled and subdued by some invisible influence. Amongst the thirty thousand souls that peopled it the day I was there not one loud noise was to be heard, not one irregular movement seen; the living tide rolls on quietly, with a deep hum like the sea heard from the distance."[30] Brontë's evocative testimony to the power of science used the familiar language of invisible forces, magic, and trances to depict its public effects. Notably, she did not identify the scientific and engineering communities themselves, or luminaries within them such as Michael Faraday or Isambard Kingdom Brunel. The power of the exhibition may have been constructed by the work of these individuals, but what captured Brontë's imagination was a sense of mysterious power. What was enchanting about science was not the intellect or the achievement of individual experts—indeed, it did not come from mere humans at all, but was the work of magical "superhuman hands."

Sciences of Mind and Society

The importance of trances and enchantment to the mastery of nature and the body was nowhere more pronounced than in the study of the mind itself. In the early nineteenth century the study of the mind became increasingly empirical, translating philosophical questions into psychological ones, and psychological questions into matters for physiological investigation. The old Cartesian unity of mind and dualism of mind and body were largely abandoned, apart from a scant lip service to psychophysical parallelism. Instead, the field of "mental physiology" straddled mental and physical phenomena, marking off a large and inchoate area of investigation into links between the two. What acted in this space was the imagination, the will, and a partly physiological, partly psychic, system of reflexes. The mind was not a simple entity but imbedded in several interrelated, but distinct, physiological components.

The structures or actions that linked brain and mind were not hidden or even obscure; one could study them by examining the outside of the body, and human behavior. Some of the more distinctive human sciences emerging in the late eighteenth and early nineteenth centuries were founded on the notion that human identity, to put it in twentieth-century terms, could be read by studying clues that literally lay on the surface of the body. In the science of physiognomy, according to Lavater, the face took the imprint of one's inner self; one's character could be "read" in its composite features. Eighteenth-century physiognomies produced indexes of human character that could be read in facial structure. The science of phrenology was based on the very different principle of "cerebral localization": the notion that psychic traits were the expression of particular organs of the brain. The result here, too, was a relief map of personality and character (fig. 7). The size of the organ determined the strength of psychic traits, as well as the shape of the skull immediately above the organ itself. Thus a trained phrenologist could read one's personality in the contours of one's skull.

Knowledge of the mind was gained not only by examining static human landscapes and by dissecting the nerves, but also by monitoring mental and social actions. Altered states of mind provided the most valuable source of overt clues to the nature of psychological powers. Dreams, madness, and drunkenness, for instance, displayed qualities that existed (but more obscurely) in the sane and sober. Like Enlightenment naturalists composing their cabinets of curiosity, natural philosophers of mind collected altered states in the form of case histories. Studying one's own mind by introspection was the most abstract form one's researches might take; among the more concrete were anatomical and physiological study of the nerves and brain, observation of different forms and treatments of insanity and other naturally occurring states of mind (including somnambulism and ordinary sleep), and experiments in the effects of mind-altering influences such as opium and hashish, alcohol, and of course mesmerism. Collectors positioned their cases along several continuums between sanity and madness, sobriety and delirium, wakefulness and unconsciousness, willed and unwilled action. During the first half of the century, they were content to demonstrate the range of mental phenomena. By the 1830s the space between mind and body, between mechanism

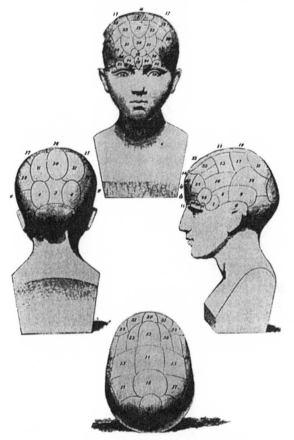

FIGURE 7 Phrenological head, viewed from front, back, top, and side. George Combe, *Elements of Phrenology* (Edinburgh: Anderson, Simpkin and Marshall, 1824).

and intention, and between sanity and madness, had become a large, diverse, and ever-expanding area of research. Studies proceeded on the assumption that one or both of two things were happening in these altered mental states: first, the restraining powers of the judgment and the will were compromised or even suspended in various states, and hence one could examine aspects of both by seeing how the mind functioned without them; and second, certain mental faculties were excited to a greater degree than in the healthy, normal state, and hence more accessible to study.[31]

Sciences of mind were not merely sets of abstracted statements. Public performances and, especially, sight, were important to what they meant. Asylums were "museums of madness" where viewers gazed at inmates acting out uncanny parodies of sanity, either emphasizing their divergence from the norm

THE PHYSIOGNOMIST.

Published by S. Dit. Fleet Street. 1831.

FIGURE 8 In this 1831 caricature the Professor addresses a disembodied audience. His raccoon hat and the collage of faces that form his body suggest that he may be an explorer or ethnologist. Iconographic Collection, Wellcome Institute.

or their eerie proximity to it.[32] In public phrenological examinations (occasions that were among the most popular forms of public science) the phrenologist explained the principles of his science using a particular individual's head as a prop. Physiognomy lectures were less frequent, and what inspired this caricature of 1831, "The Physiognomist" (fig. 8), was probably the importance of looking and of attention during public science lectures, rather than the prominence of physiognomy itself. The physiognomist's body is a collage of faces, and as he speaks he refers to an illustrated physiology textbook on his desk. Like the physiognomist, Victorians looked through physiognomic, phrenological, and, arguably, mesmeric eyes. They had habits of seeing and perceiving that required the knowledge one gleaned from these practices. From Victorian social landscapes in paintings like *Derby Day* to caricatures in popular journals like *Punch,* the human attributes and social relations that Victorians could read so clearly were visually transcribed in a physiognomic and phrenological cipher.[33]

Mesmerism was an ocular practice in a more dynamic sense than phrenology and physiognomy. It provided both a display and an account of the way displays affected audiences, an account of the power of looking as well as a powerful sight for Victorians to see. It often achieved its displays through the use of the eye, since one of the primary means of establishing the trance was through sustained eye contact. The power of looking and the relations of influence operating between the person looking and the thing being looked at were at the heart of experiments. But mesmerism not only explained what was going on in an altered state of mind; it also explained how the performance affected the audience. What was being performed explained how people reacted to it. Mesmeric performances, more openly than other forms of public display, emphasized their own status as theater. Indeed, because they promised an explanation of interpersonal influence achieved through the eye, they explored the very nature of theatricality.

Return to Mesmeria

It has become common to note that science was important during the Victorian period not only because its innovations were teaching Victorians new things but because they understood natural laws as underpinning, or having implications for, social laws. Once one appreciates the ambiguities of science and of mind in this period, it should come as no surprise that particularly vehement disagreement would focus on the way one defined mental powers and social relations. Conflicting representations proliferated of what constituted mental superiority and inferiority in society, what was the mechanism by which social influence or political power took effect.

The manifold significances of mesmerism as a science of mind, a science of sciences, and a science of society give new meaning to the satirical account of the discovery of the island of Mesmeria that introduced this chapter. It is now clear that this tale was parodic in two respects. First, it displayed twisted truths about the British state. Second, its very representational premise—that one had to be in an altered state of mind to perceive the realities of the new land— was a mocking reflection of how Victorians represented their own society. Victorians, understanding themselves to be living in a dramatically and mysteriously altered world, were attracted to the notion of altered states of mind when they sought to describe the new state of their culture. Mesmerism fascinated them partly because its phenomena answered the requirement. To many, the "mesmeric state" was a pun. Like the magnetic fluids that were thought to produce its effects, its subtle influence figured in the kinds of explanations Victorians developed of the nature of mental powers, influence, and cultural authority.

Animal Magnetism Comes to London

ANIMAL MAGNETISM DID NOT become the darling of the traditional medical elite of Britain—the courtly physicians with their noble patients. Nor was it initially adopted by the luminaries of science. The ancient universities of Oxford and Cambridge were not immediately welcoming (though, in Cambridge, animal magnetism would find its way past the porter's lodge of Trinity College by 1840). And although magnetic phenomena would eventually be discussed within the walls of the Royal Society and in its *Philosophical Transactions*, the first official discussion occurred years after it arrived. The fashionable Royal Institution would also make it the subject of evening conversaziones, but only after years of debate in which institution regulars (including its professor, Michael Faraday) observed mesmerism at other venues, or read about it from the discreet vantage point of their clubs or sitting rooms. Animal magnetism was not "clubbable." At least, not at first. It did not flow unimpeded into the august preserves of societies like the Geological or the Astronomical, whose members kept a tight rein on their new specialist fields. But if it did not immediately come to these institutions, many of their members came to it. They were drawn by the researches of a less established, but just as ambitious, group of people: a young generation of scientific and medical lecturers, professors, and medical students in the metropolis.

Animal magnetism appealed to a number of self-consciously "progressive," politically liberal and radical doctors, natural philosophers and men of letters, largely because it promised to address many of their questions about the relationship of physical forces to life. To what extent should scientific accounts emphasize matter, as opposed to vitality and spirit? Was the organizing principle of life inherent, or was it breathed in by the Creator? Was there anything essentially "vital" about living things? What was the relationship of electricity and other physical forces to the nerves and mind? And more generally, how could science and medicine use natural forces to improve individual human minds? Animal magnetism seemed to have the potential to address all of these questions, and to illuminate or to intensify connections between them. Before reconstructing its arrival and integration into 1830s London, we must therefore begin by examining the intellectual appetites of those seeking to develop a "progressive" and "philosophical" understanding of life and mind, and survey the scientific and medical cornucopia that surrounded them.

The New Sciences of 1830s London

By the 1830s London was developing a vast range of scientific and medical venues. There were old institutions like the Royal Society, the Royal Colleges of Physicians and Surgeons, and the younger but well-established Horticultural, Geological, and Astronomical Societies. But by 1840 they kept company with more than a dozen newcomers: the Zoological (1826), the Statistical (1834), the British Medical (1835), the Meteorological (1839), the Medico-Botanical, and many new venues of public science. The elite Royal Institution and the exclusive, private salons were joined by new, more accessible places to study nature and the body. Londoners could now take their pick of the Adelaide Gallery, the National Gallery of Practical Science, the Coliseum on Regents Park, the Royal Polytechnic Institution, and several private anatomy schools and museums. Such places drew performers and audiences alike from a broad range of social groups. Instrument makers, anatomists, and itinerants now had a forum, and people of all ranks of society came to see them and their creations. The supply of new medical institutions was particularly striking. A few doors down from private dissecting rooms were the new universities and their medical schools: the reformist Whig University College and its Tory rival, King's.[1]

Different practices and bodies of knowledge flourished in these places, many of them incompatible with each other. There were acrimonious debates about what was proper to science and medicine and what was not. Among them, medical reform and authority sparked particularly violent disagreements. The pages of the London medical journals simmered with complaints about the sorry state of the profession and the power of quacks, and physicians and surgeons alike wished to change the way their students related to each other and to their patients. But doing this would involve reforming not only the profession but the public as well. Key liberal reforms of the early 1830s sought to reform the human body and people's attitudes to it. The sanitary reforms suggested that moral and social well-being required a clean and healthy body; the New Poor Law was implemented not only by workhouse routines but by physical humiliations.[2] The Anatomy Act of 1834, in providing the corpses of workhouse inmates to medical schools for dissection, helped portray the human body as machine—a message that was constantly reinforced at University College after Jeremy Bentham's body was dissected and displayed in the main gallery.[3] As his corpse was being stuffed, advocates of medical jurisprudence (later "forensic medicine") were demanding legal recognition that they in their hospitals were more trustworthy than attorneys in their "red and black ink shops." Real knowledge of the body could be found only where people worshipped "natural law" instead of filthy lucre: the "Temples of Medical Science."[4] In these and other ways, claims to public authority were staked in the human body—in its tissues, fluids, nutritional requirements, and chemical processes.

More generally, reformers wanted to make the medical profession more scientific and the public more deferential to its expertise. In the opinion of Thomas Wakley (fig. 9), acid-penned leader of radical reform and founder and editor of its leading journal the *Lancet*, the old orthodoxies of medicine required no less than a demolition job: reformers had to strip the courtly physicians of their power and drive them from their positions of influence. Medicine and the management of patients would proceed on scientific principles.

The institution most likely to achieve Wakley's ambition was the recently founded University College London (UCL), one of the most self-consciously progressive of metropolitan newcomers. The faculty saw their school as an engine, instilling the rising professional classes with scientific knowledge and principle. We know a great deal about the work of the medical school of UCL and the sciences that flourished in and around it, thanks to the work of Adrian Desmond. Behind the university's classical façade was a quarrelsome population: students demanding particular lecture topics and scrambling to keep up with lecturing fees, professors fighting both to keep the newborn institution going and to drive their rivals from the faculty. Even the anatomical exhibits in the new museum were snacked upon by passing rats.[5] However precarious their position, UCL faculty took comfort in their view from the crown of the March of Intellect engine. Theirs was a future in which all obstacles in the path of reform would give way to progressive science.

Unlike the classical curriculum of the ancient universities, UCL taught discoveries so new that they would have been wild fantasies a generation earlier. Students who assembled before Dionysius Lardner (fig. 10), professor of mechanical philosophy at UCL and one of the most active and influential publicists of science of this period, heard that the powers of steam "could only have been admitted into the pages of fiction" a few years back. Even "the

FIGURE 9
Thomas Wakley, founder and
editor of the *Lancet*. Purland
scrapbook, National Library
of Medicine.

most acute and far-sighted cannot foresee" its future effects.[6] This generation, surrounded by astonishing changes wrought by science, set few limits
on the powers that might be revealed in electricity, light, magnetism, and
gases. We can find one indication of the boundaries of plausibility in the scientific horses Lardner chose to back. However marvelous the powers of
steam might be, Lardner decided, they were insufficient to enable a trans-
atlantic journey.[7] But animal magnetism would convince him both of its reality and its basis in physical force. The claim that an imponderable fluid could
pass from one individual into another, altering the processes of thought, was
astonishing, but just as worthy of serious evaluation as other great scientific
assertions.

The most provocative scientific innovations were European imports, and
many of them were funneled through UCL. They had major implications for
one's understanding of the human body and mind, and they spanned a diverse
terrain, ranging across the fields of medical therapeutics, surgery, morphol-

FIGURE 10 Dionysius Lardner, professor of mechanical philosophy at University College London, posed in cape, spectacles, and top-hat. Purland scrapbook, National Library of Medicine.

ogy, physiology, natural philosophy, and mathematics. UCL's professor of comparative anatomy, Robert Grant, was the leading importer of the comparative anatomy of Geoffroy St.-Hilaire, whose spin on Lamarck's evolutionary claims gave them radical political significance. The new mathematical analysis, imported to UCL by Augustus De Morgan, did not correspond with

FIGURE 11 John Elliotson, sketched in a series of portraits of medical heroes published in the *Lancet* (1834). One hand calls attention to his lecture notes; one leg is extended to reveal that he is clad in trousers, a new fashion.

physical reality as the old mathematics had been assumed to do, and therefore threatened the old assumption that mathematical study would confirm God's designing hand in nature.[8] And the charismatic young professor of practical medicine at UCL, John Elliotson (fig. 11), seized upon new drugs and diagnostic techniques from France and Germany, and promoted researches (notably in phrenology) that assigned an increasing proportion of human behavior to the action of bodily mechanisms instead of the will.[9]

Many of these researches addressed the question of the extent to which life and mind were mechanical and to which apparently spiritual things were governed by natural law. Phrenologists claimed to understand the relationship between brain physiology and human behavior; physiologists increasingly attended to the nerves, as a sensitive interface between the living being and the external environment; advocates of electric medicine began to see the body as a battery, storing and dispensing electric influence as needed; the new "reflex" physiology represented the human body as a system of switches and levers, reflecting incoming stimuli outward again in bodily action.[10]

As the vital sciences found machines in the body, mechanical innovations produced the signs of life and spirit. Andrew Ure notoriously celebrated the new steam-powered spinning and weaving factory machines as "instinct" with a workman's "thought, feeling, and tact."[11] Less immediately practical inventions ranged from the earthy to the exclusive: in public rooms on Pall Mall, lecturers promising the "mechanical production of life" delivered thousands of baby birds, hurried out of their shells in the spectacle of "Hatching by Steam."[12] On the other end of the spectrum was Charles Babbage's salon, where dancing automata seemed to have "grace" and "imagination," and his difference engine did arithmetic.[13] Actions that had previously seemed uniquely human no longer were so: one visitor marveled that even Babbage himself did not "profess to know all the powers of the machine," and indeed that it all seemed "incomprehensible, without the exercise of volition and thought."[14] Not only were the mental and vital produced by mechanism, but nature could even produce the (apparently) supernatural. For instance, the itinerant magician known as the Great Necromancer of the North gave popular shows that confounded the senses with displays of automatism, magic, laughing gas, and ventriloquism—all performed on the understanding that they seemed magical but came from natural causes.[15] Thus throughout London, in lectures, textbooks, salons, and popular shows, the apparently vital or mental were shown to be mechanical, the animate inanimate, and the supernatural natural.

The term "natural magic" embraced most of these inventions and researches, for they all relied on the premise that phenomena long assumed to be supernatural or spiritual were now to be demystified as natural. In 1832 David Brewster's *Natural Magic* charted a history for several phenomena, including talking machines, hallucinations, and pictures that simulated animation. Each passed through three stages, from religious delusion in the Middle Ages and early modern period, through Enlightenment amusement, to industrial production. His was the best known of several historical treatises, many of them by Scottish Evangelicals, that yoked an anti-Catholicism to a celebration of scientific progress. Many of these works discussed altered states of mind. Histories of magic and witchcraft (the most famous Scott's in 1830 and Godwin's in 1836) and studies of dreams, hallucinations, and prophecy sought to identify the mental states that people in the past assumed to be supernatural or fraudulent. The assumption was that they could now be explained using nineteenth-century knowledge. These works followed a long tradition of Protestant writings, but there was an important difference: they assumed that the "wonders" of ages past and the light amusements of the Enlightenment would become, for the first time, profitable and truly edifying once they were understood.[16] Natural magic was tantalizing not merely because its phenomena were (initially) mysterious but because the natural powers that created them were marvelous themselves.

A prime example of how phenomena associated with natural magic could illuminate force and mind was the work of Charles Wheatstone, professor of experimental physics at King's College, London. His inventions were inspired by his family's expertise in the construction of musical instruments, by new French works in natural philosophy and mathematics (such as the wave mechanics of Fourier), and by an emerging trend within philosophy of mind that treated perception as a more complex phenomenon than hitherto. His enchanted lyre (1824) used long metal pipes to connect a piano in one room with a lyre in another, with the intention that sound vibrations would be conducted from the first instrument to the second. When the keys of the piano were struck, the lyre appeared to play by itself.[17] Sound could, in a sense, be embodied in matter and moved from one place to another. It could also be transformed into another sense-perception—a phenomenon of hearing could become one of sight. The kaleidophone (1827), named after Brewster's kaleidoscope, was a means of making sound visible. Silvered glass beads set in metal rods traced the wave pattern of sound vibrations, moving so quickly that they seemed to form static geometric shapes. The eye could now see what the ear was hearing.[18] Wheatstone's stereoscope, on the other hand, explored the nature of vision. It presented two-dimensional images to the eyes in such a way that the mind perceived a single three-dimensional shape. These phenomena showed that when one looked at a single three-dimensional object, what each eye "saw" differed, both from what the other eye saw and from what the mind perceived. This experiment led to a classic paper on the physiology of vision in 1834, around the time that Wheatstone was also publishing on dreams and somnambulism.[19]

A persistent theme of his work was a distinction that some physiologists were beginning to make between sensation (defined as a stimulus to the nerves) and perception (the mind's consciousness of the stimulus or object).[20] Wheatstone's experimental juxtaposition of force and vital phenomena continued in another direction later in the decade, when he and Michael Faraday pursued the question of the "identity of the electricities" in collaborative research on the electric fish. In 1837 he developed the telegraph with Cooke, allowing the transfer of thoughts and words from one place to another, and, as we will see, collaborated with Lardner, Elliotson, and others in electric and optical experiments in animal magnetism.[21] What linked these researches was a fascination with the substitution of one sense for another, the mechanical production of human qualities, and the displacement of sound and thought through space.

A central feature of natural magic and charismatic spectacle was what one might call the "perceptual mistake." In traditional denunciations of the ostensibly supernatural, the notion of "delusion" functioned as a sort of trap door giving way beneath a discredited phenomenon. But now it became interesting in itself. These spectacles asked what was going on in the body or mind when the reality one perceived was different from the sensations that impinged on the nerves of eye, ear, and fingertip. This question made "misunderstanding" into a subject for investigation: an entire society's misunderstanding of a particular natural phenomenon, a set of beliefs instilled in an audience by a clever charlatan or priest, or, even when people rightly understood the physical manipulations taking place (such as the rapid presentation of a series of pictures), a confusion over why they created the perception they did (the impression of fluid movement of a particular image). There were also aberrant states of mind: drug-induced hallucinations, transient disorders of the senses, and even insanity. Whatever the phenomena, explanations were to be found in fast-growing fields of study: in optics and mechanical natural philosophy, combined with physiology of the mind and nerves.

This was the context in which animal magnetism first became meaningful in 1830s London. When it arrived, it was not merely a bizarre and baffling phenomenon; it was poised between spectacular automatism and the phenomena of dreams and somnambulism, and between the interests of mechanical philosophers and the ambitions of medical reformers hungry for innovative medical treatments. In 1834 Thomas De Quincey heralded its arrival by reminding his readers of the magical pedigree of *mineral* magnetism. There had never been a natural agent that "wore so much the appearance of a magical device," and no one had yet understood the "sympathy with an unknown object, which constitutes its power." And how much more mysterious, and more fascinating, was magnetism in a human being, "a world so vast and so obscure in itself; upon his diseases in the first place; next upon his volition; and, finally, upon the whole phenomena of his sentient nature." Animal magnetism, he predicted, would open "nothing less than a new world to the prospects of Psychology, and, generally speaking, to the knowledge of the human mind." [22]

New Mental Powers

By the 1830s animal magnetism had a fifty-year history of controversy. Dismissive reports by the Académie des Sciences and the Académie de Médecine branded it as quackery even before it crossed the Channel in the 1780s, and it had revolutionary associations as well. There was talk of "magnetic spies" standing on the shores of France, radiating their subversive influence into the minds of honest British yeomen, and while there was no upsurge of revolutionary mesmerism on British shores, it did catch the imagination of a number of British radicals. [23] The Shelleys and their circle made mesmeric experiments, inspiring a poem that reversed traditional relations of gender when a potent "magnetic lady" soothed a lovelorn male patient.[24] Robert Southey's *Letters from England* likened the revolutionary millenarianism of the popular leader Richard Brothers to the projects of the French mesmerist De Maineduc—with the distinction that Brothers had offered an even more exciting program and earned greater success.[25] As a medical practice, animal magnetism was associated with decadent and lascivious Regency quackeries such as James Graham's "celestial bed" and Perkins's "metallic tractors." After the first several years of the new century, almost no one was practicing animal magnetism publicly. Early Victorian doctors would later dredge up from dim memory no more than two magnetizers of earlier decades: one Miss Preston, who supposedly maintained a discreet private practice in Bloomsbury Square, and a man in Kennington, whose name no one could recall.[26]

Yet animal magnetism survived. After the Napoleonic wars it resurfaced in France transformed. By the time it crossed the Channel again in the late 1820s and early 1830s, its propagators could advertise a dramatically different set of effects. While Mesmer's patients had experienced a violent cathartic "crisis," the most influential magnetizer after him, the marquis de Puysegur, placed his patients in a calm, but dramatically altered, mental condition.[27] He could produce complete catalepsy, lack of sensation and consciousness, mimicry of the mesmerist's sensations ("community of sensation") and movements ("traction"), and a lucid state accompanied by clairvoyance and prescience. Some patients predicted the progress of their own and others' illnesses and instructed the physician as to an appropriate treatment. There were many varieties of magnetic phenomena in the 1820s and 1830s, but each involved an "altered state" of mind, a mental condition permitting experiments on the nature and possibilities of perception, thought, and communication.

The new animal magnetism also had a glittering set of credentials, including pronouncements made by leading French naturalists and natural philosophers. Laplace had refused to dismiss the possibility of animal magnetism, on the grounds that the nerves were the most "sensitive" instruments for the discovery of the "imperceptible agents of nature." The "extreme sensibility of the nerves in particular individuals" might make them receptive to the action of a particularly feeble influence, and animal magnetism might well be such an agent.[28] Cuvier went further, acknowledging that, while it was sometimes hard to tell physical causes from imaginary ones, there was no doubt that "the proximity of two animated bodies in certain positions, combined with certain movements, have a real effect [in the form of 'nervous communication'], independent of imagination."[29]

The most important part of mesmerism's early-nineteenth-century pedigree was the confidence of the Académie de Médecine. In 1820s Paris, M. Foissac,

Charles Deleuze, and Charles Dupotet made a number of mesmeric experiments at the Hôtel Dieu and the Salpetrière, and in 1826 persuaded the Académie de Médecine to convene a new committee.[30] It read reports, attended experiments, and in one case, even experienced the trance. The most striking event was a surgical operation, an amputation of the breast of one Madame Plantin by the mesmerist and surgeon Jules Clocquet. Plantin was placed in a state in which she could feel none of the usual pain of the knife (see fig. 12). The operation was considered an amazing success—despite the death of Plantin shortly afterward. Five years later, the committee concluded their investigations, judging the phenomena to be real. They confirmed the reality of effects ranging from simple (but extreme) "insensibility" to a number of astonishing new cognitive abilities and physical links in which subjects moved in an echo of the mesmerists and read without the use of their eyes. Published in France in 1831, it was translated in 1833 by the Scottish attorney J. C. Colquhoun, who then wrote his own mesmeric work. Excerpted, discussed, reviewed in the quarterlies and in penny pamphlets, these treatises put animal magnetism back on the map.[31]

Many readers immediately dismissed animal magnetism, but it drew serious attention from influential figures, notably Thomas Wakley, known to his readers as a ferocious foe of quackery. Wakley's *Lancet,* fast becoming Britain's most influential medical journal, remarked that the commissioners were "men of known respectability and veracity," and that they included François Magendie, whose works on nervous physiology were then highly influential. It was impossible to dispute the observations of such men, the *Lancet* declared, even though what they said was so extraordinary as to set all past experience "at defiance."[32] The *Lancet* excerpted experiments and urged readers to consider them seriously. As London doctors were considering how to receive animal magnetism, the first magnetizer stepped off the ferry. He was the "Baron" Charles Dupotet de Sennevoy, a figure of some prestige in France who had produced many of the celebrated phenomena in the commission's report. Londoners were slow to welcome him, but by the end of his stay some twenty months later, he was a household name in polite society, and after his return to France he claimed that his English witnesses had numbered in the thousands.[33]

The Vital Principle of Charles Dupotet

Dupotet arrived in June 1837, hired a set of rooms in Hanover Square, and hung out his shingle. But the salon culture of fashionable London was slow to respond to an unknown foreigner offering expensive tuition in the strange

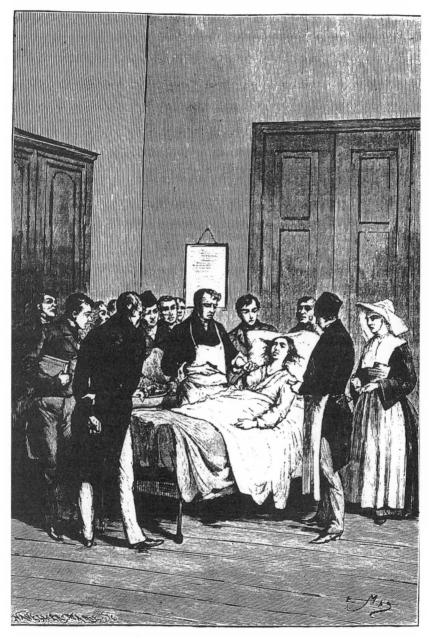

FIGURE 12 Retrospective portrayal of the operation to remove the cancerous breast of Madame Plantin in 1828. The surgeon, Jules Clocquet, is attended by a dozen witnesses. Louis Figuier, *Mystères de la Science* (Paris: Librairie Illustrée, Renaudet, 1880).

new practice. Dupotet had no connections, and he did not speak the language. He could not move smoothly through fashionable society, where social engagements might have fed him the clients he desired. Dupotet would later reflect bitterly that he might have had more success if he had brought an "ourang outang" with him and ventured into the teeming world of the London shows.[34]

But despite his faltering start, he kept visible in the press with newspaper advertisements and boastful letters to medical journals. He was already acquainted with many London doctors by the time he announced in the *Lancet* that his work proved the existence of a "new power," and that "[e]re long, no more mystery will attach to its employment than there is in electrical and galvanic apparatus." If the effects he described seemed to border on the supernatural, nothing less extraordinary could issue from the causes he claimed were at work. If "one man can penetrate another man with a part of the vital principle, which his organization conceals, the life of that individual being necessarily *mis en plus*" (fig. 13), it stood to reason that the effects should appear to have "a supernatural character, and surprise by their novelty." Soon, he promised, "thousands of your countrymen will be able to perform the wonders of which they may be witnesses, and sometimes the agents."[35]

In the autumn of 1837 he finally drew first a trickle, and then a stream, of visitors. One journalist's report to the monthly *Mirror* described what he saw when he paid a visit to Dupotet's rooms in Maddox Street, Hanover Square. An experiment was well under way.[36] Dupotet, "a man of very prepossessing appearance, with fine, dark, intelligent eyes," was seated before another gentleman, holding his hand. After some time, he "pressed his hands on the patient's shoulders, and passed lightly over his arms till their hands again touched. He repeated this two or three times, and then spreading forth his hand with the fingers closed, he moved it gently [downward]. He then continued the waving action of the hand down the stomach and legs, and, having finished the whole length of the body, returned to the brow. This was continued for a quarter of an hour." Dupotet rose from his chair, telling his audience that the mesmeric link he had established would make his patient follow him. He then took "five or six long, deliberate steps, proceeded to the lobby at the top of the stairs," looking at his patient over his shoulder as he did so. After a brief struggle the man "yielded to the influence, and cried for us to hold him, or he must follow, as if he were dragged by a strong chain!" The struggle appeared to make him "considerably excited" at his helpless situation, and when he could not be calmed, the baron declared it unsafe to continue with the experiment. They turned instead to another patient, Dupotet's domestic servant Julie.

Julie was "a quiet, simple peasant, of about forty years of age, not good look-

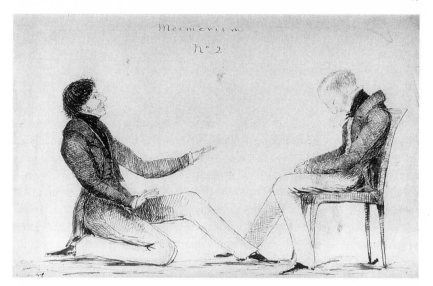

FIGURE 13 This pen-and-ink drawing was probably made during one of Dupotet's conversaziones in 1837; the magnetizer's posture recalls one of the standard techniques that Dupotet
used to transmit the vital principle from mesmerist to subject. The (unknown) artist probably
subscribed to the principles of phrenology, judging from the bulging forehead that emphasizes
the subject's intellectuality. Iconographic Collection, Wellcome Institute.

ing, and rather fat, but withall of a prepossessing appearance, and very modest, retiring manners." There was no reason to suppose that she would act in
bad faith. Before the trial she told the audience that she had been ill but was
now improving, thanks to magnetic treatment. She then seated herself, and
Dupotet began the magnetic passes. Soon she appeared to sink into a state of
insensibility, though she could still converse. One observer claimed to have a
headache and asked what medical treatment he should receive. She replied,
castor oil and chicken broth, and she dictated a recipe. Other tests followed.
Dupotet pushed "[l]arge quantities of stuff . . . into her nose without producing the least effect; pins were stuck into her arms and legs without being
noticed, and it seemed impossible to make the slightest impression on her
senses in any way." Finally, he awakened her by touching her knee, moving
his hands "crossways before her face, as if tearing aside something that covered it, and exclaiming 'Awake! awake!'" She duly woke and gazed upon the
company, looking as "simple and unconcerned" as before the trial, and apparently "quite unconscious of all that had passed."

Events like this drew Dupotet to the attention of fashionable Londoners.
Large crowds, sometimes as many as forty or fifty, assembled to see the mesmeric effects in individuals like Julie and even in themselves.[37] No consensus
was reached regarding the reality, much less the cause, of the phenomena, but

by the end of 1837 Dupotet had become a familiar topic of discussion and debate within and without scientific and medical circles.

The Temples of Medical Science

Soon Dupotet's demonstrations could be seen not only in his private rooms but in the wards of the London hospitals. First, he was invited by the physician and anatomist Herbert Mayo to give a series of demonstrations at the Middlesex Hospital. He then moved on to University College Hospital (UCH) where, for almost a year, he collaborated with John Elliotson, professor of practical medicine, in a series of treatments and public displays. Unlike Dupotet, whose purpose in London was to found a magnetic clinic, his English collaborators wished to harness animal magnetism to their own existing lines of research.

Mayo and Elliotson took opposing points of view within the fast-developing study of mind. During the 1820s and 1830s doctors were transforming the powers of the nervous system and mental phenomena. As physiology, and especially phrenology, became more prominent, it became increasingly plausible to see mental action as an assemblage of different functions with a division of psychological labor. Phrenology portrayed the brain as several distinct organs. Individually and in combination, they produced all human actions: moral, intellectual, perceptive, and motor. Marshall Hall's reflex physiology added a controversial means of displaying categories of human behavior that were structured by the reflection of incoming stimuli outward by the spine and autonomic nervous system, without sensation, and therefore entirely independent of the will.

Once the mind was an aggregate of several quasi-independent faculties, and once there were physiological mechanisms producing actions independent of the will, unusual mental states took on a new significance. An individual could have a diseased set of moral organs and could therefore be "mad," while all the other organs were healthy and intact.[38] This was the core component of "monomania," the disorder that would dominate conceptions of insanity for much of the century. One feature of the new understanding of madness was that it became more democratic. Rather than being a condition that set certain individuals permanently apart from the rest of humanity, it was a state of mind in which anyone could find themselves, and from which they could return. Madness was on one extreme of a broad continuum of altered states, a more permanent manifestation of conditions such as drunkenness and somnambulism. This new understanding of the mind and its vicissitudes made altered states of all kinds, from sleep to madness, valuable sites for medical research into the nature of thought and of the will.[39]

The nature and limits of the will became an increasingly central concern for physiologists. Over the next two decades, the issues that were emerging in the late 1830s would provoke the development of new definitions both of volition and of consciousness that would have immense social and political implications. For instance, in 1843 the MacNaughton rules of diminished responsibility for crime in cases of insanity were established using the new mental physiology, rules that have remained in place ever since.[40] In the late 1830s the physiology of human action was poised on the edge of great uncharted terrains of volitional thought and action. The question facing all physiologists was how far physiology would advance into these territories, and where might boundaries be drawn to protect the immateriality of the will, mind, and soul. Mayo and Elliotson wished to answer this question in decidedly different ways, and each thought animal magnetism offered a prime opportunity to do so.

Mayo was professor of physiology and anatomy at King's College, London, taught at the newly founded medical school of the Middlesex Hospital, and researched nervous phenomena. During the 1830s he had collaborated with François Magendie on nervous anatomy and studied the varieties of somnambulism and dreams. Mayo hoped that animal magnetism would help him prove the immateriality of the mind. He decided that the most extraordinary of mesmeric phenomena, such as the ability to foretell the future, "result from the workings of a spiritual nature, in a certain independence of those bodily organs to which it is ordinarily tied and bound." That is, mesmerism proved the independence of the (immaterial) mind from the flesh, by placing it in a state in which it could act independently of the body.[41] Canvassing for coexperimenters throughout the London community, he attracted the support of some, like Earl Stanhope, president of the Medico-Botanical Society, who also saw animal magnetism as a proof of dualism and who became an early and steadfast patron of the practice. But although some of Mayo's colleagues became actively involved in mesmeric experiments, others objected so ferociously that Dupotet's experiments were discontinued.[42]

Undaunted, Dupotet secured the patronage of the very different medical constituency at the hospital at University College, where he soon took up practice with the help of John Elliotson. Dupotet was doubly attractive to Elliotson: he offered an exciting new line of research, and, in pursuing it, Elliotson could score points against UCL's "Tory" rival. Practices claimed to have implications for the place of human beings in the natural and spiritual order were readily loaded with ideological significance in the rivalry between UCL and King's. Animal magnetism was one of several sciences of life that became political game pieces in the ideological battle between different medical constituencies. The best-known example is the field of comparative anatomy, in which rival developmental theories were championed at UCL and King's.[43]

As animal magnetism was being introduced to UCL, Robert Grant's "progressive" comparative anatomy was doing battle with the conservative Coleridgean comparative anatomy of Richard Owen at the Royal College of Surgeons, and some of Owen's staunchest supporters were on the faculty of King's. As the rivalry between the two colleges developed, animal magnetism offered itself as a timely vehicle for progressive philosophy among medical radicals.

When he met Dupotet, Elliotson was a great rising star of medicine. He was president of the Medico-Chirurgical Society of London, founder and president of the London Phrenological Society, and one of the two poles of student popularity within the medical school of UCH (the other being Robert Liston, professor of surgery). He was controversial for his radical politics, and because his phrenological claims that mind was a function of brain gave rise to suspicions of atheism. He was particularly known for using publicity and public pressure to achieve his political and professional goals and for seizing upon controversial new techniques and technologies, before they gained general acceptance. This collection of strategies and interests was spectacularly evident in 1837 and 1838, when he became animal magnetism's most intrepid and passionate researcher.

Elliotson often complained that the weakest characteristic of medical research was its failure to produce therapeutic results. He hoped that animal magnetism might be able to provide students with a more clinically based science with therapeutic application.[44] If he succeeded, he would have developed a science of life immune to one of the complaints that had been leveled at comparative anatomy, namely, that it was developed outside the hospital and brought no benefits to patients.[45] Animal magnetism certainly appealed to Elliotson because it was in some simple sense a potential therapy, but its implications were far greater than this for him. The putative physical agents that produced the phenomena gave animal magnetism the potential to aid Elliotson's medical reform campaigns and physiological research.[46] The spectacle of a doctor creating a healing trance dramatized the power of a healer at a time when doctors wished to attain a more powerful status vis-à-vis their patients. The ambiguities surrounding claims that phenomena were produced by a physical force or subtle organic emission from one body into another made animal magnetism potentially relevant to researches on the electric production of life, the pathology of hysteria, and the nature of reflexes. The conjunction of these possibilities made animal magnetism all the more exciting—and potentially dangerous—whichever side of the debates one favored.

A pivotal figure was Elliotson's close friend and ally, the radical medical publisher and surgeon Thomas Wakley, who publicized Elliotson's magnetic researches in the *Lancet*.[47] Elliotson and Wakley were close allies throughout the late 1820s and 1830s. Wakley had supported Elliotson's career from the first and became his most powerful supporter and publicist during the magnetic experiments. Wakley's *Lancet* got its start in the 1820s by publishing summaries of lectures delivered at the various teaching hospitals. Many lecturers were infuriated by this policy, because students read the reports rather than paying to attend in person. But for Elliotson, who cooperated with the *Lancet,* the publications were useful advertising: his yearly income rose from £500 to £5,000.[48] Elliotson and Wakley joined forces over phrenology, medical reform, and new therapies. They backed controversial sciences and medical causes, and many of them were soon established. The stethoscope was becoming a standard diagnostic tool, legislation was beginning to establish the legal power of medical jurisprudence, the Phrenological Society was flourishing (it became nationally based in 1838), and the medical reform movement was gaining ground.[49]

Animal magnetism could complement these enterprises and, by bringing together elements of each of them, help them to become a coherent package. Elliotson seized upon it as the crucial, dramatic test case that could establish his reductionist physiology, place mental phenomena in the hands of professional experts, and secure their place in medical reform. Within a few years it had become the crowning element in his campaign to establish "physiological science," rather than "the usages of society," as the means of deciding "the most important events in human welfare." [50]

"A Sort of Committee"

How were animal magnetic phenomena to be evaluated? They spanned the fields of science, and previous savants had failed to provide explanations that stood the test of time. Researchers from many branches of science studied the trance, but although many of them were eminent in their fields, few were willing to make extensive public statements for or against mesmerism's reality. By the spring of 1838 many London intellectuals had witnessed and participated in magnetic trials. There were attempts to assemble groups to evaluate animal magnetism in a more formal manner and, perhaps, to provide the safety of numbers. Mayo wished to convene "a sort of committee" of scientific luminaries (including William Whewell, Charles Babbage, Michael Faraday, and Charles Wheatstone), but had limited success in getting them to participate.[51] Then, during a large public demonstration of magnetism in the UCH theater on 10 May 1838, Elliotson announced that the Royal Society had appointed such a committee. It included Robert Grant, Neil Arnott, Peter Mark Roget, Herbert Mayo, Charles Wheatstone, Francis Kiernan, John Bostock, and James Joseph Sylvester.[52]

There are no records in the Royal Society either to substantiate or to contradict this claim (the appropriate sectional committee book is missing). However, there is circumstantial evidence that some such committee did exist. Elliotson's statement was delivered to an audience of hundreds, including several of the men Elliotson named, and they did not contradict him. The published summary of Elliotson's speech (including the list of committee members) appeared in the *Lancet* more than a fortnight later—leaving plenty of time to check the facts. The journal then reiterated in mid-July that the committee had confirmed the reality of the trance, and in August made reference to it again, this time with the addition of William Lawrence and the omission of Grant, Arnott, Roget, and Sylvester.

The existence of such a body would be significant not least because the sectional committees of the Royal Society were founded to help resolve a prevailing ambiguity about what was proper to the sciences, and where to draw the boundaries between different fields. The uncertainties surrounding the structure of disciplines in science and medicine spurred several efforts to define the various subdivisions and their relations with one another. In 1834 Mary Somerville published a well-received account of the "connexion" between the various physical sciences, and William Whewell, reviewing it, famously coined the term "scientist" during a complaint that science was becoming too fragmented.[53] It was in the midst of these attempts to give the sciences order and structure that the Royal Society set up the sectional committees and assigned them their disciplinary tasks.[54] The immediate provocation for the formation of these committees was the undefined status of the "spinal reflex" apparatus of Marshall Hall—that is, a highly controversial set of assertions regarding a category of nervous phenomena whose relations with the will were much at issue.[55] So the sectional committees were both scientific jury and police, and they were particularly alert to the problematic character of nervous phenomena.

With two exceptions,[56] the members of the "Magnetic Committee" came from the Physiological and Physics Sectional Committees that had been formed by the Royal Society Council on the very day of Elliotson's speech.[57] If, indeed, they were asked to evaluate his work, this would suggest that animal magnetism not only was an interesting new psychic phenomenon but also seemed to have the potential to test (for better or worse) the parameters of scientific work.

Unfortunately we know virtually nothing about what kinds of tests and conclusions the committee made. There were conflicting statements about whether and in what way its members had even been appointed, much less what conclusions it had drawn. There were conflicting reports in the press. The *Lancet* stated on 14 July 1838 that the committee had "unequivocally pronounced in favour of the reality of the coma and the somnambulism";[58] this was contradicted by the *Medical Gazette,* whose denial was reprinted in the gentleman's weekly, the *Athenaeum.*

Frustrating as the lack of definitive information may be, it is informative in another sense. The uncertainty surrounding scientific authority in this period not only affected such apparently simple questions as whether the "Magnetic Committee" had been formed, but also the question of how such a body should be constituted and how it would make decisions. Scientific claims straddling the border between the physical and the living were notoriously hard to resolve and dangerous to the reputations of those who engaged in public disputes over them. For these men to come forward as a body with the power and expertise to resolve the issue of the status of animal magnetism (which had not been settled definitively by such figures as Benjamin Franklin and Antoine Lavoisier decades earlier) was to give hostages to fortune. It is plausible that, even if no committee was formally appointed by the Royal Society, members of the Physiological and Physics Sectional Committees met informally to try to reach a private consensus about animal magnetism before taking a public stand. In short, the ambiguity over whether this body existed may have been deliberate. It would allow one to announce, after the fact, that an expert scientific jury had been appointed, had come to an authoritative decision, and had decisively validated or dismissed the practice.

One example of how scientific authority was constituted at this time in relation to particular controversial issues is the controversy that descended upon the promising young physiologist William Benjamin Carpenter when he published his first work on the life sciences. Carpenter, poised on the edge of a brilliant career, published his *Principles of General and Comparative Physiology* in 1839. Amid general acclaim, two reviews condemned his statements regarding the "lawlike" character of vital phenomena as materialist, a denial of God's agency in creation. Carpenter had consulted prestigious religious and scientific figures as he wrote the volume, showing them the passages on "lawlike" vital phenomena. To clear himself, Carpenter assembled these patrons and others into a de facto committee, and juxtaposed their supportive statements in a single document. This was published as an appendix to a supportive medical journal in the following year. The significance of this is that, however authoritative were the natural philosophers and theologians who came to Carpenter's aid, they did not, a priori, define an orthodox body. They were in fact very diverse, and while they were all luminaries in their fields, many people who would automatically have deferred to some of them would not have recognized others. It was his act of juxtaposing the names and statements of individually eminent personages that constructed them as an authoritative and definitive community. Carpenter surrounded himself with people who formed, as a composite, a body of authority tailored to accomplish immediate goals, but they existed as a unified group only for that purpose and for the temporary period in which their services were required. The incident suggests that orthodox bodies could be formed, but they did not preexist as stable communities who laid down the law on matters of science. This incident also calls attention to the ambiguities surrounding certain topics: even after Carpenter had identified his patrons, he did not know without asking them whether they would regard his claims about vital law to be legitimate or blasphemous.[59]

Although the "Magnetic Committee" was drawn from two different areas of scientific research, it was the closest thing to an authoritative body with respect to phenomena spanning so many areas of natural philosophical study. It might have functioned in a similar way to Carpenter's "jury," had it been able to come to a decision publicly. Instead, while the members of these committees met twice weekly in June and July to evaluate the effects, according to the *Lancet*,[60] they drew no public conclusions. The fate of animal magnetism at UCH was to be decided in a very different manner.

Testing the Trance

Throughout late 1837 and early 1838 the wards of UCH attracted visits from several leading intellectual figures. Charles Dickens and George Cruikshank visited on a number of occasions, and Dickens learned to produce the trance himself.[61] Michael Faraday visited on 10 February 1838. During one trial, according to the case notes, he "suggested aloud various means for rousing [the patient]: advised us in her hearing to bleed her, and then to apply a red-hot iron to stop the blood."[62] They bound her arm as if to begin this procedure, but they did not intend to continue with it. They wished to frighten the girl sufficiently to give herself away if she were feigning the trance. But according to the notes, "nothing made any impression upon her countenance or pulse, or roused her. She heard not his words, nor felt the surgeons binding up her arm." It is not clear what Faraday made of the incident, but there is evidence that he had a lasting interest in animal magnetism. He would have found magnetic phenomena difficult to adapt to his carefully managed life as a public scientist, however, because, as we shall see in chapter 3, magnetic subjects were far harder to orchestrate in the effects they produced than were Faraday's electric and chemical displays.[63]

The notion that animal magnetism straddled the mental and the physical was proclaimed by another fashionable scientific lecturer, Dionysius Lardner. In June 1838 Lardner published an account of his participation in Elliotson's experiments and his confidence in the reality of the effects. In a series of joint experiments with Elliotson throughout spring and summer of 1838, he sought to prove that the agent involved in animal magnetism would be seen to obey the same laws of reflection as light. Lardner and Elliotson reported that they magnetized a subject by making passes at her reflection in a mirror, and that she could magnetize herself by the same process. A more elaborate test followed, in which two mirrors were placed at angles of forty-five degrees from one another and at a distance of several feet from her. Elliotson made passes in one mirror; and she was "fixed" in a trance while looking at the other.[64] The hypothesis being tested was that the mesmeric influence would impinge upon the mesmeric subject only if this influence were a kind of ray, subject to laws of reflection.

In an effort to guard against imposture, Elliotson, Lardner, and their collaborators used screens made of "various opaque substances," including "pasteboard, wood, metal, & c.," to keep their experimental subject from seeing their bodily movements. Nevertheless, when the mesmerist moved, the subject echoed his gestures, duly exhibiting the phenomena of "traction." "On one occasion, the patient being placed in a chair, at some distance from a pair of folding doors which separated the apartment from an adjacent one, the operator was placed in the other apartment; the doors being closed, it was suggested by Dr. Lardner what motions should be made. The patient was affected in the usual way through the door, the motions of her limbs corresponding with those which the operator had been instructed to make."[65] To explore the power of "traction," the experimenters decided to examine how much it would enhance the body's muscular strength. The entranced patient was asked if she could hold a hundred-pound weight. She confirmed that she could, but that her arm would be damaged by doing so. Eighty pounds was the most she could lift without harming herself. Lardner and Elliotson then attached a weight of eighty-four pounds, and the magnetist extended his hand horizontally. After a struggle, she began "drawing her hand up, and extending it at the same time slightly outwards towards the operator, and lifting the weights with considerable effort." She raised the weights five or six inches off the ground, and then rose from her chair. According to Lardner's report, the shift in her center of gravity (rather than the weights themselves) made her pitch forward, bringing this particular trial to an abrupt end.

In a further trial at UCL, Lardner, Elliotson, and Phillip Crampton, surgeon general of Ireland, carried out what were later reckoned to be the most extraordinary experiments so far. They wished to explore the contention of Dupotet and other magnetizers that, in certain states of mind, one's sensory functions became displaced from their normal organs and relocated to a different part of the body. This phenomenon may sound very implausible to modern readers, but such claims had been reported in the translation of the French commission's report, and had been seriously discussed in the *Lancet* and in Thomas De Quincey's article, among other reports.[66] Lardner and his associates noticed that the magnetic subject did not seem to be able to see food with her eyes: "when a clear 'view' of the food [from the back of her hand], seemed to be obtained, she suddenly turned round the palm, and snatched the bread from the holder." [67] They gave no specific explanation for the phenomenon, apart from the suggestion that the sensory capacities of the surface of the body had been transformed by the magnetic passes.

Lardner published an account of this and other experiments, concluding with a prediction that animal magnetism might take its place among other physical and physiological forces. The "exciting cause" of magnetic phenomena was "animated matter," and the "energy of the action has a necessary relation to the quantity of animated matter in the agent." A mental operation could activate a power in the magnetizer's nervous system that could "excite the requisite action in the propagating medium, which, being conveyed to a distance, may affect the nervous system of another animated being." These nervous changes then produced "corresponding mental perceptions and emotions." [68] Lardner's hypothesis heralded a new series of experiments and lectures.[69]

One participant in this stage of the experiments was Charles Wheatstone, whose better-known work in the communication of thought by physical force—namely, the electric telegraph—had just been invented the previous year. Wheatstone and Lardner made electric tests on a number of magnetic subjects, tests that Lardner said were inspired by the "manifest connection" of electricity and animal magnetism. Lardner and Wheatstone wished to ascertain "how far the operation of electricity upon that system would be modified by it." Wheatstone prepared "galvanic and electrical apparatus" that he and Lardner attached to two magnetic subjects "in the presence of Dr. Elliotson, Dr. Roget, and a great number of medical and scientific men." They calibrated the apparatus by giving electric shocks to members of the audience—the radical MP William Molesworth among them (who had been sufficiently impressed with the UCL experiments to make a donation of 30 guineas)[70]—and producing "in each case . . . a very severe effect." But when the shocks impacted the subjects,

no visible effect whatever was produced: they held the ends of the wire steadily, and apparently without any sensation or consciousness of any particular effect. It was observed, however, that a contraction of the muscles of the hands was apparent, and the patients were not able to disengage their hands from the extremities of the wire.

Leyden vials were subsequently charged by an electric machine, and the shock taken by each of the patients without any effect, except an expression of surprise, and a burst of laughter on seeing the spark pass between the jar and their hands. These experiments were performed on the patients in the state of delirium.[71]

Lardner, now convinced of the electric or magnetic character of the effects, said so publicly in a number of lectures of late 1838. Wheatstone never went so far, but he did believe that the trance was real, and he continued to attend Elliotson's magnetic experiments in later years.[72]

Throughout July, Lardner, Elliotson, and others tried to quantify and systematize the phenomena. Their work proceeded on the assumption that the magnetic influence worked on the mucous membranes of the eyes, and that the effect was directly proportional to the visual contact of the subject with the magnetist's hand or eyes.[73] Other experiments were aimed at "bottling" the magnetic influence—either with liquid or with a metal (nickel was considered a good carrier of the magnetic influence)—to prove that it was a physical agency, rather than the immaterial will of the magnetist or the imagination of the magnetic subject.[74] While the *Lancet* continued during June and July to assure its readers that the trance was real, it found these experiments too varied in their results to be regarded as successes.[75]

Lardner concluded that the experiments were a watershed in the physical and the vital sciences. The magnetic phenomena

require the admission either of an agency in nature hitherto unnoticed, or, what is tantamount, the admission that new functions shall be ascribed to some unknown agent; that this agent is material, is propagated through space in straight lines; that various corporeal substances are pervious by it with different degrees of facility, and according to laws which still remain to be investigated; that it is reflected from the surfaces of bodies, according to definite laws, probably identical with or analogous to those which govern the reflection of other physical principles, such as light and heat; that it has a specific action on the nervous systems of animated beings, so as to produce in them perception and sensation, and to excite various mental emotions. Of these several propositions we cannot discover any grounds of doubt which would not shake all the foundations of physical science.[76]

In short, the "facts" of animal magnetism were supported by evidence "as conclusive as any of the proofs on which other physical facts repose."

The fact that animal magnetism, straddling the various fields of science and questioning the nature of evidence, was an *experimental* technique for studying the mind, suggests that it could become what one might call a "science of sciences." It could become a means of exploring the nature and relations of the sciences. People seized upon animal magnetism as a means of furthering their own research interests and expanding the scope of a particular field, not (at least initially) as an exploration of the founding assumptions of their fields of study and the boundaries between different disciplines. But these questions surfaced anyway. Animal magnetism's practitioners sought to use animal magnetism to understand better the nature of perception, reason, and communication, the three activities most fundamental to the production of knowledge.

As the fashionable physiologist Henry Holland wrote in 1840 in a work that would become staple reading for Victorian doctors, the study of mind and nervous phenomena was especially difficult not because they were inaccessible to scientific study but for the converse reason: they were accessible and relevant to too many fields of scientific endeavor. The study of the nervous system took place on a "neutral ground" between "the sciences which deal with matter in its various forms, and those which have relation to the functions of animal life and mental existence." But the studies of the physical, animate, and mental "powers" were incommensurable with each other. Hence a field of study that necessarily brought them into "common connexion" would inevitably confront enormous challenges. It was this incommensurability, Holland wrote, that gave the study of the nervous system its present "obscurity."[77] To Elliotson, Lardner, and their sympathetic collaborators, it gave their experiments that much more promise, because success in explaining mesmerism would entail success in forging new connections and commensurabilities between the sciences.

The diverse connections mesmerism involved, between subjects of scientific study, even led people who were not enthusiastic researchers in mesmerism to grapple with questions of science's structure. After people took part in mesmeric experiments, they found themselves questioning the nature of evidence and the relationship between developing areas of study. Because animal magnetism concerned the body, the mind, and a putative (but unidentified) physical force, the issues it raised straddled the life and the physical sciences.

Magnetic London

In the spring and summer of 1838 animal magnetism spread through the metropolis. One beleaguered skeptic claimed that "[i]n every house, in every society, at every dinner party, [doctors who did not practice mesmerism] are shamed with a detail of wonders which they cannot deny and cannot equal; of facts which they have not witnessed, and of phenomena which they are almost reproached for not having produced."[78]

Many London doctors found they could produce the trance and even, in one case, the more elaborate phenomena involving the reflection of the magnetic influence in the trials with Lardner.[79] Medical societies began to consider its significance: a contentious debate in the Medical Society of London pitted strongly skeptical members against equally adamant defenders of Elliotson's experiments;[80] the infirmaries of London workhouses provided new experimental subjects;[81] and members of the Medico-Botanical Society, G. G. Sigmond, Daniel Macreight, and others linked the phenomena to the production of electricity by the gymnotus (electric eel), concluding that magnetic phenomena consisted in the transmission of "some invisible aura, or electric, or electro-magnetic current . . . from the operator to the brain and nerves of the patient."[82] Elliotson's associates and students among the radical medical community took up the science, with various results.[83]

It is not hard to see the attractions of animal magnetism for young doctors and medical students, many of whom began to make their own trials in the practice. Few of them could have gained access to Babbage's salon to see, much less purchase, an automaton that could mechanically display the feminine graces; and no one but Babbage had a "thinking machine," as visitors called it. But animal magnetism allowed anyone with a servant or a curious friend to experiment in the limits of mental mechanism. Indeed, if one considers that Babbage himself had complained that everyone loved his dancer, while few noticed the difference engine, one might conclude that animal magnetism was compelling because it *combined* the salient features of a dancing automaton and a thinking machine, and did so in the body of a human being. It turned a woman into a machine and showed that the mechanical part of a human being was capable, as the difference engine was, of doing intellectual work "without the exercise of volition and thought."[84] Among the medical radicals it also had the potential to become a lawlike, "philosophical" life science based in the wards rather than in the dissecting rooms.[85] It focused on the living rather than the dead, and it offered the possibility of therapeutic application, rather than abstracted knowledge.

The magnetic influence was by no means restricted to the medical and scientific communities. Prominent liberal and radical reformers, philanthropists, and literary figures such as William Molesworth, Henry Brougham, Isaac Goldsmid, Fanny Trollope, William Harrison Ainsworth, William Macready, Moses Montefiore, and George Cruikshank took up an interest in the project, and many of them retained an involvement in animal magnetism for years to come.[86] By the summer of 1838 animal magnetism was ubiquitous in London. Londoners and the rest of the country not only followed press reports of Elliotson's experiments, but took up the issue week after week in their private correspondence and in their dinner-party conversations. Chauncey Hare Townshend, a great friend of both Dickens and Elliotson, carried out many experiments in 1838 and 1839, both in London and in Trinity College, Cambridge,

FIGURE 14 In *Oliver Twist* Oliver falls into a strange sleeplike state in which he watches the activities of the novel's villains, even though these take place several miles away. Note Oliver's extended legs, reminiscent of the rigid postures of magnetic subjects in certain stages of the trance. Charles Dickens, *Oliver Twist* (London: Bentley, 1838), 2:206.

and was soon to publish a book that would be acknowledged by the prestigious natural philosopher William Robert Grove as sensible, "philosophical," and encouraging further research on the subject.

Charles Dickens had become a particularly enthusiastic convert. He and Cruikshank attended some of Elliotson's earliest demonstrations and he became a proficient mesmerist. Some of the more extraordinary phenomena on show, such as appearing to see into closed rooms or to be aware of events occurring at a distance, probably inspired the ambiguous dream scene (fig. 14) in *Oliver Twist*. The modern reader is confused by Oliver's ability to see events occurring miles away while he is apparently asleep. Readers following the serialized novel in the spring and summer of 1838 would have had no difficulty in diagnosing this state as magnetic.[87] Animal magnetism also intervened in the high political and fiscal life of the country when the leader of the opposi-

A·NIMAL· MAGNETISM.

FIGURE 15 This was one of a series of widely distributed weekly political caricatures. Here, mesmerism explains how Peel (leader of the opposition) manages to induce Prime Minister Melbourne to abandon the Appropriations Bill that the Whigs had been about to push into law. Author's collection.

tion, Robert Peel, was represented as having used his occult powers to stop Prime Minister Melbourne from pushing through the new budget. In this caricature printed in late June 1838, Peel's arm was outstretched in a gesture that simultaneously evoked the magnetic passes and a raised hand commanding "halt." As Melbourne slumped into a trance on the front bench of the House of Commons, the Appropriations Bill slipped from his fingers (fig. 15).[88]

Given the strength and breadth of interest in the phenomena of animal magnetism and the broadening base of those involved in the science in one way or another, it is not surprising that Elliotson and his colleagues anticipated in July 1838 that animal magnetic phenomena would shortly become accepted as having physical reality. But within a few months Elliotson would become a laughing stock in the medical press, his mesmeric patients would be expelled from the hospital, and his resignation would be accepted by the council of the Medical School. The explanation for this extraordinary reversal in his fortunes centrally involves a number of individuals who have barely figured in the story thus far: a number of sickly, impoverished young girls, the magnetic subjects themselves.

CHAPTER THREE

Experimental Subjects

as Scientific Instruments

OF THE MANY PARTICIPANTS in the University College experiments, very little has been said about a group that one might regard as the most significant of all: the women and men who became the experimental subjects. Dozens, at the very least, placed themselves under the hands of the Baron Dupotet during his first months in London. When John Elliotson began his magnetic practice, he chose his subjects from the hundreds of patients who passed through his wards. Some of them, like the young domestic servants Elizabeth and Jane O'Key, drew national publicity; most remained all but unknown. Yet it was on the evaluation of them that the initial fate of animal magnetism depended. It was also in consequence of their discreditation that the UCL project collapsed.

By the end of the episode, controversy had consumed the hospital for more than a year, and faculty had almost come to physical blows. The wards had been purged of more than a dozen seriously ill patients who, regardless of their condition, were discharged because they were now deemed magnetic frauds. The slang term "O'Key," connoting a figure of charismatic deception, was coined in 1838 and retained its currency among doctors for a decade. The fury attending these controversies and their lasting presence in public memory indicate that the status of experimental subjects had implications far beyond the narrow question of the state of mind of a particular patient. Claims were even made in the medical press that a successful charade would destabilize relations of power and leadership within society more generally.[1]

Human Beings as Scientific Instruments

Elliotson drew his subjects from a group whom Victorian physicians did not regard as individuals in the same category as themselves, and possibly not as individuals at all: their charity patients. They came from the lower echelons of the working classes, including many Irish immigrants. Some were domestic servants; others, unskilled and semiskilled laborers. Elliotson was not making a virtue of necessity when he chose these people. He could have carried out his studies on medical students, on other members of the faculty, or on the rich patients he attended in his lucrative private practice. And it is easy to imagine why Elliotson might have preferred another group. He could, for instance, have expected that the cords of trust and communication between him and his peers would permit a more nuanced understanding of mesmerism's cognitive state. He used charity patients not only because they were convenient but because they had special qualities. To learn what these were, we need to begin by thinking of how these people could give, or become, forms of evidence.

Members of the working classes rarely came to the attention of professional men like Elliotson when they were not being instructed or performing their duties. A telling exception to this rule is the massive body of evidence they gave about themselves to government-appointed committees. No other groups could provide certain valuable kinds of information. The poor testified about the state of their own health, the conditions in factories, and their treatment by doctors. In giving evidence they became for the first time publicly visible. To a limited extent they were trusted to possess and to communicate facts. This was not, of course, the sort of evidence Elliotson elicited from his subjects, but the critical importance of statements of the poor in assessing such social issues established a convention in which dialogues with "specimen" individuals could become "evidence."[2]

Among the people who became Elliotson's subjects, there were important differences—differences in their perceived relation to the British social body—that affected their informative status. The many Irish patients, who included the two celebrities O'Key, deserve special consideration. The English saw the Irish poor as the lowest of the low. By their reckoning the Irish were purveyors of physical and social disease, threatening the health of the social body by their very presence in the urban centers. Indeed, the very notion of a coherent British body politic relied on such fears of alien invasion.[3] Strong physiological language was invoked to describe the Irish: they were no more than a "mass of animal organization"; their "savage habits" made them a danger to peers and employers alike.[4] However, these unsavory characteristics became assets in the hands of an enterprising physiologist. One could view an experiment on an Irish subject as the closest thing to experimenting on an animal—a primarily physiological thing.

More generally, Elliotson's charity patients came from groups who were trusted to give certain kinds of evidence about themselves, but who were also socially invisible to his peers and were compared to animals and machines. Recall that he saw mesmerism as a physical force acting on the body's machinery, manifest not only in the body but in the mind as well. To prove mesmerism's physical character, an experiment should be made to resemble standard tests of physical phenomena; the best kind of experimental subject, therefore, would be the most animal- or machine-like.[5] It was essential that the subjects should contribute little of themselves when they demonstrated in their physical actions and their words the effects of magnetic force on the nerves, spinal cord, and brain matter. But because some of the effects took place in the subject's mind, they could be manifest only through speech. One would have to trust what the subject said.

This peculiar combination of attributes made the poor and disenfranchised the best instruments for the job at hand. Middle-class patients would have brought with them an undesirable obtrusion of their own sense of identity, freedom of action, and speech into the experimental setting. Indeed, Elliotson did make a few trials on his peers, with some success, but he concluded that their own expectations led them to censor what they reported, and his inability to control their movements impeded his freedom to arrange repeat trials.[6] Charity patients were deemed to have no such problematic selfhood or freedom of action. They were useful in another respect: Elliotson's demonstrations were intended as a showcase presenting medicine as a force for reform in society and for reforming medicine itself. His patients were to be regarded as the (passive) recipients of that reform rather than active proponents of it. A true convert to Elliotson's project would find it odd even to imagine writing the history of mesmerism from the mesmeric subject's point of view. If the experiments worked, there would be no "subjective" experience to be recovered.

One way to understand the stakes involved in these experiments is to ask, what techniques did people use to make the body speak, and how did they try to interpret what it said? Animal magnetism was one of several new medical tools for interrogating the human body in the first half of the nineteenth century. Others include percussion and auscultation (tapping on the back and chest and listening for congestion in the lungs), and the techniques involved in medical jurisprudence. The public culture of scientific display relied on the overwhelming confidence people had in their instruments, artifacts, and animals. And several of these resources displayed characteristics of people, as automata replicated human work, skill, and thought. Mesmerism worked the

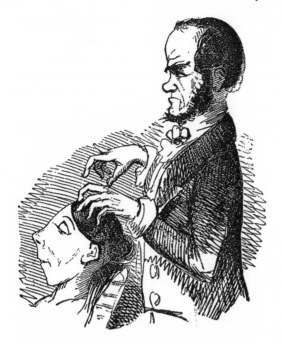

FIGURE 16 *Punch*'s send-up
of John Elliotson as a concert
pianist, appropriately attired
for the recitals that were then
becoming fashionable. He is
"playing" the phrenological
organs of a plebeian subject
as if her skull were a keyboard. *Punch* (1843).

converse transformation: a human being could be made or shown to be mechanical even in those most human of characteristics, thought and social interaction. Elliotson claimed that he could "play" the brain of a human being as
musicians played a piano, and figure 16, a caricature of the early 1840s, shows
him doing just that on an entranced plebeian woman. But while there were
many ways for the human body to speak in this culture, what it "said" would
be meaningful in the context of the mechanical culture of scientific display
only if it were thought to be produced by mechanism. Medical jurisprudence
could make bodily tissues "speak" of the processes that had placed them in
their morbid state; percussion and the stethoscope could "listen" to what bodily cavities had to tell about the fluids and gases moving within them. Elliotson dreamed of giving the speech of the magnetic subject a similar role in scientific research.

Animal magnetism could be presented as a means of interrogating the patient's body after placing it in an unusual physical condition. Elliotson and his
associates thought they produced involuntary phenomena in someone who
was rendered powerless by an altered state of mind. This view of what was going on made sense in the climate of the emerging hospital culture, and if one
accepted it, the experiments reinforced the authority and utility of the diagnostic techniques that were becoming important to hospital life. But as we
shall see, it would be difficult to regard the experimental subjects as passive

patients or scientific instruments. The usual materials of scientific display—corpses, electric instruments, and chemical apparatus—could all be expected to behave the same way whether they sat in a cupboard or were displayed before crowds in a packed anatomy theater. But the mesmeric subjects had their own ideas about what it was to be near, or on, a stage, and their own repertoire of "altered-state" performance.

A Visit to the Wards of University College Hospital

Many London doctors first learned of the UCL experiments from skeptical and fascinated narratives published in the medical weeklies. One of the earliest of such tales, sent to the *Lancet* by a medical man who had been invited by Elliotson to witness the magnetic proceedings, appeared in early September 1837. The author had a professional interest in the effects of the imagination in epilepsy, and he suspected that it played a role in the magnetic phenomena. He was also slightly acquainted with animal magnetism, his daughter having met Dupotet in Paris years earlier and placed herself under his hands for a trial. (She had, he assured readers, proved quite an "impracticable object.")[7]

In August 1837 he visited the hospital. As he approached the women's ward, he joined a company of more than twenty, composed of doctors, students, and visitors like himself. He first saw "a girl, apparently walking with difficulty, who was stated to be one of the patients on whom the experiments of the Baron had been made." She was an inpatient, about twenty years old, with dark hair, and a "heavy look as if suffering under the effect of some soporific drug." She had been admitted for epilepsy and, through her illness, had partially lost the use of her left side. Dupotet asked her to seat herself in an armchair at the center of the ward. When she had done so, he began making the magnetic "passes" near her body. He drew his hands downward over her face repeatedly, sometimes one hand at a time, sometimes both in parallel. After a quarter of an hour, when nothing seemed to have happened, he dismissed her.

The next trial was rather more dramatic. The second subject, also a young woman, was about seventeen years old, rather short, with a "fair complexion," a "profusion of flaxen ringlets," and "Grecian features." The observer pronounced her "eminently handsome," though he qualified this by noting that her ankles were "rather stouter than the Venus's," her hands were "large and red," and her figure "slightly inclining to Lord Byron's dislike" (i.e., "dumpy"). She looked to be "in the bloom of youth and health," but was actually an outpatient being treated for epileptic fits. He later noticed that she had had a seton (a thread passed through the skin to allow the discharge of bodily fluids) inserted in the back of her neck as part of her treatment. He did not know any more about her, but wrote that if he were to "hazard a conjecture, . . . I would say she was neither servant girl nor sempstress, but the daughter of an artisan or small tradesman, who scrubbed her father's stairs, washed his linen, and did the rest of the hard work of the house, but still lived in the state of freedom and enjoyment which attends on a condition so comparatively fortunate." She took her place in the central armchair, "with no reluctance, but on the contrary that appearance of self-complacency which attends on conscious eminence in any line." From the attention she received, it was clear that she was known as "the patient *par excellence*, the *prima donna* of the 'magnetic' stage."

Dupotet then began the trial. He made the usual magnetic passes, drawing his hands over the young woman in a "waving motion." The long, smooth movements were made so close that they seemed to stroke the body, but observers, on the watch for just this sort of impropriety, noticed only one or two moments when the baron's fingers brushed a lock of hair or the edge of a sleeve. Several minutes passed. Our witness noted dryly that "[t]he patient appeared disposed to doze." After some time, however, a most unusual form of sleep seemed to come over her. She grew unnaturally still and, indeed, took on "the appearance of a recent corpse." All signs of consciousness disappeared. Doctors pinched her hands, "forced snuff up her nostrils," and shouted in her ear. She lay still. When her name was called out, however, she made "movements of impatience, such as I think I have witnessed in the cases of epilepsy." After these tests had been made, the "youthful Pythoness" spoke a single sentence: "O why should blushes dye my cheek?"[8] Why indeed, when the trance gripped her too tightly to let her feel the indelicacy or discomfort of the tests?

After being "well-shaken," a more mundane pronouncement issued from her lips. She declared that she would not be "turned out, as I was before, for the servants to laugh at." It seemed that in previous experiments the hospital servants had made fun of her. One might have taken her protest as proof of partial consciousness, or at the very least of some awareness of the people around her. It is striking, therefore, that our witness did not reflect on the girl's statement. One possible reason why he did not is that the notion of "thinking while unconscious" did not yet exist as a formally acknowledged state of mind, even if this possibility was acknowledged tacitly in many experiments and discussed explicitly in some philosophical works.[9] To ask this question would have been tantamount to suggesting that the girl was fully conscious — that she was a fraud.

This is not to say that the witness did not consider the issue of her authenticity. Indeed, it was his chief preoccupation. To resolve the matter, he examined various features of her physical and social appearance. On the one hand, there was her temperament, which had an air of the "*sensible et coquette.*" This suggested sophistication and flirtatiousness, and therefore ambiguity of intention and possible bad faith. On the other hand, there were those large, red hands that "looked like vouchers for honest labour." They testified to the stolid honesty of their owner's class. Finally, in his expert medical opinion, she was "much too pretty" to be part of a fraud.

As for the mesmerist, his circumstances told against a possible deception. Dupotet knew few people in London and did not speak English. He would have needed social contacts to find a young woman with sufficiently strong powers in acting and sufficiently weak moral character to play the part. Once he had found her, she could only have learned the part after a "long drilling" with the assistance of a translator. Ironically, while Dupotet's foreignness usually enhanced people's skepticism, this witness found that it gave his performance *greater* credibility than if he had moved smoothly through London society.

In the end the witness entirely rejected the idea of collusion and fraud. The phenomena must be real. Even so, he did not believe that they were the result of magnetic or electric influence, but rather of some combination of repetitive visual stimuli and the action of the imagination. He speculated that, just as the sight of running water could sometimes make healthy people dizzy and, in epileptics, could trigger a seizure, Dupotet's hand movements produced an "action on the brain" that was "sufficient in *some* epileptic patients . . . to bring on a real repetition of the epileptic fit."[10] He could not, however, account for the speed at which she was awakened at the end of the experiment. His story left readers with the sense that what had occurred lay entirely outside the established body of medical knowledge.

This tale provides an introductory glimpse of how animal magnetism illuminated and even intensified the processes by which people evaluated one another. Its public spectacle was more than a collection of unusual mental and bodily effects; the processes people used to assess propriety and authenticity were also a central part of the experiment.[11] The evaluation consisted largely of observing and interpreting social characteristics, and judging the relationships between people. The obvious reason for this, of course, is the question of fraud. But this question leads directly onto issues of greater scope. Fraud was a central issue in these experiments because mesmeric phenomena were *made out of* social relations and social characteristics. The evaluation of those characteristics was not a separate, prior activity after the execution of which an experiment could safely proceed. Rather, it was what the experiment was all about. Deciding what the phenomena meant required that one assert what one thought social relations were, or ought to be.

The Sisters O'Key: Prima Donnas of the Magnetic Stage

When Dupotet first began to train Elliotson in mesmerism, the two conducted mesmeric experiments on several working-class patients in the male and female wards. Patients suffering from nervous disorders, especially epilepsy,[12] were thought most likely to respond to the magnetic influence.[13] Some male patients were susceptible, but women and girls seemed more responsive. An example of magnetic treatment, taken at random, is the case of Caroline O'Shea, an eighteen-year-old Irish nursery maid, who was admitted on 4 July 1837 for symptoms of hysteria and epilepsy. After many days of magnetizing, doctors were able to put her to sleep. Less than a month later she left the hospital—entirely well. The suddenness of this "cure" is as suspicious as it is typical of these cases. In cases of hysteria, epilepsy, and many other chronic problems, patients were routinely declared to be "cured" despite a lack of any indications of steady improvement. A skeptical observer might conclude that doctors seized upon a brief intermission of symptoms to rid themselves of frustrating cases, thereby conserving hospital resources and avoiding the admission of failure. Whether or not O'Shea's discharge was a matter of administrative convenience, her case and many others like it followed this pattern. After her regular fits in July and early August were treated magnetically, she was "Discharged Cured" on the fifth of the month.[14]

A rough count of the inpatients given magnetic treatment (according to Elliotson's male and female casebooks) from spring of 1837 through December 1838 suggests that about one-tenth of the women (out of about 140 entries) and only a few men (all epileptics) were treated. Most of the cases were epileptic or involved symptoms compatible with a Victorian diagnosis of epilepsy: "affections" of the nervous system involving convulsions or loss of consciousness. Among the women, several of these cases involved "hysterical" symptoms, but very few were categorized as pure cases of hysteria, which in these casebooks tended to be the diagnosis for patients presenting with numbness and paralytic symptoms. The profile of patients selected for mesmeric treatment reveals problems of the central nervous system, involving violent fits and other convulsions.[15] There is little or no evidence in these casebooks of hysteria in the later Victorian (and more familiar) sense of nervous irritability, hypersensitivity, and suggestibility.[16] If this other understanding of hysteria figured elsewhere in Elliotson's practice (perhaps in his treatment of middle- and upper-class private patients), he did not, at least publicly, regard it as suitable for mesmeric experimentation. So mesmerism, for him, was a stimulus to the brain and spinal cord, not to the imagination.

Two patients stood out among those treated with animal magnetism: Elizabeth and Jane O'Key, sisters who were among the first to receive magnetic treatment, and the last to be discharged. They lived in the wards for more than eighteen months.[17] Both were young maidservants in their teens: Jane was fifteen, Elizabeth a year older. Both had been diagnosed with hysteria and epilepsy. Their local doctor, Theophilus Thompson, had brought them to the hospital after reading the published accounts of Dupotet's work and making a few, partially successful, trials of his own.[18]

Jane's illness manifested itself in spontaneous "fits," a term that referred to a regular succession of mental phenomena that came to an end after a variable period of time. During the fit, her usual polite, reserved character (the "natural state," as the casebook put it) gave way to a new condition in which she was violent and aggressive. At these times she became unruly and "unmanageable." The fits would seize her suddenly, last for periods varying between minutes and hours, and disappear just as quickly as they had come. They were consistent in one respect at least. Jane's mind moved through three states of consciousness or "sensibility," each requisite for the next. The first was the normal one, called the "waking" or "natural" state. At this time the illness was latent, and she appeared entirely healthy. The second was the "ecstatic delirium." Jane described it, when she was awake, as a process in which she was "snatched away." The third was the "catalepsy," an unnatural sleep or "coma" that tended to follow her delirium and precede the return to normal consciousness. It was this sequence of effects that gave animal magnetism its initial therapeutic purpose. Elliotson's first attempts to magnetize Jane were intended to sober her up from the delirium, rather than to bring her into another altered state. His (unstated) logic seems to have been, if the magnetic influence put healthy minds to sleep, then infusing it into the delirious brain might move Jane from the "ecstatic" to the sleeping phase, and from there to the natural waking state.

To produce the trance, Elliotson stared continuously into Jane's eyes while, from different postures, his rigidly extended hands directed the invisible stream of magnetic fluid toward her body. Usually he stood over her, fingers aimed at her forehead. The work involved not only great quantities of putative magnetic fluid, but sustained bouts of concentration and muscular effort. After maintaining the necessary pose, trying not to blink, extending the arms, and pointing the fingers continuously for more than an hour, even the most potent mesmerist might feel a little shaky and cramped—though no one ever seems to have owned up to such weakness. Elliotson and his house surgeon, Mr. Taylor, initially alternated their efforts. After the first few times, Taylor usually had to manage on his own. The process became less onerous, because Jane seemed to grow more responsive. Her fits were as frequent and as powerful as ever, but with each repeated treatment she became more receptive, as if her skin was becoming more porous or her internal tissues more communicative. After several weeks a few minutes of eye contact and passes sufficed to bring her from the delirium to the healing sleep.

Elliotson's terminology may mislead the modern reader, for the "delirium" did not refer simply to a kind of erratic behavior or an unconscious, restless sleep, but erratic behavior accompanied by a different consciousness. Jane displayed, not an *absence* of mind, but an altered persona. The development of her new mesmeric self involved an acute sensitivity to her social environment. Her deliriums were exacerbated "if her attention or feelings are much excited by the bystanders"; Elliotson found that she became "very spiteful and mischievous" in her spontaneous delirium; and her mischief was attuned to those around her.[19] On one occasion she was so "exceedingly refractory and violent" that it required "several persons to hold her on the bed [to] make the [mesmeric] trial." On that occasion Elliotson failed, owing, he said, to her "general state of excitement."[20] Although the delirium produced tears, tremors, violence, incoherent mumblings, and restless physical movements, it also ushered in a new temperament that was as fascinating as it was exasperating.

In April 1837 Jane's sixteen-year-old sister Elizabeth joined her in the wards, admitted on the fourth for epilepsy. Elizabeth, too, received animal magnetism, but as an experimental subject she was very different. Her medical observers described her as "a housemaid of diminutive conformation,"[21] "stunted and spare" of stature, with a countenance "of a chlorotic sickliness, looking pale and melancholy." She showed no signs of having made any "approach towards puberty."[22] Elizabeth's symptoms resembled her sister's, but they were described in greater detail in the casebook, perhaps because, as later events would make clear, she was the more articulate of the two. Like Jane, she suffered from regular fits. She could tell one was coming when one of her frequent headaches was accompanied by "a sensation of coldness running up the spine, attended with numbness." When it reached her head, she had "the feeling of being stunned."[23] Then the fit would seize her. First came unconsciousness, then a new state of mind.

Elizabeth's ecstatic delirium was characterized by "convulsions chiefly of the face, and trunk." Her limbs became rigid, her face contorted. "[T]he eyes roll."[24] Convulsions came either during the initial unconsciousness or, more extensively, during the semilucid delirium following it. Then Elizabeth developed a new state of mind. Unlike her sister's delirium, this state was not violent. It was characterized more by contortions and lapses of lucidity than by "unmanageable" behavior. As Elizabeth sat or lay in her hospital bed, she could converse, albeit in a strange manner, impeded by the spasms of her face and the jarring twitches of her limbs under the bedclothes.

The first mesmeric trial to be well documented in the casebooks was made on Elizabeth O'Key, on 30 October. She was in the ecstatic delirium when the house surgeon, Mr. Taylor, began eye contact and the mesmeric postures to produce the magnetic stupor. In a few minutes she appeared to fall asleep. Her "eyes closed and [her] whole body appeared to drop[,] all spasms being for the moment relaxed[.]" At this point, however, "almost instantly she raised the eyelids and the eyes were again convulsed." Elliotson proposed that two people might have a greater magnetic effect than one, and added his own efforts. After several minutes she fell into a "profound sleep" and, shortly thereafter, "suddenly recovered from the fit in her right senses."[25] She continued "sensible" for the next few days, relapsed on 2 November and was "recovered"—presumably with the aid of magnetism. This reinforced the pattern of her mesmeric treatment for the next several months, though bleeding and drugs supplemented the magnetic therapy.[26] From November through the early months of the new year she had fits every few days and was treated magnetically by one or more of the hospital staff, depending on the extent of the delirium.

Something extraordinary happened to these girls in the fall of 1837. They stopped being merely patients and became prized experimental subjects, pivotal to medical research. One year later their names would be as well known in fashionable circles as their prestigious doctor's. At the early stage of the treatment, the case notes looked no different from those of other patients. Most case histories ran their course after a dozen or two short scribbles noting the daily or weekly progress of the patient. Most required no more than one or two manuscript folios. Elizabeth's and Jane's notes ran to more than a dozen folios spread over two books. The first sign of their change in status was an increasing attention to what happened during the course of the delirium, rather than merely the time of its start and finish. At first the notes recorded only the timing of fits and conventional treatments (cupping, silver nitrate), but by Christmas they had begun to include snippets of conversation and to describe facial expressions and emotion. On 4 January, for instance, the house surgeon noted that Elizabeth was insensible to pain during the delirium, and that a "remarkable difference also [was] observed during this delirium in the manner of expressing herself"—for instance, " 'I like you such a much,' 'It is such a big,' 'When it was just now,' 'When it is presently,' &c."[27] At this stage the purpose of the magnetizing process was still to end each fit when it occurred. It usually succeeded to this extent, but Elizabeth relapsed within hours or a few days, whereupon the treatment had to be carried out once more. The pattern was repeated, with regular success, each time a fit occurred over the next few months. [28] The case notes do not show a decline in the frequency of the fits, only a clinical judgment that in each instance the practice was able to bring them to an end.

One might conclude that Elizabeth O'Key's *mind* became increasingly visible during the winter as the magnetic treatment progressed. If, during the experiments, she could be regarded as a marionette jerked about by physical forces, it was increasingly possible to see her mesmeric self very differently: as an emerging, influential personality. During her trances she seemed to have no memory of her former life. She had forgotten where she came from and said that the "[h]ospital is her home and she has always been here[.] [Said] some of the students [are] her brothers and myself [presumably house surgeon Taylor] her Mother and Dr. Elliotson her father[.] [Said] she has six mothers." If one were to interpret her words other than in a strictly literal manner, it would not be hard to make some sense of this. A teenage girl, living for more than half a year in the enclosed space of a hospital and its small community, could conjure up a makeshift "family" out of the six house surgeons and attendants. A "home" could be made from the four white walls of the ward and its institutional furniture. This thought, however, is my own, and I suspect that it would have been too fanciful for the tastes of the exasperated house surgeon whose patience was wearing thin as he transcribed this little speech. "[I]n fact," he concluded at the end of his entry, she "talks all sorts of nonsense."[29]

The "nonsense," however little sense it seemed to make, was meticulously recorded. Whatever frustration the doctors felt was leavened by an anticipation that her words would prove to be the direct expression of physical force. Until mid-January of 1838 both sisters were magnetized only to bring spontaneous fits to an end. Elliotson departed from this routine on the thirteenth of the month, when he decided to try to create the delirium "artificially."[30] Given the role mesmerism played thus far, this may seem an odd decision, since the mesmerically induced sleep had been used for the opposite purpose. It *removed* the delirium. No justification for the apparent about-face is recorded in the case notes. One explanation is suggested by the fact that the cataleptic sleep had initially been a frequent, spontaneous sequel to the fit. Because Elliotson thought that the stages of trance (sobriety, delirium, sleep) were consecutive stages of a cycle, he may have expected mesmerism to move an individual along the psychic trajectory. Mesmerism could give the mind a push from an earlier stage to the next. There were certainly similarities between the girls' spontaneous deliriums and phenomena written up in the annals of mesmeric literature. The violent fits Elliotson had seen in Jane O'Key may have appeared very similar to the eighteenth-century mesmeric crisis, and the lucid state and strange speech of Elizabeth probably resembled the sleep-waking states produced by Puysegur, Chenevix, and Dupotet.[31] Whatever the inspiration for the trial, it was a success. Elliotson's assistant extended his hand as usual, and after twenty minutes "she opened her eyes widely and stared" just as she usually did as the delirium was coming on. While in that state, she was asked if she were in pain. She said she was well, and angrily declared that she should not be in bed. After a brief interrogation, Elliotson "extended his hand to her head for twenty minutes & she recovered as usual."[32] The state described in the passage above was similar to descriptions of the "spontaneous" fits. The only "artificial" aspect of this delirium, then, was its origin in mesmerism.

This experiment marked a turning point in Elliotson's relations with the sisters. Their delirious states were now a valued phenomenon—particularly those he produced artificially. The artificial delirium was "manageable" in the sense that its appearance was invoked by the magnetist, who then became its custodian. Once the manifestations of the disease were produced on purpose, they became valuable information about the nature of mesmeric effects and, potentially, the more general physiology of mind and body. Elliotson found he could produce a great range of the sort of magnetic phenomena documented in the literature—the French *Report* and Dupotet's book on the subject.[33] One of the last entries in Jane O'Key's case history lists some of her and her sister's feats: "All the movements of traction can be produced the same as in the Elder O'Key [Elizabeth]; the arms can be raised, the eyelids widely opened, when the operator executes the same movements in his own person. By a simple wave of the hand with only one or two fingers extended, she is rendered insensible . . . the arms & fingers remain exactly in the same position they occupied when the pass was made . . . The same movements produce the same effects when executed behind her, but not so readily."[34]

By the first of May, Elizabeth and Jane O'Key and the other subjects had developed an impressive mesmeric repertoire, and a speed in succumbing to the trance that made experiments quick and dramatic. Elliotson began to experiment with several patients at once, including Hannah Hunter, the mesmeric subject examined during Michael Faraday's visit earlier that year.

They [Elizabeth and Jane O'Key and Hannah Hunter] all three being first brought into a delirious state[,] he found that he could by moving his hand before the face of either of them (they at the same time taking hold of each others['] hands)[,] send them synchronously into a state of insensibility. When one was aroused the others spontaneously awakened. By darting his hands towards the fingers or legs of either of the trio, a distinct simulating motion was perceptible of the party operated on—this was instan[tan]eously communicated to her neighbours.[35]

The young women's behavior supported the notion that an influence passed from the mesmerist to the subject under the direction of the magnetist's will, and that it could be "communicated" from that subject to someone else who shared the mesmeric state. Behaviors could therefore be conducted from one person to another. The infectious mechanical mimicry one could produce by this process was called "simulated motion," or "traction." The passage above is one of several suggesting that, in the months following the first "artificial" production of the delirium, the psychic effects became increasingly complex and the interactions between operator and subject necessarily more extended. In addition to these physical phenomena, the young women had more to say, and as time passed people listened to them more attentively.

The Mesmeric Stage

On 10 May, Elliotson held a nationally publicized demonstration in the hospital's theater. This was its architectural and intellectual center, scene of its most important and prestigious activities. Bringing a patient from the peripheral wards to this place announced the importance of the vicissitudes of her body and mind. Jeremy Bentham's corpse had been dissected here; Robert Grant's lectures on comparative anatomy were delivered to students in these banks of seats; the knife of the master of the surgical stage, Robert Liston, did its speedy work at its wooden table. Figure 17 is a photograph taken in the theater some decades later, probably in the 1890s. If one removes the late-Victorian, hygienic surgeon and nurse from the scene, and focuses on the closely set, tiered benches, it is possible to gain some sense of what kind of a theatrical space this was for early Victorians. Audiences were placed in concentric semicircles to encourage the closest attention to the action on the stage, and the small size of the platform, coupled with the steep pitch of the rows of seats, placed observers within a few feet of the performers.

Among the hundreds who pressed into the theater's insufficient sitting room were several elite intellectual and medical figures, several members of Parliament, trustees on the UCL board, and prominent aristocratic figures.[36] Some of them, such as Dickens, Cruikshank, and Faraday, had been privy to Elliotson's private demonstrations. As for the rest, this was probably the first occasion on which they had assembled with the specific purpose of attending to the words and actions of a young working-class girl.

Elliotson chose only his most reliable and dramatic subject, Elizabeth O'Key, for this first public show. When she was carried on stage, she was already deep in the calm, sleeplike stage of the magnetic trance. With a few passes Elliotson brought her into the special state of "sleep-waking," or the

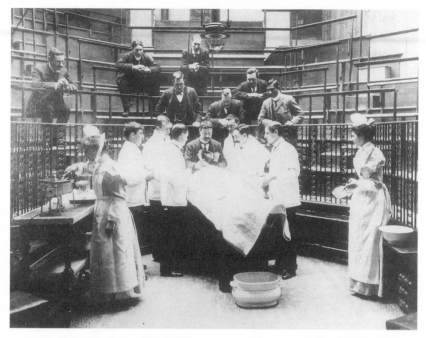

FIGURE 17 University College Hospital Theatre, c. 1890. University College London Archives.

artificial delirium, in which the magnetic phenomena appeared. At this point, according to the *Lancet,* her "dull and hippocratic" countenance changed to one of "mingled archness and simplicity." The most "accomplished actor that ever trod the stage," it concluded, "could not have presented the change with a truer show of reality."[37]

The delirium once established, O'Key displayed a number of striking phenomena. The ones that most impressed the *Lancet* were forms of "traction," produced when bodily movements by Elliotson and his assistant were made outside her field of vision. She echoed them in her own arms, legs, and face. At one point, "[t]he hands of the patient were then clasped, and she was told to keep them together, when the Doctor, from behind her, spread his arms, and, pointing to each elbow, drew his hands outwards and backwards from the body of the girl, who certainly did not see the process. After a few of these motions her arms attempted to follow, but the hands were firmly clasped. Gradually, however, her arms straightened, and the ends of her fingers, in keeping their hold, dug into the back of each hand."[38] As her hands moved apart, her "countenance [indicated] the greatest effort to prevent [their] separation." She even cried out, "[D]on't you; oh don't; pray don't," suggesting an opposition of body and mind that could only have heightened the drama of the situation.

O'Key's entranced mind contributed to the display in other ways, too. She directly engaged members of the audience in conversation and regaled them with jokes and songs—the latter despite Elliotson's instructions to the contrary.[39] Her interlocutors also included inanimate objects and parts of the body: boots, a wooden board, and her own hands. In the course of one experiment, a "mill board was . . . placed before her face for some experiment." She surprised the doctors by admonishing it. "Oh, you nasty boy," she said, "What a dirty black fellow you are."[40] However inexplicable this behavior may appear, the mesmeric literature did provide an explanation. French mesmerists had documented a phenomenon known as "transposition of the senses." During the magnetic trance, the action of certain sense organs would be displaced to other parts of the body. At times O'Key appeared to see or to hear with inappropriate bodily parts—the back of her hand, for instance, or her stomach. Confusing inanimate objects for people could be seen as a variation of a phenomenon involving changes in the geography of sensation, the difference being that this effect involved shifts in the object of sight and hearing, rather than the organ that perceived the object.[41] Accordingly, everything O'Key said and did was meticulously documented in the hope that it might be traced to the appropriate physiological cause.

Elliotson's ambition was not merely to develop plausible narrative explanations of these behaviors, but to use individual cases as a foundation for a quantitative science. At the end of the demonstration, he gave a preliminary example of how one might begin to quantify apparently qualitative effects, by counting the number of passes that were required to move his patient from one stage of the mesmeric phenomena to the next. Elliotson concluded that, eventually, one could calibrate the influence of " 'mass,' or 'surface,' and in 'numbers' " by studying the relative contributions to the effects of the mass and the exposed surface area of the magnetizer's hand. This speculation was offered as a promissory note for future demonstrations. As Elliotson brought the demonstration to a close, he made it clear that this was just the beginning of what animal magnetism could do.

The public debut of Elliotson's "new science" would seem to have been a great success.[42] The only problem was that at the moment when everyone expected O'Key would awaken, Elliotson found that he could not rouse her. Some awkward moments passed for an audience who, after sitting still for hours, knew they could not leave their seats until the star performer had left the stage. All the ordinary means failed, until, in an unprecedented development, Elliotson asked his clinical clerk, Mr. Wood, to ask O'Key herself when she would awaken and what needed to be done to accomplish this. She replied that she would come awake

"In five minutes."
"Shall you awaken yourself?"—"No."
"How then?"—"You must wake me."
"In what way?"—"By rubbing my neck."[43]

Elliotson himself carried out this procedure but to no effect. The orders had been given to Wood, and only when *he* obeyed them did she emerge from the trance. This was the most dramatic obstacle that the entranced O'Key placed in Elliotson's way. As we shall see, it foreshadowed other, more spectacular actions.

When O'Key did awaken, she was transformed. The mischievous, playful, authoritative mesmeric subject was replaced by a shy servant girl. "No two manners," reported the *Lancet,* could have differed more than "her deportment now and that which she presented during the 'delirium.'" She had been strong and outgoing during the trance; now she was "downcast and reserved." She had been lively and playful; now she showed signs of "fatigue." As she left, the "throng of persons opened to let her pass," and "many gentlemen, won by her apparent amiability, shook hands with her." O'Key acknowledged their compliment "engagingly" with a "slight curtesy, seemingly greatly wearied, depressed, and much abashed at her situation."[44]

Modern readers may find it surprising that these events were recorded by the leading medical journal of the day as pathbreaking new medical discoveries. Many will find the mesmeric phenomena implausible. Rather than dismissing the London intelligentsia as credulous, however, it is more reasonable to see the divide between our notions of plausibility and theirs as growing out of more general differences between the Victorian period and the late twentieth century. These individuals lived in a world made up of very different mental, physiological, and natural possibilities, and if their skepticism was roused differently, this was not for lack of intelligence or a critical sensibility.

Having stressed the plausibility these experiments could have for observers, I should emphasize that the phenomena they produced were very controversial. Skeptics on the medical school's council were outraged by the experiments, for reasons that will be discussed below. After a prolonged series of meetings and negotiations, the council judged that Elliotson could not use the hospital theater for future mesmeric performances.

Elliotson held a second public demonstration on the second of June, this time in a smaller room.[45] Once again, he drew a spectacular array of Londoners.[46] Many of them could not find seats, due to the change of venue. No other room was built for a large display, and the audience was crammed into a space too small for its numbers. The bishop of Norwich stood for the whole of the three-hour proceedings, and the songwriter and poet Thomas Moore, complained the *Lancet*, had to perch on a shelf, "whence, at the end of more than two hours and a half, he descended, covered with whitening from the walls."

This time Elliotson displayed several magnetic subjects, both male and female, as a warm-up group for Elizabeth O'Key. They displayed what were by now routine mesmeric phenomena: apparent sleep, insensibility, and a suspension of the will. When O'Key made her entrance, she was fully awake. Elliotson had not mesmerized her in advance, as he had done on the previous occasion, because he wished to display the full cycle of effects. These were fourfold. The first was her natural state, unaffected by magnetism or her epilepsy, when she was "reserved and quiet, rational and sensible." The audience saw this for itself. The second state was produced after the usual eye contact and extended arm movements. The *Lancet*, paraphrasing Elliotson, described it as a "harmless delirium." In this state O'Key displayed "vivacity, kindness, and familiarity of manner . . . with constant talk," as well as "brilliancy of the eye, [and] smiles." A single magnetic pass invoked the third state, when "her eyelids dropped two-thirds or more over the eyes, the eyes directed very slightly inward toward the nose, a shade of thoughtfulness appearing on the brow, and the mouth closing." Finally, a few more passes brought on the fourth state, a "deep sleep." Unlike the spontaneous delirium, which could only move progressively through its cycle, one could move from this state, as it were, both backward and forward. The subject could either be awakened or returned to the earlier delirium at the pleasure of the mesmerist.[47]

Elliotson chose to return her to the lucid state at this point, in order to show the audience still stranger phenomena than they had seen in May. At one point the doctors told O'Key to extend her arm horizontally, in order to reveal the unnatural strength and rigidity of the limbs during the trance. Her arm remained outstretched, observers confirmed, even when a weight of over fifty pounds was attached to it. In another trial suggesting that the mesmeric influence, like some physical forces, could pass through solid objects, O'Key was requested to place her hands against one side of a wooden board held vertically in front of her. When the anatomist Robert Grant placed his hands against the other side, she was "fixed" in a deep trance state.[48]

Jane O'Key then joined her sister, and both performed extraordinary feats of enhanced perception. Solid objects seemed to become transparent to their eyes: doors, boxes, even the surface of the body. There were also more instances of "community of sensation," or the sharing of the mesmerist's taste, touch, and smell. The common ground among these various effects was the erosion of the ordinary boundaries between the mind (and bodily perceptions) and other things. They claimed that they could diagnose other patients' diseases, prescribe for themselves and others, and even give a prognosis (including that of continued life or impending death).[49] They also seemed to have the ability to wield the mesmeric power themselves, placing each other, and third parties, under the influence.

How could a physiological force, acting on the brain and nerves, give someone the supernatural ability to see through solid objects, to view the internal organs of the body, and to tell the future? According to Elliotson, it didn't. The girls were only *apparently* gifted with these abilities. In truth, their ordinary senses were enhanced to extremes. Elliotson and Wood thought that the magnetic influence heightened the sensory powers to extraordinary states of sensitivity, unbeknownst to the girls themselves. For instance, in the case of mesmeric diagnosis, bodily emissions related to one's state of health impinged on the girls' sense organs—particularly the nose, one would assume. In the entranced state, the nervous system took in the stimulus and communicated to the altered consciousness of the young women the relevant information. They relayed their knowledge to others (without being aware of its source) in pronouncements that had the appearance of the supernatural. Elliotson's experiments were geared toward showing that the body's sensory capabilities could be altered by physical or physiological influences, and that in this sensorily altered state the body itself could be a diagnostic instrument of its own or others' diseases. He sought to present Elizabeth and Jane O'Key as utopian physiological apparatuses, an extreme example of the physiologist's power to make the inside of the living body accessible to research and treatment.

These were exciting developments. More phenomena were being discovered every day. But each addition to the mesmeric repertoire gave added cause for doubt, if one suspected that they were fraudulent. Elliotson needed to demonstrate an analogy between the mesmeric subject and the mechanical instruments used in most experiments, perhaps an electric machine or a chemical apparatus. But as time passed, the O'Key sisters did not merely replicate scientific phenomena in the expected manner but became increasingly unpredictable. If one were of a mind to regard them as conscious agents, the changes in their behavior would have seemed to give them more power over the proceedings. As they claimed greater access to truths about bodily and mental states, they took on the roles of their own doctors. Critics would have claimed that the experimental subjects and the researchers had even changed places. By the spring and summer of 1838 some observers were asking, who was making the experiments on whom?

Carnival, Chapel, and Pantomime

FROM THE MOMENT that Elizabeth O'Key dictated how and when she would awaken at the end of the first demonstration, it became more difficult to represent her as a living machine. Before that, her words were "nonsense" produced by the trance. But increasingly, the *meaning* of what she said became important. Her first public appearance could not conclude without attending to it; and as time passed, not only did she invert the processes of research and diagnosis in her own treatment, she extended them to the rest of the hospital. She examined other patients during her trances, prescribed therapies for them (these duly administered by the UCL doctors), and took a pivotal role in magnetic experiments. As more patients were mesmerized, the entranced O'Key even established herself as a sort of broker of mesmeric legitimacy, adjudicating whether the newcomers were truly under the influence, or only faking.[1] Rather than coming to resemble other scientific apparatuses of the 1830s as the experiment progressed, Elizabeth and Jane O'Key became, in the eyes of many observers, more independent, more authoritative, and less reliable.

Elliotson's ability to treat a human being as a scientific instrument depended on a number of changes in the representation of popular and elite cultures in the late eighteenth and early nineteenth centuries, and in the status of hospital medicine. These decades saw successive efforts by a self-defined cultural elite to construct an unauthoritative, separate popular culture, including a spate of writings on the nature of public opinion.[2] Elliotson's experimental regime and reform agendas were related to this process, because, in the most general sense, he regarded reform as an expert activity separate from and imposed upon the "common people." His experiments purported to reveal the materialist nature of mind in both normal and unusual states and could be used to dispel so-called superstitions, and in later years he would write of "cerebral physiology" as the key to social transformation through the role he saw for it in the scientific reform of education.

The changing character of the hospital provided a more immediate context for redefining human action. By the early nineteenth century, hospitals were far more withdrawn from common culture than their predecessors had been a century earlier. In the early modern period there had existed few specially designated sites at which medical practice and authority were exercised.[3] Diagnosis usually took place in the patient's or the doctor's home, and doctors advised on the basis of patients' descriptions of what was wrong with them. As medical students began to be trained in places devoted to medical study, the status of the patient's words, mind, and body changed. Instead of apprenticeships, where one visited the homes of the sick, students spent more time in anatomy rooms, learning abut the living body from the dissection of a corpse, and doing "rounds" through hospital wards with their teachers. They learned not only to value what the patient said about his or her condition, but to use new techniques and technologies to ask the body about its physiological state directly. Patient testimony became only one of several kinds of medical evidence.[4] Within these several developments, Elliotson's project was precariously and ambiguously positioned within polemical representations of the relationship between popular and elite culture, and in a volatile field of negotiation between doctors and patients.

We already have some appreciation of Elliotson's project, but what about his patient? Following Elliotson himself, we might regard O'Key as a thinking machine. Like Babbage's difference engine, this living instrument was revealing capabilities that even its inventor could not have foreseen. Alternatively, it might be possible to reconstruct the range of meanings these experiments and experiences could have for someone like O'Key herself. Studying her is far more difficult than studying her doctor, of course, because the records remaining from the UCL experiments pose the classic problems that confront all attempts to develop historical accounts "from below." The subjects of such histories—the poor, the colonized, or the young—had little access to print, and even less control over it.[5] I have been unable to find a single description of mesmerism by a working-class experimental subject. But although our knowledge of these people is mediated by the narratives of doctors and elite observers, their testimony should not been seen as fogging an otherwise clear window onto the past. The medium itself provides useful information. These narratives, drafted by doctors as they watched and listened to patients, allow one to glimpse some of the ways that the poor played a part in the representations that were made of them.

Problems of access place obstacles in the path of all studies of the poor, but in this case the mesmeric trance drops an additional veil among those already hanging between our minds and theirs. Many historians have concluded that it is simply impossible to reconstruct the intentions, motivations, and purposes of the people they study, or even that it is inappropriate to try. It is clearly harder to understand the long-dead than the living, not merely because of the dearth of information but because they lived in a different culture. To use the language of mesmerism, they lived in a different mental state. The search for meaning in the words and behavior of a mesmeric subject poses this problem in a more literal way. Some have even claimed that an entranced person had *no* motivations or purposes, so what she said in this state can provide no information about her. Even if one does not adopt this extreme position (and I do not), the historian's task is at least as difficult as the experimenters'. The approach I will take bears some similarity to the history of class resistance—of taking the measure of a disenfranchised group by studying its ability to act in ways that belied the dominance of a more powerful one—but this will not be straightforwardly an account from below or a study of resistance. Nor do I propose to offer a definitive description of the mesmeric subjects' experience, because I do not think that any such account can now be written. It is possible, however, to reconstruct the various contexts that gave (competing) meanings to what they said and did, and that is what I will do here.

This chapter reconstructs part of the world of Elizabeth O'Key, and in so doing approaches the close of the saga at UCL from a new perspective. Elliotson's fall is one of the best-known moments in the history of mesmerism in Britain, but it is usually assumed to be a moment in which one man's gigantic mistake was revealed to the world or in which one man's scientific precociousness was ignored by a hidebound establishment. The sensation caused by the UCL experiments is treated as something of a historical curiosity. If one treats the experimental subjects as historical actors themselves, bearing in mind the factors involved in representing the human mind as a scientific instrument, the broad significance and national publicity that attached to Elliotson's failure become easier to understand.

The World of Elizabeth O'Key

The notion of the carnivalesque—of the world turned upside down—is a useful starting point for studying the experiments at University College Hospital (UCH), because carnivals traditionally disrupted or even temporarily inverted the social order. They could release tensions between different ranks

FIGURE 18 Unidentified magnetic subject. It was conventional to include a few details of dress or hairstyle in medical illustrations, as in this sketch. "University College Hospital: Animal Magnetism: Sixth Report," University College London Archives.

and provide opportunities to air grievances, though they could also become truly insurrectionist.[6] By the nineteenth century, England did not have anything like the festival of carnival in the southern states of early modern Europe, but fairs and wakes contained some similar elements. On these occasions there was freedom to act out aggressions, abandonment of social restraint, familiarity between strangers, and above all, inversion of the normal rules of the social order, though these elements brought fairs under the criticism that they were demoralizing and subversive influences.[7] Descriptions of disorderly public revelry proliferated through the middle of the century.[8] But the notion of "carnival" is most useful in a looser, less literal sense. It provides a framework for understanding one part of the significance of what was going on during these experiments, and how the relationships among experimenter, experimental subject, and audience were changing over time.

We gain a vivid sense of the choices facing observers by comparing two mesmeric portraits. The first, figure 18, is a pair of sketches of an unidentified magnetic subject, published in the *Lancet* in the summer of 1838. It documents her posture during the trance, much as it might otherwise have sketched a tumor or a new surgical technique. Her face has no expression. The main difference between the two pictures is the angle of the head. She is anonymous: the primary point of interest is the change of posture. The sketches use ordinary conventions of medical illustration. They reflect doctors' confidence that,

FIGURE 19 Elizabeth O'Key. This light pencil sketch was probably executed during one of the UCH experiments. The signatures suggest that Mr. Wood, Elliotson's assistant, may have been making additional experiments in graphology. Elliotson, Female Casebook (1837–38), University College London Archives.

in some important sense, the images do not depict a specific woman. One's belief that the images portray a mesmeric phenomenon (instead of a specific person) relies on the anonymity of the woman herself.

Now, consider figure 19, a more private sketch penciled inside the back cover of Elliotson's Female Casebook for 1837–38. The light sketch, probably done by Elliotson's assistant, Mr. Wood, conveys the fascination people felt when they observed (or perhaps "met") the magnetized young woman. I find her a compelling, intelligent individual as she is drawn here, in contrast to the depersonalized figure of the earlier sketch. There is specificity to her profile, expression in her eyes and in the line of her brow. It seems plausible that whoever made this portrait was finding it difficult to sketch the mechanized apparatus Elliotson hoped to make of her.

The image brings us back to the obvious, tantalizing question: is there anything more we can learn about how she herself understood these events? For those who did not believe that mesmeric subjects were mechanical beings with no intentions of their own, it would indeed seem that O'Key took a very different view of what she was doing on the stage of UCL from the perspective of her doctors and observers. Of course, we have no means of asking her directly, nor even indirectly in the way that historians consult the written records that people of greater means left behind (diaries, correspondence, and the like). But we are not completely without resources. We can reconstruct a number of contexts for O'Key's speech and action, each involving quite different definitions of authoritative public conduct and of theatricality. These will reveal the various ways one could make sense of her so-called nonsense.

Amid the publicity surrounding O'Key's case, there were claims that she was an active participant in apocalyptic forms of evangelical religion, specifically, in Edward Irving's chapel at Islington Green, where premillenarian ecstatics spoke in tongues and predicted the date of the Apocalypse. Whether and to what extent she was involved is difficult to judge. These statements appeared in hostile press reports, whose authors regarded such affiliation as a sign of bad faith or even madness. It would be possible to conclude from descriptions of O'Key's performances either that she was influenced by Irvingite religious practices or that observers merely associated her behavior with the so-called farce of the "unknown tongues." [9] However compromised the evidence may be, the possibility is nevertheless tempting as a way of illuminating O'Key's own sensibilities.

These claims of O'Key's millenarianism are informative regardless of her real religious affiliation. They reveal, for instance, that magnetic phenomena fit a contemporary Anglican representation of sectarianism: individuals laying claim to authority on the basis of their own psychic experiences, behaving with an explicit disregard for social hierarchy, and in so doing, mounting a democratic challenge to established religion. This characterization would fit Dissenters of many kinds, from Evangelicals to Quakers, all of whom had a heightened prominence in the wake of the repeal of religious disabilities legislation. The flurry of published attacks on Dissenters and Catholics, many of them associated with natural-magic literature, usually described mental phenomena and attitudes toward the mind that were to be understood as at best blasphemous and at worst demonic. [10] Whether or not such elaborate parallels were implicit in the attribution of O'Key's millenarianism, one thing is certainly clear: it was easier for skeptical doctors to diagnose O'Key's religious enthusiasm than to decide whether mesmerism itself was real.

What could the trance have meant to O'Key if she were an Irvingite devotee? Premillenarians claimed to pass into states of mind in which divine truths came to them as gifts from God. During these trances they were conduits, conveying this knowledge to other mortals. If O'Key borrowed conventions of authority from premillenarian ecstasy, she would have had a very different understanding from Elliotson of how one obtained knowledge from altered states of mind. These were states that revealed important truths, and they gave the possessed speaker the temporary power to reveal them. In short, the significance of the trance state would have been the *opposite* for O'Key of what it was for Elliotson. For him it was a state of utter submission not only to natural forces but to the mesmerist; for her, it would have offered a state of transient authority over all onlookers. Elliotson saw it as a means of dispelling superstition, and a confirmation of his materialist views. For O'Key, if she were an Irvingite, it would have provided direct knowledge of the will of God.

Another indication that O'Key might have had a supernatural, if not specifically Irvingite, understanding of the trance is that a weekly penny pamphlet circulating in London in 1837 was dominated by stories of supernatural states, influences, and healing powers with mesmeric associations: the king's touch, the evil eye, the cures of the seventeenth-century healer Valentine Greatrakes. Figure 20 is one of the rough woodcuts printed at the beginning of each issue. Here a comatose young woman is composing (and uttering) sermons in her sleep: her attendants observe them. The series included several articles on mesmerism itself. They did not draw on the quasi-materialism of Elliotson, but on the immaterialist claims of J. C. Colquhoun and the German physiologist Jung-Stilling, both of whom located mesmerism not in the brain but in the immaterial mind and soul.[11] If O'Key or her friends had read such a work, or even glanced at the woodcuts, they would have taken away at least a general sense that mesmerism was an immaterial influence with divine associations.

There is a very different, but equally important, context in which we might understand O'Key's behavior: the theater. Working-class theatergoing involved the accepted notion that not only the official players but also the audience "performed" during the shows. In Covent Garden, working people formed a special section of the audience, and, according to contemporary reports, they rivaled stage actors in their entertainment value. They had their own idiosyncratic repertoire, and there was a regular give-and-take between them and the stage players, who accepted it as part of the show. The "stage" did not stop where the audience began, and it was not clear where "center stage" was, in the dialogues that developed between the "audiences" and the "actors." [12] Someone like O'Key might well have frequented early music halls and free-and-easies, since as many as a tenth of their clientele were younger than fifteen.[13]

During this period changes in the theater reflected shifting class relations. The ordering of seating and ticketing became increasingly hierarchical, marginalizing the plebeian members of the audience. In 1836 Cruikshank caricatured this hierarchy in a sketch, "Pit Boxes and Gallery" (fig. 21), in which the middle, upper, and working classes are neatly layered. During this period the upper classes began to remove themselves entirely from theater like melo-

LEGENDS AND MIRACLES

AND OTHER CURIOUS AND

MARVELLOUS STORIES OF HUMAN NATURE,

COLLECTED FROM SCARCE BOOKS AND ANCIENT RECORDS.

BY J. E. SMITH, M.A.

No. 8.]	Published every Saturday.	[One Penny.

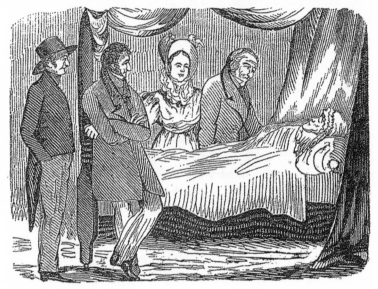

RACHEL BAKER PREACHING IN HER SLEEP.

FIGURE 20 This crude sketch of the religious invalid Rachel Baker was one of a series printed on the first page of each issue of the short-lived penny weekly, *Legends and Mysteries of Human Nature* (Smith).

drama and pantomime, thus designating these kinds of theater "popular." These changes were part of a much broader and longer-term withdrawal of a self-conscious "elite" from common culture. The riots provoked by the changes in theatrical organization in the early nineteenth century may be seen, in part, as resistance to a denigrating process of distinction. Given the charged status of plebeian theater, it is striking that the UCH performances displayed a similar ambiguity about who was performing and who had authority, among the stage players and between them and the audience. An uninitiated observer would have concluded that the people involved in the UCH performances— the doctors, patients, and members of the audiences—acted according to con-

Pit . Boxes & Gallery .

FIGURE 21 Cruikshank's 1836 caricature of London theater stacks the middle, upper, and working classes, poking fun at each class according to the stereotypes associated with it. George Cruikshank, *My Sketchbook* (San Francisco: H. H. Moore, 1836).

flicting views of how one should behave on stage, and where the center of the action lay.

There were more concrete similarities between O'Key's performances and one theatrical form that was becoming especially popular in London theater: pantomime. Pantomime has traditionally been a spectacle of defiance, disrespect, and contradiction, hence its most famous exchange ("Oh no it's not!" "Oh yes it is!"). Contradictions and insults are tossed back and forth in the dialogues of stage players and between them and the audience; the broad humor spares no one. O'Key's speeches on the UCH stage followed this pattern. They challenged the authoritative status of her interlocutors in astonishingly direct ways. Although she was relatively well spoken during her waking states, she uttered "vulgarisms" during the trance, and singled out various members of the audience to address them with "innocent familiarity." On one occasion, she remarked to the marquis of Anglesey, "Oh! How do ye? . . . White Trowsers. Dear! You do look so tidy, you do." She often mocked those around her, including Elliotson himself, telling him he was "silly" and "a fool."[14]

The published records of these speeches are careful to note that she never said such things "in her natural state."[15] Observers' confidence of the "innocence" of O'Key's "familiarity" therefore depended on their confidence in the trance. The following is a specimen exchange: "Dr. Elliotson having assured her that she had been asleep, she replied, 'Oh, Dr. Elliotson, you're mad; you're quite a baby; I haven't been to sleep; I wouldn't go to sleep in daylight; I'm going to make a parson now,' twirling her handkerchief; and before she could be prevented (a prelate and many reverend gentlemen being present) she had twisted it into a head and cassock." [16] O'Key was at liberty to speak crassly and to mock the man who was ostensibly manipulating her every state of mind and sensation, as a madman, a baby, and a fool. No one stepped in to stop her from caricaturing the aristocracy, the clergy, and the law.

The stakes were rising for Elliotson. It would be embarrassing enough to find he had been pursuing a false trail, especially now that he was so much in the public eye. It would be infinitely worse to be branded the dupe of a young servant girl, and to have been so badly deceived as to have solicited personal insults in the spectacular mistake of regarding them as valuable scientific phenomena. The likely implications of such an exposure were conjured up in a mesmeric warning, during the following exchange between Elliotson and his entranced star: "Relieved from [an] . . . experiment she placed her hands in her lap, and, leaning forward, said, with archness and good humour, amid abundant laughter, from the company seated around, which she did not at all notice, 'Poor Dr. Ellisson, would you like some sop, with some milk in it?'— 'No, for then I should be a milk-sop.' " [17] A "milksop" is an effeminate, ineffectual man,[18] and it was a striking term to use in relation to Elliotson himself. He walked a fine line between charismatic fashion and "dandyfication," and was known for his love of the latest fashions more generally: he rode the crest of all trends. First to wear trousers among his London acquaintance, first to dare new chemical treatments, first in the introduction of new instruments like the stethoscope, he cultivated a reputation for being socially and professionally intrepid. He ventured into situations that others shunned as compromising. In this case his risks were higher than ever. If O'Key were to be dismissed as a fraud and Elliotson her dupe, he would not only suffer professionally, but also risked his honor. He would become a milksop, an unmanned man.

The demonstration in which this exchange took place left its audience with another provocative term ringing in their ears. O'Key ended her performance with a song called "Jim Crow." During the 1830s the term "Jim Crow" was first becoming an adjective referring to policies of racial segregation in America. Jim Crow was also a new character in pantomime, and his song was only a few years old.[19] Jim Crow played the fiddle and danced a dazzling, heel-kicking dance (fig. 22). This song had arrived in London only in 1836, but already there were several varieties of it, judging from the specimens that have survived in broadside collections. They ranged from the silly to the subver-

The Real History of Jim Crow.

"Him so werry scientific
Him go down to L below
And ebbery one who hear him
Dance & jump Jim Crow."
(*Moncrieff's Comic Songs*)

FIGURE 22 In this engraving, one of many portraits of Jim Crow during the 1830s, he fiddles before several skeletal figures in "the land below," including Punch, a slave master, and a pirate. Mary Evans Picture Library.

sive, and it is striking that the particular version that provided O'Key's jibe involved a very particular kind of foolishness: a world turned upside down. This Jim Crow served up a crazily garbled Bible history. In his version of the Old Testament (or as he called it, his "almanack"),

... Cane was de fust man,
    Juvcome Caesar was de oder,

Dey put Adam on de treaden mill
   'Case him kill him broder

And den dat Mr. Sampson
   Was de man who built de ark,
Mr. Jonas was de fisherman
   Who swallowed down de shark.[20]

As O'Key sang, she stopped in midverse "to ask Dr. Elliotson if *he* had also "come over from Kentucky," like Mr. Crow.[21] If he answered, there is no record of his reply. O'Key then "volunteered to 'wheel about, and turn about,'" but, as the *Lancet* recorded, she was prevented—"to the manifest disappointment of many spectators." UCL was not the only venue where one could hear "Jim Crow." At the Sadler's Wells Theatre across town, a few pennies bought admission to Jefferini's daily pantomime, where this song had become an important part of the act.[22] Hostile reports of the UCH experiments took delight in pointing out the similarity of the two theaters.[23]

O'Key's song and choice of a blackface character are suggestive. She would have been familiar with blackface from shows like Jefferini's; in fact, the novelty of the character and song suggest that she could have referred to them only after seeing the show or hearing a description of it from someone who had. Both blackface and "negro" entertainers performed in the metropolis during the early Victorian period. These performers straddled the domestic and the exotic, the authentic and the fraudulent. The Jim Crow blackface characters were soon followed by "nigger" minstrels, whose popular performances were constantly appraised for their "authenticity" as specimens of "negro" or "African" culture (fig. 23). Popular caricatures supplied comical and dismissive representations of "Black" practices (fig. 24); at the same time, reports also evaluated the extent to which these performers attained European ideals of dress, manners, and artistic performance.[24] The "truly" black minstrels had to strike what may have been an impossible balance between a performance that could be judged to be "truly" exotic and one that displayed an ability to meet European aesthetic expectations. Blackface, on the other hand, connoted foolishness, alienness, or inequality, depending on the mode of performance. Such a character could therefore be translated from one form of inequality (race) to another (class and gender) in a tailor-made spectacle of disrespect.

A nexus of racial difference and authority also figured in the sisters' explanation of how their extraordinary knowledge came to them. It involved a mysterious intermediary. They did not have direct sensory knowledge of future events, but learned of them from a spirit: their "Negro." He made his first

"JUBA," AT VAUXHALL GARDENS.

FIGURE 23 "Juba at Vauxhall." A musician and dancer who performed "authentic" specimens of American "nigger" dancing. Such performers were appraised (paradoxically) according to their ability to meet Western standards of performance and their "authenticity" as specimens of Black or African culture. *Illustrated London News* (1848).

appearance in mid-May when Jane O'Key fell ill. She reported on 14 May that a spirit of this name had told her during a recent experiment "that the attack in her side was a swelling, in consequence of her ribs being strained . . . in lifting weights." A fortnight later, Elliotson's assistant described a number of premonitions of Elizabeth O'Key, in which her "Negro" accurately predicted the timing, duration, and content of her delirium.[25] The following is a published

"Natur and Naturs Laws lay hid in night,
ME Lectar to de blacks—and all was light."

FIGURE 24 In this 1850s caricature, one of a series, the artist uses English stereotypes of Black gesture to represent magnetic practice. Paraphrasing Pope's *Essay on Man*, the mesmerist proclaims, "Nature and nature's laws lay hid in night / me lectar to de blacks and all was light." Meanwhile, his light-fingered companion picks the gullible patient's pocket. Purland scrapbook, National Library of Medicine.

account of a dialogue between O'Key and a house surgeon, in which she relayed instructions from this spirit for her treatment:

Mr. Wood said to her, in the usual whisper,
    "O'Key, how do you do?"
    "I have violent pains in my head, and you will soon have to do something for it."
    "What is to be done?"
    "You will have to bleed me."
    "When?" (It was now about half-past five o'clock, P.M., Wednesday.)
    "I shall have this pain for twelve hours, and then it will be very violent, and I should be bled to stop it." [26]

The relation the "Negro" bore to the O'Key sisters paralleled their relation to medical observers. Both stood outside the social order, more knowledgeable yet less powerful than the observer to whom they conveyed information. This symmetry lends itself to the idea that the attributes of alienness and comparative weakness equipped one for being a medium or vehicle for the transmission of knowledge from somewhere else into a world to which one was only liminally connected.

I have discussed the religious and theatrical contexts for Elizabeth O'Key's behavior in the hope that they will illuminate the differences between her perceptions and those of her several audiences, and show how these differences rendered the interpretative context of the experimental trials increasingly unstable as the summer wore on. Whether or not the reports of O'Key's Irvingite past were true, they, along with the resonance between O'Key's behavior and popular theater, made it increasingly easy to construct accounts of her that differed from Elliotson's. As we shall see below, some accounts painted O'Key as a stereotypical prophetess, seductress, or actress. She turned the hospital around her into a chapel, a brothel, or a music hall. And her audiences became increasingly divided as to whether she was a physiological effect, a supernatural phenomenon, or a fraud.

A Tornado of Dispute

From the early months of 1838 UCH was consumed in disputes, as skeptics' fury intensified. Within this embattled institution, practically any project would spark disagreement, but animal magnetism was particularly contentious because of the various human performances it involved.

Elliotson clearly thought his patients were showcases of medicine's mental and social power. Animal magnetism would fuel the engines of progressive medicine by giving doctors a means of subduing, and maybe improving, the minds of the people. It could also provide a materialist complement to the radical Lamarckism of Elliotson's friend Robert Grant.

William Sharpey was one among many who became bitterly opposed to Elliotson's work, and he later remarked that Elliotson's mesmeric forays made him a "broken vessel." Whether Sharpey had ever thought that vessel sound is doubtful, given the ideological differences and personal enmity between the two men. But Sharpey was not alone in his opinion. For several UCH physicians the position of Elliotson's subjects was an affront to their basic working assumptions. Robert Carswell had trained in French anatomy and pathology, which portrayed the patient as an assemblage of bodily parts;[27] Anthony Todd Thomson was struggling to establish the field of medical forensics, in which, of course, medical experts made a corpse "speak" its cause of death.[28] For Carswell and Sharpey, to display a live, whole patient whose speech was the pivotal phenomenon was a betrayal of the basic principles of proper research and diagnosis. John Lindley and Astley Cooper were the only two members of the faculty to support Elliotson's activities, and it was only through their intervention that Elliotson was able to continue his work.[29]

It was not merely the *patients'* status that disturbed some of his enemies, but Elliotson's as well. When he stepped onto the stage of the UCH theater, he entered a space identified with surgical power, where hitherto only surgeons performed feats upon the human body. Robert Liston, the acknowledged "master" of the early Victorian surgical stage, was Elliotson's greatest competitor for students in the medical school. He regarded the mesmeric experiments as a direct challenge to his own standing and to his ambitions for surgery more generally. Liston's definition of surgical authority required that patients be seen only in highly disciplined states—for instance, under the hands of medical attendants, or strapped to the worn wooden table, through the rows of holes that were driven through its sides for that purpose. Liston, David Daniel Davis, and Thomson envisaged a future state of surgery in which a disciplined, quiescent body was subject to professionalized medical and surgical management. Elliotson's unruly magnetic subjects were literally a walking, talking mockery of those reforms.

One might protest that animal magnetism was, itself, a form of discipline. After all, it was a force imposing its influence upon the body and mind. But in order to accept this definition, one had already to believe in the reality of the phenomena; and the various forms of impropriety that Elliotson's critics saw in the patients' behavior made it hard for them to believe that they were acting in good faith. In short, mesmerism revealed something circular about how medicine defined propriety and discipline. It was hard to credit the only evidence that existed for the phenomena—the behavior of the patients—and to believe that these phenomena "disciplined" the patients' bodies, unless one subscribed to a particular definition of propriety and discipline from the start.

After a number of fraught medical school council meetings toward the end of April 1838, Elliotson had been pressured to cease the private demonstrations he had been carrying out in the first months of that year.[30] His flamboyant reply was to stage the large public demonstration on 10 May. Shortly thereafter, he wrote to the council to justify his move. Demand for a public viewing was so widespread among the "highest scientific characters of Oxford & Cambridge, of the Royal Society, King's College & of the great body of medical men engaged in private practice and in the public schools," he explained, that if he had not held such a display he would have left the hospital open to accusations of "illiberality" and secretiveness.[31] These attributes were particularly to be abhorred at UCL, which had been founded to break the "illiberal" monopoly held by the ancient universities. The council met throughout June to debate how to respond to Elliotson's demonstrations, first refusing him permission to use the theater, and then banning him from public displays entirely. He could practice mesmerism only for therapeutic purposes.[32] But Elliotson chose to interpret the meaning of both "public" and "therapeutic" creatively, and an outsider ignorant of these council decisions would have assumed that public experiments were proceeding as usual.

Even before Elliotson's first public display, people were fighting over the question of the propriety and reality of animal magnetism. From early 1838 the dispute over the status of the magnetic subjects had spread through the national press. Newspapers and medical journals had followed the experiments ever since Dupotet arrived at UCL in 1837, and the medical journals were at odds over them. The *Lancet* and the *Medical Times* supported Elliotson's work and detailed his experiments.[33] The moderate *Medico-Chirurgical Review* and *British and Foreign Medical Review* were dismissive, and the society weekly, the *Medical Gazette*, was implacably opposed. The daily *Times* and weekly *Athenaeum*, who got their medicine from the *Medical Gazette*, printed excerpts from it, although some notices in the *Athenaeum* also vouched for the reality of the effects. The *Examiner* condemned, not the experiments themselves, but the publicity attending them; the general quarterlies, while skeptical, either affirmed their confidence in a portion of the phenomena, or judged that they might eventually be proved true.[34]

Elliotson continued to hold trials of animal magnetism in June and July before smaller groups in the wards. It was during this time that Dionysius Lardner, Charles Wheatstone, Charles Dickens, and others regularly took part as witnesses or active experimenters. But as time passed, it would be tempting to conclude, as some did, that the greatest obstacles to Elliotson's success were the very people on whom it most depended: Elizabeth and Jane O'Key.

The Collapse of Elliotson's Project

During July and August, claims of mesmerism's fraudulence intensified. At the same time, people were beginning to ask about Elliotson's own mental state. To the most cynical skeptics, the mesmeric carnival had now turned the medical world completely upside down: Elizabeth O'Key was completely sane and sober; Elliotson, on the other hand, had developed a peculiar mental state in which his every professional thought was controlled by her. Ironically, those onlookers who thought O'Key was a fraud did believe her when she pronounced "Dr. Ellisson" a "fool."

The tide of medical opinion turned in mid-August, when Thomas Wakley staged a spectacular discreditation. Initially, Wakley had thrown the weight of his journal behind Elliotson's experiments, in part because he hoped they would make medicine more scientific and give doctors more authority. As the demonstrations progressed, however, it became clear that he thought animal magnetism produced the opposite of the quiescent, deferential patient of reformist medicine. The subjects, and possibly the would-be science that studied them, could not be controlled.

The fourth *Lancet* report, published in July 1838, warned that the phenomena "are not absolute, or certain." A number of mesmeric subjects—Ann Ross, Charlotte Bentley, and a few unnamed others—had confessed to pretending the mesmeric effects. While they did not have, individually, the significance of either of the O'Key sisters, a case of fraud necessarily raised questions about the whole enterprise.[35] It suggested that Elliotson was not fully in control of his experiments. The fifth report openly declared the *Lancet*'s suspicions. "A careful watching" of O'Key's "*character*" must be attempted, it warned, in order to ascertain whether her behavior was real. The journal apologized for not yet coming to a firm conclusion, but said that the character of the proceedings had made this impossible so far. The direction the trials had taken was frustrating because, it complained, "careful observers of facts" require "more exact and well-authenticated evidences"—that is, evidences for or against the O'Keys' authenticity. This was tantamount to claiming that Elliotson was incapable of controlling the experimental environment and enforcing the proper relationship between doctor and patient. The report refrained from dismissing the phenomena only because of their potentially enormous significance for that most important "department of medicine—the field of physiology."[36]

The matter was settled decisively when Elliotson agreed to bring the O'Key sisters to Thomas Wakley's home in Bedford Square for experiments. A trial was convened, its jury drawn (of course) from Elliotson's peers rather than the O'Keys'. The girls would be judged by ten gentlemen, five chosen by Wakley and five by Elliotson. The state of forensic medicine at this time gave the arrangements a special significance. Wakley, Elliotson, and many of their reformist friends were deeply involved in establishing the field of medical jurisprudence. Their efforts relied upon, and in their turn encouraged, a public acceptance of doctors as expert, trustworthy authorities, at a time when the profession was in poor esteem. Scenes like figure 25, a sober representation of Wakley presiding over a parish inquest, were part of an uphill battle to maintain that doctors used trustworthy procedures that got at the truths of the body. When the passage of the controversial Medical Witnesses Act in 1836 gave doctors a new authoritative role in the courtroom, one might have imag-

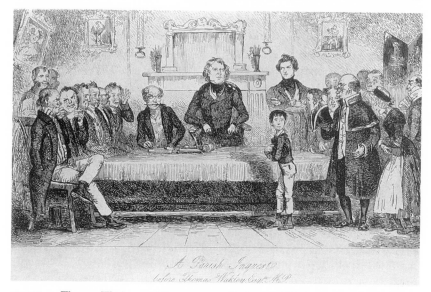

FIGURE 25 Thomas Wakley presiding over a parish inquest. Edinburgh University Library Archives (LA II.649/167/2). Reproduced with permission.

ined that it would make doctors less controversial as public arbitrators. Instead, public scrutiny of medical judgment intensified. The trials of animal magnetism therefore took place in a climate in which doctors, as much as the phenomena they were studying, were on trial in the public eye.

Before proceeding with the events of the "trial" itself, a brief word about the venue is in order. Wakley's house in Bedford Square, near the *Lancet*'s office, on the edge of a large constituency he wished to represent in Parliament, was the seat of powerful work in journalism and in politics.[37] Everything that happened there concerned medicine in some way, but Wakley would never have used his home for medical research or the training of students. The proper place for this was the hospital. He and his circle insisted, in the strongest terms, on its primacy in the making of medical knowledge. The medical school at UCH, especially, stood for a professionalizing shift away from an older patronage system, in which doctors had been taught by apprenticeship and studied illnesses in the homes of the ill. Hospitals made doctors into professionals and sick people into patients. Why, then, remove a patient from the wards? Because Wakley had already decided that O'Key was a fraud. She was not a proper hospital patient or a scientific apparatus. She was merely an impudent servant. There was no more appropriate place for her discipline than the parlor; no more appropriate parlor than one in a house that had become the hub of medical reform. In this context, a successful trial would be one that failed.[38]

On 16 August Elliotson brought Elizabeth and Jane O'Key to Wakley's home to test the mesmeric phenomena. Among these, there was one particularly contentious category of effects that on this occasion became a sort of "experimentum crucis." Recall that Elliotson wished to prove the physical character of the mesmeric influence in the same manner that other researchers were tracing the characteristics of electricity and magnetism, namely, by studying which minerals and metals conducted or resisted animal magnetism. Elliotson had accumulated a list of substances that could receive the mesmeric influence and then dispense it (water, for instance, could be mesmerized, and then entrance the individual who drank it). Of metals, nickel was thought to be receptive to the influence; lead was not. If Elliotson carried his point, he would have gone a long way to proving the reality of a physical force as the foundation of the effects. This line of research had been taken fifty years before, by a commission appointed by the Académie de Médecine in the 1780s (and composed of luminaries such as Antoine Lavoisier and Benjamin Franklin). The prestigious commission tested mesmerized water and mesmerized metals but could detect no sign of magnetism on their instruments. They then tricked patients into believing that they were being magnetized, at which point the patients duly displayed mesmeric effects. The commission concluded that the mesmeric effects were real, but that they were the result of the patients' imagination, rather than of any physical agent.[39]

Wakley's investigation followed the same pattern. Elizabeth O'Key and her sister were tested several times with mesmerized nickel and mesmerized lead. Elliotson and Wakley agreed that there were no definitive results. Then, unbeknownst to Elliotson, Wakley took aside a third party, James Fernandez Clarke, Wakley's deputy on the *Lancet* and author of some of the reports on animal magnetism. He had attended the trial at Elliotson's request, as one of his chosen witnesses. Wakley gave Clarke a sample of nickel that Elliotson had mesmerized, and told him to take it to the far end of the room while Wakley tested the effects of lead. He then approached O'Key with the lead, without identifying either to her or to Elliotson what kind of metal he was holding. By previous arrangement another bystander told him in a stage whisper not to "apply the nickel too strongly." He then applied the lead (which should have had negligible effects) to O'Key's skin. The results were dramatic: "Scarcely had these words escaped from his lips, when the face of the girl . . . became violently red; her eyes were fixed with an intense squint, she fell back in the chair, a more evident distortion of the body ensued than in the previous paroxysm, the contractions of the voluntary muscles were more strongly marked, producing a striking rigidity of the frame and limbs."[40] When Elliotson learned of the trick, he insisted on several more trials. All of them convinced Wakley of the absence of true effect; none of them convinced Elliotson.

In each case, he claimed, the experiment had been compromised. Wakley had no such reservations.

Some historians have faulted the observers for not considering the possibility of "suggestion," in the modern sense of a physical response caused by anticipation. But such causal explanations did not exist at the time.[41] In fact, they came into being in consequence of experiments like this one, over the course of the next several decades. Even though the eighteenth-century committee of the Académie des Sciences had attributed mesmeric effects to the imagination rather than to fraud, this possibility was not considered in the 1830s debates. And if it had been, it probably would not have seemed to confer scientific reality to mesmeric phenomena. The significance of "imagination" as a legitimate cause of natural phenomena did not exist during the eighteenth-century trials (their conclusions amounted to a dismissal), and it was only now beginning to emerge. Witnesses had to choose between a capriciously acting physical force and a deceitful servant. Everyone present, with the outraged exception of Elliotson, found it easy to choose the latter.

The jury did not render a verdict only on O'Key but also on Elliotson. By the time the *Lancet*'s report of the "trial" appeared, Wakley announced that he had invited Elliotson to Bedford Square not to test "the reality of the phenomena displayed" but to demonstrate the phenomena before his colleagues and to examine "the real opinions of the Doctor."[42] Wakley claimed (in retrospect) that he was sure of O'Key's fraudulence before the test. The only remaining question was the state of mind of her doctor. Elliotson, not O'Key, was the real experimental subject. Wakley therefore deceived O'Key, whom he believed to be deceptive, and Elliotson, whom he suspected of being gullible to deception. The fact that Wakley's most convincing results came from deceiving Elliotson, as well as O'Key, implied that Elliotson was not capable of keeping his thoughts from her.

To Wakley's fury, Elliotson continued his work throughout the autumn. Matters reached a crisis in December with reports that the mesmerized O'Key had been taken through the male wards to diagnose patients. The *Lancet* reporter seemed particularly distraught that her visit took place "during the twilight hours"—an especially compromising time of day, it would seem, for a young clairvoyant to gaze upon the innards of a dying man. According to the report, she passed the beds one by one, when suddenly she cried out fearfully that she could see "Great Jackie," the angel of death, hovering over a bed. "Little Jackie" it seemed, could be seen above another patient. The first man died in the night, and the second had declined markedly by morning. The episode triggered furious disputes about the connection between O'Key and the fate of the two men. The calmest critics pointed out that O'Key could easily have identified likely candidates for the attentions of "Great Jackie" and

"Little Jackie." But there was also talk that O'Key was possessed, and that the shock of hearing these pronouncements had killed one man outright and caused the "sinking" of another. Elliotson's explanation was to reiterate that the magnetic states made the senses "preternaturally acute." Morbid emanations informed her of their state of health, and she had expressed this knowledge by presenting herself with a sign of death that made sense to her.

The council decided that the best course was to expel Elizabeth O'Key and the other magnetic subjects. Elliotson submitted a letter of resignation in protest, hoping that pressure from the medical students would force the council to reinstate him. This seems to have been a possibility, because a majority vote by the student body urged the council to reject the letter, but moments before they read the results of the vote, they accepted his resignation.[43] If the long-term effects of the guilty verdict in Wakley's trial worked to the detriment of Elliotson and O'Key, they consolidated Wakley's authority. He was complimented by a wide spectrum of the London medical community, drawing grudging congratulations even from the rival journals. It is noteworthy, perhaps, that some months after his nationally publicized magnetic "trial," Wakley became coroner for Middlesex, securing his status as a power in the courts.[44]

Weak Women and Weaker Men

Once Elliotson's project foundered, its story was told as a tale of many seductions. Mesmerism became, not a science of human interaction, but a practice whose fundamental effect was to make people deceive each other and themselves, lose control of their bodies and minds, and become the means of each other's ruin. It was at this point that the *Lancet* ceased using the term "animal magnetism" and turned to "mesmerism," which became the dominant term of reference in England.[45]

In the wake of the "exposure," the other medical journals—with the single exception of the *Medical Times*, which continued to support Elliotson—took comfort in the fact that the sorry proceedings had been brought to a proper, if overdue, conclusion.[46] The remarks of the *Medico-Chirurgical Review*, although unusually colorful, are representative of the general feeling among the medical journals in early 1839. Mesmerism, its editor concluded with satisfied outrage, "enables every artful wench, under the manipulations of the magnates, or even of their brainless disciples, to set up as a prophetess . . . Every person whose brains are not in a state of magnetic coma, must see, at a glance, what irreparable mischief a PYTHIA of the modern Delphi may produce, by giving her tongue liberty to wag, and her jealousies or hatreds ample scope to victimise at the expense of others." [47] It was disgusting to think that there were physicians who believed that a "flatulent, hysterical, and impudent baggage" could "prophecy," and could "predict the operation of medicines of which she is totally ignorant!" [48]

But Wakley himself was the longest-winded on the subject of the detested young woman. In a succession of *Lancet* editorials, he furiously penned Elizabeth O'Key's demonic portrait. She was a formidable agent who exercised remarkable control, not only over her own body, but over everyone around her. Belief in mesmerism took hold in the weak and foolish, fueled by charismatic figures like her. He reminded his readers that in her *"delirium"* she had taken "strange liberties with the worthy Doctor"—a turn of phrase that gave her "familiarities" a sexual stain. She was "a genius in her line," wielding immense power "over all who have come much in contact with her." This "line," Wakley implied, was a kind of abstracted prostitution, a perverse manipulation of men's appetites for intellectual excitement. Where prostitutes spread disease, O'Key spread deception and dishonor. She was a dangerous genius, a seducer of foolish men, and a threat to society. She herself was morally weak, but her prey—men like Elliotson—were weaker still, because they gave her the power to deceive them. O'Key's career, indeed, taught astute observers what to expect from mesmerism in future. It would not die out, but would maintain a "precarious existence wherever there are clever girls, philosophic Bohemians, weak women, and weaker men." [49]

If, in the case best known to London doctors, the mesmeric subject had seduced the doctor, the danger usually lay in the other direction. But mesmerism threatened more than a figurative seduction. The practice was actually "a series of manipulations which not only injure the body but frequently lead to a loss of virtue." [50] In late 1838 Wakley relayed to English readers an alarming report that was going the rounds of the French press. A mesmerist had placed the young daughter of a wealthy French banker in a "profound sleep," whereupon "the quack stole her honour." Wakley did not believe that the young woman in question really had been placed in an altered state of mind. That was not where mesmerism's danger lay. Rather, mesmerism was a ruse. It gave "young and sanguine girls" the most dangerous of temptations, especially those "nervous and impressionable females" who were said to be most susceptible to the imaginary influence.[51] It invited them to pretend to succumb to the (pretended) power of the mesmerist, but in reality, to use the contemporary parlance for seduction, to place themselves in the (real) "power" of an unscrupulous lover. Mesmerists' "passes" were really pleasures, *"indecent assaults"* on the body that were allowed because neither party acknowledged the erotic purpose.[52] And now the *"private wards of our public hospitals"* were visited by "wealthy and, perhaps, libidinous men" seeking to witness or even take part in such assaults. "If we reflect on the *excuse* for 'going to sleep' which mesmerism affords," Wakley urged, "we must condemn unsparingly the vicious imposition."[53] Londoners had to confront these unpleasant truths, because the "Don Juan"—and who knew how many other mesmeric rakes?—had progressed to London in search of fresh meat. No one's daughter was safe.

Wakley concluded that, "in a moral point of view," one should not examine mesmerism at all. To allow situations to arise in which one could even pretend, as had the banker's daughter and Elizabeth O'Key, that they were under such an influence was "inadmissible." One could not afford to acknowledge even the possibility that mesmeric phenomena might be real. Mesmerism was a social poison. It had been the means of ruin wherever it spread, from a respected and well-educated physician to a young girl from a prosperous and protective family. Now that these truths were known, he demanded, "[w]hat father would admit even the shadow of a mesmeriser within his threshold?"[54]

Bodily Mismanagement

One way to gain a better understanding of how Elliotson became a "milksop" and O'Key a seductive fraud is by considering Victorian conventions of bodily propriety, character, and trust. Character, as opposed to rank and gentility, was becoming increasingly important in establishing honor. A "man of character" did not need the social and financial resources of a gentleman, for character was an internal state, relating to virtue and self-control.[55] In science, as in other areas of Victorian life, character began to define trustworthiness. Mastering one's own body was correspondingly important to scientific and medical credibility; conversely, negative depictions of natural philosophers and doctors portrayed their targets as physically out of control, or as subverting the self-control of others. The damaging implications of a lack of self-control figured in pejorative Victorian representations of intellect. Romantic notions of disorder and passion had been linked to genius and creativity earlier in the century, but, while they still had considerable force, they were becoming weaker than they had been a generation before. Physical descriptions of this sort increasingly connoted charismatic danger rather than awed fascination. They undermined the character and cast doubt on the intellect.

The importance of self-control posed a problem for mesmerism, because mesmeric experiments centered on less than perfectly controlled bodies—not only of the patient, but of the mesmerist, and even of the audience. Animal magnetism drew its power, in part, from the unexpectedness of bodily effects: experimenters anticipated that they would elicit unusual effects, but even they were often surprised by the proceedings, and audiences were regularly shocked out of skepticism by the phenomena they saw. The unintentional provocation of a specific trance effect was a guarantee against collusion between magnetist and subject; and, most important, the experimental subject was entirely unable to control her (or less frequently his) body. More powerful and compromising was the fact that the mesmeric influence was not contained in the relations or space between the two main parties, but spread to onlookers as well. In the process of closely scrutinizing the complex relations of magnetist and subject, other people could find themselves falling under the influence. Mesmerism's infectiousness gave even more plausibility to its effects, but it also made the experimental environment seem irrational and chaotic. From the beginning of the mesmeric experiments, people noted that to involve oneself—merely to be physically present at an experiment—threatened one's character, and to express confidence in the effects could "materially" damage it.[56]

At UCL, one of the most embattled of educational institutions, one might conclude from hostile accounts of its faculty that everyone was losing control of their bodies—that Elliotson had a great deal of company. Everyone there was consumed in some form of physical impropriety. During the period—the late 1830s and early 1840s—in which the surgeon Robert Liston was campaigning to make surgeons more skilled and personally disciplined in wielding the knife, hostile accounts described him tormenting patients with impossible demands that they control themselves. In 1840 the *Medical Times* gave a verbal "Portrait" of him pausing in the midst of an operation, demanding that a patient hold his body in a particular posture. Liston threatened to leave the operation unfinished if the patient failed.[57] In this scene, which nightmarishly portrayed Liston's vision of powerful surgeons and disciplined patients, the corrupt operator's sinister power was expressed by his control over his patient's mind, to compel the patient to discipline his own body.

If Liston's untrustworthiness could be conveyed by an account of a sadistic manipulation of others' self-control, it was just as effective to draw this conclusion from evidence that one individual made another lose this control. The "fall" of another UCL professor, Dionysius Lardner, is one of the more dramatic instances. Soon after his involvement in Elliotson's experiments, Lardner had an affair with a married woman. They fled to Paris and eventually settled in America. In 1840, however, her husband sued Lardner. There was no disputing the fact of the affair itself, but the cuckold claimed much more than this. In the sensational court case he alleged that Lardner had used science to bend the lady to his will. She had been a puppet in the events that separated husband and wife. Lardner had propelled her into the elopement, using his power as a natural philosopher. Evidence of this came to light when the husband pursued the fleeing couple to Boulogne. He found the apartment in which they had taken refuge and, searching it, found early drafts of letters from his wife addressed to him and to her father. Parts of them were written in Lardner's hand. The language of these letters, according to counsel, was "not the outpourings of a person with a troubled mind but . . . the calm, deliberate, and calculating reasonings of a mechanical philosopher." In a mesmeric mockery of the "oneness" of lovers' intimacy, Lardner's "calculated reasonings" were spoken by his victim as her own. She was *literally* his marionette. Ironically, the trial portrayed a young woman's mind as the mechanical instrument of a natural philosopher more successfully in this case than in Elliotson's, where, of course, success would have brought the mesmerist more satisfaction. The mental potency that mechanical philosophy seemed to have at this time helped to make this one of the most sensational court cases of the 1840s, and secured for the angry husband a cool £8,000.[58]

The Power of Popular Culture

The story I have told is based on elite sources. We do not have access to what the O'Keys' friends thought of Elliotson, because they were excluded from the places and publications that publicized the events, places like the surgical theater of UCH, the medical journals, and the stamped newspapers. For Wakley, Elliotson, and all the other doctors involved in the controversy, such people were to be the objects, rather than the instigators, of scientific research and social reform. They purposely excluded groups who, by virtue of their social standing and their education, constituted the vulgar and the superstitious. The O'Keys of Victorian society are consequently all but invisible among the sources available to historians today. Indeed, the reason that we have any sense of Elizabeth's physical appearance is that the details of her face and its expression were considered important in evaluating the reality and cause of the trance—and perhaps because it was impossible entirely to control her influence on experimental proceedings.

One of the many reasons that Elliotson was unsuccessful in reducing O'Key to a physiological effect was his overestimation of the ability of reformist physiology effortlessly to reconstitute deep-seated and common beliefs. His program was undermined by his working assumption that these beliefs were impotent, for it was belied by the content of what she said, the effect her prophetic stance had on other people. Not only were the common cultural views that were the target of Elliotson's mesmerism not as malleable as he needed them to be, but the sources of some mesmeric phenomena in common customs, habits, and assumptions reinforced the very views Elliotson was attempting to change.

The ambiguities surrounding O'Key's status illuminate a related issue in the history of relations between high and low culture in this period, concerning the degree of subversiveness of behavior that ran counter to elite sensibilities. In the case of the magnetic subjects of our story, the medical world was temporarily up-ended as the patients, ostensibly passive in the grip of natural forces, took increasing control of the medical stage. The experimental subjects were now directing the experiment; the medical patients had supplanted the doctor; the subjects of the experiment possessed knowledge, and the observers did not. This control never extended into patients' waking states. They became meek and confessedly ignorant once more, and, because they seemed to have no memory of the mesmeric events, there was no psychological continuity between their ordinary minds and their powerful alter egos.

If we use the notion of carnival to explore what "resistance" could mean in this context, we might initially conclude that it was just a way of releasing tensions and expressing grudges, of blowing off magnetic steam. However, a glimpse of the increasingly chaotic situation in the wards would suggest that the mesmeric subjects were sleepwalking (or, rather, "sleep-waking") their way into a real insurrection. The medical reports paint quite a picture: a poor Irish girl stands, clad in a nightgown, the center of attention in a space identified with elite, progressive science and medicine. She speaks in a familiar and even disrespectful manner to doctors, natural philosophers, members of Parliament, and aristocrats. She even tosses insults at them. If O'Key had been considered an ordinary human being, in an ordinary state of mind, this spectacle would have been an extraordinary subversion of public order. And if one sign of resistance is its ability to take effect in some real way, it is striking that half a ward of hospital patients were discharged, a prestigious physician resigned from his post, applications to the medical school dropped, and a hospital was in uproar for months.

It has become accepted that descriptions of many social phenomena the elite found fascinatingly alien, disturbing, and disrespectful are not to be understood as instances of subversion but as stories that functioned to protect and characterize an elite group by giving it an example of what it was not. In short, despite their apparent subversiveness, carnivals usually worked to stabilize an existing order. One of the most powerful reasons for believing that many "carnivalesque" occasions were not truly subversive is that they were *licensed*. If they were allowed, they could not be subversive. This perspective has been used to interpret offensive behavior in a wide range of events and communities, including the Victorian social reform movements in which Elliotson took part.

The O'Key incident emphasizes the ambiguities surrounding the cultural status of disorderly events in early Victorian Britain. If the O'Key sisters were truly mesmerized, then the experiments were licensed; if they were faking, then the events were entirely subversive. These either/or alternatives existed in 1838, and over the following years doctors continued to fight over whether the O'Key sisters had been faking—whether the experiments had been real or had been a sham. And over the years the categories of real and fake themselves became blurred and transformed; for instance, by the early twentieth century a trance state could become a vehicle of protest or resistance, and indeed, altered states have retained that scope of significance and action throughout the century. But if Victorians could not decide how to categorize the O'Keys' action, how could the experiments reinforce elite categories of high and low, self and other, in any stable manner? Similar ambiguities exist, in more subtle incarnations, in more familiar settings such as fairs and slums. There was continuing ambiguity about what was and was not permitted at country fairs, or how to describe the behavior of their participants. There was similar uncertainty about how to categorize the people who lived in the worst parts of London and the industrial cities: were they martyrs or depraved, knowledge-starved or willfully ignorant? The medical reaction to Elizabeth O'Key's performances suggests that the contested nature of mental powers and of individual agency was an important factor in limiting the extent to which the poor could be made into a sort of fun-house mirror for the ruling classes.

Only Rather Odd

Wakley and his circle were mistaken in assuming they had defeated mesmerism and dispatched to social oblivion the principals in the mesmeric drama. Elliotson himself kept many of his old patients and maintained a decent income (though nothing like what he pocketed during his tenure at UCL), and, even in the immediate aftermath of the scandal, he made new mesmeric converts. The O'Key sisters developed their mesmeric personas, and in fact, according to Elliotson, they each developed double identities: their "natural" and their mesmeric selves. The "mesmeric" O'Keys had been taught from scratch how to read, write, and work. After much tuition the sisters could function, to some extent, during their trances. They were only, Elliotson concluded hopefully, "rather odd." [59]

During this time the sisters were under Elliotson's protection and that of his friends. One of them was the novelist Fanny Trollope, who tried mesmerism as a therapy for family illnesses and took the O'Keys under her wing. She

FIGURE 26 A cruel factory owner haunted by the ghosts of the children he worked into their graves. Frances Trollope, *Michael Armstrong, Factory Boy* (London: Henry Colburn, 1840).

had just finished writing a fictional diatribe against the abuses of working-class children in the industrial north. One of its more striking episodes, drafted during the period of the O'Key experiments, combined a coincidence of working-class revenge and psychic phenomena, when the bedraggled ghosts of young factory workers haunt the industrialist who ruined their short lives (fig. 26).[60]

Neither sister would haunt their mesmeric betters in the years to come. Before 1840 both had ended their mesmeric careers. One of them, Elliotson reported, was living with her family and earning her keep as a seamstress; the other (he did not say which) was happily married. While the O'Key sisters seemed to have put mesmerism behind them, the rest of the country had barely begun to make its acquaintance. It would not only begin to prosper once again, but would thrive over the next several decades. This was not the end of mesmerism, but its beginning.

The Peripatetic Power of the

"New Science"

What an age do we live in! in matter of mind
We're leaving the ancients some cent'ries behind

. . . .

All matter is seen through, and so is all *mind*.

Opie Staite, on a "new school of the arts" [1]

WHEN THE MAGNETIC SUBJECTS were expelled from UCL and Elliotson's resignation was accepted, many people spoke as if mesmerism were a thing of the
past. The preceding year was a period of insanity, making some doctors the
horrified witnesses of mass delusion and others as mad as their patients. But
now the deception was exposed, and the participants "declared to be deceivers
or deceived." [2] Londoners could put the mesmeric incident behind them. In
1841, when news arrived that showmen-lecturers were touring the country,
the London medical journals voiced no concern about a serious resurgence
of magnetic power. [3] The "mesmero-mania has nearly dwindled, in the metropolis, into anile fatuity," one editor assured his readers, even if it "lingers
in some of the provinces with the *gobe-mouches* and chaw-bacons, who, after gulping down a pound of fat pork, would, with well-greased gullets, swallow such a lot of mesmeric mummery as would choke an alligator or a boa
constrictor." [4]

But mesmerism did not die a lingering provincial death. It gathered mo-
mentum and took the country by storm. By the mid-1840s one Nottingham

artisan would remark that "go where you would the conversation was sure to turn on the New Science."[5] The London editor's contemptuous gesture at provincial gullibility is a useful point of departure as we explore the next stage of mesmerism's history, because as people tried to understand mesmerism, they also found themselves grappling with broader questions about where intellectual authority and legitimacy lay in Britain: between the metropolis and the provinces, between professional doctors and itinerant healers, and between the classes.

A Resurgence of Magnetic Power

The magnetic fluids did not evaporate after the storms of 1838. They merely receded into the private lives of Britons, and would become publicly visible a few years later. Secret séances were convened by committed investigators like Elliotson, Mayo, and Townshend,[6] and in 1841 mesmeric currents moved through the country again, along the lecture circuits of itinerant showmen.

The early 1840s was a promising time for traveling lecturers presenting themselves as vigorous, independent-minded individuals unfettered by the stale assumption of an outmoded orthodoxy. A growing sense of provincial authority and of national connectedness was encouraged by the establishment of the penny post and the spread of the rail network; northern cities were being industrialized, educational institutions were multiplying, and people from many backgrounds and qualifications became prominent in intellectual life. Intellectual relations between London and the provinces seemed increasingly ambiguous.

One part of these changes was the growing importance of provincial communities in national scientific and medical institutions. The British Association for the Advancement of Science (BAAS) was intended as a peripatetic organization, holding annual meetings at different provincial cities. While in practice the BAAS soon came under the leadership of London elites, it was presented to and by its membership as a nationally based organization with no "center."[7] Medicine saw a parallel development in the founding of the Provincial Medical and Surgical Association (PMSA, later renamed the British Medical Association), a determinedly nonmetropolitan organization. It achieved the paradoxical feat of marginalizing the metropolis when it defeated its short-lived metropolitan rival, the British Medical Association founded by Thomas Wakley. By the early 1850s doctors would speak of the profession being run from Worcester—the base of the PMSA and its journal.

Improving societies and educational institutions were also challenging an old metropolitan dominance. For instance, the London-driven popular science program associated with the Society for the Diffusion of Useful Knowledge was unraveling. In the 1820s and 1830s the society had founded "mechanics' institutes" in the hope that "useful" knowledge (i.e., politically sanitized, class-coded, and practical) would leave no room in workers' minds for dangerous alternatives such as radical politics and irreligion. But the mechanics' institutes were now abandoning "useful" knowledge. From the earliest days the term had been treated with contempt by radicals who complained that workers sought the key to a new basis of social interaction, and that educationalists were trying to use classics, natural history, and the animal kingdom to "stop our mouths with kangaroos."[8] In the 1840s, improving institutions diversified, choosing lecture topics according to their own members' intellectual taste. Among these, sciences of mind made frequent appearances. For some audiences, mesmerism was a light amusement, but more often it was a significant (if inconclusive) intellectual event, drawing passionate and sustained debate. Indeed, its uncertain status was one of its main attractions. Its reality was an open question, its nature ambiguous, and its practice easily taught. Its nebulous character meant that it could not be defined by scientific luminaries in the same way that they put their stamp on sciences like chemistry or comparative anatomy. Mesmerism was therefore anyone's property. Taking part in mesmeric debates could affirm one's ability to engage in intellectual activity, not to be merely the passive recipient of textbook knowledge.

The individuals most responsible for mesmerism's rapid spread through 1840s Britain were the traveling lecturers. Victorian science lecturing developed out of a long-established culture of public science, and the debates over the character of the lecturer's authority waxed and waned. In the first decades of the century these issues receded, only to resurface with a vengeance in the 1840s.[9] Now, the question of what kinds of knowledge were accessible to different sectors of society was asked, implicitly or explicitly, almost every time someone stepped on a public stage. Some lecturers speaking on established branches of science (geology, for instance) represented themselves as "popularizers," diffusing established knowledge. Others presented their lectures as summaries of their own discoveries. In contrast, some controversial topics (such as mesmerism) virtually demanded that the lecturer explicitly spell out the basis of his or her authority.

During the next several years peripatetic lecturers created a new, nationally based, experimental culture prominently featuring mesmerism. They had diverse backgrounds and interests, and the only features common to all of them were their wanderlust and their mesmeric skills. Some described themselves as workingmen, some as middle-class. For most, mesmerism brought them out of a wide range of employments and into a more lucrative activity. They came from all over the country, and a few from France and Germany. Some maintained a peripatetic lifestyle for years; others were more locally based and gave regular lectures to particular improving institutions.[10] The lecturers Henry Storer, Thomas Capern, Theodysius Purland, and dozens of others (including the appropriately named Dr. Hands and Mr. Sleep) sustained careers throughout the 1840s and 1850s, giving lectures, demonstrations, and therapeutic treatments. A small but significant number, such as W. J. Vernon, Spencer Timothy Hall, Messrs. Hughes and Hagley, and William Davey, found that their lectures brought them national renown.[11] The lecturers certainly wished to make their names and fortunes, but they also wished to justify themselves intellectually. Having attained a public voice, they used it not only to proclaim the reality of phenomena they created but also to assert that science, reform, and progress were as much the property of artisans, provincials, and travelers as they were of middle-class metropolitan professionals.[12] The phenomena they produced in their demonstrations helped to shape their audiences' understanding of sensation, pain, the faculties of the mind, and the part science could play in the process of social reform.

Making Mesmeria

When mesmerism became prominent in the early 1840s, it was once again a prominent foreign magnetist who brought it into public view: the French traveling showman Charles Lafontaine. He was an exotic character, dressed in black, with a "well-set muscular frame," dark hair, and a "bold, powerful, and steady" eye. At a time when facial hair was unfashionable, his "profuse" beard "descended to his breast." People initially assumed he was either a "deluded mystic or a designing quack," but they flocked to his shows anyway.

The key to his persuasiveness lay in the initial test he used to prove the trance real: the absence of sensation. "Insensibility," as it was called, was less vulnerable to charges of fraud than were other effects. Physical tests could be, so to speak, calibrated on members of an audience. By trying the force of an electric battery or the power of smelling salts on themselves, people could be satisfied that *they* could pretend not to feel pain. During one séance Lafontaine's patient held the live wires of a battery for ten minutes after the same voltage had made members of the audience recoil immediately. When "pins" were thrust into the "vulnerable parts,"[13] large electric shocks were run through the body, pistols shot next to the ear, ammonia held under the nose, and fingers held directly above the flame of a candle, it was hard for onlookers to claim that an apparent lack of sensation was an act of fraud.[14] (Skeptics did eventually make such claims, as I will discuss below, and the result was a variety of conflicts that sometimes became physical battles over the subject's body.) Once Lafontaine had established an audience's confidence in the trance state, other experiments became more plausible. At this stage witnesses were presented with acts of clairvoyance, prescience, and "traction."

Following Lafontaine's example, domestic lecturers embarked on the lecture circuit, inflicting upon their subjects an armory of tortures.[15] Lecturers often chose to bring reliable patients with them, because it was hard to predict whether someone would respond to the mesmeric influence, and even those who did often did so only after several trials. One journalist counted as many as fifty patients traveling in a single entourage.[16] Audiences became familiar with the routines of mesmeric shows, and they grew skilled in evaluating the plausibility of the mesmeric subjects. So widespread was this lecturing empire that it became lucrative to give traveling lectures *against* the practice.[17]

For a few pennies one could attend demonstrations in temperance halls, rented rooms, mechanics' institutes, and halls of science.[18] A shilling bought admission to permanent public science institutions, such as London's Adelaide Gallery, Polytechnic Institution, and other central venues. Public houses and inns also boosted business by hiring lecturers who were passing through town.[19] In central London W. H. Halse offered electric therapy and mesmerism at Chancery Lane, near the Inns of Court, and Messrs. Hughes and Hagley gave morning and evening sessions in the Assembly Rooms near Regents Park.[20] Henry Brookes and Spencer Hall (independently) advertised from premises on Pall Mall, down the street from Buckingham Palace, St. James's, and the Royal Society of London.[21] Mesmerists may have taken particular pride in colonizing the neighborhood of Thomas Wakley, who thought he had banished them in 1838. Bedford Square sank progressively into the magnetic state. In 1845 the mesmerist N. Hale hung out his shingle there, and a few years later, the London Mesmeric Infirmary installed its premises nearby.

Lecturers passed through towns within a few days' ride of the larger cities and the major ports. Workingmen were taught the "mutual influence of mind and body" in Lynn, near Liverpool.[22] In Darlington and Hartlepool, south of Newcastle, they saw phreno-magnetic displays and bought illustrated, locally produced works to follow up the experiments in home trials.[23] Figure 27, from a Newcastle pamphlet, conveys the entertaining atmosphere of the experiments. Each scene is sketched aslant: mesmeric subjects tilt in their chairs, and mesmerists sway forward and back in alternating postures. In Chard, Somerset, the townspeople were well acquainted with popular accounts of electricity and magnetism [24] by the time William Davey arrived to teach them that "FACTS

FIGURE 27 Two views of mesmeric influence: in one scene, the mesmerist radiates the mesmeric power from his fingertips through the short space separating him from the woman he seeks to influence. In the other, the interlaced fingers of mesmerist and subject facilitate the passage of vital influence from the former to the latter. Newcastle City Library.

ARE STUBBORN THINGS" (fig. 28). Equipped with several experimental subjects and two phrenological busts (disproportionately represented, one assumes, on the broadsheet), he was confident of convincing his audience of "Mesmeric Sleep, Rigidity of the Limbs, Power of Attraction and Repulsion, and the Transmission of Sympathetic Feelings." [25]

Individual lecturers covered a substantial geographic area and addressed large groups of people at one time—from a few dozen to a few thousand. They inspired long-running disputes and experiments in local communities, as well as the founding of mesmeric classes for workingmen and others wishing to determine the facts for themselves. [26] Local newspapers reported dramatic amateur experiments. A woman in the vicinity of Bradford was put into the mesmeric state by her uncle and could not be roused until four days later, when her desperate family called in a mesmerist; [27] and a "practical joke" went badly wrong in Manchester when a boy sank deep in a trance and could not be awakened for days. [28] One H. Brookes, based in Kent, figured prominently in lectures and controversies throughout the southeast of England (see fig. 29). Over the course of several months he appeared in a number of towns around Kent, passed through London to Reading and elsewhere in Berkshire, then Bristol and its neighboring towns, and finally Hereford and Worcester. [29] In contrast, the lecturer and autodidact poet Spencer Hall, after learning mesmerism from Lafontaine, toured the Midlands and north (though also London), taking in Liverpool, Nottingham, Leicester, Halifax, Northampton, Newcastle, and Edinburgh, and drawing audiences of up to three thousand people.

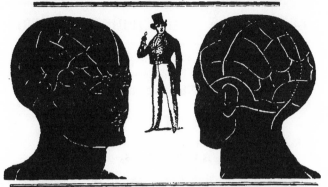

TOWN HALL, CHARD.

Mr. DAVEY

Who has just concluded a Course of Nine Lectures at Tiverton, respectfully announces to the Gentry and Public generally of CHARD, and its Vicinity, that he will deliver a Course of

THREE EXPERIMENTAL LECTURES,

ON THE UTILITY OF

MESMERISM

PHRENOLOGY,

SYMPATHY & MINERAL MAGNETISM,

AT THE ABOVE HALL, KINDLY LENT FOR THE OCCASION,

On Tuesday 8th, Thursday 10th & Friday 11th December, 1846,

TO COMMENCE AT SEVEN O'CLOCK, P. M.

That all persons may have an opportunity of witnessing the greatest wonder of the age, the price of Admission will be reduced one-half, viz. RESERVED SEATS, 1s.; SECOND CLASS, 6d.; BACK SEATS, 3d.

THE LECTURER

Will explain in his preparatory Lectures the locality, use, and abuse of the Organs, and the application of Mesmerism to human welfare, and exhibit a number of Busts, whose characters are before the Public. He will then undertake to produce Mesmeric Sleep, Rigidity of the Limbs, Power of Attraction and Repulsion, and the Transmission of Sympathetic Feelings. He will also demonstrate Phrenology, by exciting the Organs while in a state of Coma. The sleepers will perform Vocal and Instrumental Music, Dancing, Talking, Nursing, Eating, Drinking, and other feelings of mirth, imitation and independence, even up to the highest manifestations of benevolence, veneration and sublimity, while in the Mesmeric Sleep.

Mr. D. will be accompanied by Miss Henly, daughter of the late Capt. Henly, from Newton-Abbot, born Deaf and Dumb ; and he feels confident of bringing into action those faculties which have been dormant from her birth, by the aid of Pheno-Mesmerism.

"FACTS ARE STUBBORN THINGS."

FIGURE 28 Positioning his own image between two oversized phrenological heads, and above the announcement that "facts are stubborn things," William Davey encouraged prospective audiences to expect that the powerful truths of mesmerism and phrenology would force people to acknowledge their reality. Poster Collection, Somerset Records Office. Courtesy Somerset Archive and Record Service.

CROSBY-HALL

LITERARY & SCIENTIFIC INSTITUTION.

The Members and the Public are respectfully informed, that on FRIDAY the 15th, & FRIDAY the 22nd of MARCH, 1844,

Two Lectures

ON

MESMERISM

WILL BE DELIVERED BY

H. BROOKES, ESQ.

ILLUSTRATED BY EXPERIMENTS,

Showing the Sleep, Sleep-waking, Catalepsy, Phreno-Mesmerism, &c.

SYLLABUS.

LECTURE I.

Introduction—Mesmerism a Science—Definition—Effects necessarily variable—Sleep not essential—Classification of Phenomena—First stage, or half sleep—Second stage, or perfect coma—Consciousness—Memory—Sleep-waking, or double consciousness—Occasional transference of senses, or clairvoyance—Analogous phenomena resulting from disease—Of the utility of Mesmerism in surgical operations, and as a curative agency in the treatment of epilepsy, hysteria, paralysis, catalepsy, rheumatism, tooth-ache, head-ache, deafness, palpitation, insanity, and in promoting natural sleep—Cases—Experiments.

LECTURE II.

Peculiar phenomena arising from the relation established between the two nervous systems, viz. Mesmeric relation—Attraction—Catalepsy—Community of sensation—Phreno-Mesmerism—Introvision, or perception of their own internal organism, and its probable changes—Perception of disease and its remedies in others—Of the influence of metallic substances, &c.—Experiments.

To commence at 8 o'Clock.

Admission 1s. each;

Members of the Institution are entitled to a Double Ticket, admitting themselves and a Friend, at 1s. 6d. each. Tickets to be had at the Institution

Extract from Report of the Royal Academy of Medicine, Paris, 1831.

"Considered as a cause of certain Physiological Phenomena, or as a Therapeutic remedy Mesmerism ought to be allowed a place within the circle of the Medical Sciences."

Extract from the Opinion of Mr. Chenevix, F.R S., *of London.*

"It would not disgrace the greatest man whom England ever produced, to attempt an experiment or two, upon a doctrine which Hufeland, Jussieu, Cuvier, Ampere, and La Place believed. Surely, what great men believe, ordinary men may try."

FIGURE 29 A typical advertising sheet, circulated by H. Brookes to attract pupils to his weekly lecture series. Purland scrapbook, National Library of Medicine.

Defining the Powers of Body and Mind

There were several common features to the human powers developed during these demonstrations. One was a spectacle of human beings intimately connected to each other by invisible influences. Another related to the puppetlike state of the mesmeric subject: the human and the mechanical were not exactly the same thing, but disturbingly interchangeable. And the human psyche itself was shown to be elastic and progressive. It could be enhanced to explore hitherto inaccessible regions, from the inside of the body to the exotic landscapes of distant lands.

Mesmeric experiments drew upon, and contributed to, commonly held beliefs about the mind. They portrayed thought as the exercise of separate mental faculties. There was a mutual relation between mental and physical powers, and mind and brain were likened to an electric machine. Mesmerism also suggested connections between people that ran contrary to the stereotyped images we have of Victorian bodies as self-contained, discrete in their own skulls and skins. People's identities extended beyond the visible border of the body, flowing into one another.

One of the most powerful phenomena was that of "phreno-mesmerism," developed in 1842 or 1843. Phrenological examinations involved tactile contact, as trained individuals felt the contours of the skull to "read" social attributes. Mesmerists manipulated the skull, too, but with more ambitious intent. They wanted to "excite" particular organs. When mesmerists touched the place on a subject's skull corresponding to a particular phrenological organ, the entranced person manifested the appropriate sentiments.[30] One curious Edinburgh clergyman placed his daughter in a magnetic trance and then touched the places on her head corresponding to different phrenological organs: "Benevolence being excited, she put out both her hands, and with a kind expression of countenance, seemed to wish to shake hands with every one. Tune—she immediately began to hum ... Time being touched, she beat with her feet ... Veneration—she immediately put her hands together in the attitude of prayer ... Destructiveness, she pulled at and tore her dress."[31] In Nottingham an artisan tried phreno-mesmerism on the family maid: when he touched the phrenological organs of language and conscientiousness, "she began to confess to having stolen something, which I at once stopt as I did not wish her to expose herself." When he touched devotion and adoration, her face "would have been a grand subject for the painter or sculpter."[32]

Mesmerism, combined with phrenology, made for wonderful theater. The Reverend Dr. Eden, for instance, advertised a number of different kinds of mental spectacle at the Banbury Mechanics' Institute (fig. 30): performances

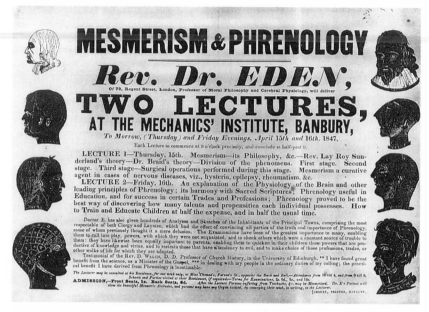

FIGURE 30 An unusually elaborate advertisement for phreno-mesmeric lectures by the Reverend Dr. Eden. The profiles decorating the margins include those of Shakespeare, Malanchton, and an anonymous idiot (judging from the size of the relevant organs). Purland scrapbook, National Library of Medicine.

of mesmeric insensibility, trials on members of the audience, and a well-rehearsed patient who displayed "the beautiful Mesmeric Attitudes." Phreno-magnetic displays such as the last item on this list gave an exotic air to established theatrical conventions, such as the "tableau vivant," which put on display idealized psychological traits or classic forms of interaction.[33] And the public musical concert, a relatively new cultural form, both took from and gave to mesmerism. In one display a hypnotic subject was placed *en rapport* with the celebrated singer Jenny Lind. She then followed Lind through the "difficult roulades and cadenzas, for which she is famous."[34]

One of the most common features of phreno-mesmeric displays was the diagnosis of mental potential that could allow parents to "quicken in their children those powers that are productive of virtue." Many such experiments were carried out in public halls, inns, and improving institutions. Here one could publicly study and debate the relationship between "the several faculties, principles, and passions."[35] Phreno-mesmerism was a particularly important phenomenon because it offered the first means of giving experimental proofs of the relationship between parts of the brain and particular behaviors. Audiences at mesmeric lectures were familiar with the various phrenological organs and the behaviors associated with them. Familiar mental faculties (such

as "veneration") were displayed as phrenological organs, and new ones discovered. The repertoire reflected the ideals of social interaction of the constituency involved. For instance, one workingmen's community discovered
the organ of *"good fellowship."*[36] Phreno-magnetic displays sometimes reflected and celebrated a prevailing social or political status quo. They could
also have implications for social change. When mesmerism enhanced the
mental powers of an individual of humble birth, experimenters speculated that
one could somehow find a way to make these changes permanent. One experiment in phreno-mesmerism could raise the possibility of large-scale cultural
engineering. As one mesmerist put it, if mesmeric effects could be "rendered
permanent and carried into the natural state," they would give society a
"mighty engine for man's regeneration, vast in its power and unlimited in its
application, rivalling in morals the effects of steam in mechanics."[37]

These powerful influences bound human beings to each other intimately, if
invisibly. It was commonly claimed that communication consisted in the transfer of vital fluids between two bodies, that people's minds and souls touched
each other (immaterially) in mysterious ways.[38] Demonstrations could display
forms of interpersonal communication and influence that seemed to dissolve
the boundaries between two people or to subsume one person's identity in another's. The manipulations of the mesmerist produced a form of mental ventriloquism or puppetry that developed a "rapport" between mesmerist and
subject. In many demonstrations, the subject shared the sensations of the mesmerist, though "somewhat modified in intensity,"[39] spoke words conceived in
his mind, and moved her limbs mechanically according to his movements.

According to mesmerists, the forces that produced these displays were the
basis of the most fundamental of connections between individuals, "the agent
of all our actions and emotions."[40] Most mesmerists located the cause of these
effects in an inequality between mesmerist and subject. Mesmerism was portrayed as an expression of where strength and weakness, or superiority and inferiority, lay in society. The particular social claims varied widely—as widely
as did Victorians' own understandings of the possibilities and proprieties of
social relations. Most experimenters and lecture audiences thought mesmerism would teach them something about the nature of social relations, but they
brought with them different expectations about what the phenomena could
mean, and drew a variety of conclusions from what they saw.

Inhabitants of the town of Halliwell, near Bolton, learned from one
W. E. Hartley that magnetic effects required the patient to have an "inferior
amount of brain" to the mesmerist.[41] Similarly, one Mr. Beattie told the inhabitants of Bury that the phenomena he could produce required "a certain inferiority of physical and nervous power on the part of the patient."[42] Yet another artisan mesmerist told the social superiors he took as his patients that

one person's ability to mesmerize another proved the mesmerist's "moral and mental superiority" to the subject.[43] More sweeping claims were made about magnetic and electric sympathies, weaving them into the social, natural, and spiritual order. Several lecturers argued that electricity or magnetism was the means by which God regulated nature.[44] Ethnographies of mesmeric phenomena—identifying them in Scottish "second sight," for instance, or the ostensible power of "Eskimos" to throw themselves into a "sleep on the approach of danger"—would provide a basis for a scientific explanation of what might otherwise have been dismissed as superstition or false testimony in other cultures or classes.[45]

Along with this portrayal of people in sensitive interaction with each other and the surrounding environment came another that might seem at odds with a science of sympathy: a similarity between human and mechanical systems. Many lecturers represented the human body as an electric machine, or as containing a machine within it. The Liverpool mesmerist Mr. Reynoldson taught that human influence was rooted in muscular energy;[46] according to the visiting American lecturer Robert Collyer, human relationships consisted in "nervo-electric influence,"[47] and the Devonshire lecturer William Davey said the brain was a "powerful battery."[48]

These claims were not a coherent body of theory but a loosely connected set of inferences from common beliefs about physical forces. For instance, readers of the *People's Phrenological Journal* tacitly accepted the notion that nervous influence could be concentrated in parts of the body by magnetic passes. They were debating among themselves "where this power [was] generated" when the mesmerist F. S. Merryweather joined the discussion. Mesmerism, he suggested, showed that the brain had both the "positive and negative powers of electricity" because, "through the medium of the nerves, [it] has the power of attracting or repulsing." The blood, Merryweather continued, was capable of carrying electric charge. It was therefore plausible that altered states of mind were produced by the attraction of an "over quantity of blood" to the head when the brain, considered as the *"galvanic battery,"* was "overcharged."[49]

Mechanism was part of the performance as well as the theory of mesmerism. Mesmerized subjects, ventriloquists' dolls, and inanimate "human automata" were literally interchangeable on the popular stage, and mesmeric displays alternated with puppetry and ventriloquism in an evening's show.[50] For instance, "The clairvoyant lady," advertised as having appeared many times at the "London Mesmeric Institution," accompanied a ventriloquist who promised to "unite" the impressive combination of "Art, Science, Mechanism, Electricity, Chemistry, Earth, Air, Fire, Water"—and "Money."[51] One automaton's "bosom" heaved as if "naturally influenced by the lungs."[52] One might wonder, upon reading promises of "rapid changes of character! . . . Imitations extraordinary" at the Regent Gallery,[53] whether these involved a ventriloquist or a phreno-mesmeric subject. It would not be clear whether an advertised "family of human automata" were made of living tissue or of wood. Mesmerism, ventriloquism, and puppetry all made living objects appear inanimate and inanimate objects come to life.

Of course, there was a fundamental difference between puppetry and mesmerism. One involved a lifeless object, the other a sentient being. People felt a consequent disorientation when the two practices were combined or when one resembled the other. Indeed, the language people used to describe the mesmeric state suggests that this disorientation played a part in the compelling, disturbing effect of the displays. A mesmeric subject could appear "as a piece of breathing organization, possessed of no independent powers, thinking, feeling, knowing, only through [the mesmerist's] will."[54] One nervous witness to a trial in Leicester foretold that there would be "animated beings standing in the street like galleries of lifeless statues."[55] The tests of insensibility mesmerists carried out were said to show not only an "absence of sensation" but even an absence "of being."[56]

This difficulty in distinguishing between the spiritual and the natural, and between the animate and the inanimate, is eloquently expressed in many fictional accounts of this period. One of the most striking examples was Edgar Allen Poe's "Facts in the Case of Mr. Valdemar," in which the lines were blurred between life and death, the animate and the inanimate, and even truth and fiction. In Poe's story a dying man asked to be placed in the mesmeric trance during his final moments. When this was done, he died, yet remained sentient. After enduring a state of "articulo mortis" for months, he implored the mesmerist to awaken him, and after a few mesmeric passes (as he cried out "dead! dead!") he suddenly rotted away into "a nearly liquid mass of detestable putrescence." When Poe's story was published in Britain, its audience took it seriously as an assertion of fact.[57] The *Hampshire Advertiser,* for instance, reproduced the story, advising readers that it had been printed in a respectable American magazine, and leaving it to them to decide how credible it was.[58] The reception of Poe's story exemplifies the sense of the uncanny that attached to representations of altered states of mind, leading them time and again to be associated with "death in life." Readers were willing to consider the possibility that mesmerism could redraw the line between life and death.[59]

These phenomena took on greater significance from prevailing concerns over the place of humanity in a society increasingly dominated by machines. The possibility of transmuting living and nonliving beings has a very long history, but these shows involved a distinctly Victorian formulation of the issue of the role of physical forces in the production and manipulation of living phenomena. Reactions to mesmerism are reminiscent of Mary Shelley's *Frankenstein*. This novel, which was partially inspired by her husband's forays into mesmerism, voiced an increasingly prevalent unease about the consequences of manipulating the powers of life.[60] Like Dr. Frankenstein, the mesmerist used his control over imponderable forces to usher the subject into and out of deathlike states. Lecturers sometimes made fairly obvious use of Shelley's story—for example, one W. Richardson's advertising broadsheet of January 1846 featured a castle whose pointed towers were assailed by jagged lightning bolts. Audiences often recalled the novel when reflecting on the issues mesmerism raised. Among the effects Richardson promised the inhabitants of Huddersfield was an electro-magnetic engine that would give "the appearance of LIFE TO A DEAD BODY" (see fig. 31).

Of course, mesmerism not only produced insensibility and forms of ventriloquism, but could also expand the powers of perception and cognition. Like the satirical Madame La Reveuse whose inspiration they had been, mesmerized clairvoyants could see events, people, and places at a geographical or chronological distance. Surveying the familiar land of Britain with a new inner eye, clairvoyants created and discovered their own country and other territories as domains of "Mesmeria." One new "territory" was the inside of the body. The stethoscope, thermometer, and percussion techniques allowed doctors an indirect means of exploring the inside of the living body, but clairvoyants claimed to see (through their closed eyes) diseased tissues and blocked canals. Magnetic subjects also claimed to be able to establish sympathetic links with people who were far away geographically or chronologically (thereby performing their "happiness, joy, [or] grief").[61]

A popular focus for this was the lost explorer John Franklin, whose whereabouts and status (living or dead) were the object of much speculation during the 1840s. One subject described her mind moving toward his over "icy mountains and the polar seas." So popular was this experiment that before she could reach him she claimed to have met " 'the spirits of two clairvoyants' who had been sent, one from England, and the other from some distant country," to check on him. They were returning from their visit and could report that he was "safe and well," and would return in five months.[62]

Part of the power of these displays was their blending of the domestic and the exotic. Mesmerism provided a literal form of armchair traveling, as the wilds of northern Canada could be visited in one's own parlor during the narratives of a clairvoyant. Such a juxtaposition formed the dramatic structure of Wilkie Collins's and Charles Dickens's play about Franklin, *The Frozen Deep*. The first act takes place in the home of the family left behind by a lost explorer; the second in the "frozen deep" where he and his crew are stranded. The two

FIGURE 31 In this broadsheet (c. 1846) a gratuitous castle tower and jagged lightning bolts advertise Mr. W. Richardson's electrifying lectures. Note that he also promises to create the "appearance of life" by running shocks through a corpse (species unspecified). Kirklees Libraries and Museums.

parts of the play are held together, as it were, by mesmeric forces: at the end of the first act, a servant in the household conveys to the rest of the family that she has been placed in contact with the explorers through the agency of "Scottish second sight." Dickens and Collins were both interested in mesmerism, and doubled up their performance of this play with Elizabeth Inchbald's eighteenth-century farce, *Animal Magnetism*.

As in the case of Elizabeth O'Key, the clairvoyant's assertion of access to knowledge was not philosophical but empathetic.[63] Clairvoyant knowledge was a direct transmission of natural (or other) truths through the mind of the subject and out into the public arena of the mesmeric trial without any intervening art or analysis. The Liverpool clairvoyant mentioned above drew support from people who argued that her story contained elements that only expert mariners and explorers could have known.[64] Better-known examples of this form of communication and knowledge include Harriet Martineau and, in fiction, one of the climactic moments of Charlotte Brontë's *Jane Eyre*, in which the heroine hears the despairing cry of the hero echoing in her mind despite the scores of miles that separate them. The more unintended the psychic event, and the more ignorant and artless mesmeric subjects were thought to be, the more their claims could be trusted.

The clairvoyant feats were the most debated of all mesmeric phenomena, although as far as I have been able to tell, their claims were never published in mainstream scientific works. For example, the major astrological journal of this period used the young clairvoyant Elizabeth Andrews as a scientific instrument to explore one of the most absorbing scientific issues of the 1840s: the nebular hypothesis.[65] After being placed in the mesmeric trance, she was requested to "travel" mentally to the Andromeda, whereupon she described a complete system of planets and stars—all inhabited. There the millennium had already begun, and different planets served different roles in the punishment, education, and reward of inhabitants.[66]

One might discount such activities as isolated curiosities or as a sort of cultural excrescence—a by-product of Victorian attitudes to the mind, but not an influence or stimulant to those attitudes. And no single individual had the prominence of the familiar luminaries of Victorian intellectual life.[67] But Victorians did not view these displays as individual events isolated from one another; they had a cumulative authority. One reason was that the lecturers' mobility gave the impression that they were ubiquitous in early Victorian society. The national presence of the platform mesmerists gave individual magnetic displays a greater significance than they might otherwise have had. Many people would have understood from what they read in the regional and national press that they were participating in a nationwide controversy. The results of a trial in one community would impact another, because lectures carried with them local news clippings describing their triumphs, and they quoted from them on broadsheets and circulated them during lectures. Everyone knew the *name* of eminent scientific figures like Michael Faraday and famous doctors like Thomas Wakley, but huge crowds, from "York to the Isle of Wight" and from "Dover to Plymouth" had actually seen and learned from the traveling lecturers *in person.*[68] In being everywhere the lecturers could not be considered "marginal" in any straightforward sense of the term. Instead of languishing on the fringes of Victorian cultural life, they suffused it.[69]

The Body as a Battleground

One could write an entire monograph on the hundreds, or perhaps even thousands, of mesmeric battles that were fought in the public spaces of England, Scotland, and Ireland during the 1840s. For my purposes it must suffice to examine a small number of them in some detail in order to understand how a consensus was reached, or failed to be reached, about both the credibility of the mesmerist and the reality of the phenomena he displayed.

Judging from the boastful advertising broadsheets, one might think that Victorian audiences were dazzled into uncritical acceptance of the mesmerist's assertions. Lecturers promised an extraordinary range of effects, and so confident were they, that witnesses could have their money back if they were not satisfied. But the actual shows describe tumultuous, embattled scenes. One unfortunate lecturer visiting Ipswich in 1843 made the crucial mistake of accepting a challenge from members of the audience to attempt to mesmerize them. They had suspected that the phreno-magnetic subject he had brought with him was a fraud, and demanded that he try his hand on someone else. After he failed to mesmerize four volunteers from the audience, there was a "great uproar," and people demanded their admission fee returned. After a "long and angry altercation" he reluctantly agreed. Even so, one "clamorous opponent" was not satisfied and demanded that the lecturer hand over "his *coat and hat!*" He retained his clothing, but was "almost bewildered" by being "hustled and assailed by showers of peas," and narrowly escaped being "kicked into the street."[70]

But such skepticism could also be transformed into resounding confidence by the end of such a demonstration, if events developed along different lines. One early example was the visit the London mesmerist W. J. Vernon paid to the Greenwich Literary Institution in January 1844.[71] Vernon had become well known from the many demonstrations he had given in London (see fig. 32, an advertising broadsheet from this period). The institution's hall was crowded with over a thousand people,[72] including "magistrates, gentry, and professional and scientific men." [73] An entranced mesmeric subject was brought on stage, and Vernon proposed to carry out tests and experiments on him. Before he could even begin, however, violent arguments, "indescribable confusion and uproar," erupted among members of the audience as to whether the subject was truly entranced and more generally whether mesmerism was a sham. One enraged individual picked up a stick, ran to the stage, and struck the patient's hand with such a powerful blow that it resounded "above the buz [sic] and noise of the meeting." The patient seemed not to feel a thing. The subject's attacker was taken away by police, and the mesmeric experiments proceeded with the full support of the community.

During the next few weeks Greenwich and nearby towns were consumed with mesmeric controversy, as mesmerists and their opponents battled it out in public, and the Greenwich residents gave mesmerism a warmer welcome than it received in Ipswich.[74] In one incident, for instance, a local surgeon's efforts to discredit mesmerism backfired badly.[75] The audience, who had welcomed the mesmerist H. Brookes some days earlier, grew restless as J. Q. Rumball began to describe how mesmerists could fake magnetic phenomena. He struggled to keep their attention, but when Brookes himself entered, the exercise was futile. Amid great applause Brookes accused Rumball of "wilfully perverting the truth" and of failing to admit that he himself had experienced mesmeric phenomena (in an experiment that had been reported in a local paper). Rumball reluctantly accepted that he had indeed experienced something during a mesmeric trial, but "no wonder," when "a fellow kept poking his fingers in his eyes for nearly an hour." After this response the audience's demands for "experiments," which had begun some time earlier, grew overwhelming. When a magnetic subject was brought on stage, Rumball "quitted the hall" in outrage and humiliation. The experiments proceeded— to the audience's apparent satisfaction—without him.

Rumball was a specimen of a new breed of scientific lecturer: the "antimesmerist." They showed how mesmeric phenomena could be faked, on the assumption that the possibility of fraud made mesmerists' burden of proof heavier. Now they would have to prove that particular kinds of fraud had *not* been perpetrated.[76] The antimesmerist T. S. Blackwell lectured on "mesmerism—a deception!!!" at the Marylebone Literary and Scientific Institution in 1844; the better-known Maskyline and Cooke, antimesmerists and "anti-spiritualists" of the 1870s and 1880s, provide a later example.[77] The convention of displaying as mysterious artifice a phenomenon that had been represented as natural law became well established during the second half of the nineteenth century. Indeed, if there had not been a preexisting culture that claimed for itself the distinction of discovering mesmerism's (and later spiritualism's) extraordinary phenomena, the feats of Houdini, who got his start by following the

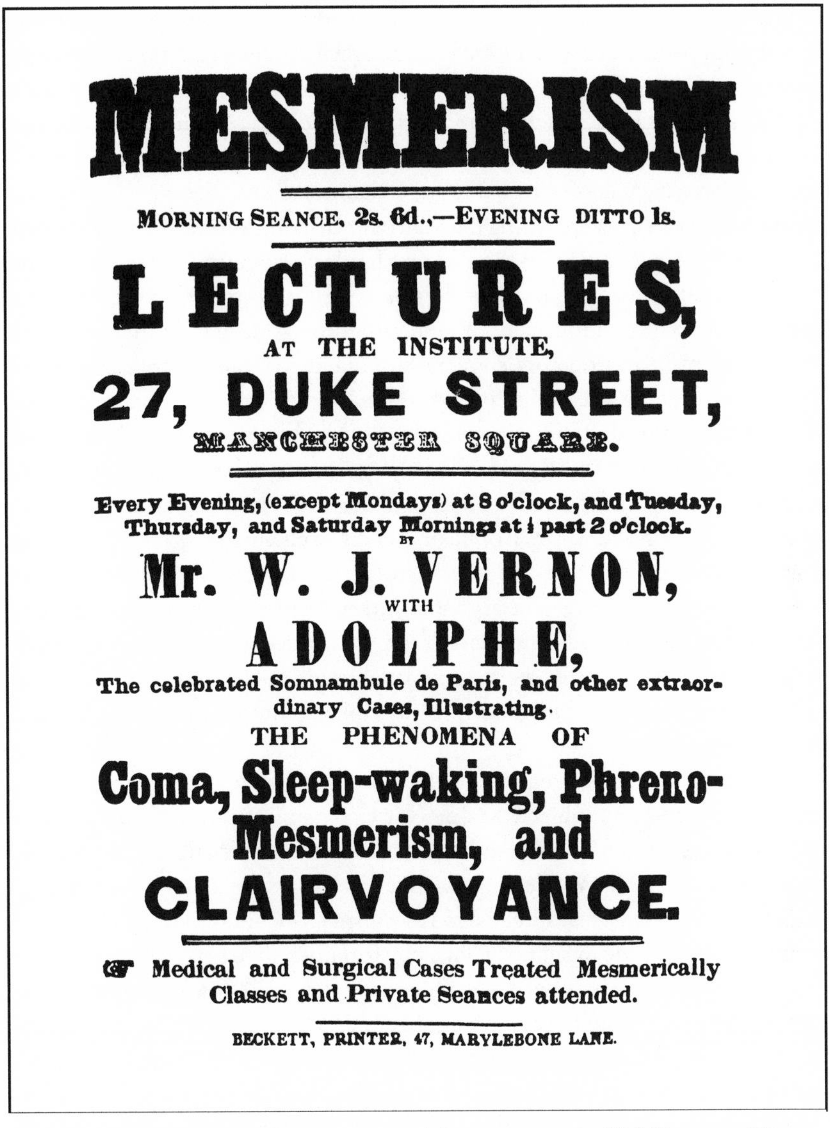

MESMERISM

MORNING SEANCE, 2s. 6d.,—EVENING DITTO 1s.

LECTURES,
AT THE INSTITUTE,
27, DUKE STREET,
MANCHESTER SQUARE.

Every Evening, (except Mondays) at 8 o'clock, and Tuesday, Thursday, and Saturday Mornings at ½ past 2 o'clock.
BY
Mr. W. J. VERNON,
WITH
ADOLPHE,
The celebrated Somnambule de Paris, and other extraordinary Cases, Illustrating
THE PHENOMENA OF
Coma, Sleep-waking, Phreno-Mesmerism, and
CLAIRVOYANCE.

☞ Medical and Surgical Cases Treated Mesmerically
Classes and Private Seances attended.

BECKETT, PRINTER, 47, MARYLEBONE LANE.

FIGURE 32 This broadsheet offered instructional demonstrations by W. J. Vernon and his professional mesmeric clairvoyant Adolphe Kiste (1844). Purland scrapbook, National Library of Medicine.

examples of Rumball, Blackwell, Maskyline, and Cooke, might have had much less of an impact. These debates helped establish a convention for discrediting experimental phenomena by showing that it was *possible* to create them fraudulently—not that in fact such a fraud had occurred. Magicians of the twentieth century have employed this convention to powerful effect and, in recent decades, have even used it to intervene in laboratory science.

Such altercations were taking place all over Britain. Antimesmerists stepped onto the mesmeric stage and entered into battle—sometimes literally—with the mesmerist for supremacy over the minds of the mesmeric subjects. Rather than shunning the demonstrations, and rather than offering polite refutations of their claims, local doctors engaged in violent struggles before audiences, sometimes even physically attacking mesmeric subjects with the goal of revealing frauds through inflicting pain. In Bolton the argument of W. E. Hartley, that one person influenced another by "corpuscular exhalation" in the same way as the lodestone affected iron filings, provoked "rather hard words" with a local surgeon, a Mr. Robinson. Their exchange triggered a "storm" of public disputation.[78] In another town the local doctors were reported to have come to the theater "in a gang," intervening in the proceedings with "clamour, clapping, yells and hisses."[79] One advertisement's pleas that participants keep their tests of the mesmeric subject "in accordance to the laws of humanity" gives some indication of the violence one could expect at these demonstrations.[80]

Some doctors exchanged their oath "to do no harm" for the mesmerist's goal of mastering the subject. At one Norwich demonstration, a furious doctor suddenly took out a lancet and "ran it deeply into the patient's finger *under the nail into the quick*." While the boy gave "no expression of pain" at the time, he "suffered a good deal after he was awakened."[81] This was clearly an attempt to "master" the mesmeric subject by forcing him to betray himself (since the doctor assumed the trance was voluntarily feigned). Such hostile maneuvers followed a principle with a long history: that one could reveal people's true nature by inflaming the passions. But this history could work to the advantage of mesmerists. In appealing to it, opponents helped establish the historical validity of tests like the one above, which, judging from the reactions of audiences throughout the period, often supported rather than undermined the phenomena.

Battles of the kinds I have described revealed profound anxieties. For some onlookers mesmerism was a dramatic subversion of the moral and social order. One outraged commentator claimed that it was a means of tearing down all the "social fences in society."[82] Experiments that produced these fears most acutely tended to be ones that addressed a crucial unresolved point.

One of the best examples of this is the experience of Jane Carlyle (wife of

Thomas) at a mesmeric *conversazione.* Carlyle recounted to her uncle how she and her husband had arrived at an afternoon tea party to find a mesmerist at work on a young lady who lay before the assembled witnesses, unconscious, "the image of death." "No marble was ever colder, paler, or more motionless." The magnetizer was also able to place her body in rigid positions, "horrid—as stiff as iron." The man, who dropped his h's and had "*dark animal-eyes,*" nevertheless claimed that mesmeric influence "consisted of moral and mental superiority." After several such feats, the magnetizer asked if his audience was convinced. Although both Carlyles conceded the reality of the phenomena, Jane denied that "any one could be reduced to that state *without the consent of their own volition.*" To emphasize her point, she challenged him to try to mesmerize her without her consent. The mesmerist asked if she thought he could not; she replied, "Yes . . . I defy you!" He then took one of her hands in one of his and darted the other toward it: "I looked him defiantly in the face as if to say, you must learn to sound your H's Sir before you can produce any effect on a woman like *me!* and whilst this or some similar thought was passing thro' my head—flash—there went over me from head to foot something precisely like what I once experienced from taking hold of a galvanic ball—only *not nearly* so violent—I had presence of mind to keep looking him in the face as if I had felt nothing and presently he flung away my hand." [83] If the experience refuted her theory of a consenting will, she concluded it also put paid to his claims that the phenomena were an index of moral or intellectual status: he "was superior to *me* in nothing but animal strength as I am a living woman!" She argued that her ability to "hinder him from *perceiving* that he had mesmerised me" proved "*my* moral and intellectual superiority." For Carlyle the experience had profound implications. Had she not been able to control her body's response to the lower-class mesmerist she would have been conceding his power—and, perhaps, his subversive claims. Carlyle's was a dramatic but by no means an unusual case. In town halls and living rooms people engaged in confrontations about the nature of the social hierarchy using this formal means of examining the impact they could make upon one another.

The point at issue between Carlyle and her mesmerist was more fundamental than whether he could produce an effect in her body. How could one tell if such an effect had been produced? And what significance would the phenomena have if one could agree that they were real? These two individuals were engaged in a contest with each other, but they were playing by different (though in each case well-articulated) rules. By his rules he won and didn't know it; by hers she won, and part of her triumph was that he did not know the true reason for her victory. This is one of ways that mesmerism became a means of affirming or destabilizing social relations. When people entered into mesmeric disputes, they often did not agree on what game they were playing and how to determine the victor. As Carlyle's story suggests, this ambiguity was what propelled some people into the mesmeric fray. Had they agreed on the rules, there would been little motivation to take part in the battle.

Spencer Hall and the Power of the "Common People"

The mesmerist Spencer Hall was unusually outspoken in using mesmerism to champion the power of the "common people." Hall first worked as a stocking maker before becoming compositor at the *Nottingham Mercury,* only to leave the paper in 1836 to start his own printing business.[84] He first learned about mesmerism when he attended one of Lafontaine's demonstrations in 1841. He then embarked on his own tours, giving demonstrations in public and at fashionable conversazione (before audiences as distinguished as George Combe, Justus von Liebig, and Robert Chambers), private tuition, and therapy, and selling copies of a mesmeric journal.

Hall claimed he spoke to and for the "common people," by which he meant provincial communities of factory workers, artisans, and small tradesmen, particularly in the provinces. Hall wished to champion these constituencies' intellectual validity.[85] The "crushing despotism"[86] of so-called professional men and academic "professors" with respect to the traveling lecturer was evidence (by being its antithesis) of the classless and professionless nature of real knowledge.[87] Hall backed up these verbal attacks by publishing the fruits of provincial, often artisan, mesmeric experimenters in his journal and by collaborating by correspondence with American democrats.[88]

The democratic character of knowledge was founded in natural law, Hall explained, because the forces of nature were accessible to everyone's senses directly. His claim that natural laws are "self-evident" recalled the rhetoric of radical agitators of the late eighteenth and early nineteenth centuries.[89] In principle, anyone could understand facts. They made their "impress" upon one's "soul" during communion with nature.[90] One's personal experiences had an authority that could not be undermined by any human agency, for they were written in the "book of Nature, the language of which is *facts.*"[91] So anyone could become a philosopher by becoming "unresisting as a child," before "Truth," the teacher.[92] The natural world Hall saw around him was fully accessible to the general public, should they choose to open themselves to it.

Wherever he went, he provided the resources for experimentation equipped with a philosophical and political justification for why "common people" could take part. Reports of researches and of the founding of experimenting clubs by many workingmen testify to the extent to which mesmerism had extended throughout the country.[93] For instance, J. S. Gee was one of a number of Northampton workingmen to form "a phreno-magnetic class" after the "sensation" caused by Hall's experiments.[94]

These individuals, however much they lauded Hall as a natural philosopher, did not necessarily adopt his perspective on mesmerism. One Nottingham cabinetmaker, James Hopkinson, was inspired by Hall to investigate mesmerism, but ultimately rejected it. His decision was probably related to a fear of compromising the self-control and personal drive for social mobility that would soon be evoked by the term "self-help." Hopkinson recounted in his manuscript autobiography how Hall's lectures had made such a "profound" impact on Nottingham that "go where you would the conversation was sure to turn on the New Science as it was called." He had attended Hall's demonstrations, studied his journal, and finally arranged to make mesmeric trials on the family servant. She was "sent," as he put it, in five minutes, and Hopkinson proceeded to perform mesmeric experiments of the kind he had seen and read about, and was a great success. After his prowess became known, Hopkinson was invited to homes throughout Nottingham to demonstrate his powers, including those of "Ladies & Gentlemen." Hopkinson became convinced that animal magnetism was "a simple natural law," underlying such everyday phenomena as the fact that we are all "attracted and repulsed by the people we come in contact with." He practiced mesmerism for three years but stopped when he became convinced that "it weakens the intelect [sic] of the persons who are sent," and cautioned his "young friends" never to "put yourselves so entirely into the power of another." [95]

Hopkinson's worries were not unique, but those who believed in the reality of the effects usually took a more sanguine view. Some prominent radicals took up mesmerism as a *reinforcement* of the power of the common will. The Chartist leader Thomas Cooper published supportive articles in his journal, framed by arguments that ran along Hall's democratic lines.[96] Similarly, the American radical "Republican" Josiah Buchanan sent correspondence to Hall's *Phreno-Magnet* that argued (among many other things) that teachers and other figures of public influence should be trained in mesmeric principles in order to become skilled at developing the mental powers of those in their charge.[97]

This understanding of workingmen's knowledge necessarily ran directly against the notion of the "diffusion" of "useful knowledge" as it was being put forward by London's professional reformers and educationalists.[98] The projects of groups like the Society for the Diffusion of Useful Knowledge wanted to distribute an easily digested, populist version of knowledge once it was discovered and validated by experts. Their publications were aimed at a "common people" who had neither the intelligence nor the education to make new

discoveries themselves. In contrast to Hall's self-motivated, intellectually discriminating workingman, the "useful knowledge" model portrayed knowledge
mechanically infusing a passive working class like water filling up a sponge.

Professional doctors, even those who practiced mesmerism, made this distinction between elite producers and the popular consumers of knowledge.
John Elliotson had continued his mesmeric work after his resignation from
UCL and in 1843 (like Hall) had founded a mesmeric journal. It was intended
as a venue for bringing together researches into the power of the mind, and to
give contributors to the journal a role to play in the reform not only of medicine but ultimately of society. Elliotson planned to make phreno-mesmerism
an experimental means of exploring how to improve education, the justice
system, and the care of the poor. Such scientific reforms would be orchestrated
by trained professional men like himself. To this extent he was in agreement
with the "Diffusors of Useful Knowledge"; the lecturers were impediments in
the path of progress and should be the object rather than the instigators of reform. Spencer Hall, perhaps because he spelled out an argument for the legitimacy of lecturers' claims to knowledge, was singled out for criticism. The
Zoist lauded Hall's motives but claimed that his lack of a "scientific education"
inclined him "to follow the promptings of an imaginative brain, rather than
the calm, persevering, philosophical course essential to the cultivation of inductive science." [99]

Hall's project, however much it claimed to ratify the ability of the "common man" against such dismissive models of knowledge, nevertheless made
certain telling distinctions. Hall portrayed factory operatives as "earnest and
philosophical," capable of becoming active interpreters of the phenomena he
demonstrated in public shows. After performing throughout Britain, he wrote
in 1845 that in no "rank" of society had he seen such "quiet and philosophical
interest" as in the "common people" of the manufacturing audiences in Yorkshire and Lancashire. [100] He referred to the several provincial societies that
were founded in the wake of his own demonstrations, and the many experiments that were tried, as evidence for their intellectual power. In contrast to
these "philosophical" operatives and potential mesmerists, Hall's mesmeric
subjects were drawn from the rural countryside, from the same environment
that he had chosen as a background for the portrait of himself that he printed
in his journal (fig. 33). Of the plowboys of the countryside around Sheffield,
he wrote that their honesty and their ignorance made them good mesmeric
subjects. The "cottage fire-side" and the "remote Yorkshire valleys" where
they lived were places whose innocence validated the research performed
there. [101] Under Hall's influence laborers spoke languages they had never
learned, recited snatches of poetry, and sang moving "country songs." The
songs were, presumably, within mesmeric subjects' ordinary mental powers,

FIGURE 33 The frontispiece to Spencer Hall's 1843 *Phreno-Magnet* gave him a simple, rural pedigree, a promise that he was "Yours, in the love of Truth," and a home address of a cottage in "Sherwood Forest."

but they emphasized the subjects' rustic origins. Through such experiments Hall sought, in part, to celebrate the plowboy. However, he did so from the superior position of the interpreter validating the interpreted. In using the ethic of the democracy of knowledge to legitimate his claims, Hall claimed to be both "one of the people" and "their" superior.

Magnetic Sympathies and Collaborations

Lecturers managed in varying degrees to interact with their allies among polite society. Some, like William Davey, a Devonshire lace maker, were very successful, perhaps because of his humility and deference to his "superiors."

He always maintained that his humble origins placed severe limits upon what he could do in the study of mind. He laid no claim to the professional territory of natural philosophers and doctors, whose business it was to trace the causes of natural phenomena. He merely had the power to heal, to demonstrate new facts, and to teach a practical skill.[102] Unlike Spencer Hall, Davey did not seek to demonstrate the intellectual legitimacy and independence of artisan lecturers (or their audiences) through his efforts as a mesmerist. Davey was well respected both by fellow lecturers and by the London professional community.[103] Davey's tour of Ireland brought him into contact with the economist and archbishop of Dublin, Richard Whately, with whom he helped to found the Dublin Mesmeric Association in 1851. When he proceeded to Scotland, he joined forces with William Gregory and Sir Thomas Makdougall Brisbane to found the Scottish Curative Mesmeric Association during the early 1850s.[104]

Spencer Hall was less successful in establishing his scientific standing. Hall introduced the journalist and popularizer Harriet Martineau to mesmerism. He also displayed mesmerism before the phrenologist George Combe, the chemist Justus von Liebig, the publisher Robert Chambers, and the radical essayist William Rathbone Greg. He helped to develop the mesmeric talents of aristocrats such as Richard Monckton Milnes and Lord Stanhope. But he could not establish his own legitimacy as a natural philosopher in these encounters. He was sporadically invited to partake in conversaziones held by more elite figures such as John Elliotson, but only as a demonstrator—not as a philosopher in his own right. Martineau's reaction was similar. However grateful she may have been to him for introducing her to the delights of mesmerism, she found him "simple-minded."[105] She dismissed him and obtained mesmeric services first from her maid and then from a respectable widow. She then added insult to injury by claiming that the itinerants had dealt mesmerism "the greatest of all injuries" and urging that professionals should take custody of it.[106]

This was demeaning enough, but Hall's experience of nobility was to be worse still. He later visited Castle Howard to teach his science to Lord Morpeth, only to be accorded the status of a tradesman. After performing experiments with Morpeth and friends, Hall was chagrined when he was sent a fee for his work. He wrote to Morpeth stressing that he mesmerized for "the love of it rather than from a mercenary motive," and enclosed his book, *The Forester's Offering*, in return for the money. "This will suit my feelings better," he wrote, adding that "the book was printed by my own hand at York—*the prose portion of it never having been written, but* 'set up' in the type as I composed it."[107] For Hall this was a validation of the ways in which his claims about nature were created—they passed directly from his experience into the media, which communicated them to others. There was no meditation, no cunning to warp truths by human prejudices.[108] And the book's preface plainly announced how Hall saw his position in relation to people like Morpeth. Hall portrayed as a triumph of democratic progress the very possibility of printing the book, and its celebration of the Prince of Thieves. The cottage, he wrote, was "beginning, not to *imitate* but to *emulate* the college, both in the acquisition and dissemination of learning." People were beginning to realize that "mankind *is one* progressive body, however diversified in its members and faculties" and that knowledge was the "common right" of "every capable mind." [109]

Morpeth, presumably, did not accept this argument, for he certainly did not treat Hall as an intellectual equal. On one occasion, after they met at a public demonstration of mesmerism, he complained in his diary that the lecturer had "claimed a 'Ustings' [i.e., 'hustings'] knowledge of me." The social and intellectual distance Morpeth saw as real and appropriate to the two did not keep him from carrying out experiments with Hall, but did give them different roles in the study of nature. On another occasion, for instance, Morpeth arranged for Hall to play the role, not of the mesmerist, but of the mesmeric subject, in his own mesmeric trials. He thereby conferred upon Hall the unauthoritative, subordinate status of the mesmeric subject (as Morpeth's circle construed it).[110] Morpeth even tried to remove Hall from the mesmeric scene entirely. During one séance Morpeth made a covert (and vain) request to his traveling experimental subject, a young boy, that he leave Hall to pursue some experiments with Morpeth and his friends elsewhere. The boy refused, fearing for his physical safety during mesmeric trials not supervised by his mesmeric custodian.[111]

The Establishment of Mesmeria

If such men as Hall did not always succeed in securing the respect of the upper classes, they certainly managed to spread enthusiasm for mesmerism. By 1844, according to one dismayed medical commentator, "every town of considerable size . . . has been visited by itinerant lecturers on Mesmerism." [112] Through demonstrations and face-to-face encounters, mesmerism gave meaning to the mind's powers. It could give "operators" and patients alike a new resource for challenging an old order at an intellectual and abstract level (a class relation, the professional authority of doctors, or the notion of provincial marginality). Conversely, it could provide a forum for people to make new assertions about human relationships—assertions that reached large constituencies, since mesmeric entourages performed before audiences ranging from the dozens to the thousands.

Intellectual histories have traditionally extrapolated Victorian understandings of the mind from the writings of figures such as John Stuart Mill and Alexander Bain.[113] Viewed from the perspective of the thousandfold audiences of mesmeric shows, this history of psychology looks too thinly drawn. Mesmerism and other experimental sciences of mind offered an exciting, new, "precise and accurate" means of "experimentalizing" on the psyche that transcended "anything of which the Olden school of metaphysicians could have conceived."[114] And these practices gave a great many constituencies of Victorian society their most striking (and in many cases their only) lessons about the mind. The lecturers had far greater contact with Victorians of most classes and both genders than most of the elite intellectuals whose names we more quickly associate with the psychology and political philosophy of this period: this culture of psychological display, alien as it may seem to traditional histories of cognitive psychology, is therefore where we must look if we wish to see which depictions of mind most powerfully expressed Victorian notions of sympathy and sensibility.

By the mid-1840s, then, the mesmerists had triumphed in one crucial respect. They had succeeded in establishing mental mastery as the test of philosophical validity; people began to describe their belief in mesmerism in mesmeric terms. It "cast a spell" on Britons that they could not "resist"[115] and had great, if indeterminate, implications for the future, according the popular writer Opie Staite:

The College, the Hall, and the School, now incrusted
With layers of dust, in a trice will be dusted;
An era of change [will] arise,
And a "New Moral World," will forthwith bless our eyes![116]

CHAPTER SIX

Consultations, Conversaziones,

and Institutions

THE PUBLIC LECTURE was only the first point of entry into mesmeric culture. Having gained an interest through lectures, or by word of mouth, many people paid for a private consultation. In the privacy of a consulting room or one's own parlor, a mesmerist could provide therapy, and a clairvoyant could give a diagnosis by touching some personal item or the body of the client. These events provide a surprising glimpse into Victorians' attitudes to the human body. Our stereotypes portray Victorians as buttoned-up, awkward in their own skins, uncomfortable with the very thought of touching each other. But in many respects they were less prudish than we are. Strangers took each other's arms; servants saw and touched the bodies of their employers; and in an age before toilets, daily baths, and tampons, the body's physical emissions were accepted (if not discussed) as part of daily life. However uncomfortable they may have been with certain kinds of human contact, they saw themselves as more extensively and delicately connected than future generations would.[1]

Victorian bodies were in fluid interaction with each other, with or without the benefit of a physical touch. Victorians were fascinated by the idea that one person's mind could reach into the intimate parts of someone else—the mind, the body, the home, or the past. As for the mesmeric passes, they were not massages or bodily rubs; they were just shy of a touch, and in that tiny space—close enough to feel each other's warmth—there was a suggestive intimacy. As we shall see, the possibilities of the mesmerist's proximity and the clairvoyant's mental explorations were tantalizing. They fueled an emerging commercial culture of psychic transactions that was established in the 1840s and continued through the end of the century. It also encouraged the notion that the most subjective of human phenomena could be understood by science. As mesmerists made converts within the medical profession, "cerebral physiologists" professed themselves "cultivators of *a science,*" declaring that "the thoughts, actions and feelings of men, can be made a subject of scientific investigation." [2]

Mesmeric Consultations

People usually approached a mesmerist only after seeing a series of public demonstrations or conferring with others who had. Lecturers distributed calling cards and advertising sheets at their shows and supplemented them with advertisements in the local papers. [3] Shyer mesmerists relied on the lecturing culture to excite people's curiosity, and restricted themselves to newspaper advertisements (sometimes anonymous ones, to avoid incurring the attacks of antimesmerists). The few women mesmerists did not give public demonstrations, perhaps because the role of mesmerist (as opposed to that of subject) was too overt a display of power. One Miss Preston of Bloomsbury Square was known by word of mouth in the 1820s; and one Isabella Litolfe (Miss) worked out of a Harley Street address and was known by reference from satisfied customers. [4] An alternate route for women was to combine the roles of healer and companion, focusing one's energies on a single individual. [5] For all mesmerists, cards and advertisements tended to include declarations of age, qualifications, or married status to defuse fear of those sexual predators that Wakley and others had warned were on the loose. [6] They often listed other services, such as phrenological exams. One of the more unusual cards was distributed by Professor Wright (fig. 34), "practical phrenologist," who advertised the unique—and perhaps alarming—combination of animal magnetism, phrenology, and taxidermy. [7]

Once the initial contact was made, the meeting could take place in either party's lodgings. Most traveling mesmerists attended patients in their own homes or met with them in the inns where they had taken up temporary residence, but some set up "mesmeric establishments," "infirmaries," or "hospitals." These provided room and board, and gave tuition and demonstrations. The platform lecturers Reynoldson of Greenwich, Hicks of Newington, and Hagley and Hale (of central London) each advertised small infirmaries, [8] and the Reverend Thomas Pyne of Kingston-on-Thames opened his "hospital" in 1845. [9] The well-known London mesmerist W. J. Vernon offered consultation,

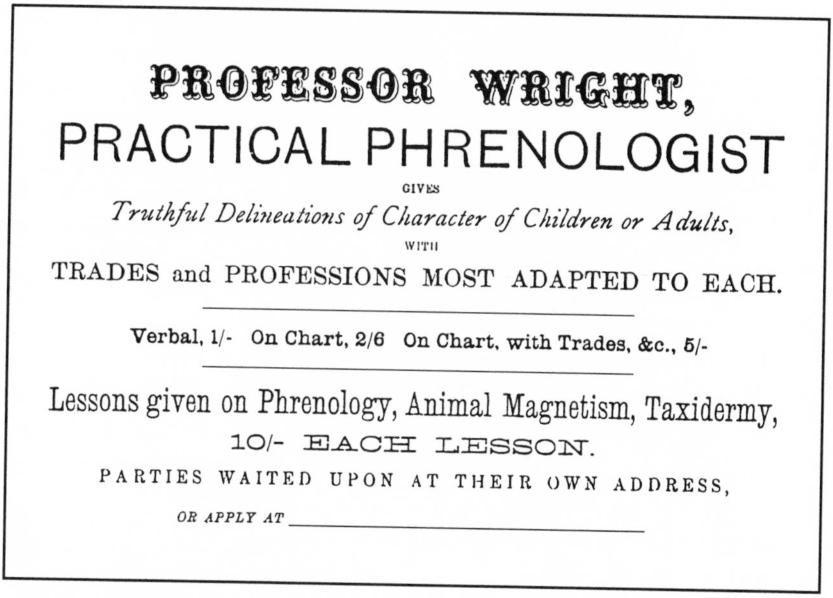

PROFESSOR WRIGHT,
PRACTICAL PHRENOLOGIST

GIVES

Truthful Delineations of Character of Children or Adults,

WITH

TRADES and PROFESSIONS MOST ADAPTED TO EACH.

Verbal, 1/- On Chart, 2/6 On Chart, with Trades, &c., 5/-

Lessons given on Phrenology, Animal Magnetism, Taxidermy,

10/- EACH LESSON.

PARTIES WAITED UPON AT THEIR OWN ADDRESS,

OR APPLY AT _____

FIGURE 34 Calling card of an unusually versatile phreno-mesmerist. Bodleian Library, John Johnson Collection (Phrenology and Chierology).

therapy, and tuition at his Regent Street premises before joining the London Mesmeric Infirmary when it opened in the mid-1840s.[10]

When mesmerist and subject did meet, they observed a number of proprieties. It is impossible to recover the etiquette of mesmeric treatment, but mesmeric instruction manuals do provide some information about how mesmerists treated patients inside the consulting room.[11] These works have the same limitations as manuals of proper conduct, being normative rather than descriptive.[12] The manuals gave detailed guidance on the mesmeric passes, the posture of the mesmerist, and who, if anyone, should be present as a witness. For example, how many people should chaperone the patient? How *few* should attend a private gathering to avoid distracting the patient? Once one had set the stage for "fastidious" treatment by choosing a "Mesmeriser . . . of character," one still needed to invite a "confidential friend or relation for a witness."[13]

Mesmeric treatments used a number of standard procedures. The patient could be mesmerized standing, sitting, or lying down—usually one of the latter two. The goal was almost always the alleviation of pain and the cure of disease. The trance could be produced by eye contact alone, but the far more usual technique was to combine eye contact with the magnetic passes. One standard technique was to make downward stroking movements from the

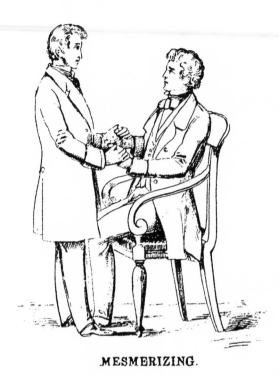

MESMERIZING.

FIGURE 35 Simple sketches of this kind demonstrated the various postures one adopted to produce the mesmeric phenomena—in this case, interlaced fingers enhanced the transfer of vital influence from one person to another. Davey, *Illustrated Practical Mesmerist*, 1st ed.

crown of the head, over the face and down the front of the body (usually without touching). This would be repeated for fifteen minutes or longer, until signs of the trance began to develop. Then the same stroking movements would be applied to the diseased part of the body.

As for the passes themselves, how close should the hands come to transmit the effect? How far away did decency require? Instructions for producing the trance were inextricable from etiquette. In contrast to the extensive body contact of eighteenth-century mesmerism, early Victorian mesmerists used eye contact or hand movements near the skin. The physical positions of mesmerist and patient also had to be judged carefully. For example, when a man mesmerized another man, they often sat with their knees touching, hands interlaced, maximizing contact so as to allow for the flow of mesmeric fluid (fig. 35). But when a man mesmerized a woman, he stood over her, either as she sat in a chair or, if she were too ill, lay on a bed. This arrangement satisfied the demands of sexual propriety, and expressed the power relations that justified the trajectory of influence between the male mesmerist and his woman patient.[14]

One of the most respected mesmeric treatises was Chauncey Hare Townshend's *Facts in Mesmerism*. Townshend was a member of fashionable intel-

P. 246.

FIGURE 36 An experiment in clairvoyance. The blindfolded mesmeric subject reads books and cards through the mesmerist's eyes. The mesmerist is clearly a gentleman, while the status of his young subject is more ambiguous—his shoes suggest gentility, but his belted coat is that of a workingman. Townshend, *Facts in Mesmerism.*

lectual circles and a friend of both Elliotson and Charles Dickens, who collaborated with him on mesmeric experiments.[15] Figure 36 depicts two men, mesmerist and entranced subject. They are in the ordinary mesmeric posture for men, the subject's knees between the mesmerist's. The mesmerist's sideburns and clothing indicate that he is a gentleman; in contrast, the subject's clean-shaven cheek suggests youth, and his leather-belted coat indicates a lower, though ambiguous, social status. The mesmerist holds a card in front of an opened book; the subject is slumped over and blindfolded, and is presumably recounting the fact that the mesmerist is holding an ace and, perhaps, is dictating some lines from the visible page in the book in the mesmerist's other hand. It is noteworthy that this experiment involved cognition, because the other illustration in Townshend's *Facts* did not.

In the second picture (fig. 37) two women have been placed in the mesmeric state and in communion with one another. The woman on the left is clearly a lady, probably gentry; the one on the right is younger and seems of a lower class. Her hair is simply arranged in two plaits; her dress is torn. Their hands are clasped, and they sit so close that their skirts blend together. The hourglass curves of their figures sketch an idealized femininity; the slight inclination of the older woman's head is symmetrical to the girl's upturned face. In contrast

FIGURE 37 This sketch of two women in mesmeric communion is particularly effective in evoking the intensity and idealism of effects in women. In communion with the lady on the left is a young girl, described in the text as her sister, although the torn dress sketched by the illustrator recalls the impoverished charity patients well known for their mesmeric potential. Townshend, *Facts in Mesmerism*.

to the cognitive activities of the first scene, this illustration portrayed the idealized relations of gentle guidance, harmony, and sweet subservience between a woman of higher social position or greater experience of the world and one of lower standing or greater youth.

Works that described mesmeric relations in such idealized terms, either verbally or visually, conceal as much as they reveal. In particular their suggestion that relations of influence in mesmerism were embodiments of idealized social relations was not borne out in practice. The mesmeric tableaux sketched in works like Townshend's *seemed* to capture an essence of social relations: the equal status of two men of equal station, the uneven power relations between men and women, the empathic, sisterly feeling of two women, and the maternal relations of mother and child. But these portrayals could be undermined by the patient's behavior or given a different interpretation by anyone at the trial. So mesmeric postures could express particular codes of propriety but could also be used to assert rival ones, all the while portraying their relations as the consequence of natural or spiritual law. Hence the explosive possibilities when the mesmerist held an ostensibly lower social position than the subject (for instance, Carlyle's mesmerist, and other workingmen with upper-class clients; and women mesmerists with male clients), and when mesmeric clairvoyants subverted the ordinary relation of authority and deference by flaunting their ability to "embody" forms of knowledge available to no one else.

The mesmeric clairvoyants of the 1840s and 1850s made a professional skill out of the varieties of psychic feat the O'Key sisters had apparently exercised spontaneously in the 1830s. Clairvoyants were placed in the trance by their mesmerists and then developed a "rapport" with the client by touching part of their body. Conveniently, this "part" did not have to be attached: a lock of hair sent through the post was sufficient. However it was created, this link enabled the clairvoyant to know, empathically in the body, what was wrong with her client. Only after he or she made, or perhaps "performed," the diagnosis with a bodily response could the mesmerist begin his therapy.[16] One critic evoked the threat posed by such mesmeric subjects in protesting that the "telescopic eye" of an "O'Key" (contemporary slang for a clairvoyant) could see "into the midst of any man's thoughts, and wrest from him the inmost secret of his bosom." [17]

The most famous mesmeric celebrity of his time was unquestionably Alexis Didier, a clerk in a Paris haulage firm whose manager, J. B. Marcillet, became his mesmerist. As the editor of one reformist medical journal complained, Alexis "came, *saw* [via clairvoyance] and conquered." [18] Figure 38, a contemporary sketch of Alexis, presented a physiognomy in which the phrenological organs associated with intellectual activity were especially developed (in the forehead area). Alexis first became known in the early 1840s, then traveled to England in 1844 and 1849.[19] Together he and Marcillet toured Europe, giving mesmeric shows everywhere in polite society, usually in arranged conversaziones or as a form of after-dinner entertainment.[20] This mode of performance fit very easily into the town-and-country circuit of fashionable socializing of the leisured classes.

Alexis had a well-established routine. He was blindfolded and then would play hands of cards, and read the titles of books. Then the blindfold would be removed. He would glance at a page of a book and then would recite a line from a page ten or twenty on from wherever it had been opened, would describe the contents of sealed boxes. After this had been done, he would perform the "mental travelling."

Alexis's performances were by no means unique. They resembled those of other clairvoyants,[21] and of magicians practicing "natural magic." But Alexis was unusually spectacular in the performances he gave. However doubtful

FIGURE 38 Alexis Didier, professional clairvoyant. Note the emphasis of the phrenological organs of abstract thinking in the curves around his eyebrows and forehead. Purland scrapbook, National Library of Medicine.

one might have been about Alexis's claims to supernatural cognitive powers, his ability to identify the contents of sealed containers and to describe landscapes or houses at a great distance challenged the most determined opponents. On the unspoken cue of a member of the audience who had been asked to focus his mind on a place of his choice, Alexis would mentally "travel" to this place and give a narrative of what he saw. If it were a home, for instance, he would enter by the front door, proceed down the halls, describe the contents of various rooms and the view from windows.

One of Alexis's most striking feats was identifying the contents of sealed containers. One incident, involving a particularly personal object, was recounted by several individuals who attended the séance, and each confirmed that no one present knew of the contents of the box or that the trial would be made. In a private party in London, one Colonel Llewellyn gave Alexis a small box resembling a surgical instrument case and asked him to identify its contents. Alexis held it in his hands, and slowly gave the following set of statements:

The object within the case is a hard substance.
It is folded in an envelope.
The envelope is whiter than the thing itself. (the envelope was a piece of silver paper.)
It is a kind of ivory.
It has a point . . . at one end (which is the case).
It is a bone.
Taken from a body—from a human body—from your body.
The bone has been separated and cut, so as to leave a *flat side*. (This was true; the bone, which was a piece of the colonel's leg, and sawed off after the wound, is *flat* towards the part that enclosed the marrow.)
[Here Alexis removed the piece of bone from the case, and placed his finger on a part, and said that the ball struck *here*.] (true.)
It was an extraordinary ball, as to its effect. You received *three* separate injuries at the same moment. (which was the case, for the ball broke or burst into three pieces, and injured the colonel in three places in the same leg.)
You were wounded in the *early part* of the day, whilst charging the enemy. (which was the fact.) [22]

One of the most striking features of this and other "identifications" was the historical or contextual information Alexis also supplied. This kind of performance—the public display of information personal to the interrogator, and the display not only of correct information about the concealed object, but also its history—was Alexis's hallmark.

This feat was a mere parlor trick in comparison with the ambitions of some of Alexis's other "explorations." His mind could stroll through an individual's past, survey the whole of his or her life, and even trace the activities of third parties who had briefly passed through it. One such case was that of Colonel Gurwood, once Wellington's private secretary, who sought the aid of a clairvoyant to restore his damaged reputation. In Napier's *History of the War in the Peninsula* Gurwood was denied the honor he claimed—of having led the assault at the siege of Ciudad Rodrigo.[23] By the time of Napier's history, everyone involved in the assault was dead except, possibly, a single French citizen who had been a prisoner of war during the siege, whom Gurwood had saved from being killed, and whose name he did not know. Gurwood sought to locate this individual, that he might bear witness to Gurwood's actions. He solicited Alexis's help, giving him no information as to the nature of his relations with this French citizen. Under the influence of mesmerism, Alexis supposedly relived the battle and located the officer in an obscure town in southern

France. The officer was indeed found, and did testify in support of Gurwood, but the affair ended in an unresolved pamphlet war, with Napier conceding that the matter was ambiguous but refusing to retract his claims.[24]

The occasions on which such discoveries were made left deep impressions on audiences' minds. Alexis was wildly popular in London during his visits of 1844–45 and 1849–50; through the activity of individuals like him, mesmerism attained a prominence in public life that kept it visible throughout the 1840s and 1850s. Through the establishment of mesmeric societies, it became in one sense increasingly established in British society.

Aristocratic Philanthropists

One mesmerist remarked in the mid-1840s that "it is among our *haute noblesse* itself that the strongest division of supporters [of mesmerism] may perhaps be found." [25] This was certainly an overstatement in demographic terms. Only a small number of aristocrats made public gestures in support of mesmerism, but this constituency did have the greatest material resources to offer. Unlike members of the professional classes, they were unlikely to be attacked by their peers for their involvement in the practice, and therefore had less to fear from the controversy surrounding it. Mesmerism offered them a form of entertainment, a philanthropic resource, and a means of expressing relations of political power.

There was a cluster of issues and projects among self-defined "progressive" groups of aristocrats that made sciences of mind of interest to them, to which one might apply the term "mental reform." This is my term rather than theirs, but it is useful because it sums up something that many aristocratic "improving" projects had in common. Several staple aristocratic projects of this period were aimed at changing other people's mental functioning, broadly construed. Many of the reformist projects of self-defined "progressive" aristocrats, including most Whigs and many liberal Tories, could be brought together under the heading of mental management because their overarching purpose was to reform the minds of the poor through skilled application of known mental and social laws. Education, lunacy reform, and prisons could all be brought together under this heading. Moreover, for at least a significant subsection of the landed classes, namely the Whig families, these improving missions extended to themselves.

While most of the aristocracy would have been exposed to mesmerism— like practically every group within Victorian society—those who were most likely to be attracted by it were groups who saw themselves as progressive. There were many such groups, but among the aristocracy they were dominated by the Whigs. The early Victorian Whigs saw themselves as guided by a new "seriousness," as trading in the old habits of personal display, the grand social rounds, and huge masquerades for philanthropic societies and Bible readings. They eschewed their fathers' and grandfathers' dandyism and styled themselves instead as sober, gentlemanly leaders. They were serious, paternal, progressive, and personally involved with the reformist projects they patronized.[26]

To old-style Whigs like Lord Morpeth, Earl Ducie, and Lord Adare, mesmerism fit into a broader project of benevolent reform and philanthropy.[27] Within these circles mesmerism was the reverse of the extreme democratizing agent it had been for the Spencer Halls of the same period. Unlike the 1830s doctors who had been threatened by the antics of Elizabeth O'Key, the gentry saw mesmeric subjects as being entirely at the mercy of the mesmerist. For example, Lord Adare, later to become president of the Bristol Mesmeric Institute, reflected that the well-known subject Anne Vials would never profit from her trance: "Poor girl," he wrote, "it will prove no advantage to her—How completely people in this state are at the mercy of the Mesmeriser.—Dr A[shburner] could get her to tell him almost anything."[28] But if it was natural for such men to see mesmerism as expressing these power relations, they tended not to reflect on the psychology of mesmerism, but rather on how it could be integrated with their philanthropic projects.

Morpeth, like most of the wealthy Whig aristocracy, ran his huge estate like an individual kingdom, regarding his tenants, servants, and families as a personal responsibility.[29] This managerial attitude toward material reform was coupled with a "liberal" (i.e., tolerant) perspective on religion and the mind in general.[30] Unlike many advocates of so-called liberal social and economic policy, for whom the ban on economic interference meant that social progress could be achieved only through attention to the minds (rather than the bodies) of the masses, the more paternalist reformers' manipulation of the material life of their charges left them "liberal" with respect to people's minds.[31] This distinction suggests why there was so little discussion of the psychology of mesmerism within these circles. Unlike most of the other mesmeric groups, while Morpeth and his circle practiced mesmerism almost obsessively and recorded the many instances of their mesmeric trials, they almost never recorded any speculations regarding the epistemological significance of their experiments.

Rather than a means of reforming the workings of the mind, mesmerism was one of many benign dispensations. The paternalist Whigs distributed mesmeric trances to their dependents the way they might on other occasions have given Bibles or medicine. Morpeth's mesmerism usually took the form of cures of tenants, servants, and beggars for headaches, rheumatism, and other ills. In such services, Morpeth wrote, was "mesmerism in good colours." [32] For example, in 1845 an impoverished woman made her way to Castle Howard, having heard of Morpeth's famous generosity with the poor, to request money to buy medicine and treatment for her breast cancer. Morpeth "preferred to mesmerise her." [33] In the past, Morpeth had merely given money and medicine to such folk, but now he ushered the supplicants into his study and mesmerized them, documenting his mesmeric forays in dozens of entries of his private journal.

Morpeth's mesmeric philanthropy found an institutional outlet when he became one of the governors of the London Mesmeric Infirmary (LMI), founded during the early 1840s and run, like an eighteenth-century hospital, according to the agendas of its lay patrons. [34] Among these circles, both in their personal efforts and in the institutions they helped to sustain, the trance was a pure essence of philanthropy disseminated by wise and benevolent masters.

One reason that mesmerism was taken into aristocratic circles so readily was that it could be made to fill a number of roles within aristocratic social life. Mesmerism's theatricality, and the challenge of interpreting the behavior of the subject, fitted neatly into the recreational habits of the stately homes. Elizabeth Inchbald's eighteenth-century farce, *Animal Magnetism,* was produced in private theatricals such as the one advertised in a playbill (fig. 39) distributed to guests at Knebworth House in 1850, who would see Charles Dickens acting in the lead role. Knebworth House was the venue for a great deal of mesmeric activity, from Bulwer-Lytton's collaborations with Chauncey Hare Townshend in mesmeric experiments, to his fictional explorations of mesmeric themes in *Zanoni,* published in 1845. There were still more illustrious venues for mesmeric spectacle: figure 40 depicts a mesmeric trial at Balmoral, in which a pistol loaded with blanks was discharged near the subject's ear to test the trance. In the 1850s one of the instruments developed to measure vital power and phrenological characteristics, the magnetoscope, became fashionable within these circles. Gladstone submitted to the operations necessary to compile a phrenological chart using the magnetoscope to measure the vital influence emitted by individual phrenological organs, and preserved the resulting document among his papers. Figure 41 is a typical specimen of such charts using the magnetoscope, whose principal practitioner was the traveling lecturer Thomas Leger. Adare, Morpeth, Ducie, and the others carried out mesmerism and its associated practices largely in their home or among an audience restricted to their own family. They tended to be repelled by venues like the Adelaide Gallery, or public shows in rented halls. [35] And at a time when the conspicuous display of the eighteenth-century nobleman was giving way to a commitment to philanthropy and the sense that one should become a good model for one's tenants, mesmerism combined these agendas.

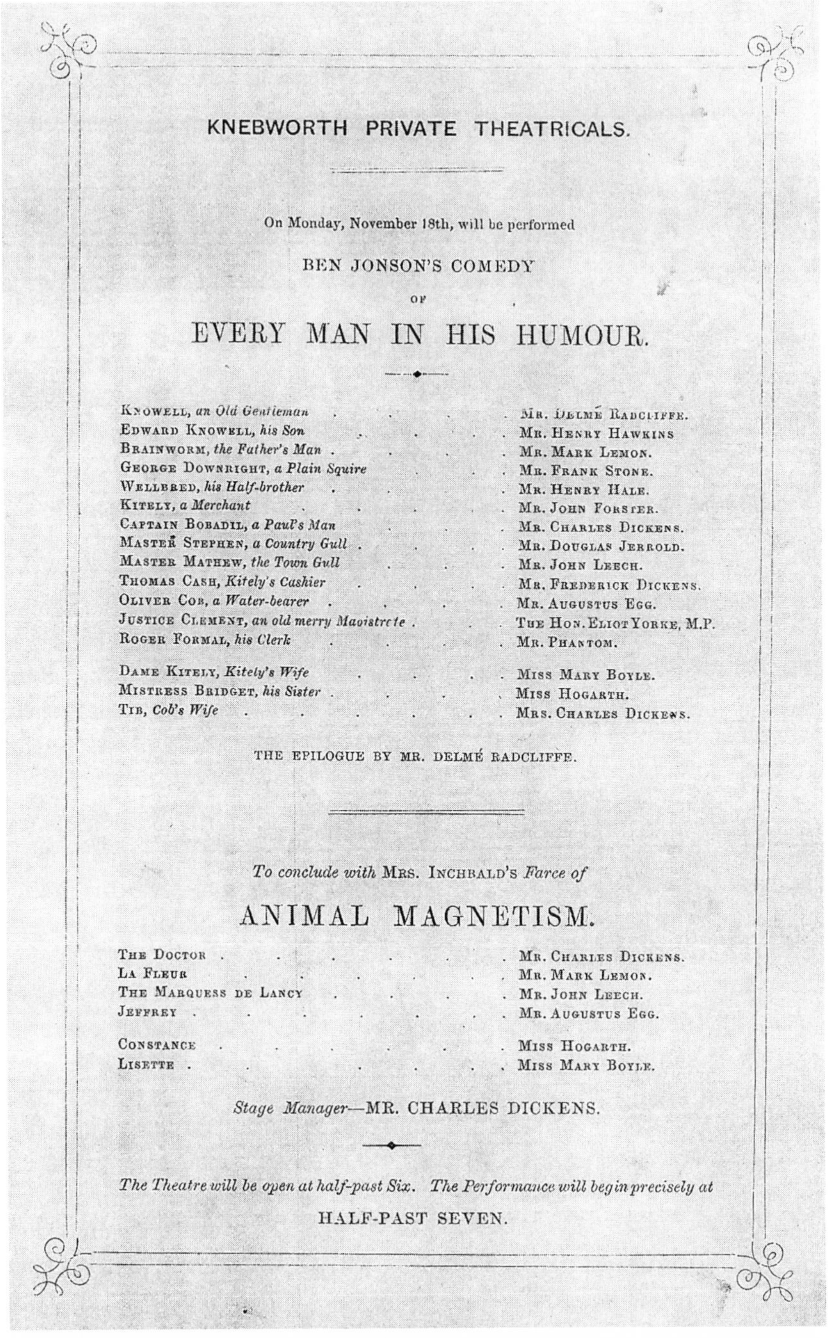

KNEBWORTH PRIVATE THEATRICALS.

On Monday, November 18th, will be performed

BEN JONSON'S COMEDY

OF

EVERY MAN IN HIS HUMOUR.

KNOWELL, *an Old Gentleman*	MR. DELMÉ RADCLIFFE.
EDWARD KNOWELL, *his Son*	MR. HENRY HAWKINS
BRAINWORM, *the Father's Man*	MR. MARK LEMON.
GEORGE DOWNRIGHT, *a Plain Squire*	MR. FRANK STONE.
WELLBRED, *his Half-brother*	MR. HENRY HALE.
KITELY, *a Merchant*	MR. JOHN FORSTER.
CAPTAIN BOBADIL, *a Paul's Man*	MR. CHARLES DICKENS.
MASTER STEPHEN, *a Country Gull*	MR. DOUGLAS JERROLD.
MASTER MATHEW, *the Town Gull*	MR. JOHN LEECH.
THOMAS CASH, *Kitely's Cashier*	MR. FREDERICK DICKENS.
OLIVER COB, *a Water-bearer*	MR. AUGUSTUS EGG.
JUSTICE CLEMENT, *an old merry Magistrate*	THE HON. ELIOT YORKE, M.P.
ROGER FORMAL, *his Clerk*	MR. PHANTOM.
DAME KITELY, *Kitely's Wife*	MISS MARY BOYLE.
MISTRESS BRIDGET, *his Sister*	MISS HOGARTH.
TIB, *Cob's Wife*	MRS. CHARLES DICKENS.

THE EPILOGUE BY MR. DELMÉ RADCLIFFE.

To conclude with MRS. INCHBALD'S *Farce of*

ANIMAL MAGNETISM.

THE DOCTOR	MR. CHARLES DICKENS.
LA FLEUR	MR. MARK LEMON.
THE MARQUESS DE LANCY	MR. JOHN LEECH.
JEFFREY	MR. AUGUSTUS EGG.
CONSTANCE	MISS HOGARTH.
LISETTE	MISS MARY BOYLE.

Stage Manager—MR. CHARLES DICKENS.

The Theatre will be open at half-past Six. The Performance will begin precisely at

HALF-PAST SEVEN.

FIGURE 39 This announcement of a play at Knebworth House was one of several stagings of *Animal Magnetism* in which Charles Dickens played the Doctor. Knebworth House Collection, Bulwer-Lytton Papers.

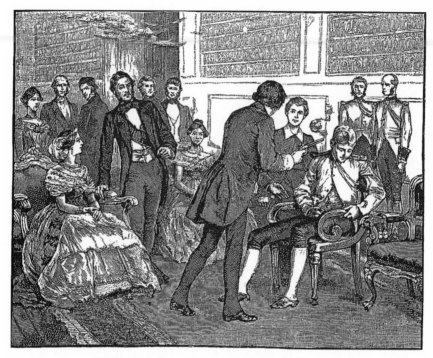

FIGURE 40 In 1849 the festivities surrounding Prince Albert's birthday included dramatic tests of mesmerism. Here the subject has been rendered immobile by the trance, unable to rise from his chair even when a pistol (loaded, unbeknownst to the subject, with blanks) is discharged in his face. *Illustrated London News* (1849).

Critics saw these projects as typical of aristocratic credulity and of the fanciful gimmickry of their "progressive" projects. For example, Edward Quillinan, Wordsworth's son-in-law, sent Henry Crabb Robinson a satirical poem he had written to Morpeth, after the style of the sonnets Morpeth and Wordsworth had exchanged in a recent controversy over the Kendal and Windermere Railway. Morpeth's interest in mesmerism had been sparked in the summer and fall of 1844, and when, in late November, he heard that the journalist Harriet Martineau had been cured of a terminal illness by mesmerism, he hurried to her Tynemouth residence to explore the phenomena himself. Quillinan caricatured his pilgrimage as a species of railway mania.

[T]hrough the Lakes at railroad speed he flies
. . . .
Away to Tynemouth! There's thy delphic shrine
    (How fair is Truth, in spite of coal and pitch!)
Go to thine own "young pythoness" divine—
As sure as thou'rt a Wizard, she's a witch.[36]

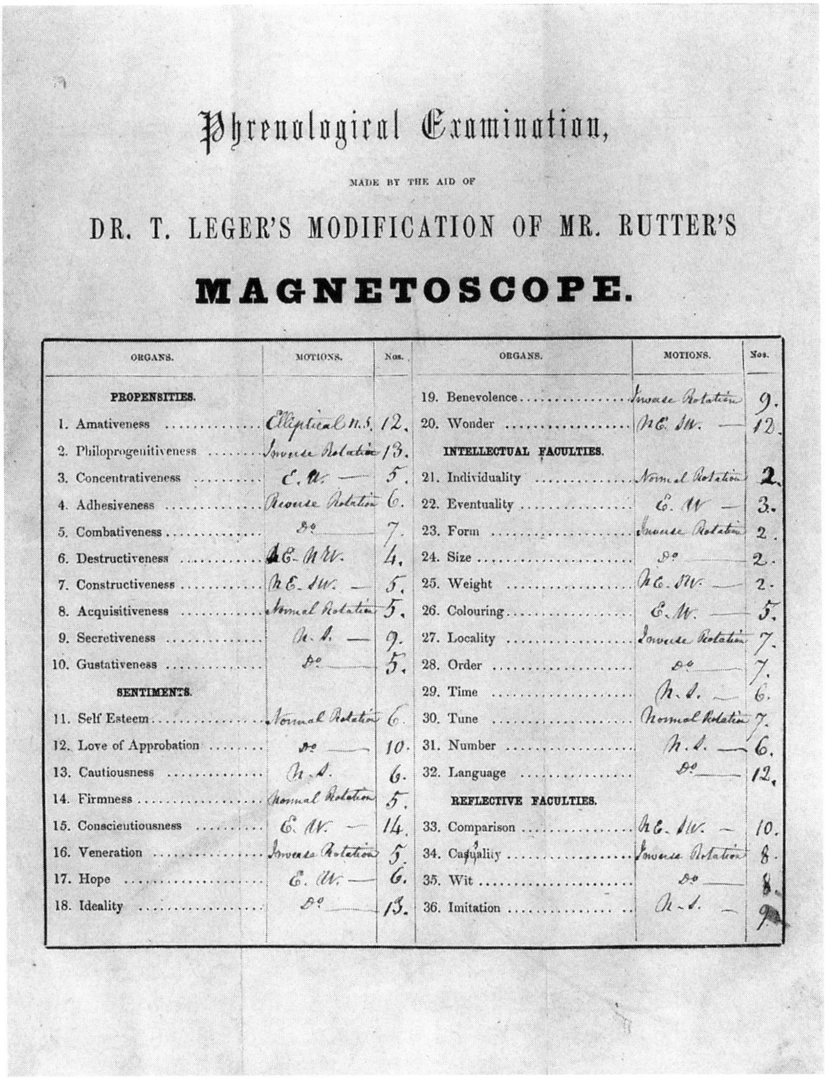

Phrenological Examination,

MADE BY THE AID OF

DR. T. LEGER'S MODIFICATION OF MR. RUTTER'S

MAGNETOSCOPE.

ORGANS.	MOTIONS.	Nos.	ORGANS.	MOTIONS.	Nos.
PROPENSITIES.			19. Benevolence	Inverse Rotation	9.
1. Amativeness	Elliptical n.s.	12.	20. Wonder	N.E. S.W.	12.
2. Philoprogenitiveness	Inverse Rotation	13.	**INTELLECTUAL FACULTIES.**		
3. Concentrativeness	E. W.	5.	21. Individuality	Normal Rotation	2.
4. Adhesiveness	Reverse Rotation	6.	22. Eventuality	E. W.	3.
5. Combativeness	Do	7.	23. Form	Inverse Rotation	2.
6. Destructiveness	N.E. N.W.	4.	24. Size	Do	2.
7. Constructiveness	N.E. S.W.	5.	25. Weight	N.E. S.W.	2.
8. Acquisitiveness	Normal Rotation	5.	26. Colouring	E. W.	5.
9. Secretiveness	N.S.	9.	27. Locality	Inverse Rotation	7.
10. Gustativeness	Do	5.	28. Order	Do	7.
SENTIMENTS.			29. Time	N.S.	6.
11. Self Esteem	Normal Rotation	6.	30. Tune	Normal Rotation	7.
12. Love of Approbation	Do	10.	31. Number	N.S.	6.
13. Cautiousness	N.S.	6.	32. Language	Do	12.
14. Firmness	Normal Rotation	5.	**REFLECTIVE FACULTIES.**		
15. Conscientiousness	E. W.	14.	33. Comparison	N.E. S.W.	10.
16. Veneration	Inverse Rotation	5.	34. Causality	Inverse Rotation	8.
17. Hope	E. W.	6.	35. Wit	Do	8.
18. Ideality	Do	13.	36. Imitation	N.S.	9.

FIGURE 41 This chart is like those commonly used in phrenology at this time (c. 1853), with the difference that the magnetoscope, rather than the eye and fingertip of the phrenologist, registers the strength of the phrenological organs (by reacting to the relative strengths of the vital influence that emanates from each). Bodleian Library, John Johnson Collection (Phrenology and Chierology).

Quillinan saw in Morpeth's pilgrimage to Tynemouth the symptoms of the so-called railway mania—the intense and often ill-fated investment in railways during these years and the reverence (which went with it) of the "delphic shrine" of technological progress.[37] Morpeth's mother, indeed, worried

The Real & the Ideal

FIGURE 42 Here the artist uses the mesmeric communion to ridicule aristocratic philanthropy: the fat landowner feasts while the poor, who are lightly sketched as shadows, move in a hollow echo of him. "Animal Magnetism in Practice."

that his involvement in mesmerism might undermine his efficacy as a politician, and urged him to "Be Cautious."[38] Quillinan's association of mesmerism and railway ideology expressed the general view of mesmerism taken by Wordsworth's circle, who saw it as one of the many expressions of a prevailing fever for the novel and technological that threatened to destroy the fragile peace, the slow pace, and the pastoral world in which life should be lived.

Amid these attacks the middle-class utilitarian press used portrayals of what they saw as the ludicrous character of aristocratic philanthropic mesmerism to deride philanthropy altogether. For instance, the *North of England Magazine* ironically suggested that one possible means of feeding the poor (the paternalists' alternative to repealing the corn laws, presumably) was to place the aristocracy in mesmeric "rapport" with the masses (fig. 42). Through the action of this "rapport," in which the subject experiences the sensations of the operator, the poor would taste the food eaten by the rich. The caricature's caption, "the real and the ideal," was not a philosophical statement in any traditional sense but a dig at the emptiness of paternalism (as this Benthamite journal saw it).[39] The accompanying poem suggested that towns establish new bylaws, such that aldermen be required to put themselves *en rapport* with "a score or two of poor at least" before dining.

What a glorious sight to see
This virtuous sympathy
Exerted on the many, by the few!
And to watch with what a stare
The poor devils find the fare
Is neither skilly, nor lobscouse, nor stew!
Oh! turbot! vermicelli! haunch! ragout!
The masses shall be fed by *smelling* you!

This dripping sarcasm was an attack on aristocracy and paternalism—not mesmerism in and of itself, which the journal supported. Indeed, among middle-class radical reformers mesmerism provided a means of direct intervention into the public mind.

The Physiology of Reform

Mesmerism raised new possibilities for the reform of mental action, especially when it joined forces with other sciences like phrenology. Once one accepted that human character and intellectual ability were formed by the interaction of inherited brain matter and the external environment, the key to social reform lay in learning how to manipulate this relationship. Phrenologists studied the skulls of executed criminals to show the exaggerated size of the phrenological organs responsible for antisocial behavior. Criminals could be portrayed as victims of their own physiology. If one could learn to mold children's social and material environment, or assign them occupations according to their phrenological profiles, one could improve the next generation. Which of these two options one emphasized depended on one's political orientation. Education and social policy would be placed on a different footing; physiological organization, rather than class, would determine what kind of education one should receive (though in practice, phrenologists' charts usually reinforced the subject's social background). All these changes would be orchestrated by doctors, the appropriate leaders of reform once reform was understood to be based in physiological law.

Phrenology could be molded to a range of political campaigns, but it flourished in movements that regarded themselves as "progressive" and "reformist." A wide range of reformers, from moderate liberals to materialist radicals, adopted it. For them, phrenology had implications for law, education, the treatment of people with nervous disorders, and in the most general sense, social and political policy.[40] When mesmerism became interlinked with phrenology, this potential became even greater—and, to opponents, even more threatening. Indeed, many doctors closely associated their fate as public authorities with the particular shape that sciences of mind came to take in the 1840s, and the degree of control they had over these sciences.

In 1842 the Phrenological Society debated the new phenomena of phreno-mesmerism. W. C. Engledue, Brighton doctor, outspoken materialist, and the society's president, argued (along with its founder John Elliotson) that phreno-mesmerism was a crucial new addition to the armory of phrenology. A heated debate ensued and the society split. Two Phrenological Societies then ran in parallel, one embracing mesmerism, the other rejecting it. In 1842 Elliotson began holding public *séances magnetiques* of phreno-mesmerism.[41] When he and Engledue founded the *Zoist* the following year, it became the major vehicle for the publication of new researches in mesmeric sciences of mind and their social implications.

According to Elliotson this process of studying the mind and applying the knowledge gained was to be done by trained professionals like him. Elliotson agreed with the so-called Diffusors of Useful Knowledge that individuals such as the platform mesmerists were impediments in the "March of Mind." Only trained experts working soberly in the privacy of the "philosopher's study" and in hospital wards could carry out reliable experiments in the nature of mental action. The lecturers, because they sensationalized sciences of mind, were not the instigators of reform but its proper objects.[42]

The purpose of Elliotson's journal, the *Zoist,* was twofold: to provide a space where researchers could publicize information, and to digest this information toward the furtherance of the "progressive" social agendas of "cerebral physiology." Everyone who contributed to the *Zoist,* from radical materialists to High Church clergymen, agreed that these sciences, properly developed, improved society. The *Zoist* regularly published new psychic truths.[43] It also extended mesmerism to the animal kingdom[44] and to the running of government affairs,[45] and linked it to exhortations on the need for progressive reform in social and educational policy.[46] And since "organic change must precede very civilised movement," the services of the "cerebral physiologist" were "pre-eminent" in designing and orchestrating social reform.[47]

The political goals of its editors—Elliotson and, especially, Engledue—were more programmatic: if the brain was the machinery of the mind, "cerebral physiology," the science that could explain its workings, was a form of mechanism that operated on the level of social change rather than of cognition. It was "the machinery" that would "work out man's emancipation." The future of the mind consisted of the "evolution" of organic material. The "evolution of thought is a vital phenomenon," the *Zoist* proclaimed, the "necessary sequence of a certain combination of atoms assuming a certain form and arrangement and having received the requisite stimulus." [48] This could provide a means of shaping the future of society by shaping a population's physiological development over generations: " 'Onward!' is the cry of our race. Progressive improvement and happiness should be the sum total of our aspirations, and the universal inculcation of the truths of Cerebral Physiology is one of the means to hasten this advent . . . With such a power in action, who will place limits to human thought, or map the boundary line which is to impede man's onward progress?" [49] At the very least, its new knowledge would allow one to make better-informed decisions regarding the social arrangements most important to the future development of an individual and, over a population, to the development of society—such as the choice of a partner for marriage or a choice of employment.

Several phreno-mesmerists saw their work as the beginning of a thoroughgoing cultural reform. Henry G. Atkinson, for instance, regarded marriage as one of the first institutions to be affected by the new knowledge.

Unions of the sexes are formed by chance, the laws of nature are neglected, and the result is, defective offspring, untimely death and misery. The rights of love and nature's laws are violated, and it is thought highly moral that man and woman should live on together, though the greatest antipathy exist, because they have been joined in "holy matrimony," whilst they were yet in ignorance of each other's dispositions, and how they would sympathize with and be happy together . . . when individuals are unsuited to each other, it is not God who put them together, but their own ignorance and perversion; and a *religious ceremony performed by an ignorant priest does not alter nature's laws.*[50]

Mesmerism and phrenology could allow a practitioner to identify the sympathetic connections between people more reliably than anyone else in society—including themselves, their family, and even their preacher. Phreno-mesmerism was also said to have vague but direct improving effects on patients' minds; for instance, in a trial reported by H. Brookes (who was discussed in chapter 5) his magnetic subject claimed to be "cleverer" than she used to be. She was said to have concluded, "I think my head must have some of yours about it." [51]

Mesmeric Institutions

By the mid-1840s there were mesmeric societies in all the major manufacturing towns, and a few specialist journals had been founded.[52] The longest-lived societies were patronized by a few scientific luminaries and wealthy philanthropists. These were founded in Dublin, Edinburgh, London, and Bristol. There were others in York, Sheffield, Nottingham, Manchester, Liverpool, Exeter, and Bradford. Some societies had the funds to maintain infirmaries and to employ permanent mesmerists and resident physicians. The Dublin Mesmeric Infirmary, run by Richard Whately, archbishop of Dublin, employed a man and a woman as mesmerists, each with a "fair share of power."[53] The Bristol Mesmeric Institute, headed by a local landed aristocrat, Earl Ducie, was run by "officers" drawn from the west of England (Bath, Clifton, Exeter) and London, and maintained a permanent mesmerist.[54] The largest, best-patronized, and probably longest-lived was the LMI. There were reports of the "Mesmeric Institute" as early as 1843,[55] but the institute as a formally constituted institution run by a set of governors and funded by subscription did not exist until 1845 at the earliest.[56] The LMI was run by an impressive spectrum of the social and intellectual elite: Whately; the mathematician and logician Augustus De Morgan; the prominent politicians Lord Morpeth and James Haughton Langston; the writer Richard Monckton Milnes; William Gregory, professor of chemistry at the University of Edinburgh; Thomas Makdougall Brisbane, president of the Royal Society of Edinburgh; the philanthropist Baron Isaac Lyon Goldsmid; and others. It was staffed by two regular mesmerists, Theodysius Purland and W. J. Vernon, with the help of a surgeon, W. J. Tubbs. They held regular demonstrations and therapeutic treatments.[57] The infirmaries declined over the 1850s and early 1860s, in large part due to the rise of spiritualism and psychic research; by the mid-1860s they had all disappeared.

At the infirmaries' annual meetings testimonies were read and recorded of patients who had experienced the most dramatic cures at the hands of employees or other mesmerists. The cases were often presented as more than instances of physiological improvement in the bodies of the ill. Some suggested the action of a powerful force in restoring moral, personal, or public order.[58] A particularly celebrated case was the amputation of the cancerous breast of one Mrs. Flowerday at the LMI in 1854. An account was published, along with the names and addresses of several witnesses. One interesting aspect of the report is the degree of personal detail it included. One might have expected that a description of the amputation and the names and addresses of the considerable number of witnesses would have been sufficient to convince readers that mesmerism had been a powerful and useful tool, but this does not seem to have been true. The operation was described in language far more personal, emotional, and moral than the authors would have used in an article for a medical journal: As the "first incision was made amidst the breathless silence . . . all eyes were directed to the face of the patient: *not a muscle moved—not a sigh! there was the same placid smile as when she closed her eyes under the mesmeric influence.*" Flowerday was so deep in the trance during the operation that afterward she climbed a flight of stairs without showing any consciousness or sign of fatigue. Photographs were taken of the patient during the entranced state and in a normal state of mind.[59] When the patient was awakened and looked down at the wound on her chest made by the amputation, she "beamed her thankfulness" to mesmerist and surgeon.[60] This language evoked a sense that mesmerism maintained bodily integrity in the most moral sense of this term: dignity and moral rectitude even when the structure of the body was being violated. It sustained *moral* fiber as the fibers of the body gave way to the knife.

One of the permanent practitioners at the London Mesmeric Infirmary, Theodysius Purland, began a scrapbook of his experiences and acquaintances in 1843. He filled it with broadsheets, letters from magnetic acquaintances, serious and satirical visual depictions of magnetic phenomena, handwriting samples of mesmeric celebrities, and other ephemera. Individuals throughout the "mesmeric world" contributed to it, sending their calling cards, advertising sheets, and offprints of their publications, broadsheets, and portraits. Visitors to the London Mesmeric Infirmary read it when they attended demonstrations or lectures or came to receive therapeutic treatment.[61] Through a consideration of its contents, then, we may gain an unusually acute sense of how such individuals represented to themselves the mental phenomena they witnessed and the sites at which they witnessed them, and how mesmeric tracts were read by their most sympathetic readers.

One of the most striking features of the scrapbook is the way in which its contents countered the most common grievance of the mesmerists, namely, the difficulty of achieving what some historians of science have called "virtual witnessing." This term refers to the crucial role played by accounts that are sufficiently detailed, and given by sufficiently trustworthy individuals, that they can be used in place of the experiment itself.[62] Mesmerists found that their work was particularly difficult to disseminate in this way. Purland's personal solution to this matter was to accentuate mesmeric accounts of all sorts in a very literal-minded manner by placing visual and narrative evidence next to them. Visitors read detailed descriptions of various experiments as they gazed at the sketches of the local landscape, or buildings in which trials had taken place, and traced the tours of various mesmerists as reports moved from town to town.

For instance, Purland closely documented the work of his colleague

W. J. Vernon. Broadsheets were consecutively arranged and interleaved with small pamphlets of his cures. They were accompanied by pictures of the lecture halls where demonstrations took place and even picturesque sketches of the cities he visited. This was a way of cherishing and keeping faith with the work of a beloved friend. Particular experimental triumphs were minutely documented so that readers of the scrapbook could visualize the location, follow the events, and read the epistolary testimonials they inspired. The last scene-setting sketch is a large representation of Nice, probably cut from the *Illustrated London News*. It is followed by one of a very few blank pages, on which Purland inscribed, in small, careful script, "Mr Vernon died in Nice."

Because Purland applied the same technique to individual written works on mesmerism as he did to the careers of his friends, this scrapbook offers us a valuable insight into what was constructed by some *readers* of mesmeric works as well as their authors and reviewers. Purland mounted the individual sheets of a number of works on the recto pages of his scrapbook, leaving the verso pages (the left-hand side of the two-page spread) blank for visual documentation. As readers turned the pages, the names of authorities cited in these works were underlined and their portraits pasted on the neighboring page. Mesmerists often expressed exasperation at the fact that it was very difficult to accept even prestigious secondhand accounts of such phenomena. The testimony of eminent savants (either in favor of mesmerism or in favor of open-minded examination of controversial new discoveries) seemed to have little impact upon audiences until they had seen the phenomena themselves. Indeed, this very problem was expressed by one much-quoted testimonial, Coleridge's declaration to a friend. He had "seen what I am certain I would not have believed on *your* telling and which in all reason, therefore, I can neither expect nor wish that you should believe on the faith of my assurance." [63] This was an argument that the friend had to see the phenomena himself, when he would find them to be real. Purland's annotation of such works changed the status of the authorities cited in the printed text. In Purland's book those heroic or wise individuals who had provided authoritative testimonials or philosophical justifications of open-minded scientific method (as well as the individuals who came in for attack in such arguments) stared up at the reader. They added the power of their presence to the words quoted in the text, in form if not in flesh.

Mesmerism and the Victorian Body

Although many doctors took up mesmerism, it was a predominantly lay practice: anyone who had the talent could mesmerize, and the practice clearly made sense, in some fundamental way, to a considerable portion of Victorian society. Mesmerism had a resolutely common character, in the sense of being accessible to all. In this respect it posed a challenge to the medical reforms that doctors were attempting to introduce to the management of illness.

The medical reform movement of the midcentury required reform of the habits and sensibilities of ordinary Victorians. One of these was the physical examination.[64] Before the early nineteenth century it had been unusual to examine a patient's body at first hand, but now new physical means of interrogating patients' bodies were being introduced. The physical examination involved an explicit suspension of modesty, the removal of clothing, and practices that were very different from other sickroom routines. Doctors complained that patients regarded exams as a breach of propriety and resisted submitting to them. They wished to introduce other changes, too, and advertised them in a number of books sold for household use on how to manage a sickroom. Such manuals of domestic medicine, written by doctors, worked to minimize the patient's freedom. They urged that household nurses be trained in hospitals, and that caregivers purchase special medical equipment for maintaining the sickroom. These and other measures would transform a sickroom into a kind of hospital ward, and bring patients under the regulated and licensed care of the profession.

This medical alternative was most systematically set out by Anthony Todd Thomson in *The Domestic Management of the Sick-Room*. Thomson argued that nurses should be trained in hospitals and receive licenses. No "unnecessary furniture" should remain in the room; a single central table was ideal. Cups, spoons, and other normal household tools were not sufficient to properly manage a medical patient. Special equipment was required—for example, a mechanical spoon to force invalids to swallow liquids and medicines against their will. Vinegar was insufficient to clean the sickroom properly, and should be exchanged for special chemicals common to hospital life. The nurse should purchase his or her supplies at the chemist's shop rather than the emporium. Thus the medical characterization of the sickroom was the scene of reform, and of the subjection of the patient to the healthy influence of medical discipline. The significance of these instructions to the control of the doctor over the patient was made explicit in an anecdote. Thomson referred to the exploits of his teacher, the eminent James Gregory of Edinburgh. On visits to a poor family Gregory always insisted that the window be left open to admit air and light to the invalid, and "generally pushed his cane through the windows" to ensure that his instructions would be obeyed.[65]

In the face of these reforms, mesmerism could actually seem conservative: a therapy and a mode of diagnosis that was less disruptive than its rivals to Victorian habits in the management of illness. Two characteristics of mesmeric practice and diagnosis worked in favor of mesmerism's application to illness. At first glance they may appear contradictory. One concerns the intimate bodily proximity involved in producing the magnetic trance; the other, the ability of the mesmeric clairvoyant to diagnose diseases and prescribe treatment at a distance.

The sickroom provided an intimacy between the invalid and caregiver—particularly family members and servants. It compelled an acknowledgment of the body and its sensations that was unusual beyond the sickroom walls. This bodily ease made the practices involved in producing the trance less of a breach of propriety than they might otherwise have been. Consider, for instance, the "passes" involved in the production of the trance. The hands "passed" down the length of the body, extremely close but not touching the skin or clothing. An invalid and her family, used to the washing and rubbing of aching limbs, would have been used to such physical proximity and even to similar kinds of motion to those involved in mesmerism. The sickroom legitimized patients' vulnerability—their exposure to, and dependency on, other eyes and other hands.

Another factor was the mesmeric diagnosis and prescription. The kinds of clairvoyant knowledge that were asserted by mesmeric subjects during these years were most influential, and more controversial among doctors, when they were used to make a diagnosis. Most clairvoyant diagnosticians were visitors from France or Germany, although there were several British clairvoyants. They included the mesmeric clairvoyants Julie, a French mesmeric patient who earned her living in London during the 1840s giving medical advice; the celebrated Alexis Didier; and Madame Von Gonnern. They claimed, like the O'Key sisters, to have cognitive access to the bodily and mental states of other people.

Mesmerism was also used to support traditional and domestic forms of knowledge at a time when doctors were trying to discredit these. For instance, one way of determining the gender of an unborn child involved hanging an object (usually the mother's wedding ring) from a piece of string over the belly of the pregnant woman; it rotated in one direction to indicate a boy, the other for a girl. This practice was said to be old in the early Victorian period, and it is still known today.[66] During the controversies over mesmerism, in which opponents demanded some instrumental means of measuring mesmeric influence, a device called the magnetoscope was introduced. This worked precisely in the manner of the original test, but used the notion of the differences in subtle vital fluids emitted by men and women to explain the movements of the magnetoscope.[67] One of the implications of this new instrument, which anyone could use, was to ratify as scientific and rational views of the body that would otherwise have been condemned as old wives' tales.

As the peripatetic mesmerists fanned out across the country, many doctors began, sometimes secretly, to try the practice themselves. One medical journal—the *Medical Times*—published articles and letters by lecturers as well as their professional "brethren." The most common stance among medical mesmerists involved two claims: on the one hand, a disavowal of the notion that a magnetic fluid was involved in the production of the trance, and on the other, a confirmation that, however the phenomena were produced, some new state of mind was elicited. One Mr. Duncan repudiated the notion of a magnetic fluid but carried out a successful demonstration of the altered states of mind.[68] J. L. Barrallier kept his distance from the theories that justified the use of "magnetic" passes, but did confirm that they worked; and a Manchester surgeon, Mr. Catlow, declared that the trance was produced, not by a magnetic force, but by the "undue continuance and repetition of the same sensible impressions."[69] An Oxford surgeon named Boyton concluded that mesmerism "strengthens the nervous system, improves the digestion, and tranquillizes the mind."[70]

In 1844 and 1845 some medical reformers fought back against the mesmeric therapists and clairvoyants, not only in theatrical public battles but in high-profile articles published in the national newspapers and major medical journals. John Forbes, medical reformer and editor of the *British and Foreign Medical Review*, published a systematic attempt to discredit the mesmeric clairvoyants in a series of articles that were published in the *Medical Gazette*, the *Lancet*, and the London *Times* and then were bound separately as a pamphlet. He described in detail the practices of clairvoyants, gave explanations for a number of the effects (explanations that involved no extraordinary mental phenomena), and described incidents in which he had discredited or at the very least cast doubt on the validity of the trial. Similar attacks were published by the phrenologist and doctor Daniel Noble, the physician Charles Radclyffe Hall, and Phillip Crampton, surgeon general of Ireland.[71]

Such well-publicized discreditations certainly had some effect, but they were not decisive, partly because mesmerism suited Victorian bodily sensibilities so much more than its rival techniques. Recall that one of the reasons that mesmeric clairvoyance was perceived as dangerous was that it adapted itself to prevailing attitudes toward the body, and in particular to the extent it was thought proper that one person could approach another. The different notions of propriety that new medical techniques wished to introduce required different bodily sensibilities.[72] The rise of hospital medicine was accompanied by a shift from the outside to the inside of the body as the focus of the medical gaze; the interior of the body was becoming "a surgical object *in potentia*."[73] It was therefore a threat to the developing medical and surgical cultures of the nineteenth century that mesmeric therapies tended to address the whole body rather than individual internal organs, focused on the outside of the body as the site of therapy, and were not as intrusive as their alternatives. Mesmerism could claim to fit the dominant sensibilities in British society better than "orthodox" medicine.

Mesmeric diagnosis and treatment were much more acceptable to many patients than allopathic treatment, and the latter could not claim a great record of success. Forbes wrote bitterly of clairvoyants' claims to diagnose internal complaints: "No doctor intrudes with his troublesome and disagreeable questions; no pulse need be felt, no tongue need be shown; no horrid *percussor* or more horrid *stethoscope* need frighten the gentle breast from its propriety. The lock is shorn . . . the dropped *Morning Post* is picked up . . . the ripple of a moment vanishes, and the surface of life is tranquil as before." [74] That is, to many members of the public, mesmerism was *more* proper than the medicine Forbes practiced. The "ripple of a moment" was all the disturbance that mesmerism would cause in the ordinary rhythm and ease of life.

This complaint pointed up a fundamental problem in extending elements of hospital culture to medical practice more generally, which would become central to doctors working in the 1840s. The stethoscope and percussion—two relatively recent innovations that asserted doctors' experimental access to the invisible parts of the body—were cultural shocks to the system. More generally, medicine was developing in ways that required the patient to become, during treatment, a quiet body, only passively involved in the procedures of diagnosis and treatment. If professionalized medicine were to succeed, doctors would have to teach the public new ways of being ill.

The Invention of Anesthesia

and the Redefinition of Pain

The gentlemen medicinal
Have of late in fury risen all

. . . .

Their courtesy punctilious
Has now grown cross and bilious.

The North of England Magazine *pokes fun at embattled doctors* [1]

BY THE MID-1840S doctors throughout Britain were torn between trying to beat the mesmerists and joining them. Each option was potentially disastrous. Defeating the mesmerists would be difficult, because they offered sick people an unrivaled benefit: relief from pain. Although opium and alcohol were traditionally used to take the edge off pain, it was dangerous to carry out surgical operations on people who had consumed large enough doses to become unconscious. When mesmerism was introduced in 1842 as a safe means of suspending sensibility, it was unique—at least at first. At a time when doctors were thought to injure as often as cure, mesmerism could plausibly be portrayed as doing no harm and as clearly succeeding in this easily tested effect. In refusing mesmerism doctors would be passing up one of the few techniques that could exert a positive influence on the patient and was guaranteed not to kill.

But joining the mesmerists was just as risky, because in the uncertain climate that pervaded early Victorian medicine, the consequences of adopting a controversial new technique were unclear. When mesmerism arrived in the medical community, medicine's future was being hotly debated, and traditional elements of medical life questioned and discarded. Physicians, surgeons, and the growing body of "general practitioners" were ostensibly run by a three-tiered hierarchy: the Royal College of Physicians, the College of Surgeons (which gained its "Royal" status in 1843), and the Society of Apothecaries in London. But the economic depression after the Napoleonic wars, competition for patients in the provinces, and the pressure of the radical reform campaign sparked several conflicting movements for change. Vigorous calls were made for improvements to medical practice and for boosts to the status of medical practitioners and institutions.[2] There was certainly room for improvement in doctors' public standing. *Punch* may have taken a particularly strong line when it portrayed medical students as a group of dissipated buffoons,[3] but feeling was widespread that many doctors were no more successful than those they branded "quacks."[4] The constant complaints about "quackery" came from so many quarters as to suggest that it was ubiquitous: there were quacks with formal medical training and without it, in the metropolis and in the provinces, and on the faculty of the universities.

By the early 1840s a wide range of campaigns and associations operated under the banner of reform.[5] Moderates would be satisfied if the colleges opened their doors to the many general practitioners without elite medical connections, and created a more meritocratic, skill-based system of medical accreditation. Radicals like Thomas Wakley wanted to abolish the hierarchical separation of medicine from surgery, and to establish state regulation.[6] Whatever one's political orientation, the proliferation of unlicensed practitioners was a major threat to doctors who had some kind of educational qualification, because the various forms of accreditation did not provide (in practice) the hard-and-fast distinction between legitimate and "heterodox" practitioners. The proposed solutions ranged from educational reforms to the introduction of legislation against lay therapists.[7]

While everyone abhorred quackery, therefore, they could not agree how to define and police it. Some doctors merely wanted to eliminate certain kinds of competition (for instance, by requiring a university degree). Others, like Wakley, thought that higher status would follow only from substantive changes in what doctors were taught. He thought it humiliating that an average doctor knew little more than his patients about "natural causes and effects." Doctors needed to "become natural and general philosophers."[8] Wakley wished to yoke such internal reforms to the regulation of quacks. This thoroughgoing package would ensure uniformity of proper practice, distinguish between qualified doctors and "quacks," and, eventually, relieve the public of a responsibility Wakley felt they were not qualified to carry out: the selection of their own medical therapies.

Many saw reform as a set of practical changes that would consolidate medicine as the arbiter of public questions about illness and the body. But securing public trust was not so straightforward. As many reformers complained, the public used different criteria to evaluate a potential therapist from those that most doctors used, or proposed to use, among themselves.[9] The public, one doctor complained, "naturally estimate a man's professional attainments," which "they cannot judge," by "the standard of his general knowledge, of which they are capable of judging."[10] Lay attitudes had to be brought into line with doctors' own definitions of expertise and legitimacy. But doctors did not agree on these definitions among themselves, and even if they could have, they still lacked the power of enforcement. At a time when medical practitioners were struggling on all these fronts, for a professional doctor to take up an intensely controversial practice was to make his position even more precarious than it already was. Doctors' reaction to mesmerism—whatever decision they made—could compromise their aspirations at a crucial moment in their collective history.

The Invention of Anesthesia

As the itinerants made their way across the country, doctors throughout Britain were confronted by physiological feats they could not match, found hard to contest, and could not explain, especially after mesmerism's anesthetic properties became known. A single, very well publicized surgical operation in November 1842 put mesmeric anesthesia into the public eye. Although this was not the first time mesmerism had been used as a surgical anesthetic, even in 1840s Britain,[11] it was the first to attain intense national publicity, perhaps because both the mesmerist and the surgeon were British, and well-respected in the community of Ollerton, near Nottingham, where the operation took place.

This case was an amputation of the leg at the thigh of one J. Wombell, a forty-two-year-old Nottinghamshire laborer "of calm and quiet temperament." The mesmerist, William Topham, was a barrister of the Middle Temple and the surgeon, W. Squire Ward, ran the Ollerton Infirmary near Nottingham. In the days before the operation, Topham placed Wombell into repeated states of diminished pain and deeper sleep. During the surgery he manifested none of the usual signs of pain except for a low "moaning." This sound was not influenced by the course of the operation; it did not change, and Wombell did not stir, when Ward cut the major nerve to the spine (the sciatic). Afterwards Wombell claimed to have felt no pain, though he did say he had *"once, felt as if I heard a kind of crunching."*[12] He recovered and lived for thirty years.[13]

Most modern readers will find it inconceivable that someone might pretend to feel nothing in such circumstances, but doctors fought violently over just this issue: was Wombell faking? Some claimed that he had colluded with the mesmerist and surgeon, and in fact had been fully conscious. That is, he had felt all the pain of the amputation but had used what muscles remained in that leg to hold it still even when the knife cut through the sciatic nerve.[14] If we are to make sense of what might seem an extraordinary line of argument, it will be useful to reconstruct the contemporary significance of the possibility of suspending sensation.

Since the 1790s at least, a wide range of drugs, gases, vapors, and techniques could suspend sensation, but until the 1840s, it seems that no one thought to use them for the suspension of pain in surgery. It is hard to imagine that doctors considered the possibility of using chemicals to suspend surgical pain for half a century but held back from doing so because they were afraid of harming the patient, because they were far more daring in experimenting with chemical cures on charity patients in hospitals. They could easily have experimented with anesthesia in the teaching hospitals. The first half of the nineteenth century saw the introduction of powerful chemicals into therapeutic treatment, many of which are ranked as poisons when used in lower doses than those used at the time for therapeutic purposes. Nor can one find an explanation in the thought that the patients themselves either were not familiar with these chemicals or could not get access to them. The perception- and consciousness-altering effects of ether and nitrous oxide routinely figured in shows at music halls and popular scientific displays. A great proportion of individuals had seen the effects of chemicals like ether, alcohol, laudanum, opium, and nitrous oxide, and had access to them.

It is extraordinary, on the face of it, that fifty years should have passed before nitrous oxide was routinely used in surgery. To understand why this should have been so, we need to begin with a rather obvious point: that sensation and insensibility had a significance in the early nineteenth century that was very different from their status after anesthesia became routine. The connection to surgery, once made and demonstrated, was obvious, but making this connection was not trivial. Otherwise, surgical anesthesia would have been developed in the late eighteenth century, when natural philosophers were most interested in developing different kinds of gases and vapors and documenting their effects on the body. Instead, the deliberate suspension of pain during surgery came as an afterthought in early Victorian mesmeric research, occurring to doctors years after they noted and debated mesmeric insensibility; and even after mesmeric anesthesia was developed, four years passed before the first official cases of chemical anesthesia.

What may be even more surprising to modern readers is that doctors' initial reaction to mesmeric anesthesia was not universal enthusiasm at the thought of suspending pain. Some were actually horrified by the idea. One medical editor protested that the idea of one person producing insensibility in another was too terrible even to admit into consideration. If pain could really be suspended, he threatened, "the teeth could be pulled from one's head" without one's even realizing it.[15] It was not the state of insensibility as such that was horrifying, of course, since alcohol and opium could dull pain and remove consciousness. But these were not dispensed by someone else; they were voluntarily consumed by the individual affected. It was the thought that one person could remove from others their sensitivity to their surroundings that was disturbing: it was an intolerable violation of the individual's agency. Recall that it was hard for doctors attending public demonstrations to believe that patients had been placed in an insensible state. Part of the moral outrage they displayed may have been directed at the supposed condition itself as well as the possibility of fraud. The horrors of the hypothetical scenario the editor laid before his readers further accentuate the difference in bodily sensibility between the 1830s and the late twentieth century.

There is no way of knowing whether the patients of such horrified doctors would have reacted similarly if the connection between the production of insensibility and its potential use in surgery had been presented to them (to any greater degree than the partial numbness imparted by alcohol), or whether, instead, they would eagerly have seized upon it. One is bound to suspect the latter, but in any case, it is certain that patients, like doctors, did not make the connections that would have given them the choice.

One factor in the changing attitude to pain was the rising power of surgeons, and their rivalry with physicians. During the early 1840s the College of Surgeons lobbied for and in 1843 received the royal accreditation that had long been the sole privilege of the Royal College of Physicians. In the late 1830s and early 1840s surgeons' drive for greater authority may have provoked, in reaction, some of the more pejorative representations of surgeons in reformist medical journals of the period. The *Medical Times,* for instance, was locked in a rivalry with the *Lancet,* which, run by the surgeon Thomas Wakley, lobbied for the cause of surgical reform.[16] In 1840 the *Times* ran a striking series of "portraits" of the master of the London surgical scene, Robert Liston. Liston was the star of the early Victorian surgical stage, preeminent for his speed and skill with the knife. But even Liston could be represented as a malicious, maladroit rogue within the reformist medical press. The *Medical Times* ran a series of hostile articles about him. Central to its sketch of a crude, cruel, and vulgar personality was the role of pain in Liston's surgical work. Pain, cast as both a sign of the surgeon's power and an indication that his status as a benign healer was suspect, was the fulcrum on which this character assassination turned.

The *Times* told of a dramatic struggle between Liston and a patient lying on the operating table. During a lithotomy the patient "attempted to close his limbs in a vain attempt to avoid stretching the gaping wound" and thereby suffer even greater pain. His surgeon shouted, "Slack your legs, man; slack your legs—or I won't go on." Then he "coolly relinquished the operation" and stated coldly, "No, I won't go on, . . . unless he loosens his limbs." Eventually the patient was able to do so.[17] Liston then proceeded with the operation and, telling the patient, "here's your enemy," removed the stone from his bladder. The article concluded with a scornful summing up: "[Liston's] element was blood, and he raised himself toward the pinnacle of professional renown upon the mangled trophies of his amputations and the reeking spoils of the operating theater." One could only pity the "trembling patients" waiting to "feel the temper of his knife." [18]

Pain had long been a sign of the surgeon's masterful status in the period before anesthesia. But in the eyes of this journalist, the surgeon was a sinister figure perversely vaulting himself to power by making a spectacle of the patient's pain and his dependent state. In this instance *mental* control of another person's body was a greater sign of surgical power than *physical* control. At the same time, though, it could be used as an indictment of the surgeon. Readers were expected to be particularly affected by Liston's insistence that the patient discipline *his own body* rather than merely calling upon attendants to do so. Thus pain and self-restraint were entangled with questions of medical and surgical authority. The broader significance of pain and self-restraint in reform debates makes it somewhat easier to understand the plausibility of some of the arguments advanced in the debate over whether J. Wombell had felt the knife as it cut through his motionless leg.

The first objection, offered by many in the audience, was most prominently stated by Sir Benjamin Collins Brodie, president of the Royal College of Surgeons. Brodie had a habit of mistrusting patient testimony, especially when the nerves were involved. In 1837 his lectures on the subject described how nervous complaints—those originating in the brain, the spine, and the nerves—could be manifest at different points and thus appear to be of local origin. Because of the existence of such cases, patients' accounts concealed more than they revealed about their problems. Only after "a diligent cross-examination"—putting the patient on trial, so to speak—could the surgeon "explain the real nature of the case." [19] Brodie regarded the sufferer as the (unwitting) deceiver of the doctor, whose professional duty lay in mistrusting his patient. Indeed, the patient had no means of understanding the real state of the body, because she or he was ignorant of the true nature of its interior: the mass of nervous connections under the seemingly simple structure of head, torso, arms, and legs. In the case of mesmerism, Brodie now argued that it was impossible to tell, from the testimony of the patient, whether she or he had experienced pain or not. Patient testimony was incapable of establishing physiological facts.

Another objection came from Marshall Hall, founder of the controversial theory of the reflex arc. He was a leading figure in a group that Elliotson sarcastically called the "reflex movement," and an opponent of Brodie on many medical matters. According to Hall's theory of the reflex arc, Wombell's leg should have jumped when the sciatic nerve was cut, independent of any sensations. It could only have lain still if he deliberately (consciously) immobilized it. Hall was supported by Wakley, Liston, James Johnson, and Brodie, an unlikely alliance formed expressly to oppose the mesmeric threat.[20]

Elliotson argued against Brodie's claims, in an 1843 pamphlet, by citing the many incidents in which a patient had pretended not to have felt surgical pain, but had been foiled by the surgeon. The implication was that a competent surgeon would see through deceit. Elliotson argued that because mesmerism was a nervous phenomenon, one could not expect the nerves to act in their usual manner (for instance, in terms of reflex action) when under the mesmeric influence.

During the next four years mesmeric anesthesia grew to be the test case for mesmerism in general. Further operations were carried out, debated, and evaluated. Long lists of successful amputations and other treatments were published in the *Zoist*, in the *Medical Times*, in local and regional papers, and then in some of the other medical journals.[21] Antagonists retaliated with anecdotes of mesmeric quackery that indicted other rival practitioners (such as bonesetters).[22] Mesmeric campaigners and critics contested and negotiated competing meanings of "anaesthesia," "pain," and the "testimony" of patients. These terms accordingly took on polemical meanings as the controversy progressed.

The Changing Meaning of Pain

The debate over anesthesia involved a major change in the representation of pain. Previously, doctors, if not their patients, did not tend to dwell (publicly, at least) on the horrors of pain, perhaps for the obvious reason that they could do little about it. If doctors ever mentioned pain, they treated it as an ordinary part of the cycle of life. But now mesmerists were subjecting "pain" to medical discipline, portraying it as horrible yet corrigible.

This campaign was fraught with difficulties, many in direct consequence of the mesmerists' solicitation of both the public and the profession at a time when medical reformers were trying to lower the authority of the general public over medical practice. Mesmerism's questions of mastery revealed prevailing uncertainties and ambivalences about the custody and care of the body. By portraying mesmerism as a physiological *discipline,* mesmerists also laid themselves open to the charge of self-promotion: the mesmerist might compete with the surgeon as the master of the surgical theater.

Mesmerists represented their craft to the public as a broadly useful social tool, not merely as a strictly medical technique, by yoking pain to disorder. After the culture of anesthesia had been created, people would look back on their experience of surgery as one physician did on his own leg amputation: a "black whirlwind of emotion, the horror of darkness, and the sense of desertion by God and man, bordering upon despair . . . which overwhelmed my heart." [23] Similarly, mesmerists portrayed the suspension of pain as a restoration of moral order—order in one's body, mind and social environment.

They who have heard, as I have heard, the dreadful shrieks, the sounds, more resembling the bellowing of a wild animal than the intonation of a human voice, which are wrung from the poor sufferer . . . can appreciate the almost overpowering thankfulness which swells the heart in return for a gift that, in a few moments, causes the shrill cry to sink into a tremulous murmur, that murmur again to become an almost inarticulate sob, and that sob to die away, at length, away into the blessed stillness of a deep restoring slumber. [24]

Some mesmerists actually claimed that mesmerism would restore the presence of God to the surgical theater—along with "solace" and "peace." Conversely, the unmesmerized surgical subject was an untamed beast in the grip of an evil influence. Pain became a sign of the surgeon's *helplessness,* rather than a necessary adjunct of his power. The surgical theater was to be seen as a spectacle of chaos or revolution, and mesmerism, in the hands of surgeons (or their mesmeric assistants), as the restorer of civilization.

One reason that mesmerists could see mesmerism as a form of bodily discipline, despite the notorious difficulty of controlling mesmeric subjects, was that anesthesia produced unconsciousness. An insensible subject could not act unpredictably in the manner made notorious to British doctors by Elizabeth O'Key. [25] In mastering the behavior of the patient, mesmerists could claim that they had subjected surgical pain to medical reform. [26] But if the patients were to be subject to medical discipline, so was the technique that imposed this discipline. Mesmeric anesthesia would succeed only if it could become a stable tool restricted to specific medical purposes and directed by professional medical practitioners.

Anesthesia, Pain, and Patient Testimony

Victorians used a dizzyingly large vocabulary for "suspended animation." [27] Sleep, coma, insensibility, catalepsy, suspended animation, transient death, human hibernation, and anesthesia were a fraction of the working vocabulary they used to describe different conditions. This linguistic cornucopia is symptomatic of the Victorians' obsession with deathlike states, and their insecurity about distinguishing one from another. Deep sleep might be mistaken for death, and sleepers might awaken in their graves. Nervous families bought coffins fitted with a rope leading to a bell above ground, to allow the undeparted to call for help. [28] In this climate it was no simple matter to label a particular behavior "anesthetized." During the anesthesia debates it was not easy to decide when a patient was "insensible." If he moaned, critics claimed he must have been awake throughout the operation. He had merely forgotten the experience. If he lay still, skeptics (like Hall) took his motionless state as an indication of conscious control of his body.

The definition of credible testimony was just as uncertain. In the case of anesthesia the challenge of evaluating the reality of the effects was complicated by the fact that the ultimate witness was also the subject of the phenomenon. The qualifications of a trustworthy witness—high social standing, say, or medical expertise—conflicted with the attributes of a good anesthetic "subject." If a subject-witness were of high standing, either in society generally or in medicine, this complicated the social geography of the experimental setting. A good experimental subject was "subject" to the authority of the experimental scene and its master. It was crucial that subjects' behavior conform to the requirements of public display and, in the context of Wakley's and Liston's reform projects, that it confirm the appropriate relations of surgeon and patient.

Moreover, critics saw the difficulties of the patient-as-witness as an inherent feature of anesthesia. A good witness must be astute and alert ("sober as a judge"), but a good anesthetic subject was influenced at just the moment when the "witness" would have to be most alert: the moment when the anesthesia took effect. Aside from all the difficulties associated with witnessing an "altered state" in oneself, the very construction of a patient-as-witness was a hindrance to the movement to discipline and control patients. To make the patient a witness was to attribute to him or her privileged access to knowledge. It would also make the therapeutic scene resemble the old patronage system in which the patient's verdict on therapeutic effects prevailed.[29] The result was an implicit compromise: the surgeons accepted the authority of the patient-as-witness but in return gained control of the therapeutic scene.

Empirical measures were deployed in attempts to bypass the problems of patient testimony: measures of pulse and breathing rates were taken in the hope of adjudicating mesmerists' claims. But since the anesthetists could not agree with their opponents on when a proper measure had been taken, or on what constituted a fair trial, the empirical tests solved nothing.[30] The same interpretive problems arose in the case of ether, but as we shall see, etherists found it possible not to address them.

The process of diagnosis posed similar problems. The activities of mesmeric clairvoyants gave the mesmeric subject the power of the doctor—namely, the ability to diagnose and to prescribe treatment. Mesmeric anesthetists hoped to bypass the issue of the cognitive possibilities of mesmerism. Their therapy rendered the subject unconscious (and therefore unable to "diagnose"). Moreover its single phenomenon, the production of insensibility, minimized the association with Martineau's patient-led mesmeric world, and stressed instead the unified power of the medical practitioners who employed it.

Ambivalent Supporters

The campaign for anesthesia soon won cautious encouragement from some doctors and natural philosophers. Indeed, one mesmeric tract that emphasized the "household" benefits of mesmerism and mesmeric anesthesia was welcomed by William Robert Grove, president of the Royal Society, who had attended some experiments. He supported the view that the "simple" effects of mesmerism such as anesthesia were real, though he dismissed the "proofs" of clairvoyance.[31] John Forbes, founder and editor of the *British and Foreign Medical Review*, argued along the same lines. The "simple" mesmeric effects—those resembling sleep and other naturally occurring phenomena—were unfeigned. Indeed, mesmeric anesthesia might become a great boon to mesmerism, if it were not proved false. In the meantime he urged doctors to evaluate mesmerism—not to ignore it.[32] And the mesmerists, "even those of the highest class, the members of the medical profession," needed to eschew the "extraordinary" phenomena, which he thought were clever frauds.[33] Forbes did not wish to drive mesmerism beyond the fringe of scientific inquiry, where he felt it existed at the moment, but to pull it into the mainstream of scientific attention, where its merits could be appraised.

Another cautious proponent was the surgeon John Chatto. He wrote to the *London Medical Gazette* to urge that mesmerism be taken up by the "profession," who could train themselves on poor patients. He warned that the rich would soon demand to be mesmerized. Surgeons would then find themselves in the dangerous position of training themselves on their most valued patients, as they struggled to catch up with their nonmedical rivals: "it seems a far more gracious circumstance that [mesmerism] should spontaneously originate with the profession, than that it should be forced upon us by the pressure of public opinion. The only difference arising from the delay shall be, that the experiment must be commenced with a different class of persons."[34] While poor patients could not demand anesthesia, the "wealthy and informed" would "naturally" insist on it. Of course, this ominous specter of market forces applied only to anesthesia, not to the wilder forms of mesmerism. Mesmerism's "ultrapretensions," such as clairvoyance, should never be allowed within the halls of a London hospital.

Although the mesmerists had several supporters among important physicians, surgeons, and natural philosophers, it was still unclear whether the mesmerist could coexist with the surgeon—both powerful performers unused to sharing a stage. Elliotson's brand of mesmerism, like his style of practicing medicine, was theatrical. The role of the mesmerist as master of the theater represented a potential conflict with the other, more established masters of theater, surgeons. If mesmerism were to succeed in British hospitals as a surgeon's tool, it would have to become a backroom activity, performed behind the scenes. Like the scientific work of Faraday, which took place in a basement laboratory before being displayed before audiences at the Royal Institution, the production of the mesmeric trance would have to disappear.[35] It remained to be seen whether British mesmerists could produce the magnetic spectacle in private.

By late 1846 mesmeric anesthesia was on the brink of gaining acceptance among medical constituencies that had long resisted mesmerism. A colonial surgeon had gained government support for his mesmeric practice, in which he used mesmeric anesthesia to perform hitherto impossible operations. British doctors, who thought of India as a laboratory for the development of new social, scientific, and medical innovations, found the Indian trials easier to believe. One claimed that Indian subjects were "scarcely intelligent enough" to have been able to pretend their invulnerability to pain.[36] Another important event was John Elliotson's Harveian Oration in the Royal College of Physicians. According to the rules of the college the youngest fellow who had not previously had the opportunity gave the oration. In 1846 this gave Elliotson the podium. He used Harvey's discovery of the circulation of the blood as an example of how discoveries with revolutionary implications could initially meet with incredulity and resistance; mesmerism's critics were likened to Harvey's misguided opponents.[37] Meanwhile, the London Mesmeric Infirmary had collected its first round of subscriptions, and rented prominent new rooms in Bedford Square (facing off, as it were, with Thomas Wakley's home and headquarters). One exasperated *Lancet* correspondent rhymed his prognosis for mesmerized medicine.

Away with the *Hall*, and away with the *College*;
Away with chirurgico-medical knowledge!
.   .   .   .
No more shall we hear the afflicted complain—
Operations will give more of pleasure than pain;
And ladies will smile, in their mesmerized trance,
As the pains of their uterine efforts advance!
.   .   .   .
And whilst sceptics their agonized vigils are keeping,
[Mesmer's] disciples will through their efforts be sleeping.[38]

Ether Anesthesia

Skeptics' "agonized vigils" were to be rewarded sooner and more dramatically than they could have hoped, when the anesthetic properties of ether vapor were discovered in November 1846. The practice of inhaling the vapor of sulfuric ether was widely popularized during the early nineteenth century as a substitute for taking nitrous oxide in pneumatic medicine (the use of vapors and gases for therapeutic, not anesthetic, purposes) and in popular science demonstrations.[39] Ether's pedigree resembled mesmerism's. It was a late Enlightenment practice, developed by political radicals (for example, Thomas Beddoes at the Pneumatic Institute), which seemed to imply that mental processes were fundamentally physical.[40] During the first several decades of the nineteenth century, they were both recreational practices that drew crowds at public science shows.[41] They were staple resources for traveling science lecturers and were both put on display at the Adelaide Gallery, London's main forum for popular science lectures. Figure 43, while it depicts nitrous oxide, evokes the kind of associations people would have had with ether, too.

During the radical medical reform agitation of the 1840s, ether was attacked as part of a general movement to clean up medical education. Medical students' fondness for consuming the inebriating vapor in "ether frolics" was undermining their education and encouraging habits of dissipation. Scenes

Laughing Gas.

"Some jumped over the tables and chairs; some were
bent upon making speeches; some were very much inclined
to fight; and one young gentleman persisted in an attempt
to kiss the ladies."

FIGURE 43 A tumultuous scene of nitrous-oxide inebriation. Cruikshank, "Laughing Gas"
(1839). Iconographic Collection, Wellcome Institute.

such as figure 44, although it depicts German medical students of this period,
capture the sense of a dangerous lack of self-control and dignity that ether
frolics represented. Wakley and others argued that, because it could disorder
the mind, ether should be used only by legitimate practitioners. Of course,
criteria for medical "legitimacy" were not at that time under seal of law. When

FIGURE 44 German medical students drunk on ether and beer. *Illustrierte Zeitung* (1847).

ether's anesthetic properties were first publicized and disseminated, etherists could not police its use, restrict its phenomena to insensibility, nor distinguish it from the practice on which it was based: mesmerism.

It was largely through the ineffectiveness of a Boston dentist, Horace Wells, both in mesmerism and in the use of nitrous oxide, that ether anesthesia was developed in 1846.[42] Wells had been experimenting for some time with mesmerism in the hope of anesthetizing his dental patients. But Wells was no mesmerist. His every effort was an abysmal failure.[43] When he noticed, during a popular science demonstration in 1845, that subjects "drunk" on nitrous oxide appeared to feel no pain, he immediately arranged a public demonstration and administered the nitrous oxide himself. He announced to his audience that nitrous oxide would usher in a "new era of tooth pulling." But the trial was a flop; the patient's sensitivity to pain remained undiminished. Wells found to his dismay that practice and skill were necessary for success. He retired in humiliation and later committed suicide after his ex-dental-partner, William Morton, received the credit for discovering inhalation anesthesia (using ether) only one year later.

Morton had been present for Wells's disastrous performance and eventually decided to try ether instead. After much practice, notably on a subject who had requested mesmeric anesthesia, Morton carefully arranged his public demonstration of ether on 19 October 1846. Morton administered the ether, and Dr. John Collins Warren performed the surgery. The operation involved a small incision to the jaw, followed by some minor dental work. According to several accounts the patient moaned and moved restlessly under the knife. Ether had not made him insensible, he later testified, though his pain had been somewhat dulled. The incision had felt to him as though a "hoe" had been "scraped" across his skin. But as Warren finished the surgery, the audience went wild. "Gentlemen," he proclaimed, "this is no humbug."

News quickly spread through Boston and America, and almost as rapidly to England. The first announcement of ether anesthesia in the medical press stressed its "medical" character by opposing it to mesmerism: "a remarkable discovery has been made. Unlike the trickery and farce of mesmerism, this is based on scientific principles, and is solely in the hands of gentlemen of high professional attainment, who make no secret of the matter or manner. To prevent it from being abused or falling into the power of low, evil minded, irresponsible persons, we are informed that the discoverer has secured a patent." [44] In this passage, ether was what mesmerism was not: it was based on "scientific principles" (however unspecified) and restricted from the start to qualified practitioners. This portrayal of ether as the inherently respectable tool of dignified surgeons was reinforced by a retrospective celebration of Morton's first operation, painted in the 1880s (fig. 45). Here the surgeons soberly execute and evaluate the anesthetized operation. In contrast to his testimony at the time, the patient is not conscious, and all traces of the unruly excitement and sensation that were described in 1846 are gone.

Criteria for Discovery

Ether's status as a heroic, revolutionary new technique was helped along by the way the Morton experiment was staged, and by the thousands of articles that celebrated ether in the medical and general press. Etherists' triumph lay not so much in a new discovery, but in securing a reputation for their anesthetic technique as both effective and legitimate. The approbation of medical onlookers went a long way toward insulating ether from the sorts of questions that plagued mesmeric anesthesia—questions that the etherists would have found difficult to answer.

Ether is known as the first anesthetic because it was the first technique to become established as a legitimate and medical means of removing pain. In understanding why ether was accepted instead of mesmerism, it is important to bear in mind the asymmetry of the processes that adjudicated each of

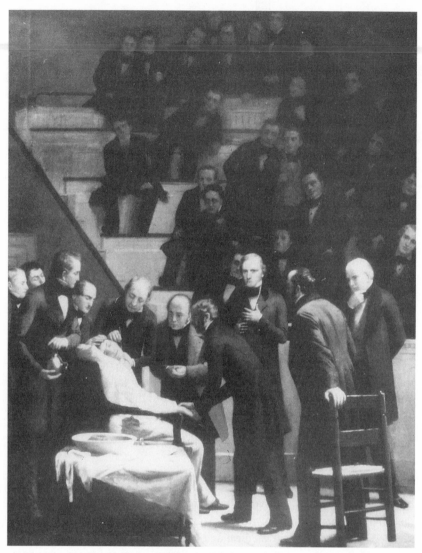

FIGURE 45 This retrospective celebration of William Morton's operation revises the accounts of the original witnesses: rather than moaning and moving under the knife, the corpselike patient now seems completely unconscious; unlike the uproar described in original accounts, these witnesses are grave, professional, and dignified. Francis A. Countway Library of Medicine, Boston Medical Library, Cambridge, Mass.

them. The following points were *not* brought against Morton and the later etherists. First, the patient moaned and mumbled during the operation. This phenomenon, when it occurred during mesmeric operations, was seen as a disqualification of mesmerism's pain-reducing claims. Furthermore, Morton's patient actually told the audience that he had felt pain, and the pain he had experienced was the result of an operation that was trivial in comparison with the leg amputation carried out by Topham and Ward. Second, the validity of the witness's testimony was not questioned. This was true of all examples of ether inhalation. More than anything else, it illustrates etherists' success in suggesting that their phenomenon had little to do with the patient. The effects produced by ether were the physician's property: the anesthetic apparatus was his means of expropriating control over the patient's body as well as over the patient's "sensibility." Third, the criticism that mesmerism required practice and that a "rapport" was necessary between subject and operator could well have been applied to the etherists, but it was not.[45] This asymmetry is particularly clear when one considers that etherists' first public attempt to anesthetize a dental subject was a complete failure, the second a partial success after much practice. Finally, it is important to remember that, both in Boston and England, the effort to establish ether as a medical agent largely ignored the task of determining *how* ether rendered patients insensible, but merely accepted the fact that it did so. Unlike the case of mesmerism, where critics had claimed that a practice was unsafe if unaccompanied by a valid causal theory, many of the same critics had no such qualms in evaluating ether.[46] At the heart of these differences is the fact that the ether anesthetists were able to secure tacit agreement from their audience that they controlled the experimental situation. Pain was treated as unproblematic because it had become the property of the surgeon, to be "conquered" by the anesthetic apparatus at will.

The spread of anesthesia through Britain was portrayed by a contemporary author as an "epidemic." The alacrity with which, as we shall see, ether was taken up by the medical profession, demonstrates that, since surgeons embraced the practice before they had any strong evidence of its effectiveness, other reasons must have prevailed in its acceptance. At every point in the brief "epidemic" of its popularity, ether was entirely defined as a substitute for mesmerism. Indeed, if a "discovery" was made during ether's reign in 1847, it was that ether could not easily be made to look sufficiently different from mesmerism to become a reputable anesthetic agent.

Both ether and mesmerism could produce an anesthetic state; both took skill to administer, and ether (like future chemical anesthetics) had what one might consider to be the distinct disadvantage of killing some of its patients. Why, then, was ether so much more acceptable to doctors? The answers have to do not with its efficacy and safety but with the way it complemented the so-cial relations surgeons wished to establish with patients.

One factor was the speed and regularity of the effects. Mesmerism could produce an anesthetic state in many, if not most individuals, but it took an indeterminate amount of time, and sometimes several sessions, to achieve a deep trance. This mattered less in a traditional "patronage" system of medi-cine, where doctors attended patients in their homes and spent considerable time with each one, than it did in the mid-nineteenth-century climate of medi-cal reform, in which many doctors and surgeons wished to model their rela-tions with patients on the authoritative relations that obtained in hospitals. A practice that involved varying lengths of time (sometimes considerable ones) ran counter to the spirit of efficient management within hospitals. Ether anes-thesia, like mesmerism, required skill, but in skilled hands it achieved the anesthetic state quickly—if sometimes fatally.

A second factor was that mesmeric effects explicitly involved the relation-ship between two people; one might even say that they *consisted of* that rela-tionship. The power of ether to produce an anesthetic state lay in a chemical, not a social, relationship. Ether avoided the disturbing, sometimes subversive associations that attended the mesmeric relationship. These criteria were re-lated to the representations that doctors made of their own authority, and they secured ether's triumph over mesmerism in 1847.

When Francis Boott, one of the first in Britain to hear about the anesthetic technique, wrote to Robert Liston, Elliotson's old rival and still professor of surgery at UCH, Liston moved quickly. He sent invitations to various medi-cal and lay acquaintances, informing them of the time and place of a planned operation two days later.[47] He consulted Peter Squire, an instrument maker, about the best techniques for effective administration of ether, and practiced several times in the interim. He selected as his patient a butler—perhaps the best compromise in the search for a good witness who was sufficiently low on the social ladder while still retaining responsibility.

Liston's operation (recorded in a painting of unknown origin, fig. 46) seemed deliberately reminiscent of landmark mesmeric feats. The operation, an amputation of the leg at the thigh, was identical to the Topham and Ward operation four years earlier; the theater of UCH, where Elizabeth O'Key had made her name, was the venue. During the operation the patient moaned and stirred restlessly, but did not cry out. Reports of the proceedings quoted Lis-ton as crowing that "[t]his Yankee dodge beats mesmerism hollow."[48] That evening he wrote to his friend, Professor James Miller of Edinburgh, exulting, "HURRAH! Rejoice! Mesmerism, and its professors, have met with a 'heavy blow, and great discouragement.' An American dentist has used ether (inhala-tion of it) to destroy sensation in his operations, and the plan has succeeded in

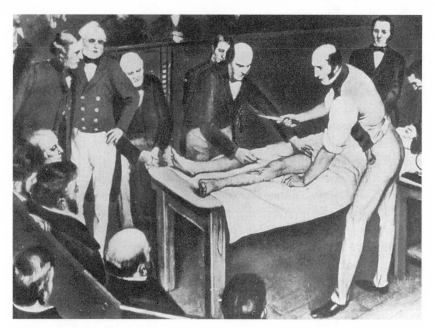

FIGURE 46 Robert Liston performs the first operation using ether anesthesia in University College Hospital Theatre. Artist unknown. University College London Archives.

the hands of Warren, Hayward, and others in Boston . . . Rejoice!"[49] Miller read the letter to his students and then made arrangements (without consulting Liston) for its immediate publication in a general magazine. At the beginning of his essay on anesthesia he announced that it was "a matter which touches all members of the human family alike."[50] There are two points to be made regarding this letter. First, the fact that news of ether anesthesia was immediately transmitted to the public indicates that public demand for mesmeric anesthesia had played an important role in making anesthesia a prominent issue. The etherists would have to not only establish ether as the respectable alternative to mesmerism, but even erase the fact that a struggle had taken place between them at all. The effort to make ether legitimate would have to become invisible, before ether could attain its status in heroic histories of medicine: of being essentially legitimate, scientific, and "an-aesthetic."

The next stage in the battle for control of anesthesia was extensive coverage in the medical and general journals. In the first six months of 1847, the *Lancet* is said to have published 112 articles on ether.[51] Wakley represented the "ethereal" phenomenon as having "a remarkable perfection" about it, especially since it would destroy, he claimed, using an appropriate metaphor, "one limb of the mesmeric quackery." His hardest task was to depict ether as the "natural" agent to fill the niche that the mesmeric campaign had worked so hard to create for mesmeric anesthesia.[52] Wakley's claim was polemical, an attempt to gloss over the difficulties surrounding etherization. Many rehearsals were required to become an adept anesthetist, and neophytes recorded many failures. Indeed, in a subsequent issue of the *Lancet* in 1847, a Dr. A. Fairbrother expressed concern regarding the many deaths from ether, and asked more than twenty questions about how to administer it.[53] Ether anesthesia was, then, far less successful in doctors' surgeries than it was in the medical press, although the hagiographic histories of anesthesia (dating from Wakley's) have made this discrepancy easy to overlook.

One of the most important aspects of the campaign was the attempt to restrict the use of ether to the medical profession, and to limit to insensibility the range of phenomena it produced. Those who responded cautiously to ether warned that it would be difficult for British hospitals to restrict it to themselves. Editorials abounded in medical journals discussing how etherization might be controlled by licensing schemes.[54] The physiologist William Benjamin Carpenter, writing as editor of the *Medico-Chirurgical Review*, claimed that the public and the medical community had been "spellbound" by ether. Anesthesia had transformed surgical theaters into fashionable "scenes of operative display," Carpenter wrote censoriously, and ether was being used "too indiscriminately" by people within and without the profession. "Already in London, chemists' shops are placarded 'painless extraction of teeth' and those in Paris, 'ici on etherize'; and, although the correctional police of the latter capital is armed with sufficient power to suppress any abuse of this kind, we fear that we have in this country no anticipatory means at our command."[55] Carpenter's concerns were related to the difficulties faced by the temperance movement, in which he was involved. The associations of ether with alcohol were strong, and Carpenter's words reflect not only his concerns but the widespread view that ether anesthesia was just another easily accessible means of becoming "dead drunk."[56] Thus the accessibility of the gas, as well as its theatrical identity, made it more difficult for crusading anesthetists to give it a medical, rather than a popular and recreational, identity.

The association of ether inhalation with drunkenness proved difficult to remove, since a great deal of skill was needed to render the patient unconscious without giving rise to effects comparable to inebriation. When Miller wished to repeat Liston's etherizations, for instance, Liston obligingly sent him the ether apparatus, a bulb with sponge and mouthpiece. But the skill of administering the vapor did not accompany the bulb. During Miller's surgery the patient was not sensible to pain, but he did remain conscious. Throughout the preparations and the operation itself, he shouted, laughed, told jokes, and predicted that he could never be made to go to sleep by a recreational substance like ether. Miller's "inebriated" subject was the norm rather than the exception, and his behavior demonstrated what surgeons called the stage of "exhila-ration" in ether anesthesia. The range and theatrical nature of "exhilarated" behavior had made ether valuable to the public lecturers, but here they were potentially disastrous. Ether's champions therefore used historical accounts to try to dissociate the present scientific use of ether from the days of "ether frol-ics," and to report accounts that played down instances where ether stimulated undesirable behavior in patients rather than knocking them out.[57]

Much of this work involved making a systematic distinction between ether and mesmerism. In early April the *Lancet* carried a long essay comparing ether to mesmerism, showing how ether avoided the traditional objections that had been leveled at mesmerism: "I myself am perfectly satisfied that nothing was feigned. The patient is neither nervous, hysterical, nor in delicate health . . . Her manner of expressing her opinion during the ether dreaming, though free from the slightest immodesty, was far removed from the reserve which a knowledge of the presence of those around would have occasioned . . . It was impossible to make the lady talk nonsense." [58] This was a compromise be-tween an admirably "controlled" patient, whose etherized state did not permit her to escape into the behavior of Elizabeth O'Key, and the need for an "inde-pendent" witness whose testimony could be trusted. The *Lancet* later used this case to demonstrate that ether resolved the problem of the patient-as-witness, which had plagued the mesmerists.

The Decline of Mesmeric and Ether Anesthesia

Elliotson was enraged at the hijacking of anesthesia by the etherists. He was particularly furious at what he saw as a campaign of silence by the medical journals, which devoted little space to antimesmeric editorials after the first months of 1847. Elliotson interpreted this as an attempt to freeze mesmerism out of medical debate altogether, and to represent to the reading public that mesmeric research had been abandoned in the wake of ether anesthesia.[59]

William Gregory, professor of chemistry at Edinburgh and one of mes-merism's most respected supporters, was horrified at the naïveté of mesmerists who regarded ether as an aid to their practice rather than its replacement. In an open letter to Elliotson, he passionately urged mesmerist anesthetists to re-spond to their rival. Mesmerism had to force its way, through brute utility, into "household uses" like the amelioration of pain. Through these practical means alone rather than the "higher phenomena" would mesmerism enter medi-cal legitimacy more generally: "I beg to suggest this investigation to you, and through you to practical mesmerists in general, because I consider it of the greatest importance to render the mesmeric action more certain of success than it is at present." [60] This advice foreshadowed the fate of mesmeric anesthesia. Although mesmerism continued to be a thriving practice outside the medical community, even to the point of the establishment of several "mesmeric infirmaries" during the late 1840s, the defeat of mesmeric anesthesia, like the O'Key incident in 1838, was widely perceived to spell the end of mesmerism's potential legitimacy. Mesmeric anesthesia was not taken into hospitals as a preparation for surgery during these years, even when first ether and then chloroform were deemed unsuitable anesthetic agents and exchanged for others.

The late 1840s saw an evanescence not only of the mesmeric fluids but of the ethereal ones that had figured in these debates. The magnetic fluids dissipated from the surgical scene during the "ethereal epidemic": ether's success evaporated as well during the late 1840s. By the end of the decade, chloroform had superseded it as the anesthetic agent of preference. According to contemporary accounts, this was because it avoided ether's tenacious stage of "exhilaration." The comparisons with drunkenness and with theatrical displays could not be eradicated as long as this entertaining phenomenon persisted, nor could the surgeon demonstrate complete control over the behavior of the subject. Chloroform, on the other hand, generally bypassed the stage of exhilaration. As one surgeon put it, "the time of the surgeon is saved [and] . . . the patient has not the same degree of tendency to exhilaration and talking." [61] One moment the patient was a conscious subject; the next, he or she was a body on the operating table.

As for the longer-term effects of anesthesia, Victorian hospital reports do not reflect a consequent increase of successful surgeries. Death rates for surgery were still extremely high from loss of blood and infection. [62] The assumption that anesthesia must have caused such a revolution is a sign of the success of the campaign to create a perfect profile for ether anesthesia in the pages of the *Lancet* in 1847, a veil dropped over the messy controversy surrounding the emergence of inhalation anesthesia. [63] The controversy over mesmerism cannot be explained in terms of a simple duel between the establishment and the fringe, since it was the construction of mesmerism as deviance that was at stake. Mesmerism, then ether, and later chloroform were seen as potentially important tools in the construction of a professional relationship between surgeon and patient; mesmerism, then ether, then chloroform were marginalized within a short time.

There is another development in the medical response to mesmerism that contributes to our understanding of how doctors tried to make trances medically acceptable during these years: the practice of hypnotism, developed in 1842 by the surgeon James Braid. Of the many consciousness-altering practices that flourished in the 1840s, hypnotism is the one that (in greatly altered form) survives today; hence it has a far more familiar ring to modern readers. However, it was only one of a great many terms associated with at least a dozen related mesmeric practices. They were distinguished from each other by different purported causes and different means of producing the trance. Braid claimed that an individual voluntarily suspended his or her will and produced the trance by a combination of imagination and attention. The phenomena, then, were produced entirely by the subject's own mind in interaction with an external sensory stimulus (visual, auditory, or tactile) rather than the insensible influence emanating from the mesmerist (magnetism, electricity, or the will). The stimulus could be a candle flame, regular drops of water falling from a faucet, magnetic passes, the eyes of another person, or perhaps the more familiar pendulum or watch fob. The object of one's attention was unimportant; what mattered was choosing to focus one's mind on one particular thing. Once this focus was maintained, the will became suspended. The intensity of focus also sharpened the senses. What people mistook for clairvoyance was actually a mental state that intensified the ordinary perceptual powers. These augmented senses transmitted information to the mind, but because the subject was not conscious, he or she was only aware of the information itself—not its (perceptual) source. A faint whiff of perfume, for instance, could convey the gender and the position of an individual standing near a blindfolded subject, who would seem to have come by the information by extraordinary means such as clairvoyance. The mesmeric subject was displaying an elaborate reflex system, taking in a stimulus and, without a conscious process of thought and analysis, reflecting it outward in another form.

Braid's "hypnotism" made three important changes to mesmerism. He removed from mesmerism its magnetic fluids, the sexual associations that attended the "passes," and the personal relationship between mesmerist and subject explicit in the claim that one person's body, mind, or will impinged on another's. Braid actively sought to denigrate the mesmerists and to distinguish his practice from theirs; he made a point of telling readers of the *Medical Times* that he had managed to use his new techniques to entrance the eminent advocate of mesmerism, the physician Herbert Mayo.[64] Braid's success in ridding his practice of some of mesmerism's controversial features was one factor in hypnotism's survival, although in the 1840s he was regarded as only one of many controversial practitioners, and drew his share of attacks.[65] Braid's version of the trance *was* unusual in providing a number of elite scientific figures with a potentially less controversial way of representing the vicissitudes of volition.

The rise of chemical anesthesia did not, of course, spell the end of mesmerism, or even (entirely) of mesmeric anesthesia. The death rates associated with the chemical anesthetics led some patients to resort to mesmerists instead, and mesmerists were still consulted for curative purposes. Most important, medicine had provided no explanation for the trance. In the absence of such an explanation Victorians continued to believe in it and to carry out researches into it. The place where mesmeric anesthesia was practiced most spectacularly and for the longest period was not Britain, however, but colonial India.

Colonizing Sensations

in Victorian India

VICTORIAN MESMERISM came to India in 1845, at the height of the controversies in Britain. Although London doctors looked to India as a sort of laboratory where anesthesia could be tested in a controlled environment, European residents in India invested mesmerism with a wider range of issues, relating to colonial power, cultural exchange, and the relative status of East and West. Colonial residents recounted their experiences of mesmerism in ways that raised and sometimes answered questions about superiority and inferiority, influence and submission between colonizer and colonized.

Mesmerism's chief colonial advocate, the Scottish surgeon James Esdaile, was fond of recounting a story that evokes these issues succinctly. According to Esdaile he and a local healer ("one of the most famous magicians in Bengal") were both summoned to the same house to minister to a patient. Esdaile arrived first and cured the patient before his rival made it to the bedside.[1] When the "magician" asked for an introduction and an explanation of the cure, Esdaile did not say that he had studied medicine at the University of Edinburgh, or that he had treated his patient with mesmerism. Instead, he gave himself the pedigree of a great Eastern mystic. He had "studied the art of magic in different parts of the world," he said through a translator, and "particularly in Egypt," where he learned "the secrets of the great Sooleymann, from the Moollahs and Fuqueers." Esdaile, in turn, queried his "brother magician" about his own techniques. Since "all knowledge" came from the East, was it not possible that their arts were the same? Each undertook to show the other what he could do.

The magician sent for a brass pot filled with water and a leafy stick. Seating himself near the patient, he "muttered" a series of "charms" over the bowl, "dipped his fore-finger into the water," and "flirted it into the patient's face." Then he slowly, repeatedly stroked the patient with the leaves from head to toe, his knuckles almost touching the body. This would continue for a half hour or more, he told Esdaile, depending on the need.

Now it was Esdaile's turn. But he wished to make his demonstration on the magician rather than his patient. When the man agreed, Esdaile asked him to lie down and to shut his eyes, so that Esdaile could not gain entry to his brain by "that inlet." Esdaile would later recount how, at this point, he chanted the song "King of the Cannibal Islands" as an "invocation," to give the proceedings a proper note of "solemnity." After Esdaile made long, stroking motions down the magician's body for a quarter of an hour, his face "became perfectly smooth and calm," and he seemed to sleep. After a few minutes, however, he "bolted up," clapped his "hands to his head, cried he felt drunk, and nothing could induce him to lie down again."

The next day the two men met once again. With true British tact Esdaile declared, "Well, you were too strong for my charm last night, I could not put you to sleep." If the magician had succumbed to Esdaile's "charm," he was immune to false flattery. "Oh! yes Sahib," he protested, "you did; I allow it; it is allowed that you put me to sleep."

On one level this tale plays out a familiar exchange, in which British colonials projected "native superstition" onto Indian culture. Victorian stories of the East scripted dramas whose Indian players performed the superstition and subordination assigned to them, confirming the power and rationality of their British masters. Esdaile's English readers assumed that it was impossible to converse with such a man without spinning a story that would accord with his expectations. But Esdaile's story relied on his own assumption that the "magician" was superstitious and gullible. He projected superstition and gullibility onto the other man so that the events could, in circular fashion, reinforce the assumptions that inspired them.

Esdaile's fictional pedigree was useful in other ways. His fraud weakened what would otherwise have been a strong association between the two practices. Mesmerism recalled the trances of traditional Indian healers, along with snake charming, the phenomenon of "fascination," opium taking, and the like. By mocking the healer in a way that only British readers could appreciate, he suggested that, although individuals like the "magician" might be able to produce the same phenomena, European science alone could discern their causes.

So far this is a straightforward illustration of how the manufacture of indigenous superstition could help manufacture Western superiority.

But mesmerism added a second dimension: when Esdaile refused to make a symmetrical show of his "charm," he was doing more than displaying his therapy in a particularly dramatic way. Turning the healer into a mesmeric subject stripped him of authority, at least in the eyes of a Western observer. And because mesmerism was a display of interpersonal power, the magician's susceptibility could look like an idealized scene of colonial power and submission. The "magician's" acknowledgment of Esdaile's power could look like a public acceptance of his allotted position in the colonial order.

When mesmerism came to India, then, it seemed to have the potential to enhance Victorian medicine's efforts to bring Western knowledge east: it would westernize even the Eastern trances and mystic arts, and convert exotic practitioners into educated medical helpers or discredited superstitious fools.

Medicine in Colonial Bengal

When he first tried mesmerism in 1845, Esdaile was running the Native Hospital in the small village of Hooghly, on the outskirts of Calcutta.[2] The circumstances of a colonial surgeon made it easier for a single individual like Esdaile to promote a new project, even though colonial doctors were more nervous than their colleagues in Britain about appearing "heterodox," particularly in association with Indian culture.

In 1845 colonial medicine was shifting gears. In medicine, as in the rest of the colonial apparatus, an old expectation of exchange and cooperation with Indian culture was being replaced by an intolerance for things "oriental" and an insistence on the one-way transfer of knowledge and culture from Britain to India as the goal of colonial life. Racial segregation was rigidly enforced in hospitals and madhouses and, beginning in the late 1830s, in medical education. Britons and Indians had studied together in the early nineteenth century, but this cooperation was broken off after the Macaulay Minute of 1835.[3]

Some features of medical life did remain cooperative. English products were often prohibitively expensive, making Indian pharmacopoeia indispensable as substitutes, and indigenous medicine continued to fascinate doctors well after intellectual exchange soured or stultified in other areas of colonial life. Indian medical workers were brought into the colonial apparatus beginning in the early nineteenth century, and their numbers rose steadily.[4]

Despite colonial doctors' ambivalence about "Britishness" in medical practice, they were freer than their British counterparts in the professional choices they made. One might have assumed that government kept a tight rein on doctors, who were ostensibly under the direct control of the Medical Board, but its activities were erratic, and doctors were accustomed to having their own way.[5] Moreover, the rapid turnover of medical staff and the long distances between practitioners made the medical community unstable and fragmented. One handbook for newcomers warned that, unless they were based in Calcutta itself, they would have little sense of community. It gave basic instructions for locating local authorities and for purchasing drugs and supplies, and warned newcomers to expect delays in receiving their instructions and their pay. One might even question whether colonial doctors formed a "community" at all.[6]

Most important, perhaps, was the medium of medical communication. Few medical journals circulated, so medical discussions relied on the general press. Members of the lay public took a correspondingly larger part in them. Many of Bengal's several thousand Europeans were part of the apparatus of the presidency, and their authoritative positions gave them a corresponding confidence in their judgment on all matters, including medical ones. The fate of any new medical project would depend on the efforts of isolated individuals and their local community. When Esdaile became an enthusiastic advocate of mesmerism, his announcements were not restricted to a small circle of professional peers, but flowed "freely over the land through the channels of the daily press, till every person of common understanding was capable of returning a reasonable verdict upon the facts from the evidence placed before him."[7]

Mesmerism Comes to Calcutta

Esdaile first came across mesmerism in an English pamphlet on anesthesia, and decided to try it himself. His first patient was one Mádhab Kaurá, prisoner in a local jail. He later reflected that if he had known more about mesmerism, he might have used a hysterical young girl, instead of a "felon of the hang-man caste." But his selection of one of "the very worst specimen[s] of humanity" proved that the experiment was not rigged. "I should," he said, "*as soon have thought of commencing operations on the first dog or pig I met on the road, as of selecting this man for his good mesmeric 'materiel.'*"[8]

Kaurá had a double hydrocele in his scrotum, a condition likened to elephantiasis. His tumor was painful but the operation to remove it far more so—indeed, sufferers would delay the operation for decades (if not forever), allowing their tumors to grow to several (or several dozen) pounds in weight. In the technique Esdaile used on this and future occasions, the patient lay down in a darkened room. Then he made passes barely above the skin, from the head down to the pit of the stomach, for a half hour or longer.[9]

When Esdaile was convinced that he had succeeded in producing the trance, he hurried over to the town hall to obtain "intelligent witnesses." One presumes that Indian medical workers did not qualify, since Chaudra Chaudhri, assistant surgeon, a Mr. Noboo, a staff doctor of the jail hospital, and Budden Chunder Chowdaree, subassistant surgeon, were already on the scene. Several British witnesses were soon brought to the hospital, including Mr. Russell, the local judge, and the local collector, the appropriately named Mr. Money.

When everyone was assembled, Esdaile then inflicted a battery of assaults on his patient. No "hallooing in his ears" could attract his attention. Esdaile made him drink ammonia, held a candle near his skin, and shone a light in his eyes. Kaurá never acknowledged any shock or discomfort. Like English subjects, he could answer questions, and, when interrogated, he claimed to feel no pain in his scrotum. Then the first of two operations was carried out. One hydrocele was removed, and again, Kaurá expressed no pain. A few days later, Esdaile made more experiments before more prestigious witnesses: the governor of Chandernagore, the local magistrate, the principal of Hooghly College, and the headmaster of the lower school. The ease with which Esdaile could assemble these witnesses was critical to his success, because, unlike his equivalents in Britain, he could round up the chief authorities of a community in a matter of minutes.

In the next few weeks Esdaile made many more experiments, always before witnesses, who found the suspension of pain a powerful spectacle. One ally, Dr. Alan Webb, professor and demonstrator of anatomy at the Calcutta Medical College, contrasted Esdaile's habits with colonial medicine's "usual managements and concealments." Doctors usually tried to shield new patients from the terrifying operating scene. But Esdaile appeared before patients " '[a]ll dabbed with blood,' a gory spectacle to those who could see," acting with a "nonchalance" with none of doctors' usual delicacy about the pain their patients would soon feel. He wielded the knife with a confidence in his patients' insensibility, even when he was cutting out a "horrible cancer." [10]

After six weeks of labor, exhausted from his mesmeric toils, Esdaile was relieved to find that he could teach the technique to others, and he soon turned the hospital into a mesmeric factory. Hospital attendants, doorkeepers, and cooks were all put to work—in effect, all the young male workers of the hospital were given mesmeric duties. "[O]ne by one, they reduced their subjects to insensibility," and when patients were ready, Esdaile would operate on them one after another.[11]

Having assembled this mesmeric corps, Esdaile turned his attention to publicity. He sent letters to the newspapers and two medical journals: the *Calcutta Medical Journal* and the *India Journal of Medical Science*.[12] The newspaper reports of mesmeric trials multiplied, and readers scattered throughout India attended and carried out mesmeric experiments, following Esdaile's widely distributed recipe for mesmeric success: "all that is necessary for success if the parties are in the relation of agent and subject, is passive obedience in the patient and a determined attention on the part of the operator, and the more the bodies of both are in a state of nature, so much the better."[13]

The Public Debates

By the time the Anglo-Indian community heard his news, they already had some acquaintance with mesmerism and its satellite practices from articles on the itinerant mesmerists and the anesthesia debates.[14] They printed mesmeric stories with a mixture of interest and incredulity, but in the early months of 1845 the balance was tipping slightly to encourage one's serious interest in the practice,[15] so that when Esdaile made his announcement, he gave a more authoritative proof of phenomena that already had some degree of plausibility in people's minds. In late May the *Bengal Hurkaru and India Gazette* announced that Esdaile's work made it "impossible" to continue to "deny that there is something more in it than we ever yet dreamt of in our philosophy." It concluded, resoundingly, "There is no resisting facts like these."[16] The *Calcutta Englishman and Military Chronicle* also urged Esdaile on. "[C]ollect, record, publish," it exhorted; "something will be learned at last."[17]

In Calcutta, Bombay, and elsewhere people were attending mesmeric experiments and making their own.[18] As people tried to make sense of these events, they inevitably focused on the usual issues of propriety and morality, and perhaps even more intently than witnesses did in Britain. These questions triggered some of the most sustained arguments regarding the natural and mental order to be published in the newspaper press during the 1840s.[19]

One example is the exchange between the *Delhi Gazette* and the *Bombay Times and Journal of Commerce*. The *Delhi Gazette* had roundly condemned the whole business of mesmerism: since the propriety of merely taking part in such experiments was dubious, one had to doubt the veracity of any witness who came forward, so mesmeric phenomena could not be verified and should not be publicized. The article triggered a shower of newsprint from defensive newspapers, including the *Bombay Times*, which thought it churlish to doubt the word of authorities like Esdaile and his witnesses.[20] As the *Bombay Times* argued for the plausibility of mesmeric phenomena as a transfer of fluid or other agent, it took the opportunity to develop a more general argument about how physical forces connected and maintained relations of influence throughout the universe. Everyone knew that each "particle of matter [in the world] is at every moment of time influencing every other particle," and that there was an "unceasing interchange of these energies" in inanimate and living phenomena alike: "No two organic bodies but attract each other . . . they cannot come together without radiating to each other Heat, nor can they touch each other without an interchange of Electricity; and did we not know that the animal tissues are themselves Magnetic, it were enough to be aware that Electric Disturbance implies Magnetic Movements, to be satisfied that they must mutually influence the Magnetic Conditions one of the other." [21] The forces of "Gravitation[,] Heat[,] Electricity[,] Magnetism etc." were the "vivifiers of matter, the agents whose union with it constitutes the Life of the Universe." One should understand that these "agents" were "energies" that worked "in and around us." Although they could be modified in form, they were "ever-present, ever-acting, ever-passing from body to body." They were "energies alike efficient and resultant—energies developed in every vital act, and at the same time requisite for its performance." [22]

Having established the importance of these energies for vital phenomena, the article argued for the importance of their circulation, mutual conversion, or exchange in human relationships. One common illustration of how "such influences do pass" from one body to another was the common habit in India of the young and the old sharing the same bed, which was commonly understood to invigorate the old and debilitate the young. Here one could see the "interchange of energies" at work, the young giving out the "stronger and more vitalizing energies at play in the juvenile constitution," and the old "radiating their enfeebled powers to their young companions."

A more healthy form of exchange was the natural pairing of men and women. If nervous influence passed between two individuals wherever there was a difference in vital powers, this might explain the mysteries of love. One of love's greatest puzzles was why people of very different types were drawn to each other. One might have expected that a "natural bias" would lead people to seek a partner similar to themselves. This would be disastrous, since parents passed their "physical, intellectual, and moral peculiarities" to their offspring, and these peculiarities would intensify over time. If humanity were to be balanced and diverse, it needed to create odd couples, and this was where the economics of nervous and vital power served a vital purpose. The fact that "two bodies brought together mutually influence each others' organization" provided "a key to much that appears mysterious in those instinctive sympathies and antipathies which individuals on a first meeting frequently entertain towards each other." The tall and the short, the thin and the fat were drawn together, and "the lady of masculine build and features becomes enamored of a smooth-faced swain, less distinguished than his fellows for those attributes which mark the Man." The anatomical and social differences between individuals were accompanied by differences in their vital influences, "be they calorific, electric, magnetic, nervous, vital, or what you will."[23] People with more or less of some agent were attracted to others with a complementary supply.

The *Bengal Times*'s last word on the subject was a warning to doctors. The limits of their own knowledge of the nervous system disqualified them from giving a decisive judgment, because doctors knew that some diseases involved "nervous impressions" but they could not actually identify them. When they did so, they would solve one of the basic mysteries of medicine and remove the "shroud" cloaking mesmerism itself.[24] In brief, the "mystery" of mesmerism was the mystery of medicine more generally.

The Government Committee

Even as the Indian territories began to buzz with curiosity about mesmerism, most Calcutta doctors turned a deaf ear, uncomfortable with its similarity to indigenous medicine and its controversial status back in Britain. But Esdaile bypassed his peers, successfully petitioning the deputy governor, Sir Herbert Maddock, for an evaluation of his work.

Maddock convened a committee to observe Esdaile's work, filled it with three lay members and three doctors, and ordered that a room be set aside in the Calcutta Native Hospital where any visitor might observe the mesmeric procedures and surgical operations. Witnesses looking through "apertures" in its door panels gazed upon a dramatic scene:

> The patient lay on his back, the body naked from the waist upwards, and the thighs and legs bare; the mesmeriser seated behind him at the head of the bed, leaning over him, the faces of both nearly in contact, the right hand being generally placed on the pit of the stomach, and passes made with one or both hands along the face, chiefly over the eyes. The mesmeriser breathed frequently and gently over the patient's lips, eyes and nostrils. Profound silence was observed. These processes were continued for about two hours each day in ten cases, for eight hours in one case in one day, and for six hours in another case, without interruption.[25]

The committee observed the treatment of ten charity patients, each mesmerized for periods ranging from two to eight hours.

Several of these patients were suffering from an ailment that Esdaile was soon to become famous for treating: hydroceles of the scrotum. Large, elephantiasis-like tumors, which grew massive as bodily fluids (mainly water) accumulated in the particular area, were discussed in works on Indian medicine as a particularly acute problem for the medical community. These tumors affected the reception of mesmeric anesthesia in a number of ways. One was that patients suffering from localized tumors like these were in fairly good overall health, and less likely to die under the knife. Another was the spectacle of the operation itself: observers could see very plainly that the cause of complaint was removed when a surgeon removed a scrotal tumor, whereas an operation on an internal complaint would be harder for a nonexpert to judge. Finally, the proof of suspension of pain was all the stronger when a surgeon could be seen cutting into the most sensitive part of a man's body. Witnesses provided vivid narrative sketches of the tumors and the operations, circulating them in newspapers and journals in India and Britain. One of the most striking cases observed by the committee was that of Hurromundoo Laha, age twenty-seven, admitted to the Native Hospital on 11 October 1846. His tumor was seven feet in circumference and two feet round its neck. After the operation, it weighed 103 pounds; Laha weighed 114.[26]

After visiting for two weeks the committee concluded that, of the first ten cases they witnessed, three did not respond and were discharged; the other seven were successes. Five tumors had been excised, one patient's leg had been amputated at the thigh, and there was one minor operation. In half of these cases, the official witnesses agreed that the patients showed no pain, and they were uncertain about the other three because the patients moaned and moved in a way that suggested discomfort, while claiming afterward to have felt nothing.

The committee validated the phenomena but rejected the practice. The committee did confirm the reality of the trance in seven of the ten cases, but further tests were necessary before they felt the procedure could be introduced to general practice—tests to see if Europeans were affected, for instance—and they could not spare the time to participate themselves. Moreover, on the basis of what they knew already, they did not welcome mesmerism. The "uncertainty of the time required" to produce a sufficiently "intense condition of the mesmeric sleep" was "very unfavourable to the general introduction of mesmeric manipulations in the practice of surgery, *especially in hospitals.*"[27]

Not everyone on the committee agreed with this verdict. One member, James Hume, publicly vouched for the reality of the effects and the importance of introducing mesmerism to hospital practice.[28] Hume was backed up by government. Maddock ordered that a mesmeric hospital be established for a year in Mott's Lane, Calcutta, beginning in November 1846, to pursue the

"A RETURN,

Showing the number of painless surgical operations performed at Hooghly during
the last eight months."

Arm amputated	I
Breast ditto	I
Tumor extracted from the upper jaw	I
Scirrhus testium extirpated	2
Colis amputated	2
Contracted knees straightened	3
Ditto arms	3
Operations for Cataract	3
Large tumor in the inguen cut off	I
Operations for Hydrocele	7
Ditto Dropsy	2
Actual Cautery applied to a sore	I
Muriatic Acid ditto	2
Unhealthy sores pared down	7
Abscesses opened	5
Sinus, 6 inches long, laid open	I
Heel flayed	I
End of thumb cut off	I
Teeth extracted	3
Gum cut away	I
Præputium cut off	3
Piles ditto	I
Great toe nails cut out by the roots	5
Seton introduced from ankle to knee	I
Large tumor on leg removed	I
Scrotal tumors, weighing from 8 to 80 lbs. removed 17, painless	14
Operations	73

FIGURE 47 Itemized list of surgical operations using mesmeric anesthesia under Esdaile's supervision, carried out at the Native Hospital, Hooghly, in 1846. "Accounts of more painless
surgical operations, communicated by Dr. Elliotson," *Zoist* 3 (1846): 196–97.

queries the committee had raised. Esdaile was to test mesmerism's medical as
well as surgical benefits, learn whether class and race variables made any difference to success, and make regular reports of his findings (see fig. 47).[29] The
hospital would be open, and members of the public (as well as a committee of
visitors) could witness the proceedings whenever they chose to visit. Spectators flowed steadily through the wards of the Mesmeric Hospital, and some
traveled great distances. The *Delhi Overland Summary* reported in March 1847
that "His Highness the Nawab Nazeem of *Moorshedabad*" visited on 10 March,
along with a number of British and Indian gentlemen. The nawab declined to
be present for the surgical operation itself, but after viewing the trance alone,
he was sufficiently impressed to donate 500 reals to the hospital.[30] Later that
year Esdaile was visited by the "prime minister" of Nepal, who was said to
have left his brother in charge of the country to journey to Bengal in order
to make his visit. On this occasion Esdaile's usual arsenal of tortures for testing the trance benefited from the clang of "Nipalese cymbals."

Despite the mesmeric performances, the hospital maintained an efficient regime. Several mesmerists prepared several patients at a time, and Esdaile dispatched them efficiently. One doctor of the Calcutta Medical College, Frederick J. Mouat, reported that the hospital had become so productive that *"scarcely a case of elephantiasis of the scrotum is to be met with in a Calcutta hospital."* [31]

Esdaile and his associates did not document the longer-term effects of the surgery, and one suspects that this is why no deaths appear in the case studies. In the absence of antisepsis, the death rates must have been very high, but Esdaile's accounts only record one. This was one Shaik Manick. Manick was an important case, because his tumor was very large and because he had demonstrated unusual psychic phenomena during one of his trances. Esdaile noted his death only in the context of another case, involving similar psychic effects to Manick's behavior in his own trial. Esdaile mentioned the dead man only because it helped him to substantiate his claim that the new patient could not have contacted him and therefore could not have imitated his behavior. [32] Esdaile's silence regarding the medium- and long-term fates of his patients suggests that we should regard his fatality rate of patients (5 percent) as valid only until the doors of the hospital swung shut behind them. [33]

Esdaile may have maintained an efficient working routine. But the great majority of his patients were impoverished Indian subjects: peasants, sidar bearers, husbandmen, and cart drivers. They created a serious dilemma for Esdaile. If his project were to succeed, he would have to extend mesmerism to elite Indian and, especially, European patients. But both groups recoiled from the necessarily intimate physical contact with hospital workers. Another problem was that the persuasiveness of his work actually *relied upon* the lowly status of his patients. They were powerless and regarded as appropriately subject to the exercise of someone else's influence. We have seen how, in Britain, it was often disturbing to see mesmeric trials display an arrow of influence that ran counter to the inequalities of society as a whole (such as working-class men mesmerizing middle- or upper-class women, or women mesmerizing men). Esdaile's patients occupied more stable places in the colonial order, at least in his perceptions and those of other Europeans. Moreover, Esdaile and those associated with him thought nothing (as we have seen earlier) of subjecting such patients to indignities and even tortures that were highly effective in validating the trance but that no high-caste Indian or member of the European community would tolerate: having a hot coal placed against the skin, being subject to intense and continuous electric shocks, and having sufficient acid poured on the skin that "the flesh became instantly white." [34]

Esdaile did manage to attract a few foreign patients among the elite Indian and Anglo-Indian communities. While it was not possible to make the home visits that most wealthy clients would have expected, he set aside private rooms in the hospital so that wealthier patients could have their mesmeric treatment in complete seclusion, and when they were ready for surgery, they could have this done at home.[35] Moreover, Esdaile did treat some Europeans—for instance, one Mr. Calder placed himself under the hands of hospital workers. After four days of trials, he finally fell into the trance, waking five hours later to find

great difficulty in raising my eyelids, or keeping my eyes open. I left the couch and retired to bed, and had my natural sleep afterwards, til six o'clock next morning. For a week afterwards, the efforts to mesmerise me were repeated for an hour daily, but without farther effect than causing a sleep of a few minutes. I however continued to enjoy my natural rest at night, found my pains abating daily, and my nerves considerably braced up; so much so, that I could walk up and down stairs without assistance, and with every confidence drive out in a buggy alone, which I could not have attempted for two years and a half previously . . . Up to the 17th of October I was thrown into a sleep, every third or fourth night, for about two hours, the effect of which you may judge of, from my being able to walk yesterday morning more than four, and this morning, more than six miles.[36]

Another patient, one Miss Gordon, had suffered for two years from "enlargement of the glands of the throat and neck." She had received no benefit from previous treatment, but was "greatly relieved by mesmerism." [37]

Other doctors also reported European cases. Mr. Blyth, curator of the Asiatic Society's museum, learned mesmerism from Esdaile himself.[38] Dr. J. W. T. Johnstone of Madras removed a tumor from the shoulder of a European woman after she had been mesmerized by a Dr. Smith, and after this success, mesmerism became fashionable within the Medical School in Madras, where "students have been mesmerizing one another under the superintendence of the surgeon." They began, it seems, by making trials "on two native pupils," worked their way up through the "apprentices," and then extended the program to everyone—"with complete success." [39] Dr. Kean of Berhampore had employed mesmerism as a treatment for madness and claimed that, after this treatment, a large number of asylum inmates were sufficiently restored to their senses to be released.[40] There were many experiments among Europeans, then, but it is important to note that these were not routine cases of hospital treatment, and their numbers were tiny in comparison to Indian charity cases.

The situation of European patients in relation to their Indian mesmerists posed a problem that was even bigger for European patients in India than in Britain: how could they reconcile themselves to the interpersonal intimacy and loss of self-control involved in the trance? There were two very strong reasons why mesmerism should have made Europeans uneasy: one was the problem of association between the races; the other was the more profound question of what coming under someone's influence meant in this context. We have almost no narratives from these patients, and it is therefore impossible to develop in the case of India the more detailed (though still very limited) understanding we have gained of how experimental subjects in Britain understood the mesmeric process and the trance. The newspaper press was uneasy about the interracial contact involved in Esdaile's hospital; such concern would have been particularly acute when mesmeric contact was made, as Esdaile put it, "in the state of nature." Physical intimacy between Britons and Indians was surely one of the greatest obstacles to Esdaile's success. But there was an additional factor: Esdaile's own understanding of the social significance of "coming under the influence" of mesmerism. Esdaile's representation of the trance did not make the link between the power of the *mesmerist* and colonial power more generally, in the way that he might have done. However, he *did* associate the vulnerability of the mesmeric *subject* with colonial subservience. As we shall see, he linked the capacity to fall "under the influence" of mesmerism to social or cultural primitiveness.

The Physiology of Colonial Power

That the British were constitutionally fit to lead, and that Indians were naturally made to serve, was obvious to Victorians, but the physical bases of these differences were not. Those seeking an explanation tended to locate the discrepancy of power and authority between the British and Indian communities in specific physiological and environmental differences. Thomas Babington Macaulay deprecated Bengalis as "enervated by a soft climate" and weak and subservient. They bore "the same relation to other Asiatics which the Asiatics generally bear to the bold and energetic children of Europe." Nowhere else, he concluded memorably, could one find a people "so thoroughly fitted by nature and by habit for a foreign yoke." Bengalis were "feeble even to effeminacy," and their inherent tendency was enhanced by their environment: the "vapour bath" in which they were steeped. The Bengali's habits were "sedentary," his limbs "delicate," and his movements "languid." No wonder that foreigners had "trampled" them underfoot over the ages; what little their constitution provided to them in the way of raw materials for independence and honesty their environment helped to corrode.[41]

Macaulay's words, published only two years before mesmerism came to Calcutta, would become staple reading for colonial and Indian students for

decades. Not only did Europeans imbibe and propagate this notion of effeteness, but the Bengali elite read, accepted, and, it has been argued, internalized
such colonial representations. British and Indians alike understood Indian
subservience and colonial degradation in an unusually physical manner.[42] It
should come as no surprise, therefore, that Bengal, of all Britain's colonial territories, should have been a fertile ground for a practice that displayed power
physiologically, and in gendered terms.

In contrast to the wide variety of altered states of mind in British mesmerism, Indian mesmerism focused on the erasure of consciousness. The goal was
not to alter mental action but to remove it altogether. This made the seat of
power far less ambiguous than it was in Britain, where mesmeric subjects,
rather than the mesmerists, sometimes appeared to be in charge. There are
various ways that people could see this loss of consciousness, or, in the current
parlance, "sensibility," as a display of colonial power. The most obvious was
also the most powerful: the ability to subdue the body and mind of another
person, or to deputize that ability to someone in one's charge. Others were
more potent in India. One of the greatest aspirations of a colonial doctor was
to triumph over those bizarre and horrifying diseases, unknown in Britain,
that he found in India.[43] Mesmerism offered the possibility of carrying out
operations on a number of indigenous disorders that had been virtually inop-
erable before anesthesia.[44] Whereas in Britain the subject's surrender to the
mesmerist was the most potent display of power, in India there developed a
more abstracted notion of "mastery" of the body, involving understanding the
nature of the trance, and its management in a population of hospital patients
rather than a single individual.

Esdaile differed from British mesmerists in his views about what mesmeric
effects revealed about social relations more generally. British mesmerists drew
what one might call "relational" conclusions about power from their experiments. It was common for mesmerists to argue that their power to create the
trance was a sign of their superiority over the person who succumbed to them.
In Britain there was an obvious and symmetrical relationship between power
and superiority, on the one hand, and weakness on the other. This symmetry
of power and submission did not exist in Esdaile's system. Anyone, he claimed,
could produce the mesmeric trance, regardless of their status in society. Race,
class, and, one might assume (though he did not state it), gender made no
difference. There were variations in susceptibility, but everyone could, in
time, feel mesmeric effects. Indian patients were in one sense the most difficult
subjects to mesmerize, and in another the easiest. The subgroup of Indian subjects he most frequently encountered was the least psychologically sensitive of
the race. "Felons of the hang-man caste" and other members of the lowest

orders of society made the "most unfavorable subjects for psychological experiments." They were the least attuned to others, the least nervous, the least delicate—and therefore the least responsive to nervous influence. His power of mesmerism over these people testified to the fact that it could have some effect over practically anyone.

In order to understand what Esdaile thought the trance revealed about human relations more generally, let us consider how it fit into his philosophy of medicine. His ideal of medical practice was one of seeking subtle ways of augmenting the body's natural powers of recovery. A good doctor tried to "induce nature to interfere and take up the case of his patient; and when he sees signs of her gracious presence, he only reverentially looks on, and confines himself to removing impediments in her way." Most practitioners, however, did not aspire to the ideal. They stuffed their patient full of "pills, powders, and potions." If he recovered, these got all the credit. A healer who claimed to be able "to cure disease by the unassisted powers of nature . . . is called quack, imposter, or fool, and hunted down." [45]

Mesmerism met Esdaile's ideal. The physician mobilized the body's inherent healing powers—his and his patient's both. This was not a bond of sympathy or a cord of communication. It was a physical transmission "exerted by one animal over another, under certain circumstances and conditions of their respective systems" stemming from an "irregularity in the distribution of nervous energy," a "transfusion" of a "vital agent from the one body into the other." [46] Perhaps nervous force could flow into the space just beyond the surface of the body. If the will could make the nerves pass vital influences to the "ends of the fingers," why not one small increment further? Esdaile speculated that mesmerism dissolved the edges of the body in this way; the skin was no longer a fixed border between one self and another. When the mesmerist made his magnetic passes, his "organs of sense" discharged the "nervous energy" that then radiated outward from his skin for a short distance—far enough to be received into the body of another person, if the two were very, very close.

This description of energy transfer suggested that every human being could be affected by mesmerism. However, some were affected more readily than others. Among the "human family" Indians were one of the more susceptible races. [47] The main reason for this was not that they were lacking in vital power but that they were more culturally primitive. A determining factor in a people's responsiveness to the trance was their "closeness to" or "distance from" the natural order. In India one found "simple, unsophisticated children of nature." When they lay down for a mesmeric treatment, Esdaile found them "neither thinking, questioning, nor remonstrating, but passively submitting to my pleasure, without in the smallest degree understanding my object or intentions." Esdaile's portrayal translated into mesmeric terms a familiar representation of indigenous peoples as comparatively animallike. European civilization, Esdaile claimed, was in damaging respects "artificial." Westerners had "so far deserted Nature, that, in return, she has renounced us as unnatural children, and left us to our self-sufficiency and artificial resources." These resources were mere "palliatives." Progressive medicine could bring matters full circle and teach "artificial man" to respect "the steady and enduring curative powers of nature, when properly understood and brought into action." The fact that Europeans could succumb to the trance at all meant that this process of removal from nature was not irreversible. If the "proud sons of civilisation [would] condescend to return for a moment to the feet of their mother Nature," they would find that her powers of natural healing would work once again in their bodies and minds.[48] Europeans had to become primitive (temporarily) in order to be natural. They had to make themselves unsophisticated in mind so that they could be healthy and strong in body. If we think back to Esdaile's early exhortation that the more the patient was "in the state of nature, the better," we can now appreciate that much more than literal nakedness was called for.[49]

If the ability to mesmerize was not a sign of power in itself, colonial power relations were nevertheless crucial to the production of trances in Esdaile's hospital. No mesmerist in Britain would have had the patience or stamina to mesmerize someone (especially a charity patient) for several hours daily, over a period of two or three weeks. Once one appreciates the importance of using Indian labor to produce the trance, it also becomes clear that there were strong incentives for Esdaile to make a theoretical separation between the power to produce the trance and the tendency to succumb to it, which played an important role in justifying the organization of mesmeric labor in the hospital. He could not have used a mesmeric corps of servile workers yet claim that the power to mesmerize was a sign of social, intellectual, or cultural superiority. He therefore discerned a mutually reinforcing relationship between the economy of his mesmeric hospital and the physiological and psychological structure he saw at work in it.

Once mesmerism was carried out by hospital dressers, it could be carried out both intensively and cheaply. Esdaile's wards became a surgical assembly line.

All that is *necessary* for the surgeon to do, is to look in at his hospital daily at the most convenient time, and if any patient allows him to stick a pin into his nose, pinch his nipple, or apply live-charcoal to any part of his body without resenting it, he may proceed to cut him up upon the spot without any of the coaxing, coughing, choking, vomiting, convulsions, and anxiety, usually, more or less, attendant upon ether and chloroform operations; not to speak of the frequent disagreeable and occasional fatal consequences. In this way, I have disposed of four patients in twenty minutes in one forenoon, and a few days ago, I had three men all ready at once for the knife. If the patient is not ready, you have only to call again to-morrow till he is, and if very obstinate, it may be allowable to *chloroform him* as the last resource. But so far from *delay doing any harm, it will, in nine-tenths of the operations, do good*, from the nervous system being soothed and refreshed by the process.[50]

Esdaile's hospital would become a training ground for the "mesmeric corps" who would be apprenticed with him for a month in preparation for work at other hospitals. Once trained, these individuals could further spread the practice: "one properly instructed mesmeriser can make a hundred more." The members of this corps were subalterns, rather than charismatic leaders of the sort that British mesmerism often suggested. A mesmeric empire would soon fan out over the face of India.[51]

Esdaile's system also had ethnological, or archeological, implications. Because the more primitive races were in a more "natural" state than Europeans, it was easier for them to discover their bodies' "latent curative powers" and develop them "for the cure of disease." Thus mesmerism turned up among the "medicine men of America," the "Mumbo Jumbo men of Africa," and the "charmers of this country." Mesmerism's long history among an unchanging people suggested that Indian charming produced a present-day example of what other, more advanced races might have done in the past—for instance, Indian charmers had practiced it since "time immemorial, like every other custom in this immutable society."[52] Scenes like figure 48, an eighteenth-century English rendition of religious healing in India, contributed to the image of Indian superstition that Esdaile was drawing on. Indigenous healing arts were living specimens of social archeology. Esdaile told of Dr. Davidson, a resident doctor at Jeypore, who had encountered cures of this sort when one of his patients had failed to get well.[53] Some years later, Davidson wrote to the *Zoist*, chronicling the incident to which Esdaile had referred. A patient suffering from rheumatism had left Davidson unsatisfied, only to return, four or five days later, claiming to be cured. The man said he had consulted two "*ẓâ-doo wâlees*" (Davidson translated this as "dealers in magic") from the local bazaar. After he had paid them the equivalent of twopence each, he lay down on a low bed. In Davidson's paraphrasing and translation of what his patient told him, "one sat at each side of me, and both passed their hands over my body, so (describing long mesmeric passes), and thus they set me to sleep, and

A SICK PERSON presented to IXORA, an Indian Deity for the recovery of his Health.

FIGURE 48 An invalid brought before the deity Ixora in the hope of a cure. Hurd, *Religious Rites and Ceremonies*.

I slept soundly; when I awoke I was free from rheumatism, and am now perfectly well."[54] The man also told Davidson that Bengal was a region particularly known to mountain dwellers as a place full of "sorcerers."

Accounts such as these portrayed indigenous healing power as a disguised form of mesmerism. But a combination of ignorance and greed led indigenous healers to dress up their power in magical stories. "Savages" had neither the intellectual sophistication necessary for developing scientific explanations nor the social responsibility that would lead them to refrain from manipulating nature for their own selfish purposes. They lacked both knowledge and the wisdom to use it.

Esdaile's remarks implied a cultural scale, in which one's place was assigned by one's power of understanding. An individual's degree of knowledge, and of control over one's own intellect, was an index of one's position in the human family. People who succumbed most easily to the mesmeric influence were closer to a "state of nature," with the simplicity of mind that the term implied. They might or might not make good mesmerists, but in either case they could not understand what was going on. This difference made complete honesty impossible between these people and more sophisticated beings. It was necessary for those who *did* understand to produce a palatable fiction, to construct a common ground for interaction with one's inferiors. For instance, Esdaile used the term "belatee muntur," or "European charm," in explaining to his Indian assistants the process they were carrying out.[55] Only the most civilized and progressive could know the "real" nature of the phenomena.

Stealing Men

Like all powerful forces, mesmerism had destructive as well as beneficial uses, and Elliotson's mesmeric project involved policing the use of psychically potent practices. One day, as Esdaile drove through the Hooghly bazaar, he came upon a crowd. The bystanders told him that a boy had nearly been kidnapped some moments before and that, after his rescue, the child recounted that the kidnapper had done something to his mind that compelled him to accompany him without protest. The accused kidnapper was arrested. During the preliminary hearings Esdaile was called in as an expert witness and asked whether such a thing was possible. He told the magistrate's court that he was sure it was, because he had done it himself. When the case came to trial, however, he found it "utterly impossible" to convey "even a glimpse of my meaning" to the "minds" of the Indian law officers who had to try the case. The judge therefore requested that he demonstrate the phenomena in the courtroom. As mesmerists liked to quote Othello, only the "ocular proof" would do.[56]

Esdaile accepted the challenge. On the day of the demonstration, news of the mesmeric "trial" packed the court with curious observers of both East and West. Esdaile's first subject, one Nazir Mohamed, was brought into the courtroom and placed at the bar: "I mesmerised him in a few minutes, and led him, with his arms catalepsed, out of the court, and set him walking down the road for some distance, making his arms rigid in any position, as long as I pleased. I then replaced him at the bar where the judge and Moulavies all loudly addressed him, without his paying any attention to them; and they were obliged to ask me to awake[n] him." The judge eventually asked Esdaile to awaken Mohamed. This was easily done, and a second demonstration on another subject was equally successful. No one denied that Esdaile, as he put it himself, "stole the men." The kidnapper, too, was convicted of mental theft: he had "stolen" the child. He was sentenced by the jury to nine years' imprisonment with labor in irons, though he was later pardoned by the government, who felt that Esdaile's display had exercised an unfair influence over the "mind of the court"—that he had, in effect, stolen the court as he had stolen his mesmeric subject.[57]

The Fate of the Mesmeric Hospital

At the end of the probationary year, Esdaile's project was declared a success. The new deputy general, Lord Dalhousie, rewarded his success by promotion to presidency surgeon from January 1848. Ironically, this actually made his work more difficult, because no hospital came with the position, and Dalhousie refused to fund a permanent infirmary. Dalhousie was a Peelite free marketer with a distaste for government intervention in philanthropic concerns, including matters of public health that affected one sector of society more than another.[58] Mesmerism, known for its aid in the removal of diseases thought particularly to afflict the Indian community, fell into this category. Withholding support would teach Indians "to help themselves" in medical matters.[59] Several editorials in the colonial press echoed Dalhousie's views. One suggested that a major donation from "one of our Calcutta Millionaires" might be forthcoming; such a gift would be "of far greater utility than that of erecting a bridge, building a ghat, or digging a tank." [60]

When the hospital closed in January 1848, protests came from a cross-section of the Calcutta communities. One response was a petition submitted to Dalhousie, organized by influential Indian commercial and intellectual families and signed by between 300 and 400 Bengalis.[61] Several signatories joined with a number of British citizens to organize a private subscription for the continuance of the Mesmeric Hospital. The hospital closed for some months while these funds were being organized. One reason given for the delay was the collapse of the Union Bank (which was thought to be making people tighter with their cash).[62] The Mesmeric Hospital reopened in September 1848, when it became part of the services provided by the Sukeas Street Dispensary. Esdaile became its superintendent, and the Hospital Committee was divided between prominent British and Indian members of the Calcutta community. This charity dispensary seems to have used mesmerism for surgery and therapy in only about sixty cases each year out of almost a thousand, perhaps because it could afford to employ only a few mesmerists.[63]

This new arrangement brought mesmerism into regular hospital practice, but at considerable sacrifice, for this was a clear step down in the medical world. The enterprise had previously enjoyed a set of self-contained rooms in a prime Calcutta location. It was now a subset of a poor charity dispensary, far from the center of town.[64] An inscription on the side of a "dingy and neglected" building announced to visitors that this was "the Mesmeric Hospital and Sukeas Dispensary." One visitor reported that a "peepul tree" growing on the roof had run its large roots all the way down the sides "to the very foundation." On the trees outside the compound wall, "large flocks of bats were hanging from the half-withered branches, like rows of soda-water bottles."

The sight one saw on entering was no better. The rooms were large and covered by a "curious ceiling of carved wood," but they were dark and dirty. Patients "in all stages of recovery" filled the close-set beds. Most of these had been "operated on in the mesmeric trance." Their beds, though covered for the occasion of his visit with white sheets, were "filthy." The patients themselves were described in exotic, grotesque terms.

One had lately been freed from an extraordinary tumor, as big as his head, and projecting from his neck or rather his lower jaw, which was still hideous with large bags of skin; the arm of another which had grown into his side, had lately been dissected out; the rest seemed cases of those monstrous elephantoid tumors for which the hospital is celebrated. On this occasion, or the week after, I forget which, I saw one poor man in a side room ward, who seemed anchored on his bed, or rather moored to a great buoy—a tumor apparently heavier than the rest of his emaciated body. In these extreme cases, the outline of a man approximates to that of a gigantic wasp.

The most striking part of his account was the surgical process itself. In one ward the visitor could see, "through the gloom," three patients, "each with a mesmeriser at his head brooding over him." As the visitors entered, *"a flood of the brightest light poured into the room, without disturbing the proceedings."* The mesmerists were all "vigorous young men." With a "serious earnest expression of countenance, [each] bent over his subject's face, as though about to kiss it, breathed on the eyes, and laid his hands on the pit of the stomach, or moved them with hooked fingers before the brow." One patient was pricked with a "sharp pointed knife" on the most "sensitive parts of the body" and had a "live coal" dropped on the "inside of the thigh," but showed no sign of consciousness or sensation.

The mesmerists "then went to the second and third beds, and treated their sleeping occupants to the same experimentum crucis of fire and steel. *There was something awful in the imperturbable repose, which stood out against this."* The surgical instruments resembled "murderous weapons"—especially the bistouri, a "long thin reaping hook"—and the doctor's clothes warned of a gory event: oilskin trousers, fisherman's boots, and an apron up to the neck.

The first tumor, the size of a cow's udder, was laid bare, and the bistouri introduced. It was a sickening yet wonderful sight, to see the long knife slashing through the mass, and yet avoiding, as by a miracle, the parts to be preserved; and the fingers of the assistants who pounced eagerly on the spouting blood vessels. The *long deep preliminary gashes, the careful dissection out of parts hidden in the centre of the mass, the severance of the tumor, when these were secured, the tying up of nearly twenty blood-vessels*—all did not occupy, by my watch, three minutes. While this was going on, the mesmeriser, doubled up at the head of the bed, was pouring his whole soul into the patient's face, who *continued to slumber like an infant.*

This account was tinged with a salaciousness about the violence being done to the patient's body. The report was suffused as much by disgusted fascination with the dirt and decrepitude of the infirmary, the exotic squalor the visitor perceived in the wards, as with the efficacy of the medical technique he had come to observe. Mesmerism, for him, became partly horrifying and partly awe-inspiring. It had taken on the "magic" and "wonder" that Esdaile's original mesmeric project had sought to reform.

By this time, Esdaile had left. He retired in 1851 and was succeeded by Alan Webb, professor of demonstrative anatomy at the Calcutta Medical College. At this point, Webb had a subassistant surgeon, two compounders, one dresser, three mesmerizers, nine inferior servants, and assorted other workers.[65] Well over three thousand patients were treated at the dispensary during the second half of 1851 (i.e., the first six months of Webb's tenure), and a similar number in the first six months of 1852. Although the source of these numbers, Webb's report on the work of the dispensary, implies that all or most patients received mesmeric treatment, this is unlikely. There were only three mesmerists, and each mesmerist would have had to work for hours at the very least to prepare each patient for surgery. There were sixty-seven inpatients in the second half of 1851—a more manageable number. Almost all were charity patients. Only the "respectable" patients who paid for their treatment were named in the infirmary's annual report: Gopaul Chunder Bose, a writer for the Bengal Secretariat; Rammohun Roy and Isser Chunder Sircar, Calcutta merchants; and Nufferloll Ghosain, priest to the maharajah of Burdwan.[66] While the hospital continued to function, by the mid-1850s it attracted almost no publicity and its activities were restricted almost entirely to those of a charitable dispensary; before the end of the decade it had closed.

The career of the Mesmeric Hospital suggests that mesmerism could have a role in *removing* the exotic from the management of Indian bodies, rather than being an exotic influence itself. Before the introduction of mesmerism, Calcutta hospitals showcased instances of morbid anatomy that could only be examined and classified—not cured. In this respect they resembled "cabinets of curiosities," collections made by British naturalists and travelers of the eighteenth and nineteenth centuries. These collections often included specimens of pathological anatomy brought to England from the East. The value of such specimens arose from an Orientalist taste for the Eastern exotic. British representations of tumors such as hydroceles of the scrotum that, according to medical writings of the period, were rarely to be found in the West were influenced by this perspective. Figure 49 depicts one of the patients whose

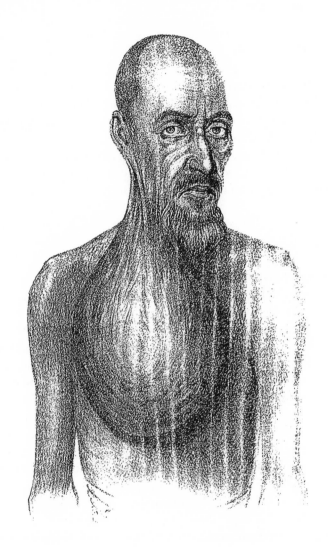

KHANOO (MOSSULMAN) AGED 42.

The tumor had been growing for 10 years, and weighed 5 lbs. It was cut away during the mesmeric trance without his knowledge by D. Webb in Calcutta Oct 20th 1851 and he was discharged well at the end of December

F. P. 280 & 282.

FIGURE 49 This sketch of a man suffering from a tumor of the face and neck was made in the Mesmeric Hospital in 1851 and later published in the *Zoist*. The tumor (the result of ten years' growth) weighed five pounds after it was excised while the patient was mesmerized. Elliotson, "Account of the mesmeric hospital," plate opposite page 282.

hydrocele (in this case, a facial tumor) was removed in the Mesmeric Hospital. In the middle decades of the nineteenth century, when the older Orientalist notions were being replaced by the "diffusionist" spirit evoked by the Macaulay Minute, mesmerism promised to make hospitals into spaces displaying, not the exotic, but instances of British reform. Indian bodies that would have been the object of morbid fascination at the mysteries of the East became models of moral and physiological sanitary reform disseminated from Britain. After Esdaile left, mesmerism and the disorders with which it was associated were more easily portrayed in terms of the exotic and mystical, as in the British visitor's description of the Sukeas Street Dispensary in 1852.

India as a Laboratory

During the period of these events in Bengal, the controversy over mesmeric anesthesia was heating up in Britain, and Esdaile's work had a significant impact on it. Elliotson gave Esdaile's work visibility, reprinting Indian mesmeric publications in pamphlet form and in the *Zoist*. Esdaile's project made mesmeric anesthesia look more plausible and potentially acceptable back at home. But one is bound to ask why trials made at such a distance should have been credible, when many skeptics stipulated that they could never believe a mesmeric trial they had not carried out themselves. One reason is that before and during this period India was regarded as a controlled environment, safely set apart from the center of Victorian society. It was treated as a vast laboratory in which to develop a variety of sciences and technologies, prominent among them the study of social institutions and mental phenomena.[67] The Lancastrian system of education was developed in Madras before it was brought to Britain;[68] and the first statistical office was founded in Calcutta in the 1820s before the Statistical Section of the BAAS was founded by a colonial statistician. Moreover, the strongest associations Victorians made with India involved trances (opium poppies, superstitious peasants, ecstatic religious states); it was easy to think of this territory as fertile ground for the cultivation of altered states of mind.[69]

To Victorians on their own soil, the problems of racial mixing and the conflation of mesmerism and magic were not disturbing. A broad consensus on the subservient status of indigenous peoples made the notion of an Indian being placed in the mesmeric trance (whether by another Indian or by a Briton) far less controversial than any domestic trial. It did not inspire the same anxious or outraged reflections that followed from the sight of the prone figure of any British subject, regardless of class and gender, in the context of a public debate in Britain in which so many competing claims regarding the map of worth and authority could flourish. Mill reflected in the wake of the Indian Mutiny that the English regarded Indians as "dirt under their feet," that they felt it was "monstrous that any rights of the natives should stand in the way of their smallest pretensions," and that they were appalled by "the simplest act of protection to the inhabitant" against English power.[70] While some range of opinion surely existed on the status of Indian subjects, every British subject could concur in the perception of the Indian as being naturally subject to the exercise of another's power. This combination of factors helps explain why, from the vantage point of Britain, an Indian mesmeric trial had a trustworthiness that domestic trials lacked. Even those editors of medical journals who had remained fiercely skeptical of domestic mesmeric experiments softened substantially (with the inevitable exception of Thomas Wakley) when they read Esdaile's reports. Several regarded his hospital's work as the decisive incident in the campaign to gain mesmerism acceptance into hospital practice, and at the very minimum as a focus of research, before the advent of chemical anesthesia.[71]

The Decline of Colonial Mesmerism

Esdaile's use of public displays to establish the reality of mesmeric phenomena has figured in the work of Gayan Prakash as an example of the problem for British science of "going native" in nineteenth-century India.[72] On the one hand, science's practitioners tried to distinguish it from "magic" and "wonder"; on the other, these very practitioners used conventions associated with magic in establishing scientific claims in this period. Because one of the most important functions of public activities associated with science was to set it apart from the wonderful, the use of these conventions suggests that this process of differentiation was doomed, or at least that it was fraudulent in a certain sense: magic was a resilient part of the public life of knowledge in India.

Mesmerism is a particularly striking example, because of its strong affiliations with precolonial Indian culture. It had to be exported to Britain and brought back to India in order to become knowledge. Yet the process of proving the validity of this knowledge involved a return to the world of magic and wonder from which the excursion through Western science had been intended to distinguish it. Esdaile used a vocabulary of magic and wonder in the public demonstrations of his work, as his initial encounter with the "magician" in the beginning of this chapter reveals, and as his repetition, even reinforcement, of the representation of mesmerism by his Indian interlocutors in the courts further illustrates. This difficulty had its equivalent in Britain—the claim that people were mesmerized by mesmerism—but here the significance of "wonder" was a more loaded term, because of the racial distinctions that came with it. In consequence, what was a general problem for science was more acutely so for mesmerism because of its association in Western eyes with Indian superstition and primitiveness.

If Esdaile was promoted and celebrated for his mesmeric accomplishments, and mesmerism provided a cheap and highly effective medical treatment, why did mesmerism not survive in colonial India? One reason is relatively straightforward. Once chemical anesthetics were available, many doctors claimed that mesmerism served no purpose, for while Esdaile had claimed that it had curative as well as palliative properties, these were far more controversial. Mesmerism also encouraged, and in some respects *required*, a substantial degree of interracial association that, as Waltraud Ernst argues, worried potential patrons. Such association was intolerable to those constituencies whose involvement and financial support were essential to the continuation of mesmerism as a colonial project. After the founding of the Mesmeric Hospital, complaints appeared in the colonial press about the degree of association between Europeans and Indians in the process of soliciting patients, working over their bodies, and witnessing surgery. Worse, concerning those few Europeans who had been treated in the mesmeric infirmary, some newspaper editorials expressed a sense of horrified incredulity that "native assistants" were practicing mesmerism.[73]

It is ironic that mesmerism failed to become established in India, because Esdaile succeeded in doing to mesmerism what reformist doctors were trying to do to medicine generally during these years, and feared that mesmerism would prevent them from doing: he made it a means of producing row after row of docile patients in his wards. But if Esdaile failed to establish mesmerism in India, he nevertheless spent his final years in a mesmeric environment. Illness drove him from India, and when he retired in 1851 he returned to his family home in Perth, Scotland, where his family's mesmeric nursing eased his old age. During the same years when Esdaile's Calcutta Mesmeric Hospital was dying a lingering death, it is a further irony that Esdaile spent his own last years in a space where, as we shall see in the next chapter, mesmerism thrived: the Victorian sickroom.

CHAPTER NINE

Emanations from the Sickroom

Never did I dream of experiencing in this life that most awful, yet most calm consciousness—
the inkling of new faculties,—the distinct consciousness of their incipient exercise! . . .
no words can tell the impression of the serene region of translucent intellectuality from w^h
I derived these ideas,—a state in w^h all things seemed to become clear.

Harriet Martineau on the diagnostic powers she discovered in the mesmeric state[1]

It would be somewhat odd for the *disease* to give itself a *name*.

A scathing medical response to Martineau's assertions[2]

FROM THE 1840s through the end of the century mesmerism was recommended as a therapy for family members—a means of lulling a child to sleep, of soothing an invalid, and of easing chronic complaints of all kinds. It could ease the ordinary aches and pains of childhood and adulthood and the agonies of serious illnesses, and the publicity surrounding mesmeric anesthesia made it increasingly acceptable. By the mid-1840s some women delivered their infants while mesmerized, and families eased the pain of the dying by applying the mesmeric influence.[3]

Mesmerism was associated with the sickroom for less practical reasons, too. The trance, like the sickroom and its inmate, was poised between consciousness and unconsciousness, between life and death, between this world and the next. The mesmeric subject and the invalid were reminiscent of one another: their weakness conferred an indirect kind of power, and access to an unusual kind of knowledge. Invalids used their delicacy to control their social environment by negotiating who could enter the sickroom, how much privacy they enjoyed, and which healer offered the best advice.[4] The acute awareness of the abnormal states of their bodies often led them to claim that they knew themselves and their illnesses better than anyone else. Like the magnetic subject in her altered state, their unusual state of sensitivity allowed them to examine themselves as others could not. One of the more flamboyant of intellectual invalids even claimed that her body was "an experimental laboratory always about me, and inseparable from me," within which she could experiment upon herself.[5]

Among the middle and upper classes the female invalid's powers faintly resembled the mesmeric subject's: strength through weakness, and authority through submission. The sickroom might seem the last place where women would have developed powerful ways of representing themselves, displaying as it did the characteristics of idealized Victorian femininity: here could be found a fragile creature, confined to the domestic sphere, her weak body making her dependent on others while simultaneously enhancing her spirituality. But for these very reasons, the Victorian sickroom displays how malleable and intertwined were notions of femininity and illness. In the sickroom one's body and mind were in an altered state. The significance of that state, in relation to what a woman could do with her mind, was open to definition.

Intellectual women had particular reason to reflect on this relationship, because contemporary physiology represented their minds and bodies as mutually compromising. A woman's intellect was unreliable because it could be overthrown by the imagination. Women's bodies were apparently subject to nervous influences that overstimulated the imagination and prevented them from being free agents in the evaluation of evidence. However, opponents of women's intellectual activity also claimed that their bodies were not strong enough to harness intellectual powers in order to generate authoritative knowledge. They could create only fancy. Worse still, intellectual women were likely to overstrain their delicate bodies, producing madness or other distempers. These kinds of worries provided the framework for a wide range of debates over women's education, moral fortitude, and mental health.[6] Many claims were made in these debates about the compromising tendency of women's physiology, but it was also possible to make the converse argument, that women's imaginative tendencies could be enabling rather than destructive. Fundamentally, the female body was vulnerable to overthrow by the mind, and the mind equally vulnerable to overthrow by the body.

The portrayal of women as powerfully imaginative could support the notion that they were particularly suited to the most creative kinds of intellectual work. The claim that some women were in thrall to their imaginations could be positively transformed if it were adapted to the traditional role of the prophet or oracle. Such a transformation was both difficult and dangerous, as we shall see, but it was also potentially very rewarding. It became possible to describe femininity as embodied imagination, attributing to certain women a level of insight unattainable by less fanciful individuals. Such possibilities were realized by a number of women invalids—for instance, Harriet Martineau, Elizabeth Barrett Browning, and Florence Nightingale—who used invalidism as an experimental resource of great value. Many invalid women reflexively studied their bodies and minds, to ascertain how their sickly states affected their intellectual and creative powers, and even their public authority.[7]

The Magnetic Sickroom

When mesmerism entered the sickroom, the various meanings of delicate feminine states and mental situations were epitomized in a more explicit and visible way than they were in ordinary life. An assertion made in the context of a mesmeric trial, of how a particular woman should be treated or the character of her intellect, was often treated as a test of what all women, or at least all women of her rank, might be able to do. Recall the two ways that mesmerism displayed or conferred authority. The mesmerist could infuse or mobilize others with vital influences. Men's superior physical strength and intellectual powers were often given as reasons why they were usually the mesmerists and women usually the subjects, though there were many important exceptions to the rule. But the mesmeric subject could also find authority in the trance state. The traditional role appropriate to this state was the oracular authority, the mesmeric subject whose body was freighted with information. This latter representation would supply the convention that would be taken over by spiritualist mediums later in the century. Women usually occupied this role, although several prominent mesmeric clairvoyants were men.

The campaigns by itinerants and mesmeric doctors to introduce mesmerism into early Victorian sickrooms were facilitated (or, for some potential patients, impeded) by a few celebrated, exotic cases. During this period a number of women invalids were said to have been placed in extraordinary states by mesmerism. One well-known case was that of a Bavarian peasant woman, the so-called Seeress of Prevorst, chronicled by the novelist Catherine Crowe. Her deathlike magnetic state blinded her to her immediate physical environment but put her in contact with what she called the "real world" invisible to everyone else (fig. 50).[8] A domestic specimen was Elizabeth Squirrell of Shottisham, who suffered since early childhood from a number of serious ailments, including a climactic twenty-five-week stint of lockjaw at the age of eleven when she could consume only fluids (fig. 51).[9] Animal magnetism first sustained her, then cured her of her illness, and finally gave her extraordinary

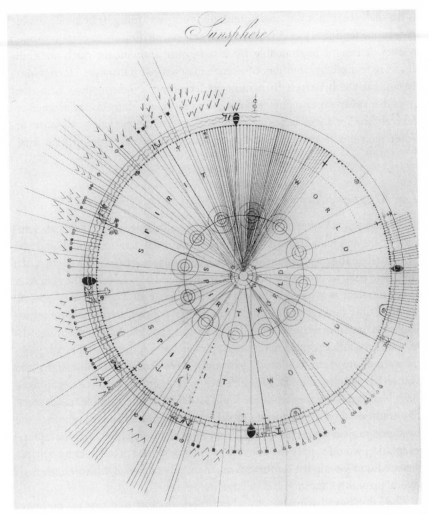

FIGURE 50 Map of the "spirit world" as dictated by the Seeress of Prevorst. Kerner, *Seeress of Prevorst.*

new cognitive abilities during the trance.[10] Animal magnetism extended the conventions that represented the invalid as sensitive and authoritative, both in extraordinary stories of exemplary invalids such as these and in many individual experiences, some recorded in the press and some not, across Victorian Britain.

These are unusual examples, but many ordinary invalids tried mesmerism themselves, often in desperation at the hopelessness of other treatments. One convert eschewed the practice until a member of his family was deathly ill. When all else failed, he called in a mesmerist: "I was sitting at a distant part of

FIGURE 51 Elizabeth Squirrell of Shottisham, one of several otherworldly invalids of the 1840s. During a several-week fast, Squirrell's increasingly insubstantial body became increasingly sensitive to nervous and spiritual influences. Squirrell, *Autobiography*.

the room, silently watching the patient in her slumbers . . . my attention was suddenly arrested, by observing her hand following the hand of the Mesmeriser, as by the force of attraction. Never shall I forget the feeling with which I started from my chair, ejaculating to myself, '*there is then something* in Mesmerism.'"[11] One successful trial in such circumstances could make an advocate out of a family member. Numerous stories not only of the relief of pain, but of cures of otherwise fatal diseases and the production of extraordinary mental phenomena, "emanated," to use the contemporary term of choice, from British sickrooms.

There are two, superficially contradictory, reasons that mesmerism suited certain aspects of the management of illness within a domestic setting. One was that the intimate bodily contact involved in producing the magnetic trance was less of a breach of propriety when it was carried out within the sickroom, because the invalid was used to extensive physical contact with nurses and other caregivers. The other is that the mesmeric clairvoyant had the power to diagnose diseases and prescribe treatment with no such intimate contact. Clairvoyant diagnosis put allopathic doctors at a disadvantage. One contributing factor was that the qualities that gave the clairvoyant her authority—a delicacy of body and mind that connected her consciousness with the physical and mental conditions of others—were present in slighter, less visible form in existing attitudes to invalids and the sickroom. The suffering, immobilized invalid was sensitized to her own inner states of body, mind, and soul, and even to the dynamics of the external world—if not to its most material workings, to the more important currents that structured them.

Harriet Martineau and the Reform of the Invalid

One of the best-known invalids of the 1840s, and certainly the most controversial, was the journalist Harriet Martineau. In 1844 she wrote an influential exposition of the invalid's role from her sickbed. As the work rolled off the presses, she stunned readers by making a spectacular recovery from her supposedly terminal illness after mesmeric treatment.

During the early and mid-Victorian period, Harriet Martineau (fig. 52) was one of the best-known journalists and documentary writers in Britain. She was celebrated for her descriptions of social life and social issues, from the conditions in factories to the state of American society. She was one of the most prolific popularizers of Benthamism and was "lionized" in London for her wildly popular *Illustrations of Political Economy*. People differed in their attitudes to her hard-line Benthamite political views, but most respected her as a commentator on social and political life. By the 1840s she was one of the most authoritative witnesses of Victorian society; as one hagiographic poem put it, "Truth is her law, and reason is her guide." [12] She was also represented as Britain's most "mannish" woman: sensitive enough to perceive the nuances of what she witnessed, yet strong enough to journey long distances to reach the scene of her investigations, and unflinchingly to record harsh, unpalatable, or indelicate truths.

In the early 1840s she had the opportunity to report on a new realm of human experience, one in which the authority of personal testimony was more precarious than in any of her previous inquiries. In 1839 she fell ill and retired to the home of her brother-in-law, Edward Michael Greenhow, in terrible pain and immobilized on her sickbed. He examined her and diagnosed a malignant uterine tumor. Within two years her plight was nationally known; friends and admirers organized "testimonials" to her great services to Britain to provide funds for her last days. [13]

When Martineau became an invalid, her independence was under threat—but not for long. [14] She moved from her sister's house to rooms of her own, hired her own nurse, and, a few years later, wrote a normative treatise on invalidism. [15] This defended the invalid's authority over her environment and made a case for the advantages invalidism could confer upon the life of the mind. The space she described was no clinic or hospital ward, but neither was

FIGURE 52
Harriet Martineau, c. 1834.
The hand cupped to her
ear represents her deafness
and perhaps her populism.
*Harriet Martineau's
Autobiography*, vol. 1.

it an ordinary bedroom. Her sickroom was a liminal space whose inhabitant was poised between the passivity of the ill woman and the assertiveness of a public figure.

Martineau built on those existing conventions that accentuated the authority of the ill and minimized those that undermined it. There were "hints" that boosted the invalid's power relative to doctors and nurses,[16] but the most significant argument in view of her later conversion to mesmerism related to the invalid's powers of observation and understanding. These were enhanced by suffering and isolation: "We may be excluded from much observation of the outer life of men; but of the inner life, which originates and interprets the outer, it is scarcely possible that in any other circumstances we could have known so much. Into what depths of opinion are we not let down! To what soaring heights of speculation are we not borne up! What is there of joy or sorrow, of mystery and marvel, in human experience that is not communicated to us!"[17] Martineau likened the invalid to a seraph, poised outside the "real" world and looking on.[18] What the "seraph" saw was a soothing shoreline view: fig. 53 is the landscape visible from her sickroom window, a middle-class, pastoral scene of families and workers walking peacefully near the mouth of the Tyne. The invalid's removal from the "affairs of men" conferred authority. She could see whole truths that were undistorted and unfragmented by the bustle of life surrounding the healthy. In the context of an extensive medical

FIGURE 53 Martineau's sickroom window looked onto a distinctly middle-class scene: strolling families, grazing cows, ships entering and leaving the Tyne. Martineau, *Autobiography*.

literature urging reforms of the sickroom that tried to make the invalid more passive, Martineau's success in asserting her sanity and authority was a significant achievement. It was a success that was both strengthened and challenged by her later involvement in mesmerism.

Most of her friends were inspired by the volume, and so was the wider readership.[19] Several letters amid her pile of fan mail described moral revolutions in the souls of her readers.[20] One lawyer had read *Life in the Sickroom* "at the Reform Club, where, in a corner of a green velvet sofa, he wept and prayed,—and on returning home c^d not sleep, till he had emptied his soul" in a letter to her. The man had a "horror of being drawn downwards by his profession and the world," she wrote exultantly to her friend Henry Crabb Robinson, "and he entreats my prayers."[21] The popular journalist and minor poet Richard Horne, in his 1844 *New Spirit of the Age*, wrote that the book had intensified the "moral influence emanating from her sick room."[22]

Sickroom was not universally acclaimed. The "serious" Evangelical readership, Martineau told Robinson, thought its "suppositions of self-reliance" "dangerous"; another warned that it assumed that the intellect and will were, as Martineau quoted one critic, "adequate to more than it is safe to suppose."[23] Doctors, of course, tended to see it as a challenge to their custodial role. Of the few critical reviews, the most striking appeared in the *British and Foreign Medical Review*. This addressed the work as if it were a piece of pathological evidence—a compilation of notes taken by an anonymous surgeon on Martineau's behavior and nervous symptoms. In lieu of access to the patient, the anonymous reviewer performed a medical examination upon her book. He diagnosed a "dissatisfaction" stemming from a "morbid" vanity; the "unhealthiness" of mind "spoilt" the book as a literary work. The cure was "unconditional submission"—presumably to her fate.[24] The reviewer also emphasized that he was writing not as a member of the general public eager to be instructed, but from a position of authority higher than she deserved: he was a "pathologist," and his job involved "elucidating the effects of diseases of body on the mind." His readers were medical professionals. This shift of audience transformed the book's significance. No longer an authoritative statement, it became the object of authoritative study; where it had been a body of knowledge, it became a piece of contingent evidence.

This reviewer was only expressing the views of most of the medical community, but the shift of authority he made in the course of the review foreshadowed other, more extensive challenges that were shortly to be directed against this view of invalidism. For Martineau the authority on the experience of somatic diseases, and even, potentially, on the nature of the disease itself, was the invalid.[25] In contrast, the reviewer sought to retain the experiences of the ill, and their bodies, under medical jurisdiction. One of his conclusions was that "advice offered to the individual by his intellect is very incapable of correcting these disordered states of the feelings." This was the rhetorical framework in which Martineau's highly public confrontation with the medical profession was shortly to be carried out.

Queen of Mesmeria

Throughout her convalescence Martineau had been urged by several acquaintances, including Basil Montague and Edward Bulwer-Lytton,[26] to try the practice. She had consistently refused, despite her increasing interest in the science, because Greenhow had stipulated that she must either be "without it or him."[27]

But the situation changed drastically in 1842 and 1843 with the spread of mesmeric anesthesia and dozens of itinerant lecturers traversing the country. Many local doctors were now convinced of mesmerism's efficacy and usefulness. They also worried about the damage to their practices if they did not at least covertly explore the possibilities of incorporating mesmerism into their work. At this time (1842 or 1843) Greenhow became more open to the science, perhaps reassured by the fact that Martineau's other brother-in-law, the Liverpool physician Alfred Higginson, had begun to use mesmerism to anesthetize his patients. When Spencer Hall reached Newcastle during one of his northern tours, Greenhow witnessed a demonstration and (without revealing in advance the identity of his patient) brought him to Martineau's bedside for a trial.

Martineau's first experience was slight but definite. She later described how she had been sent forth by the creative hand of her mesmerist to feel the walls of her room "dissolve," the barrier of a lifetime's partial deafness melt, and her senses expand to take in new sights and sounds.[28] After the first session she had a "strong persuasion that I am capable of more—much more—than I have experienced yet."[29] The trial was a success, and after several others with different mesmerists, Martineau reported a dramatic improvement in her condition. Her pain and lethargy drained away and eventually vanished. She began to take exercise, sometimes walks of five miles or more, and claimed that even her deafness had improved.[30] She abandoned her opium habit, which had become intense during her illness, exchanging its "hot heavy comfort" for mesmerism's "fresh, cold stimulus."[31]

Martineau's authoritative status changed even faster than her health. Initially, Greenhow had considered that *he* was performing an experiment upon Martineau and that he would evaluate it, but he soon learned that she considered this to be her job. He expected to be the judge of the success of the trial, and whether further trials, and eventual publications, should be ventured. However, Greenhow's experimental subject considered that she alone had that right. As we shall see, Martineau and Greenhow differed not only on whether the experiments had been a success but, in retrospect, on what had been wrong with her in the first place.

Martineau soon dismissed Hall, replacing him first with her maid and then with a genteel woman's companion, Mrs. Montague Wynyard. Wynyard came with a mesmeric pedigree. She had been "married to abominable husband, paid all his debts twice, refused a third time, for wch she was much abused by his family; got into wretched health, was mesmerised . . . and entirely cured."[32] Wynyard became a close companion for the next several years, and Martineau wrote that "I cordially respect & love her."[33]

In their mesmeric sessions the goal was for Wynyard's will temporarily to overwhelm Martineau's: "To have her will uppermost is just what I want."[34] Martineau's description of the process must be qualified by the social position of dependence she chose in her mesmerist: a genteel lady's companion fallen on hard times. Wynyard was a woman of similar social background to Martineau but without her financial independence. This helped make her a safe figure to whom to "submit" temporarily, in a way that Hall, because of his gender, his lower social standing, and his itinerancy, was not (he could be expected to use his trials on Martineau as the basis for public lectures at some future point; and indeed he did refer to the experiments in newspaper advertisements). Martineau was happy to surrender her will only to a subservient member of her household, who did not threaten to undermine, as a male mesmerist might, her recent success in establishing her independence and authority.

In addition to these two women, Martineau also enjoyed in a lesser capacity the mesmeric services of the phreno-mesmerist and philosopher Henry G. Atkinson, with whom she would later write a notorious philosophical work.[35] Its content was partly inspired by Martineau's mesmeric experiences. Under the influence of her mesmeric coterie, she claimed to have developed a dramatic corpus of mesmeric knowledge. The trance placed Martineau "in a higher plane of existence," which gave her "ideas and insight (religious and philosophical) wch are to me worth more than any former experience":[36] "Never did I dream of experiencing in this life that most awful, yet most calm consciousness—the inkling of new faculties,—the distinct consciousness of their incipient exercise! I retain *four ideas*—distinct, pregnant,—awful beyond description, but as clear & expansible as any proposition in reasoning ... no words can tell the impression of the serene region of translucent intellectuality from w^h I derived these ideas,—a state in w^h all things seemed to become clear."[37] It is appropriate that a natural, physical force, rather than learned critical study or other possible means of achieving wisdom, supplied the means of learning fundamental truths. Martineau was known for a proto-materialist view of mind[38] and a strong commitment to phrenology. She found it plausible that a natural influence could enhance the physiological capabilities of the brain. Indeed, this force, like those driving the development of mankind itself in the many sciences of progress of this period, would enable her to view the advancement of mankind and beliefs. She declared, in language reminiscent of the book of Revelation, that "I *saw* the march of the whole human race, past, present, and to come, through existence, and their finding the Source of Life. Another time, I *saw* all the Idolatries of the earth coming up to worship at the ascending series of life-fountains, while I discovered these to be all connected,—each flowing down unseen to fill the next,—so that all the worshippers were seen by me to be verily adoring the source."[39]

Here was the philosophical summit of her mesmeric experiences, and indeed her intellectual life more generally. Through the direct action of a force of nature on her nervous system, Martineau had attained access to the "very laws of life"[40] and the source of all beliefs about the world, and was able to understand how they related to one another. But these were dangerous developments in Martineau's mesmeric career: the content of her vision, even had it been expressed outside the context of mesmeric trances, would have been controversial among the Unitarian community of her family and friends. It might have seemed to deny the very notion of idolatry, since whatever lesser stream of the "life-fountain" one worshipped, one was "verily adoring the source." Martineau announced that she had her "foot on the shoulder" of the "mysteries" not only of mesmerism but of the basis of life and of human belief.[41]

Everything about these experiences was controversial, from the content of the vision to the means by which it had been produced. However compelling Martineau found her mesmeric thoughts, they had to remain "unuttered" (to the general public) lest she be declared "insane." [42] Nevertheless, she persevered with her investigations, soon discovering that "*I* have the power [to mesmerize others],—& not inconsiderably." [43] She also arranged for Mrs. Wynyard to mesmerize Jane Arrowsmith, the young niece of Martineau's landlady, with remarkable results. Arrowsmith was "a sweet, innocent, upright, conscientious girl of 19," whom Martineau had known for years, and even when she began to show signs of clairvoyance, Martineau had no doubt about her credibility. On one occasion the entranced girl saw a violent storm pounding the shoreline hundreds of miles away, and described a shipwreck. The shipwreck, it later emerged, had indeed taken place, but the news was thought not to have reached Tynemouth until after the experiment.[44]

Martineau decided to publicize her mesmeric experiences in a series of letters to the *Athenaeum* in late 1844.[45] But even before they appeared, rumors flew across the country along the transmission lines of Martineau's correspondence network.[46] The "Martineau incident" became public property long before it was officially announced, and "all manner of invalids and medical strangers," each begging to know "all particulars," began to contact her.[47] By her own report she was "buried" under a mass of letters asking for verification of the news. She told them all that "*[m]esmerism is true to the full extent:*— I mean, human beings have, under certain conditions, a power of Prevision and Insight, alternating with ordinary states of the mind." Once she had time to make further tests she would "throw the whole weight of my character, intellectual and moral, into my testimony to this truth." [48] Despite the qualms of friends, Martineau's *Athenaeum* articles described her full experiences.[49]

Martineau's was the most significant claim to a mesmeric cure so far. Henry Crabb Robinson reported that it was having "the wildest effect," because Martineau had "credit for possessing the too rare faculties of observing justly and reporting faithfully." [50] Thomas Arnold's widow Mary concurred: Martineau's "name, combined with her power as a writer, will make her Evidence . . . very effective; and we may expect to hear of a Mesmeriser kept as a regular part of one's establishment." [51] Here was evidence that Martineau might achieve what other mesmeric subjects had not: credibility as witnesses despite their status as experimental subjects.

These events took place in the autumn of 1844; the published account appeared first in the *Athenaeum* in late November and December and was issued as a book some months later. By late November it seemed as if all of polite society was following Martineau's example. Séances were convened in middle-class parlors, in stately homes, even in the dowager queen's court.[52] Popular lectures replicated her findings—and remained popular for years. Newspapers printed summaries of her letters to the *Athenaeum,* and amateur mesmerists negotiated pilgrimages to visit her.[53] Martineau's acquaintance, she wrote, not only enjoyed "witnessing my return to life,—but they are everywhere curing the 'incurable,' practising mesmerism with their hands with fine success."[54] Martineau's case had generated an enormous popular sensation throughout the country, as "sick and suffering strangers, & inquiring doctors," sent her "[l]apfulls of letters" for information, attempted their own experiments, and debated their significance.[55]

Many members of the intelligentsia were fascinated as well—particularly those interested in questions about the extent and character of natural law. Wynyard carried out a successful experiment on the publisher and scientific writer Robert Chambers, whose anonymous *Vestiges of the Natural History of Creation* had just rolled off the presses.[56] After a few passes near his forehead "the effect was immediate and unmistakable." Chambers "continued in a deep mesmeric sleep or stupor until a few dispersive passes dispelled the influence."[57] Martineau's sister, Rachel, was successful at mesmerizing Hall's traveling subject, a young boy,[58] and Lord Morpeth, a leading Whig politician, carried out a number of successful experiments on Jane Arrowsmith.

The key to Martineau's success was the great degree of public support on which she could draw. She was a major public figure, adored by a large proportion of the middle-class readership. Her celebrated powers of observation had set the seal of truth on an issue that had already captured the imagination of polite society. Moreover, her moral powers had assessed the controversial practice, and had approved it. From December 1844 onward, a high-profile public debate took shape, which, in addressing the key problems of mesmerism, necessarily brought out important issues regarding the nature of private and public space and discourse. The debate precipitated conflicting images of what it was (or should be) to be a woman, to be ill, and to be a medical practitioner.

The Medical Opposition

Even as Martineau's account went to press, the *Athenaeum*'s editor, Charles Wentworth Dilke, commissioned a critical reply. This anonymous article was credited by Charles Darwin to Sir Benjamin Collins Brodie, president of the Royal College of Surgeons. Brodie attacked Martineau on three fronts.[59] First, he claimed (contrary to Greenhow's diagnosis) that her disease was hysterical.[60] A change of mood would easily make her feel better. Thus no curative effects could be ascribed specifically to mesmerism. Second, as a member of the public she could not testify because she had not the necessary expertise.[61] Finally, she could not witness natural phenomena for the simple reason that she was part of the phenomena herself.

Brodie already had a history of distrusting even the most dramatic of patient testimonies in relation to mesmerism and nervous phenomena. Recall that in previous work he advised that the doctor should always distrust what his patients said when nervous phenomena of any kind might be involved. Martineau's claims to knowledge threatened to subvert his model of medical diagnosis, inasmuch as they asserted the primacy, importance, and authenticity of the patient's experiences. Brodie also headed an institution whose traditional conventions of privilege and patronage were under threat by the radical reform movement. He had been intimately involved in the progress of the various reform bills that had spared the Royal College of Surgeons from the threat of a unified faculty. Adrian Desmond has shown how corporation conservatives, in particular Richard Owen (who was championed by Brodie in 1837),[62] fought to generate a "conservative" physiology and anatomy sophisticated enough to do battle with the radical coterie.[63] Brodie's work in the Royal College of Surgeons kept the engine of conservatism running during the 1840s. His response to Martineau was part of this project. In divesting her of authority over her own medical case, he was combating a supporter of the very social reforms that, taken up by the radical medical reformers, threatened his institution.

Among many *Athenaeum* readers Brodie's letters succeeded in casting doubt upon Martineau's claims, but not in demolishing them. Among some scientific specialists they were more decisive. Charles Darwin identified Brodie as the author by way of cautioning his cousin C. J. Fox, who was inspired by Martineau to embark upon a mesmeric course of his own. Darwin warned him that a "tendency to deceive is characteristic of disordered females," and furthermore that "[m]y father has often known mania [to] relieve incurable complaints." So Martineau's improved health might itself be a symptom of madness. The answer was to avoid women altogether. Animals were less likely either to be duped by their own bodies or to fool people: "*keep* some cats *yourself* & do get some mesmerizer to make experiments upon them."[64]

Darwin could have drawn on the pioneering work of a doctor who had, he reported, made trials on a number of cats—along with several other species of animals. After the O'Key sisters were discredited, John Wilson, physician to the Middlesex Hospital, experimented on these creatures in 1838 and 1839 to avoid just those problems of testimony that worried Darwin. With a methodical thoroughness that Darwin himself would have endorsed, he published full particulars of the experiments: dates, locations, details of practice, and even the names of his experimental subjects. He began with cats. Wilson "made the passes on Kitty and Fuzzy, both for the first time, and both were put to sleep in about a quarter of an hour." After this remarkable success he progressed successively to dogs, a drake, three ducks, a pool of fish, and a pair of "healthy, fat" pigs, which he mesmerized in their sty ("at each pass, spasmodic convulsions of the ear, snout, and whole body were strongly developed"). He then traveled to the Zoological Gardens in Surrey, where, after two or three (ambiguously) "unsuccessful" trials on a leopard and leopardess, he labored for nearly a week on a pair of Ceylon elephants. At length he could report progress: one of them "yawned thrice, wide and long." Wilson concluded his efforts at this stage, prudently reluctant to discover "what the consequences might be" if the animals passed through the stage of sleep and into the state of "delirium." [65]

Whether Fox followed Wilson's example is unknown, but Darwin did at least succeed in dissuading him from visiting Martineau in the winter of 1845. Other doctors were also made chary of mesmerism in the wake of Brodie's statement, judging from the response of the major medical journals. The *British and Foreign Medical Review* and the *London Medical Gazette* both supported him; so did Thomas Wakley, whose opposition to mesmerism only intensified with time. Because they were fellow radical reformers, one might have expected Wakley's scheme of medical "reform" to coincide with Martineau's. That it did not shows the malleability of what radical reform meant in practice. Martineau's *Sickroom* and *Letters on Mesmerism* were aimed at spreading a network of patient-controlled treatment throughout Britain. Martineau used radical reform policy to use the self-help ideology that had first established her reputation for the advantage of sickroom inmates. Thus her project could easily be seen as subversive by those who, like Wakley, wished to restrict the production and adjudication of knowledge to a specific and limited authority.

Wakley's written condemnations concentrated on restricting Martineau, physically and intellectually, to the invalid's couch, from which mesmerism had temporarily, and dangerously, freed her.[66] One correspondent to the *Lancet* summed up the radical medical reformers' case by noting that the "nature of the disease was not described in the paper of Miss Martineau. It would be somewhat odd for the *disease* to give itself a *name*."[67] Martineau could not participate in medical debates, or perhaps any debates, for that matter, because there could be no distinction made between her and her disease.

As the medical attacks mounted, Greenhow became uneasy. As a medical man he should have prevented, much less taken part in, the mesmeric experiments. If these events had taken place a few years later, Greenhow might have benefited from the notorious advice of Robert Brudenell Carter, who became known for his insistence on controlling the hysterical patient and placing her "under his roof, as only there can she be described as under his treatment." Otherwise the patient might "damage his reputation, and certainly not add to it."[68] Greenhow was indeed worried that Martineau had placed his professional standing at risk, and he took the controversial step of publishing his own version of the case.[69] He related specific details of Martineau's physical condition, including a vaginal examination, that many readers (not to mention Martineau) considered highly indiscreet and repulsive. He also made a claim that Martineau denied, that he had diagnosed her condition as nervous and likely to improve suddenly and without apparent provocation. Greenhow printed his pamphlet in a cheap English edition, announced in the introduction that he had secured Martineau's permission, and put it on general sale. The medical journals reprinted it, but the public also purchased it and discussed Harriet Martineau's uterine tumor at their leisure. Greenhow's choice of a cheap English edition for his pamphlet is significant partly because it indicates the lack of consolidation and authority within the medical profession, at least in the northeast of England, during this time; if the general public had not played an important part in the decision over the status of mesmerism, there would have been no need for such a publication.

Martineau was horrified. She claimed that she had given permission for her case to be discussed only within the medical community. She later explained that she did not object to the publication per se, but to its accessibility. She expected the pamphlet to be published in a medical journal or in Latin (it is interesting that the choice of language provoked much discussion despite the fact that almost all medical works were now published in English), and never expected the price to be low enough for all middle-class readers to afford. Greenhow's pamphlet appeared to Martineau and many of her acquaintances (not necessarily those supportive of mesmerism) as a betrayal of family loyalty and privacy, and beginning in January 1845, she broke off all contact with the Greenhows.

Martineau quickly learned to distrust doctors; in January she wrote, albeit lightheartedly, of wishing to avoid "doctors" who might "persecute us."[70] The persecution she felt most strongly was, of course, Greenhow's. Partly in reaction against him, Martineau published her letters in a book, which sold out in four days. She introduced the bound edition with a word of encouragement for those doctors prevented by discretion or fear from speaking out: "Besides the natural reluctance to come forward alone, a humane and gentlemanly feeling towards their patients keeps them silent,—prevents their exposing their charge to . . . impertinences and injurious imputations." She wished to reach these isolated individuals, invalids, and provincial mesmerists, "hitherto scattered," and bring them "into co-operation."[71] As in her *Morals and Manners,* which advised that "no fact is without its use," she now heralded the birth of a new inductive science. Mesmeric truths would spread over the face of Britain, forever changing the nature of convalescence and the care of invalids.

Martineau was confident that those same principles of supply and demand that she had popularized for her political patrons during the 1830s would now come to work for her.

[T]he elements of the supply are all abundant, and only wait to be brought together. There is the mesmeric power,—there is the desire for employment . . . [I]f only half a dozen Mesmerists were to meet for mutual information, trial, and practice,—there would presently be such an accession of numbers and force as would meet much of the existing need. A succession of Mesmerists and nurses would go out . . .—men and women of education . . . who would first directly, then as a consequence, change the aspect of half the sick-rooms of the land.

Marching troops of mesmerists and nurses would teach the sick of Britain not only new methods of cure, but new ways of being ill. Fulfilling the vision of Martineau's *Life in the Sickroom,* they would change the "aspect" of illness, such that mesmeric principles and therapies could take a central place in the restoration and preservation of health—and thus attain the status of a fundamental corpus of laws governing the nature of the body.

Martineau's efforts did not go unrewarded. While the opposition cast doubt on her claims, especially on her reports of experiments in clairvoyance and prescience,[72] the medical campaign against her, especially the article by Brodie and the pamphlet published by Greenhow, was met with outrage by many commentators outside professional medical circles. The *London Medical Gazette*'s casual explanation of Martineau's testimony as evidence that she was at "the turn of life" was met with contempt by a writer in *Chambers's Edinburgh Journal,* who complained, "[O]ne cannot but be amused to see extremes return upon themselves, and scepticism pretend to an oracular power far beyond the ordinary stretch of the grossest superstition."[73]

One popular rendition of the Martineau episode is especially revealing of the public status of her mesmeric experiences. In 1845 the novelist Horace Smith published a novel inspired by his own mesmeric experiences, containing a heroine inspired jointly by Jane Arrowsmith, Martineau, and perhaps Elizabeth O'Key.[74] The heroine's lack of education was a sign of purity, her humble social position a security against corruption; and her invalidism and hysteria rendered her especially sensitive to invisible forces. In one scene she lectured her father on mesmerism, using knowledge that came to her in a trance: "What is it that makes the lodestone attract the needle? what is the secret of electricity? who can account for the shock of the galvanic battery, or of the electric eel, or for the phenomena of crystallisation? why does opium produce sleep . . . all these come from God, so do I believe that Mesmerism and its prodigies . . . are of divine origin." [75] Mesmerism revealed natural law to be a public property. The mystery surrounding mesmerism kept it from being, as many physical forces were becoming, the property of the scientific or medical elite, and taught people to treat the claims of elite science as being less certain than they might otherwise have assumed. The heroine's monologue demonstrates the public fascination with the oracular figure of the hysteric rendered sensitive by her illness, which paved the way for the success of spiritualism in the 1850s. Apart from these public evidences of the continuing interest in mesmerism, within the correspondence of Martineau's circle it is clear that her experience triggered an intense interest in experimentation into altered states of mind. [76]

Ada Lovelace

Victorian intellectual women were, almost by definition, oddities. Their individuality was one of the few things they all shared. So we must not take Martineau's case as representative of how intellectual women tended to make meaning from illness, nervous phenomena, and altered states. Rather, her story illustrates some of mesmerism's possibilities, and one of the most influential examples that others observed and evaluated.

Another, quite different example of how an intellectual invalid might try to gain knowledge by monitoring herself, and the ambivalent role that mesmerism could play in such ambitions, is Ada Lovelace, Byron's daughter and a prominent intellectual figure during the 1840s (fig. 54). During the early 1840s Lovelace wished to study mathematics, and her family and friends thought she had the ability to excel in the field. But the eminent mathematician and logician Augustus De Morgan, who was tutoring her by correspondence, worried that his pupil had mental powers too great for her bodily health. In 1844 he wrote to Lady Byron to warn that her daughter's body and mind were headed for a life-threatening conflict. De Morgan's worries expressed a common opinion about mathematical work: the process of making new advances in mathematical knowledge required large expenditures of bodily energy. These stretched the limits of strong athletic men. This was the assumption upon which the athletic regimes of the mathematical tripos of mid-

FIGURE 54 Ada Lovelace, dressed in one of the costumes that earned her a "fantastic" reputation—a far cry from the more conventional tight waists and leg-o'-mutton sleeves. © British Museum.

Victorian Cambridge would soon be laid in the 1850s through the 1870s. These regimes were maintained on the assumption that strengthening the body made it a more powerful engine with which to supply energy to the mind, and a stronger vessel for the containment of the mental energy deployed in mathematical thinking.[77] A woman, conventional wisdom had it, was doubly disadvantaged by a smaller frame and the need to reserve energy for reproduction. De Morgan warned that, if Lovelace encouraged the development of her mental powers to the necessary extent, they might become so great that her body would no longer be able to contain or to harness them.

According to De Morgan, Lovelace was highly unusual among Victorian women in having a mind capable of grasping "strong points and the real difficulties of first principles." However, De Morgan told her mother, he had never acknowledged this to Lovelace because he felt ambivalent about whether she should be encouraged in her efforts not only to "reach but to get beyond, the present bounds of knowledge." It was precisely because she had great mental powers that it was dangerous for her to use them. Her body, perhaps any woman's body, was too delicate to cope with the rigors it would have to endure to fulfill her potential as an original mathematician. De Morgan told Lady

Byron that encouraging her daughter would endanger the health of her body and mind. The "very great tension which [mathematical studies] require is beyond the strength of a woman's physical power of application. Lady L. has unquestionably as much power as would require all the strength of a man's constitution to bear the fatigue of thought to which it will unquestionably lead her."[78] De Morgan's warnings suggest that great mental powers could be turned on or off. In contrast to Martineau, who denied that one could "hush" creativity as one could "pat a dog to sleep," De Morgan thought one could choose whether to awaken and unleash one's mental energy or to let it remain neutral or dormant. Applying oneself to hard work, one surmises, revved up a machine whose activity might be too overwhelming for its delicate structure. Lovelace herself, and her mother, responded with a rival representation of uncontrollable energy, but a somewhat different one. Both mother and daughter claimed that Lovelace's mathematics was a force welling up in her. The creative process would occur regardless of her wishes, whether or not she threw herself into her work. Bottling it up, therefore, was dangerous. Lady Byron assured her daughter, "no one who has seen you could imagine a *discontinuance* of mathematics necessary."[79]

But De Morgan's worries might seem to have been well-founded: Lovelace's health, always precarious, faltered disturbingly in the mid-1840s. She was bedridden for much of 1843 through 1845, and intermittently before and after this. Lovelace, like the mesmeric oracles mentioned earlier, regarded her state of illness as providing her with new intellectual powers and possibilities, but she differed from them in the effects she thought mesmerism had on the body. For them it improved or sustained their health; for her it had the reverse effect. Lovelace had experimented in mesmerism in 1842 and 1843, shortly before the onset of her three-year bout of nervousness, digestive problems, hot flashes, and excruciating headaches. She drew different conclusions from it than did Martineau: when she experienced "unnatural feelings bodily and mental" over the next few years, she attributed these to her mesmeric experiences.

Lovelace used her sickroom as a way of keeping other people (mainly her mother) at bay. She reflected on the intellectual significance of her illness and decided that her ailing body provided her with a valuable intellectual opportunity. She began to regard her body as a "molecular laboratory," offering her the means of studying the relationship between nervous physiology and the development of knowledge. Having sensed the workings of this process in the welling-up of knowledge, she could carry out scientific study of this process by carrying out introspective researches inside her own skin. Studies of mesmerism, though not with herself as experimental subject, were part of her researches. Lovelace did correspond at length on the possibilities of using her

FIGURE 55. Ada Lovelace on her deathbed, sketched by her mother. Bodleian Library, Lovelace Collection, Noel-Byron Papers.

"molecular laboratory" to develop, as she put it on one occasion, a "Calculus of the Nervous System," but she never developed any such corpus of knowledge or theory.

If mesmerism did not yield new truths about the brain and body, she did not give up on it entirely. In 1852, suffering from her most serious disorder yet, a severe ovarian tumor, mesmerism was one of the therapies she tried in a desperate, and vain, attempt at a cure. Even on her deathbed (fig. 55) she was writing to her mother that she was on the edge of the extraordinary discoveries she sought through introspection. She left no such intellectual legacy. In late 1852 she died. The *Times*'s obituary recorded her age, family connections, and the husband and children she left behind. No mention was made of her intellectual work.

Elizabeth Barrett

Lovelace was unusual in her confidence that her illness would give her knowledge and power, and in her frankness about her bodily states; Martineau was unusual in the publicity she solicited from within her sickroom and the strength of will she displayed in publicizing her cure. Few Victorian women would have been able to empathize with their ability to relish the experience of succumbing to nervous influences. Even among the small group of women whom we would think of as "intellectuals," several found Martineau's publicity jarring and Lovelace's ambitions incredible. To gain a better sense of the spectrum of the possible views of mesmerism, let us now consider the experiences of a very different intellectual. She, too, used her sickroom as a source of authority and a means of asserting control over her life and social acquaintance. But she developed a very different account of the relationship between states of the body and the intellect and will, and a radically different attitude to mesmerism itself.

In the early 1840s one would not have expected Elizabeth Barrett to have before her anything but a life of the mind. A spinster in her late thirties, she had been sickly and reclusive for years. But these frailties gave body and will a prominent place in her ruminations as she monitored the state of her nerves. In 1843 and 1844 a conjunction of personal and intellectual developments made the question of bodily influence and the public status of intellectual women particularly significant to Barrett when she first encountered mesmerism and began to follow the controversy over Martineau's cure. The nature of the will (hers and others') was a clear preoccupation in a family where her father exerted an extreme degree of authority over the movements of his children (even by Victorian standards). In 1843 and 1844 Barrett struggled against her frailty as she prepared a manuscript that, once published, became immensely popular just as the controversy over Martineau broke. Barrett met the poet Robert Browning at the end of 1844. During 1845 she was preoccupied in her correspondence on mesmerism with the question of how one person could "possess" another, and reflected on more personal issues of "possession" in her secret courtship with Browning.

Barrett's situation was in some ways very similar to Martineau's, and these similarities make the differences between their attitudes to illness stand out. They were invalids during the same period, and their readers had a powerful sense that their frailties informed their writing. Both were, broadly speaking, "reformers" and came from professional families. They were both very familiar with altered states of mind, and each had had an opium habit for years. However, they could not have been more different in their understandings of the physical and sensory dynamics of their intellectual lives and personal identities. Martineau prided herself on placing "reason over passion" and was touted as one of Britain's most "mannish" women. She was certainly one of the most public and well traveled. Barrett thought of herself as driven by feeling, was becoming known in this period as one of the most womanly of writers, and was extremely reclusive.

Although Barrett's sickroom was a source of authority to her, it functioned in a very different way from Martineau's. Martineau ushered a stream of people through her sickroom during her five-year illness, making the sickroom in some degree a public space controlled by its inmate. The invalid directed her nurses, vied for authority with her doctors, and had, in principle, more public authority than those walking the streets of Britain. Barrett, in contrast, used her invalidism to fend off other people. The display of strength in other people made her feel proportionately weaker, and when she was forced to be near other people's bodies, she thought of the experience as an "assault" on her nerves.[80] She engaged in lengthy negotiations with friends and acquaintances wishing to visit her in the flesh, often begging them to stay away.

Her longing to be safely "separated from all life & its emotions" had a physiological cause: the east wind, she told friends, had "shaken me, & 'jangled' my nerves."[81] They were "all broken on the rack, & now hang loosely . . . quivering at a step and breath."[82] It was as if her years of illness had worn away her skin or made it porous, making her nerves sing at the slightest breeze. Barrett, nursing her nerves in the still air of her cloistered bedroom, portrayed the invalid as engaging with abstract, ethereal truths in her solitude. She mediated her interactions with other men and women by ink, paper, and the penny post. While she relished the immense (and often very intimate) acquaintance she maintained in epistolary correspondence, she was too delicate to tolerate *physical* proximity. The differences between Barrett and Martineau regarding the function of the sickroom and the management of nervous delicacy foreshadowed their different reactions to mesmerism. Martineau welcomed mesmerism as a liberating, or, to use a modern term that is growing a little stale, an "empowering" force; Barrett feared it as a form of personal obliteration, the extreme manifestation of the threat of subjection to other people that so terrified her.

Nervous States of Creativity

Barrett, like many early-Victorian intellectual women, understood her creativity as depending on a delicate balance or tension of nervous states in her body. She felt a "need of utterance" borne of words that seemed to be "actually lying within" her.[83] Self-expression was therefore not entirely a volitional act, but a welling-up of knowledge, which was in large part unwilled. But while her poetic power was accentuated by her sensitivity, the strength she needed to articulate this verse, to realize it in words and stanzas, was limited by nervous weakness. The very nervousness that facilitated this internal poetry also made her too weak to sustain the process of articulating it without suffering ill health; conversely, this ill health validated the poetry by confirming it as the product of "genuine" sensibility.

One consequence of the fact that creativity was only partly volitional was that the maladies related to intellectual life could not be understood fully by medical doctors. Barrett and Martineau corresponded over this matter. Martineau, as a fellow literary invalid, communed over them with Barrett and offered a prescription. Doctors could not understand the physiology of creativity because they were not similarly creative, and only personal knowledge of this state could allow one to know it. One might recommend writing "as an amusement," Martineau wrote ruefully, assuming that "one could take it up like wool-work & with no more wear & tear"; another would forbid "all excitement & intellectual labour, as if one could hush one's mind, as you pat your dog to sleep." While it would be better that Barrett's "pulses" should get themselves "in order" than that "more poems [utter] themselves," the former could not occur without the latter. Barrett would not recover while she was "keeping a burning & thrilling weight of poetry on [the] heart & brain." She had to "empty" herself of that poetry she could feel "lying within." Once having done so, Martineau advised, she should seek out activities that "less deeply affect your nerves & brain." [84] Martineau's advice was about purging the mind in the same way that Victorian medicine emphasized purging and eliminating things from the body. The difference was that, unlike the matter produced by digestion, what was being purged was not inert. The poetry was an active entity within her, "uttering itself," pushing its way out in a manner similar to a traditional representation of creative production as reproduction.

Jangling Nerves and Creeping Blood

Barrett's unusual sensitivity to the physical presence of other people made it more plausible to her that one person's body could exert a powerful influence (even at a distance) over another's. It also made mesmerism more frightening. A science whose purpose was to demonstrate the influence that operated between individuals, and that dissolved certain cognitive boundaries (both of knowledge and of independent action) between them, was a nightmarish extreme of what she already dreaded in ordinary interaction. She first became convinced of the reality of mesmerism in 1843 when her friends began experimenting in the science. Although she witnessed no experiments and recoiled from the thought ever of experiencing the effects herself, she wrote extensively of mesmerism in her correspondence, regularly pumping her friends for information and exchanging references to articles in the general and medical press. One friend, she reported to another, was "thrown" into the magnetic sleep, and "slept & talked & tasted just as her Mesmeric master was pleased to command—& made faces when *he* drank vinegar, & started aside, when *he* was pricked by a pin, . . . seemed to adopt in fact his senses for her." [85] Many other such reports were to follow, from credible sources such as close friends and members of her family.[86] When she heard of Martineau's experiences, she reported them exultantly to her friends: "Consider what a case it is! No case of a weak-minded woman and a nervous affection; but of the most manlike woman in the three kingdoms . . . and suffering under a disease which has induced change of structure and yielded to no tried remedy! Is it not wonderful, and past expectation? . . . her experience will settle the question of the reality of magnetism with a whole generation of infidels." [87] Barrett's fascination was purely an abstract, intellectual interest, not a personal and practical one. She had no plans to try mesmerism for her own ailments. In cases "such as mine," she confided to her intimate friend Mary Russell Mitford, "the remedy has done harm instead of good, by over-exciting the system." [88] She did not specify what such cases were, but one presumes that they were included in the large but ambiguous category of nervous disorders into which many complaints fell during these years.

As the Martineau debate progressed, Barrett and Mitford followed it closely, intensively debating the proprieties and possibilities of mesmerism between themselves.[89] As they passed the latest mesmeric news back and forth and traded opinions on how credible each incident was, Barrett complained that it was hard to walk the line of rational appraisal between automatic dismissal of new phenomena and unthinking credulity. "It is easy to say 'humbug,'" she wrote, "and perhaps as easy to swallow the world & its follies whole by an 'omnivorous' credulity. But not to be either a stupid infidel or a credulous *hoaxee*, is really hard,—where one's experience & what one calls one's philosophy, lie on one side, & a heap of phenomena on the other." [90] When the predictions of Martineau's mesmeric servant, Jane Arrowsmith, were being debated, Mitford asked how anyone could pay attention to the "wild notions of a girl of nineteen." Barrett replied that the notions were unimportant in themselves but might reveal "the extent of the agency." [91] Mitford thought mesmerism might be acceptable as a medical treatment or anesthetic but was appalled by experiments in prophecy and the other "higher" phenomena; Barrett found the idea of giving mesmerism a practical application before its nature was understood more frightening than "to wring prophecies from it in a spirit of objectless curiosity." Fundamentally, Barrett was unwilling to make a priori distinctions between categories of information that mesmerism could illuminate. Since Arrowsmith had been believed by many witnesses when she gave mesmeric diagnoses and seemed to have the ability to converse in languages she had never learned, how could those same individuals refuse to consider the possibility that she could perceive events happening at a geographical or chronological distance? "A housemaid who speaks anatomy by revelation, may speak divinity, by the same—may she not?" [92]

Although Barrett championed Martineau's courage in putting her case forward, and argued in abstract terms about the need to investigate the phenomena, she was personally appalled by the idea of mesmerism. The kind of bodily influence it involved filled her with a "creeping" and a "shrinking of horror" in the blood. The widest range of mesmeric phenomena felt, to Barrett, like forms of possession, even apparently innocuous practices such as the use of a lock of hair for clairvoyant analysis. When friends asked her to give them a lock of her hair to be given to a French clairvoyant (probably Alexis Didier, who is discussed in chapter 6) in order to obtain a diagnosis of her condition, she was terrified. She imagined lying on her sickbed "at the mercy of my imagination," mentally following the lock of hair into the clairvoyant's consulting room hundreds of miles away. Relinquishing a part of herself in this way would make her feel that the clairvoyant had "hold of me by a lock of hair" as surely as if he were standing by her and grasping a living part of her body.[93] Mesmerism was the incarnation of her worst fears regarding Victorian society, and she agonized over the question of how one could possibly retain one's identity in the presence of such a power.

Whereas Martineau had the luxury of temporarily suspending her will and giving herself up to the control of another person, one suspects that this was because she defined the "giving up" as being limited in a way that Barrett feared it would not be. Martineau did not conceive that she could be truly possessed by another person; Barrett was convinced that she could. Barrett shrank from "the idea of subjecting my will as an individual to the will of another" because for her this meant "merging my identity (in some strange way which makes my blood creep to think of)" in that of someone else. Her difficulty with magnetism was that it required her "[t]o submit myself soul & body to another will" and that was "revolting to my apprehension; & few considerations in the world w^d induce me to do such a thing."[94]

Magnet or No Magnet, I Have Been Brought Back to Life

Although Barrett was clearly desperate to keep other people physically at bay in the early 1840s, in 1845 she began to contemplate the most extreme form of intimacy: married love. Barrett began her acquaintance with Robert Browning at just this time. She actively considered both the phenomena of mesmeric intimacy and of lovers' closeness in 1845, and in expressing her developing feelings for Browning she sometimes used the language of mesmerism. Love laced with mesmerism, it would seem, altered Barrett's bodily sensibilities. By the autumn of 1845 she had a completely different attitude to the erasure of the boundaries between two people. Instead of obliterating her, as she had so feared before late 1844, it did the opposite: it "brought" her "back to life." [95]

Barrett had long admired Browning's poetic "passion," and in the volume of poems she published in late 1844 she told him so. In "Lady Geraldine's Courtship," she included two lines of praise to him which he interpreted as an invitation to get in touch: in early 1845 they began a correspondence which almost immediately developed into courtship (on his side at least; she held him at bay a little longer). [96] Despite this growing intimacy, or perhaps because of it, Barrett was desperate to postpone or to avoid entirely meeting Browning face to face. When she gave in to his requests to visit, she warned him that she would find it terrifying and painful. After meeting him she described the meeting in strikingly mesmeric terms. He had "influenced" her as no one else had. The very ease with which he persuaded her to meet him was a sign of his power. And once he arrived, she told him afterward, "you never went away— I mean I had a sense of your presence constantly . . . I said to Papa . . . the next morning . . . 'it is most extraordinary how the idea of Mr Browning does beset me . . . it haunts me . . . it is a persecution . . .' Do you know that all that time I was frightened of you?—frightened in this way. I felt as if you had a power over me & meant to use it, & that I could not breathe or speak very differently from what you chose to make me." [97] Later, reporting a friend's claim that love was identical to animal magnetism, she told him, "I say in my heart, that, magnet or no magnet, I have been drawn back into life by your means & for you." [98]

Over the following year Barrett overcame her fears of intimacy and physical proximity. This process involved a redefining not only of closeness but of mesmerism. Barrett and Browning used mesmeric language in their courtship and debated the practice between themselves. On discussing mesmerism with Browning, Barrett found him skeptical of mesmerism's most fervent advocate, John Elliotson. She acknowledged, "[There is] something ghastly & repelling to me in the thought of Dr Elliotson's great boney fingers seeming to 'touch the stops' of a whole soul's harmonies—as in phreno-magnetism." [99] Barrett now described what horrified her about mesmerism in somewhat different terms from those she had used to Mitford and other friends in earlier correspondence. What was distasteful about the effect of Elliotson's "great boney fingers" was not the merging or communion of two people, possession in the sense of extreme intimacy and "oneness"; rather, it was possession in the sense of the deliberate manipulation of another person's being, mind, or soul. This presents a stark contrast with her reference to the possible link between love and mesmerism and her claim that love, with or without the ingredient of mesmerism, had brought her back to life. The contrast between the two representations suggests that her attitude to phenomena associated with mesmerism was dividing into two distinct categories. There was the control of one person by another person, which she still associated with obliteration. But this was increasingly distinct from the phenomenon of the blending of two people, which she now associated with love and life.

The fact that, in 1845, Barrett and Browning were using mesmerism to make a distinction between the blending of two people and the control of one person by another suggests that it may have been part of the gestation of a poem that Robert Browning was to publish a decade later.[100] "Mesmerism" is a dramatic poem of mental possession, which portrays animal magnetism as a disturbing combination of puppetry and the power of devotion. The narrator describes how he conjures his love in a trance before him, as Daniel Karlin recounts: "first hallucinating her image and then compelling her by occult power to 'inform the shape' he has imagined with her living presence." At the end of the poem, when she opens her arms in an acknowledgment of his power, he does not narrate the process of taking final control of her. It is the potential to possess her, the claimed ability to do so, rather than the actual carrying out of it, that is valued. "The speaker's authority is, in one sense, absolute," as Karlin comments, "but in another sense this very authority is what makes the narrative fantastic and unreliable."[101] Some critics have represented the narrator of the poem as mad—imagining the power he has over a woman, when neither the power nor the woman is real. A more convincing reading is that of Karlin, who suggests that there is a deliberate ambiguity about the status of the narrator's words: is he hallucinating, or is he really stretching out his invisible will to draw his lover to him?[102] This ambiguity is resonant with the similar ambiguities that both Barrett and Browning perceived in mesmerism in 1845, and that it had more generally in Victorian debate.

It is easy to see why Browning would have written the poem, harder to understand the timing. By the time he published it, a decade after the events recounted in this chapter, the mesmeric phenomena surrounding Britons at home and on the Continent were very different from those evoked in his poem. As I shall discuss in chapter 11, 1850s phenomena involved individuals in conscious states of mind. One of them, the practice of "electrobiology," was a form of mental domination, but unlike mesmerism it had no emotional or erotic associations, involved no dreamlike states, and did not receive accusations that it was a form of possession.[103] The phenomena that figured in the poem were visible and salient in 1845, not 1855, which is not surprising because in writing it, Browning drew heavily on his correspondence with Barrett during 1845, on the depictions both of mesmerism specifically and of a mental link maintained at a distance, which were recurrent subjects of their letters of this time.[104] The proper context for Browning's "Mesmerism," then, was the mid-1840s.

One of the most plausible reasons why it was not written until the early 1850s was that "Mesmerism" would have posed a threat to Barrett's changing attitude to intimacy. Browning's letters and visits by turns excited and soothed Barrett's nerves, rather than "assaulting" them as the approach of most other human beings did. Over the course of many months he overcame her fears by combining an inexorable determination to approach her with an acute sensitivity to her nervousness. It would have been counterproductive, to say the least, to have given Barrett a tale of mental possession by a man of the woman he loved. If Browning had written the poem when the resources for doing so were at their freshest and the cultural context gave the greatest resonance to the tale, he would have threatened the new bodily sensibility Barrett needed to develop if they were to be together.

Women Turned Inside Out

One of Barrett's chief concerns while following the controversy over Martineau's cure was a sense of outrage at the way in which her friend's authority and character were being attacked. Martineau's disclosure that her illness had been uterine had been the subject of intensive discussion in the weekly and medical press. Barrett found the coverage "most unpleasant" and had been told by her father that they "quite turned her inside out." [105]

Barrett was ambivalent about this, for, while she would never want such publicity as Martineau had deliberately sought, she regarded Martineau's actions as heroic, and considered the attacks she had incurred as an indication of the unfair treatment of women intellectuals—or more particularly, women who placed their minds and representations of their bodies in the public domain for legitimate intellectual purposes. There were many such attacks, as I have indicated above, but one that most strikingly illustrates the quality of condemnation that perturbed Barrett is evoked by an editorial in the *Lancet* published some eighteen months later. The following passage was part of a sweeping dismissal of women who claimed to have knowledge of their own physiology and felt the need to communicate this knowledge directly to a wide audience.

Affected by a depraved appetite, like that which impels certain descriptions of patients to eat the dirt of the most loathsome corners, and to devour with greediness the most unnatural substances, so these semi-patients & semi-dupes, affected by a moral pica,[106] delight to dwell upon disgusting or indelicate details, which otherwise would never meet the public eye. In this way the celebrated authoress of the preventative check [i.e., Martineau] parades her diseased vagina and *os uteri* as it were in a public speculum before the general gaze, and other ladies write and publish pamphlets about their uterine symptoms and their disorders of sex, in a manner to have made our grandmothers sink into the earth for shame.[107]

The writer was in effect suggesting that the wish to give testimony about one's body was a diagnostic criterion for insanity. This was convenient, of course, given that in the 1840s diseases of the sexual functions and nervous system (presumed to be linked in women) were a major area of development in medicine. The argument of the *Lancet*'s editorial redefined a potential challenge to medical authority to make it a new area of medical research. The editorial therefore made the activity of women who spoke out as Martineau had done into a reinforcement of an authoritative medical role. More generally, it represented doctors as public moral guardians. This passage, with its reference to a previous generation of women with more delicate sensibilities, indicted Victorian womanhood as prone to talk about their pathologies with a shamelessness unknown to previous generations of femininity.

This was only the most extreme manifestation of a far more general backlash against women's staking public claims to authority. The mesmeric controversy made more visible to Barrett a state of affairs in public culture in which women's coming forward with personal revelations in the cause of truth was not tolerated. What was honorable about Martineau was the sacrifice, so many kinds of sacrifice, that her public statement entailed. The case was distasteful to Barrett, but it was not Martineau herself who inspired this feeling. The "locality and character" of Martineau's disorder made all the greater her "moral courage" in coming forth to declare the efficacy of a treatment she believed in. Barrett thought she would not have been able to come forward if she had had the same experiences, but this was not because she had a greater sense of propriety but because she was a "coward." "What I admire in her," Barrett wrote to Mitford, "is her courage in speaking the truth at the expense of the personal exposure, which, if she is a woman at all, must be painful to her— a more miserable exposure, I deeply agree with you, than Godiva's own." [108] Barrett confessed in strict confidence that she would have preferred Martineau's immobilizing illness to the "exposure" Martineau had brought on herself by her public statements regarding her cure.[109] But this reaction itself made her admire Martineau "all the more!! I mean, all the more for being brave beyond my capacity." Martineau's courage was a striking and inspiring exception to what Barrett saw as a prevailing "tendency to exalt the form above the substance, the figment above the essence, I see everywhere, & with indignation & fear. Is reputation to be dearer than virtue? [110] If the Godivas are to sit at home, it must be on that principle. It is painful too to observe how the tendency of women is to glorify themselves in their weakness & deficiencies, both of the body & mind." [111] Martineau's predicament moved Barrett to an emotional declaration of the problems posed by the seeming incongruity of femininity and strength in women of letters. She wrote to Mitford that she would not have confessed her feelings to "a common woman" but Mitford was "a woman & man in one." Her public life, from the recognition brought by her well-known novel, *Our Village,* and her lifelong prominence in literary circles, had made her well acquainted with the problems of being at once a woman and an authoritative figure. While Mitford had managed the difficult balance of power and femininity which allowed her to be "forgiven for her strength by her grace," other women were not so fortunate. Sometimes there was "too much strength in proportion to the grace—and then . . . " Her allusion to Martineau's imbalance in this respect, and the vilification it brought, moved her to exclamation: "O miserable woman!—The abuse which even I, with my narrow notions of society, have heard lavished on that poor, noble Harriet Martineau, is beyond my repeating! And the why!—the why!—And surely we do owe, as women, our righteous indignation to such 'villainie.'" [112]

An ironic postscript to this intensive series of reflections on mesmerism in 1844 and 1845 came a decade later, in the last letter Mitford would read of the thousands that she received from Barrett from the time their correspondence began in the 1830s. In 1845 the two had been divided over the extent to which it was proper to explore and apply mesmerism: Mitford thought mesmerism's medical application as a therapy and anesthetic might be acceptable, but drew the line at the so-called higher phenomena—the experiments in prediction, clairvoyance, and the like. Barrett did not wish to see mesmerism used for any practical purpose until its nature was better understood, but supported all lines of investigation. But in March 1854 Mitford grew terribly ill. Barrett engaged her in an impassioned plea to try mesmerism, which, evidently (for we have only Barrett's half of the correspondence) she resisted. Barrett told her she was "wrong" about mesmerism. The mesmerist Spencer Hall, with whom Mitford had become friendly in the late 1840s, had evidently weakened himself through mesmeric exertions, and Mitford was reluctant to try it herself lest she become weaker. But, Barrett argued, Hall had weakened himself through expending mesmeric influence, "the active putting-forth——& not being mesmerized." She meant that Hall was expending his energy in mesmerizing others and not receiving any in return. This was an entirely different activity from the "passive

244 CHAPTER NINE

recipiency" she wished Mitford to try. Even "unbelievers in the spiritual phenomena," Barrett urged,

admit the good done physically by such means—and, as Mr May seems to have exhausted his resources & to promise nothing very confidently, I can't conceive why
you should not make an experiment *attended with no risk to you* . . . for, observe if you
fail to get benefit from mesmerism, you can at least get no injury . . . I do earnestly
wish you would give the thing a trial . . . for the sake of those who love you, if for
no other reason—I have heard of wonderful cures in cases of a similar character—
and really with every respect for the ancient medical authorities, one cant go so far
as to reverence them for their *failures* CAN one now, with reason? Dearest Miss
Mitford. . ." [113]

It is unclear whether Mitford agreed to a mesmeric trial, but it seems unlikely.
In any case, this was the last letter of Barrett's that she would read; the next arrived shortly after her death.

Nervous Economies

Martineau, Lovelace, and Barrett shared a sense that an economy of power is
involved in intellectual activity. Their precise understanding of this economy
differed, but they were agreed that their intellects were tightly enmeshed in
the production, distribution, and dissemination of vital energy of one kind or
another. By the middle decades of the century, the notion of the conservation
of bodily resources or energy had become central to discussions about mind/
body relations in women, and the idea that only a very strong body—a man's
body—could provide sufficient power to support sustained intellectual functioning was growing influential.[114] It was common to assert that a woman, by
virtue of her smaller body (and the fact that it had to sustain a reproductive
system, too), possessed insufficient strength to cope with intellectually strin-
gent demands. In a healthy woman, these limitations of the female physiology disinclined her to intellectual work. Conversely, intellectual activity could
compromise a woman's capacity to reproduce. In extreme cases, the mutual
strains between body and mind ostensibly produced insanity, sterility, cancer,
or unhealthy offspring.

Barrett's remark that Martineau had been "turned inside out" provides a
useful clue to how Victorian women could justify their ability to do intellectual work. The prevalence of arguments against the healthiness of women's
intellectual activity created a context in which intellectual women often—

perhaps usually—felt the need to explain how their bodies could support intellectual activity. This was a primary reason why the bodies of women intellectuals were so often discussed in their correspondence and even in their public lives.

No wonder, then, that it was hard to be excused one's strength by virtue of one's grace, as Barrett had complained. To establish their strength, many women used physiological imagery or even systematic arguments about the vicissitudes of their own bodies in relation to their minds. Ada Lovelace construed her body "not as a snail shell but a molecular laboratory"; this suggested that it was (metaphorically) a space within which natural philosophers developed scientific knowledge—something that by definition was public and publicly evaluated. Elizabeth Barrett wrote constantly about the state of her nerves in relation to her intellectual activities and, like Lovelace, claimed that her delicacy—her feminine frailties—facilitated rather than constrained her intellectual activity. Martineau's mesmeric discoveries could only be justified by the frankest description of her uterine tumor and its amelioration, giving the most literal meaning to the *Lancet*'s retrospective complaint about the display of one's body in the "public speculum." Intellectual women displayed their insides, to varying extents and with respect to a variety of different interlocutors or readers, as a way of explaining how in their case, and perhaps in any case, feminine knowledge was not a contradictison in terms. Turning oneself inside out, as Martineau, Barrett, and Lovelace each did in different ways, was a powerful, if dangerous, convention for characterizing feminine intellect during the 1840s.

CHAPTER TEN

The Mesmeric Cure of Souls

Call not the gift unholy; 'tis a fair, a precious thing,
That God hath granted to our hands for gentlest minist'ring.
Did Mercy ever stoop to bless with dark, unearthly spell?
Could impious power whisper peace, the soul's deep throes to quell?

A young poet defends mesmerism's piety[1]

There shall be false Christs and false prophets, and shall shew great signs and wonders;
insomuch that if it were possible, they shall deceive the very elect.

A millenarian warns of mesmerism's satanic deceptions[2]

ONE OF MESMERISM's most tantalizing prospects was the cure of disease. In religious contexts "cure" took on an evocative pair of meanings that were particularly appropriate to mesmerism: "custody" and "healing." Mesmerism, too, joined them in a single word. It held out the tantalizing possibility of teasing apart proper and improper, spiritual and satanic, legitimate and false, forms of influence over the sinful, sick, and suffering. One reason was mesmerism's similarity to forms of possession and divine inspiration. Indeed, witnesses usually mentioned it on their first viewing of the trance. But there was a broader range of associations between mesmeric states and religious ones. Belief in mesmerism, people often said, was a "faith," a "dogma," a "creed." The testimonies people gave to their mesmeric experiences often read like narratives of conversion. Life-changing crises provoked one's first hesitant explorations—a brush with death, perhaps, or a family illness. Then followed agonies of confusion, consultations with authorities in the new faith, and a searching of one's inner self. Finally, one would be overwhelmed with thanks and wonder when hopes turned to certainties. Whether the conversion involved mesmerism or religious affiliation, the change brought a dramatically different perception and understanding of the world. Onlookers watching these transformations then confronted an issue that provoked ferocious and protracted disagreement: whether the old or the new state was the more enlightened, the more virtuous, or the more spiritual.

And what about the sage or healer who helped one attain this new state? To people who were hostile to the faith at issue, preachers and mesmerists were false prophets or charlatans. To those who revered them, the "consecrated character" of the preacher was not so different from that of the mesmerist.[3] Both had a special quality, related to their psychic or spiritual role. They were part of the social order, yet also, by virtue of their power or spirituality, set apart from it. From this liminal position—neither wholly in nor out of the world—they lifted or lowered others into a new state. And the connections went beyond metaphor. Mesmerism could complement the preacher's role as a spiritual guide, adding a physiological component to Christian empathy. Figure 56, a sketch of the process of mesmerizing published by a visiting mesmeric American preacher, could have been mistaken for a portrayal of one man counseling and empathizing with another. The mesmerist could share his patient's feelings in the most literal sense, in an intense moment of spiritual or psychological blending.

What made these parallels so suggestive in the early- and mid-Victorian period was a prevailing anxiety about spiritual influence. Evangelicalism peaked within Anglicanism during the 1830s and 1840s, and the Catholic Church grew more prominent. Amid calls for a "broad church" sensibility embracing everyone, there were defections to Nonconformity and "Popery." Radicals intensified their secularist agitation. Some preachers, such as Thomas Chalmers and Edward Irving, were credited with the power to alter the mental states of their congregations, but by and large the figures most credited (or rather discredited) with this power were Roman Catholic priests. To Anglicans, the whole Roman Catholic faith was based on images and superstitions that depersonalized laypersons and subjected them wholly to the will of the priest. The power to reaffirm or to change someone's religious states of mind was therefore a major preoccupation for Victorian preachers worried about the dispersal of their flock, seeking to add to it or wishing to infuse complacent members with renewed piety.

Mesmerism offered a technique that was relevant to these concerns, in its incarnation as what one might call a "pastoral science." The use of mesmerism as a healing practice could help individual preachers, or individual sects, extend

{THE PROCESS OF MAGNETIZING.}

FIGURE 56 The process of magnetizing. Frontispiece to John Bovee Dods, *Six Lectures*.

their authority. Preachers began to investigate the subject from the mid-1840s onward, just as the debates over medical mesmerism had spread news of the practice through most parishes, and as the ferocity of medical debate over mesmerism began to wane. Clerical mesmerists dreamed of making it an "engine in education,"[4] a tool for missionaries working abroad,[5] and a means of discrediting both nonconformity and popery.[6] Spiritually potent and infinitely malleable, mesmerism could appear to be an ideal complement to the preacher's social, spiritual, and intellectual tools.

Even if one did not become a practicing mesmerist, it was still useful—and often unavoidable—to investigate its claims so as to be able to take a stand as to its nature. Central to what has been called the Victorian "crisis of faith" was the status of various kinds of evidence—of Scripture and of God's action in the mortal world. The rising public status of Catholicism and Nonconformity after the religious disabilities legislation of the late 1820s spurred an increase in historical and psychological literature on the supernatural and natural in mind. There were attacks on claims of supernatural events, either in the form of Evangelical "enthusiasm" or popish excesses; less prominently, there were also defenses of the reality of cures and supernatural powers. These warring pamphlets were not just affirmations and discreditations of the reality or fraudulence of particular states. Rather, they contributed to a growing field of debate in which altered states of mind could be made meaningful spiritually and through scientific study in a greater range of ways (particularly secular ones) than hitherto.

These issues were very tangible when one contemplated mesmerism, or dared to examine it directly, since mesmeric states were so similar to religious ones. The relationship between the two was tantalizingly ambiguous. Add to this the fact that issues of evidence were unusually pronounced during mesmeric experiments, and that these phenomena could be produced on command (with luck and skill) in one's own home, and it is not hard to see mesmerism's appeal. People who were actively trying to distinguish the natural from the supernatural, the pious from the impious, found mesmerism hard to ignore.

As people debated the "natural" or "supernatural" character of mesmeric phenomena, the experiments and controversies themselves altered the meaning of these two terms. Most mesmeric preachers claimed to be pursuing a "scientific" study of a "natural" phenomenon. There was no consensus on how these terms should be defined, and indeed the way they were used calls our attention to the way the categories of "natural" and "supernatural" have hardened over time; many mesmerists, for instance, claimed that their "natural" mesmeric phenomena were also essentially "spiritual." A smaller number of others saw their enterprise as "supernatural." These terms did not refer to areas of agreement among those who subscribed to them; rather, they were nodes of debate in themselves.

The spiritual status of mesmerism and "altered states" became a node of public debate from the 1830s onward, intensifying in the mid-1840s and early 1850s. Harriet Martineau and other prominent mesmeric figures were accused of possession and satanism; Unitarians, deists, and atheists translated a "natural history" of supernatural events into mesmeric terms, making miracles and divine inspiration into a natural (if unusual) state of the brain; and premillenarian Evangelicals debated whether mesmeric phenomena warned of the coming of the Apocalypse. Mesmerism was used by a number of divines—including Thomas Arnold, master of Rugby; Henry Wilberforce, son of William, and a prominent high churchman; and the political economist Richard Whately, archbishop of Dublin—in comparisons and contrasts with miracles. Finally, while all these issues bore some relation to the cultural status of the church in Victorian society, some people made mesmerism central to this issue by spelling out the implications of altered states of mind for clerical authority. In the late 1840s and early 1850s the historian and onetime secretary to the archbishop of Canterbury, Samuel Maitland, used mesmerism as a case in point in the use of church history to fortify the authority of the church both in general society and in competition with science for authority over new spiritual and natural truths.

A Pastoral Science

Mesmeric trances were new theological and scientific territory for Victorian preachers, and an opportunity to guide the many individuals who were working in the open spiritual sea of mesmeric experimentation: the itinerants who had often introduced them to it; medical antagonists who deprecated it and medical secularists who practiced it impiously; the professional clairvoyants who did not employ it in the proper sober spirit.[7] Once guided by religious hands, mesmeric phenomena could extend one's pastoral constituency both intellectually and professionally. A number of Anglican preachers took up the practice, including Samuel Wilberforce, soon to be bishop of Oxford; William Scoresby, vicar of Bradford; George Sandby, vicar of Flixton, Suffolk; Thomas Pyne, incumbent of Hooke, Surrey; and Robert Holdsworth, vicar of Brixham. One of the most celebrated itinerants, William Davey, was a Wesleyan preacher.[8] What mesmerism meant to them varied, but in broad terms, it was used to harness "nature" as the property and authoritative force of evangelical Anglicanism.

Preachers were drawn to investigate mesmerism by members of their flock, when parishioners or family members demanded a verdict on its spiritual status. They needed to come to a decision in order to advise whether it was safe to witness or take part in experiments.[9] This was how Samuel Wilberforce became acquainted with the science in late 1844. Six months later he would be appointed bishop of Oxford; fifteen years on and he would become renowned—or notorious—for his defenses of religion against the onslaught of Darwin's natural selection.[10] In the 1840s, however, he did not see a sharp demarcation of religious from scientific authority, not even in relation to mesmerism, with its obvious potential for materialist interpretations. Indeed, like most mesmeric clerics, his concern was whether it was real and whether it was natural or supernatural. His attention was drawn to mesmerism in late 1844, when members of his family wished to use it as a medical therapy. He threw himself into an investigation of the subject with characteristic energy. On New Year's Eve of 1844 he barely managed to dash off a note to his sister after being closeted all day with the well-known itinerant lecturer H. Brookes.[11] A few days later, he told her, he would continue his investigations with another mesmerist.[12] By early 1845 he was "very deep in mesmerism," but he could find "no solid foot-hold."[13]

Nevertheless, he saw nothing inherently impious about it, and his developing knowledge turned out to be useful in the care of his parish. In January 1845 one of his parishioners "opened his mind" to him. He had been "all his life a deep, & dissatisfied searcher after knowledge: going through pursuit after pursuit & then casting unfiled each book[?] away." In 1842, during the initial sweep of magnetic lecturers through the country, his attention had been called to the science. He "[m]agnetised his daughter; found her the most first rate of clairvoyants," and concluded from her entranced pronouncements that alchemy, one of his pursuits, was really "magnetism"—animal, that is. The "Philosopher's Stone was the power of creating, by being placed en rapport with creative power . . . *he* knew how to attain it, & could make gold, &c &c." He was a "very clever man," Wilberforce confided to his sister, but "nearly mad." Wilberforce had caught his charge just in time, for the poor man was "on the verge of developing for himself the Gnostic heresies." But Wilberforce, with his own knowledge of mesmerism and with "great sympathy," judiciously applied, was able to point him away from his heretical tendencies. Here one saw, Wilberforce concluded, "a great gentleman of pastoral treatment." As he counseled him, he burrowed through the man's trove of mesmeric literature in search of "what mesm'm is." If he ever found out, he never said so, but this did not stop him from becoming an effective mesmerist over the next six months with the help of various practitioners. Appropriately enough, during this time he gave a lecture on the importance of religion to science to the meeting of the BAAS meeting in Cambridge, which he recounted to his sister almost as an afterthought at the end of a letter describing his latest mesmeric forays.[14]

Many clergy became involved in mesmerism as Wilberforce had, in an effort to vet its pious status for someone in their moral charge. Once having done so, they often used their new skill to extend their authority more widely. Henry Wilberforce, Samuel's brother, also converted to the magnetic cause and saw it as a crucial stepping-stone for the clergy. They needed to exert their authority to medical matters in order to stem the "injurious" influence that medicine was exerting "to the faith." In 1847 he exhorted readers of the High Church *Christian Remembrancer* that no "great instrument" (of whatever sort) should be left in "evil hands," that is, those of "unbelievers."

Has no harm been done, when science has been left in the possession of those who longed to employ it against God and His Church? Has any good come of the abandonment of history during the last century to the infidel party? . . . Animal magnetism, indeed, has no necessary or even natural connexion with unbelief . . . But it is equally true that some of its ablest advocates in this country are evidently unbelievers, and desirous of using it as an instrument against Christianity. Under these circumstances, is it wisest to leave it in their hands, or to employ it ourselves?[15]

Henry Wilberforce was speaking of radicals and secularists like Elliotson and his materialist ally W. C. Engledue. Engledue recognized himself as a target and responded in kind. Henry Wilberforce and his clerical friends were making a "sly" move, he charged, putting out a "feeler" for clerical authority in matters that lay beyond "the limits their profession prescribes for them." Henry Wilberforce's well-known Catholic sympathies had led him "to substitute a seductive mannerism for increasing intelligence." [16] Neither side was to triumph in this matter, for the London Mesmeric Infirmary was maintained throughout the 1840s and 1850s by an alliance of aristocrats, clerics, doctors, wealthy Jewish philanthropists, and tradesmen.

If Wilberforce's ambitions were not to be realized, it was certainly possible to extend one's authority as a healer of the body in settings where one's status as a healer of the spirit was already established. Mesmerism offered an appropriately spiritual means of healing not only the soul, but the flesh and the mind as well. Clerical mesmerists like Pyne, Sandby, Dods, and Whately lulled patients to sleep with mesmeric anesthesia; they claimed to have cured nervous diseases, insanity, and internal disorders. Unlike the platform mesmerists their power lay not in producing a striking display in the bodies of strangers or before their eyes, but by extending, and even *performing*, the bonds of sympathy and guidance that already existed in their local communities.

If these activities sound more modest than those of the platform mesmerists, they were not necessarily conceived on a small scale. Thomas Pyne, a humble incumbent of Hooke, a village near Kingston-on-Thames, had grand aspirations. In 1844 or early 1845 he established a "Hospital" for "Vital magnetic and general medical and surgical treatment." [17] Small as it probably was, the infirmary attracted large numbers of patients and several eminent visitors. One of them reported that Pyne's cases numbered as many as "one to two hundred three times a week." [18] His cottage was "surrounded by patients of every age . . . [the] infirm and crippled patients waiting on the porch, on benches, under sheds." When Lord Morpeth and Samuel and Robert Wilberforce came to visit in June 1845, Pyne was so exhausted by the end of the afternoon's mesmeric sessions that he had not the strength to treat his last patients. The three visitors volunteered to do so themselves. Samuel, proficient after months of practice, placed two patients under the influence on his first trial; Morpeth succeeded as well, though more slowly. Robert Wilberforce, stung at being the odd man out, ascribed his own failure to a "want of luncheon." [19]

As patients accepted their treatment, they also heard a theological explanation or biblical pedigree for the practice. Pyne told his patients that the eye contact that produced the trance caused an "emanation" of vital influence to pass from him to them.[20] They were taught that their experiences had, though not a miraculous, nevertheless a biblical pedigree. Pyne looked to the book of Kings for evidence of mesmerism in the Old Testament, and offered patients and students the following labored translation (in parentheses) of an incident of spiritual healing in 2 Kings 5:11: "Thus, Naaman said, when seeking for the prophet's aid, 'I thought he would surely come out to me, and stand and call on the name of the Lord his God, and strike his hand over the place, (move his hand up and down—Hebrew), and recover the leper.'"[21] He assured patients and readers that this was not a miracle; the gospel of Paul carefully distinguished miracles from healing in his enumeration of spiritual gifts as being gifts of God, but not individual instances of divine intervention. Pyne "distinguished between the miracles of Scripture and Magnetism" by stipulating that "[i]n the Lord's miracles . . . an effect was produced . . . the blind or the withered arm restored received." What was special in miraculous healing was not only the production of "new power" but "a fresh mental development for its adequate and instantaneous use."[22]

Mesmerism often seemed to produce an "essence" of some human quality or relation. For Elliotson it had been the subtle materials of interaction; for Dugald Stewart it had been the immaterial relations of "sympathetic imitation" or "mental impressibility" by which human beings learn from one another. For those clerical mesmerists who regarded mesmerism (whether supernatural or natural) as in some way spiritual, it involved an intensification of spirituality. Pyne's patients were taught that mesmerism could never undermine morality because the process of mesmerism was itself a spiritual event. It placed the soul, according to Pyne, in a state of "highest mentality": mesmerism suspended the physical instincts and allowed one's pure, untrammeled conscience to "fully work."[23] Pyne drew on the work of Bishop Warburton (author of *Divine Legation of Moses*) in defining the conscience as "moral instinct" and therefore, in moral terms, an agency that was the more potent when its automatic action was not impeded by the conscious intentional mind, with the sinful distractions and delusions to which it was subject. Pyne also supplied a chemistry of these various spiritual states: "just as in the curious laws of crystallization, after the severest chemical changes the body returns not only to defined particles, but to these in normal forms . . . so the arrangements of the subtile aether may be found superior to dissolution, and remain the vesture of the soul in that happy eternity, in which 'Mind shall with mind direct communion hold, / And kindred spirits meet to part no more.'"[24] This chemical argument, and others like it, supply a reason why the British public were able to find a physics of the soul plausible later in the decade when they encountered spiritualism and psychic research. They already had a generation's experience of such phenomena and similar arguments. Séances, as "sittings" where one could do experiments with spiritual states, and explanations of the phenomena that combined spiritual and physical influences, had been familiar for more than a decade by the time the first spiritualist mediums set up shop in the mid-1850s. What made such arguments plausible in their immediate environments was the local authority and familiarity that individuals like

Pyne enjoyed with his audience and patients. In such settings as Pyne's "hospital" in Surrey, clerical mesmerists could build local environments that validated their custodial authority and accentuated the pastoral influence they exercised over the mental state of those under their care not only through the actual act of mesmerism but through the theological explanations of what patients were experiencing.

Magnetic Evangelicalism: William Scoresby

If mesmerism expressed relations of influence and care in a vague and general sense, it could also take on a more specific role in the elaborate economies of matter and spirit in which mesmerism played a crucial role, and in the process of developing particular definitions of science and scientific authority. A striking example is the Reverend William Scoresby (fig. 57). By the 1840s and 1850s, when he became involved in mesmerism, Scoresby was nationally respected as a heroic, pious model for Britain and Britain's youth, renowned during these years as a moral, spiritual, and scientific authority.[25] His life story was dramatic, and he publicized it fully in his sermons and lectures. Scoresby had been a celebrated whaler in the 1810s, until he experienced a dramatic, providential spiritual regeneration in the Arctic seas. He embarked on a career as an evangelical Anglican clergyman and a program of research in natural philosophy. He took a special interest in magnetism, one of the "ordained . . . servants" of God by which the system of the universe was "controlled" and "bound together."[26]

In fashioning his public image as an Evangelical preacher, Scoresby drew strongly on his reputation as a heroic ship's captain and natural philosopher. For Scoresby the "shipwreck of the soul" and similar biblical allusions, such as the three shipwrecks of St. Paul, were in his case literal experiences. His first chaplaincy was aboard the Liverpool Mariner's Church, a decommissioned man-of-war floating in Liverpool harbor. From the three-tiered pulpit in its hull (fig. 58) he belted out inspiring sermons that made analogies between the compass's magnetic guidance "through the tractless deep" and the guidance given by the "Spirit of CHRIST" through the "manifold perils of this mortal life."[27]

For Scoresby the study of nature was a heroic expression of one's religious calling. Conversely, the spiritual influence was comparable to the magnetic power that guided the compass needle.[28] Scoresby also characterized as intensely spiritual the practices that made up his scientific research, such as the pounding of metal to make magnets. Both activities—preaching and pummeling—channeled God's influence through the natural world. This was

FIGURE 57
William Scoresby, c. 1850.
From Scoresby-Jackson,
Life of William Scoresby.

no simply analogical relation, but a strong and real identity. The two aspects of spiritual action were perhaps most clearly united in the practice of animal magnetism, or mesmerism, to which he dedicated much of his time beginning in the mid-1840s.

The forces manifest in mesmerism, he claimed, functioned within the economy of nature as a "mysterious and subtle agency," by "means of which, as the servant of the Great Creator, He appears to regulate and subordinate the creation to His will." This agency was perceptible in other phenomena, such as (most notably) electricity and magnetism, but in mesmerism its essential characteristic—the guiding power of the Creator over his creation—was most visible. To Scoresby mesmerism revealed the underlying character of divine influence: of the magnet over iron filings, of the earth's poles over the needle of the compass, of the preacher over his flock, of the social reformer over the community. The phenomena of "retentive magnetism," which he

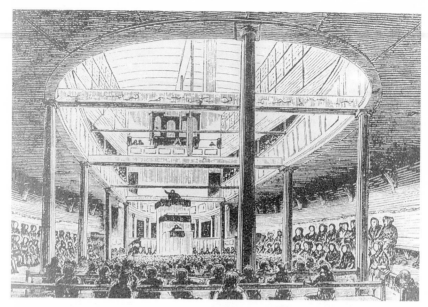

FIGURE 58 The Mariner's Church, c. 1830. The preacher is gesturing from the three-tiered pulpit at the center. Note that the upper level of the ship is also filled with pews, and toward the bow of the ship (the back of the space presented here) a great organ is perched on a high platform, near one of the ship's masts. Courtesy *Sea Breezes Magazine*.

regarded as central to navigational problems, had their exact equivalent in the human phenomena of mesmerism, in the form of the "mastery" of one magnetic orientation by another. That is, in the case of competing influences over a piece of "formless" matter, the one whose magnetic powers were stronger not only would succeed in ordering matter in "conformity" with itself, but would force the rival magnet to bow to its will.[29] Hence mesmerism played a crucial part in the identity of Scoresby's investigations as religious acts, as a means of "experimentally" realizing God's will working within oneself.

In pursuing his "zoistic" investigations Scoresby worked systematically to reproduce via mesmerism many of the magnetic phenomena that the platform mesmerists produced. He described, for example, "a sort of *polarity* in Zoistic Magnetism, with sensibilities of an electrical nature, apparently, of exquisite delicacy."[30] He also observed that his subjects could be "insulated" by non-conducting material from frissons of electricity, thereby drawing evidence of an alliance between the electric sensations of magnetized subjects and the posited magnetic nature of the phenomena themselves. Further experiments established the existence of magnetic poles, of attraction and repulsion, and of the communication of magnetic fluid from one person to another. Scoresby concluded that God designated a mysterious ethereal fluid or fluids (among many such agencies, no doubt) that enforce his will on earth. These fluids are conducted among his subjects to varying degrees. They are better conducted by "stronger, more tempered" guiding figures and to a lesser extent by "weaker, untempered" ones. Those who are properly quickened with God's spirit are better conductors of his will.

Scoresby claimed that the magnetic fluid works literally to bring the weaker soul "into conformity" with the stronger one, in the same manner, for example, as Scoresby himself had formed his experimental apparatus.[31] Hence Scoresby drew from animal magnetism, a practice known since its inception for harnessing magnetic theory to programs of social control, the perfect vehicle for the amalgamation of his various interests. Zoistic magnetism became a single complex theology with the potential to solve both his administrative problems as spiritual leader and the task he had set himself, as ecclesiastical reformer, to revitalize or "quicken" institutions in which he was involved, such as the shipping industry, the church, and the BAAS. In Scoresby's hands, then, zoistic magnetism contributed to a vision of an evangelical social order in which ethereal fluids were material servants of God. Individuals struggling to raise their pious standing also improved their magnetic disposition, thereby becoming fit politically to govern others. Those more susceptible to magnetic influence were both naturally guided by their moral and social superiors and more vulnerable to sinful thoughts.

Scoresby's success is evidenced by the testimony of his mesmeric subjects, though the only available narrative was clearly solicited (and presumably influenced) by Scoresby himself. By 1845 Scoresby was lecturing on and practicing mesmerism as he carried out his other scientific work (see fig. 59), for instance as part of a series of lectures on work presented at the BAAS meeting of that year. One of Scoresby's patients described first hearing about mesmerism at a lecture he gave during this meeting of the BAAS. She did not expect to be able to meet him, so she asked a friend, Mrs. Cary, to try to produce the effects. She "succeeded in putting me to sleep but I felt she could do no more." Through the efforts of another friend she secured a meeting with Scoresby. Although she was nervous at first, she claimed that

the moment I was settled on the sofa, with my hands in his—all apprehension vanished, a calmness, a delightful resignation to his will came over me. My eyes were irresistibly drawn to his and in vain did I combat the superior power of my Mesmerist. A pleasant thrill ran from my fingers throughout my body towards my feet—my heart pounded with joy . . .

The faces and figures of those around me dissolved, one melting into another until the last vision of them seemed to vanish in Dr. Scoresby's eyes. He was no longer Dr. Scoresby to me, but my all, part of myself; what he wished, I wished. In fact the

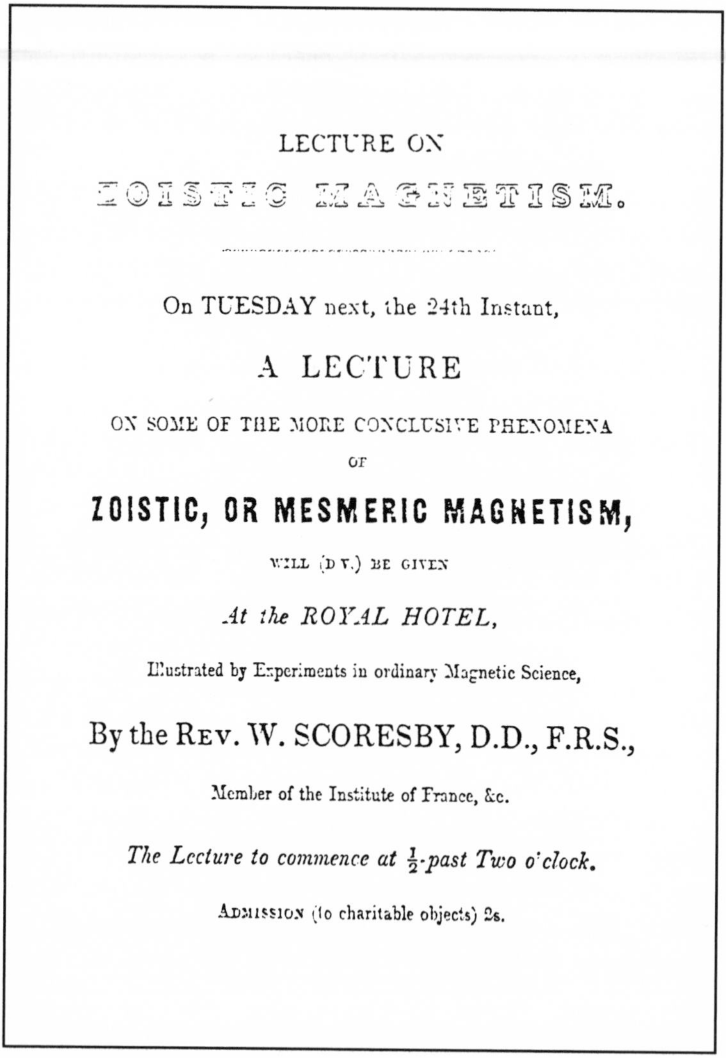

LECTURE ON

ZOISTIC MAGNETISM.

On TUESDAY next, the 24th Instant,

A LECTURE

ON SOME OF THE MORE CONCLUSIVE PHENOMENA

OF

ZOISTIC, OR MESMERIC MAGNETISM,

WILL (D V.) BE GIVEN

At the ROYAL HOTEL,

Illustrated by Experiments in ordinary Magnetic Science,

By the REV. W. SCORESBY, D.D., F.R.S.,

Member of the Institute of France, &c.

The Lecture to commence at ½-past Two o'clock.

ADMISSION (to charitable objects) 2s.

FIGURE 59 Handbill advertising Scoresby's lectures on zoistic magnetism, c. 1849. Author's collection.

attraction astonished me. The cares, the interest in this life ceased. I felt no longer a common mortal but infinitely superior and yet felt my Mesmeriser far superior to myself.[32]

In her "resignation to his will" and her sense of being made "superior" by a yet more "superior" being, she described her experience much in the way Scoresby would have wished her to. The narrative also implied the existence of a hierarchy of spiritual power: Mrs. Cary could produce only a slight effect, while Scoresby could lift up his subject to a spiritual state "infinitely superior" to her ordinary one. While the significance of this testimony is limited by the fact that it is the only first-person account I have been able to find, it nevertheless suggests that he was able to extend his mesmeric project to the very way in which his subjects characterized their own experiences.

As Scoresby developed the social and spiritual dimension of his magnetic system, he simultaneously worked toward putting into effect the moral regeneration of public institutions—for example, the BAAS. Throughout the 1830s and 1840s he had given papers and sermons to meetings of the association, but the sermon he gave at the 1850 meeting incorporated elements of his mesmeric work. It was a discourse on scientific piety. One's proper goal consisted of trying to "magnify" the Creator, tracing his will as it is manifest on earth, back to its holy source.[33] This was similar to the agency of mesmerism as Scoresby understood it, since mesmerism intensified, made larger and more visible the means by which God ordered and "subordinated" his Creation. Science should have an explicit, pious purpose, and the figure of the mesmerist—as Scoresby embodied it—was a role-model of heroic scientific inquiry.

If some of his patients, at least, shared his view of the moral and spiritual order displayed by magnetic effects, to what extent was he able to extend his perspective to a wider audience? It is certainly clear that Scoresby was somewhat successful in bringing his project to the attention of the scientific elite— Lord Rosse, for instance, president of the Royal Society of London, talked "frequently" with Scoresby on the subject and had his own copy of Scoresby's book.[34] But outside such private networks of correspondence, how would Scoresby's system have fared in a national debate? Scoresby himself never engaged in a public controversy over the phenomena of mesmerism, but many of the crucial elements of his system—especially the spirituality and leadership of the heroic natural philosopher and the primacy of individual experience in scientific research—came to the fore when he engaged in a debate with the astronomer royal, George Airy, over the question of the deviation of the compass in iron ships. In this debate, which was carried on in the national press for over a decade, Scoresby was successful in putting forward his own characterizations of scientific expertise and authority despite the strongest opposition from Airy, and despite all the authority of the metropolitan scientific elite that Airy represented.[35]

Scoresby is an unusual figure inasmuch as he articulated such an elaborate role for mesmerism and such a self-consciously worked-out cosmology. Most people did not construct entire "cosmologies" within which to live. But he was representative inasmuch as he used mesmerism to unify spiritual and physical, the spirit and the flesh, in a guiding and healing role as preacher.

Supernatural Truths and Deceits

The poem excerpted at the beginning of this chapter devoted pages of painful couplets to the plea that Victorians should "[c]all not the gift unholy; 'tis a fair—a precious thing." Whether or not anyone took it to heart, the issue was certainly fraught in the 1840s and 1850s, only to intensify when spiritualism joined the fray. At a time when there was fear that the Church might fail to maintain its strength in industrial cities, Anglicans were concerned about loss of faith. Despite the most reasonable or sentimental rhetoric, mesmerism was dogged by fears that it was impious—if not a form of possession, some lesser corruption of the soul. Claims that mesmerism and its associated phenomena were supernatural (whether a form of divine ecstasy or satanic influence) provoked a number of skirmishes in the press and anxious private ruminations from the 1840s onward.

It was unusual for those who regarded mesmerism as supernatural to approve of it. The exceptions were a small number of "optimistic" premillenarians, those who believed that the end of the world and the return of Jesus Christ was imminent, and anticipated the prospect with intense pleasure rather than fear and dread, and among these, mesmerism was a tool of supernatural experimentation and prognostication. For example, during a mesmeric séance in Trinity College Dublin, one H. Hill Hardy heard a mesmerized clairvoyant relate "that great changes are now being effected in the spirit-world" and that "previously existing relations between men and angels appear to be changing."[36] But by and large, the work of individuals like Pyne, Scoresby, and other Evangelical preachers was the last straw for some of their "brethren" who had watched the development of platform mesmerism with horror, only to see fellow pastors join the fray. The more common response among Evangelical premillenarians was, then, to condemn mesmeric phenomena as diabolical. The Evangelicals Charlotte Elizabeth Tonna, Lord Ashley (later the earl of Shaftesbury), and others—termed "diabolists" by the *Zoist*[37]—made widely distributed statements that mesmerism was satanic.[38]

One of the earliest and most influential of these attacks was a sermon preached by Hugh M'Neile in Liverpool in 1842, which claimed not only that mesmerism was the work of the Devil but that it was a particularly striking instance of a more general phenomenon. He preached that mesmerism, if natural, must be the product of constant natural law, and therefore uniform in action. If not, it was not a natural phenomenon. If it were a natural power, like steam or electricity, then there should be clear, carefully worked-out laws that were said to govern them. Such laws existed for steam, whose power varied with its compression. Similarly, the shock of electricity was "proportioned to" the charge given to the battery.[39] But if it were not sufficient grounds for suspicion that the professors of mesmerism could offer no such laws, other claims were being made about mesmerism's *divine* character, which, on their own, were cause for alarm. M'Neile described one such claim by the prominent Catholic Lord Shrewsbury. His account of Ecstatica, a woman who was fixed in adoration of the Virgin and who showed similar insensibility to pain and other stimuli as magnetic subjects did, was offered as proof of the divine source of Catholicism.[40] Ecstatica, M'Neile claimed instead, was clearly mesmerized.

When a phenomenon was, on the one hand, "pleaded by a popish writer as proof of divine influence [and] divine origin of his creed" and, on the other, claimed as a science when no natural law could explain it, was this not "an exploit worthy of Satan?" Satan fooled men into thinking they were "philosophers" when he had, in reality, turned them into "necromancers"; he "put forth the power which it is permitted him to exercise in men's bodies" not simply to produce madness but to attract the attention of "learned men" and to lure "professional gentlemen" to witness and then to proliferate the phenomena.[41]

Mesmeric phenomena provided the occasion to make the case for Satan's continuing presence in the bodies of the vulnerable and, consequently, the importance of clerical authority in distinguishing somatic disorders from supernatural influences. M'Neile compared biblical cases of possession with the sights one could see in a nineteenth-century lunatic asylum to argue that medicine's constraints did not allow doctors to identify possession when they saw it. Doctors would say "that there was some disorganization of the poor creature's brain"; this was because their philosophy was limited to "organized or disorganized matter." [42] But if he "who can see into the spiritual world entered one of our lunatic asylums, he would see what our doctors cannot see . . . that the devil is there." Just as doctors could not diagnose possession in these maniacs, so were they unfit to decide if there was anything supernatural going on in mesmerism. Neither the "searching knife" nor the medicines that course "through all the pores and alleys of the body" could locate Satan: "he works unseen." [43]

M'Neile's protest was one of the best-known, but by no means the only, exhortations of this kind. George Corfe, a clergyman and surgeon at the Middlesex Hospital, finally snapped after thirteen years in which at least two of his colleagues at the hospital, John Ashburner and John Wilson, maintained continuous mesmeric practice on "incurable" patients there. In 1848 Corfe could be silent no longer. Mesmeric phenomena, he claimed in a fat pamphlet, were neither natural states nor divine inspiration. They were forms of possession, similar in kind to the outpourings of those misguided premillenarian ecstatics who spoke in tongues (as Elizabeth O'Key had been claimed to have done) in Edward Irving's Caledonian Chapel. Corfe concluded passionately that "the terrific events which have passed before my eyes compel me to say, beware how you plunge farther into this awful delusion of the devil's chicanery."[44] Similarly, in late 1844, in the aftermath of Harriet Martineau's cure, the well-known Evangelical writer Charlotte Elizabeth Tonna wrote an "open letter" to her warning that she was flirting with Satan. Martineau did not respond publicly to the attack, though she commented derisively about it to her friends. Nor did others engage Tonna publicly. But her charge, and others like it, intensified anxious ruminations.

Elizabeth Barrett, whatever her personal sympathies for Martineau and her fascination with mesmerism, was horrified at its possible religious implications. Within weeks of Martineau's announcement, Barrett would write to Mary Russell Mitford to announce that "my worst fears are justified in another direction" because a new "religious sect" had been formed at Cheltenham. Its members, she related, "receive their theological system wholly from mesmerized subjects, and call the agency 'the third revelation.'"[45] While this might be dismissed as a mere "abuse," such a dismissal made too little of the difficulty of drawing "a line between the physical & spiritual." For once having accepted someone as a witness to something as extraordinary as seeing "through the wall of a house," it was only a short step to accepting their testimony of seeing through the "veil of the flesh."[46] That is, "[o]ne percipiency is not more contrary to our ordinary experience . . . than the other. Mesmerized persons profess to see *both* the spiritual & the natural. Now for me & for you to receive what we like & leave out what we dislike, may prove more than we can do logically, however we may attempt it." For Barrett the solution was to proceed cautiously, and not to employ mesmerism as a remedy before its nature as a power was understood; for Tonna the only safe course was to leave the subject alone entirely.

A similar set of issues were to surface during the 1850s, when the phenomenon of table-turning became a focus for controversy over the existence of supernatural agency in the mortal world. The phenomenon was produced when a table, placed under the hands of several "operators," began to move without being pushed—the most common explanation for the motion being the action of an imponderable agent of some kind (such as electric or magnetic force produced or channeled through the human body). This practice was very fashionable in the major European cities beginning in late 1851, and popular journals in France and Britain published sketches of table-turning soirées

FIGURE 60 One of dozens that survive, this sketch of a table-turning trial presents the experiment in a middle-class domestic setting, with parents and children taking part together. Mary Evans Picture Library.

(fig. 60). The *Times*'s first announcement of the table-turning obsession came from its Vienna correspondent, and clearly revealed his view that the phenomenon was caused by an electric or magnetic force: "Round the table three ladies and five gentlemen placed themselves, and formed a magnetic chain, which is effected by each person laying his hands lightly on the margin of the table and placing the little finger of his right into his neighbor's left . . . All rings and bracelets in the case now described were removed."[47] The experiment was successful. After more than an hour, the table began a movement "so violent" that members of the audience stepped forward "to relieve the original actors," who had grown tired chasing after it.

Table-turning spread rapidly among the well-educated, leisured classes. Whatever one thought was making the tables spin—a natural or supernatural, electric or spiritual force—one trusted one's own senses as to whether one's dining-room table were moving by the agency of an imponderable of some kind or by the mechanical influence of one's hands. During the 1850s there was a sense of confidence among the middle and upper classes about their ability to pass judgment on such matters, and this confidence fueled a storm of controversy over table-turning.

When people began to find that the tables not only turned, but appeared to supply a link to a conscious agency of some sort (i.e., one could ask it questions), premillenarian clergy sat down in their dining rooms to take matters into their own hands. The Reverend N. S. Godfrey, incumbent of the village of Wortley, near Leeds, sat down with his wife and curate one evening in June 1852, placed their hands on a small mahogany table and found that after forty-five minutes it began to move.[48] Godfrey rounded up the two family servants and the local schoolmaster as witnesses and carried out a series of experiments. He found that he could will the table to move in various ways—and its movements were sinister. At one point he "caused the table to revolve rapidly and gave the signal—the bible was quietly laid upon the table, and it stopped! We were horror struck!" He could also converse with it—and its conversation sent chills through the assembled group. He commanded the furniture that "'If there be not a devil, knock twice': *to our horror, the leg slowly rose and knocked twice!* I then said, 'In the name of the Lord Jesus Christ, if there be *no* devil, knock twice:' it was motionless."[49] Presumably, the invocation of Christ's name prevented the spirit from lying on the second occasion, and the effort needed to make the table tell the truth made the experiment even more frightening than it might otherwise have been. Needless to say, this evidence of a conscious entity meant that the phenomena could not be the mere mechanical result of bodily electricity impinging on an inanimate object. The nature of this agency was also clear: the table's denial of the existence of Satan was itself evidence of his presence. Other experimenters reinforced these findings with similar results. In Bath the Reverend Gillson asked his table if it were a soul in torment, and was answered *"by a sort of writhing motion which no natural power could imitate!!!"* In Islington the Reverend William Vincent's table tapped out messages from the damned, which terrified its owners. *Punch's* sendup of two Greenwich clergymen (fig. 61) might give the impression that they were easily dismissed as credulous idiots, but several were men of authority and good reputation.[50]

These men were not carrying out physiological experiments in the production of electric influence and mechanical motion. They were trying "the spirits, whether they are of God" (1 John 4:1). They had revealed "the spirits of Devils, working miracles" (Revelations 16:14). The sudden appearance of so much satanic influence in the world, particularly in phenomena involving "the will,"[51] suggested that these were days immediately preceding the Apocalypse, the final effort to "overthrow Christ's Kingdom" when "'The King,' the heading up of the iniquity of man and devil, 'shall do *according to his will*' [Daniel 9:36]."[52] Britain needed to know that "the spirits of Devils working miracles '*are already going forth—Hence the great day of God Almighty*' is at hand!!"[53] The table-turning phenomena "are a warning to you," Godfrey told the thousands of readers who bought the several editions of his pamphlet: "they are signs of the times."[54]

One's dining-room table became the scene of epic struggles. After-dinner experiments placed people's fingertips in direct contact with demons. For these

CONCLUSIVE TABLE-TURNING EXPERIMENT MADE AT
GREENWICH.

"THERE, OLD FELLA ! HOPE YOU'RE SATISFIED IT GOES ROUND NOW."
"OH YESH ! THERE'S NO MISTAKE !"
[*These subjects are submitted, very respectfully, to the Reverend (!)
Gentlemen who hold so much conversation with Furniture.*

FIGURE 61 *Punch's* contemptuous portrait of clerical experiments in table-turning. Note the shadowy figure crouched under the table, presumably turning it as the drunken, speech-slurred reverends deem the trial a success. *Punch* (1852).

authors, the dining rooms of table-turners staged struggles between good and evil. Moments like these might make someone an unwitting victim to Satan during this intermediary period, for it was highly dangerous to assume that God was *constantly*, rather than eventually, interventionist and all-powerful.[55] That is, dabblers might become casualties in the final battle: God would eventually be triumphant, but not necessarily *initially* so, and in the interim those in contact with Satan might be lost. In the struggle that preceded the eventual destruction of Satan, many mortal souls could be lost.

Apocalyptic characterizations of trance phenomena and table-turning were often published in the printed transcripts of sermons delivered in parish churches. They, along with literature instructing would-be researchers of the principles of table-turning, were very popular and went through many editions. The struggle over the natural or supernatural character of mesmerism, table-turning, and early spiritualism developed into a pamphlet war during the early 1850s, in which moderate Evangelicals, doctors, and scientists put forward evidence of the natural character of the phenomena against the claims of premillenarians.[56] While there were many different views of the nature of mesmeric phenomena, they were united in their opposition to the "diabolists."

The most famous attempt of this kind was made by Michael Faraday in 1853 in a controversy that launched an extended discussion of the state of "public judgment" that will be discussed in chapter 11. Faraday was exasperated to receive a great many letters from experimenters demanding his confirmation that table-turning was produced by electricity generated by the group encircling the table.[57] In response he published instructions for an experiment that proved (he claimed) that the researchers unconsciously pushed the table. That is, the will of the researcher (who naturally wished to see the table go round) caused the effect through muscular movement alone.

His experiment, and the issue of table-turning more generally, was taken up by a wide range of writers, for some of whom phenomena associated with mesmerism helped delineate the miraculous and the natural. Francis Close, dean of Carlisle, used mesmerism and table-turning as examples of natural phenomena which might appear to be of divine origin, but which could be shown, through operations like Faraday's, to involve no "Divine interference."[58] The rash, "speculative and dogmatic teaching" of the premillenarian sectors of the Evangelical party was destructive: it was damaging to the "public mind" and made Christians "predisposed . . . to catch the infection of any baneful religious epidemic which may arise among us."[59]

While Faraday's experiment was enough to persuade some experimenters that neither a supernatural nor a physical force was involved in mesmeric phenomena, many remained unconvinced. We might have expected this to be a straightforward refutation of the table-turners' claims, but it was not sufficient reassurance to a number of worried millenarians and other experimenters. One could not make mesmeric phenomena innocuous simply by making them the product of the will. For the will itself was one of the most controversial focuses of religious discussions of mesmerism. While mesmerists like Pyne referred to the subjection of the patient's will to the mesmerist's as an aid in missionary work, it was common for mesmeric opponents to warn of the dangers of trusting oneself to another, or of weakening one's will in any respect. Given Evangelical emphasis on the personal struggle to become, and remain, saved, it should come as no surprise that many argued that with the weakening of the will went a decreased ability to determine one's spiritual fate.

The difficulty went deeper than the *protection* of the will—it extended to its *definition*. The concept of a voluntary or willed action being carried out *unconsciously* was not only objectionable to many Evangelicals but even unimaginable. To make what were in effect unconscious choices would make it impossible to be on one's guard against satanic influence. A postscript to Godfrey's pamphlet stated that he had been given Faraday's description of his experiments, and that these were irrelevant to Godfrey's arguments. The individuals in Faraday's experiments "imparted the motion, he tells us, *which we did not.*" The notion that Faraday's apparatus was designed to show involuntary and unperceived yet nevertheless willed actions (by definition, those that the individual would not think he had carried out) passed Godfrey by.

Given that there were so many different ways of representing these states, it should come as no surprise that polemical representations of the magnetic trance were used to discredit other creeds.[60] Narratives of trances and visions were of course an established genre of validation and conversion among Dissenters and Catholics. For example, Lord Shrewsbury and Lord Stanhope, both Catholic sympathizers, collected stories of conversions to Catholicism involving what they saw as supernatural trance states (including mesmerism, somnambulism, spiritualism, and ecstatic convulsions).[61] For such men trances imparted an overarching knowledge of the world which was inaccessible through mere science. In this sense the term "science" was itself quite misleading. For Stanhope in particular, such emblematic sciences of the Victorian period as geology were "fiddle faddle."[62] In his opinion mesmerism validated those very truths of spiritual reality—the possibility of prophecy, the immortality of the soul, and the immateriality of mind—that radicals like Elliotson hoped it would expunge.[63]

Nor was its utility restricted to Catholic sympathizers. Samuel Wilberforce, Sandby, Pyne, and others stored up accounts of mesmeric conversions to Anglicanism from atheism, Catholicism, and Nonconformity.[64] Sandby cited a case of a girl raised by "Socialist parents, and brought up in an ignorance and unbelief of Scripture." When mesmerized by a man of "strong religious feelings," she demonstrated a great knowledge of the Bible and could discover "the deepest meaning in the most abstruse chapters."[65] For these Anglican mesmerists, scientific method was the means by which trance phenomena were to be rescued from the misguided views of the unenlightened, in whose "enthusiasms" a physiological state was taken for a supernatural one. According to Sandby, one should interpret as "natural Mesmerism," or "hysteria," the convulsions and ecstasies of religious states.[66] Such interpretation directly opposed that of Catholics looking for spiritual events. This was the true interpretation, for example, of the behavior of the Wesleyan woman who prophesied after she was supposedly dead. Pyne agreed with M'Neile that Ecstatica was in a mesmeric trance, but differed from him in using this claim, implicitly, to validate mesmerism and show up Catholicism as superstition.[67]

Natural Histories of Psychic States

There was another way in which mesmerism could undermine the presence of spiritual agency in the world, namely, in debates about church and Scriptural history. Mesmerism had long been seen as a potential agent of atheism. The closest any mesmeric figure came actually to yoking mesmerism to atheism was W. C. Engledue, whose materialist psychology helped split the London Phrenological Society over the theological significance of mesmerism. Unitarians were already speculating that the "bearing of this Mesmerism on Revelation is one of its most interesting features." [68] Thus, even if one were not placed directly under the mesmeric influence, the science threatened to weaken Christian beliefs *indirectly* by the variety of dangerous theological arguments it might serve.[69]

Given the similarity of mesmeric cures to the biblical miracles, believers worried that they might provide evidence that miracles were not divine but merely natural phenomena whose causes were not understood at the time. According to Strauss's *Life of Jesus*, for example, the "miracles" were miraculous only in the sense that they were instances of knowledge known before its time; and some readers of Strauss interpreted his claims as threatening Christ's divinity.[70] It was certainly very easy to portray Christ's miracles as a feat of mesmerism. A picture of Christ (fig. 62), printed in a French mesmeric journal, associated mesmerists with Christ by claiming that mesmerism's opponents would imprison Christ for fraud, were he to return to modern society. More frequently, mesmerism could easily fit within the campaign of German rationalist literature to portray the miracles of the New Testament as instances of skillful medicine: as natural events mistaken for supernatural ones.

The radical mesmerist Thomas Chandler, Huxley's teacher and a colleague of John Elliotson, constructed a history of "mesmerism in antiquity" and attributed to it several supposedly divine cures by the early saints. For example, the cures of St. Ewald the Fair were characterized by Chandler as cases in

Jésus guérissant l'aveugle de Jéricho.

Comme Jésus passait , il vit un homme aveugle dès sa naissance.
. . . . . . 3° . . . . . 4° . . . . .
Pendant que je suis au monde, je suis la lumière du monde.
Ayant dit cela, il cracha à terre, et de sa salive il fit de la boue, et
il oignit de cette boue les yeux de l'aveugle.
Et il lui dit : Va, et te lave au réservoir de Siloé (ce qui signifie en-
voyé), et il y alla donc et se lava, et il en revint voyant clair.
(*Evangile selon saint Jean*, chap. IX.)

FIGURE 62 This sketch of Jesus healing the blind man of Jericho was used by Charles Dupotet in his French journal to complain that, were Jesus walking the streets of 1840s Europe, he would be castigated as a fraud. Dupotet, *Journal du Magnétisme*.

which "maniacs" were cured by "mesmerism," and used by the *Zoist* to naturalize as insanity historical cases of possession (fig. 63).[71] Similarly, Theodysius Purland's scrapbook at the LMI included early modern prints of spiritual healing as well as witchcraft: both were explained as instances of unrecognized mesmerism.

Even when mesmerists themselves set out in painstaking detail the differences between mesmerism and miracles, they could easily seem to be emphasizing the similarities. For example, Sandby's long passages contrasting mesmerism with Christ's cures at a distance and the creation of wine from water[72] may not have convinced those who had themselves watched mesmerized subjects actually perceive water as wine, and seen trances created by mesmerists in another room, or even another house.[73] One of Sandby's more interest-

ST EWALD THE FAIR, HEALING A POSSESSED WOMAN

IN PRESENCE OF RADBRAD, DUKE OF FRIESLAND.

AFTER BERNARD VON ORLAY.

FIGURE 63 This sketch of St. Ewald the Fair was copied from a painting by Bernard D'Orslay. The incident was used as an example of a consistent history in which mesmeric phenomena were mistaken for supernatural events. Chandler, "Mesmeric Scene."

ing arguments was that miracles were fail-safe because they were the work of an omnipotent being. Mesmerism, however, was proved to be the result of natural law because it *did not* work each time and *was not* universally effective: it was the product of ordinary human labor mobilizing a not-yet-understood force of nature.[74] Sandby's argument, ironically, coincided with the argument made *against* mesmerism by certain medical and scientific opponents, that mesmerism must not be the result of natural law, since it did not work every time, or universally. Indeed these two conflicting conclusions illustrate how open to interpretation were all trials of mesmerism, inasmuch as even those refutations that might have seemed the most obvious—the objections that it did not always work—could be made to support mesmerists' most ambitious objectives. In the context of these arguments, then, opponents often claimed that *any* involvement in mesmerism was dangerous because it could undermine the legitimacy of biblical miracles.

But this perceived threat could also be turned on its head to place mesmerism in the service of faith. Thomas Arnold, master of Rugby, used the fear of mesmerism as the occasion to give a definition of miracles that protected them against the encroachments of secular representation. He had become convinced of the reality of even those mesmeric phenomena that so far departed from the "known laws of nature" that they seemed "more extraordinary than some things which we might call miracles." He preached that to perceive mesmerism as a threat to Christianity was already to have given up the battle. That is, to claim that mesmerism had the power to "shake our faith in miracles" was "far more unreasonable and dangerous to our Christian faith than any belief in the facts of magnetism." The crucial part of Arnold's argument was the claim that the doctrine validated the miracles, rather than the other way round. For "these [mesmeric] facts are mere wonders in our own state of knowledge; at a future period, perhaps, they may become the principles of a new science." But this could never erode the miraculous nature of the New Testament miracles. Their miraculous character lay not in their status as "wonders," but "because he [Christ] wrought them."[75] The first part of Arnold's argument, that is, the transient status of the "wondrous," is strikingly reminiscent of Charles Babbage's treatment of miracles in his *Ninth Bridgewater Treatise*, first published in 1837. Babbage argued that apparent miracles were only a sign of a more sophisticated, more general natural law as yet undiscovered. The fact that other comments on animal magnetism by Arnold date his interest to the late 1830s suggests that he may have seen mesmerism as a means of saving miracles from the threat posed by Babbage's argument, while preserving the progressive character of human knowledge that Babbage proposed.

Another, quite famous argument aimed at retrieving miracles from skeptical attacks was also readily turned to mesmerism's purposes. Richard Whately, archbishop of Dublin, used the same arguments to validate mesmeric phenomena that he had used decades earlier to defend the biblical miracles against the onslaught of Humean skepticism in his *Historic Doubts Relative to Napoleon Bonaparte*.[76] There Whately argued that the reality of Napoleon Bonaparte was more difficult to establish than the validity of assertions of miracles in the Bible. Those using Humean arguments to support skeptical stances toward miracles could not trust their belief in one of the most culturally visible figures of their day. Whately brought the same argument to bear on the question of the reality of mesmeric phenomena: "Hume's chief argument against miracles universally is, that there are plenty of sham ones: he might as well have argued from the numbers of forged bank notes that there are none genuine. I wish to adopt finally the conclusions that shall imply the least credulity. But when will people be brought to understand that credulity and incredulity are the same?"[77] It was as "credulous" to refuse to accept the evidence of massive testimony and personal experience in "unaccountable" cases as it was to be too easily convinced. Whately became an enthusiastic mesmerist and mesmeric patient. He was president of the London Mesmeric Infirmary in the 1850s, founded the Dublin Mesmeric Infirmary,[78] and involved his family members in the science at a time when he was centrally involved in British social science.[79] In 1852 his wife claimed to have restored the sight of a woman who had been blind for twenty-six years;[80] and when Whately's health began to decline, he not only had himself treated mesmerically, but left instructions, in the event that he lost the power of speech or consciousness, that no allopathic doctor was to be brought to his bedside.[81]

Supernatural Histories

As these kinds of arguments demonstrate, it was crucial to enforce a distinction between mesmerism and miracles. But this business was delicate, since many of the arguments one might make for or against mesmerism might be used in the same manner with respect to miracles. Throughout the 1840s and 1850s the distinction between mesmerism and miracles proved quite difficult to sustain. This was one factor in Henry Wilberforce's campaign to place mesmerism under clerical authority. He concluded that, if, as it seemed, Christ "was pleased to employ some means very close to those employed in magnetic cures" in the miracles of the New Testament, one should not be surprised, since one might expect to see a "resemblance between the mode of His acting and that of His creatures," though the mode of action of human beings would be of a much lower order.[82] The author pointed to science and to biblical history as endeavors that undermined Christianity when abandoned to the whims or malign campaigns of "the infidel party."[83] Thus whatever the status of mesmerism, he concluded, the new science, like any other potent social force or influence, was safe only when carefully supervised and controlled by the church.

One attempt to define the significance of mesmerism with respect to church authority was that of Samuel Maitland, onetime secretary to the archbishop of Canterbury, and an eminent historian of the church. Maitland became involved in mesmeric disputes after reading the references to the account of the role of the clergy in the Inquisition in the second edition (1848) of Sandby's *Mesmerism and Its Opponents*. Sandby got his Inquisition from Combe's *Constitution of Man*, which used an account of a horrific and unnecessary Inquisition to portray the state of society in the late sixteenth century as "little better than a large suburb of Pandemonium." It was also an example of the "insufficiency of mere theological knowledge" to protect people from "practical errors."[84] Combe, in turn, had drawn his information not from primary sources but from the article "Daemonology and Witchcraft" in the *Foreign Quarterly Review*, in which the Europe of the late sixteenth century was characterized by a catalogue of Inquisition horrors in which the "clergy displayed the most intemperate zeal."[85] Sandby linked Combe's, and, indirectly, the *Foreign Quarterly* reviewer's, portrayal of a prejudiced clergy of an earlier period to the religious opposition to modern mesmerism. Indeed, in those cases where witchcraft had seemed most likely in the early modern period, "the charge . . . too commonly arose out of the medical success of the offender."[86] This terrible pedigree was the inheritance of the clerical opponents of mesmerism, some of whom "enthralled" the "weakest members of their flock" by claiming that mesmerists were "victims of satanic cruelty!"[87]

Maitland was convinced of the reality of table-turning as based in more than unconscious muscular action, and indeed his admission of the validity of the phenomena was used by mesmerists as support of the practice.[88] However, he condemned mesmeric practices through a complex etymological argument that linked quite specific mesmeric phenomena—especially the "transposition" of the senses, in which mesmerized subjects would see and hear with parts of the body (especially the stomach) other than their eyes and ears—to specific passages in the Hebrew Bible condemning witchcraft.[89]

Maitland's attitude toward mesmerism reflected his stance on the history of the church and the implications of this history for the position of the church in modern society. Maitland's *Dark Ages* had portrayed the clergy of the ninth through twelfth centuries as a sensible, unsuperstitious, and authoritative body. According to Maitland the Inquisition had been an orderly, necessary process carried out by beleaguered administrators whose duty it had been to arbitrate claims of witchcraft. Maitland agreed that many unusual phenomena recorded during this period should be diagnosed, retrospectively, as mesmeric.[90] But while Sandby had concluded from the mesmeric character of these phenomena that they contravened no biblical admonishments against witchcraft, Maitland's new biblical translations suggested that mesmerism was expressly forbidden in Scripture.

Maitland's links between trance phenomena of the medieval and early modern period lent rhetorical force to his use of mesmerism as a case in point with respect to the role of the clergy as authorities in modern society. He attacked the romantic vision of the Inquisition epitomized by the anonymous reviewer (whom he reckoned to be Sir Walter Scott, on the basis of textual comparisons between the article and Scott's *Letters on Demonology and Witchcraft*)[91] and the Evangelical portrayals of men like Sandby, who used the notion of a bloody Inquisition as a stick with which to beat the clerical antimesmerists.[92]

Maitland also used the controversies over mesmerism and table-turning to undermine the rise of scientific authority at the expense of the authority of the church.[93] In particular he attacked Michael Faraday. Faraday's attacks on the table-turners had rested on a distinction between religious and "ordinary" knowledge, between the weight of testimony of the general public and that of scientific experts, and between what is possible and impossible in natural phenomena. He had also exhorted the public to recognize the "*deficiency*" of their "*judgment*" with respect to nature.[94] But Maitland refused to exclude religious authority from any realm of debate. Individuals who were creditworthy in general society, including (and perhaps especially) in the church, were fit to judge facts of nature. Maitland challenged Faraday to give a precise definition of what was possible and impossible in the world. He spoke for many when he wrote that table phenomena "are a stumbling block to science in its railroad course. It is utterly at fault; and its misfortune is not merely that it has been unable to explain, but that in rushing out 'to inflict a mortal wound on the monster superstition' it has exposed its weakness." It has allowed the ostensibly educated public to glimpse the limits of its explanatory power.[95] Many felt as Maitland did, that Faraday and other would-be authorities rejected the obvious reality of trance phenomena as experienced by many experimenters, without supplying a satisfactory explanation. Indeed, this stalemate would be one of the motivations for the individuals who considered themselves the leaders of the scientific community, such as Michael Faraday and William Whewell, to discuss among themselves how the public mind could be reformed so as to be able to recognize "proper" scientific authority and accept "proper" scientific explanations.

Defining the Categories of Nature and Spirit

Maitland's attack on mesmerism suggests that "science," whatever individual Victorians thought the word meant, had not established its ascendancy with respect to questions about nature, even as late as the 1850s, in certain religious circles. It was still possible to challenge the validity of individual scientific programs and groups of scientists; further, one could even cast doubt on the assumption that the scientific enterprise had privileged and trustworthy access to nature. The strategy of emphasizing the supernatural was to construct a rivalry between science and religion where one did not exist, and to construct a privileged authority for religion over phenomena that otherwise would have come under the jurisdiction of science.

More generally, this chapter has shown how a practice of spiritual influence stimulated various religious constituencies, provoking people to question the distinctions they made between the natural and the supernatural, between piety and impiety, and between virtue and vice. Most important, it provided a new means of exploring the character of different kinds of influence at a time when the clergy were exercised about its nature, about how they could positively influence their charges, and about the threat of charismatic influences (especially those emanating from Rome) that might threaten members of their fold. In every case, mesmerism acted as a catalyst, forcing people to explore the categories they were using to understand themselves, their relations with one another, and the worlds of nature and spirit.

These individuals made spiritual matters their primary concern and even their livelihood. But even as the "diabolists" railed against mesmerism as a demonic force, most of mesmerism's practitioners continued to have ambitions for making it a science. It should not be surprising, therefore, that the categories that mesmerism brought into question most insistently of all continued to be those of science itself.

Expertise, Common Sense,

and the Territories of Science

MESMERISM EXASPERATED those scientific skeptics who saw themselves, however paradoxically, as an unrecognized body of leaders. To them mesmerism
was a dramatization of the mental cloddishness of a population who were so
unfit to make scientific judgments that they were oblivious to their own inep-
titude. One might assume that this state of affairs was a problem of reception.
Legitimate doctors and scientists knew who they were and could distinguish
between proper and improper lines of inquiry. Their challenge would lie in
teaching the public to make the same identifications and distinctions, thereby
banishing the intellectual cockiness that sciences like mesmerism encouraged.
But in fact the problem was more fundamental. Prestigious scientists needed
to define their communities, to define their publics, and to define the rules of
behavior appropriate to each.

Critics saw mesmerism as alien to science and medicine, yet well-known
doctors and natural philosophers engaged in debates and experiments. And
even people who despised it were drawn in when they were called upon for an
opinion: if they failed to give one, they were said to have no explanation to offer, yet any opinion they did give became the *beginning* of a discussion rather
than a final judgment. So fluid was the relevant vocabulary that assertions
about the relationship between physical forces and living or mental phenomena could be taken as support for mesmerism. For example, Michael Faraday
told his audiences that the human body was "diamagnetic"; many listeners
took this to mean that the body was a living magnet, and that one body could

"magnetize" another body. Similarly, when the prestigious physiologist Carlo Matteuchi claimed that muscular contractions produced electric currents, some readers concluded that human interaction involved an electric circuit. Virtually any claim about life and physical force could be appropriated to serve a wide range of purposes. In this state of affairs, scientific luminaries were celebrated and were called upon to explain new phenomena, yet they were not the ultimate arbiters. In fact, one could go further to say that even the most obedient-minded Victorian would have to learn how to defer to scientific authority, because the channels of communication between "authorities" and their audiences were not stable. The claims that left the podium during Faraday's public lectures were different from the ones that took shape in the minds of his listeners.

In the twentieth century the common ground between scientists and the general public has become even smaller, but, by and large, scientists do not struggle daily to define their authority. Unlike Victorians, people of the late twentieth century no longer feel that cutting-edge science can be understood and should be appraised by anyone with, say, a college education. This change in conventions of authority came about partly as a result of a rise in specialist knowledge and the invention of the professional scientist. The walls of the laboratory closed around scientific labor during the second half of the nineteenth century, and scientific innovation has become increasingly removed from public culture ever since. Controversies over mesmerism, and especially the debates addressed in this chapter, helped catalyze the creation of the enclosed, austere world of modern science by providing a testing ground where people could try out their answers to one of its central questions: what makes a science?

Magnetism, Perception, and the Correlation of Forces

In 1845 the German natural philosopher Karl von Reichenbach announced that he had discovered a new force of nature, as the result of experiments on "sick sensitives," women with unusually sensitive constitutions. When magnetic or crystalline materials were placed near their bodies, they described sensations similar to those of some mesmeric subjects: they saw flames emitted from the ends of magnets, felt warmth or cold, and saw a diffuse aura issuing from objects. Reichenbach concluded that crystals—and any polar structure—gave out an as-yet unidentified imponderable agent that was related to physical phenomena and to life. It could be conducted, like the putative mesmeric fluid, through magnetic and organic matter. It also seemed to be contained in some chemicals and metals. It had polar qualities: one pole provoked a chill when placed near the skin, while the other seemed to impart a feeling of warmth. These effects were so slight that they could be perceived only by individuals in enhanced nervous states—mesmeric subjects or people who were constitutionally sensitive. The new imponderable was named "Od" (in English, "odyle"). Reichenbach's announcement was published in 1845 in one of the most prestigious German natural philosophical journals, Liebig's *Annalen der Chimie und Pharmacie*,[1] and an "abstract" in translation was made in 1846 by William Gregory, professor of chemistry at the University of Edinburgh and an active mesmerist.

Meanwhile, an English researcher was conducting his own examinations of the relationship between light and magnetism, and would shortly announce one of the most important discoveries of the decade. Six months after Reichenbach's claims appeared in the *Annalen*, Michael Faraday announced that light could be polarized. The Royal Institution philosopher had demonstrated a particular connection between two natural forces—magnetism and light—that had hitherto been assumed to be independent. This discovery also had implications for the structure of the sciences. It added a new "correlation" (between light and magnetism) to the process of "correlating" the forces of nature—a process that was crucial for the understanding of how different scientific disciplines related to one another.

Because Reichenbach's claims made a link (if an ambiguous one) between light and magnetism, Faraday's announcement helped boost the credibility of the experimental study of mind and nervous sensibility. Faraday's and Reichenbach's researches were likened to one another. For instance, the rhymed "complaint of a sunbeam against Michael Faraday" gave his discovery a mesmeric glow:

You've heard how Alexis electrified London,
    And Elliotson doct['']red the Misses O'Key,
How Wheatstone's "Express" have time and space undon[e]
    And finally, Faraday's magnetized me.[2]

Faraday's achievement recalled earlier ones: Elliotson's, Alexis's, and Wheatstone's, and most recently Reichenbach's. According to the "sensitives" whose experiences preceded Faraday's discovery, magnets emitted light. One might have asked if this light could be related to the "magnetic fluid," as magnetism was still commonly described, but if so, one would have expected a curving or undulating stream. Instead, the flames were perpendicular or parallel to the magnet bar itself, suggesting a polar phenomenon (see fig. 64). Could these sensitives be perceiving a manifestation of Faraday's phenomena, perhaps a

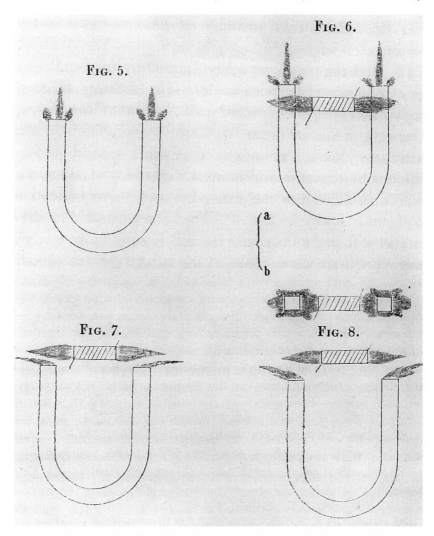

FIGURE 64 Four examples of the odylic phenomena, in which sensitives described light issuing from magnets (and other substances) in patterns such as these. Reichenbach, *Abstract*.

more general set of effects? The mutual relations of light, magnetism, and vitality could form the basis of a sweeping set of correlations, extending them to the nervous system and the mind itself.

Over the next decade, Reichenbach's phenomena were taken up by a number of stock-taking works on the sciences. In 1846, when William Robert Grove's laboratory assistant, George Thomas Fisher, wrote a review of new discoveries in magnetism, he grouped together Reichenbach's *Abstract* and

Faraday's announcement of the polarization of light. The timing of Reichenbach's work gave it a plausibility that would otherwise have been compromised by its proximity to mesmerism. But because Reichenbach's claims preceded Faraday's and they concerned strikingly similar, hitherto unknown phenomena, Fisher suggested that the two lines of investigation should be considered in tandem.[3] Five years later, when the eminent physiologist William Benjamin Carpenter published a major paper attempting to bring the life and the physical sciences together in a grand set of correlations, his reference to Reichenbach sounded the same note: "the discoveries of Prof. Faraday in regard to the universal operation of the magnetic force, and its relation to light and to the polar force of crystals," suggested that Reichenbach's work required serious consideration, particularly because Faraday's "had not been made when the phenomena observed by Baron von Reichenbach were first made public" (746). The simultaneous discoveries of Faraday and Reichenbach confirmed each other and provided further empirical grounds for studying how living phenomena could produce physical phenomena, and vice versa.

The "Reichenbach phenomena" were the subject of much dispute and experimentation for the next several decades.[4] Reichenbach continued his researches in Germany, arguing that his new imponderable was at once a physical and a living force. Substantial translations were published in the 1850s, motivating a number of different groups of researchers.[5] Some wished to explore the relationship between mental and vital phenomena and physical forces (for instance, the study of reflexes), others, the "correlation" that William Robert Grove had developed for the physical forces to vital phenomena.[6] In the last decades of the century the phenomena became one of the fundamental areas of investigation leading to the founding of the Society for Psychical Research.[7]

Modern readers would probably ask if Reichenbach's sensitives could have perceived the flames, the changes in temperature, and the light merely because they expected to do so. Reichenbach was not assailed by queries of this sort. Only one person made such a challenge: James Braid, the inventor of hypnotism and the man who established the term "suggestion" for certain categories of mental influence. In a short pamphlet of 1846, Braid claimed that, in experiments on subjects he considered nervous, they perceived what they expected to perceive, and demonstrated the mesmeric phenomena that mesmerists attributed to the action of physical forces.[8] By manipulating their expectations he could alter their sensations. They saw flames, felt heat, and felt cold according to their expectations. The people were not frauds; their sensations were real, but they came not from physical stimuli but from an internal nervous response to the influence of the imagination. Braid implicitly relied on the notion of an unconscious cognitive process—an innovative notion that, however familiar and powerful it would become by the century's end, was new and anti-intuitive at the time. Braid's argument did not, therefore, have the force for contemporaries that it would have when there was a physiology of unconscious action to support it. The latter only emerged in the second half of the century, as the *result* of researches and debates along these lines.

Turning the Tables of Electric Authority

Over the next several years, physiologists were fascinated by the prospect of magnetic or electric character of the nerves and mental action. New terms and new practices appeared, and new phenomena were produced and debated. Some of them produced a veritable hurricane of public dispute. The first of these was "electrobiology." In 1850 and 1851 American showmen introduced Britons to the practice of electrobiology, in which social relations were treated as an electric circuit. A coin made up of a core of copper, surrounded by zinc, would produce an electric circuit through the air that would suspend an individual's will while leaving him or her conscious and fully cognizant of all that transpired.

Electrobiology was disseminated principally by the itinerant American lecturers, of whom the best known were H. G. Darling, G. W. Stone, Theophilus Fiske, and H. E. Lewis (who attracted particular attention because he was "of African descent"; see fig. 65, a representative broadsheet). This technique was not intended to induce an altered mental state, merely to remove the will and leave the consciousness intact. It swept through Britain in 1851 and 1852, when it was eclipsed by table-turning and spiritualism.[9] Lewis produced his effects by maintaining eye contact with his subjects for several minutes, or by staring at them while they kept their eyes fixed on an object nearby. He had an "energetic concentration of will," according to one commentator, "which I have never seen so strongly developed [in anyone else]."[10] Darling used a different technique. He asked several people to gaze for ten to fifteen minutes "on a small coin, or double convex mass of zinc with a small center of copper, placed in the palm of the left hand." During this time they had to maintain "perfect stillness," "entire concentration," and a "perfectly passive will, or state of mind." After several minutes, Darling instructed the subjects to close their eyes, and then, touching the forehead, would declare it impossible for him or her to open them. If this seemed to be the case, he proceeded with further experiments. If not, he waited a few minutes and tried again. When the practice worked the way it was supposed to, patients experienced the assertions of the biologist as if they were reality. These assertions were not commands of what subjects *should* do ("do not open your eyes"), but assertions of what they *could* do ("you cannot open your eyes"). Biological subjects

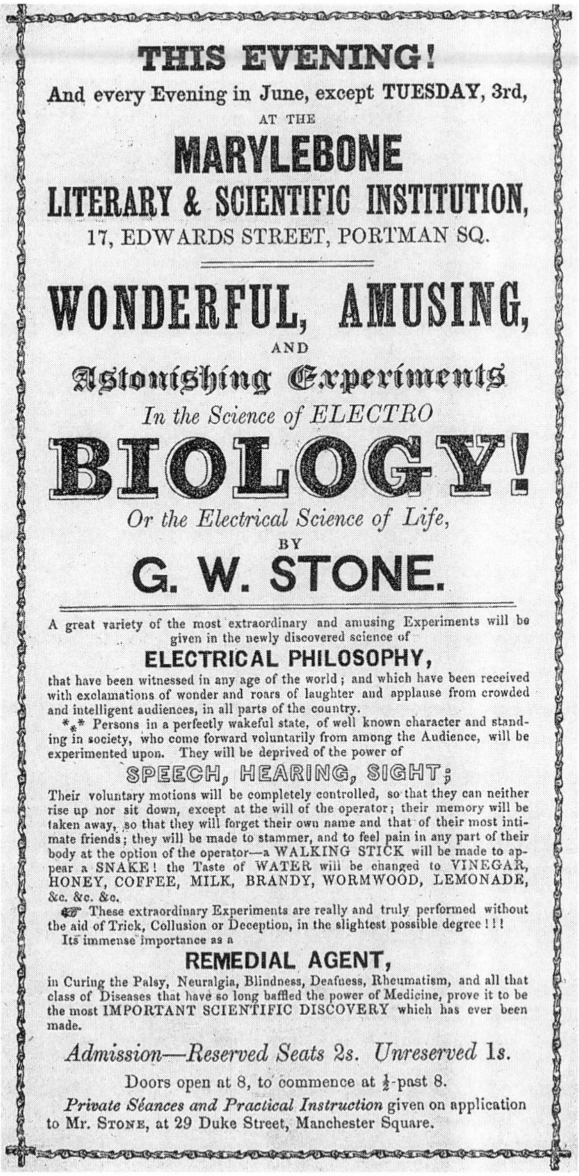

THIS EVENING!

And every Evening in June, except TUESDAY, 3rd,

AT THE

MARYLEBONE

LITERARY & SCIENTIFIC INSTITUTION,

17, EDWARDS STREET, PORTMAN SQ.

WONDERFUL, AMUSING,

AND

Astonishing Experiments

In the Science of ELECTRO

BIOLOGY!

Or the Electrical Science of Life,

BY

G. W. STONE.

A great variety of the most extraordinary and amusing Experiments will be given in the newly discovered science of

ELECTRICAL PHILOSOPHY,

that have been witnessed in any age of the world; and which have been received with exclamations of wonder and roars of laughter and applause from crowded and intelligent audiences, in all parts of the country.

*** Persons in a perfectly wakeful state, of well known character and standing in society, who come forward voluntarily from among the Audience, will be experimented upon. They will be deprived of the power of

SPEECH, HEARING, SIGHT;

Their voluntary motions will be completely controlled, so that they can neither rise up nor sit down, except at the will of the operator; their memory will be taken away, so that they will forget their own name and that of their most intimate friends; they will be made to stammer, and to feel pain in any part of their body at the option of the operator—a WALKING STICK will be made to appear a SNAKE! the Taste of WATER will be changed to VINEGAR, HONEY, COFFEE, MILK, BRANDY, WORMWOOD, LEMONADE, &c. &c. &c.

These extraordinary Experiments are really and truly performed without the aid of Trick, Collusion or Deception, in the slightest possible degree !!!

Its immense importance as a

REMEDIAL AGENT,

in Curing the Palsy, Neuralgia, Blindness, Deafness, Rheumatism, and all that class of Diseases that have so long baffled the power of Medicine, prove it to be the most IMPORTANT SCIENTIFIC DISCOVERY which has ever been made.

Admission—Reserved Seats 2s. Unreserved 1s.

Doors open at 8, to commence at ½-past 8.

Private Séances and Practical Instruction given on application to Mr. STONE, at 29 Duke Street, Manchester Square.

FIGURE 65 G. W. Stone's broadsheet advertising electrobiological demonstrations. Purland Scrapbook, National Library of Medicine.

experienced these assertions as fact. Darling could control sensation by asserting that "one hand, or one arm, [had no] . . . feeling, and [rendered] it utterly insensible to the most acute pain; or he [could make] his subject feel a cold pencil-case burning hot, or himself freeze with cold." Central to his dramatic productions was the suspension of the will.

[Dr. Darling] controls the will, so that the subject is either compelled to perform a certain act, to fall asleep in a minute, or to whistle, &c. &c., or is rendered unable to perform any act . . .

Dr. Darling further controls the memory. He causes the subject to forget his own name, or that of any other individual: or to be unable to name a single letter of the alphabet, &c &c.

Moreover, he causes him to take any object to be what Dr. Darling says it is, a watch for a snuff box, a chair for a dog, &c . . .

Again, he will cause the subject to imagine himself another person, such as Dr. Darling, . . . Prince Albert, or the Duke of Wellington, and to act the character in life.[11]

There were a number of rival explanations for the effects: that the copper and zinc coin established an electric circuit, or that because eye contact and concentrated attention could produce the same effect, it was a minor form of mesmerism or hypnotism.[12] Whatever explanation one preferred, central to it were the suspension of the will and acceptance of assertions as reality.

Electrobiology displayed in its effects the difficulties of adjudicating it. Its phenomena were double: the confused judgment of the experimental subject and (according to skeptics) the confused judgment of its advocates. Electrobiology's own nature questioned whether the public mind could be trusted to discriminate between a charlatan's assertions and the truth. The notion that there was something worryingly amiss in the state of people's judgment was intensified by the fact that the people involved were among the most educated in the country: the faculty and students of the Scottish universities. Indeed, at least one faculty member, William Gregory, was an enthusiastic and extremely public mesmerist, and carried out experiments on his students and on local school children.[13] An appalled John Hughes Bennett, professor of theory of physic at Edinburgh, claimed that these activities were more than misguided—they produced real nervous disorder on a massive scale. "Fashionable parties have been converted into scenes of experiments on the mental functions," he recorded, and a cross-section of fashionable society, "[n]oblemen, members of the learned professions, and respectable citizens, have been amusing themselves in private."[14] Everyone had been

FIGURE 66 The only self-controlled individual in this scene is the mesmerist, who extends his arm to throw six women and a young girl into a somnambulic "ecstasy" before a dozen witnesses (c. 1850). Mary Evans Picture Library.

seized by a "mania," even the elite doctors to whom one might have turned for treatment: "On one occasion the Royal Medical Society was operated on; and if a proof of the correctness of the facts to be described is required, it will be found in the circumstance, that the nervous aberrations noticed, were really exhibited in some of its most sceptical members."[15] All educational establishments were afflicted, from elementary schools to universities. In elementary schools, "girls and boys throw themselves into states of trance and ecstasy, or show their fixed eyeballs and rigid limbs, for the amusement of their companions." And in universities, students were "incapacitated from following their ordinary occupations and obliged . . . to absent themselves from their classes." Electrobiology brought learning and enlightenment to a shuddering halt.

One thing that added to the social threat of electrobiology was that mesmeric practices of all kinds were now staged using a larger number of people. Instead of the one-on-one practice of previous years, many mesmerists were staging group experiments, entrancing many individuals at once. There were reports of roomfuls of swooning somnambulists; figure 66 shows a contemporary French sketch of the "extase somnambulique." So threatening to the social and rational order were the psychic phenomena that they were compared to "what occurred in the middle ages." They earned a title of their own, as a notorious watershed in public life: the Mesmeric Mania of 1851.

Sitting in Judgment

Electrobiology might have flourished longer in Britain but for the arrival of the still more accessible experimental practice of table-turning from Vienna, Paris, and New York. It spread through Britain with astonishing speed. Within weeks, thousands of middle-class dinner tables were being tickled by the fingertips of expectant diners who linked hands (fig. 67). Table-turning attracted even wider attention than had mesmerism when it first arrived, because there was no taint of sexual impropriety associated with it, because the practice was self-explanatory ("link hands, let your fingertips touch the table, and wait"), and because every British dining room came equipped with the appropriate instrument.

The table-turning "epidemic," as people called it, shows how easily mid-century scientific knowledge could become common property. Decades of public conversaziones such as the one held at Apothecaries' Hall in 1851 (fig. 68) gave people the confidence to trust the evidence of their own senses, especially when they were presented with a new experimental phenomenon that seemed to be an extension of what they already knew about natural powers. Most people knew that the body carried and produced electricity: authorities like Michael Faraday had told them so. They might even have carried out their own experiments to see the muscles of a frog generate a galvanic current. It was commonly understood that air carried electricity and that electricity played a role in the formation of natural structures. Dozens of cheap pamphlets explained the role of physical powers in daily life, and dozens of natural philosophers and doctors intoned on such subjects. But further conclusions were now to be matters of sustained public debate.

The mesmerists were divided about the reality of the effects. The *Zoist*'s initial response was contemptuous, and, in case readers lacked imagination, it published a sketch of a table leg being nudged by a fashionably clad foot. But one of the most "philosophical" of mesmerists, Chauncey Hare Townshend, wrote from Paris to declare that careful and extensive experimentation had convinced him the effects were real. Townshend devised a few simple tests to distinguish between mechanical and imponderable influences. He placed a delicate piece of tissue between the hand of each table-turner and the table. If it were twisted or torn, the table had been pushed (and vice versa). Similarly, he placed thin, flat objects (such as a sheet of smooth wood) between the hand and the table: if the wood slid in the direction of the table's movement, the trial was a failure, and if it moved the other way, a success. There were some "successes" among his many trials, and he concluded that an imponderable influence did indeed exist.

TABLE MOVING.

FIGURE 67 A table-turning experiment. Men and women alternate here, as they would at a dinner party, but in this case the arrangement is supposed to enhance the flow of vital influence. *Table-Moving by Animal Magnetism.*

FIGURE 68 This sketch of a conversazione at Apothecaries' Hall evokes the Victorians' enthusiasm for examining nature themselves. A woman in the foreground (apparently under instruction by her male companion) and other browsers examine the exhibits and look through the microscopes. *Illustrated London News* (1851).

Skeptics—and there were many—took one of two stances. Either they followed the *Zoist*'s claim that this was simple fraud, or they gave a more complex explanation along the lines of the complaint of James Braid in "The power of the mind over the body": the individuals were acting *unconsciously* according to their preconceptions, producing the effects they expected to see. Indeed, Braid himself used this argument against the table-turners. He conducted his own trial, and arranged to judge an evening trial of table-turning in a city hall in Manchester. Although he used almost exactly the same simple test apparatus as Townshend's, he obtained the opposite results. Sometimes the tissues were torn, sometimes slightly wrinkled if the table moved; just as often they remained pristine after a trial in which the experimenters failed to agree among themselves whether the table had budged. The tests continued for several hours, but no one could agree whether any were successful. Braid's own summary of events used the same argument he had applied to mesmerism and the Reichenbach phenomena. In a trial where there was no positive proof of the existence of magnetic fluid, the experimenters had acted under the influence of suggestion. As the disputes continued, they provoked increasingly elaborate accounts of the nature and relations of the will, the judgment, and human action.

Sciences of Volition and the Powers of Judgment

How could a conscious person act unconsciously? Claims about unconsciousness were not unknown during this period, but the idea of unconscious action *during consciousness* was unfamiliar and controversial. In the late 1840s and 1850s it became prominent in the work of several physiologists and doctors, among them James Braid, Thomas Laycock, and William Benjamin Carpenter. Carpenter was most directly responsible for developing a psychological claim, in reaction to the table-turners and electrobiologists, that used the notion of "mental reflexes" to develop a physiology of authority. Mental reflexes soon became immensely influential as a basis for explaining human action and in particular as a psychology of authority.

Carpenter was the leading physiologist of his generation.[16] He was very widely known from the hundreds of public lectures he gave to audiences ranging from skilled artisan communities in Manchester to the fashionable clientele of London's Royal Institution. His general scientific views had a broad base from his many textbooks and popular encyclopedias, the most widely distributed of which, published anonymously in the early 1840s, sold more than 70,000 copies.[17]

His career began with efforts to make comparative physiology more law-like, and during the late 1840s and early 1850s he became increasingly interested in the mind.[18] In the early 1850s, passages on mind and will in his treatises ballooned into hundreds of pages, many of them concerning altered states of mind and mental reflexes[19] and indebted to the work of Marshall Hall, James Braid, and Karl von Reichenbach. In Hall's reflex system, a considerable proportion of bodily action was produced when the spinal cord (or brain) reflected incoming stimuli outward in behavior. Reichenbach's claims provided an empirical forum for exploring the relation between the reflex apparatus and the apparently augmented perceptions of mesmeric subjects. James Braid's new science of "hypnotism" was helpful because unlike mesmerism it used physical stimuli such as points of light to create the trance.[20] While Braid had designed this technique as an attack on the fluid theory of the mesmerists, his choice of stimulus served Carpenter's needs for different reasons: the incoming stimulus of light and the manifestation of trance could be claimed to be a mental manifestation of the reflex arc that Hall asserted with respect to the spinal column. Mesmerism, according to Carpenter, produced in an artificial form the same kinds of phenomena that appeared naturally in the mentally ill: the mental reflexes became more influential than in people in ordinary mental states. Hypnotized and insane subjects could smell, hear, and see things that normal people could not, because the suspension of consciousness brought an exaggerated sensitivity.

Carpenter's colleague Thomas Laycock (who would later claim a share of the credit for the notion of mental reflexes) provided a similar explanation for how a change in the state of attention could alter the nerves of sensation: "an act of attention may be, and often is, involuntary and instinctive, when it is to be classed . . . with the excito-motory phenomena. Point at a nervous female, and she will complain of a sensation as if cold or warm air were blowing [on the relevant part] . . . The sensation probably depends upon changes in the central terminations of the sensitive nerves, excited by the act of attention."[21] But the nervous reflexes were far more powerful than these phenomena suggested. Laycock also described a case in which a ventriloquist foretold the death of a guest at a soirée: "such was the impression made, that it actually took place."[22] In the context of the work of Laycock, Hall, and Braid, one might think of hypnotism as beheading the will from the experimental subject, who then played out the variations of stimuli in "automated" behavior.

While Laycock wished to study nervous phenomena as part of his researches on hysteria, Carpenter's work on *mental* reflexes supplied both an explanation for all kinds of mesmeric phenomena (including table-turning and electricity) and the fundamental component of an altered portrayal of human agency more generally. Carpenter attributed trance behavior to the act of con-

centrating on an external stimulus, which severed the mental connections between the mental reflexes and the will. Electricity was not involved in the
phenomenon: the act of concentration alone caused the effects. As a result,
the "biologised" subject's "voluntary control over the current of thought is
entirely suspended, the individual being for the time (so to speak) a mere
thinking automaton, the whole course of whose ideas is determinable by suggestions operating from without."[23] Ideas were the external stimuli that, impinging upon the brain, were directly "reflected" in what Carpenter labeled
"ideo-motor" actions. These actions were either *nonvolitional* acts, when the
will was entirely suspended (this was the case in electrobiology) or *semivoli-
tional* acts, when the will was partly suspended (as in the case of table-turning).
During a table-turning experiment the subjects' wish for the table to move was
the internal stimulus that was unconsciously reflected in pushing the table
around. This claim was indebted to David Hartley's psychology, in which
nerve fibers set up permanent connections between different centers in the
brain, and mechanically linked sensations and ideas.[24]

The notion of mental reflexes became a central part of Carpenter's emerging mental physiology, which extended the notion of "consensus" from the
region of sensation to that of intellectual stimulus, from "sensori-motor" to
"ideo-motor" actions.[25]

[A]ctions, being dependent upon the prompting of sensations, are "sensori-motor" or
"consensual."—But further, there is evidence that even the Cerebrum may respond
(as it were) automatically to impressions fitted to excite it to "reflex" action, when
from any cause the Will is in abeyance . . . Thus in the states of . . . Somnambulism
[etc.] *ideas* which take possession of the mind, and from which it cannot free itself,
may excite respondent movements; and this may happen also when the force of the
idea is morbidly exaggerated, and the will is not suspended but merely weakened, as
in many forms of Insanity.[26]

Carpenter moved "consensual" phenomena into the realm of ideas and integrated them into a hierarchy of self-command and judgment, in which different levels of the will and higher reflexes were stripped away by different
trance-inducing practices. Hypnosis could demonstrably remove the will from
the experimental scene, thereby revealing the extent to which behavior could
proceed without it.[27] During trance periods, sensory impressions led directly
to ideas and thence to action, entirely bypassing volition. Naturally occurring
examples of related phenomena included dreams, drunken behavior, insanity,
and forms of hysteria.[28]

It was only through natural philosophy of mind that the various levels of
the mental hierarchy could be traced. Carpenter laid out this hierarchy in a

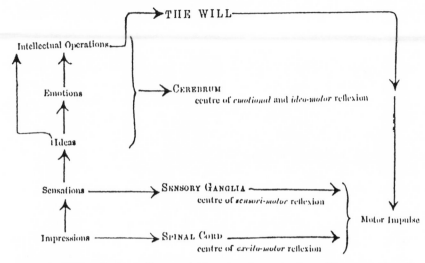

FIGURE 69 William Benjamin Carpenter's hierarchy of mental reflexes. The arrows show the various courses of incoming impressions as they are transformed into outward action. Carpenter, "On the Influence of Suggestion."

chart of mental functioning (fig. 69). In this context altered states of mind bared the underlying apparatus of mental functioning. The mesmeric subject became an anonymous machine, devoid of authority and even individual character, whose experiences and testimony were excised from the process of understanding the phenomena. The natural philosophers who could explain this process thereby became the custodians, not only of natural knowledge, but of public judgment itself.

Disciplining Willful Experimenters

Table-turners turned to the national expert on electricity to help resolve matters. Michael Faraday was the preeminent authority on electricity during the early Victorian period, and one of the most eminent natural philosophers in the country. In the early months of 1853, he was besieged by letters demanding his opinion of table-turning. Exasperated when his correspondents would not let the matter rest with a dismissive flourish of his pen, Faraday took refuge in experiment: he designed an apparatus to prove that mechanical influence alone was moving the tables.

In letters to the *Times* (4 January) and the *Athenaeum* (27 June) Faraday described two apparatuses. The first was similar to those of Chauncey Hare Townshend, James Braid, the editors of the *London Medical Gazette*, and

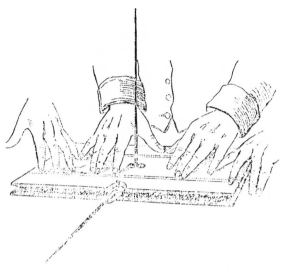

FIGURE 70 Michael Faraday's instrument for detecting muscular effort during table-turning experiments. It was published in the *Illustrated London News* in 1853, along with instructions for replicating the instrument at home.

countless other contenders who wrote to local papers to describe their researches. The second apparatus, which he displayed at an instrument maker's shop, employed a more sophisticated version of the same principle. Two very thin, parallel boards were separated from each other by horizontal glass cylinders (fig. 70), which let the boards move in opposite directions from each other. A single pin was pushed vertically through both boards, in such a way that if the top board moved with respect to the bottom board, the pin would slant in the direction of the movement. Last, a long, thin straw was attached to the pin and to the top board, such that the movement of the top board with respect to the bottom board would be illustrated, in amplified form, by the movement of the straw. The apparatus was kept together by two rubber bands.

During the experiment the fingertips rested on the top board rather than on the table. If, as the table moved, the straw pointed in the direction of the table's movement, witnesses could conclude that the hand was not exerting muscular force to push the table, since the straw's position would indicate that the hand was dragging behind. If the straw pointed in the direction contrary to the movement of the table, one could conclude that the hand was pushing the table. Faraday's experiments with this apparatus proved largely inconclusive, but in a few cases, according to Faraday, the straw swung in the direction opposite to the table's movement. Drawing on Carpenter's notion of "ideomotor" action, Faraday concluded that table-turning could be attributed only to what he called a "quasi-involuntary muscular response" on the part of the table-turners: they pushed the table without realizing it. It is unclear how many individuals tried to build Faraday's apparatus; it appears that no one published a claim to this effect; but, as we shall see, this did not mean that the table-turners deferred to Faraday's opinion on the nature of the phenomena.

One useful aspect of the concept of ideo-motor action was that it provided a means of discrediting people without casting doubt on their honor. Faraday's challengers were people whose word on matters of fact could not be challenged in the way that working-class mesmeric subjects, itinerant lecturers, and foreign therapists could be. The educated Victorian public thought themselves well able to judge experiments themselves. Whether or not their estimation was well founded, the experimenters of polite society could not be dismissed as unscrupulous liars and frauds. An explanation that claimed that these people acted without intending to or being aware of doing so discredited them without questioning their honor. This explanation therefore had the potential to deal with a large population of witnesses whose veracity could not be questioned, but whose claims were unacceptable to Faraday and his colleagues. This solution literally removed from experimenters' authority and responsibility the physical movements that supplied the evidence for their claims. By placing the hand movements of perfectly sentient table-turners under the aegis of a physiological theory that deemed them "involuntary," the table-turners themselves became part of an experiment run and interpreted by others—namely, their opponents.

Faraday's was not the only intervention of this kind. The physiologist who had supplied him with the concept of "ideo-motor action," William Benjamin Carpenter, energetically put it to work in the adjudication of mesmeric researches. In 1852 his lecture "On the Influence of Suggestion" at the Royal Institution used ideo-motor action to explain both the Reichenbach phenomena and the phenomena of table-turning. Reichenbach's subjects and the experimenters who placed their hands on tables in the expectation that they would begin to spin, acted unconsciously either in producing sensations in their own minds, or in exerting mechanical force. The following year, Carpenter commissioned from James Braid a review of the mesmeric literature that appeared in the medical journal he edited throughout this decade. In his review "Odyle, Mesmerism, [and] Electro-Biology," [29] Braid complained that Reichenbach had not realized that his sensitives were to be regarded as scientific instruments. They needed to be calibrated. "What the thermometer and the telescope are to the chemist and the astronomer," Braid told Reichenbach, "Mlles. Reichel, Maix, and the other 'sensitives,' are in the hands of the inquirer into the laws and properties of odyle—*mere instruments of research.*" Reichenbach had mistakenly treated them as partners in his investigation of nature, and listened to them as he might a fellow experimenter. This was "fatal" to Reich-enbach's "high character" as an experimental philosopher, for his experiments should not have required him to trust his subjects straightforwardly as wit-nesses. Braid concluded by urging the medical readership to "investigate— not mesmerism,—but the phenomena which it has appropriated, and so trans-fer them to the domain of pure science." [30]

The notion of unconscious action quickly became a conventional response to psychic researches of the 1850s and 1860s, but this did not mean that it was definitive or even very successful in dissuading people from pursuing these lines of research and finding electric explanations plausible. The table-turning incident set a precedent in how to deal with future practices that propagated theories that involved manipulation of the principle of life. Spiritualism was imported into Britain along with table-turning. Many table-turners explored the phenomena of "spirit-rapping," in which the spirits of the dead spelt out messages by tapping out a cipher on the table. Of course, mesmeric and elec-tric phenomena were marshaled to account for spirit-rapping as well, and so table-turning, which was at first more popular with members of the educated classes than any of its predecessors, brought out the most explicit involvement yet of any electric theory with questions of spirit. In the mid-1850s there is no doubt that many table-turning experimenters were discouraged from mak-ing further experiments. But there were many, too, who refused to accept the notion of ideo-motor action or who thought it did not apply to their experi-ences, like the Reverend N. S. Godfrey of chapter 10, who stood by his apoc-alyptic theories. Carlo Matteuchi's claims about the muscular production of electricity, and his (and others') experiments showing that muscular power could generate a slight electric current, kept debate running as well. In 1854 the lecturer J. O. N. Rutter published a pamphlet laying out an argument us-ing Matteuchi's work, among other things, to defend electrobiology, table-turning, and other satellite practices of mesmerism from Faraday's dismissal (see fig. 71).

A succinct postscript on the skirmish between Faraday and the table-turners came from the young James Clerk Maxwell, who, at work on his own reflections on mechanical movement and elusive physical powers, had fol-lowed the incident closely. Faraday had proved that the tables had moved by muscular action, he told a correspondent, and this had been done without im-pugning the honesty of the experimenters. But the result was not the end of debate but the opening of a Pandora's box: "letters are being written to Faraday boastfully demanding explanations of this, that, and the other thing, as if Faraday had made a proclamation of Omniscience. Such is the fate of men who make real experiments in the popular occult sciences,—a fate very easy to be borne in silence and confidence by those who do not depend on popular

FIGURE 71 This experimental subject clenches her fists around an underwater wire, producing a slight electric current that registers on the instrument. The experiment was used as evidence that muscular effort could produce movement electrically, rather than through mechanical force. Rutter, *Human Electricity*.

opinion, or learned opinion either, but on the observation of Facts in rational combination." [31] Instead of ending the table-turning controversy and consolidating the public influence of scientific specialists, Faraday had intensified his public's self-confidence. In fact, table-turning had become more an experiment in public judgment than a study of physical and vital influences. The results of the experiment were to reveal "what the state of the public mind is with respect to the *principles* of natural science." [32] "Our anti-scientific men," Maxwell concluded, "triumph over Faraday."

Mental Education

One curious feature of these debates is their timing. Why did Faraday not confront the mesmerists in 1838, when he saw his first mesmeric trial and when researchers were linking mesmerism to his researches on the gymnotus, or in 1845, when the polarization of light was linked to Reichenbach's sensitives, or in 1851, when "electrobiologists" described their electric circuits? One factor that gave a sense of urgency to the issue of the public's powers of scientific judgment was a more general debate about the reform of education that was taking place at the same time. Beginning in the 1850s, there were several rounds of debate about educational reform and several government-sponsored investigations, culminating in the 1870s with the funding of major new provisions for laboratory science in the schools and universities. The two sets of controversies—education and the status of the mesmeric sciences—fueled one another in a circular fashion.

During the first half of the nineteenth century there was a growing debate over the structure of university teaching and research. Reformers objected to the fact that university teaching posts were a stopping point for orthodox Anglican parsons in the interim between ordination and a provincial living. They wished to see permanent posts for scholars within the university. For many, this aim was not an end in itself; it was part of a campaign to make the liberal arts curriculum of classics give way to a more career-oriented program, which many felt could not be accomplished without the provision of an adequate domain for scholarly work in the form of a secure position and a good salary. The debate culminated in the appointment, in 1850, of a royal commission to evaluate the university teaching system, itself the first of four reviews that took place over the next several decades.[33]

The Royal Institution lectures of 1854 were a major contributor to these debates during the 1850s. They took place in the wake of the report of the first commission on university education in 1852, and in the year the second study began. They were also an explicit response to the table-turners. Faraday's invitations to speakers for the series bemoaned the state of public judgment as revealed by the apparent plausibility of table-turning, and his letter to the *Times* ended with a disappointed verdict on the "condition of the public mind." People did not realize that they were not "learned enough" to pass judgment on such matters, and the problem lay in their own schooling: "the system of education which could leave the mental condition of the public body in the state in which this subject has found it, must have been greatly deficient in some very important principle."

Faraday personally organized the series of lectures on "mental education" at the Royal Institution in early 1854. The speakers were Faraday himself, Charles Daubeny on chemistry, James Paget on physiology, W. B. Hodgson on economics, John Tyndall on physics, and William Whewell on the history of science.[34] Daubeny, Tyndall, and Hodgson used the platform to argue for the salutary effects of their respective sciences on the mental powers of ordinary citizens; so did Paget, though he also hoped to increase the numbers of practicing physiologists and to enhance the status and rigor of the field. But the convener of the lectures—Faraday—and the first speaker—the conservative savant William Whewell—included more specific remarks about the sorry state of public judgment, evidenced by the status of mesmerism and table turning. Indeed, this problem was a major incentive to participate: Faraday's invitation to Whewell gave as a sign of the event's importance the "social phenomena" of table turning (i.e., public credulity), proof that for those "who esteem themselves amongst the fully educated there is still an education of the mind required."[35]

In the first lecture, Whewell argued that the measure of a science was whether it could raise man "above himself," that is, above the "rudeness, dimness, confusion, laxity, insecurity," and other vices that are the natural conclusion of undisciplined thought.[36] In the inductive accumulation of scientific truths toward generalizations, the great challenge was to maintain control of scientific language. Scientific words had a "fixed and definite" meaning, and should always be used according to the sense "conveyed" by the discoveries that generated them. They must remain the property of the scientific elite, and not fall into the hands of those rude, dim, confused, lax, and insecure amateurs who could pervert their true meaning by using them in an "unlawful" manner.

Whewell was alarmed that people pursuing nonscientific "fancies" thought it possible to use these privileged terms in any way they pleased. The researches and practices associated with mesmerism formed his prime area of complaint: "*Magnetism* and *Electricity* [are in particular appropriated] and applied in cases in which we know that the sciences from which the names are conveyed have not the smallest application. Is Animal Magnetism anything? Let those answer who think they can, but *we* know that it is not *Magnetism*. When I say we, I mean those who are in the habit of seeing in this place the remarkable—exhibitions of what magnetism is, with which we have long been familiar." Whewell's "we" was his small elite group of associates. The meaning of "magnetism" and "electricity" was safe among them. But how could they create a public culture in which nonscientists would respect the language of science they now misused so frivolously?

Whewell's analogy between science and law provides a possible answer. The public should become more "cultured," since only a "cultured" mind could properly appreciate scientific terms. The liberal arts curriculum Whewell considered indispensable to both law and science would be the means of such enculturation. The educated public would be awakened to their proper attitude to scientific theory, and would in consequence defer its adjudication to the experts.

Faraday made more specific prescriptions for how the "condition of the public mind" might be improved. His own lecture, "On Mental Education," suggested that the answer lay less in a classical liberal arts education than in a rigorous self-education and voluntary self-restraint. Faraday introduced his talk by asserting that the public most lacked a good sense of "discipline" or judgment. And they were not even aware of this deficiency. This "unconsciousness" with respect to mental training led them into misjudgments that could only be avoided through the establishment of mental "government."

Faraday had begun his discussion by warning that questions of the "spirit," or of man's "future," were beyond what man could explore through science. And an ability to recognize and respect such boundaries was one sign that an educated person had acute powers of judgment. Another important quality of the educated man was, of course, deference to proper authority. A good scientist should always justify new theories by placing them in relation to older ones; likewise, the general public should defer to the judgment of experts like Faraday himself. Table-turning was symptomatic of an advanced state of chaos in the relations between science and its public, a sign of which "the many who watch over the interests of the community" should take note.

The remedy was to teach people to discipline their own judgment. It was unhealthy for the British public to "occupy itself" with questions about the physical world and to judge "them as common things." Physical phenomena were not accessible to untutored common sense. They were special and could only be explained by specialist inquiry. One of the first steps Faraday recommended in addressing this problem was to encourage in members of the public a sense of their own ignorance in the face of experts' knowledge. Such humble self-consciousness would leave them *"open to correction upon good grounds in all things."*

The minds of the public and the study of science should both be *"under government."* Scientific results must not be released until the well-disciplined judgment "has been exercised upon it." Table-turners were an example of the unhealthy relations of "two classes" of experimenters, namely "those who decline to educate their judgments in regard to the matters which they decide, and those who, by self-education, have endeavoured to improve themselves; and upon the remarkable and somewhat unreasonable manner in which the latter are called upon, and occasionally taunted, by the former." [37] Faraday himself was a self-made man. He learned chemistry by attending Humphry Davy's lectures at the Royal Institution, and earned Davy's patronage by presenting to him sets of meticulously transcribed lecture notes. Faraday had risen in the scientific world by carefully mastering experts' knowledge and deferring to their authority. He was therefore a perfect example of the workings of that lubricant of Victorian social mobility that was more celebrated in the 1850s than in his struggling early years: the notion of "self-help." His own life was an example of how he wished the public to behave—to cultivate in themselves a clear sense of humility and deference to established authority—and the directive role of scientific experts in providing the educated classes with guidance about how they could become self-educated.

Faraday's experimental work also set the tone for part of this policy. He always emphasized that one must never tamper with the "principle of life." Living phenomena could be studied after they had begun to develop, but one must not intervene in the more fundamental vital principle itself. In his researches on the electric fish, he stated that, while one must steer clear of such interventions, vital phenomena produced by the principle of life were fair game. A researcher having "more knowledge than the fish" could piece together the relationships of the vital and physical forces involved in the gymnotus's production of electricity.[38] The foundation of Faraday's own conception of "self-help" was that the love of knowledge, like the "principle of life" itself, must not be "determined." Only after the love of knowledge had given rise to the effort to educate oneself could the student be helped; and indeed, at this stage guidance was essential. Just as those scientists who had "in that point of view more knowledge than the fish" could guide the electric fish's production of electricity, they could ensure that those seeking to become self-educated be properly governed by the elite protectors of the growth of knowledge.

In flagrant violation of Faraday's admonitions, new schools of mesmeric fish soon produced new variations of electric, "odylic," and magnetic forces. Once the turning tables began to "rap," spiritualist researchers found it possible to interrogate the inhabitants of the spiritual world, and after two decades of spiritualist researches, the Society for Psychical Research was founded.[39] If these psychic successes were not enough, Faraday himself was to take back his opposition some decades later. Years after his death, a spiritualist medium transcribed a message dictated by his spirit. His prohibitions against studying the principle of life were reversed.[40]

William Benjamin Carpenter would not have been surprised at Faraday's failure to instill "mental discipline" merely by announcing to mesmerists and mediums that they were not qualified to make the claims they were making. He taught that it was not sufficient to contradict believers in mesmerism (and other dubious sciences). Instead, would-be intellectual authorities needed to educate themselves as to the nature of various "consensual" effects (such as mesmerism and credulity). Second, they should design programs to help people to identify proper authorities.

One characteristic of "consensual" and "mesmeric" phenomena was that they not only explained how individuals interacted or might interact, but also supplied tools that individuals like Carpenter could use to intervene in real situations in order to establish their authority in a specific case. On a larger scale, these interventions had a resonance with the practices they sought to eradicate.

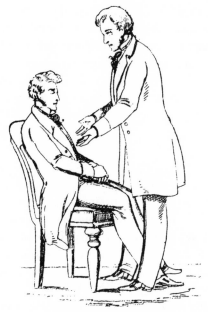

DEMESMERIZING.

FIGURE 72 Demesmerizing. The mesmerist's hands are slowly raised to draw the influence out of the subject. Davey, *Illustrated Practical Mesmerist.*

Mesmeric manuals devoted a great deal of attention to the process of de-mesmerizing (fig. 72). One typical piece of advice was that one must first "apprise" the subject of one's intentions, and "advise him to participate in them; one-half of the business will be done as soon as he will have a wish to awaken." Passes were then made in the reverse direction of the ones that had created the trance in the first place. Handkerchiefs were shaken in front of the individual's face. But often the subject would not realize that she was mesmerized, and would resist this necessary sobering process. Arguing with the subject was no good, for arguments would only be interpreted within the subject's existing delusional state. Indeed, events could easily degenerate into "a quarrel, and sometimes a regular combat." [41] It was necessary, even if force was required, to make the necessary psychological interventions which, through acting directly on the subject's mind, would restore her to an ordinary mental state.

Carpenter, Faraday, and other self-appointed custodians of science all faced the same challenges. Carpenter's psychology was used for decades in controversies over mesmerism and spiritualism. Although their work succeeded in disillusioning some people with these sciences, it was far from the panacea that they might have hoped for. When Carpenter used his project to intervene in séances, he saw himself as correcting a situation that was subversive of healthy political order, and doing so without the cooperation of the individuals who would most benefit from his intervention. The reform of education and the institutionalization of various forms of pedagogical discipline were used by one influential group of scientific naturalists in an attempt to reverse a process of mental weakness and unhealthy "consensus" that had prevailed in the early nineteenth century: as a sort of "demesmerism," to use Victorian terminology, of society.

A New Breed of Scientist

The mid-Victorian period saw a number of important changes in the authoritative status of the sciences and medicine. Medicine became increasingly (though by no means definitively) regulated, partly in consequence of the Medical Registration Act of 1857 and reforms in university education. These reforms affected science as well, producing a professional class of scientists much more clearly separated from a newly "lay" public than their predecessors. What would become recognizable as emergent modern science, an activity broken up into clearly demarcated disciplines (such as physics, chemistry, and biology) arguably did not exist before there was a means of training individuals to ask similar questions and pursue similar lines of investigation in answering them. The claims made by spiritualists and psychic researchers over the next few decades built on the mesmeric claims of the 1840s and 1850s, but they were also transformed by the energy physics and laboratory culture of the later century. And while the psychological dismissals for each new phenomenon (by individuals like Carpenter) were fairly consistent, there was one important change in the context in which the explanation was made: an increasingly professionalized and demarcated state of science.

One shift that this story will illuminate is the change from a culture of public science to one of increasingly professionalized laboratory science. In the first half of the century, the sites of scientific work were the field museum, the lecture hall, the hospital, and the theater. Everyone, including natural philosophers, learned about nature by attending shows and lectures and by venturing into nature to experience it directly.[42] Increasingly, in the second half of the century, science was dominated by experimentalist disciplines based in universities—the physiological laboratory of Michael Foster, for instance, and the Cavendish Laboratory, both in Cambridge University.[43] Educational reforms (such as the revised natural science tripos at Cambridge) were geared toward disciplining students to think and ask questions in a particular way, and to learn particular skills in the sites where they would use them in future.[44] Science was becoming a profession one learned on the job, and workplaces of science now became the university laboratory and the field station. Historians of science are aware of this shift and of the mechanics of how it came about (how laboratories were built, for instance) and of the differences in the making of knowledge between them. However, we have only the beginnings of an appreciation of the motivations of those individuals whose careers and aspirations spanned this shift. Such individuals—Faraday, Whewell, and Carpenter among them—were closely involved in setting up the educational structures that made later Victorian science a pedagogically disciplined activity. Their responses to mesmerism and its allied practices reveal some of the central motivations for the construction of disciplined science in the mid-Victorian period. The walls of the laboratory were built to keep out certain problematic and troublesome natural phenomena.

One consequence was that it became easier to claim that only people whose training gave them expertise about very specific and delineated patches of nature could speak about issues that belonged to their territory. This had two broad implications that need to be considered carefully in relation to sciences of mind and influence. One was that accepting the power of science in its increasingly "disciplined" form undermined an earlier confidence in nature's accessibility to intelligent inquiry. The other was that phenomena that did not fit into the emergent scientific disciplines were often entirely abandoned as areas of scientific inquiry.

Ironically, the same psychology that helped to redefine the scientist was catalyzed by the mesmeric debates. Between the early decades of the century and the later ones, there was a marked shift in how leading scientific figures defined the necessary capabilities for doing scientific work. In the earlier period there was a broad consensus that scientific creativity was an innate gift. Natural philosophers were born, not made. William Whewell maintained that it was not possible to *teach* the mind to "hit upon a right supposition." [45] The cognitive powers that produced new ideas and new avenues of thinking were the lucky gift of those individuals who had been born with them. But in the 1850s and 1860s the liberal scientific educators who helped to construct a professional role for scientists armed themselves with a very different notion of the psychology of scientific work. According to them scientific thinking was just a disciplined form of common sense; and conversely, scientific thinking was a role model for good thinking. This meant that everyone could benefit from a scientific education, because science could discipline the mind. All, in principle, could make themselves useful in scientific research, if they would only subject their minds to proper training and discipline.

Mental reflexes provided a physiological foundation for this new notion of scientific work. In the most general sense, Carpenter had argued that reflexes were the key to rational self-determination and proper educational policy.

The ill-educated were like riders asleep on their horses, or engine drivers collapsed at the controls. They stumbled through life "played upon" by external stimuli and their own inner cravings, instead of using a strong will and healthy judgment to control their destiny. Carpenter claimed that mesmeric advocates and subjects had fallen into a state in which their judgment and will were suspended, and in which their minds operated according to the mechanism of mental reflexes. Thus a "consensual" state would be one in which one's higher mental powers were suspended, and incoming suggestions were reflected consensually in outgoing expressions of belief. Advocates of mesmerism, and individuals who tried their hand at table-turning, *believed* they had the power of free choice and were exercising it informedly, but in fact the circumstances and assumptions in which they evaluated mesmerism made it impossible for them to exercise their critical faculties properly, leaving them vulnerable to the charismatic influence of the science and its quack practitioners.

There was a Lamarckian evolutionary component to consensual psychology, too, because Carpenter asserted the hereditary character of acquired psychic traits. The implication was that people whose minds were undisciplined were a danger not only to the present polity, but also to Britain's future. According to Carpenter's view of popular education and mental evolution, mesmerism was made to look like the *reverse* of mental progress. Mesmerism stripped the public of its ability to determine its own mental fate, and made it more difficult for it to be guided by "legitimate" scientific educators. Moreover, mesmerized subjects were placed in a more primitive mental state, which Carpenter felt was analogous to that of animals or to the more "primitive" tribes of man.[46] Within Carpenter's system, mesmerism became an *archeology* of the mind. This archeology was also, in some sense, embodied in the spectrum of humanity, because individuals who were more susceptible to mesmerism represented an older mental state.

Writers on mental physiology like Thomas Henry Huxley, Henry Maudsley, Herbert Spencer, and Alexander Bain shared an emphasis on reflexes as the foundation of human action: they all taught that the building of one's mental reflex apparatus was the key to proper mental functioning. One part of this notion of mental discipline as the development of certain mental reflexes was a new definition, in physiological terms, of common sense. Common sense was the automatic sense of what was right and sensible, and what was automatic about this was the action of one's reflexes—in fact, common sense was a form of "consensus" in the physiological sense, because information was impinging on the sensory nerves, and an automatic judgment was coming out. This made "scientific" thinking into something that anyone might do. For instance, Huxley taught that science improved the finer feelings by making people more alert and observant, by imposing a mental discipline: "the training an strengthening of common sense." Indeed science is "nothing but trained and organised common sense, differing from the latter only as a veteran may differ from a raw recruit." [47] Scientific thought processes were merely a more disciplined, specialized form of ordinary thinking.

This new emphasis on the powers of a disciplined mind democratized science. Everyone could partake in some way because everyone could build a disciplined common sense within themselves. One's constantly developing structures of automatic thinking could be taught to make, automatically, the kinds of distinctions that had eluded the table-turners. Once the strictures of scientific inference and evidence were internalized by proper education, the educated could not be played upon by passing crazes because their internal mechanism would react with discomfort to pseudoscientific fads.

This notion of mental functioning became very widespread. Carpenter gave hundreds of lectures, at venues ranging from the Royal Institution to Sunday lectures to workingmen's associations in the industrial north; his textbooks sold in the five figures during the middle decades of the century. Other influential figures, those mental physiologists mentioned above, adopted similar stances and, to varying extents, publicized them among a broad middle-class readership.

In the late 1860s and 1870s a number of government-sponsored investigations and reports into the state of British science dramatically transformed science teaching. The Devonshire Commission on Scientific Instruction took evidence from leading scientific figures as to how scientific provision should be made, and what effect it should have on students in schools and universities. One recurrent theme of their testimony was the notion that scientific training could promote a kind of mental culture or discipline.[48] No one set out explicitly what the nature of this state was, but it is likely that it was something akin to the notion of mental discipline that Carpenter and his physiological associates described. Carpenter himself was one of the experts who gave testimony. One of the worst aspects of the present system was that it ignored "that exercise of the mind which science alone gives." A good teacher did more to structure the mind than to fill it with particular pieces of information: "A good teacher . . . will connect the abstract ideas with the objective realities." He said that he knew "from Heads of Colleges, whose own teaching was classical, that they had observed a great improvement in the mental activity of many of their pupils after these pupils had applied themselves to the study of chemistry." [49] When Carpenter told the Devonshire commissioners that scientific education was a mental discipline, he had a very specific set of mental processes in mind, namely the reflex action and the phenomena of "consensus." In short, the physiological notion of "consensus" contributed to definitions of scientific thinking that were fundamental to the creation of the professional scientist;

the history of consensus was part of the same process that constructed a scientific community that had been *designed* to be "consensual." The epistemological history of agreement was linked to creation of communities that were able to agree in new ways on what kinds of questions one ought to ask and what practical means there were of answering them.

The Decline of Mesmerism

In a series of articles on mesmeric practices published in 1867, Carpenter used the notion of mental reflexes to dismiss them all. Common sense and ordinary, or even unusually strong, intelligence provided insufficient tools to study psychic phenomena or nature more generally. Training in a particular field was required, lest one come under the irrational influence of a "prepossession" in mind which would prejudice one's study of nature and make it impossible fairly to judge the facts: "Nothing is more common than to hear it asserted that these are subjects which any person of ordinary intelligence can investigate for himself. But the Physicist or the Chemist would most assuredly demur to any such assumption in regard to chemical or physical inquiry; the Physiologist and Geologist would make the same protest against the judgment of unskilled persons in physiology and geology." [50] Carpenter claimed that psychic researchers who had distinguished themselves as natural scientists had strayed from their areas of expertise (the physical world) into a very different one (physiology). Obvious examples were William Crookes and Oliver Lodge, both of whom treated the study of the spirit world as a branch of physics. They were insufficiently skilled and discriminating in this unfamiliar area of study to be able to evaluate the phenomena correctly.

But Carpenter was no more successful in his attacks on spiritualism in the 1860s and 1870s than he had been in his attacks on table-turning and the Reichenbach phenomena in the 1850s. He convinced some people, certainly, that the phenomena that were claimed to be the result of physical force were forms of self-delusion, but the Society for Psychical Research had a thriving membership throughout the late nineteenth century and into the twentieth. This is not to say that some of his claims regarding the fences being drawn round the different territories of science had no force or validity. What they reflected was not a landscape in which the questions raised by mesmerism, spiritualism, and psychic research found proper explanations (though very different ones from those offered by the practitioners of those sciences). Rather, it was one in which certain questions could no longer be asked, and where certain lines of inquiry could no longer be pursued.

In 1859 Robert Chambers published an irate pamphlet on the status of testimony in relation to the natural world.[51] He complained that science was increasingly dominated by the model of physics, in which phenomena that could not be tested by the instruments of the modern laboratory sciences were no longer admissible as areas of scientific investigation in the manner that, he claimed, they had been in the past. The chief category of phenomena was that which was mainly accessible through introspection and personal testimony. The emerging scientific disciplines left no place for testimony on new scientific truths, unless it was subservient to laboratory apparatus or specimens of new species. Chambers's complaints were confirmed by Carpenter, who argued that testimony of the sense was not to be admitted as scientific evidence when it concerned dramatic new phenomena that were not already accepted as features of the natural world. Testimony that something had occurred that was known to occur was acceptable; testimony to new startling truths was not admissible on its own.

Thus the new divisions between the sciences left no space for the lines of experiment and inquiry that mesmerism involved. Natural philosophy of mind had centrally involved the processes of introspection and the making public of the evidence of one's inner thoughts. Physiology and physics, the disciplines most relevant to its areas of inquiry, were now laboratory sciences far less connected to each other than their predecessors had been earlier in the century, and designed to exclude the very phenomena that had been central to the investigation of mesmerism and its satellite practices.

As Carpenter's frustration indicates, it was no good merely arguing with a general public mesmerized by philosophies like mesmerism. These kinds of techniques might, at best, resolve individual debates. What was needed was a means of changing the structure of the mind such that it would be led by proper authority, yet become immune to the temptations of philosophical quacks. And what this entailed was no less than a shift in the structure of society. One of the intriguing developments that began to take place in the second half of the century, when a developing intellectual elite was preoccupied with finding secure means of coming to valid forms of consensus in public debate, was a change in the concept and terminology of consensus itself. The resolution that embattled members of the scientific elite—and other cultural, social, and political leaders—anticipated for their dilemmas would lie in nothing less than a redefinition of agreement.

CHAPTER TWELVE

The Social Body

and the Invention of Consensus

THE HISTORY OF MESMERISM in Victorian Britain is a history of discord. People failed to come to terms with each other regarding the nature of evidence and authority, and those who considered themselves indisputable experts found their views confidently disputed. Victorian intellectual life, viewed through a mesmeric lens, was as disunited and quarrelsome as it was enthralled by the powers of matter and mind. But in a very different sense, mesmerism and similar cultural phenomena are part of a history of agreement. They displayed a cord that bound people together: an influence that coordinated their thoughts or actions, or a sympathetic current that united a population. The ties that bind have always been mysterious, but these practices offered a means of studying them. Remarkably, this remained true even if one thought the practices themselves illegitimate or dangerous. In retrospect, mesmerism and associated cultural phenomena offer a history, not of how people reached consensus in controversial matters, but of how they defined agreement itself.

One might say that mesmerism provided the solution to itself. In the 1830s and 1840s it posed enormous and varied questions about the nature of authority, influence, and communication. Attempts to resolve its nature actually intensified existing ambiguities, because experimenters brought with them conflicting assumptions about authority and evidence that became explicit as an experiment proceeded, and that became the occasion for dispute on issues that did not tend to be discussed openly. Mesmerism's very flexibility, which made it accessible to so many different groups throughout Victorian culture, also made it extremely difficult to reach a consensus about its nature at a time when people felt fundamentally at odds. And mesmerism's challenges did not go away because people stopped practicing it. In fact, the subscription list to the LMI actually lengthened in the 1850s and 1860s,[1] and encyclopedias and domestic medicine manuals began routinely to acknowledge the reality of the mesmeric state throughout the second half of the century. Mesmerism became increasingly widespread as a medical therapy and more acknowledged as a real phenomenon. But at the same time, it became less of a catalyst or spur to fights about the nature of authority and evidence. What had changed was its political and intellectual status.

One reason for the change was the emergence of a very popular physiology of mental reflexes that itself was catalyzed by mesmerism. The notion of a mental reflex may seem so fundamental that it is hard to imagine it as a reaction to a specific practice such as mesmerism. But this seems to have been the case. Before 1851 there was only a very restrictive notion of how reflexes could act in the brain, and even that was controversial because of its materialist associations. It was only in 1851 and 1852, in response to electrobiology and table-turning, that claims were made (first by William Benjamin Carpenter, and then by many others) that *thinking* could be a reflex act. There were a number of reasons for this: the mesmeric practices of these years provided the most striking phenomena yet of human automatism and "consensual" phenomena, in the physiological sense described in chapter 11: involuntary actions provoked from without. But mesmerism also provided the opportunity for representing reflexes as a positive science of mind, by providing it with a foil. Presented as an alternative to mesmerism, reflexes became a contrast to the materialist and subversive scientific challenges that mesmerism represented, and to the unhealthy social and political incorporation associated with it.

When reflexes in the processes of thought were positioned in this manner, they could become a means of salvaging the will and supporting the possibility that experts could lay down the law on matters of psychological evidence. The developing science of reflexes was also put to work in explaining social cohesion on a larger scale. It was part of a much more general set of changes in how Victorians understood human relations, as an increasingly compartmentalized society, equipped with an energetic scientific community, developed a number of very systematic descriptions of the relationship of the individual to the aggregate social body. The mass was no longer undifferentiated (and necessarily unthinking or dangerous), but a coordinated body that could be brought under good management. The various ways in which one portrayed this strange conglomerate of individual, group, and mass involved an implicit or explicit psychology justifying how an individual could become a "consensual" part of the whole.

I have used the notion of "consensual" action only to refer to Victorian physiology's understanding of a reflex act, but it had a much wider currency, even though no one yet used "consensus" in English in its modern sense. The English usage began only in the Victorian period, and did not become widespread until the end of the century. In the intervening decades "consensus" was one of the many terms that recurred in descriptions of collective phenomena. It could refer to a number of very different forms of "agreement": the coming together of different elements into one system, or, in the work of physiologists like Carpenter and his circle, the coordination of different parts of a living thing by stimulus or sensation. The Victorian citations in the entry for "consensus" in the *Oxford English Dictionary* are diverse. One of the earliest for the nineteenth century is the (1838) English edition of a physiological work of the influential German physiologist Johannes Müller, who used it to describe the coordinated action of different bodily parts. Around the same time, John Stuart Mill's *Logic* (1843) used "consensus" to refer to the coordinated thinking of large groups of individuals. A few years later, George Cornewall Lewis used it to refer to the agreement of experts in his *Essay on the Influence of Authority* (1849). In the 1850s an attack on Comte's positivism declared that he "resolves to see only a vast consensus of forces" in a godless universe. And in the 1860s the Whig historian Goldwyn Smith used the term to evoke the "general connexion between the different parts of a nation's civilisation."[2]

Why should "consensus" have had these resonances, and how did it come to have the stable meaning it attained by the end of the century? One part of the answer lies in the physiology of influence and the will, which increasingly focused on collective action. "Consensus" was an old term in physiology referring to the coordination of different bodily parts by sympathy. In the 1830s the reflex arc supplanted "sympathy" with a network of nerves and nervous influences (akin to electricity) as the causes of "consensual" phenomena (coughing and blinking were standard examples). During the 1840s physiologists moved reflexes up the spinal cord and into the brain and, in the 1850s, during mesmeric controversies, applied them to ideas and social action. The will of the "biological" subject was suspended, reducing him to a reflex system. The table-turners were in a state of "reverie" that allowed their desire for the table to spin to be expressed in the push they unconsciously gave it.

The notion of mental reflexes had far-reaching implications. After providing ammunition to elite scientists during the "mental education" debates of the mid-1850s, it contributed to a sweeping change in the understanding of mental and social action. One consequence was the creation of the professional scientist, as we saw in chapter 11. But "consensual" social and psychological phenomena pervaded mid-Victorian culture. In this final chapter I would like to follow mesmerism and mental physiology into some of the cultural, social, and intellectual developments to which they were most important. These were either midcentury innovations in which groups of people were "stimulated" (to use Victorian physiologists' terminology) or events that involved "cultural consumption" (to use a term current in cultural history). Three in which mesmerism and the physiology of sensation played a particularly explicit role were the invention of the baton conductor and the rise of the public concert, the representation of reading in the new genre of sensation fiction, and the liberal political writings that sought to develop a new understanding of the constitution in an emerging age of mass democracy.

The Conductor and the Unifying Power of the Eye

The mesmerist and the orchestral conductor looked like refracted images of one another in the middle decades of the nineteenth century, partly as a result of a shared vocabulary of influence. When Victorians spoke of musical or mental power, they often retooled an ancient analogy between the organization of the mind and the design of a musical instrument. One of the most influential physiological works of this period portrayed the major nerves of the body lining up in sequence in the brain, played upon by the will in the same way as a player struck the keys of a piano.[3] Mesmerists commonly portrayed the phrenological organs as a keyboard: mesmerizing a particular "key" would make the brain sound the appropriate psychological "note" (recall *Punch*'s sketch of Elliotson "playing" a plebeian woman [fig. 16]).[4] Equivalent analogies were put to use in explaining what the conductor did to the orchestra, as when, in 1845, the celebrated pianist Ignaz Moscheles asked the London Philharmonic to feel as if they had become "the fingers of an admirably trained pianoforte player's hand." He, of course, would be "the hand which sets these fingers in motion, and imparts life to them."[5]

The role of the baton conductor was established by the midcentury, but it had been created decades earlier. Before 1800 a pair of individuals managed the players in what was known as the "double-direction system." The "conductor" (often the composer) sat in the back at the piano; the "leader" at the front was either a timekeeper (clapping his hands or tapping the beat with a roll of music), or the first violinist, setting an example by his own performance. The time was kept by ear—by following the piano, the violin, the roll of music, the clapping hands. In the early nineteenth century, however, the orchestra grew dramatically larger, in response to demands for new kinds of civic celebration by the growing populations of the major European cities. Up to three times as many players were needed for Berlioz as had been for Mozart, and audiences grew at an even faster pace. Music was becoming a business in the nineteenth century, and eventually a phenomenon of "mass culture." [6] Histories of the orchestra teach that as it grew, this system of divided management became unworkable. Orchestras increasingly opted for a single leader whose guidance made sight predominant over sound in unifying the players. The eye, "so much quicker than the ear," could be "attracted" by the *baton*, thereby allowing players to be "more strictly regulated." [7]

The baton conductor was soon established on the Continent, but in Britain his most fundamental feature—the powerful ability to unite and direct a group—made him controversial. In 1820 the celebrated composer Louis Spohr brought conducting to London when he alarmed the governors of the London Philharmonic by planting himself in front of the orchestra and whipping out his baton. But, according to his own account, after some initial jitters the players paid "more than usual attention" to their conductor and showed an unprecedented "spirit and correctness." The newly unified body, inspired by its potential for harmoniously coordinated action, ignored the reluctance of its official directors, "expressed aloud its collective assent to the new mode of conducting," and promptly "over-ruled all further opposition." [8] This was a subversive event. Spohr assembled the players into a collectivity and then provoked an insurrection. The resemblance that he and future conductors bore to problematic figures such as the Napoleonic demagogue and the mesmerist suggests one reason for a feature of conducting history that has long puzzled historians of music, namely, that Britain was slow to accept such an obviously useful technique. The London Philharmonic and other British orchestras clung to the double-direction system for decades. [9]

From the 1820s onward, the succession of visiting charismatic foreigners who amazed audiences with the power of their waving hands was as fascinating and almost as controversial as that of their fellow travelers, the Continental mesmerists. They drew similar descriptions. One could be dismissed as a "tricksy professor of charlatanerie" [10] or resented as a potent predator— as when the twenty-year-old Felix Mendelssohn visited London in 1829, "mounted the orchestra and pulled out my white stick." Although the press confirmed the powerful "*discipline*" of that stick, leading violinists resented how it "completely usurped" their "authority." [11] An Englishman visiting Berlin the following year confirmed that the new system was superior to the old,

FIGURE 73 Louis-Antoine Jullien conducting at Drury Lane, c. 1850. Author's collection.

but despite his personal approval of "despotism in musical governments," he feared "that the British constitution will not admit such a mode of rule." [12]

The governors of British orchestras did regard the baton as a blow to their constitution, but after three contentious decades, it was finally established around 1850. The decisive moment is traditionally said to be 1846, when Michael Costa refused to join the London Philharmonic without "sole and undivided control," [13] but the conductor who established the role in the public eye during the 1840s was a popular showman, Louis-Antoine Jullien (fig. 73). He became particularly known for vast performances in the Promenades and Covent Garden, assembling huge audiences using an apparently mesmeric power. *Musical World* said that this "soul of the great poly-body" (whose prescient parents had loaded him with forty-one names) [14] was a "wizard"; his "necromatic baton" was elsewhere said to contain a "mysterious virtue," like mesmerism's "secret influence." [15] His shows had other elements in common with mesmeric spectacle; for instance, they often included sideshows of "tableaux vivans." [16] Reviewers noted elements of "quackery" in his performance, but the generous ones forgave this as a necessary aid to uniting many diverse individuals into one satisfied audience.[17] *Punch* evoked a similar image when it described Jullien's musical "shop" crammed with a collective "JOHN BULL." [18] As Jullien's reputation soared, his dress, posture, and gestures were copied by other public performers: mesmerists, lecturers, and entertainers dressed "à la jullien" and commissioned advertising broadsheets depicting them in his characteristic poses (e.g., fig. 74).[19] From midcentury, populist performances from music to science were beginning to adopt common conventions that conveyed charismatic unification and management.

In the 1840s and 1850s the scenes that drew some of the most vivid and self-conscious descriptions of how leaders could unite a population were concerts by celebrity composer/conductors. While Felix Mendelssohn was the most beloved in Britain, Hector Berlioz and Richard Wagner—a *real* demagogue in 1848—drew the most striking descriptions of powerful leadership.[20] Neither was very proficient on wood, wind, or keyboard, but each was a master on the collective human instruments he brought into being with his baton.[21] Each had republican and revolutionary associations, albeit passing ones, and these were represented in 1850s London as adding spice to their British careers[22]— a portrayal that would have been impossible in the previous decade. Both therefore had a number of credentials associated with mesmerism, and in fact an 1864 caricature represented their rivalry as a magnetic duel (Wagner was the more powerful mesmerist in this case; see fig. 75). The music critic Francis Hueffer was struck by the "immediate *rapport* established between Wagner and his orchestra as soon as he raises his baton." Each individual player was "equally under the influence of a personal fascination, which seems to have much in common with the effects of animal magnetism. Every eye is turned towards the master; and it appears as if the musicians derive the notes they play, not from the books on their desks, but from Wagner's glances and movement." [23] From the conductor radiated an influence that coordinated and transformed a group of individuals into a performing body.

This new way of describing an assembled collectivity could be seen in representations of orchestra and audience alike. The orchestra was a living aggregate of equivalent individuals influenced in the same powerful way by a unifying figure. The notion that Wagner was pouring the music from his body into theirs was a powerful way of evoking the emerging sense that the conductor realized the work of music (from its abstracted potential in the score), by uniting the orchestra into one functioning entity. Changes in audience behavior displayed a similar sensibility, though to a far lesser extent. From the perspective

Lecture Hall, Carter Street,
WALWORTH.

For One Night Only !
MONDAY EVENING, APRIL 1st, 1850.

THE WIZARD OF WIZARDS
GREAT MODERN MAGICIAN,
PROFESSOR OF EXPERIMENTAL PHILOSOPHY,
VENTRILOQUIST and IMPROVISATORE,

Mr. JACOBS,

Respectfully announces his performances as above. The very great success that has invariably attended him is a sufficient proof of his attractive powers; and, in making his Entertainment known on the present occasion, he has now to introduce some of the most

EXTRAORDINARY EXPERIMENTS

possible to imagine. The peculiar nature of Mr. JACOBS' profession is, that he deceives the public. This he admits in a professional point
of view, and does not mind the mask being withdrawn from his practices by those who have eyes sufficiently quick to detect them; but with all
his deceptive tricks, he never deceives his Friends with his announcement, whenever they honour him with their presence; whatever he promises, he performs. In these wonderful times of discovery, of Literature and Art, it requires no mean talent to be able to

ASTONISH THE WORLD!!

Yet this lot has fallen to the great Ambidextrous Prestidigitator JACOBS. Many may read these assertions and fancy them puff, exaggeration,
and stuff, but let them once place themselves within view of his

INCOMPREHENSIBLE WONDERS!

And they will immediately feel the influence of those extraordinary powers which have caused so much wonderment, talk, and amusement to all
who have been spell-bound by the Cabalistic Experiments exhibited before them. If this has been accomplished in the nineteenth century, what
would have been the surprise of our ancestors, could they only take a peep at this

FIGURE 74 The mysterious Mr. Jacobs (probably a pseudonym), advertising an April
Fool's show (1850), portrayed himself prancing down a catwalk, the center of attention.
Guildhall Library. Corporation of London.

FIGURE 75 Berlioz and Wagner take each other on in a mesmeric battle, score in one hand and baton in the other. Wagner triumphs as the entranced Berlioz's head sinks to his chest. *Revue Trimestrielle* (1864).

of composers and conductors, early-nineteenth-century audiences were shamefully ignorant of how they ought to behave at a concert. They often chatted with each other, or, if they were silent, they did not take in the music in the way that composer, conductor, and orchestra intended them to.[24] They had to be taught how to hear. The model of musical "reception" that conductors wished to realize in their listeners, and that, to some extent, developed over the course of the century, was one of silent, unified attention. As a single group intently focused on the performance, they were able to receive the music in a way that was likened to a physical transmission. A visual portrayal of how music influenced its audience, reminiscent of the description of Wagner's mesmeric creation of notes in the bodies of his performers, is the *Charivari* caricature of 1868 (fig. 76). Here, as Wagner conducts (with a violin bow instead of a baton), the notes fall like rosin dust from its horsehair into the mouths and ears of listeners.

The content of the music that was pouring into these increasingly quiet assemblies was itself infused with mesmeric and mental physiological themes. For instance, Wagner brushed up on animal magnetism to prepare for writing

FIGURE 76 All we see of Wagner in this caricature is his hand, but the shower of notes from his bow suggests that he, personally, has created the music that hails down into his audience. *Charivari* (1868).

a number of his operas. Jenny Lind, one of the best-loved Victorian singers, posed for sketches as Amina in *La Sonnambula*, a role that suggested that her mesmerizing performances were enhanced by a real magnetic trance (see fig. 77);[25] and, in the most enduring musical use of mental physiology, Berlioz adapted the physiology of monomania to the structure of his compositions. In 1830, when he was writing the *Symphonie fantastique*, he gave the name "idée fixe" to a recurrent musical phrase, threaded into the music in a manner that was supposed to sustain and intensify the listener's attention.[26] The idée fixe

FIGURE 77
An entrancing portrait of
Jenny Lind as Amina in the
opera *La Sonnambula*.
Bodleian Library, John
Johnson Collection
(Musicians and opera
singers).

itself became a recurrent theme of musical composition throughout the nineteenth century.

If Wagner's performances were likened to the vital influence of animal
magnetism, Berlioz's bore a greater similarity to electricity. Observers portrayed his influence as a mechanical link that drew players together and coordinated them. This impression could only have been enhanced by an invention that came to be known as "the electric baton." From the late 1840s
onward, Berlioz staged massive performances using such large numbers of
performers that he could not maintain direct eye contact with all of them. In
preparation for the 1855 Paris Exhibition in the Palace of Industrial Products,
when he was called on to perform *L'Impérial*, Berlioz used the relatively new
technologies of the metronome and the electric telegraph to invent a new conducting technique.[27] As his right hand directed those immediately before him,
his left tapped the same rhythm into a master metronome. It was connected by
telegraph wires to a set of subsidiary metronomes, each hooked up to its own

(human) "sous-chef." Berlioz thereby turned his metronome into an extension of himself—into a mechanical conductor—and his sous-chefs into living metronomes and telegraph systems. They received, through their fingers, the signals that passed from Berlioz's mind, down his arms, and through the metronome-telegraph system; they then "conducted" the impulses into the players and through them into the audience.

Berlioz's musical technology would have reminded onlookers of the international telegraphic networks that were being celebrated at this exhibition. The use of human beings in Berlioz's "electric baton" made his instrument similar to other experiments in recent years using groups of living things as collective scientific instruments. The inventor of the Tempest Prognosticator, which made its debut at the English Great Exhibition, suggested that simple animals (in this case leeches) responded to electric changes in the atmosphere.[28] A still more ambitious claim was made in 1850 for the powers of the humble snail. The connections of sympathy, electricity, and animal magnetism acting between their bodies were so intense that if they came near each other they would become permanently locked in a pattern of parallel movement (like the "communion" of mesmerist and subject). This was sustained even over vast distances. One such pair was separated in 1850 to prove the long-distance power of sympathy: one was ensconced in Paris and the other taken to New York. A respected Paris newspaper announced that a message traced out by one snail was echoed by the other. The "snail telegraph" was a success.[29] It was a timely achievement: the first telegraph cable to connect Britain and France had been laid across the Channel earlier that year, and it was not working properly. Now the scientific luminaries and engineers struggling with the problems of international telegraphy could relax. Communication by "galvano-terrestrial-magnetic-animal-adamic force" would make their technology obsolete.

After a number of serious reports, the snails' custodians revealed that they had carried out a hoax. But the idea was clearly plausible to the many reporters and readers who had been taken in, and one reason was the currency of the notion of consensus: the idea that similar and separate entities could be mechanically coordinated. Both the musical and the snail telegraph inspired a number of caricatures with imperial themes, for instance figure 78, in which an empire is maintained by wires draped over the globe (Berlioz stands at the top, with players coordinated at their locations in Africa, Turkey, and elsewhere). The imperial theme is even stronger in a Daumier print (fig. 79) in which a Berlioz-like system of subconductors is poised over a massive crowd of bourgeoisie, who do not realize that their thoughts and movements are being conducted. The assertion, presumably, is that the electorate of the Second

FIGURE 78 Berlioz's electric baton creates a global empire, as telegraph wires connect the Master (the tousled figure holding the baton at the top of the globe) with figures in various costumes elsewhere on the planet. *Charivari* (1855).

Empire is ignorant of the influence of the dictatorship to which they have subjected themselves.

Despite the many associations between mesmeric and conducting systems, there were crucial differences between them that paralleled the representation of unhealthy versus healthy forms of incorporation. In the orchestra, players consented to the leadership of the conductor and were aware of how they were being led. Unlike the absolute mental and bodily ventriloquism that sometimes featured in mesmerism, conducting invited the surrender of only *part* of one's autonomy. It could sustain togetherness without seeming to destroy the individual, as mesmerism often did. When musical performers seemed to grow more expressive as they took inspiration from the baton, this was a sign of the conductor's success—not, as often was the case in mesmerism, of the

FIGURE 79 In Daumier's "Sous-Chefs," the figures in the foreground carry on earnest discussions as if they controlled their own lives, but in reality they are directed by the anonymous sous-chefs towering above them. *Charivari* (1859).

mesmerist's loss of control. Like the models of healthy minds and social interaction suggested in some of the mental physiologies of the period, performers were simultaneously individuals and part of the collective body.

Conducting was an example of a more general phenomenon, the development of ways of representing a central harmonizing influence. They used elements of mesmerism (the idea of a vital connection or electric stimulus between people, and of coordination at a distance, perhaps using the nerves). But these elements were put to work in a very different manner, using an understanding of influence that was less amenable to subversion than in mesmerism (when, for instance, mesmeric subjects could up-end the experiment, and opportunistic charismatic figures could seize control of vulnerable "subjects"). The notion of a harmonious group coordinated by a single, centralized influence was so widespread that it would require a separate study to make a thoroughgoing examination of it. However, we can get a better sense of it by looking at two other examples: the significance attached to conducting encouraged the extension, to nonmusical contexts, of the notion of "conducting" in the sense of charismatic leadership of a coordinated group, and the notion of "harmonious" society as developed in the liberal political philosophies of the 1860s and 1870s.

The Orchestration of Reading

The orchestra was only one of a number of places where conducting took on new associations in the Victorian period—other examples include the train, the omnibus, and the tramcar. What such conductors shared was a role in managing groups of people during a process of transmission—physical, from one place to another, or musical, as the potential encoded in a score was realized in performance and delivered to the ears of a listening audience. This kind of custodial activity could also be seen in new efforts to manage an ever-growing population of readers. Along with the dramatic increase in reading matter in the 1850s and 1860s, and the perception that there were more working-class readers than ever before,[30] there were the usual anxieties about how to manage a collective reading public or publics.

One part of this change was a shift in what it could mean to "conduct" a journal. Earlier in the century, it was harder to present oneself as a powerful, charismatic figure yet also a benign one as the controlling editorial voice of a magazine. There had certainly been individuals who were prominent masters of their periodicals—Cobbett was the master hand of *Cobbett's Journal,* and T. J. Wooler ran the *Black Dwarf.* But outside radical constituencies these men were regarded as literary demagogues, creators of unhealthy forms of incorporation.[31] Journals such as Knight's *Penny Magazine* and *Chambers's* were also run by powerful master spirits, but their proprietors worked behind the scenes, unobtrusively running the show. Although Robert Chambers put his name on the title page, he worked diligently to hide how much he controlled his journal's content, writing in a variety of styles to keep readers from hearing a single voice in the text.[32] The *Penny Magazine* was associated less with its real master, Knight,[33] than with Henry Brougham and the Society for the Diffusion of Useful Knowledge. Jon Klancher has argued that the "corporate" character of middle-class journals helped construct a middle-class general readership, encouraging people to learn to read in a particular way and to think of themselves as part of a general community of readers.[34] But if a "consistency of tone" was crucial to this corporate character,[35] a consistency of "voice" could be damaging, because it could have demagogic associations in a period when the creation of one social body by one master was strongly associated with unhealthy political states.

When Charles Dickens founded *Household Words* in 1850 as a rival to *Chambers's Journal*, he gave himself a very different role from that of Chambers. Dickens was very much the master spirit of the journal, and he instructed prospective authors that their anonymous articles would read as if one voice was speaking.[36] But he was going to be a very visible master spirit. His decision to call himself "conductor" may have been related to the kind of influence this term connoted in musical contexts, where the charismatic, powerful leader was no longer threatening. While this term had long been used by proprietors of journals and institutions, its new associations could help to portray him as an organizer, medium, director, and companion-guide all at once: an "orchestrator" of British reading.

In 1849, as he ruminated about what kind of a journal to have and how he should define his position in it, he considered (and discarded) the conceit of a "spirit" omnipresent in London, an omniscient source of information and guidance.[37] It may have seemed too inconspicuous, since he then toyed with *CHARLES DICKENS. A weekly journal designed for the instruction and entertainment of all classes of readers, CONDUCTED BY HIMSELF.*[38] In the end *Household Words* offered itself as a "friend of many thousands of people, of both sexes, and of all ages and conditions." As readers sped along on the railways, each weekly act of reading was supposed to help an individual form "associations" with the diverse people "among whom he passes like the wind." The result: a "multitude moved by one sympathy."[39]

Of course, there was not one multitude out there, but many. The thousands of readers Dickens hoped to reach with *Household Words* were nothing to the invisible "monster audience" his close friend and collaborator Wilkie Collins discovered gobbling up the sensational penny weeklies eight years later. Writing in *Household Words*, he announced that this population represented an incredible opportunity for literature. They had barely begun to read as he understood the term. If they could be incorporated into the literate classes, taught to exchange their fodder for *Household Words*, the result would be a mutual transformation of literature and reading.[40]

As Collins was writing his essay, Dickens himself, an enthusiastic liberal reformer, was launching his own incorporative project. As Helen Small has shown, his series of platform readings were intended to hasten this process.[41] They are now remembered partly for the extreme behavior of their audiences. The organizers of these events worried—on good grounds, it would seem— about a problem that threatened all collective gatherings: they might produce disorder and irrationality. Years later, people would remember how they were driven to laughter, screams, and tears. Furniture was broken and clothing torn. The audience sometimes seemed to teeter on the edge of collective madness. On one occasion, Dickens wrote to his friend John Forster, he had been in full flow before a very full house. The listeners packed into the passages were "tearing mad" when a lantern was knocked to the ground. Suddenly, a "lady in the front row of stalls screamed, and ran out wildly towards me." There was a "terrible wave in the crowd." [42]

But the people did not form a mob, and Dickens took credit for saving the event. How he did so suggests what kind of influence he thought he was exercising. Listeners found Dickens's readings "magnetic" and "contagious," and in fact he had long practiced mesmerism,[43] but on this occasion he acted more like a conductor. A mesmerist would have quelled disorder by erasing his subjects' wits, by suspending their powers of reason. Dickens did not subdue the woman by the power of his will, voice, or eyes, but "half-asked and half-ordered her to sit down again; and in a minute, it was all over." [44] The lady half-decided and was half-compelled to return to her proper place, in a manner that recalls the semiwilled state that the mental physiologists saw as a fundamental part of deference to leadership, forming the flexible bond that kept the orchestra in order. Some of Dickens's publicity enhanced this association. The *Illustrated London News* chose to position him standing behind the reading desk, gesturing with a pencil as he spoke (fig. 80). The accompanying text described his power to give life to the story and infuse its meaning into his listeners through intonation and efficient gesture. It is hard to imagine why he would have needed a writing implement during a public reading, except to emphasize his authorial role and to focus listeners' attention on the rhythm of what he was trying to convey. Dickens and his admirers alike saw the "Master of Art" [45] as being at once a charismatic and an ordering influence. However magnetic his words, he did not so much enchant his public into dazed fascination as conduct it through the tale.[46]

A larger-scale example of socially potent fiction is the publication of the work that is traditionally accepted as launching the genre of middle-class sensation fiction, Wilkie Collins's *Woman in White*. The response of readers as the novel appeared in 1859 and 1860, week by week in *All the Year Round*, was unprecedented. People took bets about Sir Percival Glyde's "Secret," babies were named after the more admirable characters, and besotted readers fantasized about marrying them.[47] The novel quickly became one of the most popular of the century.

One striking feature of the "sensation" caused by this novel was the collective way that people experienced it. Earlier novels had been much celebrated, cried over, and talked about, but there was a new character to the reception of *The Woman in White*. Previously, people used the moral sciences to describe their experience of reading. They reflected on the characters, sympathized

MR. CHARLES DICKENS READING "LITTLE DOMBEY," AT ST. MARTIN'S HALL.
(SEE NEXT PAGE.)

FIGURE 80 The *Illustrated London News* (1859) accompanied this sketch of Dickens by describing him "directing the force of [his words] . . . and impressing their true meaning on the mind of his auditors by their proper emphasis and the vital interpretation of gestures and his own natural elocution."

with them, and decided whether they deserved their fates. Even when readers strongly empathized with characters, their feelings were mediated by their judgment and imagination. They might have said that they felt "as if" they were in the same situation as a character, or could share his emotions. In the case of *The Woman in White*, many readers described a response that bypassed this intermediary stage of reflection: the route from page to nerve was direct. Readers did reflect on and sympathize with characters, but they also reported a direct physiological response that was prior to, and perhaps in many cases more powerful than, self-conscious thought. Readers reported involuntary reactions and excited states of mind. Their responses were also treated as individual instances of a more general phenomenon. Everyone had a set of nerves, and they all thrilled when their owners read the "sensation incidents." The reviews, good and bad alike, used a common pool of physiologically charged terms: the novel was "thrilling"; it provoked an "over-mastering excitement" and an "extraordinary fascination."[48] The print holds the reader "fast and holds him . . . long," according to the *Spectator*, and the *Saturday Review* likened the experience of reading *The Woman in White* to a spell of "rapt attention" (from which, however, it said the reader awakened disappointed).[49] When Edward Fitzgerald was forced (by illness) to stop midway through, he told his friend W. F. Pollock that from the cupboard where he had locked it away, the novel still drew him with "a sort of magnetism."[50]

The most detailed and vivid reflection on what it felt like to read the novel came from Mrs. Oliphant in *Blackwood's Magazine*. The writings that had helped create the genre of sensation literature over the past few decades had used "fantastic" and unnatural topics (like "mad psychology," mesmerism, and the supernatural) to shock readers. She praised Collins for restricting himself to "common human acts." But Oliphant's description of the experience of reading the novel implicitly associated the *power* (if not the content) of the narrative with the phenomena she was so relieved not to see in the story. *The Woman in White* laid a "spell" on the reader, and this was a large part of what one got out of reading it, for Oliphant did not think much of the characters themselves. Readers did not so much dwell on the characters, as dwell *in* the feeling provoked by reading the "sensation incidents."[51]

To make her point, Oliphant guided readers through several passages. Two years after the first bound edition of the novel, she could assume that this would not be the first time people had seen them. Her purpose was not to chronicle the plot, nor to call attention to nuances in the choice of language (she did not discuss this). She wanted to make readers feel certain sensations. Indeed, in the care with which she introduced and concluded the passage, Oliphant was "conducting" her readers through their experience of it. The first passage was taken from the moment when the "woman in white," Anne

III.

THE heat had been painfully oppressive all day; and it was now a close and sultry night.

My mother and sister had spoken so many last words, and had begged me to wait another five minutes so many times, that it was nearly midnight when the servant locked the garden-gate behind me. I walked forward a few paces on the shortest way back to London; then stopped, and hesitated.

The moon was full and broad in the dark blue starless sky; and the broken ground of the heath looked wild enough in the mysterious light to be hundreds of miles away from the great city that lay beneath it. The idea of descending any sooner than I could help into the heat and gloom of London repelled me. The prospect of going to bed in my airless chambers, and the prospect of gradual suffocation, seemed, in my present restless frame of mind and body, to be one and the same thing. I determined to stroll home in the purer air, by the most round-about way I could take; to follow the white

winding paths across the lonely heath; and to approach London through its most open suburb by striking into the Finchley-road, and so getting back, in the cool of the new morning, by the western side of the Regent's Park.

I wound my way down slowly over the Heath, enjoying the divine stillness of the scene, and admiring the soft alternations of light and shade as they followed each other over the broken ground on every side of me. So long as I was proceeding through this first and prettiest part of my night-walk, my mind remained passively open to the impressions produced by the view; and I thought but little on any subject—indeed, so far as my own sensations were concerned, I can hardly say that I thought at all.

But when I had left the Heath, and had turned into the by-road, where there was less to see, the ideas naturally engendered by the approaching change in my habits and occupations, gradually drew more and more of my attention exclusively to themselves. By the time I had arrived at the end of the road, I had become completely absorbed in my own fanciful visions of Limmeridge House, of Mr. Fairlie, and of the two ladies whose practice in the art of water-colour painting I was so soon to superintend.

I had now arrived at that particular point of my walk where four roads met—the road to Hampstead, along which I had returned; the road to Finchley; the road to West End; and the road back to London. I had mechanically turned in this latter direction, and was strolling along the lonely high-road—idly wondering, I remember, what the Cumberland young ladies would look like—when, in one moment, every drop of blood in my body was brought to a stop by the touch of a hand laid lightly and suddenly on my shoulder from behind me.

I turned on the instant, with my fingers tightening round the handle of my stick.

There, in the middle of the broad, bright high-road—there, as if it had that moment sprung out of the earth or dropped from the heaven—stood the figure of a solitary Woman, dressed from head to foot in white garments; her face bent in grave inquiry on mine, her hand pointing to the dark cloud over London, as I faced her.

FIGURE 81 A thrilling passage from Collins's *Woman in White. All the Year Round* (1859).

Catherick, startled the main character, Walter Hartright, by laying her hand on his shoulder in the dead of night. At the end of the passage, Mrs. Oliphant concluded that few readers could "resist the mysterious thrill of this sudden touch." Her evidence was the sensations of her own readers in *Blackwood's*, who had presumably felt this "thrill" a moment before. Figure 81 reproduces the passage as it appeared in *All the Year Round;* readers may wish to try the experiment themselves. The way Oliphant described the link of sensation between reader and character recalled the mesmeric "community of sensation" that removed the boundaries between people: "The silent woman lays her hand upon our shoulder as well as that of Mr. Walter Hartright." [52]

Oliphant did not reflect in any detail about the agency that was involved in her nervous response, but her description of how the book "played" on her nerves suggests a carefully calibrated instrument, built to have as "delicate" a touch as its author, working upon her nerves as her eyes scanned the page. The notion of a mechanical process of influence accords with the way that Collins himself saw the relationship of ink to eye, and with reviewers' reference to the novel's line-by-line excitement. One reviewer noted as a mark of Collins's authorial power the "desire that . . . possesses [the reader] to go through every line of it continuously," even though its pages were up to twice as dense as those of most circulating-library fare.[53] This compulsion was not the result of a lucky hit or a peculiar gift for storytelling, but of extensive effort by the author. Collins was acutely concerned to keep and manage his readers' attention, and understood this challenge as one of micromanagement. One of Dickens's few criticisms was that Collins did not trust his readers enough to refrain from "forcing" points on readers' "attention." [54] In fact, Collins not only paced his verbal cues in a way that Dickens called "dissective," but even tried to control how readers' eyes would take in the print. He took great pains over typographical effect. According to John Sutherland, Collins told the printer exactly where he should use "small capitals, 'white lines' (the breathless gaps that punctuate the narrative), and italics." [55] As readers' eyes made passes down each page, the optical sensations created by the running pattern of black and white were coordinated by the novelist.

Collins claimed that the novel was an experiment in narrative—specifically, in the use of a series of first-person testimonies. While there has been dispute from the first about whether he was justified in his claims to originality, it is worth considering whether another experiment was going on in a work that Henry James said was more "science" than "art": [56] an experiment, not in narrative structure, but in physiological response. Collins had actually carried out experiments in altered states of mind and nervous influence in 1852.[57] During his trials of mesmerism, the subject could be made to have sensory experiences at Collins's pleasure, and to conceive, in her mind, thoughts that originated in his. She even seemed to have the power to mesmerize *him*. During an attempt to establish a mesmeric communication between Collins and the entranced subject, her hand was laid on his arm to facilitate the connection between them. From the point of contact came a recurrent shock to his nerves that he regarded as the early stages of the mesmeric state (he would later be mesmerized by his lover, Caroline Graves).[58] Later in the decade, mesmerism was still on Collins's mind. He had recently collaborated with Dickens on *The Frozen Deep,* a play whose two acts are held together by Scottish second sight. The play would have reminded audiences of the mental journeys mesmeric clairvoyants made in the 1840s and 1850s in search of John Franklin, the lost explorer who had inspired it. The coauthors performed the play themselves in January 1859, in a double bill with Elizabeth Inchbald's *Animal Magnetism.* Dickens played Mesmer.[59]

Without meaning to suggest that Collins set out literally to mesmerize his readers, I do think it plausible that this was an experiment in mental influence and nervous stimulus in a more literal sense than readers might assume.[60] And whether or not he was making such a deliberate effort, it is possible to piece together a very specific sense of how Collins and his readers might have understood the nervous phenomena that could be produced by the act of reading. Upper-middle-class, professional, and intellectual readers shared a vocabulary and a framework for understanding the psychological and physiological phenomena that accompanied reading in general, and certainly the sort of intense reading activity that surrounded *The Woman in White.*

What was actually going on in Mrs. Oliphant's nerves when she felt Anne Catherick's touch? There was a widely known, well-established and growing body of physiological literature that could supply an answer. If Collins himself had wished to give one, he would probably have consulted the two physiologists whose work he would use a few years later when he was composing *The Moonstone.* One of them, William Benjamin Carpenter, was the most prestigious and influential physiologist working at this time; the other, John Elliotson, was the most controversial and notoriously materialist.[61] Others included G. H. Lewes, Herbert Spencer, Alexander Bain, and, from the mid-1860s onward, Henry Maudsley and Thomas Henry Huxley. They had their differences, but they agreed on the important role of mental reflexes in the complex relationship of attention, perception, and action. Carpenter's work was very widely publicized in the mid-Victorian period in scores of lectures and a large collection of papers in the quarterly and monthly journals.[62] Major works by Spencer, Lewes, and Bain were published between 1855 and 1860, and over the next decade, as their publications multiplied, Maudsley and Huxley began to publish in these areas as well.[63] Huxley's textbook of 1867, a staple in schools, explained unconscious reflex action using the example of reading: "In this case, the whole attention of the mind is, or ought to be, bent upon the subject-matter of the book; while a multitude of most delicate muscular actions are going on, of which the reader is not in the slightest degree aware . . . And yet every one of these muscular acts may be performed with utter unconsciousness, on his part, of anything but the sense of the words in the book. In other words, they are reflex acts."[64] Most middle-class and professional readers would have had at least a very vague acquaintance with this kind of notion, and many would have been quite familiar with it. Even if they had no specific knowledge of the work of Carpenter or Huxley, a great many would have shared a perspective informed by their basic physiological assumptions.

Drawing on the mental physiologists, one would make the following diagnosis of Oliphant: her attention was intensely focused on the story, to the exclusion of everything else. Such a "rapt" state of locked attention (as it had been described by one of the reviewers) was a physiological condition similar to that of the table-turner and the electrobiological subject. Because the judgment and will required the attention in order to act, in its absence they were suspended. This explained the book's "hold" on the mind, the fact that one could not put it down. The will and judgment could not respond to signs of fatigue or hunger (or any other stimulus besides the book) until these reached an unusual intensity. When they did penetrate the reader's concentration, they could produce a shock. The same kinds of nervous influences were in play among the fictional characters as between the reader and the book. For instance, in the passage Oliphant chose, Walter Hartright was in a state of "reverie," his mind "played upon" by random thoughts, and this is why Anne Catherick's touch startled him.

As for the sensations the book aroused, readers were possessed by the experiences recounted in the narrative. The act of extreme, sustained concentration severed the connection between the perceptual powers and the discriminating judgment, dissolving the distinction between a verbal assertion and a physical reality. Words appearing in a less "gripping" passage would have entered the conscious mind and been accorded their "meta" (as it were) status as descriptions of a fictional reality. But in the reverie of these readers, they were "reflected," in the physiologist's phrase, into the nerves of sensation as if they had a physical existence—as if they impacted the body as physical stimuli striking the nerves. The (miscoded) stimulus then traveled to the sensorium in the brain, where the conscious mind was informed (in the case of the first passage Oliphant chose) that the shoulder had been touched.

Reflex physiology could also explain how the reading of sensational material was communal. One presumes that the readers who consumed Collins's novel were equipped with similar reflex systems. Reflexes did vary from individual to individual, but the differences were most pronounced in the higher strata of mental functioning—the moral faculties, the processes of abstract reflection, and so forth. In fact, in the context of this physiology of mind, one could argue that *only* a literature that affected the lower and intermediary

mental reflexes could be a collective activity in a literal sense, because it operated on aspects of mental life that were similar in all readers. A literature that
appealed primarily to the reflecting, moral powers would address mental faculties that differed most across a population. When the thousands of readers
who bought *All the Year Round* stepped into the railway carriage or the parlor,
settled into their seats, and began to read, their nerves jumped together, their
pulses raced at the same rates, and their breath caught in their throats at once.
This state of "attention," in the physiological sense, extended over a vast population to form one giant reflex in the social body of readers. I have deliberately pushed this explanation to its extreme, in order to show how detailed and
literal a physiology of reading the very widely known and well-established literature could support.

Was it healthy to read sensational material? This question was central to
worries about the health risks of reading that reached their peak in the 1880s,[65]
after the demise of sensation fiction proper, but in the late 1850s and early
1860s a thrill to the nerves was not as alarming as it would later become. A
"semi-volitional" state like Oliphant's could be good or bad, according to the
liberal psychologists, depending on the specifics: repeated experiments in electrobiology, for instance, could weaken the will, but placing oneself in a reverie
by focusing on intellectual work could build up habits of mental discipline and
logical thinking. It was important to choose with care, because each mental
act had a permanent effect on the reflex system. The "secondary automatic"
actions—those created by habit, which could be controlled if one paid attention to them—evolved over time. They were reinforced by repetition.
Whether one tended automatically to act in a virtuous or responsible manner
depended on whether one had built a reliable set of reflexes. The reflex system
was no less than the sum total of life. In other words, it was an embodied form
of memory. This doctrine applied the homily of "you are what you eat" to the
psyche. Later complaints about sensation reading would speak of "overfeeding," [66] but the mid-Victorian physiologists were more concerned with quality than with quantity. And the quality of these novels (in relation to states of
the mind and brain) was an open question.

This kind of physiology—and it was predominant from the 1850s through
the early 1870s—supplied the framework for the question of how reading was
going to affect an increasingly literate society. There was a gathering storm
over whether reading was becoming a "disease," and it took its vocabulary
and its frame of reference from mental physiology. In 1867 *Sharpe's London
Magazine* published an anonymous essay, "Reading as a Means of Culture." It
complained that readers often read with no particular "purpose in view," [67]
leaving to chance how print would form their habits instead of designing a set

of habits for themselves. The proper way to read was not merely to "surrender to the print" but to examine oneself first, identify deficiencies (not merely of knowledge but of mental discipline and moral strength), and deliberately choose a reading stimulus that could redress them. The essay provided a list of possible weaknesses and literary prescriptions.

A few years later, Alfred Austin published a scathing attack on British reading habits in terms borrowed from the mental physiologists, many of whom had published major works (or new editions of existing ones) in 1873 and 1874. He complained that some books were "so exciting to the attention, to the imagination, to the passions, that they produce a mental debauch." In reading such books "the mind is often in nearly a passive state, like that of dreaming or reverie, in which images flit before the mind without any act of volition to retain them." In such contexts, it was the print that played upon the nerves and mind of the reader, rather than the reader who actively focused on a written work to learn a new truth or to apply a critical perspective to an argument. The context for much of this anxiety was the proliferation of the mass periodical press.[68] Another factor in Austin's particular grievance was probably his own frustrations, since Austin, later to distinguish himself as a contender for the century's worst poet laureate, was at this time fighting a losing battle to sell his novels in an uncongenially pulpy climate.[69]

But in addition to the personal factor in Austin's case and the broader issue of particular forms of publication, there was yet a more general basis for these kinds of complaints. The fact that Oliphant, who was contemptuous of mesmerism itself, described her experiences in terms strikingly reminiscent of mesmeric phenomena, suggests that these terms were part of a repertoire for describing influence and communication that did not depend on whether one subscribed to mesmerism. The prominence of themes of madness in mid-Victorian novels has justifiably encouraged literary historians to emphasize madness and mental pathology in descriptions of the cultural context in which these books were written and read. But this emphasis can lead one to assume that Victorians thought about reading and writing in physiological terms only when these activities were carried out in an unhealthy way. I think it would be fairer to say that most readers approached their books with an understanding (whether implicit or explicit) of reading as a physiological activity that transformed the ink on the paper into meaning in the brain. The specificity of this repertoire in the mental physiology of the 1850s and 1860s also suggests that many — possibly most — of the physiological terms that are often used casually or metaphorically in modern literary criticism in relation to Victorian literature could be understood more literally. If we could ask Collins's readers what they thought a "hystericized" reading response might be, or if they could explain the "coordinated nature of late Victorian fiction's reflex action," they could have come up with an answer, though it would probably be quite different from what the literary critics who used these phrases meant to convey.[70] And the meaning these terms would have had was intimately related to the very wide range of discussions that used the physiology of volition to explore how individuals could be part of a "mass" experience without losing their sanity or identity.

The Politics of Sensation

As readers of *Sharpe's London Magazine* were reading about the dangers of indiscriminate literary consumption, they could learn elsewhere just how much power over their minds an unscrupulous "literary adventurer" could achieve. An article in the *Economist* described the successes of an unscrupulous master of literary creation, whose greatest strength was an extraordinary understanding of "the obvious momentary part of English society." His writings described them beautifully, and he was as good at turning the real phenomena to his advantage. With his particular combination of charismatic skills, this novelist had perpetrated a singularly successful "fraud" upon the minds of the English people, catapulting himself, upon his deception, to the highest position in the land: prime minister.[71]

Benjamin Disraeli had succeeded in the fraudulent role he played in the passing of the Second Reform Act because he was skilled at manipulating the evanescent, from the fleeting power of his "vivid" novels on the many readers who consumed them, to the momentary passions of a campaign. In a society whose political body was expanding, the only way for good leaders to protect the people from such charlatans was to become masterful in managing social sensation in all its forms. This challenge became one of the chief preoccupations of the most influential liberal political writer of his generation, Walter Bagehot.

Bagehot devoted many of his political writings to the question of how to make the "mass" into a healthy part of the modern state. This was one of the dominant challenges of the second half of the century. Before the mid–nineteenth century there were many benign representations of crowds,[72] but the most powerful image was a destructive one, established in conservative reactions to the French Revolution. The revolution, it was claimed, was provoked by demagogues who led French subjects astray. The rule of the masses was actually the rule of the demagogues. When people were united into a single body (often by an "electrical" or "magnetic" process), they lost their power of independent judgment. They became insensitive to proper guidance yet vulnerable to illegitimate political leaders. There was also uncertainty about who was really in charge. As the constant change of revolutionary leaders illustrated, rival leaders or the masses themselves could be revealed as the ones truly in power. Versions of this story were told in attacks on English sympathizers with the French Revolution, Irish insurrectionists in the 1790s, and intermittently from the 1810s to the 1840s, with respect to English radicalism, Irish issues, and early trade unionism. Above all, they were inspired by the Continental revolutions of 1848, which reinforced a link between the question of how to manage the charismatic individual and the question of how safely to absorb into the formal political process previously alienated groups.

The social unrest of the 1840s and the 1848 revolutions on the Continent inspired particularly vivid descriptions of a collective body in a morbid or monstrous state. Charlotte Brontë spoke with a sort of horrified fascination of the French people's "spasms, cramps and frenzy-fits."[73] Her friend Elizabeth Gaskell likewise portrayed the uneducated poor in *Mary Barton* as a Frankenstein's monster that could suddenly "rise to life." It was "powerful" but "ungifted with a soul, a knowledge of the difference between good and evil." Lack of education made people vulnerable to "all that is commonly called wild and visionary," because movements like Chartism and Communism offered people a way out of soulless oblivion.[74]

As for the charismatic leaders of such movements, vulnerability to them was a fact of life, no matter how socially destructive this propensity might be. In 1841 Carlyle deplored hero worship, but thought that the only answer was to choose one's heroes well.[75] In 1848 the conservative savant William Whewell reflected on the problem soon after the revolution had been brought home to him when the deposed provisional premier Guizot turned up on his doorstep as a refugee. In a letter to his brother-in-law, who was thinking of writing a book on great men, he warned him that, though institutions could lose spirit and need to be revived, it was dangerous to celebrate the individuals who took it upon themselves to do this because it could lead one to "speak as if . . . revolution were good and great, in general and in the abstract."[76] But trying to thwart incorporation by suppressing hero worship and using "taxes on knowledge" or bans on public assembly looked futile after the revolutions. People would inevitably form collective bodies, so it was necessary to find ways of making them benign.

A persistent theme in Bagehot's writings was that the powerful effects of charisma, sensation, and contagious irrationality were inevitable, manageable, and even essential to modern political life. Trade unions should be legalized, he consistently argued, because the power of combination they had when illegal was "mysterious," "secret," and more potent than when they were exposed to full public examination. The proliferation of (more but weaker) trade unions would make them less damaging to the working classes, and the very "framework of society might in consequence be much benefitted." [77] Similarly, his answer to the financial "panics" of the 1840s and the 1850s (in which the Bank of England had been forced to take the illegal step of printing more currency than was permitted by Peel's act of 1844) was new legislation. Britain needed a legal framework that could accommodate and manage the emotional vicissitudes of the market. A modern state needed to accept the reality of the "panics" and "feelings" of its members, manifest on a mass scale. [78]

As for the charisma of the demagogue, the manipulation of sensation he used to gain power was not only inevitable, but even constructive, if it was done by a good leader in a healthy political system. Charisma was indeed dangerous where it was unharnessed, as in America, that unhealthy laboratory of democracy. There, government was the creature of the masses, whose powers of judgment were undisciplined. It was a crude reflex system, immediately reacting to the stimulus of the moment. In America, power lay in the hands of the *"just-taught* classes"—that is, the classes whose knowledge was fresh and raw, whose minds had not matured. The leveling effect of making "[r]eading and writing" into "the property of everybody" was a defiant cockiness. And although Americans had a "sharp, 'smart' sense" about things that came within their daily experience, one could not expect from them "the balanced sense, the exercised judgment, the many-sided equanimity, which are necessary to form a judgment on elaborate controversies, and on difficult foreign relations." America had created, on a national scale, what the British ruling classes feared from their crowds: "They go too quick . . . They are the ready victims of incendiaries." [79]

In contrast, Britain had a structure of government that made the power of the public speaker a positive political tool, and a critical one for the modern state. A distinctly new style of leadership would be necessary to govern modern Britain, one emphasizing public oratory over parliamentary eloquence. A landmark moment in the emergence of this new mode of leadership was Gladstone's speech at Greenwich in 1871, which was the first time a prime minister had ever addressed the public directly. [80] Bagehot celebrated it as marking a "new era" in English politics. From now on, the prime minister would "exert a control over the masses . . . *directly* by the vitality of his own mind." This skill could be learned, and it was essential that future leaders take care to study it as Gladstone had done. He had come to appreciate by painful experience that "the speech of the head of a great administration declaring and expounding his policy" to voters had to be delivered very differently to voters from how one would speak to Parliament. It was impossible to trace the "fine lines of a national policy" before an audience of 25,000. Gladstone's electrifying oratory was the result of carefully taking the measure of the masses, suiting the words to the occasion. By judicious management of public sensation, he had consolidated his political power and his national credibility.[81]

What was it that distinguished Gladstone's statesmanship from American demagoguery? To answer this, Bagehot needed to explain how healthy political influence could operate on a massive scale. He had an early acquaintance with sciences of interpersonal influence, for he had been a paying pupil under the instruction of William Benjamin Carpenter in the early 1840s, and attended a number of mesmeric trials.[82] Twenty years on, he developed an account of the British constitution that was striking in the degree to which it resembled contemporary physiologies of mental reflexes, sensation, and consensual phenomena.

Bagehot was particularly concerned to resolve the fundamental question of how the franchise could be extended without producing a democracy. He addressed this issue systematically in the work that became the most important political treatise of the mid-Victorian period, his *English Constitution*. From the vantage point of 1867, it was clear that "a change has taken place in society exactly similar to the change in the polity. A republic has insinuated itself beneath the folds of a Monarchy" (61–62). This was not a dangerous development but an essential one for political progress: constitutional monarchy acted "as a disguise . . . [which] enables our real rulers to change without heedless people knowing it. The masses of Englishmen are not fit for an elective government; if they knew how near they were to it, they would be surprised, and almost tremble" (66).

For Bagehot the characteristic of British government that kept the country stable while other nations collapsed into an unhealthy democracy was the split between what he called the "efficient" and the "dignified" parts of the constitution. The dignified parts, such as the monarchy, "excite and preserve the reverence of the population," thereby procuring power from the people. The parts that actually wielded it were the efficient parts: Parliament, the cabinet, and the judiciary. The reason that getting power had to be separate from using power was that the most effective way of securing power was through appeals to the senses, and this required forms of theatricality that were incompatible with the processes best suited to putting this power to use.

The task of the "dignified" parts of the constitution was to create consensus, both in the modern sense of the term—a sense of agreement about a particular issue (in this case the propriety of a certain form of rule)—and in the sense of a unified body of people formed into one consenting "mass." If people easily and naturally agreed on their needs and how to meet them, there would be no need for such an influence, but this was not the case. The world was "organized far otherwise," so governments needed a way to make people agree to a collective purpose. To motivate the "ruder sort of men" one could not appeal to the issues—the "real needs"—that Parliament would wish to address. Rational argument was impotent compared to an appeal to the senses and passions. The "ruder" men would sacrifice anything, "even themselves," for a moving idea, an "attraction which seems to transcend reality" (65). The way to unite a population was to play on their senses, to enchant them with occult ideas, to dazzle them: "The elements which excite the most easy reverence will be the theatrical elements—those which appeal to the senses, which claim to be embodiments of the greatest human ideas, which boast in some cases of far more than human origin. That which is mystic in its claims; that which is occult in its mode of action; that which is brilliant to the eye; that which is seen vividly for a moment, and then is seen no more . . . [this is the only sort] which yet comes home to the mass of men" (66). So the dignified parts of government served the function of theatrically producing consensus in a way that the untheatrically efficient parts could not do.

A fudge was necessary to sustain a healthy polity, because the best-intentioned leaders had to act in ways that, if they did so in their own clubs or around their own dining-room tables, would seem manipulative, specious, or at least a form of bad faith. For instance, the monarchy's representation of leadership "by a single will, the fiat of a single mind" was erroneous. But it was crucial to government, because the easily understood notion of the leadership of a single individual surreptitiously achieved the highly complex and, as Bagehot put it, "unseen formation of a guiding opinion." In the most general sense, consensus required an environment in which the views and allegiances of the general public would be theatrically oriented in a particular manner, such that the unseen workings of a separate and truly potent political structure could be protected.

Theater was important not just for the lower "ruder" classes but for all of society. The "active voluntary part of a man is very small"—even in "the most intellectual of men," he felt compelled to spell out—"and if it were not economized by a sleepy kind of habit, its results would be null." "Sleepy" habits were essential to human life, because without them people could not accomplish anything individually, and they could never act together: "One man . . . would go off the known track in one direction, and one in another, so that when a crisis came requiring massed combination, no two men would be near enough to act together." Here the "dignified" elements of the constitution went to work. The role of "traditional" forms of society was like the "secondary automatic" (mental reflex) system of the physiologists. Traditions had been built up over long periods of time, functioned automatically, and took effect naturally because people were built to respond to them. Such an influence could "*take* the multitude," that is, "guide by an insensible but an omnipotent influence the associations of its subjects" (66–67).

Tradition, understood as a "secondary automatic" reflex, bound people together who were otherwise separated by different degrees of evolutionary development. Britain, like all "great communities," was like a mountain, with "primary, secondary and tertiary strata of human progress; the characteristics of the lower regions resemble the life of old times rather than the present life of the higher regions." One could find "crowds of people scarcely more civilized than the majority of two thousand years ago . . . [and] others, even more numerous, such as the best people were a thousand years since" (65).

These strata could be examined in one's home. To learn where the cook sat on the evolutionary scale, one asked her an easy question and measured how big a gap of communication was evident in her confused reply. In fact, Bagehot suggested that such an exercise should drive home the important function of ceremony and theater to social cohesion. The mental gulf between the different members of society, people differently positioned on the evolutionary scale, made rational intercourse impossible. Only a theatrical influence, one that worked on the senses and the reflexes rather than on the conscious processes of thought, could maintain cohesion. Without such an influence, the members of the higher strata might be overwhelmed by the (more numerous) creatures of the lower.

A few years later Bagehot examined the developing reflex system of the body politic more systematically. In *Physics and Politics* he built both his argument and the origins of the modern state on the reflex system. "No one," he warned in his opening pages, "will ever understand the 'connective tissue' of civilisation" without studying the reflex system and the nervous power flowing through it. This alone was the "connective force which binds age to age" (8). Before proceeding with the evolutionary history of the polity he was about to develop, he painstakingly acquainted the reader with the spinal reflex apparatus, and, especially, with mental reflexes. The work as a whole was an application of evolutionary theory to the history of states and their political organization, but the driving force within that evolutionary system was nervous influence, "playing upon the nerves of men and, age after age, making nicer music from finer chords" (9).

The scientific founders of this work were the mental physiologists, especially Huxley and Maudsley. The mental physiologists all thought that reflexes were the key to mental evolution, however much they might disagree on the finer points of the matter. For Carpenter, the least materialist of the lot, the possibility of using the will to harness the rest of the mind was the key to preserving the notion of individual responsibility while emphasizing that most action was a reflex; it also gave physiologists a powerful role to play in creating a population equipped with healthy, responsible minds. Huxley taught that the very "possibility of all education" relied on the ability of the mind to build an unconscious reflex system.[83] In lecture tours in the 1860s and 1870s, Carpenter exhorted his listeners to monitor closely the automatic selves they were building in their own brains. Initially, our "early habitudes of Thought and Feeling are determined *for* us, rather than *by* us." Early education, he advised in a rather blunt analogy, "has to be conducted upon exactly the same method as that of a Dog."[84] But once the "special" human attribute of self-consciousness and self-direction emerged, one's responsibilities began. The "consciousness of power, is the foundation of all effort . . . The "I AM," "I OUGHT," "I CAN," "I WILL," of the Ego, can train the mental as well as the bodily Automaton, and make it do anything it is capable of executing."[85]

One psychological invention of this period provided a means of making everyone the same without removing the individuality created by this personal shaping of the reflex system. This was the "personal equation." It was the creation of the German physiologist and psychologist Wilhelm Wundt, and it was put to work in Britain in the Royal Greenwich Observatory as a way of coordinating a community of scientific researchers. It measured the variations in the speed at which different researchers reacted to the same stimulus (such as observers marking down the moment at which they noted the appearance of a celestial body). Each researcher was assigned a different "equation" based on his own speed, and a central manager used it to factor out the differences in data collected by a group of individuals. A much more ambitious (if vaguer) use of this notion was possible if most of the functioning mind was reckoned to be a reflex. In this case one could, in principle, produce a "personal equation" for most human action. Carpenter used it to develop a psychology of belief that could explain how people made very different sense of the same phenomena. One stimulus went into many different mental reflex systems; out came many different conclusions. If one could take the measure of a whole population in this way, one could develop ways of leading a group that unified them. By understanding and managing the individual differences between them, one could make them identical in their coherence while remaining unique in their individual qualities of mind.[86]

Bagehot used the same scientific resources to emphasize the aggregate rather than the individual in his history of the polity. The distinctive feature of early civil society was a sort of mental mush in the skulls of its members:

an "instability" of mind that placed "ante-political" men "at the mercy of every impulse and [saw them] blown by every passion." As the modern state emerged, one of its fundamental features was its composition in a "*like* body of men, because of that likeness capable of acting alike, and because of that likeness inclined to obey similar rules." [87] The way such a collective was produced was through the "inherited drill." Individual members of society built up their internal systems of automatic thinking. The habits they developed as individuals changed the nature of the "germ" and were passed on to their children in a Lamarckian social evolutionary system. In Carpenter's physiology of mind, and probably in Bagehot's system as well, the political policy maker and educator should be (ideally) a conductor figure, designing policies that would progressively improve the "germ." As an aggregate, people's individual changes contributed to a collective and evolving reflex apparatus, in which each generation passed on greater structure, strength, and discipline to the next.[88]

Gladstone's Glamour and Svengali's Sorcery

In the last decades of the century, depictions of social "coordination" and "harmony" by a central influence took on a heavier character, even as the word "consensus" passed into common usage to refer to spontaneous agreement. While the "inherited drill" might have been expected to make structure triumph over the inchoate instability of "ante-political" man, Bagehot's friends feared an impulsive and passionate future for the British nation. The increasing pace of democracy would make it impossible for the balance of dignified and efficient parts of the constitution to protect the political system.

After the second edition of *The English Constitution* was published, the earl of Carnarvon wrote to Bagehot to congratulate him on a brilliant work. He feared that it would not have "the weight it deserves," however, because these days people were less able to "weigh the reasons of things." There was a taste for "sensational legis[latio]n," and there was a "criminal tendency of politicians to satisfy it from a conscious or unconscious sense of their own interests also growing greater; whilst the mobility of the classes wh. are thus courted appears to be on the increase." [89] Carnarvon may have meant "mobility" in two senses: in the sense that remains in use today, connoting "activity," and in a usage that has died out since the nineteenth century, connoting the converse of "gentility." That is, the class of Britons who were most likely to form a mob were also those who were becoming more active, and the English government was becoming the creature of its most unhealthy members.

Of the many projects aimed at stemming the tide of mass degeneration, one was the proliferation of benevolent societies and charities that were aimed at propping up the respectable classes, and here, too, one can find examples of "consensual" systems at work. One of the more unusual examples I have come across is a musical performance celebrated in the *Graphic* in 1887, the Christmas concert of a charity school for the children of professional families who were down on their luck.[90] The school was founded to help stem the tide of social deterioration by helping these children to stay in their parents' class. The *Graphic* published a sketch of a circle of children playing Haydn's Toy Symphony. The centerpiece of the scene was a Maypole-like system of ribbons tied to the top of a pole held by the teacher; each girl held the end of her own ribbon. This contraption, which served no purpose besides displaying the performers as a unified group, dominates the picture. To some modern eyes it might have seemed like a particularly weird example of the Victorian taste for sentimental ornament; to others it might reek of the oppressiveness they associate with Victorian charities. In 1887 many would have interpreted this publicity piece as it was surely intended: to suggest that the institution was staging on a small scale the social harmony and moral rectitude of respectable society, encoding these vital ingredients into its charges.

But would coordinating influences such as those suggested by the *Graphic* actually produce psychological order in the modern state? In the uneasy nerviness of the fin de siécle, the conductor-mesmerist could no longer be the benign "soul of the great poly-body" in the way, for instance, that Jullien seemed in 1850. It now seemed appropriate that he died alone, impoverished, and insane. The charismatic images of the 1880s and 1890s that were the inheritors of the midcentury conducting and mesmerism systems were oppressive, ambivalent, or perverse. Gladstone, the great healthy unifier in the rhetoric of Bagehot, was portrayed during the home-rule controversies of the 1880s as a slick, American-style quack. A satirical poster sketched him standing on the back of his traveling carriage-shop selling potions—they could have been drawn with a degree of physiological knowledge, because Gladstone was acquainted with Carpenter's physiological works and had written to him on the subject.[91] The contents of one flask, marked "Gladstonian Glamour," presumably removed the judgment of his customers (fig. 82).

The ultimate figure of this kind, however, was Svengali, in George Du Maurier's *Trilby*. In the famous scenes of the novel, Svengali not only "conducted" the heroine, Trilby, in her extraordinary singing performances (of which she was incapable without his influence), but actually erased her. In taking mesmeric possession of her, he made her into the ultimate human instrument (see fig. 83). The sinister role of the conductor-mesmerist as a malevo-

THE TRAVELLING QUACK.

FIGURE 82 William Gladstone portrayed as a traveling quack. Gladstone stands on the back steps of his coach, which is equipped with everything a political quack could desire, including an anatomy of the "capacity of radical voter's stomach," and a flask of "Gladstonian Glamour" to entrance his listeners into buying his jars of "Infallible Home Rule Ointment." Iconographic Collection, Wellcome Institute.

FIGURE 83   A famous image of Trilby in Svengali's power. George Du Maurier, *Trilby* (London: Osgood McIlvaine and Co., 1895).

lent demagogue in *Trilby* here involved a far more frightening image of mental control and the destruction of individual identity than had ever appeared earlier in the century.

Morbid Masses and Healthy Consensus

In the mid-Victorian period there was a marked change in the way that social cohesion was portrayed, and it was related to the question of how groups of people acted in concert. Throughout the early nineteenth century there were signs of the emergence of "mass" phenomena that would become very pronounced from the midcentury onward: the first census in 1801, the statistical movement from the 1830s onward, and in the same decades the emerging phenomenon of a "mass" reading public.[92] During these years there were sustained debates about how to manage public debate and how to produce a harmonious society, but there was little agreement about how this could happen. There was no way of representing a collectivity that simultaneously preserved individuals within it and explained how they were bound together as a coherent social unity. Depictions of "mass" phenomena referred to vast, undifferentiated groups even when their authors also wished to acknowledge that these were made up of individuals. But during the mid-Victorian period new representations of harmonious groups attempted to show how individuality could survive within a "mass"—representations to which, in their most general forms, a great many people subscribed.

During these years Britons attended the Great Exhibition, passed the Second Reform Act, founded cooperative societies and legalized trade unionism, funded dozens of government studies of education, and consumed a dizzying array of new periodicals. So one would expect to find works describing and reflecting on the behavior of large numbers of people. But it is striking that many of them described a process one might call "incorporation," meaning by it a much broader and looser notion of the "making of many people into one" than the old legal meaning of this term implies. This process was pivotal to cultural innovations such as the invention of the orchestral baton conductor, social developments like the emergence of a "mass" reading public, and political issues such as how people outside the formal political process could safely be absorbed into the franchise.

Mid-Victorian sciences of mind and social relations tended to see incorporation as a fundamental feature of society. There were healthy and unhealthy forms of it, and by studying them one could learn how the bad could be avoided and the good encouraged. Many descriptions of "mass" phenomena assumed that one could guide the activity of a collective body, usually by managing how sensations impinged upon its members. People placed themselves in situations that connected them to the group by a partial suspension of their will or judgment, and by a coordinating stimulus that acted where the will did not. Unlike mesmeric subjects, people in these roles were to some considerable extent conscious of their situations and had consented to them.

For people trying to explain these phenomena, mesmerism was both a problem and an opportunity. It was a problem because, before the 1850s, it was the dominant example of unhealthy incorporation: it made two people one, erasing the boundaries between them, and it supplied a vocabulary and an explanation (sometimes figurative, sometimes literal) for descriptions of madness in crowds. But it was also a resource. In the 1850s and 1860s its phenomena, and others associated with it, became fundamental to respectable, "benign," mid-Victorian accounts of how one could be made out of many.

The physiology of mind had great potential as a science of personal management at a time when society was increasingly deemed to be an aggregate of similar individuals responsible for their own actions and their own contribution to the common good. If the "glory of a state" issued, ultimately, from the "power of universal self-management and self-reliance," [93] mental physiology had a crucial role to play in explaining this power. Armed with a new understanding of the mind and social interaction, leaders could hope to give people a set of mental tools they could use to live more responsibly. People would become part of a consensus, healthily coordinated with each other, immune to dangerous influences yet sensitive to proper leadership. The physiology of agreement involved an input-output system—stimulus going in, action coming out. The propriety of the action depended on the internal mechanism that turned input into output.

There are as many possible routes for studying Victorian notions of "incorporation" as there were examples of social cohesion. Many of them have been mapped out by social histories: transport, imperial propaganda, business organization, the civil service, education, elections. We know a great deal about the history of many of the changes that occurred in these areas during the second half of the century, but we are less familiar with the notions of agreement that underpinned them all. It is perhaps ironic that a book that has traced a series of cascading disagreements pervading a diverse culture should end by suggesting an understanding of what some of these notions of agreement were, and how they came to be.

The Day after the Feast

IN 1857 WALTER BAGEHOT characterized the mid-Victorian decades as the "day after the feast," a feast to which those living in the first half of the century had been invited. "They did not know what was coming but they knew it was something gorgeous and great; they expected it with hope and longing."[1] Now, many felt deeply that "something had come, and something had gone." But the nature of this "something" was not at all clear. And if the Victorians did not know in advance what was to transpire at the banquet, they were just as confused the next morning.

Like the evanescent feast, mesmerism was one of those "gorgeous and great" things to which the Victorians looked with such longing, and which they found it so impossible to define. In fact, mesmerism was as much about promise—about expectation—as it was about the mind. Its fascination ultimately lay not in its ability to establish particular psychological truths but in staging events that offered a way of exploring mental, social, and scientific potential.

Mesmerism, one might say, was a science of possibility. Its every feature was suggestive, but what was being suggested was not easy to determine. Dozens of tracts stipulated rules for "what mesmerism is, and what it is not"—but these rules were often mutually exclusive. Mesmerism's very name, marking a dismissal of "animal magnetism," was a negation. No staple set of practices produced the mesmeric effects—which was just as well, since no one could agree on what these effects were, and, both in principle and in specific instances, there was just as much disagreement about whether the effects were real. If one were lucky enough to get a room of witnesses to confirm the success of a particular trial, they would be very unlikely to agree on its implication.

If mesmerism was one of the most slippery and ambiguous of Victorian practices, its ambiguity and its enormous possibilities reinforced each other. And these twin features make it in retrospect into a peculiarly useful diagnostic tool for understanding Victorian intellectual life. Wherever mesmerism flourished—in the sense of attracting interest and becoming the focus of controversy—the nature of influence and authority was rendered particularly uncertain. If we follow mesmerism into these places and look at the sense people tried to make of it, we learn about the potential as well as the actual status of science, say, and the imagined as well as experienced position of women. We learn, not just the concrete realities of Victorian life, but what Victorians thought they ought to be. In particular, we apprehend what people thought the status and mutual relations should be (and might be in future) of scientists, doctors, women, working people, colonial administrators and Indian subjects, and the clergy.

Of course, mesmerism cannot take us everywhere in Victorian culture. It was catalytic particularly to disputes about intellectual authority (including authority in science and medicine), the relative status of the classes and genders, and the vicissitudes of the human mind, body, and spirit. In these areas mesmerism became a resource for drawing new geographies of authority within British society, and can therefore reveal important features to the modern historian. But alone it cannot, for instance, lay bare the intricate stratagems of high politics, even if it can teach us that those involved (figures like Morpeth and Gladstone) took an interest in the physiology of mind and influence. Nor can it unlock the experience of those many thousands of toiling poor for whom land was everything, even if we can use it to study how the power of the "common people" was championed to factory operatives in the industrial north.

With mesmerism as an escort, we see how diverse constituencies of Victorian Britain tried to define and harness the powers of mind and influence, often in contradictory ways. In the hands of John Elliotson, mesmerism expressed, and seemed to have the potential to put into action, an agenda of reform led by metropolitan radicals. But the very people whom Elliotson and his friends intended to reform turned mesmerism to their own purposes. Elizabeth O'Key made the stage of UCH into a combination of a pantomime and a millenarian chapel; Spencer Hall and other itinerant lecturers saw mesmerism as a tool for exposing the fraudulence of professional claims to authority on intellectual matters. For doctors struggling to combat these challenges, what was most revolutionary about chemical anesthesia was not its ability to suspend pain but its power to eliminate sources of professional discomfort: the animation of the patient and the activity of lay mesmerists who had relied on mesmerism's uniqueness. In India mesmerism seemed to have the potential to reinforce the authority of colonial medicine, by adding to the resources it could use to heal the sick. Its primary advocate, James Esdaile, also saw knowledge of the natural laws underpinning mesmeric phenomena as an index of one's civilized status. But Indian mesmerism undermined the very things it was supposed to accomplish: the threat of interracial contagion made it impossible to extend the practice to Europeans, and Esdaile himself, in a circular fashion, used a crude fiction to explain the trance to the natives he assumed were too "superstitious" to understand the truth as he understood it.

Mesmerism was more successful, depending on how one defines success, in the sickroom, where it helped transform the invalid's weakness into a source of otherworldly authority. Its prophetic powers, and the powerful influence of the mesmerist, provoked religious figures to investigate it: the results ranged from a "pastoral science" in which mesmerism was thought to enhance the preacher's power, to warnings that it provided a conduit for satanic influence into the mortal world. The ambiguities mesmerism identified in relation to science—to the fields of scientific inquiry and the boundaries between expert and amateur—contributed to the development of educational philosophies and mental physiologies that were aimed at producing a new generation of scientists and their publics. Finally, one of the ironies of mesmerism's history is that, through all this ambiguity, diversity, and discord, it catalyzed the development of a physiology of agreement that contributed to a distinctly new and influential resource for portraying social cohesion in the second half of the century.

Mesmerism therefore epitomized both the longing to achieve great answers to fundamental questions about nature and society and, at the same time, the difficulty of doing so. It expressed the lack of resolution in various areas of inquiry, but it could also propel into public view issues that were previously taken for granted.

There is another light in which we might see mesmerism's relationship to Victorians' own perception of their culture. We could adopt the language of the times to portray it as a "spirit of the age." The early decades of the nineteenth century saw the development of a sense that there was a *Geist* or a character typifying a culture at a particular stage of development. This distinctive character was summed up or contained in some way in the lives of representative individuals, events, or trends. They were often called "spirits of the age," presumably because a single spirit (in the sense of an individual person) was thought to evoke the culture, and because what was being evoked was its essence.[2] In 1831 John Stuart Mill made the recursive claim that this very notion was peculiar to an age of change such as the present. The spirit of the 1830s, he suggested, was the state of becoming aware that one was in the midst of change and that there was a distinctive "spirit" to the new times.[3]

Always literal-minded, the early Victorians enlisted a variety of real spirits to tell themselves about the state of their society. The Ghost of Christmas Present, of course, transported Scrooge through the metropolis in 1843 for an uncompromising look at the state of the hearts, minds, and stomachs of Londoners; a few years later, as he prepared to launch *Household Words,* Charles Dickens imagined a "SHADOW," binding his concerns together and giving readers the sense that it was moving through every house knowing the secrets of every heart.[4] Victorians also appointed real people to the status of "spirits of the age." Victoria herself was the ultimate choice, of course, but it is suggestive that two official "spirits" were those otherworldly invalids, Elizabeth Barrett and Harriet Martineau, who were portrayed as "emanating" their influence over the land.[5] Mesmerism, one might say, was particularly good at displaying salient features of the early Victorian "spirit," even if people could not agree about what those features were. This was why it was tempting to call Britain an "island of Mesmeria," and why this island was a mysterious place inviting intrepid exploration.

Mesmerism's fluidity and its catalytic role are helpful in understanding how and why it declined from prominence. Catalysts disappear when the reactions they facilitate are complete; fluids are absorbed into their surrounding environments. In the second half of the century mesmerism was absorbed into a variety of different disciplines and projects. In the process mesmerism itself was divided and became historically invisible, and its practice lost the provocative role that it had once played in intellectual debate. The "Other World" became, in the hands of men like William Crookes and Oliver Lodge, a branch of physics. Surgeons crafted the "anesthetic" state into a stable means of disciplining patients. In figure 84, a late-Victorian scene of two doctors standing on either side of a surgical patient holding a bag of nitrous oxide, the artist has made it clear that anesthesia is no laughing matter. The other "altered states" were parceled off between medicine and surgery, the spiritualism industry, and psychoanalysis. In psychoanalysis, for example, the fact that the information imparted in the mesmeric state was unconscious and unintentionally expressed by the subject became a central part of consulting-room culture.

Within these new disciplines, retrospective accounts of what the early Victorians had called "mesmerism" became not so much critiques as pedigrees. One history, graphically portrayed in figure 85, led to the modern showman hypnotist. In this poster of the early twentieth century his ancestry lies with the shamans and Indian healers, then skips to Mesmer in the eighteenth century and Braid in the nineteenth. Alternatively, mesmerism was reconstrued as quackery in hagiographic histories of anesthesia. Later historians of the "discovery of the unconscious" crowned Mesmer as a previous incarnation of

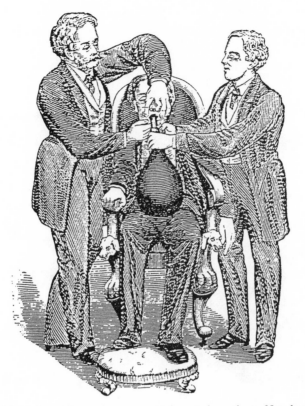

FIGURE 84 A late-nineteenth-century portrayal of surgical anesthesia. Note how sober and disciplined the participants are as they apply the "laughing gas" to their somber patient. F. R. Thomas, *Manual of . . . nitrous oxide* (Philadelphia: S. S. White, 1870).

Freud, and historians of physics portrayed the "Ether" as the "Other," the false grail, of prestigious late-nineteenth-century physics.[6]

The figure of the mesmeric subject came to be stabilized, too. Figure 86 is an image printed on one side of an early twentieth-century patent medicine advertisement. It portrays an entranced, late-Victorian woman being examined by several gentlemen. They have abandoned their pencils and notebooks; the trance has distracted them. The setting is not a parlor or a bedroom but a teaching laboratory, with laboratory equipment, a blackboard, and several chemical flasks; the one nearest to her contains a clear liquid, perhaps water (though there is no glass). The scene is also full of sexual cues: the gentleman who seems to be taking her pulse is, on closer inspection, stroking her forearm. Another man seems to be examining her eyes—perhaps checking the size of the pupils—but a second look reveals him to be drawing closer in fascination. Another gentleman seems to be looking not at her face but at her

FIGURE 85 Here the showman hypnotist's pedigree begins with ancient shamans, progresses through Indian healers, Mesmer in the eighteenth century, and Braid in the nineteenth. Bodleian Library, John Johnson Collection (Entertainments Folder 7).

FIGURE 86 The original sketch that inspired this image was published c. 1890. This version was published in the early twentieth century, on the reverse side of an advertisement for a patent medicine. Iconographic Collection, Wellcome Institute.

chest, and there is rather more bosom exposed than any respectable Victorian woman would have permitted.

One instructive feature of this scene is how easy it is for us to make sense of it. Most readers, if they were presented, say, with figure 37, would find it hard to come up with an account of was going on. But in figure 86 we have no difficulty in identifying the setting, the activities, and even their ostensible purpose. It is also easy to propose an alternative story to accompany the picture, in which the experiment is tainted by sexual opportunism. The scene is readily deciphered not only because it takes place in a setting closer to our own (chronologically and culturally) but also because the signs or conventions of evidence became more concrete. It is easier to tell if one person is taking another's pulse than it is to identify a state of psychic rapture.

Many forms of human evidence became more tangible toward the end of the century. While early Victorian invalids would claim to be ambiguously, but delicately, connected to nature by tighter cords than the rest of humanity, one late-nineteenth-century French hysteric made her body write the words "La Nature" on her back (fig. 87), perhaps to leave no doubt in readers' minds that the words were the result of natural law. In the decades that saw the introduction of fingerprinting to Europe and America, spirits were thoughtful

FIGURE 87 In the phenomenon of "autographisme," a hysterical patient of Dr. Mesnet is induced to produce the words "La Nature" on the surface of her own body, a phenomenon that was ironic in several respects, because the "natural" status of hysterical and mesmeric phenomena was continually contested, and because hysterics and mesmeric subjects were thought to be more powerfully influenced by natural influences; even the status of the image was ambiguous, because this sketch was made from a photograph, a controversial practice in relation to its ability to represent nature. One might even see the phenomenon as an advertisement for the journal in which its picture was published. *La Nature* (1890).

enough to leave thumbprints in clay or plaster during séances, providing mediums with permanent relics of their visit.[7]

Yet these pieces of evidence were often nearly as evanescent as they were concrete. Specimens of Victorian psychic evidence were elusive, fleeting, and fragile. Ghosts had bad breath, for instance, and regional accents. An example that still allows examination is an experiment that used a locked box containing chalk and chalkboard. During the experiment one could hear the scratching of chalk against slate. Afterward, when the box was opened, one saw that a message had appeared. Some of these boxes survive today, their delicate messages intact; one slip of the reader's fingers would erase them.[8] What is most evanescent about these pieces of evidence, as about mesmerism, has to do with the ways of seeing, hearing, touching, and interpreting that made them plausible. Plausibility is one of the hardest things for historians to reconstruct in a satisfying manner, perhaps because it involves not merely a set of logical propositions but also a visceral response to sensory phenomena. Mesmerists and psychic researchers not only emphasized different kinds of arguments from ours, but they used their eyes, ears, and noses differently.

Ironically, the discrepancy between the day before the feast and the day after—between the tales mesmerists (or their subjects) had to tell and those told of them by their descendants—resembles the interpretative problems raised by the difference between the trance state and the waking state in mesmeric practice: a sense of expectation, promise, and ambiguity and a set of possibilities would become nearly invisible when one looked back from the vantage point of a cultural hangover or a professionalized discipline. The world of the mesmerists, the state of the entranced mind, and the possibilities of early-Victorian intellectual culture all suggest fundamental challenges of retrospective interpretation. Historians are not mesmerists, but all concerned in mesmerism had to become historians in their fashion. Individuals experiencing the mesmeric trance for themselves were in no state of mind to communicate it to others; but upon waking, it was all too frequently the case that these experiences were lost forever. Either the subject was unable to summon words adequate to her experience, or, worse, she could remember nothing of what had passed. She was in the position of the soul as described by Wordsworth, "And the soul, remembering how she felt, / But what she felt remembering not."

Mesmerism, like the "island of Mesmeria" explored by Madame La Reveuse, provided a means of discovery. It was imagined as a discovery of a new place, but, both in the experiment of Madame La Reveuse and in mesmerism's own career, it became the cause of its own obliteration. Recovering this world therefore remains partial, problematic, impeded at every step. Mesmeria survives in the record it has left us of the collaborations and rivalries of those who believed they had come to know something about it. That record does exist, but it is conditioned by circumstances of custom, language, class, and gender, as was the conclusion of the imaginary mesmeric experiences of Madame La Reveuse on the island of Mesmeria. In fact, we might turn in closing to *The Island of Mesmeria* one last time to recall the exchange that ended her mesmeric explorations.

Signor Phantasio: What discoveries I have made! I shall be honoured like Columbus!
Madame La Reveuse: I think I am the discoverer.
Signor: Of what?
Madame: I know not. I have no recollection.

⤞ N O T E S ⤝

Introduction

1. Ryals and Fielding, *Letters of Thomas and Jane Welsh Carlyle*, 18:282–84.
2. "University College Hospital: Animal magnetism," *Lancet*, 26 May 1838, 285.
3. The pathbreaking study was Robert Darnton's *Mesmerism and the end of the Enlightenment in France;* the social history of mesmerism in France and England at the turn of the eighteenth and nineteenth century is Fara, "Attractive practice."
4. Kaplan, "Mesmeric mania"; Palfreman, "Mesmerism"; Quen, "Three cases"; Parssinen, "Mesmeric performers"; Parssinen, "Medical fringe"; Basham, *Trial of woman.*
5. Barrow, "Medical heretics."
6. For a more extended discussion of the literature on this subject, see Winter, "Construction of orthodoxies."
7. Daston and Galison, "Image of objectivity."
8. Chambers, *Testimony*, 10.
9. Poovey, *Making a social body*, 55–77.
10. Burn, *Age of equipoise.*
11. Owen, *Darkened room;* Oppenheim, *Other world;* Cooter, *Cultural meaning of popular science.* My account tries to fulfill some of the historical "promise" described in Cooter's "History of mesmerism in Britain."
12. The definitive study is Alan Gauld's *History of hypnotism;* see also Crabtree, *From Mesmer to Freud.* For an argument tracing key elements of modern cognitive psychology to Victorian mesmerism, see Miller, "Going unconscious."
13. The classic work is Ellenberger's *Discovery of the unconscious.* (On the history of this book and its influence, see Hacking, *Rewriting the soul.*) The work that most blatantly uses the Mesmer-reincarnated-as-Freud gimmick is Buranelli, *Wizard from Vienna.* These books form two poles of sophistication and empirical "thickness" in this literature.

14. Parssinen, "Medical fringe"; Palfremen, "Mesmerism and the medical profession"; Quen, "Three cases."

15. For a discussion of what "unconscious" could mean in early Victorian physiology, see Miller, "Going unconscious."

16. See Collingwood *(Idea of history)* on the Albert Memorial—a monument so ugly that it is proof that the culture that produced it must be incommensurable with ours. See also Jardine, *Scenes of inquiry,* opening paragraphs.

Chapter One

1. "Discovery of the island of Mesmeria."

2. This was a reference to the Society for the Diffusion of Useful Knowledge, founded in the 1810s to "diffuse" knowledge to the minds of working people.

3. White, *Month in Yorkshire,* 103–4, transcribed the popular song "The railway to heaven," which ends as God urges, "give me thy heart; / Make haste, or else the train will start." Shaftesbury described rail as satanic in 1839, quoted in Hodder, *Life of Shaftesbury,* 1:257.

4. John Leech's "Railway juggernaut of 1845," discussed in Dods, *Age of paradox,* 22.

5. Mill, "Spirit of the age I," *Collected works,* 22:227–34, 228.

6. Froude, *Carlyle's life in London,* 1:310–12.

7. "Dipsychus," in Clough, *Poems and prose remains,* 109–73; Young, *Portrait of an age,* 24. Young's quote from Clough ("animal sensibility") is not footnoted, and I have not identified its source.

8. Carlyle, *Sartor Resartus,* 129, 142, 148.

9. Carlyle, *Past and present,* 1–2; Chesney, *Victorian underworld,* 11–37.

10. William Huskisson's death famously cast a pall over this moment in the "march of mind."

11. Somerville, *Autobiography,* 360–61.

12. [Gallenga], "Age we live in."

13. "Religion is . . . the spirit of spiritless conditions. It is the opium of the people" (critique of Hegel's *Rechtphilosophie,* in Marx and Engels, *Collected works,* 3:175–76).

14. On the sixteen-year-old O'Key, see chapters 3–4; Reichenbach, *Abstract;* Atkinson and Martineau, *Letters on the laws.*

15. Mary Howitt to William Howitt, in Howitt, *Autobiography,* 2:99.

16. Clarke, *Autobiographical recollections,* 161.

17. Lafontaine, *Mémoires,* 1:272; Hall, *Mesmeric experiences,* 1; Gauld, *Hypnotism,* 163–65, 203–4, 281.

18. "Animal magnetism: Letter from Baron Dupotet."

19. *Vandeleur, or Animal magnetism,* excerpt printed in *Times,* 20 October 1836; Romer, *Sturmer.*

20. [Wakley], "Animal magnetism," 450; [Wakley], "Virtues of animal magnetism," 413–14.

21. Carlyle, *Past and present*, 23.

22. "To Sir Rhubarb Pill." For similar portraits of Peel as a demagogue, see Richard Monckton Milnes, "Mesmerism," commonplace book 6, xxiii, Houghton Papers, Trinity College; "Animal magnetism in practice."

23. The best-selling example was Chambers's *Vestiges*. See Secord, *Books of Creation*.

24. Somerville, *Connexion;* Gooding, "Faraday, Thomson"; Morus, "Correlation."

25. Yeo, "Intellectual authority," 9.

26. Eliot, *Mill on the Floss*, 238.

27. Faraday, "Observations on mental education," 474.

28. Faraday (attributed to), identified on title page as "late electrician and chemist of England," *Relations of science to the phenomena of life*. This was published in Massachusetts and distributed in England as well.

29. Lewis, *Authority and influence*, 55.

30. Charlotte Brontë to her father, 7 June and 8 October 1851, in Jennings, *Pandaemonium*, 262.

31. Cooter, *Cultural meaning of popular science;* Smith, *History of the human sciences.*

32. Scull, *Most solitary of afflictions;* Showalter, *Female malady.*

33. Cowling, *Artist as anthropologist*, 121–81, 370.

Chapter Two

1. The new scientific and medical enterprises of 1830s London have been described in Desmond, *Politics of evolution*, 101–51; Morus, Schaffer, and Secord, "Scientific London"; Morus, "Currents from the underworld"; and Ginn, "Philosophers and artisans," chapters 1, 3–4.

2. For instance, the shaving of inmates' heads (Groth, "Christian radicalism," chapter 2).

3. Richardson, *Death, dissection, and the destitute*, 159–61, discusses Bentham's ultimate Utilitarian message: his will instructed that his own body provide an example that human bodies were machines, and could continue to be of use when their original owners no longer needed them.

4. Quoted in Cawthorn, "Thomas Wakley," 197. See also Crawford, "Scientific profession."

5. Desmond, *Politics of evolution*, 83.

6. Quoted in Hays, "Rise and fall," 534.

7. Hays, "Rise and fall," 539.

8. On the significance of the French Analysis in England, see Ashworth, "Memory," 634–37.

9. Porter, "Physical examination"; Robert Liston's model of the live surgical subject on the dead anatomical one, in *Practical surgery*, 3.

10. Cooter, *Cultural meaning of popular science*, 111–13; Combe, *Constitution of*

man; Smith, "Background of physiological psychology"; Leys, "Background to the reflex controversy," 8, 34; Miller, "Going unconscious."

11. Ure, *Philosophy of manufactures,* as cited in Jennings, *Pandaemonium,* 192.

12. "Extraordinary novelties . . . Eccaleobion," advertising sheet, c. 1837, Guild-hall Library.

13. Baum, *Calculating passion,* opening paragraphs.

14. Ticknor, *Life, letters, and journals,* 12 July 1835, 1:407–8.

15. "Necromancer of the North," broadsheet, Guildhall Library.

16. Brewster, *Natural magic;* Scott, *Demonology and witchcraft;* Godwin, *Lives of the necromancers;* and the less well known Upham, *Lectures on witchcraft;* T. S. F., *Demonologia;* [Moir?], "Daemonology and witchcraft"; Newnham, *Essay on superstition;* Prichard, "Somnambulism and animal magnetism." An influential German source was Jung-Stilling, *Theory of pneumatology.* Godwin, *Lives of the necromancers,* addressed many of the subjects of natural magic but to a slightly different purpose: to document the power of the human imagination.

17. Wheatstone, "On the transmission of musical sounds"; Bowers, *Wheatstone,* 32–38.

18. Wheatstone, "Description of the kaleidophone."

19. Wheatstone, "Contributions to the physiology of vision"; Brewster and Wheatstone, *Brewster and Wheatstone on vision;* Wheatstone, "Some remarks on dreaming, somnambulism, and other states of partial activity of the cerebral faculties," *Lancet,* 31 March 1832, 30 January 1832, cited in Cooter, *Phrenology in the British Isles.*

20. See Smith, *Trial by medicine;* Taylor, *Secret theatre of home,* chapters 1–2. This distinction was new, but it would soon become standard.

21. The "identity" question was whether electricities from different sources are the same. On research with Faraday see Faraday, *Experimental researches in electricity,* 420–21, 455; on the telegraph see Hubbard, *Cooke and Wheatstone,* 37–57; Bowers, *Wheatstone,* 63–86.

22. De Quincey, "Animal magnetism," 456, 473.

23. Porter, "Under the influence." Fara's "Attractive practice" describes mesmerists and their practices between the 1780s and the 1810s. See also Gauld, *Hypnotism,* 197–99.

24. Shelley, "The magnetic lady to her patient" (1822), in Shelley, *Poetical works.* See Leask, "Shelley's magnetic ladies."

25. Southey, *Letters from England,* letter 52. J. F. C. Harrison (*Second coming,* 74) speculated that mesmerism complemented William Sharp's Swedenborgianism. On radical careers between the 1790s and the 1830s, see McCalman, *Radical underworld;* McCalman, "Popular irreligion."

26. Elliotson, *Human physiology,* 1:663. I have found one more, but no one seems to remember him at all: Loewe, *Animal magnetism.*

27. Crabtree, *From Mesmer to Freud,* 40–45, 90–91; Gauld, *Hypnotism,* 39–40, 111–18. For a contemporary example of what readers knew of Puysegur, see Hall, "Rise, progress," 151.

28. Laplace, *Théorie analytique,* as quoted in Lardner and Bulwer-Lytton, "Animal magnetism," 28–29.

29. Cuvier, *Comparative anatomy,* 2:29.

30. The committee's members were MM. Bourdois, Itard, Gueneau, de Hussy, Guersent, Fouquier, Leroux, Magendie, Marc, Thillaye, and Husson. Laennec was an original member but withdrew because of illness.

31. Colquhoun, *Report,* 207; De Quincey, "Animal magnetism"; Colquhoun, *Isis revelata.*

32. "Animal magnetism," review of Colquhoun's translation of French commission report, 177. The *Lancet* failed to note that Magendie, while present on the committee, abstained from signing the final report. See also "Animal magnetism," *Monthly Chronicle;* Colquhoun, *Isis revelata.*

33. Dupotet, *Magnétisme opposé,* 186–262.

34. Dupotet, *Magnétisme opposé,* 186.

35. Dupotet, "Letter to the editor," 905–6.

36. "Animal magnetism, in London, in 1837." The next several quotations come from this source. See also "Animal magnetism," *Mirror,* 18 March 1837, 169: "it would be unjust to assert . . . that all the learned and independent men who supported it [at the Académie] are either fools or knaves." Compare " 'Animal magnetism,' from the *Comic Annual,*" which mocked the experiments.

37. "The humbug of animal magnetism," *Times,* 18 October 1837.

38. This was the central tenet of monomania, which became widely used in reference to any obsession. Initially, it referred only to obsession with a particular idea, but James Cowles Prichard developed from it the notion of moral insanity. See Scull, *Solitary affliction;* Smith, *Trial by medicine.*

39. Altered states of mind exaggerated the mental faculties. When a person was drunk, for example, "his qualities, good or bad, come forth without reserve" because drink weakened the "power of volition, that faculty which keeps the will subordinate to the judgment" (Macnish, *Anatomy of drunkenness,* 44). On the similarity between dream states and insanity, see Macnish, *Philosophy of sleep,* 43–44.

40. On the insanity defense see Smith, *Trial by medicine.*

41. Mayo, Untitled passage.

42. I have not been able to discover the nature of the objections that ended Dupotet's work at the Middlesex. Mayo's sympathetic colleagues included John Wilson and Daniel Macreight. Macreight lectured on *materia medica* and therapeutics at Middlesex and published a *Manual of botany.* Wilson practiced animal magnetism at the Middlesex during the next several years. For Mayo's interests see *Outlines of human physiology,* 186, 92–93, 169–201.

43. Desmond, *Politics of evolution,* 230–35, 274–75, 383 n.

44. "Dr. Elliotson on clinical instruction."

45. E.g., Desmond, quoting *Medical Gazette,* in *Politics of evolution,* 181.

46. On Elliotson see Clarke, *Autobiographical recollections;* Cooter, *Cultural meaning of popular science,* 52, 363; Miller, "Gower Street scandal"; Williams, *Doctors differ,* 155–94.

47. See Sprigge, *Life and times of Wakley;* Schwartz, *Wakley and the "Lancet";* Richardson, *Death, dissection, and the destitute;* Peterson, *Medical profession,* chapters 1−3. Most of the relevant *Lancet* articles are reproduced in Kaplan, *Elliotson on mesmerism.*

48. Williams, *Doctors differ,* 161.

49. Cooter, *Cultural meaning of popular science,* 100.

50. Elliotson, "Education as it is," 351.

51. Mayo to Whewell, n.d., Whewell Papers, Add MS a 29929, Trinity College. The others, Mayo told Whewell, were to be "Babbage, Faraday, & Wheatstone." See Mayo to Babbage, 19 March 1838, 21 March 1838, British Library, Additional Manuscripts, 37910, Babbage Correspondence, folios 398, 400; James, *Correspondence of Michael Faraday,* 2:498−99. Faraday's visit to the UCH wards was recorded on 10 February 1838, University College, Hospital Casebooks, MR/1/16.

52. "University College Hospital: Animal magnetism," *Lancet,* 26 May 1838, 283. George Mills was said to have written many, if not all, of these reports in the *Lancet* (see " 'Animal magentism,' or 'Mesmerism,' " 805). See also *Athenaeum,* 21 July 1838, 515; "Animal magnetism," *Lancet,* 25 August 1838, 780: "A committee, consisting of some distinguished members of the medical profession, having been formed to investigate the subject of Animal magnetism . . . consists, among others, of Dr. Bostock, Mr. Lawrence, Dr. Roget, Mr. Mayo, Mr. Kiernan, and Professor Wheatstone."

53. Somerville, *Connexion;* Whewell, review of Somerville's *Connexion.* On these issues see Yeo, "Intellectual authority"; Secord, "Extraordinary experiment"; Winter, "Construction of orthodoxies."

54. Council Minutes, 10 May 1838, Royal Society of London; Hall, *All scientists now.*

55. See Desmond, *Politics of evolution.*

56. They were Elliotson's friend Robert Grant and Neil Arnott, who was a physician and a natural philosopher and had recently (1836) become a member of University of London Senate and more recently Fellow of the Royal Society (FRS; 1838).

57. Hall, *All scientists now.* The Physiological Sectional Committee included Charles Bell, Thomas Bell, John Bostock, Benjamin Collins Brodie, William Clift, Francis Kiernan, William Lawrence, William Sharp Macleay, Herbert Mayo, Richard Owen, Wilson Phillip, James Cowles Prichard, Peter Mark Roget, and Robert Bentley Todd. Thomas Bell was surgeon at Guy's Hospital and professor of zoology at King's. Bostock was president of the Geological Society in 1820s. Clift was a naturalist and caretaker of the Hunter Collection, Royal College of Surgeons.

58. "University College Hospital: Animal magnetism: Fifth report," 549.

59. Winter, "Construction of orthodoxies."

60. "Animal magnetism," *Lancet,* 25 August 1838, 780.

61. In fact, Dickens became deeply involved in mesmerism. See Kaplan, *Dickens and mesmerism.*

62. Elliotson, Female Casebook, 1837−38, MR/1/16, 10 February 1838, University College London, Hospital Casebooks.

63. Faraday never distanced himself from animal magnetism the way he did from

claims regarding the electric production of life, and he preserved a sheaf of papers from the 1840s relating to animal magnetism. However, he never publicized this or any other experiment, except for table-turning. On Faraday's displays see Gooding, "In nature's school"; Morus, "Different experimental lives."

64. "University College Hospital: Animal magnetism: Conclusion of second report of facts and experiments," 403.

65. Lardner and Bulwer-Lytton, "Animal magnetism," 21.

66. [De Quincey], "Animal magnetism"; "Animal magnetism," review of Colquhoun's translation of the French commission report.

67. "University College Hospital: Animal magnetism: Sixth report," 385–88, 587.

68. Lardner and Bulwer-Lytton, "Animal magnetism," 30.

69. According to brief press notices and private gossip, the experiments and lectures were carried out; however, I have not been able to locate records of them.

70. Molesworth believed that "the researches now being made . . . will add considerably to our knowledge of the phenomena of Nature, extend the bounds of science, and afford explanations of numerous facts previously inexplicable" ("University College Hospital," *Lancet*, 26 May 1838, 320).

71. Lardner and Bulwer-Lytton, "Animal magnetism," 26.

72. Toole, *Ada;* Elliotson, *Numerous surgical operations,* mentions an experiment in 1840 with Wheatstone and with Neil Arnott (at Arnott's request).

73. They tried making passes with one, two, and three fingers, varied the number of passes, and tried experiments with the patients' eyes partly versus completely open (*Lancet*, 23 June 1838, 445).

74. Their efforts to prove the existence of a physical agency involved "magnetizing" fluids such as water and various mild acids by placing the magnetizer's finger in the fluid for a short period of time, and then asking the subject to drink the fluid; alternatively, a range of different metals were found to convey the magnetic influence from magnetist to subject (nickel was a good conductor while lead was not).

75. "University College Hospital: Animal magnetism: Sixth report," 585.

76. Lardner and Bulwer-Lytton, "Animal magnetism," 29–30.

77. Holland, *Medical notes;* the discussions of mental phenomena were so popular that they were reprinted separately as *Chapters on mental physiology.*

78. Forbes, "History of animal magnetism," 303.

79. Sharpe, "Animal magnetism." The doctor used the object glass of an achromatic telescope and a couple of mirrors to make similar experiments in reflection. He claimed that the magnetic influence was capable of reflection and obeyed "those laws of caloric that relate to its double and single refraction and polarisation" (454). One associate of Sharpe wrote to the *Lancet* to dissociate himself from the "impious and immoral" science (Bromet, "Animal magnetism").

80. "Medical Society of London."

81. J. N. Bainbridge, letter to the editor, *Lancet*, 28 April 1838, 168–69.

82. "Medico-Botanical Society," 367–71.

83. E.g., Chandler, "Rheumatism."

84. Ticknor, *Life, letters, and journals*, 12 July 1835, 1:407–8.

85. *Medical Gazette*, quoted in Desmond, *Politics of evolution*, 123.

86. William Macready thought the patients were partly under a "morbid influence and partly lend themselves to a delusion"; William Harrison Ainsworth thought the effects "truly surprising—almost magical" (Kaplan, *Dickens and mesmerism*, 29).

87. See Sutherland, *Is Heathcliffe a murderer?* 42–45.

88. Caricatures in this series were a regular form of political commentary and were routinely discussed in the *Times*. I am very grateful to Jim Secord for this document.

Chapter Three

1. E.g., "Animal magnetism," *Medico-Chirurgical Review*, 1 October 1838, 635–36.

2. "Evidence relating to the medical relief of the sick poor," *Lancet*, 1 April 1837; "Evidence relating to medical relief of the sick poor," *Lancet*, 13 May 1837, 264–68; [Wakley], editorial, *Lancet*, 11 November 1837. "Treatment of the sick-poor" transcribes verbatim a poor patient's description of his medical treatment.

3. Poovey, *Making a social body*. On the Irish, see 55–72. Engels's Irish guide, Mary Burns, provides another useful point of comparison to the Irish magnetic subjects discussed in this chapter. See Kiernan, foreword to Engels, *Condition of the working class*, 13.

4. James Phillips Kay, quoted in Poovey, *Making a social body*, 55–72. On Irish "savagery" see Engels, *Condition of the working class*, 123–26.

5. Barnes and Shapin, "Head and hand."

6. Elliotson, *Human physiology*, appendix.

7. "Animal magnetism: Experiments of the Baron Dupotet."

8. "Animal magnetism: Experiments of the Baron Dupotet." I'd like to thank Nigel Leask for identifying the reference to Byron's taste in women's bodies *(Don Juan)*.

9. The closest thing to a discussion of unconscious thinking for this period is Brown, *Philosophy of the human mind*.

10. "Animal magnetism: Experiments of the Baron Dupotet," 837–38.

11. Other examples from this stage of the experiments include the exchange between Elliotson's clinical clerk William Wood and an anonymous Eye-Witness. See Eye-Witness, "Trials of animal magnetism"; Wood, "Animal magnetism in London," 163–65; Eye-Witness, "Mesmerism at University College Hospital." The Eye-Witness conceded the validity of some of the effects but said they were a form of hysteria.

12. On what was meant by diagnoses of epilepsy and hysteria, see Shorter, *From paralysis to fatigue;* Micale, *Approaching hysteria;* Showalter, *Female malady.*

13. Kaplan, "Mesmeric mania," discusses Elliotson's experiments of this period. See also "Abstract of a clinical lecture on sleep waking"; "Dr. Elliotson on clinical instruction"; Wood, "Animal magnetism in London," which discussed the fact that male patients were far less susceptible to the magnetic influence than female ones, but also described a striking male case.

14. Caroline O'Shea, 18, admitted 4 July 1837, Elliotson Female Casebook, 1837–38, MR/1/9, 203–4.

15. The presenting symptoms of women patients treated with mesmerism included "affection of the head," chorea, delirium, *tic douloureux*, and (especially) epilepsy. Approximately twenty-five patients were diagnosed with hysteria during this period, and only two were recorded as having been treated with animal magnetism. Several of the mesmeric subjects did show hysteric symptoms, but only as a subsidiary part of a more complex or different set of symptoms (University College London, Hospital Casebooks, MR/1/5, MR/1/9, MR/1/16).

16. On the changing symptomatology of hysteria, see Shorter, *From paralysis to fatigue;* Micale, *Approaching hysteria.*

17. Jane was initially admitted 14 February 1837, discharged 6 June, and readmitted months later. Elizabeth was admitted 4 April 1837 and discharged along with her sister, in late December 1838.

18. Theophilus Thompson had recently written a work echoing Wakley's calls for mental and professional discipline (*On the improvement of medicine*, 17–19). It was reviewed around this time in the *Literary Gazette*, a slight but favorable notice.

19. Elliotson, Female Casebook, 1837–38, MR/1/16, 24.

20. Elliotson, Female Casebook, 1837–388, MR/1/16, 18 March 1838, 26.

21. Elliotson, Female Casebook, 1837–38, MR/1/9, 4 April 1837, 142.

22. "Animal magnetism," *Lancet*, 18 August 1838, 727. Her prepubescent appearance was misleading; the casebook (MR/1/9, 179) recorded that she menstruated for the first time on 28 June 1837.

23. Elliotson, Female Casebook, MR/1/9, 142.

24. Elliotson, Female Casebook, 1837–38, MR/1/9, 142.

25. Elliotson, Female Casebook, 1837–38, 30 October 1837, 246.

26. For instance, see entries of Elliotson, Female Casebook, 1837–38, 251–52: 7, 9, 11, 18, 23, 25, 27 November. On the twenty-seventh the clerk referred to the free discharge emitted from a blister: "Blood buffed and cupped coagulum softer. After the bleeding . . . head was relieved but she felt exceedingly weak."

27. Elliotson, Female Casebook, 1837–38, MR/1/16, 4 January 1838, 273.

28. For examples of typical relapse and recovery, see the entries of 3, 5, 9, 12, 14, 16, 18 September 1837, Elliotson, Female Casebook, 1837, 209.

29. Elliotson, Female Casebook, 1837–38, MR/1/9, 273.

30. Elliotson, Female Casebook, 1837–38, MR/1/9, 13 January 1838, 274. The clerk wrote "spontaneously," presumably out of habit, then crossed it out and wrote "artificially" above the line.

31. On these see Gauld, *Hypnotism*, 39–44, 128–29, 174–75, 199–200; Ellenberger, *Discovery of the unconscious.*

32. Elliotson, Female Casebook, 1837–38, MR/1/9, 13 January 1838, 274.

33. Dupotet, *Introduction to animal magnetism.*

34. Elliotson, Female Casebook, 1837–38, MR/1/16, 1 May 1838, 29.

35. Elliotson, Female Casebook, 1837–38, MR/1/16, 8 April 1838, 27.

36. They included the marquis of Anglesey, Sir Charles Paget, the earl of Burling-

364 NOTES TO PAGES 73–76

ton, the duke of Roxburgh, Earl Wilton, Lord Dinorben, Dr. Michael Faraday, Sir Joseph De Courcy Laffan, and Sir J. South ("University College Hospital: Animal magnetism," *Lancet*, 26 May 1838, 282).

37. "University College Hospital: Animal magnetism," *Lancet*, 26 May 1838, 284. Kaplan, in "Mesmeric mania" and *Dickens and mesmerism*, discusses the public demonstrations and the controversy attending them. The *Lancet* reports are reprinted in Kaplan, *Elliotson on mesmerism*. An interesting point of comparison as to what the "most accomplished actor" might have been thought to accomplish in the way of an altered state of mind was the Irish actress Harriet Smithson, who was becoming wildly popular during these years for her portrayal of Ophelia (among other things; Berlioz, *Memoirs*, 109–13). After seeing Smithson playing *Hamlet* for the first time, Berlioz developed a "nervous condition like a sickness, of which only a great writer on physiology could give an adequate idea. I lost the power of sleep, and with it all my former animation" (58).

38. "University College Hospital: Animal magnetism," *Lancet*, 26 May 1838, 285–86.

39. O'Key sang several psalms and "The green hills of Tyrol": "'Pray don't sing,' said the Doctor. 'Don't sing,' she replied; 'Where does sing live? I *may* sing 'Buy a Black Sheep,' for Mr. Wood told me so" ("University College Hospital: Animal magnetism," *Lancet*, 26 May 1838, 286).

40. "University College Hospital: Animal magnetism," *Lancet*, 26 May 1838, 286. Little historical attention has been given to portrayals of race in Britain during this period, and certainly too little to know whether and to what extent "Black" would have been a racially specific term for O'Key. Given the importance of the character of a "Negro" to the O'Key sisters soon after this experiment, I suspect that it was. This issue will be discussed below.

41. Mayo as quoted in "Animal magnetism," *Athenaeum*, 1838; "Animal magnetism," *Medico-Chirurgical Review*, 1 October 1838, 635. On France see Gauld, *Hypnotism*.

42. The *Lancet* drily summed up the reactions of the nonmedical observers: "'Marvellous!' murmured the astonished commoners. 'Very odd concern,' observed the carriage company, who arrived by turns, and saw the phenomena by bits'" ("University College Hospital: Animal magnetism," *Lancet*, 26 May 1838, 286).

43. "University College Hospital: Animal magnetism," *Lancet*, 26 May 1838, 287–88.

44. "University College Hospital: Animal magnetism," *Lancet*, 26 May 1838.

45. "University College Hospital: Animal magnetism: Second report."

46. They included the anatomist Robert Grant; the poet Thomas Moore; the bishop of Norwich; Philip earl of Stanhope; Isaac Lyon Goldsmid, who was one of the founders and trustees of UCL; the eminent philanthropist and sheriff of London, Moses Montefiore; and many members of Parliament. Other eminent observers included the earl of Wilton, the earl of Mansfield, Colonel Yorke (probably Phillip James Yorke, chemist), and the theologian (sympathetic to the apocalyptic evangeli-

cal preacher Edward Irving) Henry Bulteel ("University College Hospital: Second report").

47. "University College Hospital: Second report."

48. "University College Hospital: Second report," 383.

49. Although these feats were reported in the press for the first time in the summer, they occur in the case notes earlier. For instance, O'Key was reported to have mesmerized Hannah Hunter, one of the youngest patients (Elliotson, Female Casebook, MR/1/16, 31 January 1838, 31–34).

Chapter Four

1. "Our weekly gossip," Athenaeum 560 (1838): 515. The *Athenaeum* used such an incident to cast doubt on O'Key's veracity: O'Key (while entranced) accosted another magnetized patient. She "thundered forth with alarming gesticulations—'Arise, or I'll limb you! Get up! I say, or I'll limb you! You asleep indeed!'"

2. Shiach, *Discourse on popular culture*, 73.

3. Jewson, "Medical knowledge"; Jewson, "Disappearance of the sick man"; Nicolson, "Metastatic theory of pathogenesis"; Fissell, *Patients, power, and the poor.*

4. On the complex early history of doctor/patient relations, see Fissell, *Patients, power, and the poor;* Porter, "Physical examination."

5. E.g., Sharpe, "History from below." In the history of science there have been attempts to reconstruct even less accessible perspectives: those of the nonhuman entities studied by scientific experiments (Latour, *Pasteurisation of France*).

6. Bakhtin, *Rabelais and his world;* Burke, *Popular culture in early modern Europe,* 192.

7. Reid, "Interpreting the festival calendar," esp. 227 ff.

8. R. and G. Cruikshank, "The grand carnival," in Egan, *Life in London.* For a later example see "Carnival in Lewes" (*Illustrated London News,* no date [midcentury], on file under "Carnival" in Mary Evans Picture Library), in which top-hatted gentlemen and their ladies look on from the shadowy margins as night revelers with animal masks and torches sweep through the streets.

9. Clarke, *Autobiographical recollections,* 163–164 n: "She was, I believe, one of the foremost actors in the farce of the 'unknown tongues' . . . in the séances of that remarkable preacher Edward Irving" at Islington Green, after he left Hatton Garden. On Irving's meetings, see the (hostile) account by Baxter, *Narrative of facts.*

10. For instance, Baxter's *Narrative of facts.* The religious disabilities legislation, established in the Restoration, prevented non-Anglicans (Catholics and Dissenters) from participating in any office connected with the state.

11. Smith, *Legends and miracles.*

12. Baer, *Theatre and disorder,* 166–88; Barker, "Chartists, theatre, reform"; Booth, "East End and West End"; Mekeel, "Social influence."

13. Bailey, "Custom, capital, and culture," 180–208.

14. "University College Hospital: Animal magnetism," *Lancet*, 26 May 1838, 284–85.

15. At one point O'Key woke in a state of delirium from a deep sleep and, when asked, claimed she hadn't "been nowhere" ("University College Hospital: Animal magnetism: Second report," 381).

16. "University College Hospital: Animal magnetism: Second report," 381.

17. "University College Hospital: Animal magnetism," *Lancet*, 26 May 1838, 286–87.

18. *OED:* "an effeminate and spiritless man or youth; wanting in courage or manliness." For a contemporary usage, see "Noctes Ambrosianae," *Blackwood's Magazine* 32 (1832): 392: "This new dandyfied era of milksoppism."

19. "Jim Crow" was written by Thomas D. Rice in 1832, according to Woodward, *Strange career of Jim Crow*, 7 n.

20. "Jim Crow" (1836), Madden Collection of Broadsides, Cambridge University Library, 9:202.

21. "University College Hospital: Animal magnetism," *Lancet*, 26 May 1838, 286–87.

22. Presumably the dance O'Key offered to make figured in the popular pantomime routines of the late 1830s that used the character Jim Crow. On Jim Crow at Sadler's Wells see Salberg, *Once upon a pantomime*, 15–16.

23. "Our weekly gossip," *Athenaeum* 569 (1838): 699: "Sadler's Wells is the only fit arena for a more protracted discussion; and heavily do we feel the loss of our old favourite Grimaldi, who would have been so admirable a professor to pit against the magnetists."

24. "Juba at Vauxhall," *Illustrated London News*, 1848, Mary Evans Picture Library; "The Ethiopian serenaders," *Illustrated London News*, 1848. "Juba at Vauxhall" evaluated this man's performances at the Vauxhall Gardens in 1848. The published sketch (fig. 24) depicts him in a posture reminiscent of Jim Crow (suspended in the air, one knee bent). His was a "national dance" (i.e., a "Nigger dance") that "we can believe in" because it combined a dizzying speed and dexterity of movement that no European could match with the air of natural movement: "how could Juba enter into their wonderful complications so naturally?" The "Ethiopian serenaders," on the other hand, were more ambiguous. They dressed in "dandy costume, *à la Jullien*" and performed their Western airs in so "grotesque" a manner that they cast doubt on the "authenticity" of the African airs.

25. See Kaplan, *Dickens and mesmerism*, 43, for further discussion.

26. "University College Hospital: Animal magnetism: Sixth report," 590.

27. Robert Carswell's single major work, *Forms of disease*, was published in 1837. "Dr Elliotson on medical instruction" indicates an existing rivalry for students.

28. Anthony Todd Thomson, professor of medical jurisprudence at UCL, had just joined Wakley's campaign for coroners to be medically trained, and his lectures on medical jurisprudence appeared weekly in the *Lancet*.

29. Lindley attended his demonstrations throughout the spring and summer,

though there is no indication that Cooper did; Lardner and Bulwer-Lytton, "Animal magnetism," 28, reported that Lindley, Grant, and Graham attended regularly.

30. On 1 May 1838 Thomson, Davis, and Liston called a faculty meeting to discuss whether Elliotson's demonstrations were "detrimental to the character and the interests of the College and the Hospital" (University College London, College Correspondence 1838:102). At Lindley's urging, the council made no formal request, but hinted to Elliotson that he should desist (extract of minutes of meeting held Monday, 12 April 1838, College Correspondence 1838:4280).

31. University College London, Council Minutes, 9 June 1838.

32. Over the course of several specially convened meetings (6, 9, 13 June), the council took an increasingly strong line: on 13 June it resolved that the "public demonstration" of animal magnetism was "foreign to the objects of the hospital" and, in response to a protest from Elliotson, prohibited demonstrations to "any parties whatsoever" (University College London, Council Minutes 1838:165).

33. Palfreman, "Mesmerism."

34. "Animal magnetism," *Quarterly Review*, 61; "Animal magnetism," *Tait's Edinburgh Magazine;* [Palmer], "Animal magnetism."

35. "University College Hospital: Animal magnetism: Sixth report." See also Leeson, "Objections."

36. "University College Hospital: Animal magnetism: Fifth report."

37. See Sprigge, *Life and times of Wakley.* Sprigge described Wakley's move to Bedford Square in 1828 as a triumphant conclusion to professional and personal struggles of the 1820s.

38. Secord, "Extraordinary experiment," has discussed a similar strategic discreditation of controversial experimental findings during this period, in the case of Andrew Crosse's electric production of life.

39. Darnton, *Mesmerism,* 64–66.

40. "'Animal magnetism,' or 'Mesmerism,'" 806.

41. "Suggestion" was, however, an important term in the psychology of cognition as developed by Thomas Brown in 1820 (connoting a positive role for the imagination and intellectual faculties in changing the character of a sensation before it was presented to the conscious mind in the act of perception). While this was very different from suggestion in the hypnotic sense of the term (beginning in the 1840s), Brown's notion was an important contributor to its development.

42. "'Animal magnetism, or 'Mesmerism,'" 805.

43. These events are chronicled in Kaplan's *Dickens and mesmerism.*

44. Wakley put on trial and condemned other doctors routinely. For a timely example of a case of alleged malpractice and alleged misrepresentation of what had transpired, see the editorial in the *Lancet,* 16 December 1837, a condemnation of Samuel Cooper of UCH, who was accused of causing a patient's death.

45. As we shall see in future chapters, "mesmerism" could be used for the positive reason that it was agnostic about the causal agency involved, but its initial usage emphasized an association between the early Victorian practice and the supposed charlatanism of the science's founder.

46. Jon Palfreman's "Mesmerism" claims that the *Medical Times*'s support for animal magnetism in the wake of the Wakley incident was a calculated move in a rivalry with the *Lancet*.

47. "Animal magnetism," *Medico-Chirurgical Review*, 1 October 1838, 635. Pythia was priestess of Apollo at Delphi. Women who held this position were suddenly inspired by the sulfurous vapors that issued from the temple. In altered states of mind they would speak the oracles of the gods, often with howling and cries, while priests transcribed their utterances and put them into order.

48. "Animal magnetism," *Medico-Chirurgical Review*, 1 October 1838, 636.

49. [Wakley], "Experiments on the two sisters." Many of the articles that were published on mesmerism in the *Lancet* were not supplied with formal titles. In these cases the running head on the page is given as a working title.

50. [Wakley], "Virtues of animal magnetism."

51. [Wakley], "Immoral tendency of animal magnetism," 450–51.

52. [Wakley], "Virtues of animal magnetism."

53. [Wakley], "Immoral tendency of animal magnetism," 450–51.

54. [Wakley], "Immoral tendency of animal magnetism," 450.

55. Collini, "Idea of 'character.'"

56. "Animal magnetism [second notice]," 438, review of an attack on animal magnetism by Edwin Lee: Lee had, they claimed, "materially damaged the character of the witnesses in its [magnetism's] behalf, whose haste and credulity he has so effectually exposed."

57. "Medical portraits: Robert Liston." See also below, 168.

58. "Chronicle," *Annual Register* (1840): 293, 304; on the incident see Hays, "Rise and fall," 540–41.

59. Elliotson, *Human physiology*, 1166.

60. Trollope, *Michael Armstrong*. On Trollope's interest in Elliotson, mesmerism, and the O'Keys, see Ransom, *Trollope*, 130. Ransom reports that Trollope's involvement with the O'Keys was motivated at least as much by concern that they were not being treated properly (by Elliotson) as by interest in the mesmeric phenomena. A letter from Trollope concerning the care of the O'Key sisters and arranging a séance is in the Townshend Papers, Wisbech Museum. See also Elliotson, *Human physiology*, 1165–66.

Chapter Five

1. [Staite], *Mesmerism*, 7–8.

2. Forbes, "History of animal magnetism."

3. Wakley, "Mesmeric phenomena in Paris"; "Secrets of mesmerism unveiled"; "Dr. Elliotson's mesmeric exhibitions."

4. "Mesmerism: Its pretensions and effects."

5. Hopkinson, *Victorian cabinet maker*. The best account of the traveling mesmerists is Parssinen, "Mesmeric performers."

6. E.g., Mayo to Elliotson (late April? 1838) arranging a meeting in 1840 (Elliotson Correspondence, Townshend Papers); Elliotson to unknown correspondent, Morgan Papers, Pierpont Morgan Library. One of Elliotson's collaborators wrote a description of their mesmeric experiments in a pamphlet whose title sarcastically replicated Wakley's warnings about mesmeric rape. See Eye-Witness, *Full discovery*.

7. Morrell and Thackray, *Gentlemen of science*.

8. Quoted in Barnes and Shapin, "Head and hand."

9. Golinski, *Science as public culture*, traces the history of this issue up to the 1820s.

10. Parssinen, "Mesmeric performers," 89–90.

11. One medical mesmerist lauded William Davey for rising from a lace maker to a scientific lecturer through mesmerism. See Haddock, *Somnolism and psycheism*. See also Barrow, "Socialism is eternity."

12. The lecturers were self-conscious heirs to Priestley's ideal of communally legitimized knowledge. See Golinski, *Science as public culture*.

13. M'Neile, "Satanic agency," 147.

14. E.g., the *Times*, 20 July 1841, reported some of these tests as having been carried out on a subject of Lafontaine's and on 24 July 1841 called for further tests of mesmerism. See Gauld, *Hypnotism*, 164–65, 203–4, for more on Lafontaine.

15. Sandby, *Mesmerism and its opponents*, 1st ed., 112; "Exeter mesmeric record," *West Exeter and Plymouth Gazette*, 11 August 1849; "Abstract of a lecture on electrobiology"; Gregory, *Letters to a candid inquirer;* "Mr. Spencer Hall and the new organs"; "Lectures on phrenology"; "Phreno-magnetic cases"; C. Holmes, "Animal magnetism," 14 July 1843, Chelmsford, broadsheet, Purland Papers, National Library of Medicine.

16. "Recent demonstrations of animal magnetism," 205.

17. That is, either the reality of the phenomena or the validity of the theories the lecturers attached to them.

18. Jabez Inwards, 18 July 1843, Mechanics Institution, Holborn, admission 6p, handbill; E. Taylor, "Mesmerism, or vital magnetism," 20 and 27 November [1843?], Temperance Hall, Tottenham Court Road, admission 2d, handbill; J. N. Bailey, 19 July 1843, Hall of the National Association, High Holborn, admission 2d, broadsheet; Henry Marshall, 29 February 1844, Hall of Science, Finsbury Place, admission 3d, broadsheet. See also the broadsheet "This is Truth, though opposed to the Philosophy of Ages," 29 November, and 2 December 1852, Hall of Science, Finsbury Square: Gerald Massey was the mesmerist, his wife the clairvoyant diagnostician. All in Purland Papers.

19. Henry Marshall L. Sharpe, Angel Inn, Islington, admission 1s; Robert Collyer, City of London Literary and Scientific Institution, Aldersgate Street, admission 1s, broadsheet; H. Brookes, 13 May 1844, Lecture Hall, 57 Pall Mall, West, admission 1s, broadsheet; W. Brookes, May 1844, Eastern Lit and Scientific Institution, Hackney Road, admission 1s, broadsheet. All in Purland Papers.

20. W. H. Halse, "The wonders of mental magnetism," City Hall, Chancery Lane, admission 1s, handbill, Purland Papers; Hughes and Hagley, 31 January, broadsheet,

370 NOTES TO PAGES 113–119

Purland Papers. Hughes and Hagley were nationally known ("Mesmerism: Its dangers and curiosities").

21. H. Brookes, 13 May 1844, Lecture Hall, 57 Pall Mall, West, admission 1s, reserve seats 2s, broadsheet, Purland Papers; Mr. Spencer T. Hall, practical and consulting mesmerist and phrenologist, 59 Pall Mall, advertisement, Purland Papers.

22. Poster Collection (PPT), KL471.990.23, SHIC 1.619, Lynn Archives.

23. Mr. Brownless, "Phrenomesmerism," lecture at the Sun Inn, 29 August 1843, poster, Tyne and Wear Archives Service, 963/49/2 C16587. This poster was also used for a lecture at Hartlepool.

24. Mr. Stringfellow, "A lecture on electricity, electro-magnetism, and magnetic electricity," Chard, poster, Poster Collection, DD/SAS c/909 159, Somerset Records Office. One lecturer produced a model volcano whose chemical eruption was "ignited by a Spark from the Electrical or Galvanic Battery." The lecturer was Mr. Aldridge (Poster Collection, DD/SAS c/909 167/13, Somerset Records Office).

25. William Davey, Poster Collection, DD/SAS c/909 159, Somerset Records Office.

26. Hall, *Mesmeric experiences*, 22–24.

27. "Caution to amateur mesmerists," *Halifax Guardian and Huddersfield and Bradford Advertiser*, 28 December 1844, 6a.

28. "Mesmerism, serious practical joke," *Manchester Guardian*, 6 February 1842.

29. "Lecture on mesmerism," *Maidstone Journal and Kentish Advertiser*, 27 December 1842; "Lectures on mesmerism," *Maidstone Journal and Kentish Advertiser*, 3 January 1843; "Mesmerism," *Reading Gazette*, 18 February 1843; "Mesmerism," *Bucks Herald*, 30 March 1843; "Mesmerism," Bristol news clipping, May 1843, Purland Papers; "Mesmerism," *Hereford Times*, 9 December 1843.

30. "Recent demonstrations of animal magnetism."

31. "Recent demonstrations of animal magnetism."

32. Hopkinson, *Victorian cabinet maker*, 53.

33. Phrenology had become so deeply integrated in Victorian culture that paintings and caricatures depicted human characters using phrenological rules; artists could assume that viewers would read these signs appropriately. See Cooter, *Cultural meanning of popular science;* Cowling, *Artist as anthropologist*.

34. "Jenny Lind and hypnotism."

35. Jackson, *Lectures on mesmerism*, 51.

36. Horne, "To the editor of the *Mesmerist*," 30. Horne described how Hall discovered (and phreno-magnetically displayed) the organ of "good fellowship" and taught his audience the motto "science belongs to no class, sect or party." Hall is discussed at greater length below.

37. "Prospectus," 3.

38. E.g., Stanhope, "Reflexions on a future state," Stanhope Family Papers, Kent Records Office.

39. Davey, *Illustrated practical mesmerist*, 1st ed., 55.

40. "Mesmerism," *Bolton Chronicle and South Lancashire Advertiser*, 11 May 1850, 5a.

41. "Mesmerism,"*Bolton Chronicle and South Lancashire Advertiser*, 11 May 1850, 5a.

42. "Mesmerism," *Bury Post*, 20 June 1849.

43. Jane Welsh Carlyle to John Welsh, 13 December 1844, in Ryals and Fielding, *Collected letters*, 18:282–83.

44. Dods, *Six lectures*, 32–33: matter was "electrically and magnetically suspended and moved by the immediate energies of the Divine Mind." Similarly, Scoresby, *Zoistic magnetism*, 118, claimed that magnetism was "the means by which He appears to regulate and subordinate the creation to his will."

45. "Mr. Spencer T. Hall on mesmerism," *Bolton Chronicle and South Lancashire Advertiser*, 7 March 1846, 4c.

46. Back in Liverpool, Reynoldson had run a Medical Mesmeric Society in the 1840s. The influence that produced the trance involved a "transfusion" of "nervous or muscular energy." Voluntary control over this energy was the basis of the mesmeric practice known as "electrobiology" ("Saturday evening entertainments," Western Institute, 47 Leicester Square, admission 1s, broadsheet, Purland Papers). Reynoldson was still practicing in the 1850s, e.g., "Mesmerism applied to the cure of diseases," lecture, 31 October 1853, town hall of Lynn (near Liverpool), handbill, Poster Collection (PPT), KL471.990.20, SHIC 1.619, Lynn Archives.

47. Collyer was a one-time student of Elliotson, self-proclaimed discoverer of phreno-mesmerism, and recent expatriate to America, late physician to the Marine Hospital, New Orleans. He offered "Lectures on the philosophy of mesmerism, and its application to human welfare" (23 April–7 May, City of London Literary and Scientific Institution, Aldersgate Street, broadsheet, Purland Papers).

48. Davey, *Illustrated practical mesmerist*, 1st ed., 18.

49. Merryweather, "Remarks on cerebro-magnetism."

50. On puppetry see Speaight, *English puppet theatre;* see also Taylor, *Death and resurrection show*, 103–11.

51. C. Sinclair, "Wizard of all the wizards," broadsheet, and "Clairvoyant lady," news clipping, 5 September 1855, Linwood Gallery, Leicester Square, John Johnson Collection, Bodleian Library. See also "Mental magnetism, a novel and mysterious séance by Mr. Devant, aided by his sister Dora Devant," Royal Victoria Theatre and Pavilion, John Johnson Collection.

52. "Automata," Exeter, [1840s–50s], broadsheet, Collection of Printed Ephemera, Guildhall Library.

53. Mr. G. Hodson, "My Irish portfolio," 4 September 1854, broadsheet, John Johnson Collection.

54. *Morning Herald*, 3 October 1851, on M. Lassaigne and Mlle Prudence.

55. E. T. Hicks, "Mesmerism," letter to the editor, *Leicester Journal*, in George Sandby, scrapbook of press cuttings, 2:25, Library of the Society for Psychical Research, Cambridge University Library. Numbers preceding a page number refer to separately paginated sections of Sandby's scrapbook.

56. "Mr. Duncan's lecture."

57. Fuller, *Mesmerism and the American cure of souls*, 38, quotes Elizabeth Barrett

Browning as saying that the story was "going the rounds of the newspapers," throwing everyone into "dreadful doubts as to whether it may be true."

58. *Hampshire Advertiser*, 1846, Purland Papers.

59. Another example is Henry Cockton's popular novel *Valentine Vox*, the story of a capricious ventriloquist who humorously subverted public order. In an earlier, more disturbing tale by E. T. A. Hoffmann, "The sandman," the hero mistook for a living woman a wax doll. He fell in love with her, then was driven mad by realizing his mistake. One of Hoffmann's nineteenth-century readers defined the uncanny as the state of being uncertain as to whether a thing presumed inanimate might actually be alive (and vice versa). See Freud's essay "The 'uncanny.'"

60. Leask, "Shelley's magnetic ladies." On romantic connections of mesmerism, electricity, mind, and vital phenomena, see Tatar, *Spellbound*, 45–120.

61. Sandby press cuttings.

62. "A night with the clairvoyants," *Liverpool Mercury*, 10 May 1850, bound in Sandby, press cuttings, 1:35. A similar incident (this time in Bolton) was described in "Sir John Franklin," Sandby, press cuttings, 1:29. For other cases see Forbes, *Illustrations of modern mesmerism*, 39–45. The author of the account was convinced by this not only of Franklin's safety, but also of the evangelical utility of mesmerism: the "revelations" of "this unlettered maiden" were at least as persuasive regarding the "immortality of the soul," he argued, as "the thoughts of the most learned men."

63. E.g., Kerner, *Seeress of Prevorst*, 3–4.

64. This special knowledge included the time difference between Britain and Hudson Bay, for instance, and the fact that Hudson Bay was a very likely distance for Franklin to have reached, were he in good health ("Sir John Franklin," Sandby, press cuttings, 1:29).

65. See Schaffer, "Nebular hypothesis." Richard Whately described another somnambulist who had made mental excursions based, he thought, on Chambers's *Vestiges* (Whately to George Combe, 7 February 1848, Combe Papers, National Library of Scotland). Another case, in which a mesmerized girl gazed into a glass of water and saw "small insects" that were "struck down as if struck by electricity," is reminiscent of the published claims of Andrew Crosse, described by Secord in "Extraordinary experiment." See Pearsall, *Table rappers*, 22.

66. One of the educational planets was, appropriately enough, called "Herschel"—presumably after John rather than William (critique of *Zadkiel's almanack for 1845*, Sandby, press cuttings, 2:65–66). I have not located the article in the almanac to which this review made reference. On "Zadkiel" see Curry, *Confusion of prophets*, 61–108; Anderson, "Prophecy and power."

67. Spencer, incidentally, published on phreno-mesmerism during these years. See Spencer, "Discovery of a new phrenological organ."

68. Sandby, *Mesmerism and its opponents*, 1st ed., 86.

69. On the "mobility" (social and geographical) of scientific lecturers in this period, see Inkster, "Marginal men."

70. Untitled news clipping, *Ipswich Journal*, 11 November [1844], Purland Papers.

71. W. J. Vernon, 4 January 1844, Lecture Hall, Greenwich, admission 1s, broadsheet, Purland Papers.

72. "Greenwich Literary Institution," Purland Papers. The style of this sketch suggests that it may have been taken from the *Illustrated London News*.

73. Untitled news clipping, *Morning Herald*, 1844, Purland Papers.

74. Broadsheet, 8 January 1844, Purland Papers; handbill for 7 February 1844 (Purland Papers), when Messrs. Taylor and Hagley held a meeting on "animal magnetism" at the "sacred harmonic society."

75. "Greenwich Lecture Hall," February 1844, news clipping, Purland Papers.

76. This mode of attempted discreditation began a convention that persists to the present day. A recent example is the case of the Paris physiologist Benveniste, whose laboratory researches tended to support certain claims of homeopathy. When Benveniste sent a paper describing this work to *Nature*, the journal hired a magician, the Amazing Randi, to travel to Paris and find a fraudulent means of replicating Benveniste's work (Picart, "Scientific controversy as farce").

77. T. S. Blackwell, "Mesmerism: A deception!!!" handbill, Purland Papers; "Maskyline and Cooke, Anti-spiritualists," handbill, John Johnson Collection.

78. "Mesmerism and clairvoyance," *Bolton Chronicle and South Lancashire Advertiser*, 27 April 1850, 5c. Hartley, a Bolton resident, was lecturing in the Bertinshaw schoolroom, Turton.

79. "Retrospect," 163.

80. W. J. Vernon's "Mesmeric Matinees," Adelaide Gallery, advertisement, John Johnson Collection. Vernon was the mesmerist of Adolphe Didier, brother of the well-known clairvoyant Alexis. See also Forbes, *Illustrations of modern mesmerism*.

81. Sandby, *Mesmerism and its opponents*, 1st ed., 160–61 n.

82. "Animal magnetism," *Medico-Chirurgical Review* (1838): 634–38.

83. Jane Welsh Carlyle to John Welsh, 13 December 1844, in Ryals and Fielding, *Collected letters*, 18:282–83.

84. Hall, "Sherwood Forrester." On the use of the figure of Robin Hood to give a historical pedigree to plebeian authority and virtue, see Barczewski, Ph.D. dissertation, Yale University, 1996.

85. Hall, *Mesmeric experiences*, 22–24. A more extensive discussion of Hall's use of mesmerism in defining the intellectual powers of the "common man" is presented in Winter, "Mesmerism and popular culture."

86. Davey, *Illustrated practical mesmerist*, 1st ed., vi.

87. See also Hall's tactful "Gross stupidity in a professional man." Similarly, a Dr. Owens ("Dr. Owens on mesmeric experiments") gave a classical pedigree for itinerant mesmerists in supplying "the intellectual wants of the community."

88. For example, Josiah Buchanan, editor of the *Journal of Man*, and La Roy Sutherland, editor of the *Magnet*. On American mesmerism see Fuller, *Mesmerism and the American cure of souls*.

89. McCalman, *Radical underworld*.

90. Hall, *Mesmeric experiences*, 4. Mesmeric phenomena reminded him, with his Quaker background, of the "unusual clearness yet expansion of spirit, like that

described by the primitive Quakers in their meetings" (16). For other Quaker accounts see Warrenne, "Curative power"; Lloyd, "Case of lock-jaw."

91. Hall, *Mesmeric experiences*, 18.

92. Hall, *Mesmeric experiences*, 4. For a similar representation of other lecturers see "Messrs. Jackson and Davey"; Mr. Cobbold, letter to the editor, *Norfolk Chronicle*, 7 April 1849.

93. Spurr, "Phrenological investigations"; "Mr. Potchett's phreno-magnetic notes"; Horne, letter to the editor, *Mesmerist* 1 (1843): 30–32. Other accounts of mesmerism among the working classes include Powell, *Life incidents*. Powell was an Owenite who became a spiritualist after mesmeric forays in the 1840s; Wallis, *Autobiography*, claims that he practiced mesmerism; see also Factory Girl, *Unfortunate genius*, for a psychic experience the narrator associated with mesmerism. For middle-class converts made by itinerant mesmerists, see "Exeter mesmeric record: No. XXI," *Woolmer's Exeter and Plymouth Gazette*, 23 December 1848; Sandby, *Mesmerism and its opponents*, 1st ed., 88–97.

94. Gee, "Letter to the editor of the *Mesmerist*."

95. Hopkinson, *Victorian cabinet maker*, 52–55. Similarly, T. S. Arthur's novel *Agnes* warned that influencing another person's will (mesmerically) did them a profound injury.

96. Cooper, "Testimony" and "Philosophy of mesmerism."

97. Buchanan, "Impressibility," 321–30.

98. On this issue see Johnson, "Really useful knowledge."

99. "Lecture mania," 99.

100. Hall, *Mesmeric experiences*, 22.

101. Hall, *Mesmeric experiences*, 6–7.

102. Davey, *Illustrated practical mesmerist*, 1st ed., introduction.

103. Elliotson, "Messrs. Jackson and Davey," 305.

104. An excerpt of the report of the Scottish Curative Mesmeric Association is printed in an appendix to Davey's *Illustrated practical mesmerist*, 2d ed.

105. Harriet Martineau to Richard Monckton Milnes, 2 July 1844, Houghton Papers, 1668.

106. Martineau, *Letters on mesmerism*, 48. See also Cooter, "Dichotomy and denial."

107. Hall to Morpeth, 5 June 1845, Papers of George William Frederick Howard, Seventh Earl of Carlisle, Howard (Morpeth) Papers, Castle Howard, J19/1/39, 65. Hall exercised unusual control over his texts by printing them by hand. As James Secord discusses in *Books of creation*, one of the most dramatic consequences of steam technology was the need for capital in publishing; Hall was asserting his independence from the hegemony of the steam press.

108. This may have been part of a nonconformist tradition, for early Quakers printed this way. Hall's printing practices also resembled the automatic writing of spiritualist mediums, with respect to the ways in which they legitimized the texts they created. On the ways in which automatic writing validated claims about nature, see Owen, *Darkened room*, 79–83; Oppenheim, *Other world*, 148, 239, 242, 266.

109. Hall, *Forester's offering*, preface. This was the kind of statement that got "progessive" mesmerists in trouble with conservative clergy. See Sandby, *Mesmerism and its opponents*, 2d ed., 86.

110. Hall, *Mesmeric experiences*, 78. This is not to say that being mesmerized was always to be placed in a subordinate role, but rather that Hall made himself vulnerable to having this role imposed on him by Morpeth and his friends, who certainly defined the mesmeric subject in this way. See also G. W. F. Howard, diary, 19 April 1845, Howard (Morpeth) Papers, J19/8/7, 10.

111. G. W. F. Howard, diary, 4 June 1845, Howard (Morpeth) Papers, J19/8/7, 38.

112. Allison, *Mesmerism*, 5.

113. The most recent intellectual history of psychology for this period is Richards's *Mental machinery*, which succeeds admirably on its own terms; the danger lies in the potential for readers to take such works as evidence of how broader constituencies of Victorians understood the mind.

114. Jackson, *Lectures on mesmerism*, 51–52.

115. L. Ritchie, "Literature: Mesmerism," *Indian News*, 7 May 1844, in Sandby, press cuttings, 2:12, Library of the Society for Psychical Research.

116. [Staite], *Mesmerism*, 20–21.

Chapter Six

1. On Victorian sexual attitudes see Masson, *Making of Victorian sexuality*, 38–40, 117–19, 122–33; Davidoff and Hall, *Family fortunes*.

2. L. E. G. E., "Cerebral physiology."

3. "Mr W. H. Parsons, medical mesmerist, 44 Clarence Sq, Brighton," [1852], calling card, Purland Papers; George Barth, Mesmerist and Medical Galvanist, No 4 Mornington Crescent, calling card, Purland Papers. Barth advertised his tract, *The principle of health transferrable*, on such cards. He also acted as broker for Mrs. Wagstaff, wife of Mr. P. W. Wagstaff, who was placed in the trance *"for purposes of diagnosis only."*

4. Miss Isabella Litolfe, mesmerist, Harley Street, calling card, Purland Papers.

5. E.g., Mrs. Wynyard, mesmerist to Harriet Martineau. See chapter 9.

6. "Mesmerism: Nervous diseases: A married physician . . . ," [1849], newspaper advertisement, Purland Papers.

7. Leonard Wallington, medical mesmerist, calling card, John Johnson Collection.

8. "Mesmeric Establishment. Mr. Reynoldson, Medical Mesmerist, 4 Romney Terrace, Greenwich," n.d., broadsheet, Purland Papers. Reynoldson could "accommodate a few mesmeric patients with board." One Mr. Hicks advertised "Phrenology and Mesmerism in [Stoke?] Newington," June 1848. N. Hale advertised "The Adamic Infirmary of Animal Magnetism," 18 Store Street, Bedford Square (broadsheet, Purland Papers). Meetings (admission free) were held every Wednesday evening, supported by voluntary subscription. Hale claimed to have been practicing for twenty-five years.

9. Thomas Pyne, incumbent of Hook, Kingston-on-Thames, "Hospital: Vital magnetic and general medical and surgical treatment," June 1845, short pamphlet, Purland Papers.

10. "Phrenology and mesmerism," c. 1850, 11 Warwick Street, Regent Street, 1 guinea for the public class, broadsheet, Purland Papers.

11. Barth, *Mesmerist's manual;* Barth, *Principle of health transferable;* Barth, *What is mesmerism?* Buckland, *Handbook of mesmerism;* Davey, *Illustrated practical mesmerist; Hand-book of curative mesmerism; Handbook of vital magnetism;* Saunders, *Mesmeric guide for family use;* Teste, *Practical manual of animal magnetism.*

12. On the difficulties of interpreting etiquette manuals, see Curtin, *Propriety and position;* St. George, *Descent of manners.*

13. Sandby, *Mesmerism and its opponents,* 1st ed., 191; Teste, *Practical manual of animal magnetism,* 151; Saunders, *Mesmeric guide for family use,* 17–18.

14. Saunders, *Mesmeric guide for family use,* 19–20; Davey, *Illustrated practical mesmerist,* 1st ed., 11–12. These may have been largely gestures toward propriety, for other sections of mesmeric manuals often ignored them. Teste, *Practical manual of animal magnetism,* 152, advised, "[T]humbs on the pit of the stomach, and the other fingers below the ribs. Then you will descend slowly along the body as far as the knees." Such instructions recall Wakley's warnings ("Virtues of animal magnetism," 413–14).

15. See Kaplan, *Dickens and mesmerism,* 57–59. For Townshend's mesmeric correspondence with Dickens, see Townshend to Dickens, 11 May, 7 June, 24 July 1841, all in Huntington Library.

16. E.g., mesmerists promised to heal organs such as the heart, stomach, and pancreas (Earnest Searcher after Truth, *Pain of body and mind removed*).

17. "Mesmerism and Dr. Bushnan," *Medical Times,* 6 April 1850, in Sandby, press cuttings, 1:33, Library of the Society for Psychical Research.

18. Forbes, *Illustrations of modern mesmerism,* 1.

19. Gauld, *Hypnotism,* 235. Didier charged about 24 shillings for appearing before a private party.

20. "Mesmerism: On the subject of Messrs. Marcillet and Alexis," *Cheltenham Free Press,* 20 September 1845, in Sandby, press cuttings, 2:55, Library of the Society for Psychical Research.

21. Gauld, *Hypnotism,* 236.

22. Elliotson's transcription, as quoted in Gauld, *Hypnotism,* 237.

23. The challenge to Gurwood's status was made in Maxwell, *Extracts from the life of Wellington,* 2:439; Napier's sympathetic reference to it was made in the sixth volume of his *History of the war in the Peninsula* (1840); a compilation of the various claims, plus testimonials and Gurwood's version of the case, appeared in the *United Service Magazine* in 1845 and then in a separate pamphlet, Gurwood, *Major General Napier.*

24. See "Colonel Gurwood and mesmerism," *Cheltenham Free Press,* in Sandby, press cuttings, 2:51–54, Library of the Society for Psychical Research; Adare, mesmeric journal, 1:30–31, Dunraven Papers, Belfast Public Records Office.

25. Sandby, *Mesmerism and its opponents,* 1st ed., 266.

26. Mandler, *Aristocratic government.*

27. Morpeth may have encountered mesmerism when he visited America and met the Unitarian divine Dr. Channing, who was reportedly engrossed with mesmerism (Martineau to Monckton Milnes, 2 July 1844, Houghton Papers). For Adare's views see Adare to W. R. Hamilton, 25 July 1844, and Hamilton's response, 16 August 1844, Hamilton Papers, D3196/F/1 275, D3196/F/1 296, Trinity College Dublin; Adare, mesmeric journal, vols. 1 and 2, Dunraven Papers. See also Oppenheim, *Other world,* 451 n. 102. Ducie was the patron of the Bristol Mesmeric Institute, which was supported by the eminent chemist William Herapath, professor of toxicology at Bristol Medical School, among others. See *Bristol Mesmeric Institute;* "Mesmerism in the west of England."

28. Adare, mesmeric journal, Friday, 5 July 1844, 1:87, Dunraven Papers. Lord Morpeth, when he mesmerized his friend H. S. Thompson, wrote that he felt like "what the Duke of Wellington was, and Dr. Johnson was not, 'Vanqueur du vanqueur de la terre'" (Morpeth diary, 8 July 1845, Howard [Morpeth] Papers, J19/8/8, 15).

29. Mandler *(Aristocratic government)* divides the aristocratic Whigs into "plain," or "Foxite," Whigs and the liberals who began to emerge from the late 1820s onward.

30. Hilton, "Whiggery."

31. The "liberal" attitude toward the mind by the groups that Peter Mandler has characterized as "Foxite Whigs" is discussed in Hilton, "Whiggery," 10.

32. Morpeth diary, 19 April 1845, Howard (Morpeth) Papers, J19/8/7; see also Olien, *Morpeth,* 271–73; Morpeth diary, 3 July 1844. Morpeth had a frightening experience when he mesmerized his sister-in-law. A few passes turned her rigid, and even after she awakened, she acted very strangely (Olien, *Morpeth,* 288 n. 42). See also Morpeth diary, 29 September 1845, J19/8/9, 1.

33. Morpeth diary, 3 July 1845, J19/8/8, 8 ff. Morpeth saw his services as doing what doctors could not: see Morpeth diary, 1845, J19/8/8, 18. On Whig paternalism, see Mandler, *Aristocratic government,* 80.

34. For example, the patients were referred to the infirmary by the governors. See *London Mesmeric Infirmary: Annual reports,* Society for Psychical Research Collection.

35. *Spectator,* 30 June 1849, in Sandby, press cuttings, 1:22, Library of the Society for Psychical Research, on clairvoyance séances at Ducie's house; Morpeth diary, c. 18 June 1845, Howard (Morpeth) Papers, J19/8/7, 52–53, gives an evocative account of such a séance.

36. Quillinan to Robinson, 23 March 1845, Robinson Papers, Dr. Williams's Library. This poem inspired an angry exchange between Henry Crabb Robinson and Quillinan, whom Robinson accused of attacking Morpeth merely because he was a Whig. Quillinan denied the charge.

37. The poem is evocative of a caricature reprinted in Dodds, *Age of paradox,* 226. A terrified passenger holds on for dear life as he is carried along by the runaway Railway Juggernaut of Speculation.

38. She did not think he was "sufficiently on your guard to avoid ridicule . . . do

not you rather think you have it in your power to be of some—nay of great use in your generation—is it right to diminish this power of usefulness?" (to Morpeth from his mother, 7 June 1845, Howard [Morpeth] Papers, J19/1/39, 66).

39. "Animal magnetism in practice," 74. More often, aristocratic interest in mesmerism and table-turning was seen as just another sign of aristocratic gullibility, e.g., "Select spiritual rapping soirée."

40. Cooter, *Cultural meaning of popular science;* Gauld, *Hypnotism.*

41. "Mesmerism," *Medical Times* 6 (1842).

42. "Lecture mania," 99.

43. For the range of discoveries see Adams, "Remarkable mesmeric phenomena"; Baldock, "Cure of severe affection of the stomach"; Burq, "Nervous affections"; Childs, "Severe nervous disease"; Holdsworth, "Case of asthma"; Gregory, "Case of vision at a distance."

44. Elliotson, "Successful result of two cases of lock-jaw"; "Cerebral sympathy and clairvoyance in brutes."

45. Prideaux, "On the application of phrenology."

46. [Elliotson], "Education as it is"; [Elliotson], "Education as it is, and as it ought to be."

47. L. E. G. E., "Cerebral physiology," 21.

48. L. E. G. E., "Cerebral physiology," 14.

49. L. E. G. E., "Cerebral physiology," 13, 24.

50. Atkinson, probably written for the *Zoist* of 1845−46, as quoted in "Doings and sentiments of the phrenologists."

51. Brookes, "Case of external soreness." Brookes encouraged others to follow his example ("Mesmerism: Modes").

52. *Zoist,* 1843−57; *Phreno-Magnet,* 1843, edited by Spencer Hall; *Mesmerist,* 1843; *Phreno-Magnetic Vindicator,* 1843, edited by Thomas Beggs; *Journal of Zoomagnetism,* edited by J. C. Colquhoun. Apart from the *Zoist,* each journal folded the year it began. There was a *Journal of Mesmerism* (excerpts from it exist in the Purland Papers), but I have found no full copies.

53. "The Dublin Mesmeric Association," printed advertisement, Purland Papers. The first president was Falconer Miles, Esq., and the second Richard Whately, archbishop of Dublin.

54. *Bristol Mesmeric Institute.* The main mesmeric practitioner at the Bristol Mesmeric Institute was Henry Storer. See "Electro-Biology and mesmerism, by Dr. Storer, physician to the Bristol Mesmeric Institute," broadsheet, Purland Papers. This included favorable notices by all the Bristol papers: *Bristol Mercury, Bristol Gazette, Bristol Times,* and *Bristol Mirror.* This suggests that there was more of a consensus supporting mesmerism in Bristol than elsewhere. See also Storer, *Mesmerism in disease.*

55. Morpeth diaries, Howard (Morpeth) Papers, J19.

56. At this point the infirmary was based in premises at Duke Street, Manchester Square, but within two years it had moved to Bedford Square. By the early 1850s its

annual meetings drew 600–700 people. See *London Mesmeric Infirmary: Annual reports*, Society for Psychical Research Collection.

57. "Extraction of teeth in the mesmeric state," a description of Theodysius Purland's mesmeric anesthesia at the "Mesmeric Institute," 5 May 1845; the *Times* ran an advertisement for the institute on 24 March 1845.

58. For instance, the use of mesmerism in quickly subduing a madwoman with a strength greater than "two powerful men." The annual report of the Bristol Mesmeric Institute said how one mesmerist "advanced to her, fixed his eye upon her, took her hand, and she at once fell down under the influence" (*Bristol Mesmeric Institute*, 10).

59. Included with Flowerday's photographs are those of Vernon and Tubbs, two of the mesmeric gentlemen involved in the operation (Purland Papers).

60. Purland Papers.

61. Correspondence with Purland, included in this scrapbook, indicates its status as a publicly accessible document.

62. On "virtual witnessing" see Shapin and Schaffer, *Leviathan and the air pump;* Shapin, "Pump and circumstance."

63. One of the many discussions that printed this statement was Lardner and Bulwer-Lytton, "Animal magnetism."

64. Porter, "Physical examination."

65. Thomson, *Domestic management*, 105, 116, 112. Thomson was one of Elliotson's opponents during the UCL controversies in 1838. See "Medical journals and medical men," 283 n.

66. There seems to be a curious sympathy for certain mesmeric tenets even among modern scientists: when I described this effect to a Cavendish physicist friend in Cambridge, he nodded over his pint and replied, "There's nothing so natural as left and right."

67. Rutter, *Magnetoid currents*. See also T. Léger to Monckton Milnes, 16 May 1853, Houghton Papers, uncat. MSS, for an example of how one procured such an apparatus.

68. "Medical news: Animal magnetism"; "Mr. Duncan's lecture."

69. Barrallier, letter to the editor; "Mr. Catlow's discoveries."

70. Boyton, "Surgeon's experience of mesmerism."

71. Forbes, *Illustrations of modern mesmerism;* [Noble], *Mesmerism true, mesmerism false;* Hall, "Rise, progress." Hall's article was a response to the fact that "the public now expect the medical profession to investigate mesmerism." His list of discreditations is given on page 118. See also Crampton, "Frauds called 'mesmerism' and 'clairvoyance'"; "Mesmeric frauds."

72. Shuttleworth, "Female circulation."

73. Lawrence, "Democratic, divine, and heroic." See also the discussion of "unveiling" nature in nineteenth-century anatomy in Jordanova, *Sexual visions*, 102–10.

74. Forbes, *Illustrations of modern mesmerism*, 108.

Chapter Seven

1. "Animal magnetism in practice."

2. Peterson, *Medical profession,* 5–39, 136–93; Waddington, *Medical profession,* 53–95; Loudon, *Medical care and the general practitioner,* 129 ff.

3. Desmond, *Politics of evolution,* 167.

4. See Barrow, "Medical heretics"; Porter, *Health for sale,* 222–39.

5. See Desmond, *Politics of evolution,* esp. chapter 8.

6. See Sprigge, *Life and times of Wakley;* Schwartz, *Wakley and the "Lancet";* Wakley, editorial, *Lancet* 2 (1832–33): 576.

7. Waddington, "General practitioners."

8. Wakley, "On obstacles to medical reform." See also Crawford, "Scientific profession"; Warner, "Idea of science in English medicine."

9. For example, the *Athenaeum* urged its readers to help define proper medical behavior. See "Medical etiquette."

10. Greenhow, "General practitioners"; Collins, "Sketches of the present state."

11. E.g., Clocquet's operation on Madame Plantin; and, according to Lafontaine, his aid during a leg amputation in Sheffield in 1842 (quoted and discussed in Gauld, *Hypnotism,* 240 n).

12. Topham and Ward, *Successful amputation,* 5, 14, 15. It was reprinted in the *Medical Times* (7 [1842–43]: 177), and in regional papers such as the *Hampshire Telegraph.* A more detailed account of mesmerism and the history of anesthesia is provided in Winter, "Ethereal epidemic."

13. Captain John James, cited in Gauld, *Hypnotism,* 220, 240 n.

14. The Medico-Chirurgical Society refused to publish any account of this matter, but Elliotson published a summary that was not contradicted in the medical press. See Elliotson, *Numerous surgical operations.* The individuals who convened this meeting were Dr. John Scott of Glasgow, the Edinburgh surgeon William Tait, William Chambers (probably the publisher), James Simpson, and James Nasmyth. See also Packman, "Mesmerism in Paris."

15. "Animal magnetism," *Medico-Chirurgical Review* (1843).

16. Palfreman, "Mesmerism."

17. "Field day in Gower Street."

18. "Medical portraits: Robert Liston."

19. Brodie, *Nervous affections,* 7.

20. See Elliotson, *Numerous surgical operations.*

21. Elliotson, "More painless amputations," on a Cherbourg amputation, 490–92; Hall, "Rise, progress," mentions a leg amputation; see also "Extraction of a tooth."

22. "Signal failure of mesmerism," reprinted from the *Provincial Medical and Surgical Journal,* chronicled the failure of clairvoyants to identify the details of a £100 note sealed in an envelope (anyone who did this could have the note); Hall's "Rise, progress" was a response to the mesmeric experiments inspired by Harriet Martineau's advocacy of mesmerism.

23. Massey, "First public operation."

24. Townshend, *Facts in mesmerism.*

25. James Johnson wrote that one of mesmerism's great liabilities was that it gave the subject's tongue "liberty to wag." See Johnson, editorial, *Medico-Chirurgical Review* (1839): 634–35.

26. This vision of the medical patient is aptly described by Michel Foucault's term "docile bodies" (Foucault, *Discipline and punish*).

27. Stevenson, "Suspended animation."

28. Richardson, *Death, dissection, and the destitute;* Stevenson, "Suspended animation."

29. Benjamin Collins Brodie, in disqualifying both Wombell and, two years later, Harriet Martineau, argued that only doctors could be witnesses, and only patients could tell if the mesmeric effects were true, so validating mesmerism was impossible.

30. Hall alluded to the "real" status of his polemical theory in order to assign "unreal" status to the presumed "insensible" subject. In the case of Harriet Martineau and mesmerism, fluctuating pulse and breathing rates were treated as evidence against a subject's claims to have been insensible, whereas Wombell's steady pulse was claimed to be peripheral to the Topham-Ward debate. Compare Greenhow, *Medical report.*

31. See Townshend, *Facts in mesmerism;* review by [Grove], "Mesmerism."

32. Forbes's introduction to [Noble], *Mesmerism true, mesmerism false;* Forbes, *Illustrations of modern mesmerism.* The *Illustrations* was a compilation of papers originally published in the *Medical Gazette* and the *Athenaeum.*

33. *Illustrations of modern mesmerism* recounts Forbes's involvement. See also Forbes, "On mesmerism."

34. Chatto, "Mesmerism applied to surgical operations." On relations between doctors and working people, see Green, *Working-class patients and the medical establishment.*

35. See Gooding, "In nature's school."

36. "Mesmerism in India"; "Dr. Esdaile on the application of mesmerism."

37. Wakley, editorial, *Lancet,* 4 July 1846, 16–17. Wakley claimed that during the oration Elliotson tried surreptitiously to mesmerize his colleagues in the audience "under cover, not of the bedclothes, but of his gown" (an allusion to the indecent assaults he considered mesmerism to involve). Wakley reprinted the article describing his "exposure" of the O'Key sisters, 18–21 of the same issue.

38. "Mesmeric hospital." See also "Mesmeric infirmary," *Lancet;* "Mesmeric infirmary," *Times,* 14 July 1846.

39. Smith, *Under the influence;* Lawrence, "Power and the glory."

40. On Beddoes's practice see Porter, *Doctor of society.*

41. For a sense of the close associations between mesmerism, ether, and the more powerful consciousness-altering drugs, see De Quincey, *Confessions of an English opium eater;* [De Quincey], "Suspiria de profundis"; [Eagle], "Few passages on omens"; Parssinen, *Secret passions, secret remedies.*

42. For contrasting pedigrees of ether anesthesia see Smith, *Under the influence;* Fulop-Miller, *Triumph over pain;* Nuland, *Origins of anaesthesia;* Cartwright, *English pioneers;* Duncum, *Inhalation anaesthesia;* Thatcher, *History of anesthesia.*

43. See esp. Thatcher, *History of anesthesia,* chapters 1 and 2.

44. Cited in Sykes, *Essays,* 1:48.

45. One author claimed that "it requires no 'rapport' for its administration than that, of a tube connected with the bottle holding the ether vapour" (*London Medical Gazette* 39 [1847]: 395).

46. In response to a highly successful example of surgery on a mesmerized subject, the *London Medical Gazette* rejected the case because the mesmerists could not give a cause for the anesthetic effects: "no one can doubt that" the medical community "requires causes" of candidate medical practices ("Mesmeric surgery"). With respect to ether see, e.g., Forbes, "On etherization."

47. Liston did not invite Boott, and in his letter thanking Boott for the information, he claimed that the operation had not been planned at all. The *Lancet* collaborated in this attempt to establish Liston as the single heroic British "discoverer" of the technique. See Ellis, "Robert Liston's letter."

48. Squire, "On the introduction of ether."

49. [Miller], "Painless operations," 176–77.

50. [Miller], "Painless operations," 169.

51. See Sykes, *Essays,* vol. 1, "In the beginning."

52. [Wakley,] editorial, *Lancet* 1 (1847): 16.

53. Fairbrother was senior physician to Bristol General Hospital. He could not produce the ethereal effects and asked for precise descriptions of the apparatus, the conditions of the surrounding environment, and the expertise of the operator. See Fairbrother, "Fatal administration of ether."

54. During its brief reign, ether was also used as an agent of "policing" generally; for example, the *Lancet* described how it could differentiate between "real" and "feigned" disease in the case of curvature of the spine and contractions of muscles. See "Practical application of ether."

55. [Carpenter], editorial, 530.

56. For example, see the anonymous, untitled article in *Athenaeum* 1 (1847): 22.

57. E.g., Gardner, "On ether-vapour."

58. Hall, "Rise, progress," 437.

59. Elliotson, "On the art," 48–49.

60. Gregory, "On the probability," 382.

61. Mortimer, "Chloroform as a means of producing insensibility."

62. See Green, "Anesthesia and the development of surgery," for London and Edinburgh hospital statistics for 1846–96.

63. Youngston, *Revolution in Victorian medicine.*

64. "Animal magnetism," *Medical Times,* 283.

65. "Mesmerism," *Medical Times* 9 (1843–44): 495. Braid and Catlow engaged in a particularly long and sustained antagonism. See "Animal magnetism in practice"; "Mr. Catlow's discoveries."

Chapter Eight

1. This and the next several quotations are from Esdaile, *Mesmerism in India* (1846), 21–23.

2. Crawford, *History of the Indian medical service*, 2:153. For a description of Esdaile's practice and a succinct account of the history of the mesmeric hospital, see Ernst, "Under the influence in colonial India." A brief introduction to Esdaile's mesmeric practice is provided in Winter, "Ethereal epidemic"; Prakash, "Science 'gone native,'" gives a brief but illuminating discussion of Indian mesmerism.

3. Ernst, *Mad tales from the Raj*. The Calcutta Medical College, founded in 1839, was to be the sole site of Bengali medical training (Bala, *Imperialism and medicine*, 50 ff.).

4. Arnold, *Colonizing the body*, discusses the use of indigenous practitioners to popularize Western medicine via the cooperative funding of dispensaries by wealthy westerners and wealthy Indians. See Ramasubban, *Public health;* Harrison, *Public health;* Raj, *Social and cultural context*.

5. Ernst, *Mad tales from the Raj*.

6. Gordon, *Handbook*.

7. Esdaile, "Reports of the Mesmeric Hospital," 26.

8. Esdaile, *Mesmerism in India* (1846), 40–41.

9. This and the next several quotations are from Esdaile, *Mesmerism in India* (1846), 44–45.

10. Webb, published letter quoted in Esdaile, *Introduction of mesmerism* (1852), 19.

11. Esdaile, *Introduction of mesmerism* (1852), 17.

12. "Mesmeric facts, reported by James Esdaile, M.D., Civil Assistant Surgeon, Hooghly," *Bombay Times and Journal of Commerce*, 4 June 1845, 370–71. This was reprinted from the *India Journal of Medical Science* and circulated in several other papers, e.g., "Dr. Esdaile's mesmeric facts," *Bengal Hurkaru and India Gazette*, 11 June 1845, 246; "Mesmeric facts, reported by James Esdaile, M.D., Civil Assistant Surgeon, Hooghly," *Bombay Times and Journal of Commerce*, 28 June 1845, 428–30; "Mesmeric facts, reported by James Esdaile, M.D., Civil Assistant Surgeon, Hooghly," *Calcutta Englishman and Military Chronicle*, 11 June 1845; "Mesmeric facts, reported by James Esdaile, M.D., Civil Assistant Surgeon, Hooghly," *Bengal Hurkaru and India Gazette*, 17 May 1845.

13. Esdaile, "Mesmeric facts" (Calcutta, 1845), as quoted in *Mofussilite*, 9 August 1845, 22: "Mesmerism is no longer to be laughed at"; "Weekly summary of the news: Mesmerism," *Mofussilite*, 23 August 1845, 63, similarly: "The man must be a good actor indeed who can play a serene, and composed part, while a doctor is taking off his leg, or arm." Untitled article in *Bombay Times and Journal of Commerce*, 23 July 1845, 482, advertised a forthcoming pamphlet by Esdaile on mesmerism.

14. "Dr. Mesmer's first essays in animal magnetism at Vienna: Translated from the 'Memoirs of Caroline Pickler,'" *Bengal Hurkaru Weekly Supplementary Sheet*, 578. This was a serious description of mesmeric effects in Vienna during the 1770s. In

contrast see the mocking "Letter from Albert Smith, 24 April 1845," *Bengal Hurkaru and Indian Gazette,* 10 June 1845. This comical article dismissed the mesmeric effects and mentioned Spencer Hall and Harriet Martineau. "Miss Harriet Martineau's mesmeric revelations," *Friend of India,* 30 January 1845, 73–74, was similarly dismissive. See also "Indian news: Madras: Galvanic rings," *Mofussilite,* 9 August 1845, 28. The report, which was reprinted from the *Record* of 22 July 1845, claimed that galvanic rings had been shown to cure cholera.

15. "Illustrations of mesmerism," *Atlas of India,* 24 March 1845, advocated serious attention to Spencer Hall's work. "Medical statistics: Mr. Spencer Hall, the mesmerist, in London," *Atlas of India,* 8 March 1845, claimed that Hall's work gave "universal gratification, even to the most sceptical"; "Advertisement for Mesmeric Infirmary," *Calcutta Englishman and Military Chronicle,* 2 January 1847, 1, listed subscribers and described the organizational meeting for the infirmary.

16. Untitled article, *Bengal Hurkaru and India Gazette,* 17 May 1845. This lauded Esdaile's "humane" efforts where existing medical capability could give "no alleviation."

17. *Calcutta Englishman and Military Chronicle,* evening edition, 11 June 1845.

18. Letter from W. Ewin, 2 June 1845, "Another very successful and authenticated case of mesmerism," *Calcutta Englishman and Military Chronicle,* 12 June 1845, described a test in which "unbelieving gentlemen" used a "cruel" series of tests (e.g., "burning him with the ends of lighted cigars"). But each one "proved ineffectual." An account of Mr. Scott's trials is given in "To the editor of the *Englishman,*" by L. A. Pholipsz, Salaam medical student written from Chinsurah, *Calcutta Englishman and Military Chronicle,* 28 May 1845.

19. For one such conflict between (medical and nonmedical) witnesses and skeptical doctors, see the following exchanges: "Mesmerism: Letter to the editor of the *Englishman,*" *Calcutta Englishman and Military Chronicle,* 23 January 1847, 2; "Misrepresentation exposed: To the editor of the *Englishman,* signed No Doctor," 23 January 1847, *Calcutta Englishman and Military Chronicle,* 25 January 1847, 2; "Mesmerism: To the editor of the *Englishman,* by Edward Edlin, M.D.," 23 January 1847, *Calcutta Englishman and Military Chronicle,* 25 January 1847.

20. "Dr. Esdaile and his critics," *Bombay Times and Journal of Commerce,* 21 June 1845, 412. See also *Calcutta Englishman and Military Chronicle,* 12 June 1845; "Spirit of the Indian Press: Mesmerism," *Bombay Times and Journal of Commerce,* 25 June 1845, 422. "Spirit" is a reprint of articles published in the *Calcutta Englishman,* 12 June 1845.

21. "Mesmerism," *Bombay Times and Journal of Commerce,* 14 June 1845, 392–93.

22. "Mesmerism," *Bombay Times and Journal of Commerce,* 14 June 1845, 392–93. This newspaper was more generally interested in electricity and medicine: for instance, "Application of galvanism to horticulture," *Bombay Times and Journal of Commerce,* 2 July 1845, 440. In a letter to *Bombay Times and Journal of Commerce,* 2 July 1845, 436, one Cherry Wilkins wrote to ask if the galvanic rings could help with her complaints of "giddiness."

23. "Mesmerism," *Bombay Times and Journal of Commerce,* 14 June 1845, 392.

24. "Mesmerism," *Bombay Times and Journal of Commerce*, 14 June 1845, 393.

25. Elliotson, "Report of the committee," 52, 51. The article lists patients and results. The committee consisted of James Atkinson, inspector general of hospitals; E. M. Gordon; John Jackson, surgeon to the Native Hospital; Duncan Stewart, presidency surgeon; James Hume, police magistrate; A. Rogers, Esq.; and William Brooke O'Shaughnessy, M.D. O'Shaughnessy was secretary of the committee.

26. Elliotson, "More painless surgical operations," 564–66.

27. Elliotson, "Report of the committee," 56–57.

28. Hume, quoted in Elliotson, "Report of the committee," 58.

29. Elliotson, "Report of the committee," 62. See also "Correspondence: Monthly report of the Calcutta Mesmeric Hospital," *Calcutta Englishman and Military Chronicle*, 20 January 1847, in which Esdaile announced that he would publish "monthly reports"; the first of these was "Monthly report of the Calcutta Mesmeric Hospital," *Calcutta Englishman and Military Chronicle*, 21 January 1847, 2: "It is undoubtedly very desireable that every form of disease which requires the knife of the surgeon should be in turn treated by Mesmerism."

30. As quoted in Esdaile, "Dr Esdaile's first monthly report," 186.

31. Reprinted in Esdaile, *Introduction of mesmerism* (1852), 21–22.

32. Esdaile, "Dr Esdaile's first monthly report," 180–82.

33. Statistics for 200 cases of scrotal tumors of 10–103 pounds (Esdaile, *Introduction of mesmerism* [1852], 28).

34. Esdaile, "Dr. Esdaile's first monthly report," 184.

35. Elliotson, "Report of the committee," 69.

36. Esdaile, *Mesmerism in India* (1846), 153–55. The testimonial was signed J. Calder, 28 October 1845.

37. Elliotson, "Report by Dr Elliotson on 'A record,'" 32.

38. Esdaile, *Introduction of mesmerism* (1846), 121.

39. Johnstone, *Notes of a case*. Johnstone was late president of the Royal Medical Society, and a member of the Medico-Chirurgical Society, Edinburgh. This report described a successful surgery and cases in which patients in the local male asylum were treated for internal diseases (not, it seems, for their madness).

40. "Mesmerism in the treatment of insanity," pamphlet or offprint, Purland Papers, vol. 4. This document quoted Kean as saying that, of seventy-four patients treated mesmerically in his asylum in 1847 and 1848, sixty-four had been cured and discharged; Elliotson, "Mesmerism in the East," relayed Kean's claim that "since the employment of mesmerism almost all difficulty in the management of patients has vanished . . . Now the whole are as orderly as an equal number of persons in another house." Elliotson further reported Kean as anticipating that he could increase his inmate population tenfold (in terms of his ability to manage it) with the use of mesmerism; see also Capern, *Mighty curative powers of mesmerism*, xii.

41. Quoted in Brantlinger, *Rule of darkness*, 79.

42. Rosselli, "Self-image of effeteness."

43. Arnold, *Colonizing the body*.

44. Goodeve, "Fatal case."

45. Esdaile, *Mesmerism in India* (1846), 39.

46. Esdaile, *Mesmerism in India* (1846), 132.

47. Esdaile, *Introduction of mesmerism* (1852), 7.

48. This series of quotations is from Esdaile, *Mesmerism in India* (1846), 14–15.

49. Esdaile, "Mesmeric facts."

50. Esdaile, "Reports of the Mesmeric Hospital," 29.

51. Esdaile, "Reports of the Mesmeric Hospital," 29.

52. This series of quotations is from Esdaile, *Mesmerism in India* (1846), 20. For an earlier claim of this sort in the British medical press, but by a colonial surgeon, see A Retired East India Surgeon, "Practice of Hindoo Mesmerism."

53. Esdaile, "Second half-yearly report," 361–62.

54. Davidson, "Mesmerism in human and brute inhabitants," 3.

55. Prakash, "Science 'gone native,'" 161.

56. Esdaile, *Mesmerism in India* (1846), 86–94.

57. Esdaile, *Mesmerism in India* (1846), 91, 92, 93, 94.

58. Dalhousie was known for his patronage of communications technology during this period: telegraph, postal system, and rail; a confirmed "Benthamite," according to the *New Cambridge history of India*, he drew a distinction between state support for such innovations and paternalistic treatments of the weak and suffering (which he would not have favored, and among which he would have placed mesmerism).

59. Esdaile, *Introduction of mesmerism* (1856), 26.

60. *Christian Advocate*, as quoted in Elliotson, "Triumph and reward," 116.

61. The families were Roy, Bahadoor, Ghosal, Jeebun, Deb, Sal, Cowasjee, Ghose, Sein, Mullick, Chatterjee, Chowdry, and Mitter. The text of the petition (though not the names of signatories) was printed in Elliotson, "Triumph and reward," 119–20. "[T]he continuation of re-establishment solicited will be thankfully received by us as an indication that your Lordship is disposed to bear in mind the expressed wishes of the native community on a point where . . . they have a direct interest in a science, [whose value] . . . they have learnt to appreciate from the evidence of their own senses." The involvement of Debendranath Tagore, son of the recently deceased Brahmo leader Dwarkanauth Tagore, is suggestive, because it would not have been hard to link mesmerism with Brahmo campaigns for humanitarian reform and their interest in bringing together Indian intellectual traditions with Western thought (in this case, the locating of mesmeric practice in traditional Indian medicine).

62. Elliotson, "Triumph and reward," 120.

63. Esdaile, "Second half-yearly report." The hospital committee consisted of Sir H. M. Elliott, James Hume, Rev. M. La Croix, Dr. Martin, Rajah Kali Krishna, Rajah Sutt Churn Ghosal, Rajah Chunder Sing, and Baboo Ramapersaud Roy. Elliotson, "Second half-yearly report," 353, records thirty-one cases in each half-yearly period of 1849, six of them tumors of forty to ninety-six pounds, and all "but three" were "discharged cured."

64. Elliotson, "Account of the mesmeric hospital." The next several quotations come from this source.

65. Webb, "Report of the Mesmeric Hospital." The staff included a European superintendent, a subassistant surgeon, two compounders, one dresser, three mesmerizers, and nine inferior servants.

66. Webb, "Report of the Mesmeric Hospital." In the second six months of the year the infirmary saw 3,646 "outdoor" patients, of whom 3,270 were said to have been relieved (6 incurable, 327 "absconded"). There were 67 inpatients, 40 of whom were said to have been cured, and the others either continued as patients, left the hospital "incurable," or died (5 deaths were recorded). The numbers given for inpatients are approximately double those Esdaile provided for his own involvement in the hospital, and it is likely that they (as opposed to those for "outdoor" patients) represent the patients treated with mesmerism.

67. Baber, *Science of empire*, 8.

68. Leask, *British romantic writers and the East.*

69. Milligan, *Pleasures and pains.*

70. Mill, quoted in Brantlinger, *Rule of darkness*, 82.

71. "Mesmerism in India," 558–8; "Indian report on mesmerism."

72. Prakash, "Science 'gone native,'" 162. For a discussion of the cluster of issues relating to the maintenance of "difference" and authority in colonial relations, see Bhaba, "Signs taken for wonders."

73. *Mofussilite*, 9 August 1845, 22: "Native Doctors at Hooghly are permitted to practice Mesmerism . . . we would suggest an interference on the part of the government—for its suppression;" see also Ernst, "Under the influence."

Chapter Nine

1. Martineau to Monckton Milnes, 27 October [1844?], Houghton Papers, 1678(2).

2. Pathologist, "Correspondents," *Lancet* 2 (1844): 304.

3. "Report of a woman giving birth while mesmerised, at Manchester Lying In Hospital." The surgeon was M. R. Whitehead *(Manchester Guardian)*. See Lynell, "Labour in the mesmeric state." Mesmerism was more commonly used to ease the pain of dying. See Sandby, *Mesmerism and its opponents.*

4. For instance, see Browne, "I could have retched."

5. Lovelace to Lady Byron, 11 November [1844], cited in Toole, *Ada.*

6. Showalter, *Female malady;* Schiebinger, *Mind has no sex?* Jordanova, *Sexual visions;* Poovey, *Uneven developments*, 36–38.

7. On Nightingale see Showalter, *Female malady;* Nightingale, *Cassandra and other selections.*

8. Crowe, *Night side of nature;* Kerner, *Seeress of Prevorst.*

9. Squirrell, *Autobiography.* Her disorders included "ossification of the heart" and "violent epileptic fits." When she was eleven, she temporarily lost her sight, hearing, and smell.

10. Squirrell, *Autobiography*, 269, 292–94, 297–98.

11. Sandby, *Mesmerism and its opponents*, 1st ed., 65.

12. Robertson, "Consistency."

13. "Meeting of Miss Martineau's admirers at the Rotunda, Blackfriars Road" *Times*, 2 November 1842, 6.

14. Cooter, "Dichotomy and denial."

15. As a sickroom journalist Martineau was "wholly lifted up,—from being ministered to to ministering" (Martineau to Monckton Milnes, 22 December [1843], Houghton Papers, 1650[5]).

16. Martineau to Monckton Milnes, "Saturday" [1843?], Houghton Papers, 1654(3); Martineau, *Sickroom*, v.

17. Martineau, *Sickroom*, 211.

18. "[A] Seraph, poised on balanced wings, watching the bringing out of a world from chaos, its completion in fitness, beauty and radiance, and its first motion in its orbit." Martineau attributed this image to Akenside and to Milton's *Paradise lost* (Martineau, *Sickroom*, 64).

19. Martineau to Edward Bulwer-Lytton, 26 January 1841, 8 February 1844, Bulwer-Lytton Papers, D/EK C4/5-20, Hertfordshire Record Office. Monckton Milnes sent her a poem dedicated "to Harriet Martineau," and Garrison was also moved to write a sonnet to "the name, the worth, the works, of Harriet Martineau" (Pope-Hennessy, *Monckton Milnes*, 128; Westman, "Memorial," in Martineau, *Autobiography*, 3:250–51). See also Henry Crabb Robinson to Thomas Robinson, 5 October 1844, Robinson Papers.

20. See Martineau to Henry Crabb Robinson, 14 December 1843, Robinson Papers.

21. A post-*Sickroom* correspondence with a suicidal man brought "the poor sufferer to his knees"—he "arose a softened man," she wrote triumphantly (Martineau to Henry Crabb Robinson, 14 December 1843, Robinson Papers).

22. Horne, *New spirit of the age*, 2:66. The similar reviews are "Life in a sickroom," *Westminster Review;* "Life in the sick-room," *Tait's Edinburgh Magazine;* "Thoughts of an invalid."

23. Indeed, *Sickroom* claimed that the soul "is adequate to all that is required from it" (Martineau to Henry Crabb Robinson, 3 January 1844, Robinson Papers). The quote was from a Mrs. Stanley, probably Emma Stanley, wife of Edward Stanley (1799–1849), bishop of Norwich. See also the curt dismissal in "Life in a sick-room," *Literary Gazette*.

24. "Life in a sick room," *British and Foreign Medical Review*, 477.

25. "I care most for the chance of being found capable of clairvoyance, whereby I might obtain that dear knowledge of my condition wch the doctors cannot afford" (Martineau to Monckton Milnes, [July 1844], Houghton Papers, 1667[1]). Martineau worried that her political activities would be compromised by claims that "my mind is weakened by illness" (Martineau to Monckton Milnes, May 31 [1843?], Houghton Papers, 1629).

26. Bulwer-Lytton sustained a mesmeric correspondence with Chauncey Hare Townshend from 1840 throughout the 1860s (26 February 1840, Bulwer-Lytton Pa-

NOTES TO PAGES 221−224 389

pers, Hertfordshire Record Office, C6/11). Townshend claimed that Bulwer-Lytton's "German depths" would help plumb those of mesmerism.

27. Martineau to Monckton Milnes, [July 1844], Houghton Papers, 1667(2); Martineau, *Autobiography*, 2:191.

28. Martineau, *Letters on mesmerism*.

29. Martineau to Monckton Milnes, 2 July [1844], Houghton Papers, 1668.

30. Martineau to Monckton Milnes, Tuesday, n.d., Houghton Papers, 1677; Martineau to Monckton Milnes, n.d., Houghton Papers, 1680.

31. Martineau to Monckton Milnes, [1844], Houghton Papers, 1673.

32. Morpeth diary, 4 January 1845, Howard (Morpeth) Papers, J19/8/6, 24−25. The mesmerist was Henry G. Atkinson.

33. Martineau to Monckton Milnes, 27 October 1844, Houghton Papers, 1678(2).

34. Martineau to Monckton Milnes, [1844], Houghton Papers, 1673. Morpeth described Martineau being mesmerized. Wynyard mesmerized her so "intensely and grasped her so mentally tight, that she was frightened, got away at last and locked herself up in her own room" (Morpeth diary, 4 January 1845, Howard [Morpeth] Papers, J19/8/6, 25).

35. Atkinson and Martineau, *Letters on the laws*.

36. Martineau to Morpeth, 4 July 1845, Howard (Morpeth) Papers, J19/1/39, 70.

37. Martineau to Monckton Milnes, 27 October [1844?], Houghton Papers, 1678(2).

38. E.g., Mrs. Hamilton lectured on the "materialist" doctrines of Martineau in comparison with the "spiritualist" doctrines of Catherine Crowe (1850, broadsheet, Guildhall Library).

39. Martineau to Monckton Milnes, 2 February 1845, Houghton Papers, 1661. She wrote of the same vision to Morpeth, 4 July 1845, Howard (Morpeth) Papers, J19/1/39, 70.

40. Martineau to Monckton Milnes, 27 October [1844?], Houghton Papers, 1678(2).

41. Martineau to Monckton Milnes, 27 October 1844, Houghton Papers, 1678.

42. Martineau to Morpeth, Howard (Morpeth) Papers, J19/1/39, 70; Martineau to Morpeth, 4 July 1845, Howard (Morpeth) Papers, J19/1/39, 70. Morpeth decided that the phenomena displayed "a highly wrought reflex[?] of her ordinary turn of thought" (Morpeth diary, 22 July 1845, Howard [Morpeth] Papers, J19/8/8, 24).

43. Martineau to Monckton Milnes, 23 May [1845], Houghton Papers, 1662(2); Martineau to Morpeth, 29 June 1845, Howard (Morpeth) Papers, J19/1/39, 68.

44. Martineau, *Letters on mesmerism*. Arrowsmith, like O'Key, used the trance state as a borrowed cloak of authority.

45. Martineau, "Miss Martineau on mesmerism."

46. E.g., MacPherson, *Memoirs of Anna Jameson*, 205−9.

47. Martineau to Monckton Milnes, 27 October 1844, Houghton Papers, 1678.

48. Martineau to Robinson, 6 October 1844, Robinson Papers.

49. See Mitford to Barrett, 27 November 1844: "If mixed up with the details of a

marvellous nature she will only get wrecked upon the sharp edges of prejudice in every corner . . . For certainly what is wanted of Mesmerism is, not the wild notions of girls of nineteen, but the power to alleviate disease and perform operations without pain" (L'Estrange, *Life of Mary Russell Mitford,* 3 : 181).

50. Henry Crabb Robinson to Thomas Robinson, 5 October 1844, Robinson Papers.

51. Mary Arnold to Henry Crabb Robinson, 11 October, 27 November 1844, Robinson Papers.

52. Martineau to Monckton Milnes, 15 December 1844, Houghton Papers, 1681.

53. Articles in the press include "Miss Martineau," *Times,* 20 November 1844, 6; "Miss Martineau and mesmerism," *Times,* 25 November 1844, 8; "Miss Martineau and mesmerism," *Times,* 30 November 1844, 3. Charles Darwin's cousin C. J. Fox was one of many who contemplated a visit. See Darwin to Fox, 20 December 1844, 13 February 1845, Fox Papers, Christ's College, Cambridge. Others were William Gregory, professor of chemistry at the University of Edinburgh, and Henry G. Atkinson, whose mesmeric experiments on Martineau culminated in their *Letters on the laws of man's nature and development* in 1851.

54. Martineau to Monckton Milnes, 23 May [1845], Houghton Papers, 1662(2).

55. Martineau to Monckton Milnes, 23 May [1845], Houghton Papers, 1662(1); Martineau to Monckton Milnes, n.d., Houghton Papers, 1677.

56. On Chambers and *Vestiges* see Secord, "Behind the veil."

57. Chambers later spoke of his sensations as being of "a dim, impalpable character without any desire to use effort, or, as he supposed without any power to carry out either mental or bodily effort." This was the account given by his friend Thomas Sopwith, who had accompanied him on a trip to Tynemouth on 6 October 1844 (extracts from Sopwith diaries 1828–78, no folio number, Special Collections, Robinson Library, University of Newcastle). I am very grateful to Jim Secord for this reference.

58. Martineau to Monckton Milnes, 2 July 1844, Houghton Papers, 1668.

59. [Brodie], "Few words by way of comment." In a letter to Fox, Darwin wrote that Brodie was the author of the piece (20 December 1844, Fox Papers). I consider this to be a plausible (though not certain) attribution and, with this proviso, will henceforth refer to the work as Brodie's.

60. There is a large literature on the politics of diagnosis and therapy in hysteria. See, for example, Smith-Rosenberg, "Hysterical woman"; Russett, *Sexual science;* Masson, *Dark science.* Sally Shuttleworth's discussion of medical advertising on uterine complaints ("Female circulation") is striking in light of Martineau's case, since Martineau was popularizing a very different way of being ill and a very different notion of treatment for the same complaint.

61. [Brodie], "Few words by way of comment," 1199. See also "Absurdities of mesmerism," which lamented mesmerism's status, particularly its "rapid progress and its singularly enthusiastic reception among the excitable and uncontrolled masses"; "Clairvoyance."

62. Brodie, *Hunterian Oration of 1837,* 35. Brodie also published, much later, his own tract on mind and brain, *Mind and matter.*

63. See Desmond, *Politics of evolution*, 236–75.

64. Darwin to Fox, 20 December 1844, Fox Papers.

65. Wilson, *Trials of animal magnetism*, 10–11, 14, 35–36, 41–42, 46, 47–48.

66. E.g., [Wakley], "Mesmerism, Miss Martineau." Other articles in the *Lancet* during the Martineau controversy include Hall, "Rise, progress."

67. Pathologist, "Correspondents," 304.

68. Carter, *Pathology and treatment of hysteria*, 106.

69. Greenhow, *Medical report*.

70. Martineau to Morpeth, January 1845, Howard (Morpeth) Papers, J/19/1/39, 15.

71. Martineau, *Letters on mesmerism*, viii. The next two quotations are from vii and ix–x.

72. The fights appeared in the following *Athenaeum* articles: "Miss Martineau in reply to the *Athenaeum*"; "Miss Martineau and mesmerism."

73. "Miss Martineau's case." It is plausible that this article was written by Robert Chambers. His views on mesmerism changed from skepticism to belief after experiences at Martineau's séances. On Barrett's outrage see below and Barrett to Mitford, 14 December 1844, in Browning, *Elizabeth Barrett to Mary Russell Mitford*, 229.

74. Smith, *Mesmerism*. On Smith's own mesmeric experiments, see his preface, iv–v. The author may have learned of animal magnetism by the works of the Reverend George Sandby, to whom several characters refer in the course of the novel.

75. Smith, *Mesmerism*, 82.

76. See Isabella Fenwick to Henry Crabb Robinson, 29 January 1845, Robinson Papers. She told Robinson that her friend Mrs. Villiers recounted observations like those of Martineau. See also Hall, *Mesmeric experiences*, 63–75.

77. A more extended discussion of this issue in relation to Lovelace and De Morgan is presented in Winter, "Calculus of suffering." On the physical regimes of mathematical Cambridge, see Warwick, "Exercising the student body."

78. De Morgan to Lady Byron, 21 January 1844, Lovelace Collection, Bodleian Library, 344.

79. Lady Byron to Ada Lovelace, 17 January [1844], Lovelace Collection, 57 folio 3.

80. Browning, *Elizabeth Barrett to Mary Russell Mitford*.

81. Browning, *Elizabeth Barrett to Mary Russell Mitford*.

82. Browning and Browning, *Letters*, 1:41.

83. Browning, *Elizabeth Barrett to Mary Russell Mitford*.

84. Browning, *Elizabeth Barrett to Mary Russell Mitford*.

85. Browning, *Elizabeth Barrett to Mary Russell Mitford*, 3 August 1843, 2:277.

86. Barrett found Elliotson an "able & honest man" but took his testimony less seriously than did those of her immediate circle because "there is a 'speculation in his eyes'" (*Elizabeth Barrett to Mary Russell Mitford*, 279). The quote is *Macbeth*, act 3, scene 4, line 94.

87. Karlin, "Browning, Elizabeth Barrett, and mesmerism," 68; Browning, *Letters of Elizabeth Barrett Browning*, 1:196–97.

88. Karlin, "Browning, Elizabeth Barrett, and mesmerism," 68.

89. Browning and Browning, *Brownings' correspondence*, 9:163.

90. Browning, *Elizabeth Barrett to Mary Russell Mitford*, 3 August 1843, 277.

91. Browning, *Elizabeth Barrett to Mary Russell Mitford*, 20 November 1844, 19.

92. Browning, *Elizabeth Barrett to Mary Russell Mitford;* similarly, Barrett to Kenyon, 8 November 1844, "Why shouldn't Miss Martineau's apocalyptic housemaid tell us whether Flush has a soul, & what is it's 'future destination'?" (Browning and Browning, *Brownings' correspondence*, 9:220).

93. Browning, *Elizabeth Barrett to Mary Russell Mitford*, November 1844.

94. Browning, *Letters of Elizabeth Barrett Browning*, 1:219.

95. Browning and Browning, *Letters*, 1:488–89.

96. Browning and Browning, *Letters*, 1:41.

97. Browning and Browning, *Letters*, 1:488–89.

98. Browning and Browning, *Letters*, 2:680.

99. Karlin, "Browning, Elizabeth Barrett, and mesmerism," 69–70. Barrett was probably referring to *Punch*'s caricature of Elliotson (fig. 16).

100. Robert Browning, "Mesmerism," in Browning, *Men and women* (London, 1855).

101. Karlin, "Browning, Elizabeth Barrett, and mesmerism," 76–77.

102. Karlin, "Browning, Elizabeth Barrett, and mesmerism."

103. There were, as we shall see, apocalyptic claims made in relation to table-turning, but as far as I am aware no claims were made that electrobiology was a form of possession.

104. Karlin discusses this theme of Browning's letters, e.g.: "You *know* by this that it is no shadowy image of you and *not* you, which having attached myself to it in the first instance, I afterward compelled my fancy to see reproduced, so to speak, with tolerable exactness to the original idea, in you, the dearest real *you* I am blessed with" (15 March 1846, in Browning and Browning, *Letters*, 1:538).

105. Browning, *Barrett to Mitford*, 20 November 1844, 19.

106. The urge to eat dirt or feces.

107. "Mesmeric deceptions," 178–79.

108. Browning, *Barrett to Mitford*, 11 December 1844, 32.

109. Martineau understood herself in the same terms (Browning, *Elizabeth Barrett to Miss Mitford*, 11 December 1844, 32).

110. This phrase is probably a reference to Mary Wollstonecraft.

111. Browning, *Barrett to Mitford*, [24] December 1844, 40–42.

112. Browning, *Barrett to Mitford*, [16] December 1844, 38.

113. Browning, *Barrett to Mitford*, 19 March 1854, 404.

114. Burstyn, "Education and sex"; Conway, "Stereotypes of femininity"; for an American example see Smith-Rosenberg, "Beauty, the beast."

Chapter Ten

1. Poem printed in Capern, *Pain*, 34.

2. Mark 13:22−23, Matthew 24:24−25, as quoted in *Satanic agency and table-turning*, 9.

3. As quoted in Heeney, *Different kind of gentleman*, 11. On debates over the social function of the church in the decades preceding these debates, see Hole, *Pulpits, politics, and public order*, 187 and passim.

4. "Yorkshire clergyman's opinions of mesmerism," 201−3.

5. Pyne, *Vital magnetism*, v.

6. See esp. Sandby, *Mesmerism and its opponents*, discussed below.

7. Sandby *(Mesmerism and its opponents*, 1st ed., 1−2) wrote that lecturers brought mesmerism into "discredit."

8. Sandby identified himself as Evangelical by stating that his doctrinal views were broadly similar to those of the Evangelical minister Hugh M'Neile of Liverpool, in *Mesmerism and its opponents*, 1st ed., 7; Holdsworth, "Case of asthma"; Jackson, introduction to Davey, *Illustrated practical mesmerist*, 2d ed.

9. Sandby, *Mesmerism and its opponents*, 1st ed., 2, 6.

10. Samuel Wilberforce's famous debate with Thomas Huxley over evolutionary theory has been described most recently in Browne, "I could have retched," and Desmond and Moore, *Darwin*.

11. This is the H. Brookes of chapter 5.

12. "I write in much haste having all this afternoon been closetted with Mr Brooke the Mesmerizer who was at Romsey . . . to search into the System. I am going on Thursday to have another bout at it with [69v] the help of Dr Richardson & ce. At present I am much more disposed to think it a lawful remedy" (Samuel Wilberforce to Louisa Noel, 31 December 1844, Wilberforce Collection, d.43, folio 69, Bodleian Library).

13. "I am endeavouring by reading at present, really to master it. My present inclination is to think of it as quite allowable but some points still perplex me: too long to write out" (8 January 1845, Wilberforce Collection, d.43, folios 72−73).

14. "I have never got quite light enough to feel fine about Mesmm but my mind is greatly more disposed to believe that used with the limitations & curative purpose you would use it with & for it must be lawful" (11 February 1845, Wilberforce Collection, d.43, folios 82−83). See also Ashwell, *Life of Wilberforce*, 1:260−61. Wilberforce continued his mesmeric experiences at least into the 1850s: see *Table-moving by animal magnetism*.

15. "Animal magnetism," *Christian Remembrancer*. The attribution of Wilberforce's identity as author was made by the *Zoist* in an angry rejoinder article: see L. E. G. E., "'The *Christian Remembrancer*,' or Arrogance unmasked," 315 n.

16. L. E. G. E., "'The *Christian Remembrancer*,' or Arrogance unmasked," 314. It was shocking to find, in the middle of the nineteenth century, a "species of religious crusade against a small knot of natural philosophers" whose efforts were aimed at finding new means of "alleviating the miseries of suffering humanity."

17. Pyne advertised the hospital in a leaflet attached to his pamphlet "Vital magnetism."

18. Morpeth diary, 5 June 1845, Howard (Morpeth) Papers, J19/8/7, 48–49.

19. Morpeth diary, c. 14 June 1845, Howard (Morpeth) Papers, J19/8/7, 48.

20. Pyne, *Vital magnetism*, 59–60.

21. Pyne, *Vital magnetism*, 18.

22. Pyne, *Vital magnetism*, 20–22.

23. Pyne, *Vital magnetism*, 57–59. Pyne's argument was an example of mesmeric claims that the mind "gains juster notions, to have quite a new sense of spiritual things, and to be lifted nearer the fountain of all good and of all truth," as an opponent sarcastically summarized the view. See Hall, "Rise, progress."

24. Pyne, *Vital magnetism*, 55.

25. See Stamp and Stamp, *William Scoresby;* Scoresby-Jackson, *Life of William Scoresby.*

26. Scoresby, *Magnetical investigations*, 1:4; Scoresby, "Description of a magnetometer"; Scoresby, "Experiments and observations."

27. *Story of Scoresby*, 91–92.

28. Scoresby, *Discourses to seamen*, 28.

29. Scoresby, *Zoistic magnetism*, 118 and 9.

30. Scoresby, *Zoistic magnetism*, 55.

31. Scoresby's museum bequest refers to the construction of "subordinate" magnets by a single great "master" magnet (Scoresby-Jackson, *Life of William Scoresby*, appendix, "Bequest").

32. Untitled MSS, n.d., in collection of manuscripts organized under the heading of "Zoistic magnetism," Scoresby Papers.

33. Scoresby, *Jehovah glorified in his works*, 14.

34. Lady Rosse to William Scoresby, 1850, Scoresby Papers.

35. Winter, "Compasses all awry"; Cotter, "Early history of ship-magnetism," provides a different account of this controversy.

36. Hardy, *Analytic researches*, viii. Hardy dedicated his mesmeric tract to the Jews. On Israelism, see Wilson, "British Israelism"; Cahagnet, *Celestial telegraph.* Through this means a subject could be placed in a state in which she maintained, over years of experimentation, a parallel spiritual life during her trances in which she "lives with the beings of the other world" and could communicate between specific deceased individuals "at will." Cahagnet's Heaven resembled a complete panopticon, elucidated by mesmeric ecstatics. See Cahagnet, *Celestial telegraph*, 53; Hilton, "Whiggery."

37. A. B., "Review of the Rev. Dr. Maitland's book."

38. [Tonna], *Mesmerism;* Corfe, *Mesmerism tried;* M'Neile, "Satanic agency." Monckton Milnes referred to Ashley's views in "Mesmerism," a newspaper cutting [1843?] pasted into his commonplace book, Houghton Papers. I am very grateful to Miss Diana Chardin for finding this reference for me. On M'Neile's influence in Liverpool, see Moore, "This Whig and Tory ridden town," 53. "Satanic agency," *Zoist* 3 (1845): 532–35, gives a taste of radical mesmerists' attitudes toward such attacks.

These were just the forerunners of decades of such claims; see Oppenheim, *Other world*, 66–67.

39. M'Neile, "Satanic agency," 149. M'Neile was noticed not only in religious circles; see "News of the week."

40. Talbot, *Letter descriptive of the Estatica*. This went through a number of editions in the 1840s, as well as provoking a small pamphlet war over the status of the Estatica. She even failed to blink or wince when a fly crossed "her open eye, walking over the ball," according to a later account (Pyne, *Vital magnetism*, 23). There were other very striking instances of this kind for those who visited the Continent—for instance the celebrated visionary Bernadette Soubirous. See Ruth Harris's forthcoming study of Soubirous and religious healing in France during this period.

41. M'Neile, "Satanic agency," 150.

42. M'Neile, "Satanic agency," 143.

43. M'Neile, "Satanic agency," 150–51.

44. Corfe, *Mesmerism tried*, 44. Corfe quoted the Reverend Thelwall, *Refutations of Irving's heresy* (1836), as saying, "Oh! take warning while it is called today." A similar attack was made by Baxter, *Narrative of facts*.

45. Browning, *Elizabeth Barrett to Miss Mitford*, 11 December 1844, 3:32.

46. Browning, *Elizabeth Barrett to Miss Mitford*, 11 December 1844, 3:32. The last quote is from Dryden, "The hind and the panther," 1:134.

47. *Times*, 3 March 1852.

48. Godfrey, *Table-moving tested*, 20.

49. Godfrey, *Table-moving tested*, 23.

50. Close, *Testers tested*.

51. Godfrey, *Table-moving tested*, 28.

52. Godfrey, *Table-moving tested*, 28.

53. Gillson, *Table-talking*, quoted (in a rebuttal) in Close, *Testers tested*, 28; see also Close, *Table-turning not diabolical*. Gillson replied to Close in *Whose is the responsibility?* Another opponent of Close published *Satanic agency and table-turning*. Other pamphlets in this genre include Vincent, *Satanic influence;* Dibdin, *Table-turning*, and Kotch, *Table-moving and table-talking*. A number of pamphlets, running to several editions each, were published by the Reverend N. S. Godfrey, e.g., *Table-moving tested; Table-turning the Devil's modern masterpiece*.

54. Godfrey, *Table-moving tested*, as quoted in Close, *Testers tested*, 18. N. S. Godfrey also wrote *A Watchman's appeal, with especial reference to the unexampled wonders of the age*. See also Vincent, *Satanic influence*.

55. See also *Art of spirit rapping;* Banton, *Table moving by the power of the will*.

56. These debates parallel a crisis in French psychiatry that involved similar issues. See Vandermeersch, "Victory of psychiatry over demonology."

57. G. W. Cooke to Faraday, 12 May 1853; J. Allen (archdeacon of Salop) to Faraday, 16 May 1853, Press Vicarage, Shrewsbury; W. E. Hickson (from Fairseat, Wickham, Kent) to Faraday, 17 May 1853; Hickson to Faraday, 19 May 1853; F. W. M. to Faraday, 8 June 1853, Misc. 219; F. W. M. to Faraday, 11 June 1853, Misc. 219. All in Archives of the Institute of Electrical Engineers.

58. Close, *Lecture on the nature of miracles*. He reiterated his argument in the wake of the Faraday experiments in Close's *Table-turning not diabolical*, 35–36, in which he attributed mesmeric phenomena to the will.

59. Close, *Testers tested*, 32.

60. Pyne, *Vital magnetism*, v.

61. See Binns, *Anatomy of sleep*, 441–503; Sandby, *Mesmerism and its opponents*, on Shrewsbury. For an example of the use of mesmerism by a Wesleyan preacher, see Davey, *Illustrated practical mesmerist;* Shrewsbury contributed to Binn's *Anatomy of sleep* (460–62) a letter passed on to him by a Catholic priest, describing how ghostly experiences converted a Presbyterian woman to Catholicism. See also Talbot, *Letter descriptive of the Estatica*.

62. As quoted in Charles Darwin to Charles Lyell, 2 September 1844, in Burkhardt and Smith, *Correspondence of Charles Darwin*, 4:252. I am very grateful to Anne Secord for this reference.

63. See Stanhope, "Reflections on a future state," n.d., Stanhope Family Papers, U1590 C124, U1590 C215, 9. He claimed that the ability to speak foreign languages in an altered state of mind proved the immortality of the soul. Against Elliotson, Stanhope argued that mesmerism proved the immateriality, rather than the materiality, of the mind. See Binns, *Anatomy of sleep*, appendix, 452. Stanhope's copy of Binns's *Anatomy of sleep* is in the Society for Psychical Research Collection, Cambridge University Library, Hunter, d.84.7.

64. Morpeth cited a "case of a young man (Gardiner) who had been converted by it [mesmerism] from infidelity" and another in which a woman was induced, while mesmerized, to postpone plans to enter a nunnery (a plan that horrified her Protestant parents). See Morpeth diary, c. 14 June 1845, Howard (Morpeth) Papers, J19/8/7, 49; 8 July 1845, J19/8/8, 13.

65. Sandby, *Mesmerism and its opponents*, 1st ed., 257.

66. Sandby, *Mesmerism and its opponents*, 1st ed., 243. Sandby also referred to the work of R. Young, *The entranced female*, which went through twenty-seven editions, as an example of mesmeric phenomena misclassified as supernatural. Young's and other trance works were condemned by Philo-Veritas, *Modern miracles condemned by reason and Scripture*, which Sandby did not find adequate.

67. Pyne, *Vital magnetism*, 23. See also *Magic and mesmerism*, a novel of scandalous mesmerism among Jesuits, nuns, and somnambulic would-be saints (reviewed in "Magic and mesmerism").

68. Henry Crabb Robinson to Thomas Robinson, 17 January 1845. Crabb Robinson cited Greg as remarking that mesmerism must be "brought within the sphere of science" and "taken" from that of miracles. See also Miss Fenwick to Henry Crabb Robinson, 19 January 1845, Robinson Papers. See also "Mesmerism satanic or the gift of God," 544: "The German neologians have invented a system, and proceed upon the strength of it to 'rationalize' (as they call it) the pages of Divine revelation. In like manner Mesmer invented a system about the mysterious influence of magnets upon the human frame." Sandby, *Mesmerism and its opponents*, 1st ed., 207–9, acknowl-

edged the link made by "unbelievers" between the raising of the dead and the revival of entranced people.

69. A Christian, *Veil uplifted*, wrote of mesmerism's danger as a materialist system that denied the existence of the soul.

70. However, the uses of Strauss by such readers must be distinguished from his own views on the implications of his *Life*. The first translation of Strauss's *Life of Jesus* appeared in 1847, but the *Life* was known even before its translation. See Chadwick, *Victorian church*, 487–88; Doodd, "Strauss's English propagandists"; Pals, *Victorian "lives" of Jesus*, 53 n: in 1846 it was selling more than any other book on the market, and by 1848 (28) there was talk of the existence of a band of secret Straussians.

71. Chandler, "Mesmeric scene," 226, 237.

72. See Sandby, *Mesmerism and its opponents*, 1st ed., 201–18.

73. Such demonstrations were quite common, including the specific command to the mesmeric subject to perceive wine as water. Morpeth recounts such an incident, in c. 15 December 1844, Howard (Morpeth) Papers, J19/8/6, 6; in published accounts, authors tended to list practically everything *but* wine in their accounts of what subjects were made to believe they were consuming. For example, Gregory, *Letters to a candid inquirer*, 348: "milk, coffee, rum, whiskey, or wormwood . . . after drinking it [water] as whisky, they were told that they were drunk, and in a minute or two became . . . very drunk indeed." Similarly, Stone, *Electro-biology*, 42.

74. Sandby, *Mesmerism and its opponents*, 1st ed., 212.

75. Thomas Arnold, "Our hope toward God in Christ," sermon 19, in Arnold, *Sermons*, 169–70. In 1838 Arnold was actively seeking news of mesmerism, which, he claimed, "has always excited my curiosity" (Arnold to W. A. Greenholl, in Stanley, *Life of Arnold*, 2:81). Elsewhere during the same year he argued that "above all Animal Magnetism" would eventually make possible knowledge of the "principle of animate life" (Arnold, *On the divisions and mutual relations of knowledge*, 410). Arnold's reference to the principle of life in 1838 is significant in that it was made in the context of current debates over the electrical production of life. See Secord, "Extraordinary experiment"; Arnold, in "Our hope toward God in Christ," argued that "[t]here exists a lurking fear of these phenomena, as if they might shake our faith in true miracles; and therefore men are inclined to disbelieve them in spite of testimony; a habit far more unreasonable to our Christian faith than any belief in the facts of magnetism."

76. Several editions were published in the 1840s and 1850s (e.g., 9th ed., 1849) and were used, along with more general references to Whately's name and reputation, to legitimate mesmerism. For example, Elizabeth Barrett used Whately's support to sanction mesmerism in correspondence with Mary Russell Mitford; see Porter, *Through a glass darkly*. Sandby also used Whately's arguments, summarizing them as "we are obliged to believe something that is very wonderful, in order to avoid believing something else that is still more wonderful" (review of Cahagnet's *Arcanes de la futur devoilés*, 421).

77. Whately, *Life and correspondence of Richard Whately*, 235.

78. *London Mesmeric Institute: Annual reports;* Davey, *Illustrated practical mesmerist.*

79. For instance Whately chaired the section on statistics at the BAAS meeting in 1852.

80. "Report of a woman, blind for twenty-six years, restored."

81. Whately to Charles Brent Wale (his son-in-law): "I cannot say I find any after-effects of Mesmerism. The disorder continues to gain ground; especially since that great storm I had to encounter about the Irish-town missions[?]. The disorder is very much dependent on whatever affects the mind, but not at all on any medicine or diet, or weather" (Whately Papers, MS 216420, February 1858, folios 202–3, Lambeth Palace Library). See also "Memorandum," n.d.: "In case of my being seized with any disorder that deprives me of speech or of reason: my earnest desire is that none of the ordinary—or as they are called, Allopathic—practitioners may be called in; but that Homeopathy may be resorted to, if any one can be found to so prescribe, & if not, I may be left to Nature. And in case of my death, this memm may be produced as a vindication of my attendants" (Whately Papers, MS 216420, folio 239).

82. [Wilberforce?], "Animal magnetism," 388–89. His source for mesmeric information was William Newnham, a doctor in Farnham, Surrey, who wrote many tracts on mesmeric phenomena, including *Essay on superstition* and *Reciprocal influence of body and mind*. Newnham's work was used to claim that religious influence was a medical concern. See "Mr. Newnham on the influence of body and mind."

83. [Wilberforce?], "Animal magnetism," 389. This was probably a reference to German rationalist criticism and, in particular, to Strauss's newly translated *Life of Jesus*.

84. Combe, *Constitution of man*, 315, 314.

85. [Moir?], "Daemonology and witchcraft," 41.

86. Sandby, *Mesmerism and its opponents*, 2d ed., 103.

87. Sandby, *Mesmerism and its opponents*, 1st ed., 39.

88. *Mesmeric phenomena*.

89. Maitland, *Illustrations and enquiries relating to mesmerism*, part 1, 54–64. (No further parts were published.) His argument is too complex to enter into here, but it involved new translations of the term "aub" (among others), which was ordinarily translated as "familiar spirit" (he referred to Isaiah 8:9 and 1 Samuel 28:7 in his translations), such that the term seemed to bear directly on various phenomena of mesmerism; and this formed the Scriptural source for mesmerism's illegal status. The *Zoist* used Whately's *Historic doubts* to attack this argument. See "Review of Dr. Maitland's book," 398.

90. Maitland, *False worship*, 234.

91. The *Wellesley index* (2:144) attributes this article to G. Moir. What Maitland saw as the similar mistakes between Scott's *Letters* and the article may merely indicate that the former was a source for the latter. Maitland's complaints about Sandby and Combe appeared in "On the conduct of the clergy," 165.

92. Maitland, "On the conduct of the clergy." See Smith, *Gothic bequest*, 198–99, on Maitland's agendas and his antagonism to the Evangelical view of the medieval church.

93. Maitland, *Superstition and science*, 69. He cited the second edition of Prichard's

work on table-turning *(Few sober words of table talk)*, in which Prichard abandoned his confidence in Faraday's tests, as support for his own dismissal of Faraday.

94. Faraday, "Observations on mental education," 464–65.

95. Maitland, *Superstition and science,* 74. Against Maitland see [Clericus], *Spirit-rapping and table-turning.*

Chapter Eleven

1. Reichenbach subsequently published his experiments as *Physikalisch-physiologische Untersuchungen.* Reichenbach's work was first abridged and translated by William Gregory in 1846 as *Abstract of physical researches.* The full text was translated twice, first by John Ashburner as *Physico-physiological researches . . .* , 2 vols. (1850–51), then by William Gregory as *Physico-physiological researches . . .* (1851).

2. "The complaint of a sunbeam against Dr. Faraday," manuscript poem, author unknown, Owen Papers, British Library. The poem went on to warn the other forces of nature to keep away from Faraday if they did not wish to be "converted."

3. Reichenbach's work was related to Faraday's discovery of the polarization of light in [George Thomas Fisher], "Researches in magnetism," 293. Fisher supported it despite his acknowledgment that "we are treading on dangerous ground; we are approaching the confines of . . . animal magnetism." I am very grateful to Iwan Morus for the reference to this paper and for identifying its author.

4. Regular reports were printed in the *Zoist* and in separate pamphlets on these phenomena; for instance, "Popular letters on the od force"; see also Reichenbach, *Odic-magnetic letters.*

5. Reichenbach, *Physico-physiological researches.*

6. Carpenter, "On the mutual relations," 746.

7. On the Society for Psychical Research, see Oppenheim, *Other world;* Noakes, "Cranks and visionaries."

8. Braid, *Power of the mind over the body.*

9. According to Gauld *(Hypnotism,* 231), G. W. Stone brought the first medium, Mrs. Haydon, to Britain.

10. Gregory, *Letters to a candid inquirer,* 154–55.

11. Gregory, *Letters to a candid inquirer,* 192–93.

12. Gauld, *Hypnotism,* 233, quotes Elliotson: "The phenomena resulted from imagination, excited by suggestion in a slight degree of mesmerism."

13. At the University of Edinburgh, William Gregory, professor of chemistry, was an active researcher in mesmerism during this time and practiced mesmerism on his students. Gregory's manuscript "Mesmeric journal" survives in the papers of the Society for Psychical Research, Cambridge University Library, SPR Z1850.11. He attended many electrobiological lectures and demonstrations and in 1851 published detailed accounts of the methods and phenomena *(Letters to a candid inquirer).*

14. Bennett, *Mesmeric mania of 1851,* 6.

15. Bennett, *Mesmeric mania of 1851,* 5.

16. E.g., see his role in *Reports from commissioners*, 28. Carpenter's *Animal physiology* and Huxley's *Lessons in elementary physiology* were the texts in the City of London school. In Taunton School they used Huxley's *Physiology*.

17. *Chambers's course of study on zoology; Chambers's information for the people;* entry on "Zoology" in Conolly, Forbes, and Tweedie, *Cyclopedia of practical medicine.* Carpenter's more specialist textbooks were staple reading for medical students, and, at the time of the Devonshire commission's survey of scientific instruction in the early 1870s, his *Zoology* and *Physiology* were being taught in London schools.

18. Jacyna, "Physiology of mind"; Jacyna, "Immanence or transcendence"; Winter, "Construction of orthodoxies."

19. The successive editions of Carpenter's *Principles of human physiology* show a dramatic increase in the attention given to mental phenomena.

20. See Braid, *Observations on trance;* Braid, *Neurypnology.*

21. Laycock, *Nervous diseases*, 111. On Laycock see Leff, "Thomas Laycock and the cerebral reflexes"; on Laycock and Marshall Hall see Jacyna, "Scientific naturalism," 164–80.

22. Laycock, *Nervous diseases*, 112.

23. Carpenter, "On the influence of suggestion," 147.

24. See Carpenter, *Systematic education*, 2:271–72.

25. See esp. Carpenter, *Human physiology*, 3d ed., 800.

26. Carpenter, *Human physiology*, 3d ed., 672.

27. See [Carpenter], "Correlation of forces."

28. Carpenter's concept was widely adopted to explain these phenomena. One of the earliest doctors to employ it was Robert Brudenell Carter, in an explanation for hysterical muscle action (*Pathology and treatment of hysteria*, 63–64; on Carpenter's priority in developing this notion, see 64 n).

29. Braid reviewed Mayo, *On the truths contained in popular superstitions.* Included in the review was Wood, *What is mesmerism?*

30. Braid, "Odyle, mesmerism," 388–89, 431.

31. James Clerk Maxwell to Charles Benjamin Taylow, 8 July 1853, in *Scientific letters and papers of James Clerk Maxwell*, 1:221.

32. James Clerk Maxwell to Lewis Campbell, 14 July 1853, in *Scientific letters and papers of James Clerk Maxwell*, 1:222.

33. Engel, *Clergyman to don;* Heyck, *Transformation of intellectual life.*

34. The lectures were published by the Royal Institution in 1855 *(Lectures on education),* and several were reprinted in 1867 in Youmans, *Modern life.*

35. Faraday, "Observations on mental education," 485–86.

36. Whewell, *On the influence of the history of science on intellectual education,* 19–20. The next several quotes come from this source.

37. Faraday, "Observations on mental education," 485–86.

38. Faraday, "On the production of electricity in the gymnotus"; see also Secord, "Extraordinary experiment."

39. Oppenheim, *Other world;* Owen, *Darkened room.*

40. Faraday (attributed to), *Relations of science.*

41. Teste, *Practical manual of animal magnetism*, 176.

42. Pickstone, "Ways of knowing"; Pickstone, "Museological science."

43. Crowther, *Cavendish laboratory;* Sviedrys, "Rise of physics laboratories"; Geison, *Michael Foster.*

44. Sviedrys, "Rise of physics laboratories"; Smith and Wise, *Energy and empire,* 128–35.

45. Layton, *Science for the people,* 141.

46. Their "condition resembles that of the dreamer, the somnambule or the insane patient, in all of whom . . . voluntary control is suspended and who [may be] 'played upon' by the suggestion of ideas" (Carpenter, *Human physiology,* 3d ed., 672); an animal "may be . . . compared to an automaton; in which particular movements, adapted to produce a given effect, are produced by touching certain springs" (Carpenter, *Principles of general and comparative physiology,* 4th ed., 687). On the contemporary anthropological literature see Stocking, *Victorian anthropology.*

47. Huxley, "On the educational value of the natural history sciences," in *Collected essays,* 3:45, 59; see also Heyck, *Transformation of intellectual life,* 103.

48. Royal Commission on Scientific Instruction, *Appendix [2] to sixth report,* statement by Professor G. C. Foster, 68–70: science training was the perfect mental discipline for life (physics was the ultimate example). Physics is useful as a means of "*educating the judgment,* or the faculty of drawing true conclusions from the direct observation of our senses . . . [it is a] mental discipline [that tends] *toward the power of thinking definitely and correctly* . . . instruments of mental education . . . The function of education . . . is not so much to excite increased mental activity as to discipline that which exists."

49. Royal Commission on Scientific Instruction, *First, supplementary, and second reports,* "Questions put to William Benjamin Carpenter," 1:541–42, para. 7864–7092.

50. Carpenter, *Mesmerism* (1877), 5–6.

51. Chambers, *Testimony.*

Chapter Twelve

1. LMI Reports, 1852–67, Library of the Society of Psychical Research.

2. Müller, *Physiology;* Mill, *System of logic;* Lewis used "consensus," italicized to indicate a foreign term, only in the table of contents, not the text, so it is difficult to judge what he meant by it, but the notion of (psychological) agreement is plausible; Comte did not know "whence they flashed into being, what power sustains them, or what their mighty movements mean" (Brimley, "Comte," 317–36); Goldwyn Smith, *Modern history.* On 'consensus' see also Poovey, *Social Body,* 28, 35, 47.

3. This treatise by the physiologist Johannes Müller also supplied the *OED* with its reference to "consensus," and the metaphor was repeated among his English followers. The relevant sections of his *Physiology* were so popular in England that the publisher reprinted them, bound separately as *Physiology of the senses.*

4. A more sophisticated version of this metaphor helped Elizabeth Barrett express

just what was so horrifying about phreno-mesmerism, when she took the materialism out of phrenological "organs" by imagining Elliotson's "boney finger" touching "the stops of the soul" (Barrett to Browning, 1845, in Browning and Browning, *Courtship correspondence*).

5. Ryan, *Recollections;* Moscheles, *Life of Moscheles*. Similarly, Sir Charles Hallé described Berlioz's power by likening the players to a single instrument, played "as a pianist upon the keyboard" (Carse, *Orchestra,* 375).

6. Weber, "Wagner, Wagnerism, and musical idealism." On this increasingly "massive" phenomenon, see Weber, *Music and middle-class society.*

7. Quoted in Carse, *Orchestra,* 354.

8. Galkin, *History of orchestral conducting.*

9. On the Philharmonic in this period, see Nettel, *Orchestra in England,* 203–16. Galkin, *History of orchestral conducting,* 502, quotes a number of sources on the slow establishment of baton conducting in Britain, compared to the Continent.

10. "Monsieur Jullien," *Punch* (1841): 15.

11. Carse, *Orchestra,* 300, 323.

12. J. T., "Notes of a musical tourist," quoted in Carse, *Orchestra,* 322.

13. Foster, *History,* 193.

14. This count was made from Jullien's full name as listed in Carse's *Life of Jullien,* treating hyphenated names individually.

15. *Musical World,* 1842; Carse, *Orchestra,* 380–82. Jullien wore white kid gloves as he conducted, and these were brought to him at the beginning on a silver platter. His stick was jeweled, and he sat on a throne (Galkin, *History of orchestral conducting*).

16. Broadsheet advertising Jullien's show, reproduced in fig. 73.

17. *Athenaeum,* 1851, quoted in Carse, *Orchestra,* 378.

18. *Punch,* 1852, as quoted in Carse, *Life of Jullien,* 75.

19. "Mr. Jacob," 1 April 1850, broadsheet, Guildhall Library; "Ethiopian singers," *Illustrated London News* (1846).

20. Wagner and Berlioz could not compete with Felix Mendelssohn for popularity in Britain more generally; on Mendelssohn's popularity see Weber, *Music and middle-class society.*

21. Galkin, *History of orchestral conducting.* Galkin calls attention to the contrast between the passionate, romantic notion we now have of Berlioz and his reputation in the nineteenth century as being wedded to strict regularity of time.

22. Francis Hueffer, *Musical Times,* 26 December 1855.

23. Hueffer, *Richard Wagner,* 294–95; on Wagner's style more generally, Galkin, *History of orchestral conducting,* 565–68.

24. See Johnson, *Listening in Paris,* "The social roots of silence," 179–205.

25. During a trial of hypnotism in the 1840s, Lind participated in hypnotic experiments in which she was placed in "communion" with another woman, who was thereby enabled to follow Lind through the incredibly difficult arpeggios and scales that had made Lind famous (for being uniquely able to carry out such technical performances). On Lind's own mesmeric status see Benét, *Enchanting Jenny Lind* (on *La*

Sonnambula, 287–92); Bulman, *Jenny Lind* (esp. 157–238); Holland and Rockstro, *Memoir,* 2:81–91.

26. The notion of an idée fixe was that the mental faculties could become so intently focused on a specific idea or topic that they could not break free. On monomania in France during this period, see Goldstein, *Console and classify.*

27. On the history of the metronome, see Saint Phalle, *Le métronome;* Harding, *Metronome and it's* [sic] *precursors.* On telegraphy see Morus, "Electric Ariel"; Morus, *Frankenstein's Children.*

28. Merryweather, *Essay explanatory,* 44. Several leeches were kept in glass jars, in which pieces of wood hung by a string, which itself dangled from a bell. Changes in the atmosphere before a storm, Merryweather hypothesized, would compel the leeches to try to leave the jars, thereby making the string move and the bells ring.

29. Baring-Gould, "Snail telegraph." M. Jules Allix, in an article in *La Presse,* announced the discovery of "a new system of universal intercommunication of thought" by the French inventor, M. Jacques Toussaint Benoît (de l'Hérault).

30. Sutherland, *Victorian novelists and publishers,* 53; Altick, *English common reader.*

31. These journals used the same vocabulary to celebrate mass power as conservatives used to condemn it. For instance, the "spark of patriotism runs with electric swiftness from pulse to pulse, until the whole mass vibrates in unison . . . Then, despots, tremble" (T. J. Wooler, *Black Dwarf* 3 [1819]: 695). I am grateful to Kevin Gilmartin for this source. More generally on how crowds were depicted in such journals, see Gilmartin, *Press politics.*

32. Secord, *Evolution for the people,* chapters 3–4. On the variety of journalists' anonymous "authorial personae," see Brake, *Subjugated knowledges,* 10.

33. Anderson, *Printed image,* 71–80.

34. Klancher, *English reading audiences,* chapter 3.

35. Brake, *Subjugated knowledges,* 11.

36. Letter inviting Mrs. Gaskell to contribute, in Dickens, *Letters,* vol. 6, January 1850.

37. Dickens, *Letters,* 5:622–33, 7 October 1849.

38. To John Foster, 31? January 1850, in Dickens, *Letters,* 6:25. A longer list of possible titles is to be found in Dickens to Foster, 1 February 1850, 26.

39. [Dickens], *Household Words,* no. 1 (1850): opening pages.

40. Collins, "Unknown public," 221, 220, 222, discussed in Small, "Pulse of 124."

41. Helen Small argues for this in a paper to which I am very indebted in this discussion. See Small, "Pulse of 124," 268.

42. Dickens to Forster, November 1861, in Dickens, *Letters,* 3:261, quoted in Small, "Pulse of 124," 281–82.

43. Small, "Pulse of 124," 283; Kaplan, *Dickens and mesmerism.*

44. Dickens to Forster, November 1861, in Dickens, *Letters,* 3:261, quoted in Small, "Pulse of 124," 281–82.

45. "Master of Art" was Mrs. Oliphant's term.

46. For other examples of Dickens's confidence in the possibility of sustaining, or

creating, peaceful order in this period, compare the riot scenes in *Barnaby Rudge* and *A tale of two cities*.

47. Sutherland, introduction to *The Woman in White*, vii–viii. See also Davis, *Life of Wilkie Collins*, 216; Robinson, *Wilkie Collins*, 137.

48. *Critic*, 25 August 1860; Thackeray, *Cornhill*, August 1862; *Times*, 30 October 1860; all in Page, *Wilkie Collins*, 82, 122, 102.

49. Page, *Wilkie Collins*, 92, 84.

50. Edward Fitzgerald, *Letters*, 11 November 1867, in Page, *Wilkie Collins*, 125.

51. Oliphant, "Sensation novels," 566, 570. Of course, those readers who were besotted with Collins's heroine would have protested at Oliphant's dismissal of the characters.

52. Oliphant, "Sensation novels," 572–73. For a discussion presenting the identification of reader and character as a complex process of hysterical response, see Miller, *Novel and the police*, esp. 160.

53. *Spectator*, 8 September 1860, 864, in Page, *Wilkie Collins*, 92.

54. Dickens to Collins, 7 January 1860, in Page, *Wilkie Collins*, 80.

55. Sutherland, introduction to *The Woman in White*, xiii.

56. Page, *Wilkie Collins*, 123–24. However, James was saying that Collins's novels were intellectually engaging in the way a scientific treatise (not an experiment) would be.

57. [Collins], "Magnetic evenings at home."

58. [Collins], "Magnetic evenings at home," letter 4, *Leader*, 28 February 1852, 207–8: "I felt the magnetic influence communicating itself from her to me. The sensation was precisely like that produced by a mild shock from a galvanic battery—*i.e.* a slight feeling of *tingling* in the hand, and of numbness all up the arm. Whenever I felt this sensation at all on the increase, I changed the hand I gave to V—— [the mesmeric subject]; otherwise . . . I should have been soon thrown into the magnetic state myself."

59. *The frozen deep*, 6 January 1859, was followed by *Animal magnetism* with Dickens in the starring role. For the playbill, see Brannan, introduction to *Under the management of Mr. Charles Dickens*.

60. It would be possible to give a thoroughly mesmeric reading of this novel, casting the characters in the roles, states of mind, and experiences of mesmerists and their subjects. The closest thing to such a reading is Jenny Bourne Taylor's illuminating study of Collins, *In the secret theatre of home*.

61. In 1852 Collins would have encountered this physiology, because it was relevant to the dispute Collins was having with G. H. Lewes over mesmerism, and had in fact been developed during similar disputes. Lewes (in "Fallacy of clairvoyance") argued that clairvoyants mistook a "*dreaming* power for a *seeing* power." The "suggestions of external stimulus" created a false belief that these "suggestions" were realities. Collins published a rebuttal ("Incredible not always impossible") but was wary of psychic phenomena in future. Collins later used the treatise that first systematically described mental reflexes when he needed a complex mental physiology for the pivotal scenes of *The moonstone*. Collins needed the more elaborate notion of mental

action that Carpenter was developing at this time, and earlier works would not have met his needs. See Carpenter, *Human physiology*, 4th ed., 807–8, for *The moonstone* passage.

62. Lewes and Spencer were also known for their critical essays; Lewes was particularly prolific, but Spencer had published two influential essays on taste during the 1850s, and his *Law of progress* supplied a physiological explanation for the expansion and differentiation of the periodical press. See "Popular literature."

63. Spencer, *Principles of psychology;* Bain, *Emotions and the will;* Bain, *Mental and moral science* (this became a school and college textbook); Bain, *Mind and body;* Lewes, *Physiology of common life;* Maudsley, *Physiology and pathology of the mind;* Maudsley, *Body and mind;* Huxley, *Lessons in elementary physiology.*

64. Huxley, *Lessons in elementary physiology,* 284–86.

65. According to Mays, "Disease of reading."

66. Mays, "Disease of reading," cites C. H. Butterworth, "Overfeeding," *Victorian Magazine* 14 (1870): 501.

67. "The act of reading terminates in itself. Reading is itself a state of mind" ("Reading as a means of culture"). For a fuller discussion of this essay and its context, see Mays, "Disease of reading."

68. Mays quotes and discusses Austin's amazing essay at length. See Mays, "Disease of reading," 171 ff.

69. The elegant (and funny) demolition job on Austin in the *Dictionary of National Biography* lists with relish the literary figures Austin dismissed (including Hugo, Tennyson, Browning, Morris, Arnold, Clough, and Swinburne). The last novel Austin actually owned up to was published in 1867, but anonymous works continued to appear in the 1870s.

70. Miller, *Novel and the police,* 160; Stewart, *Dear Reader,* 344.

71. Bagehot, "Why Mr. Disraeli has succeeded."

72. E.g., Harrison, *Crowds in history,* 168–76.

73. Brontë to Margaret Wooler, quoted in Shuttleworth, *Charlotte Brontë,* 34–36.

74. Gaskell, *Mary Barton,* 199. Gaskell offered *Mary Barton* as a lesson in the "agony" that "convulses this dumb people," a lesson made more timely and pertinent by events on the Continent (xxxiv).

75. Carlyle, *Heroes and hero-worship.*

76. Todhunter, *Whewell,* 2:344.

77. Bagehot, "Trades unions and reform," 1175. Similarly, "Working of trades unions": "Persecute a sect and it holds together, legalise it and it splits and resplits, till its unity is either null or a non-oppressive bond."

78. Bagehot, "What a panic is": "we require *more* bank notes, just because the *feeling,* the confidence which made *few* bank notes effectual has disappeared." See also Bagehot, "Panic." Bagehot was also developing an accompanying psychology of belief, in which an emotional component (not just a logical one) was necessary for beliefs to be strong enough for one to feel confident in acting on them. See Bagehot, "On the emotion of conviction."

79. Bagehot, "Inconvincible governments."

80. Before this period, prime ministerial speeches had been published, of course; what was new was the phenomenon of a prime minister establishing his authority and credibility by social contact with the general public.

81. Bagehot, "Mr. Gladstone and the people." On the other mode of political action, the "unsensational" one, see "Unseen work of Parliament." Parliament works because "the nation is not inclined to require excitement from it." It can work only if the theatrical elements are displaced elsewhere. It is ironic that when television was brought into the House of Commons in the 1980s, politicians' worries sounded, superficially, quite similar to these: their activities could not sustain public gaze. But they worried about a very different problem: that, rather than looking too abstruse, formal, or stuffy, the "unseen work" of Parliament would not look like work at all, when viewers could see how few members of Parliament regularly sat on the long, empty green benches, and could hear how awkward, petty, and inefficient were the ordinary speeches of backbenchers.

82. Bagehot to Edith Bagehot, 2 May 1842, on mesmerism, in Bagehot, *Collected works*, 12:148–49.

83. Huxley, *Lessons in elementary physiology*, 286.

84. Carpenter, "On the hereditary transmission," 312.

85. Carpenter, *Doctrine of human automatism*, 31–32.

86. On the "personal equation" as a means of calibrating scientific researchers, see Schaffer, "Astronomers mark time"; Carpenter, "Psychology of belief," 128–29.

87. Bagehot, *Physics and politics*, 19, 18, 21.

88. Bagehot, *Physics and politics*, 7; identical claims were made by Carpenter, Maudsley, Huxley, et al.

89. Carnarvon to Bagehot, 1872, in Bagehot, *Collected works*, 2:xxx.

90. "Performance of Haydn's 'Toy Symphony.'" The charity equipped children "to regain the superior position lost by their parents."

91. Carpenter, *Nature and man*, reprints Gladstone's letter reflecting on Carpenter's essay "On the hereditary transmission."

92. Poovey, *Making a social body*, chapter 1; Porter, *Rise of statistical thinking;* Klancher, *English reading audiences*, 76–97.

93. Quoted in Poovey, *Making a social body*, 34.

Conclusion

1. Bagehot, *Works*, 2:323, quoted in Burn, *Age of equipoise*, 55.

2. Chandler, *England in 1819*.

3. Mill, "Spirit of the age." Mill referred, implicitly, to Hazlitt's collection of biographical studies, *The spirit of the age*, whose epigram advises, "To know another very well is to know oneself."

4. Dickens to Forster, 1849, in Dickens, *Letters*.

5. Horne, *New spirit of the age*.

6. Thatcher, *History*, xiii; Buranelli, *Wizard from Vienna;* even Ellenberger's otherwise extremely useful *Discovery of the unconscious*.

7. Oppenheim, *Other world;* Noakes, "Cranks."

8. The elusiveness as well as the tangibility of late-nineteenth-century psychic phenomena was brought home to me during research for this book, when a librarian took me into the basement of Cambridge University Library to examine a valuable specimen of ectoplasm. The medium had been strip-searched to prevent a fraud, and during the proceedings a damp cottonlike substance was produced (believers claimed it was a by-product of spirit materialization; skeptics, that the cotton was hidden in a bodily orifice). For a century it had been preserved in the archives, but now the librarian was unable to lay hands on it. "I've a nasty feeling," he concluded at length, "that it's gone astray."

BIBLIOGRAPHY

Primary Sources

Airy Papers, Royal Greenwich Observatory Collection, Cambridge University
    Library, Cambridge
Babbage Correspondence, British Library, London, Additional Manuscripts
Bakken Library, Minneapolis
Bulwer-Lytton Papers, Hertfordshire Records Office, Hertford
Bulwer-Lytton Papers, Knebworth House, Hertfordshire
Carlisle Correspondence, British Library, London, Additional Manuscripts
Chambers Papers, National Library of Scotland, Edinburgh
Collection of Printed Ephemera, Guildhall Library, London
College Correspondence, University College London, London
Combe Papers, National Library of Scotland, Edinburgh
Council Minutes, Medical School, University College London, London
Dunraven Papers, Belfast Public Records Office, Belfast
Edinburgh University Library Archives, Edinburgh
Faculty of Medicine, University College London, London
Faraday Papers, Royal Institution of Great Britain, London
Fox Papers, Christ's College Library, Cambridge
Glynne-Gladstone Manuscripts, Flintshire Records Office, Hawarden, Flintshire
Hospital Casebooks, University College London, London
Houghton Papers, Trinity College, Cambridge
Howard (Morpeth) Papers, Castle Howard, North Yorkshire
Huntington Library, San Marino, Calif.
Institute of Electrical Engineers, London
John Johnson Collection of Printed Ephemera, Bodleian Library, Oxford
Kirklees Libraries and Museums

Library of the Royal College of Surgeons, London
Liverpool Records Office, Liverpool
Lovelace Collection, Noel-Byron Papers, Bodleian Library, Oxford
Madden Collection of Broadsides, Cambridge University Library, Cambridge
Mary Evans Picture Library, London
Newcastle Public Library
Nottinghamshire Records Office, Nottingham
Owen Papers, British Library, London, Additional Manuscripts
Pierpont Morgan Library, New York
Poster Collection, Lynn Archives, Liverpool
Poster Collection, Somerset Records Office, Taunton, Somerset
Purland Papers, National Library of Medicine, Bethesda, Md.
Robinson Papers, Dr. Williams's Library, London
Royal Society of London, London
Scoresby Papers, Whitby Museum, Whitby, North Yorkshire
Society for Psychical Research, library and archives, Cambridge University
    Library, Cambridge
Somerville Papers, Bodleian Library, Oxford
Sopwith Diaries, 1828–1878, Special Collections, Robinson Library, University
    of Newcastle, Newcastle
Stanhope Family Papers, Kent Records Office, Maidstone
Townshend Papers, Wisbech Museum, Wisbech, Cambridgeshire
Trevelyan Papers, University of Newcastle Library
Tyne and Wear Archives Service, Newcastle
Wellcome Institute for the History of Medicine, London
Whately Papers, Lambeth Palace Library, London
Whewell Papers, Trinity College, Cambridge
Whipple Library, University of Cambridge, Cambridge
Wilberforce Collection, Noel-Byron Papers, Bodleian Library, Oxford

NEWSPAPERS

The Atlas
Bengal Hurkaru and India Gazette
Bolton Chronicle and South Lancashire Advertiser
Bombay Times and Journal of Commerce
Bristol Gazette
Bristol Mercury
Bristol Mirror
Bristol Times
Bucks Herald
Bury Post
Calcutta Englishman and Military Chronicle
Delhi Gazette
Edinburgh Courant

Forres Gazette
Halifax Guardian and Huddersfield and Bradford Advertiser
Hampshire Advertiser
Hampshire Telegraph
Hereford Times
Ipswich Express
Ipswich Journal
Leicestershire Mercury
Liverpool Mercury
Maidstone Journal and Kentish Advertiser
Manchester Guardian
Mofussilite
Morning Chronicle
Morning Herald
Norfolk Chronicle
Reading Gazette
Record
Times
West Exeter and Plymouth Gazette
Woolmer's Exeter and Plymouth Gazette

PUBLISHED SOURCES

A. B. "Review of the Rev. Dr. Maitland's book." *Zoist* 7 (1849–50): 395–407.

Abdy, Mrs. "The mesmerist." *Metropolitan Magazine* 40 (1844): 286.

"Abstract of a clinical lecture by Dr. Elliotson, on remarkable cases of sleep waking and on the effects of animal magnetism on patients with nervous affections." *Lancet,* 9 September 1837, 866–73.

"Abstract of a lecture on electro-biology." *Edinburgh Medical and Surgical Journal* 76 (1851): 239.

"The absurdities of mesmerism." *London Medical Gazette* 2 (1843–44): 705.

Acland, ——. "The galvanic disc delusion dispelled." *Zoist* 10 (1852–53): 48–67.

Adams, ——. "Remarkable mesmeric phenomena." *Zoist* 7 (1849–50): 79–80.

Allison, J. *Mesmerism: Its pretensions to a science physiologically considered.* London, 1844.

"Animal magnetism." *Christian Remembrancer* (1847): 366–91.

"Animal magnetism." *Medical Times* 5 (1841–42): 283.

"Animal magnetism." *Medico-Chirurgical Review,* 1 October 1838, 634–38.

"Animal magnetism." *Medico-Chirurgical Review,* 1 October 1843, 496–97.

"Animal magnetism," *Mirror,* 18 March 1837, 169.

"Animal magnetism." *Quarterly Review* 61 (1838): 273–301.

"Animal magnetism." Review of Colquhoun's translation of French commission report. *Lancet,* 4 and 11 May 1833, 175–83, 205–18.

"Animal magnetism." *Tait's Edinburgh Magazine* 9 (1838): 460–67.

"Animal magnetism and its scientific abettors." *London Medical Gazette*, n.s., 13 (1851): 762.

"Animal magnetism: Experiments of Baron Dupotet." *Lancet*, 2 September 1837, 836–40.

"'Animal magnetism,' from the *Comic Annual*, by Thomas Hood." Excerpted and reprinted in *Mirror*, 17 December 1837, 410–13.

"Animal magnetism, in London, in 1837." *Mirror*, 6 September 1837, 185–86.

"Animal magnetism in practice." *North of England Magazine* 1 (1842): 72–74.

"Animal magnetism: No. IV, What animal magnetism is, and what it is not." *London Saturday Journal* 17 (1839): 257–61.

"'*Animal magnetism*'; or, '*mesmerism.*' Experiments performed on Elizabeth and Jane O'Key, at the house of Mr. Wakley, Bedford-Square, in August, 1838." *Lancet*, 1 September 1838, 805–14.

"Animal magnetism [second notice]." *Athenaeum* 556 (1838): 436–38.

Arnold, Thomas. *On the divisions and mutual relations of knowledge.* Rugby: Combe and Crossley, 1839.

———. *Sermons.* 3d series. New ed. 2 vols. London: Reeves and Turner, 1876.

Arthur, T. S. *Agnes, or The possessed: A revelation of mesmerism.* London: J. S. Hodson, 1852.

The art of spirit rapping, and table-turning; also researches in somnambulism, &c., with an appendix on witchcraft demonology and thought-reading . . . . Colchester, [n.d., 1850s].

Ashburner, John. *On the connection between mesmerism and spiritualism, with considerations on their relation to natural and revealed religion and to the welfare of mankind.* London, 1859.

———. "On the silent influence of the will." *Zoist* 6 (1848–49): 96–110.

Ashwell, A. R. *Life of the Right Reverend Samuel Wilberforce, D.D. . . . with selections from his diaries and correspondence.* 3 vols. London: John Murray, 1880.

Atkinson, Henry G., and Harriet Martineau. *Letters on the laws of man's nature and development.* London: John Chapman, 1851.

Babbage, Charles. *The ninth Bridgewater treatise: A fragment.* 2d ed. London: John Murray, 1838.

Bagehot, Walter. *The collected works of Walter Bagehot.* Ed. Norman St. John–Stevas. London: Economist, 1989.

———. *The English constitution.* London: Chapman and Hall, 1867.

———. "Inconvincible governments." *Saturday Review*, 21 June 1856, 167–68.

———. "Mr. Gladstone and the people." *Economist*, 4 November 1871, 1330–31.

———. "On the emotion of conviction." *Contemporary Review* 17 (1871): 32–40.

———. "The Panic." *Economist*, 19 May 1866, 581–83.

———. *Physics and politics.* 2d ed. London: Henry S. King, 1873.

———. "Trades unions and reform." *Economist*, 22 October 1859, 1174–75.

———. "The unseen work of Parliament." *Economist*, 9 February 1861, 141–42.

———. "What a panic is and how it might be mitigated." *Economist*, 12 May 1866, 554–55.

————. "Why Mr. Disraeli has succeeded." *Economist,* 7 September 1867, 1009–10.

————. "The working of trades unions." *Economist,* 27 April 1867, 468–69.

————. *The works and life of Walter Bagehot.* 9 vols. Ed. Russell Barrington. London: Longman's, Green, 1915.

Bain, Alexander. *The emotions and the will.* London: J. W. Parker and Son, 1859.

————. *Mental and moral science: A compendium of psychology and ethics.* London: Longman's, Green and Co., 1868.

————. *Mind and body: The theories of their relation.* London: H. S. King, 1873.

Baldock, Thomas. "Cure of severe affection of the stomach with mesmerism." *Zoist* 3 (1845–46): 337–38.

Banton, George. *Table moving by the power of the will: Similar manifestations obtained by the divining ring: Being a statement of original experiments, reprinted from the "Kentish Independent" newspaper, of Dec. 25 1852, and March 10 1853.* London: Strange, 1853.

Baring-Gould, S. *Historic oddities and strange events.* London: Methuen and Co., 1891.

Barrallier, J. L. Letter to the editor. *Medical Times* 5 (1841–42): 187–88, 248.

A Barrister. "Remarks on phreno-magnetism: The Sherwood Forester and animal magnetism." *Provincial Medical and Surgical Journal* 5 (1843): 398–402.

Barth, George. *Mesmerist's manual of phenomena and practice: Directions for applying mesmerism to the cure of diseases . . . intended for domestic use . . . .* 3d ed. London: H. Bailliere, 1852.

————. *The principle of health transferable.* London, 1852.

————. *What is mesmerism? The question answered by a mesmeric practitioner, or Mesmerism not miracle.* London, 1853.

Baumann, A. M. F. *Curative results of medical somnambulism, including the somnambule's own case and cure.* London, 1849.

Baxter, Robert. *Narrative of facts, characterizing the supernatural manifestations in members of Mr. Irving's congregation . . . and formerly in the writer himself.* London: J. Nisbet, 1833.

Bennett, J. H. *The mesmeric mania of 1851, with a physiological explanation of the phenomena produced.* Edinburgh: Sutherland and Knox, 1851.

Berlioz, Hector. *Memoirs of Hector Berlioz, including his travels in Italy, Germany, Russia, and England, 1803–1865.* Trans. D. Cairns. New York: Dover, 1969.

Binns, Edward. *The anatomy of sleep . . . second edition, with annotations and additions, by the Earl Stanhope.* London: John Churchill, 1845.

Blakiston, P. *Clinical reminiscences.* London: J. and A. Churchill, 1878.

Bostock, John. *Elementary system of physiology.* 3d ed. London: Baldwin and Cradock, 1836.

Boyton, W. "A surgeon's experience of mesmerism." *Medical Times* 7 (1842–43): 362.

Braid, James. "Abstract of a lecture on electro-biology, delivered at the Royal Institution, Manchester." *Edinburgh Medical and Surgical Journal* 76 (1851): 239–48.

————. *Braid on hypnotism: Neurypnology, or The rationale of nervous sleep . . . .* Ed. A. E. Waite. London: G. Redway, 1899.

————. *Neurypnology, or The rationale of nervous sleep considered in relation to animal magnetism.* London: John Churchill, 1843.

————. *Observations on trance, or Human hybernation.* London: John Churchill, 1850.

————. "Odyle, mesmerism, electro-biology, &c." *British and Foreign Medical Review,* n.s., 8 (1851): 378–431.

————. *The power of the mind over the body.* London: John Churchill, 1846.

————. *Satanic agency and mesmerism reviewed, in a letter to the Rev. H. McNeile....* Manchester: Simms and Dinham, 1842.

Brewster, David. *Letters on natural magic.* London: John Murray, 1832.

Brewster, David, and Charles Wheatstone. *Brewster and Wheatstone on vision.* London: Academic Press for Experimental Psychology Society, 1983.

Brimley, George. "Comte." In George Clark, ed., *Essays.* Cambridge: Macmillan, 1858.

Bristol Mesmeric Institute: Report on the first public meeting. Bristol, 1849.

[Brodie, B. C.?]. "A few words by way of comment on Miss Martineau's statement." *Athenaeum,* 7 December 1844, 1198–1200.

————. *The Hunterian Oration, delivered in the theatre of the Royal College of Surgeons in London, on the 14th of November 1837.* London: Longman and Co., 1837.

————. *Lectures illustrative of certain local nervous affections.* London: Longman and Co., 1837.

————. *Mind and matter, or Physiological enquiries....* New York: Putnam, 1857.

Bromet, William. "Animal magnetism." *Lancet,* 7 July 1838, 527.

Brookes, H. "Case of external soreness over the organs of time and tune after excessive excitement." *Medical Times* 6 (1842): 170–71.

Brookes, W. [H.?]. "Mesmerism: Modes of conducting the operation." *Medical Times* 6 (1842): 325.

Brown, Thomas. *Lectures on the philosophy of the human mind.* Edingburgh: W and C Tait, 1820.

Browning, Elizabeth Barrett. *The letters of Elizabeth Barrett Browning to Mary Russell Mitford.* 3 Vols. Waco: Baylor University, 1983.

————. *The letters of Elizabeth Barrett Browning.* Edited with biographical additions by E. G. Kenyon. 2 vols. New York: Macmillan, 1898.

Browning, Robert. *Men and women.* London, Chapman and Hall, 1854–55.

Browning, Robert, and Elizabeth Barrett Browning. *The Brownings' correspondence.* 13 vols. Ed. Phillip Kelly and Ronald Hudson. Winfield, Kans.: Wedgestone Press, 1984–91.

————. *The letters of Robert Browning and Elizabeth Barrett, 1845–1846.* 2 vols. Ed. Elvan Kintner. Cambridge: Belknap Press, 1969.

————. *Robert Browning and Elizabeth Barrett: The courtship correspondence, 1845–1846.* Ed. Daniel Karlin. Oxford: Clarendon, 1989.

Buchanan, Josiah. "Impressibility." *Journal of Man* 1 (1849): 321–30.

Buckland, Thomas. *Handbook of mesmerism, for the guidance and instruction of all per-*

sons who desire to practice mesmerism for the cure of diseases . . . . 2d ed. London: H. Bailliere, 1850.

Burq, V. "Nervous affections, metallo-therapy, or metal cure: New properties of metals illustrated through mesmerism." *Zoist* 10 (1852–53): 121–40, 230–78.

Bushnan, J. S. *Miss Martineau and her master.* London: John Churchill, 1851.

Bushnell, H. "Unconscious influence: A sermon." Edinburgh: W. P. Kennedy, 1849.

Cahagnet, L. A. *The celestial telegraph, or Secrets of the life to come revealed through magnetism.* 2 vols. in one. London: G. Pierce, 1850.

Capern, Thomas. *The mighty curative powers of mesmerism: Proved in upward of one hundred and fifty cases of various diseases.* London: H. Bailliere, 1851.

———. *Pain of body and mind relieved by mesmerism: A record of mesmeric facts.* London: H. Bailliere, 1861.

Carlyle, Thomas. *On heroes and hero-worship.* London: J. Fraser, 1841.

———. *Past and present.* Ed. A. M. D. Hughes. Oxford, 1918.

———. *Sartor Resartus: The life and opinions of Herr Teufelsdröckh.* London: Saunders and Otley, 1838.

———. "Signs of the times." *Edinburgh Review* 49 (June 1829): 439–59.

Carlyle, Thomas, and Jane Welsh Carlyle. *Collected letters of Thomas and Jane Welsh Carlyle.* 24 vols. Ed. C. L. Ryals and K. J. Fielding. General ed. C. R. Sanders. Durham, N.C.: Duke University Press, 1970–95.

Carpenter, J. Estlin. "William Benjamin Carpenter: A memorial sketch." In J. Estlin Carpenter, ed., *Nature and man: Essays scientific and philosophical,* 4–154. New York: D. Appleton, 1888.

Carpenter, Lant. *Systematic education.* 2 vols. London, 1840.

Carpenter, W. B. "Alison, Bushnan, Swainson, on instinct." *British and Foreign Medical Review* 11 (1841): 90–103.

[———]. "Correlation of forces, physical and vital." *British and Foreign Medico-Chirurgical Review* 8 (1851): 206–38.

———. *The doctrine of human automatism: A lecture.* London: Sunday Lecture Society, 1875.

———. "Dr. Moreau's psychological discoveries on hachish and on mental derangement." *British and Foreign Medical Review* 23 (1847): 217–36.

[———.] Editorial. *Medico-Chirurgical Review,* 1 April 1847, 530.

———. "Electro-biology and mesmerism." *Quarterly Review* 93 (September 1853): 501–57.

———. *Epidemic delusions.* Science Lectures for the People. London: Science Lectures for the People, 1871.

———. *Mesmerism, spiritualism, &c., historically & scientifically considered.* London: Longman's, Green and Co., 1877.

———. *Mesmerism, spiritualism, &c., historically & scientifically considered: Being two lectures delivered at the London Institution with preface and appendix by W. B. Carpenter.* New York: D. Appleton, 1887.

———. *Nature and man: Essays scientific and philosophical.* Ed. J. Estlin Carpenter. London, 1888.

————. *On the fallacies of testimony in relation to the supernatural.* London, 1875.

————. "On the hereditary transmission of acquired psychical traits." *Contemporary Review* 21 (1873): 778–93.

————. "On the influence of suggestion in modifying and directing muscular movement, independently of volition." *Proceedings, Royal Institution of Great Britain* 1 (1851–54): 147–53.

————. "On the mutual relations of the vital and physical forces." *Philosophical Transactions* 140 (1852): 727–57.

————. "The phasis of force." *National Review* 9 (1857): 359–94.

————. *Principles of general and comparative physiology.* 4th ed. London: John Churchill, 1854.

————. *Principles of human physiology.* 3d ed. London: John Churchill, 1853.

————. *Principles of human physiology.* 4th ed. London: John Churchill, 1855.

————. *Principles of mental physiology.* 1st ed. London: H. S. King and Co., 1874.

————. *Principles of mental physiology . . . .* 6th ed. London: C. Kegan Paul, 1881.

————. "On the psychology of belief." *Contemporary Review* 23 (December 1873): 123–45.

————. "Remarks on some passages of the review of 'Principles of general and comparative physiology' in the Edinburgh Medical and Surgical Journal, January, 1840, by William B. Carpenter." *British and Foreign Medical Review* 9 (1840): appendix.

[————]. *Temperance and teetotalism.* London: Churchill, 1847.

————. *The unconscious action of the brain.* Science Lectures for the People, ser. 3. London: Science Lectures for the People, 1871.

————. *What is common sense?* London, 1872.

Carter, R. B. *On the pathology and treatment of hysteria.* London: John Churchill, 1853.

"Cerebral sympathy and clairvoyance in brutes." *Zoist* 9 (1851–52): 392–97.

Chambers, Robert. *Testimony.* London, 1859.

[————]. *Vestiges of the natural history of creation.* London: John Churchill, 1844.

Chambers's course of study on zoology. Edinburgh, 1838.

Chambers's information for the people: Zoology. Edinburgh, 1841.

Chandler, Thomas. "A mesmeric scene a thousand years ago." *Zoist* 9 (1851–52): 225–37.

————. "Rheumatism, with periodical fits of delirium, treated by animal magnetism." *Lancet,* 14 April 1838, 81–83.

Chatto, John. "Mesmerism applied to surgical operations." *Medical Gazette* 35 (1844–45): 354–55.

Chenevix, Richard. "On mesmerism, improperly denominated animal magnetism." *London Medical and Physical Journal* 61 (1829): 219–30, 491–501; 62 (1829): 114–25, 210–21, 315–29.

Childs, C. "Severe nervous disease cured with mesmerism." *Zoist* 3 (1845–46): 36–39.

A Christian. *The veil uplifted and mesmerism traced to its source.* London, 1852.

"Clairvoyance." *Provincial Medical and Surgical Journal* 9 (1845): 70–72.

Clarke, J. F. *Autobiographical recollections of the medical profession.* London: J. and A. Churchill, 1874.

"Clerical table-turners and spirit-rappers." *Punch* 25 (1853): 266.

[Clericus]. *Spirit-rapping and table-turning: Remarks on Dr. Maitland's "Superstition and science."* London, 1856.

Close, Francis. *A lecture on the nature of miracles, delivered to the members of the Church of England Association . . . 20 November 1845.* Cheltenham, 1845.

———. *Table-turning not diabolical: A tract for the times.* 2d ed. London: J. Hatchard, 1853.

———. *The testers tested, or Table moving, turning, and talking, not diabolical: A review of the publications of the Rev. Messrs. Godfrey, Gillson, Vincent, and Dibdin.* London: J. Hatchard, 1853.

Clough, Arthur Hugh. *Poems and prose remains.* 2 vols. London: Macmillan, 1869.

Cockton, H. *The life and adventures of Valentine Vox, the ventriloquist.* London: R. Tyas, 1840.

Collins, J. "Sketches of the present state of the medical profession in the provinces; and more especially in Liverpool and its vicinity." *London Medical Gazette* 14 (1834): 96–99.

Collins, Wilkie. "The incredible not always impossible." *Leader,* 3 April 1852, 328–29.

[———]. "Magnetic evenings at home." *Leader,* January–April 1852.

———. "The unknown public." *Household Words* 439 (1858): 217–22.

Collins, Wilkie, with Charles Dickens. *The frozen deep. A drama. In three acts.* London, n.p., 1866.

Collyer, Robert. "Etherology." *Lancet* (1837): 866–73.

———. *Psychography, or The embodiment of thought.* Philadelphia, 1843.

Colquhoun, J. C. *The fallacy of phreno-magnetism detected and exposed.* Edinburgh: W. Wilson, 1843.

———. *An history of magic, witchcraft, and animal magnetism.* 2 vols. London: Longman, Brown, Green, and Longman's, 1851.

———. *Isis revelata: An inquiry into the origin, progress, and present state of animal magnetism.* 2d ed. 2 vols. Edinburgh: Maclachlan and Stewart, 1836.

———, ed. *Journal of ZooMagnetism.* Edinburgh, 1839.

———, trans. *Report of the experiments on animal magnetism made by a committee . . . of the French Academy of Sciences.* Edinburgh: Robert Cadell, 1833.

Combe, George. *The constitution of man, in relation to external objects.* 4th ed. Edinburgh: William and Robert Chambers, 1836.

Conolly, John, John Forbes, and Alexander Tweedie, eds. *The cyclopaedia of practical medicine.* 4 vols. London: Sherwood, Gilbert and Piper, 1833–35.

Cooper, Thomas. "Philosophy of mesmerism." *Cooper's Journal* 1 (1850): 225–29.

Cooper, Thomas. "Testimony to the value of mesmerism." *Cooper's Journal* 1 (1850): 60–62.

Corfe, George. *Mesmerism tried by the touchstone of truth: Being a reply to Dr. Ashburner's remarks on phrenology, mesmerism, and clairvoyance.* London: Hatchard and Son, 1848.

"Correspondence between Geo[rge]. Combe, Professor Reid, and Dr. Laycock." *Lancet*, 23 August–20 September 1845, 231–33, 255–58, 283–84, 308–9, 347–48.

Crampton, Philip. "On the frauds called 'mesmerism' and 'clairvoyance.'" *Lancet*, 14 November 1846, 542–44.

Crowe, Catherine. *The night side of nature*. 2 vols. London: T. C. Newby, 1848.

"Cure of hysterical epilepsy, somnambulism, etc., with mesmerism." *Zoist* 3 (1845–46): 39–79.

Cuvier, Georges. *Lessons on comparative anatomy*. Trans. William Ross. 2 vols. London: Longman and Rees, 1802.

Darwin, Charles. *The correspondence of Charles Darwin*. Vol. 4. Ed. Frederick Burkhardt and Sydney Smith. 10 vols. Cambridge: Cambridge University Press, 1985–97.

Davey, William. *The illustrated practical mesmerist, curative and scientific*. Edinburgh: for the author, 1854.

———. *The illustrated practical mesmerist, curative and scientific*. 6th ed. Introduction by J. W. Jackson. London: J. Burbs, 1862.

Davidson, C. J. E. "Mesmerism in human and brute inhabitants of India." *Zoist* (1851–52): 1–10.

Davis, D. D. *The principles and practice of obstetric medicine*. 2 vols. London: Taylor and Walton, 1836.

Deleuze, J. P. F. *Practical instruction in animal magnetism*. Trans. T. C. Hartshorn. Rev. ed. New York: D. Appleton, 1846.

[De Morgan, Augustus]. Preface to [Sophia E. De Morgan], *From matter to spirit*. London: Longman, Green, Longman, Roberts and Green, 1863.

De Quincey, Thomas. "Animal magnetism." *Tait's Edinburgh Magazine* 4 (January 1834): 456–74.

———. *Confessions of an English opium eater*. London: William Smith, 1845.

[———]. "Suspira de profundis: Being a sequel to *the Confessions of an English opium eater*." *Blackwood's Magazine* 57 (March, April, and June 1845): 269–85, 498–502, 739–51.

De Tocqueville, Alexis. *Journeys to England and Ireland*. Trans. George Lawrence and K. P. Mayer. New Haven: Yale University Press, 1958.

Dibdin, R. W. *Table-turning: A lecture*. London: Aylot [1853].

Dickens, Charles. *Letters of Charles Dickens*. Ed. Graham Storey and Katherine Tillotson. 9 vols. Oxford: Clarendon, 1965–98.

Didier, Adolphe. *Animal magnetism and somnambulism*. London: T. C. Newby, 1856.

"Discovery of the island of Mesmeria." *New Monthly Magazine* 73 (1845): 125–29.

Dods, John Bovee. *Six lectures on the philosophy of mesmerism*. New York and Wells, 1843.

"Doings and sentiments of the phrenologists." *Lancet*, 11 July 1846, 50–52.

"Dr. Davey and mesmerism at the Colney Hatch Lunatic Asylum." *Medical Times* 25 (1852): 87–89.

"Dr. Elliotson on clinical instruction and its improvements; the exployment of new remedies; good and bad experiments; and animal magnetism." *Lancet*, 21 October 1837, 122–24.

"Dr. Elliotson on medical instruction." *Lancet*, 14 April 1838, 84–86.

"Dr. Elliotson's mesmeric exhibitions." *Lancet*, 18 September 1841, 897–900.

"Dr. Esdaile on the application of mesmerism, &c." *British and Foreign Medical Review* 22 (1846): 475–87.

Du Maurier, George. *Trilby*. London: Osgood, McIlvaine and Co., 1895.

Dupotet de Sennevoy, Charles, "Animal magnetism: Letter from Baron Dupotet." *Lancet*, 16 September 1837, 905–6.

———. *An introduction to the study of animal magnetism*. London: Saunders and Otley, 1838.

———. *Le magnétisme opposé à la médecine: Mémoire pour servir à l'histoire du magnétisme en France et en Angleterre*. Paris: A. Réné, 1840.

Eagle, J. "A few passages on omens, dreams, apparitions, e&c., in a letter to Eusebius." *Blackwood's Magazine* 58 (1845): 735–51.

[Eagles, John]. "What is mesmerism?" *Blackwood's Magazine* 70 (1851): 70–83.

"Edinburgh University. Clinical lectures in Medicine, by Dr. Duncan." *Lancet*, 22 May 1830, 277–84.

Egan, R. *Life in London*. London, 1821.

"Electricity a cure for Tetanus." *Lancet*, 2 June 1838, 350–51.

"Electric lady." *Punch* 24 (1853): 14.

"Electro-biology." *Westminster Review* 55 (1851): 312–28.

Eliot, George. *The mill on the Floss*. Ed. Carol T. Christ. New York: Norton, 1994.

Elliotson, John. "An account of the mesmeric hospital in Bengal since Dr. Esdaile's departure from India." *Zoist* 10 (1852–53): 278–93.

———. "Accounts of more painless surgical operations." *Zoist* 4 (1846–47): 5–59.

[———]. "Conclusion of the *Zoist*." *Zoist* 13 (1855–56): 441–44.

———. "Cures of palsy by mesmerism." *Zoist* 1 (1843–44): 300–349.

———. "Death of Miss Barber." *Zoist* 7 (1849–50): 323–26.

———. "Dr. Esdaile and mesmerism in Perth." *Zoist* 11 (1853–54): 419–27.

[———]. "Education as it is." *Zoist* 1 (1843): 351–69.

[———]. "Education as it is, and as it ought to be." *Zoist* 2 (1844): 1–20.

———. *Harveian Oration . . . with an English version and notes*. London: H. Bailliere, 1846.

———. *Human physiology*. 5th ed. 2 vols. London: Longman, Orne, Brown, Green, and Longman's, 1840.

———. "An instance of sleep and cure by imagination only." *Zoist* 12 (1854–55): 396–403.

———. "Instances of double states of consciousness independent of mesmerism." *Zoist* 4 (1846–47): 157–87.

[———]. "Introduction to volume XI of the *Zoist*." *Zoist* 11 (1853–54): 1–17.

———. *John Elliotson on mesmerism*. Ed. Fred Kaplan. New York: Da Capo, 1982.

———. "Mesmeric phenomena in brutes, as effected by the duke of Marlborough and the rev. Mr. Bartlett." *Zoist* 8 (1850–51): 295–99.

————. *Mesmerism in India: Second half-yearly report of the Calcutta Mesmeric Hospital, from 1 March to 1 Sept. 1849.* London, 1850.

————. "Mesmerism in the East . . . ." *Zoist* 7 (1849–50): 121–37.

"Messrs. Jackson and Davey." *Zoist* 9 (1851–52), 304–10.

————. "More of Alexis Didier." *Zoist* 3 (1845–46): 389–98.

————. "More painless amputations and other surgical operations in the mesmeric state." *Zoist* 3 (1845–46): 490–508.

————. "More painless surgical operations in the mesmeric state." *Zoist* 4 (1846–47): 193–218.

————. "More painless surgical operations: Report of a committee at Calcutta in favour of the truth and utility of mesmerism." *Zoist* 4 (1846–47): 563–83.

————. *Numerous cases of surgical operations without pain in the mesmeric state . . . .* London: H. Bailliere, 1843.

————. "On the art of suddenly restoring the moral feelings and intellect to activity in large masses of mankind." *Zoist* 5 (1847–48): 44–50.

————. "Report by Dr Elliotson on 'A record of cases treated in the Mesmeric Hospital.'" *Zoist* 6 (1848): 1–42.

————. "Report of the committee appointed by government to observe and report upon surgical operations by Dr. J. Esdaile . . . ." *Zoist* 5 (1847–48): 50–69.

————. "Reports of various trials of the clairvoyance of Alexis Didier, last summer, in London." *Zoist* 2 (1844–45): 477–529.

————. "Review of an abstract of researches on magnetic and certain allied subjects . . . by Baron von Reichenbach . . . ." *Zoist* 4 (1846–47): 104–24, 277–84, 346–61.

————. "Review of an abstract of researches on magnetic and certain allied subjects . . . by Baron von Reichenbach." *Zoist* 5 (1847–48): 234–53.

————. "Successful result of two cases of lock-jaw or tetanus in horses, treated with mesmerism . . . ." *Zoist* 9 (1851–52): 49–51.

————. "Triumph and reward of Dr Esdaile." *Zoist* 6 (1848–49): 113–20.

Engels, Friedrich. *Condition of the working class in England.* Ed. Victor Kiernan. Harmondsworth: Penguin, 1987.

Engledue, W. C. "Cases of mesmeric clairvoyance and sympathy of feeling." *Zoist* 2 (1844–45): 269–73.

————. *Cerebral physiology and materialism.* London: H. Bailliere, 1842.

————. "Introductory address." *Phrenological Journal* 15 (1842): 291–314.

Esdaile, James. "Dr Esdaile's first monthly report." *Zoist* 5 (1847–48): 178–87.

————. "Dr. Esdaile's first monthly report of the Calcutta Mesmeric Hospital . . . ." *Zoist* 5 (1847–48): 178–87.

————. *Hypnosis in medicine and surgery, originally entitled "Mesmerism in India."* Introduction and supplemental reports on hypno anesthesia. 1846. Reprint, New York: Julian Press, 1957.

————. *The introduction of mesmerism as an anaesthetic and curative agent, into the hospitals of India.* Perth: Dewar, 1852.

————. *The introduction of mesmerism into the public hospitals of India.* 2d ed. London: W. Kent, 1856.

————. "Mesmeric facts." Reprinted in *Bombay Times,* 4 June 1845, 370–71.

————. *Mesmerism in India, and its practical applications in surgery and medicine.* London: Longman, Brown, Green, and Longman's, 1846.

————. *Mesmerism in India: Second half-yearly report of the Calcutta Mesmeric Hospital, from 1st March to 1st September 1849* . . . . London: H. Bailliere, 1850.

————. "On the operation for the removal of scrotal tumours." *London Medical Gazette,* n.s., 11 (1850): 449–54.

————. *A record of cases treated in the Mesmeric Hospital, from June to December 1847, with reports of the official visitors.* Calcutta: W. Ridsdale, 1848.

————. *A record of cases treated in the Mesmeric Hospital, from November 1846, to May 1847, with the reports of the official visitors.* Calcutta: W. Ridsdale, 1847.

————. "Reports of the Mesmeric Hospital, Calcutta." *Zoist* 7 (1849–50): 24–44.

————. "Second half-yearly report of the Calcutta Mesmeric Hospital . . . ." *Zoist* 7 (1849–50): 353–63.

————. *Two lectures on mesmerism, delivered in the City Hall, Perth, at the request of the directors of the Anderson Institution, on March 10 and 17.* London: H. Bailliere, 1853.

"The Evidence relating to the medical relief of the sick poor in the parochial unions." *Lancet,* 1 April 1837, 49–54.

"The Evidence relating to the medical relief of the sick poor . . . ." *Lancet,* 13 May 1837, 264–68.

E. W. C. N. "The medical journals and medical men." *Zoist* 2 (1844–45): 273–88.

"Extraction of a tooth during mesmeric sleep." *Medical Times* 9 (1843–44): 323.

"Extraction of teeth in the mesmeric state." *Zoist* 3 (1845): 214–16.

Eye-Witness. *A full discovery of the strange practices of Dr. E on the bodies of his female patients! At his house . . . with all the secret experiments he makes upon them . . . .* London: n.p., 1842.

Eye-Witness. "Mesmerism at University College Hospital." *Lancet,* 4 November 1837, 210–11.

————. "The trials of animal magnetism, at University College Hospital." *Lancet,* 14 October 1837, 99–101.

Factory Girl. *The unfortunate genius.* 2d ed. London: The Booksellers, 1853.

Fairbrother, A. "The fatal administration of ether to Mrs. Parkinson." *Lancet,* 3 April 1847, 370.

Faraday, Michael. *The correspondence of Michael Faraday.* 3 vols. Ed. Frank A. J. L. James. London: Institute of Electrical Engineers, 1991–96.

————. "Observations on mental education." In *Experimental researches in chemistry and physics,* 463–91. London, 1859.

————. "On the production of electricity in the gymnotus." In *Experimental researches in electricity,* vol. 2, pars. 1749–95. London: R. and J. E. Taylor, 1844.

Faraday, Michael (attributed to). *The relations of science to the phenomena of life.* Star Publishing Co.

"Faraday on table-turning." *Medical Times and Gazette*, n.s., 7 (1853): 42–43.

Ferrier, J. "An introduction to the philosophy of consciousness." *Blackwood's Edinburgh Magazine* 43 (1838): 437–52, 784–91, 234–44; 44 (1838): 539–52.

"Field day in Gower Street." *Medical Times*, 11 July 1840, 181.

[Fisher, George Thomas]. "Researches in magnetism." *Westminster Review* 45 (1846): 281–303.

Forbes, John. "History of animal magnetism." *British and Foreign Medical Review* (1839): 303–52.

———. *Illustrations of modern mesmerism from personal investigation*. London: John Churchill, 1845.

———. "On etherization, &c." *British and Foreign Medical Review* 1 (1847): 547–70.

———. "On mesmerism." Review of fourteen mesmeric tracts. *British and Foreign Medical Review* (1845): 428–65.

Froude, J. A. *Thomas Carlyle: A history of his life in London, 1843–1881*. 2 vols. London: Longman's, 1891.

[Gallenga, Antonio]. "The age we live in." *Fraser's Magazine* 24 (1841): 1–15.

Gardner, J. "On ether-vapour, its medical and surgical uses." *Lancet*, 3 and 24 April 1847, 349–54, 431–34.

Gaskell, Elizabeth. *Mary Barton*. Ed. Edgar Wright. Oxford: World's Classics, 1987.

Gasking, Elizabeth. *The rise of experimental biology*. New York: Random House, 1970.

Gee, J. S. Letter to the editor. *Mesmerist* 1 (1843): 64.

Gillson, E. *Table-talking: Disclosures of satanic wonders and prophetic signs: A word for the wise*. London, Bath: n.p., 1853.

———. *A watchman's appeal, with especial reference to the unexampled wonders of the age*. London: n.p. 1853.

———. *Whose is the responsibility? A letter to . . . F. Close . . . in reply to his pamphlet "The testers tested."* London, 1855.

Godfrey, N. S. *The conflict and the triumph, or The things that are coming on the earth*. London: Partridge, Oakey and Co., 1855.

———. *Table-moving tested, and proved to be the result of satanic agency*. London: n.p., 1853.

———. *Table-turning the Devil's modern masterpiece, being the result of a course of experiments*. London: Partridge, Oakey and Co., 1853.

Godwin, William. *Lives of the necromancers*. London: Frederick J. Mason, 1834.

Goodeve, H. H. "Fatal case of removal of an enormous tumour." *Lancet*, 18 August 1838, 718–21.

Gordon, Charles Alexander. *Handbook for medical officers, of H. M. Service, in India: Describing the phenomena and treatment of the principal diseases, and the official routine peculiar to the Indian service*. London, 1851.

"Government of Bengal to J. Atkinson, Esq., Chairman, and W. B. O'Shaughnessy, Esq., secretary of the committee appointed to observe and report on Dr. Esdaile's mesmeric experiments." *Zoist* 5 (1847–48): 60–62.

Greenhow, E. "General practitioners." *London Medical Gazette* 13 (1833–34): 357.

Greenhow, Thomas Michael. *Medical report of the case of Miss H―――M―――*. London: S. Highley, 1845.

Greg, W. R. *The creed of Christendom: Its foundations & superstructure*. London: J. Chapman, 1851.

Gregory, William. "Case of vision at a distance." *Zoist* 9 (1851–52): 422–24.

―――. *Letters to a candid inquirer on animal magnetism*. London: Taylor, Walter and Moberly, 1851.

―――. "On the probability of the discovery of physical agents able to produce the mesmeric state." *Zoist* 4 (1847): 380–82.

Grimes, J. S. *Electrical psychology*. N.p., 1851.

[Grove, W. R.] "Mesmerism." *Blackwood's Magazine* 57 (1845): 219–41.

[―――]. "Physical science in England." *Blackwood's Magazine* 54 (1843): 514–25.

Gurwood, John. *Major General Napier and Colonel Gurwood*. Author, 1845.

Haddock, J. W. *Somnolism and psycheism, or The science of the soul* . . . . London, 1849.

―――. *Somnolism and psycheism, or The science of the soul* . . . . 2d ed. London: J. S. Hodson, 1851.

Hall, Charles Radclyffe. "On the effects of ether inhalation in reference to mesmerism." *Lancet*, 24 April 1847, 436–37.

―――. "On the rise, progress, and mysteries of mesmerism in all ages and countries [in 10 parts]." *Lancet*, 1 February 1845, and subsequent weeks, 112–18, 149–52, 179–32, 206–8, 233–36, 256–59, 281–83, 309–15, 345–47, 369–72, 403–6, 435–37, 459–62, 493–95.

Hall, Spencer T. *The forester's offering*. London [the author]: Whitaker and Co., 1841.

―――. "Gross stupidity in a professional man." *Phreno-Magnet* 1 (1843): 165.

―――. *Mesmeric experiences*. London: H. Bailliere, 1845.

―――. "The Sherwood Forrester." *Chambers's Edinburgh Journal* 11 (1842): 6–7.

Hand-book of curative mesmerism. Edinburgh: Thomas Grant; London: Houlston and Stoneman, 1854.

Handbook of vital magnetism, or mesmerism . . . . London: Bartlett, 1844.

Hardy, H. H. *Analytic researches in spirit magnetism*. London: G. Pierce, 1852.

"History of animal magnetism in France, Germany, and England." *British and Foreign Medical Review* 7 (1839): 301–52.

Hodder, Edwin. *The life and work of the seventh earl of Shaftesbury*. 3 vols. London: Cassell and Co., 1886.

Hoffmann, E. T. A. *The tales of Hoffmann*. Ed. M. L. Levine, G. C. McNamee, and Daniel Greenberg. New York: Bantam Books, 1970.

Holdsworth, Robert. "Case of asthma cured with mesmerism." *Zoist* 2 (1844): 465–67.

Holland, G. C. *The philosophy of animated nature*. London: John Churchill, 1848.

―――. *Vital statistics of Sheffield*. Sheffield: n.p., 1843.

Holland, Henry. *Chapters on mental physiology*. London: Longman, Brown, Green, and Longman's, 1852.

Hood, Thomas. "Animal magnetism." In *Comic annual*, 97–111. London, 1838.

Hopkinson, James. *Victorian cabinet maker: The memoirs of James Hopkinson, 1819–1894.* Ed. J. B. Goodman. London: Routledge and K. Paul, 1968.

Horne, James. "To the editor of the *Mesmerist.*" *Mesmerist* 1 (1843): 30–32.

Horne, Richard H. *New spirit of the age.* 2 vols. London: Smith, Elder, and Co., 1844.

Howitt, Mary. *An autobiography.* 2 vols. London: W. Isbister, 1889.

Hueffer, Francis. *Richard Wagner and the music of the future.* London: Chapman and Hall, 1874.

Humanitas. "Treatment of the sick-poor under the union medical contract system." *Lancet,* 18 November 1837, 278–79.

Huxley, Thomas. *Collected essays.* New York: D. Appleton and Co., 1909–10.

———. *Lessons in elementary physiology.* London: Macmillan, 1868.

Ikin, J. I. "Gross malapraxis and ignorance of a quack." *Lancet,* 27 January 1838, 630–32.

"Illustrations of political economy." *Athenaeum,* 11 February 1832, 95.

"Indian report on mesmerism in reference to surgical operations." *London Medical Gazette* 39 (1847): 347–51, 392–95.

"Intelligence." *Phrenological Journal* 18 (1845): 94.

Investigator. "Mesmerism in Leicester." *Medical Times* 11 (1844–45): 257–58.

Jackson, J. W. *Lectures on mesmerism, delivered at the Rotunda, Dublin.* Dublin: James McGlashan, 1851.

"Jenny Lind and hypnotism." *Phrenological Journal* 20 (1847): 456–58.

Johnson, James. Editorial. *Medico-Chirurgical Review* (1839): 630–31.

———. Editorial. *Medico-Chirurgical Review* 39 (1843): 147–50.

[Johnstone, Christian]. "Animal magnetism." *Tait's Edinburgh Magazine* 9 (1838): 460–67.

Johnstone, J. W. T. *Notes of a case of painless surgical operation performed while the patient was under the influence of mesmeric agency.* Madras, 1847.

J. T. "Notes of a musical tourist." *Harmonicon* 8 (January 1830): 5.

Jung-Stilling, Johann Heinrich. *Theory of pneumatology, in reply to the question, what ought to be believed or disbelieved concerning presentiments, visions, and apparitions.* Trans. Samuel Jackson. London: Longman, 1834.

Kerner, J. F. *The Seeress of Prevorst: Being revelations concerning the inner-life of man* . . . . Trans. Catherine Crowe. London, 1845.

Kiste, Adolphe. *Mesmerism, or Facts against fallacy.* London: H. Bailliere, 1845.

Kotch, C. *Table-moving and table-talking reduced to natural causes, with especial reference to E. Gillson's recent pamphlet.* London, 1853.

Lafontaine, Charles. *Mémoires d'un magnétiseur* . . . . 2 vols. Paris: Germer Bailliere, 1866.

Lang, W. *Mesmerism: Its history, phenomena, and practice, with reports of cases developed in Scotland.* Edinburgh, 1843.

Lardner, Dionysius, and Edward Bulwer-Lytton. "Animal magnetism." *Monthly Chronicle* 1 (1838): 288–307; 2 (1838); 11–17.

Laycock, Thomas. *Mind and brain, or The correlations of consciousnes and organisation:*

Systematically investigated and applied to philosophy, mental science, and practice. 2 vols. Edinburgh: Sutherland and Knox, 1869.

———. "On the reflex action of the brain." *British and Foreign Medical Review* 19 (1845): 298–311.

———. *A treatise of the nervous diseases of women: Comprising an inquiry into the nature, causes, and treatment of spinal and hysterical disorders.* London: Longman, Orme, Brown, Green, and Longman's, 1840.

"The lecture mania." *Zoist* 2 (1843–44): 95–100.

Lectures on education delivered at the Royal Institution of Great Britain. London: John W. Parker and Son, 1855.

"Lectures on phrenology." *Phrenological Journal* 20 (1847): 87.

Leeson, John. "Objections to the reality of phenomena in animal magnetism." *Lancet*, 18 August 1838, 727–28.

L. E. G. E. "Cerebral physiology." *Zoist* 1 (1843): 5–25.

———. "The *Christian Remembrancer*, or Arrogance unmasked." *Zoist* 4 (1847): 313–31.

Léger, Thomas. *Animal magnetism, or Psychodynamy.* New York: D. Appleton, 1846.

———. *The magnetoscope* . . . . London: H. Bailliere, 1852.

L'Estrange, A. G., ed. *Life of Mary Russell Mitford, related in a selection from her letters to her friends.* 3 vols. London: Richard Bentley, 1870.

Lewes, G. H. "The fallacy of clairvoyance." *Leader*, 27 March 1852, 305–6.

———. *The physiology of common life.* London: Blackwood and Sons, 1859–60.

Lewis, G. C. *An essay on the influence of authority in matters of opinion.* London: J. W. Parker, 1849.

"Life in a sick room." *British and Foreign Medical Review* 18 (1844): 472–81.

"Life in a sick-room." *Literary Gazette*, 20 January 1844, 39.

"Life in a sick-room." *Westminster Review* 41 (1844): 608–11.

"Life in the sick-room." *Tait's Edinburgh Magazine* 15 (January 1844): 131–35.

Liston, Robert. *Elements of surgery.* London: Longman, Rees, Orme, Brown, Green, and Longman's, 1831.

———. *Practical surgery: With one hundred and twenty engravings on wood.* London: Longman, Rees, Orme, Brown, and Longman's, 1837.

Lloyd, W. "Case of lock-jaw in a youth successfully cured." *Zoist* 11 (1851–52): 52–54.

Loewe, M. *A treatise on the phenomena of animal magnetism, in which the same are systematically explained according to the laws of nature.* London: G. Schulze, for the author, 1822.

Lynell, J. P. "Labour in the mesmeric state." *Zoist* 2 (1844–45): 121–23.

Macaulay, T. B. *Speeches by Lord Macaulay, with his minutes on Indian education.* 1835. Reprint, London: Oxford University Press, 1935.

Mackay, Charles. *Memoirs of extraordinary popular delusions.* 3 vols. London: Richard Bentley, 1841.

Macnish, Robert. *Anatomy of drunkenness.* Glasgow: W. R. M'Phun, 1840.

———. *The philosophy of sleep.* Glasgow: W. R. M'Phun, 1830.

MacPherson, Geraldine. *Memoirs of the life of Anna Jameson*. London: Longman and Co., 1878.

Macready, W. C. *Reminiscences, and selections from his diaries and letters*. 2 vols. Ed. F. Pollock. London: Macmillan and Co., 1875.

Macreight, Daniel. *Manual of British botany: In which the orders and genera are arranged and described according to the natural system of De Candolle*. London: Churchill, 1837.

Magendie, François. "On the physical phenomena of life [vital hydraulics]." *Lancet*, 16 December 1838, 412–14.

"Magic and mesmerism." *Tait's Edinburgh Magazine* 10 (1843): 484–92.

Magic and mesmerism: An episode of the eighteenth century and other tales. 3 vols. London: Saunders and Otley, 1843.

Maitland, S. R. *The Dark Ages: A series of essays, intended to illustrate the state of religion and literature in the ninth, tenth, eleventh, and twelfth centuries*. London: Francis and John Rivington, 1844.

———. *False worship: An essay*. London: Rivingtons, 1856.

———. *Illustrations and enquiries relating to mesmerism*. Part 1. London: W. Stephenson, 1849.

———. "On the conduct of the clergy with regard to magic and sorcery." *Theological Critic* 2 (1852): 163–91.

———. *Superstition and science: An essay*. London: Rivingtons, 1855.

Martineau, Harriet. *Harriet Martineau's autobiography, with memorials by M. W. Chapman*. 3 vols. Ed. M. W. Chapman. London, 1877.

———. *Harriet Martineau's letters to Fanny Wedgwood*. Ed. E. S. Arbuckle. Stanford: Stanford University Press, 1983.

———. *Letters on mesmerism*. 2d ed. London: E. Moxon, 1845. Reprinted from "Miss Martineau on mesmerism," *Athenaeum* 23 November 1844, 1070–72; 30 November 1844, 1093–94; 7 December 1844, 1117–18; 14 December 1844, 1144–145; 21 December 1844, 1173–74.

[———]. *Life in the sickroom: Essays by an invalid*. London: E. Moxon, 1844.

———. "Mesmeric cure of a cow." *Zoist* 8 (1851–52): 300–303.

[Martineau, James]. "Mesmeric atheism." *Prospective Review* 7 (1851): 224–62.

Marx, Karl, and Friedrich Engels. *Collected works*. Trans. Richard Dixon et al. 47 vols. New York: International Publishers, 1975–97.

Maudsley, Henry. *Body and mind: An inquiry into their connection and mutual influence*. London: Macmillan, 1870.

———. *Physiology and pathology of the mind*. London: Macmillan, 1867.

Maxwell, J. C. *Scientific letters and papers of James Clerk Maxwell*. Ed. P. M. Harman. 2 vols. Cambridge: Cambridge University Press, 1990, 1995.

Maxwell, W. H. *Extracts from the life of Field Marshall His Grace the Duke of Wellington*.

Mayo, Herbert. *On the truths contained in popular superstitions with an account of mesmerism*. 3d ed. Edinburgh: Blackwood, 1851.

———. *Outlines of human physiology*. 4th ed. London, 1837.

————. *The philosophy of living*. London, 1837.

[————]. Untitled passage attributed to Herbert Mayo. *Lancet*, 1 September 1838, 811–13.

Medical directory for Great Britain and Ireland. London, 1845.

"Medical journals and medical men." *Zoist* 2 (1844–45): 273–88.

"Medical news: Animal magnetism." *Medical Times* 5 (1841–42): 155–56.

"Medical portraits: Robert Liston." *Medical Times*, 4 July 1840, 169.

"Medical Society of London." *Lancet*, 23 June 1838, 457–58.

"Medico-Botanical Society: Animal magnetism." *Lancet*, 9 June 1838, 367–71.

Merryweather, F. S. "Remarks on cerebro-magnetism, or mesmerism." *People's Phrenological Journal* (1844): 167–70.

Merryweather, George. *Essay explanatory of the tempest-prognosticator*. London: John Churchill, 1851.

"Mesmeric cure of blindness of 26 years' duration: By a Lady." *Zoist* 7 (1849): 81–86.

"Mesmeric deceptions: The Whipton prophetess." *Lancet*, 13 February 1847, 178–83.

"Mesmeric frauds." *Lancet*, 26 December 1846, 703.

"The mesmeric hospital." *Lancet*, 8 August 1846, 164.

"Mesmeric infirmary." *Lancet*, 18 July 1846, 82–83.

"Mesmeric infirmary in London." *Phrenological Journal* 19 (1846): 390.

"The mesmeric mania." *Illustrated London News* (1843): 407.

Mesmeric phenomena: Their reality and importance attested by Dr. Maitland, the "Edinburgh Review," and others. London, 1851.

"Mesmeric surgery: Cause of the success of quackery," *London Medical Gazette* 37 (1846): 1106.

"Mesmerism." *Medical Times* 6 (1842): 74.

"Mesmerism." *Medical Times* 9 (1843–44): 495.

"Mesmerism." *Medical Times* 22 (1850): 262.

Mesmerism and media, with full instructions how to develop the alleged spiritual rappings in every family. London: H. Bailliere, 1855.

Mesmerism considered. Glasgow: W. Mackenzie, 1852.

"Mesmerism in Edinburgh." *Medical Times and Gazette* 23 (1851): 129–30.

"Mesmerism in India." *Medico-Chirurgical Review*, 1 October 1846, 558–59.

"Mesmerism in the west of England." *Zoist* 7 (1849–50): 152–64.

"Mesmerism: Its dangers and curiosities." *Punch* 2 (March 1844): 124.

"Mesmerism: Its pretensions and effects, &c." *Medico-Chirurgical Review* 38 (1843): 577–78.

"Mesmerism satanic or the gift of God." *Christian Observer* 69 (1843): 538–49.

Mesmerism solved . . . . London: Jones, 1853.

"Mesmero-phrenology." *Medical Times* 6 (1842): 324–25.

"Messrs. Jackson and Davey." *Zoist* 11 (1851–52): 304–10.

Miles, F. *Mesmerism and the diseases to which it is most applicable . . . .* Dublin: author, 1854.

Mill, John Stuart. "The spirit of the age." In *Collected works*, 22:227–316. Toronto: University of Toronto Press, 1986.

————. *A system of logic, ratiocinative and inductive: Being a connected view of the principles of evidence, and methods of scientific investigation.* London: J. W. Parker, 1843.

[Miller, James]. "Painless operations in surgery." *North British Review* 7 (1847): 169–206.

"Miss Harriet Martineau's mesmeric revelations." *Friend of India,* 30 January 1845, 73–74.

"Miss Martineau and mesmerism." *Athenaeum,* 15 March 1845, 268–69, 290–91, 310–11, 333–35, 361–63.

"Miss Martineau and mesmerism." *Mirror of Literature, Amusement, and Instruction,* n.s., 6 (1844): 351–54.

"Miss Martineau in reply to the *Athenaeum.*" *Athenaeum,* 4 January 1845, 14.

"Miss Martineau's case." *Chambers's Edinburgh Journal,* 7 January 1845, 16.

M'Neile, Hugh. "Satanic agency and mesmerism: A sermon preached at St. Jude's church, Liverpool, on Sunday evening, April 10 1842." *Penny Pulpit,* nos. 599–600 (1842): 141–52.

[Moir, George?]. "Daemonology and witchcraft." *Foreign Quarterly Review,* no. 11 (1830): 1–47.

"Monsieur Jullien." *Punch* 1 (1841): 15.

Mortimer, W. H. "Chloroform as a means of producing insensibility to pain." *Edinburgh Medical and Surgical Journal* 69 (1848): 243–49.

Moscheles, Charlotte. *The life of Moscheles.* 2 vols. Trans. A. D. Coleridge. London: Hurst and Blackett, 1873.

"Mr. Catlow's discoveries." *Medical Times* 5 (1841–42): 249–50.

"Mr. Duncan's lecture on animal magnetism." *Medical Times* 5 (1841–42): 187.

"Mr. Newnham on the influence of body and mind." *British and Foreign Medical Review* 15 (1843): 413–29.

"Mr. Potchett's phreno-magnetic notes." *Phreno-Magnet* 1 (1843): 177–79.

"Mr. Spencer Hall and the new organs." *Phrenological Journal* 18 (1844): 8–14.

Müller, Johannes. *Physiology.* Trans. William Baly. London: Taylor, Walton and Maberly, 1838.

————. *The physiology of the senses.* Trans. William Baly. London: Taylor, Walton and Maberly, 1848.

Napier, W. F. P. *History of the war in the Peninsula and in the south of France from the year 1807 to the year 1814.* 6 vols. London, 1828–40.

Neilson, W. *Mesmerism in its relation to health and disease, and the present state of medicine.* Edinburgh: Shepherd and Elliot, 1855.

Newnham, William. *Essay on superstition: Being an inquiry into the effects of physical influences on the mind, in the production of dreams, visions, ghosts, and other supernatural appearances.* London: J. Hatchard and Son, 1830.

————. *Human magnetism: Its claims to dispassionate inquiry.* London: John Churchill, 1845.

————. *The reciprocal influence of body and mind considered.* London, 1842.

Nicholles, J. "Extraction of a tooth without pain. . . ." *Medical Times* 9 (1843–44): 323.

Nightingale, Florence. *Cassandra and other selections from suggestions for thought*. Ed. Mary Poovey. New York: New York University Press, 1992.

[Noble, David]. *Mesmerism true, mesmerism false: A critical examination of the facts, claims, and pretensions of animal magnetism*. Ed. John Forbes. London: John Churchill, 1845.

"Notices of some new works." *Medico-Chirurgical Review* 31 (1839): 497–98.

"Obscene quackery." *Lancet*, 26 December 1846, 702.

Oliphant, Margaret. "Sensation fiction." *Blackwood's Magazine* (May 1862): 564–84.

"On the present state of animal magnetism in Germany." *Blackwood's Edinburgh Magazine* 2 (1817–18): 36–38.

Owens, J. D. "Dr. Owens on mesmeric experiments." *Medical Times* 11 (1844–45): 450–51.

Packman, F. "Mesmerism in Paris." *Medical Times* 8 (1843): 300–301.

[Palmer, J. F.]. "Animal magnetism." *Dublin Review* 4 (January 1838): 202–32.

Pasley, T. H. *The philosophy which shows the physiology of mesmerism and explains the phenomena of clairvoyance*. London: Longman, Brown, Green, and Longman's, 1848.

Pathologist. "Correspondents." *Lancet*, 30 November 1844, 304.

"Performance of Haydn's 'Toy Symphony' by children of the Royal Asylum of St. Anne, Redhill." *Graphic*, 18 June 1887, 637–38.

Philo-Veritas. *Modern miracles condemned by reason and Scripture*. London, 1843.

"Phreno-magnetic cases." *Phrenological Journal* 17 (1844): 172–77.

A Physician. *A short sketch of animal magnetism* . . . . London: J. Hatchard, 1838.

Poe, Edgar Allen. "The facts in the case of Mr. Valdemar." In *Complete tales of Edgar Allen Poe*, 656–63. New York: Knopf, 1964.

———. "Mesmeric revelation." In *Complete tales of Edgar Allen Poe*, 2:543–50. New York: Knopf, 1964.

"Political electro-biology." *Punch* 22 (1852): 212.

"Popular literature: The periodical press." *Blackwood's Magazine* 85 (February 1859): 180–95.

Powell, J. H. *Life incidents and poetic pictures*. London, 1865.

———. *Spiritualism . . . facts and phases*. London, 1864.

"Practical application of ether to medical jurisprudence, to distinguish feigned from real disease." *Lancet*, 17 April 1847, 411.

"The present comet." *Monthly Chronicle* 2 (1838): 118–26, 136–44, 253–60.

Prichard, J. *A few sober words of table talk about table-spirits and the Rev. N. S. Godfrey's incantations: Second edition, with the detail of a series of experiments, conclusively proving the motive agency upon matter of electric currents, transmitted by contact with the fingers*. Leamington, 1853.

Prichard, J. C. "Somnambulism and animal magnetism." In John Forbes and A. C. Tweedie, eds., *Cyclopaedia of practical medicine*. 4 vols. London: Sherwood, Gilbert and Piper, 1833–35.

Prideaux, J. S. *Dr. Carpenter and the anti-phrenological physiologists: A New Year's gift to the medical profession*. London, 1847.

―――. "On the application of phrenology in the choice of parliamentary candidates." *Zoist* 3 (1845–46): 399–416.

"Principles of general and comparative physiology." *Medico-Chirurgical Review* 31 (1839): 165–70.

"Prospectus." *Zoist* 1 (April 1843): 1–4.

Purland, Theodysius. *Cures of St. Vitus's Dance: Deafness cured and the dumb made to speak: Mesmeric tract 6.* London, 1856.

Pyne, Thomas. *Vital magnetism: A remedy.* London: S. Highley, 1845.

"Reading as a means of culture." *Sharpe's London Magazine,* n.s., 31 December 1867, 322.

"Recent demonstrations of animal magnetism." *Chambers's Edinburgh Journal,* 15 July 1843, 205–6.

Record of cases treated in the Mesmeric Hospital from November 1846 to May 1847, with reports of the official visitors. Calcutta, 1847.

Reichenbach, Karl L. von. *Abstract of "researches in magnetism."* Trans. William Gregory. London: Taylor and Walton, 1846.

―――. *Odic-magnetic letters.* New York: C. Blanchard, 1860.

―――. *Physico-physiological researches on the dynamics of magnetism, electricity, heat, light, crystallization, and chemism, in their relations to the vital force.* 2 vols. Trans. John Ashburner. London: H. Bailliere, 1850–51.

―――. *Physikalisch-physiologische Untersuchungen.* 2 vols. Braunschweig: F. Vieweg, 1849.

―――. "Popular letters on the odic force." *Zoist* 11 (1853–54): 101–28, 274–94, 329–49.

―――. *Researches on magnetism, heat, light crystallization, and chemical attraction in their relation to vital force.* Trans. William Gregory. London: Taylor, Walton and Moberly, 1850.

Report of the committee appointed by government to observe and report upon surgical operations by Dr. Esdaile upon patients under the influence of alleged mesmeric agency. Calcutta: W. Ridsdale, 1846.

Reports from commissioners, inspectors, and others: Endowed schools: Scientific instruction and advancement of science. Session 5 February–13 August 1875. Parliamentary Papers London: Spottiswoode, 1875.

A Retired East India Surgeon. "Practice of Hindoo mesmerism." *Medical Times* 10 (1844): 292–93.

"Retrospect." *Phreno-Magnet* (1843): 161–64.

"Revelations of a clairvoyant." *New Monthly Magazine* 53 (1838): 301–9.

Review of "Medical etiquette, compiled exclusively for the profession, by Abraham Banks." *Athenaeum* 652 (1840): 330.

Review of Thompson, *On the improvement of medicine. Literary Gazette* (1838): 341.

Ricard, J. J. A. *Physiologie et hygiène du magnétiseur . . . .* Paris: Bailliere, 1844.

Ritchie, L. "Literature: Mesmerism." *Indian News* 2 (1844): 12.

Robertson, E. "Consistency." *North of England Magazine* 2 (1843): 355.

Robertson, J. "A disciple of Mesmer." *Lancet,* 1 March 1845, 248.

Romer, Isabel. *Sturmer: A tale of mesmerism, to which are added, other sketches from life*. 3 vols. London: Parry, 1841.

Royal Commission on Scientific Instruction and the Advancement of Science. *First, supplementary, and second reports, with minutes of evidence and appendices*. Vol. 1., Parliamentary Papers 28. London: Spottiswoode, 1872.

Royal Commission on Scientific Instruction and the Advancement of Science. *Sixth Report of the Royal Commission . . .* Parliamentary Papers 28. London: Spottiswoode, 1875.

R. S. S. "Animal magnetism and neurohypnotism." *Fraser's Magazine*, June 1844, 681–99.

Rutter, J. O. N. *Human electricity: The means of its development illustrated by experiments*. London: J. W. Parker, 1854.

———. *Magnetoid currents, their forces and directions: With a description of the magnetoscope*. London: J. W. Parker and Son, 1851.

Ryan, Thomas. *Recollections of an old musician*. New York: E. P. Dutton and Co., 1899.

Sandby, George. "Can Professor Faraday never be wrong? or Is table-turning all a delusion?" *Zoist* 11 (1853–54): 320–24.

———. *Mesmerism and its opponents*. 2d ed. London: Longman, Brown, Green, and Longman's, 1848.

———. *Mesmerism and its opponents: With a narrative of cases*. London: Longman, Brown, Green, and Longman's, 1844.

———. *Mesmerism the gift of God*. London: W. E. Painter, 1843.

———. Review of Cahagnet's *Arcanes de la futur devoilés*. *Zoist* 7 (1849–50): 414–31.

"Satanic agency." *Zoist* 3 (1845): 532–35.

Satanic agency and table-turning: A letter to the Rev. Francis Close. London, 1853.

Saunders, S. D. *The mesmeric guide for family use: Containing instructions for the application of mesmerism as a curative agent*. London: H. Bailliere, 1852.

Savory, J. *A compendium of domestic medicine*. 4th ed. London, 1848.

Scoresby, William. *Discourses to seamen*. London: J. Nisbet, 1831.

———. *Jehovah glorified in his works: A sermon preached . . . on occasion of the meeting of the British Association for the Advancement of Science at Edinburgh*. Edinburgh, 1850.

———. *Zoistic magnetism: Being the substance of two lectures descriptive of the original views and investigations respecting this mysterious agency*. London: Longman, Brown, Green, and Longman's, 1849.

Scoresby-Jackson, R. E. *The life of William Scoresby*. London, 1861.

Scott, Walter. *Letters on demonology and witchcraft: Addressed to J. G. Lockhart*. London: John Murray, 1830.

"Secrets of mesmerism unveiled." *Lancet*, 14 August 1841, 725–27.

Sharpe, James Birch. "Animal magnetism." *Lancet*, 23 June 1838, 454–55.

Sharpey, William, and Allen Thomson. *A tale of three cities: The correspondence of William Sharpey and Allen Thomson*. Ed. L. S. Jacyna. London: Wellcome Institute for the History of Medicine, 1989.

Shelley, Mary Wollstonecraft. *Frankenstein, or The modern Prometheus*. The 1818 text. Ed. Marilyn Butter. London: William Pickering, 1993.

Shelley, Percy. *Poetical works of Shelley*. Ed. Thomas Hutchinson. 2d ed. London: Oxford University Press, 1975.

A short catechism of mesmerism, intended to develop the first principles of the science, in the form of question and answer. 2d ed. London, n.d.

Sidgwick, H., E. M. Sidgwick, and A. Johnson. "Report on the census of hallucinations." *Proceedings of the Society for Psychical Research* 10 (1894): 25–422.

Sidgwick, H., E. M. Sidgwick, and G. A. Smith. "Experiments in thought-transference." *Proceedings of the Society for Psychical Research* 6 (1889–90): 128–70.

"Sidney Smith on animal magnetism." *Phreno-Magnetic Vindicator* 1 (1843): 11–16.

Sigmond, G. G. "Address delivered before the Medico-Botanical Society of London." *Lancet* 24 February 1838, 769–76.

Simms, W. G. "Mesmerides *[sic]* in a stage-coach, or Passes en passant." *Godey's Lady's Book* 31 (1845): 111–19.

Slatterie, E. *A brief account of mesmeric-phrenology, its origin, progress, &c*. North Shields, 1843.

Smee, Alfred. *Elements of electro-biology*. London, 1849.

———. *Instinct and reason: Deduced from electro-biology*. London, 1850.

Smethurst, Thomas. "Mesmerism unmasked." *Medical Times* 9 (1843–44): 145–47.

Smith, C. M. *On the law of servant and master*. London, 1852.

Smith, G. E. *Legends and miracles of human nature*. London, 1837.

Smith, Goldwyn. *Modern history*. London, 1861.

Smith, Horace. *Mesmerism: A mystery*. Vol. 3, pp. [35]–360 of Horace Smith, *Love and mesmerism*, 2 novels in 3 vols. London: H. Colburn, 1845.

Smolnikar, Andreas. *Lecture: Of the dreadful abuse of human magnetism (improperly called mesmerism) in the mysteries of the Roman Church and her daughter*. Salem, Ohio: author, 1851.

Snewing, W. "An instance of the effect of maternal impression upon the offspring before its birth." *Zoist* 10 (1852–53): 379–85.

Somerville, Alexander. *The autobiography of a working man: By "one who has whistled at the plow."* London: C. Giltin, 1848.

Somerville, Mary. *The connexion of the physical sciences*. London: John Murray, 1834.

Southey, Robert. *Letters from England: By Don Manuel Alvarez Espriella, translated from the Spanish*. 2d ed. 3 vols. London: Longman, Hurst, Rees, and Orme, 1808.

Spencer, Herbert. "A theory concerning the organ of wonder." *Zoist* 2 (1845): 316–25.

———. "A new view of the functions of imitation and benevolence." *Zoist* 1 (1843): 369–85.

———. *Principles of psychology*. London: Longman, Brown, Green, and Longman's, 1855.

Sprigge, S. S. *The life and times of Thomas Wakley, founder and first editor of the "Lancet"*. . . . London: Longman's, Green and Co., 1897.

Spurr, J. "Phrenological investigations." *Phreno-Magnet* 1 (1843): 2–54.

Squire, W. W. "On the introduction of ether inhalation as an anaesthetic in London." *Lancet*, 22 December 1888, 1220–21.

Squirrell, E. *Autobiography of Elizabeth Squirrell of Shottisham, and selections from her writings, by one of her watchers.* London: Simpkin, Marshall and Co., 1853.

[Staite, Opie]. *Mesmerism, or The new school of the arts.* London, 1844.

Stanley, A. P. *Life and correspondence of Thomas Arnold.* 2 vols. London: John Murray, 1881.

Stewart, Dugald. "Law of sympathetic imitation." In *Collected works of Dugald Stewart*, 10 vols., ed. William Hamilton. Edinburgh: Constable and Co., 1854–60.

Stone, G. W. *Electro-biology, or The electrical science of life.* Liverpool, 1850.

Storer, H. *Mesmerism in disease: A few plain facts, with a selection of cases.* London: [Bailliere], 1845.

Table-moving by animal magnetism demonstrated. 3d ed. N.p., n.d.

Talbot, John. *Letter from the earl of Shrewsbury to Ambrose Lisle Phillipps, descriptive of the Estatica of Caldaro, and the Addolorata of Capriana.* 2d ed. London: C. Dolman, 1842.

Teste, Alphonse. *A practical manual of animal magnetism.* Trans. D. Spillan. London, 1843.

Thelwall, A. S. *Refutations of Irving's heresy.* London, 1836.

"Thirtieth annual meeting of the British Medical Association." *British Medical Journal* 2 (1862): 144–53.

Thompson, H. S. "On the silent power of the will of one person over another." *Zoist* 5 (1847–48): 253–60.

Thompson, Theophilus. *On the improvement of medicine.* London: J. Hatchard and Son, 1838.

Thomson, A. T. *The domestic management of the sick-room, necessary, in aid of medical treatment, for the care of diseases.* London: Longman, Orme, Brown, Green, and Longman's, 1841.

———. "Lectures on medical jurisprudence." *Lancet*, 25 March 1837, 1–9.

———. "Lectures on medical jurisprudence." *Lancet*, 12 November 1836, 241–46.

"Thoughts of an invalid." *Chambers's Edinburgh Journal*, 17 February 1844, 107–10.

Ticknor, George. *Life, letters, and journals.* 2 vols. London: Sampson, Low, Marston, Searle, and Rivington, 1876.

Todhunter, Isaac, ed. *William Whewell: An account of his writings, with selections from his literary and scientific correspondence.* 2 vols. London: Macmillan, 1876.

[Tonna], Charlotte Elizabeth. *Mesmerism: A letter to Miss Martineau.* London, 1844.

Topham, William, and W. Squire Ward. *Account of a case of successful amputation of the thigh during the mesmeric state, without the knowledge of the patient.* London: H. Bailliere, 1842.

"To Sir Rhubarb Pill." *Punch* 1 (1841): 123.

Townshend, C. H. *Facts in mesmerism with reasons for a dispassionate inquiry into it.* London, 1840. Reprint, New York: Da Capo, 1982.

———. "Recent clairvoyance of Alexis Didier." *Zoist* 9 (1851–52): 402–14.

Toynbee, G. *A sketch of the administration of the Hooghly District from 1795 to 1845.* Calcutta: Bengal Secretariat Press, 1888.

T. S. F. *Demonologia, or Natural knowledge revealed: Being an exposé of ancient and modern superstitions, as connected with the doctrine [of] caballa and jargon.* London: A. K. Newman, 1831.

Tweedie, A. C. *Mesmerism and its realities further proved: By illustrations of its curative powers.* Edinburgh: Paton and Ritchie, 1857.

Tyndall, John. "Science and the spirits." In *Fragments of science: A series of detached essays, addresses, and reviews,* 444–52. London: Longman's, Green and Co., 1879.

"University College and Hospital: Expulsion of Elizabeth O'Key: Resignation of Dr. Elliotson: Meeting of students." *Lancet,* 5 January 1839, 561–62.

"University College Hospital." *Lancet,* 26 May 1838, 320.

"University College Hospital: Animal magnetism." *Lancet,* 26 May 1838, 282–88.

"University College Hospital: Animal magnetism: Conclusion of second report of facts and experiments." *Lancet,* 16 June 1838, 400–403.

"University College Hospital: Animal magnetism: Fifth report of experiments and facts." *Lancet,* 14 July 1838, 546–49.

"University College Hospital: Animal magnetism: Fourth report: Remarks and experiments." *Lancet,* 7 July 1838, 516–19.

"University College Hospital: Animal magnetism: Second report of facts and experiments." *Lancet,* 9 June 1838, 377–83.

"University College Hospital: Animal magnetism: Sixth report of experiments and facts." *Lancet,* 21 July 1838, 585–90.

Unwins, T. "Moral benefits of mesmerism." *Zoist* 2 (1844–45): 33–36.

Upham, Charles W. *Lectures on witchcraft, comprising a history of the delusion in Salem, in 1692.* Boston: Carter, Hendee and Babcock, 1831.

Ure, Andrew. *The philosophy of manufactures.* London: C. Knight, 1835.

Vincent, William. *Satanic influence: Its probable connexion with table-talking.* London, 1853.

Wagner, A. *Facts and fallacies of mesmerism: Demonstrated to its friends and opponents.* London: Stevenson, 1845.

[Wakley, Thomas.] "The animal magnetism fraud and humbug." *Lancet,* 1 December 1838, 380–81.

[———]. "Desecration of the College of Physicians." *Lancet,* 20 June 1846, 687–88.

[———]. Editorial. *Lancet,* 27 July 1833, 574–77.

[———]. Editorial. *Lancet,* 11 November 1837, 234–35.

———. Editorial. *Lancet,* 16 December 1837, 429–33.

———. Editorial. *Lancet,* 25 November 1837, 314–17.

[———]. Editorial. *Lancet,* 4 July 1846, 16–17.

[———]. Editorial. *Lancet,* 2 January 1847, 16–17.

———. Editorial. *People's Phrenological Journal* (1844): 170–72.

[———]. "The experiments on the two sisters, O'Key." *Lancet,* 15 September 1838, 873–77.

[————]. "Immoral tendency of animal magnetism." *Lancet,* 15 December 1838, 450–51.

————. "Mesmeric phenomena in Paris." *Lancet,* 7 August 1841, 692–94

[————]. "Mesmerism, Miss Martineau, and the 'great new idea.'" *Lancet,* 30 November 1844, 291.

[————]. "On obstacles to medical reform." *Lancet,* 4 February 1843, 685–88.

[————]. "The virtues of animal magnetism." *Lancet,* 8 December 1838, 413–14.

Wallis, Thomas Wilkinson. *Autobiography of Thomas Wilkinson Wallis: Sculptor in wood.* Louth: J. W. Goulding, 1899.

Warrenne, William. "Curative power of mesmeric influence proved by its successful application in a variety of extreme cases." *Medical Times* 12 (1845): 385–86.

Webb, Alan. "Report of the Mesmeric Hospital." *Zoist* 10 (1852): 280–81.

Whately, E. J. *Life and correspondence of Richard Whately.* New ed. London: Longman's, Green, 1875.

Whately, Richard. *Historic doubts relative to the reign of Napoleon Bonaparte.* 9th ed. London: J. W. Parker, 1849.

Wheatstone, Charles. "Contributions to the physiology of vision." Reprinted in Wheatstone, *Scientific papers,* 187–89.

————. "Description of the kaleidophone." *Quarterly Journal of Science, Literature, and Art* 1 (1827). Reprinted in Wheatstone, *Scientific papers,* 21–29.

————. "On the transmission of musical sounds through solid linear objects." Reprinted in Wheatstone, *Scientific papers,* 47–63.

————. *The scientific papers of Sir Charles Wheatstone.* London: Taylor and Francis, 1879.

Whewell, William. *On the influence of the history of science upon intellectual education: A lecture delivered at the Royal Institution of Great Britain, Saturday, April 29, 1854.* Boston: Gould and Lincoln, 1854.

————. Review of Mary Somerville's *Connexion of the physical sciences. Quarterly Review* 51 (1834): 54–68.

White, Walter. *A month in Yorkshire.* London: Chapman and Hall, 1858.

Wigan, [A. L.] "The duality of the mind." *Lancet,* 4 and 11 October 1845, 366–77, 387–89.

Wigan, A. L. *A new view of insanity: The duality of the mind proved by the structure, function, and diseases of the brain, and by the phenomena of mental derangement ....* London: Longman, Brown, Green, and Longman's, 1844.

[Wilberforce, H.?]. "Animal magnetism." *Christian Remembrancer* 13 (1847): 288–89.

Wilson, John. *Trials of animal magnetism.* London: Sherwood, Gilbert and Piper, 1839.

Wood, A. *What is mesmerism? An attempt to explain its phenomena on the admitted principles of physiological and psychical science.* Edinburgh: Sutherland and Knox, 1851.

Wood, W. "Animal magnetism in London: Reply to the letter of an eye-witness." *Lancet,* 28 October 1837, 163–65.

"A Yorkshire clergyman's opinions of mesmerism." *Phreno-Magnet* 1 (1843): 201–3.

Youmans, Edward. *The culture demanded by modern life: A series of addresses and arguments on the claims of scientific education.* New York: Wheeler, 1867.

Young, R. *The entranced female, or The remarkable disclosures of a lady, concerning another world.* 14th ed. London: T. M. Inchbold, 1842.

Secondary Sources

Altick, Richard Daniel. *The English common reader: A social history of the mass reading public, 1800–1900.* Chicago: University of Chicago Press, 1957.

———. *The shows of London.* Cambridge Mass.: Belknap Press, 1978.

Anderson, Katherine. "Practical science: Meteorology and the forecasting controversy in mid-Victorian Britain." Ph.D. thesis, Northwestern University, 1994.

———. "Prophecy and power." *History of Science,* forthcoming 1999.

Anderson, Patricia. *The printed image and the transformation of popular culture, 1790–1860.* Oxford: Clarendon, 1991.

Arnold, David. *Colonizing the body: State medicine and epidemic disease in nineteenth-century India.* Berkeley: University of California Press, 1993.

Ashworth, W. J. "Memory, efficiency, and symbolic analysis: Charles Babbage and the industrial mind." *Isis* 87 (1996): 622–53.

Baber, Zaheer. *The science of empire: Scientific knowledge, civilization, and colonial rule in India.* Albany: State University of New York Press, 1996.

Baer, Marc. *Theatre and disorder in late Georgian London.* Oxford: Clarendon, 1992.

Bailey, Peter. "Custom, capital, and culture in the Victorian music hall." In R. D. Storch, ed., *Popular culture and custom in nineteenth century England,* 180–208. London: Croom Helm, 1982.

Bailin, Miriam. *The sickroom in Victorian fiction: The art of being ill.* Cambridge: Cambridge University Press, 1994.

Bakhtin, Michel. *Rabelais and his world.* Cambridge, Mass.: MIT Press, 1968.

Bala, Poonam. *Imperialism and medicine in Bengal: A socio-historical perspective.* New York: Sage, 1990.

Barker, Clive. "The Chartists, theatre, reform, and research." *Theatre Quarterly* 1 (1971): 3–10.

Barnes, Barry, and Steven Shapin. "Head and hand: Rhetorical resources in British pedagogical writing, 1770–1850." *Oxford Review of Education* 2 (1976): 231–54.

Barrow, Logie. *Independent spirits: Spiritualism and English plebeians, 1850–1910.* London: Routledge, 1986.

———. "Socialism is eternity: The ideology of plebeian spiritualists, 1853–1913." *History Workshop* 9 (1980): 37–69.

———. "Why were most medical heretics at their most confident around the 1840s? The other side of mid-Victorian medicine." In Roger French and Andrew Wear, eds., *British medicine in the age of reform,* 165–85. Cambridge: Cambridge University Press, 1991.

Barton, Ruth. "The X Club: Science, religion, and social change in Victorian England." Ph.D. thesis, University of Pennsylvania, 1976.

Basham, Diana. *The trial of woman: Feminism and the occult science in Victorian literature and society.* New York: New York University Press, 1992.

Baum, Joan. *The calculating passion of Ada Byron.* Hamden, Conn.: Archon Books, 1986.

Beer, Gillian. "Problems of description in language." In George Levine, ed., *One culture: Essays in science and literature,* 35–56. Madison: University of Wisconsin Press, 1987.

Bellot, H. H. *University College, London, 1826–1926.* London: University College London Press, 1929.

Benét, Laura. *Enchanting Jenny Lind.* New York: Dodd, Mead and Co., 1940.

Berg, Maxine. *The machinery question and the making of political economy, 1815–1848.* New York: Cambridge University Press, 1980.

Bhaba, Homi. "Signs taken for wonders: Questions of ambivalence and authority under a tree outside Delhi, May 1817." *Critical Inquiry* 12 (1985): 144–64.

Booth, Michael. "East End and West End: Class and audience in Victorian London." *Theatre Research International* 2 (1977): 98–103.

Bowers, Brian. *Sir Charles Wheatstone, FRS, 1802–1875.* London: H.M.S.O., 1975.

Brake, Laurel. *Subjugated knowledges: Journalism, gender, and literature in the nineteenth century.* New York: New York University Press, 1994.

Brannan, R. L., ed. *Under the management of Mr. Charles Dickens: His production of "The frozen deep."* Ithaca: Cornell University Press, 1966.

Brantlinger, Patrick. *Rule of darkness: British literature and imperialism, 1830–1914.* Ithaca: Cornell University Press, 1988.

Brown, S. J. *Thomas Chalmers and the godly commonwealth in Scotland.* Oxford: Oxford University Press, 1982.

Browne, Janet. "I could have retched all night: Charles Darwin and his body." In Christopher Lawrence and S. L. Shapin, eds., *Science incarnate: The physical presentation of intellectual selves,* 240–87. Chicago: University of Chicago Press, 1998.

Buckly, Jerome Hamilton. *The Victorian temper: A study in literary culture.* Cambridge: Harvard University Press, 1951.

Buranelli, Vincent. *The wizard from Vienna.* London: P. Owen, 1976.

Burke, Peter. "History of events and the revival of narrative." In Peter Burke, ed., *New perspectives on historical writing,* 233–48. Cambridge: Cambridge University Press, 1991.

———. *Popular culture in early modern Europe.* London: T. Smith, 1978.

Burn, W. L. *The age of equipoise: A study of the mid-Victorian generation.* London: George Allen and Unwin, 1965.

Burstyn, Joan. "Education and sex: The medical case against higher education for women in England, 1870–1900." *Proceedings of the American Philosophical Society* 117 (1973): 89–97.

Bynum, W. F., and Roy Porter, eds. *Medical fringe and medical orthodoxy, 1750–1850.* London: Croom Helm, 1987.

Cannadine, David. "The context, performance, and meaning of ritual: The British monarchy and the 'invention of tradition,' c. 1820–1977." In Eric Hobsbawm and Terence Ranger, eds., *The invention of tradition*, 101–64. Cambridge: Cambridge University Press, 1983.

Carse, Adam. *The life of Jullien, adventurer, showman-conductor, and establisher of the Promenade Concerts in England, together with a history of those concerts up to 1895.* Cambridge: Heffer, [1951].

———. *The orchestra from Beethoven to Berlioz: A history of the orchestra in the first half of the nineteenth century, and of the development of orchestral baton-conducting.* New York: Broude Brothers, 1949.

Cartwright, F. F. *English pioneers of anaesthesia.* Bristol: Beddoes, J. Wright, Davy, and Hickman, 1952.

Cawthorn, E. "Thomas Wakley and the medical coronership: Occupational death and the judicial process." *Medical History* 30 (1986): 191–202.

Chadwick, Owen. *The Victorian church: Part 1, 1829–1859.* London: A. and C. Black, 1966.

Chandler, James. *England in 1819.* Chicago: University of Chicago Press, 1997.

Chesney, Kellow. *The Victorian underworld.* London: Maurice Temple Smith, 1970.

Collingwood, R. G. *The idea of history.* Oxford: Clarendon, 1946.

Collini, Stefan. "The idea of 'character' in Victorian political thought." *Transactions of the Royal Historical Society* 35 (1985): 29–50.

Collini, Stefan, Donald Winch, and J. Burrow. *That noble science of politics: A study in nineteenth-century intellectual history.* Cambridge: Cambridge University Press, 1983.

Conway, Jill. "Stereotypes of femininity in a theory of sexual evolution." *Victorian Studies* 14 (1970): 47–62.

Cooter, Roger. *The cultural meaning of popular science: Phrenology and the organisation of consent in nineteenth-century Britain.* Cambridge: Cambridge University Press, 1984.

———. "Dichotomy and denial: Mesmerism, medicine, and Harriet Martineau." In Marina Benjamin, ed., *Science and sensibility: Gender and scientific enquiry*, 144–74. Oxford: Basil Blackwell, 1991.

———. "The history of mesmerism in Britain: Poverty and promise." In H. Schott, ed., *Franz Anton Mesmer und die Geschichte des Mesmerismus*, 152–62. Wiesbaden: F. Steiner, 1985.

———. *Phrenology in the British Isles: An annotated historical biobibliography and index.* Metuchen: Scarecrow Press, 1989.

Cotter, C. "The early history of ship-magnetism: The Airy-Scoresby controversy." *Annals of Science* 34 (1977): 589–99.

Cowling, Mary. *The artist as anthropologist: The representation of type and character in Victorian art.* Cambridge: Cambridge University Press, 1989.

Crabtree, Adam. *From Mesmer to Freud: Magnetic sleep and the roots of psychological healing.* New Haven: Yale University Press, 1993.

Crawford, Catherine. "A scientific profession: Medical reform and forensic medicine in British periodicals of the early nineteenth century." In Roger French and Andrew Wear, *British medicine in an age of reform*, 203–30. Cambridge: Cambridge University Press, 1991.

Crawford, D. G. *History of the Indian medical service.* 2 vols. London: Thacker and Co., 1914.

Crowther, J. G. *The Cavendish laboratory, 1874–1974.* New York, 1978.

Curry, Patrick. *A confusion of prophets: Victorian and Edwardian astrology.* London: Collins and Brown, 1992.

Curtin, Michael. *Propriety and position: A study of Victorian manners.* New York: Garland, 1987.

Darnton, Robert. *Mesmerism and the end of the Enlightenment in France.* Cambridge: Harvard University Press, 1968.

Daston, Lorraine. "Enlightenment calculation." *Critical Inquiry* 21 (1994): 182–202.

Daston, Lorraine, and Peter Galison. "The image of objectivity." *Representations* 40 (Fall 1992): 81–128.

David, Dierdre. *Intellectual women and Victorian patriarchy: Harriet Martineau, Elizabeth Barrett Browning, George Eliot.* Ithaca: Cornell University Press, 1987.

Davidoff, Leonore, and Catherine Hall. *Family fortunes: Men and women of the English middle class, 1780–1850.* London: Hutchinson, 1987.

Davis, Natalie. *Fiction in the archives.* Stanford: Stanford University Press, 1987.

Davis, Nuel. *Life of Wilkie Collins.* Urbana: University of Illinois Press, 1956.

Dawson, F. R. *The first Latin American debt crisis: The City of London and the 1822–1825 loan bubble.* New Haven: Yale University Press, 1990.

Decker, Clarence Raymond. *The Victorian conscience.* New York: Twayne Publishers, [1952].

De Giustino, David. *Conquest of mind: Phrenology and Victorian social thought.* London: Croom Helm, 1975.

Desmond, Adrian. *The politics of evolution: Morphology, medicine, and reform in radical London.* Chicago: University of Chicago Press, 1989.

Desmond, Adrian, and J. R. Moore. *Darwin.* London: Michael Joseph, 1994.

Dingwall, E. J., ed. *Abnormal hypnotic phenomena: A survey of nineteenth-century cases.* 4 vols. London: J. and A. Churchill, 1967–78.

Dodds, J. W. *The age of paradox: A biography of England, 1841–1851.* New York: Rinehart, 1952.

Doodd, A. "Strauss's English propagandists and the politics of Unitarianism, 1841–1845." *Church History* 50 (1981): 425–29.

Duncum, Barbara. *Development of inhalation anaesthesia.* London: Wellcome, 1976.

Ellenberger, H. F. *Discovery of the unconscious: The history and evolution of dynamic psychiatry.* New York: Basic Books, 1970.

Ellis, J. R. H. "Robert Liston's letter to Francis Boott: Its reappearance after 135 years." *History of Medicine and Allied Sciences* 38 (1987): 546–49.

Embree, Ainslee T. "Bengal as the image of India in the late eighteenth and early nineteenth centuries: Notes towards the definition of an imperial experience." In Martin Davis, ed., *Bengal: Studies in literature, society, and history*, 131–41. East Lansing: Asian Studies Center, Michigan State University, 1976.

Engel, A. J. *From clergyman to don: The rise of the academic profession in nineteenth-century Oxford*. Oxford: Oxford University Press, 1983.

Epstein, James. *The lion of freedon: Feargus O'Connor and the Chartist movement, 1832–1842*. London: Croom Helm, 1982.

Ernst, Waltraud. *Mad tales from the Raj: The European insane in British India, 1800–1858*. New York: Routledge, 1991.

———. "Under the influence in British India: James Esdaile's Mesmeric Hospital in Calcutta and its critics." *Psychological Medicine* 25 (1995): 1113–23.

Falk, D. V. "Poe and the power of animal magnetism." *Publications of the Modern Languages Association* (1969): 539.

Fara, Patricia. "An attractive practice: Animal magnetism in eighteenth-century England." *History of Science* 33 (1995): 127–77.

Fissell, Mary. *Patients, power, and the poor in eighteenth-century Bristol*. Cambridge: Cambridge University Press, 1992.

Foucault, Michel. *Discipline and punish: The birth of the prison*. Trans. A. M. Sheridan. London: Allen Lane, 1977.

Freud, S. "The 'uncanny.'" In *Standard edition of the complete psychological works of Freud*, 17:217–52. Trans. James Strachey. London: Hogarth Press, 1955,

Froude, J. A. *Carlyle's life in London*. 2 vols. London, 1891.

———. *Thomas Carlyle: A history of his life in London, 1834–1881*. 2 vols. London: Longman's, 1891.

Frow, Gerald. *"Oh yes it is!" A history of pantomime*. London: British Broadcasting Corp., 1985.

Fuller, R. C. *Mesmerism and the American cure of souls*. Philadelphia: University of Philadelphia Press, 1982.

Fulop-Miller, René. *Triumph over pain*. London: Bobbs-Merrill, 1978.

Galkin, E. W. *A history of orchestral conducting: In theory and practice*. New York: Pendragon Press, 1988.

Gallagher, Catherine, and Thomas Laqueur. *The making of the modern body*. Berkeley: University of California Press, 1987.

Gauld, Alan. *A history of hypnotism*. Cambridge: Cambridge University Press, 1992.

Geison, G. L. *Michael Foster and the Cambridge school of physiology: The scientific enterprise in late Victorian society*. Princeton: Princeton University Press, 1978.

Gilmartin, Kevin. *Press politics*. Cambridge: Cambridge University Press, 1996.

Ginn, W. T. "Philosophers and artisans: The relationship between men of science and instrument makers in London, 1820–1860." Ph.D. thesis, University of Kent, 1991.

Ginzburg, Carlo. *Ecstasies: Deciphering the witches' sabbath*. Trans. R. Rosenthal. Ed. G. Elliot. New York: Pantheon, 1991.

———. *Myths, emblems, clues*. Trans. J. and A. C. Tedeschi. London: Radius, 1990.

Goldstein, Jan. *Console and classify: The French psychiatric profession in the nineteenth century*. Cambridge: Cambridge University Press, 1987.

Golinski, Jan. *Science as public culture: Chemistry and Enlightenment in Britain, 1760–1820*. Princeton: Princeton University Press, 1992.

Gooding, David. "Faraday, Thomson, and the concept of the magnetic field." *British Journal of the History of Science* 13 (1980): 91–120.

―――. "In nature's school: Faraday as an experimentalist." In David Gooding and A. J. L. Frank James, eds., *Faraday rediscovered: Essays on the life and work of Michael Faraday, 1791–1867*, 105–36. Basingstoke: Macmillan, 1985.

Green, D. G. *Working-class patients and the medical establishment: Self-help in Britain from the mid–nineteenth century to 1948*. New York: St. Martin's Press, 1985.

Green, N. M. "Anaesthesia and the development of surgery, 1846–1896." *Anesthesia Analgesia* 58 (1979): 5–12.

Groth, Eileen. "Christian radicalism in Britain, 1830–1850." Ph.D. thesis, University of Cambridge, 1993.

Hacking, Ian. *Rewriting the soul: Multiple personality and the sciences of memory.* Princeton: Princeton University Press, 1995.

Hall, Mary Boas. *All scientists now: The Royal Society in the nineteenth century.* Cambridge: Cambridge University Press, 1984.

Hall, V. M. D. "The contribution of the physiologist William Benjamin Carpenter (1813–1885) to the development of the principle of the correlation of forces and the conservation of energy." *Medical History* 23 (1979): 129–55.

Harding, Rosamond E. M. *The metronome and it's* [sic] *precursors.* Henley-on-Thames: Gresham Books, 1983.

Harrison, J. F. C. "Early Victorian radicals and the medical fringe." In W. F. Bynum and Roy Porter, eds., *Medical fringe and medical orthodoxy, 1750–1850*, 198–215. London: Croom Helm, 1987.

―――. *The second coming: Popular millenarianism, 1780–1850.* New Brunswick, N.J.: Rutgers University Press, 1979.

Harrison, Mark. *Crowds and history: Mass phenomena in English towns, 1790–1835.* Cambridge: Cambridge University Press, 1988.

―――. *Public health in British India: Anglo-Indian medicine, 1859–1914.* Cambridge: Cambridge University Press, 1994.

Hays, D. "Rise and fall of Dionysius Lardner." *Annals of Science* 38 (1981): 527–42.

Heeney, W. B. D. *A different kind of gentleman: Parish clergy as professional men in early and mid-Victorian England.* Hamden, Conn.: Archon Books, 1976.

Heyck, T. W. *The transformation of intellectual life in Victorian England.* New York: St. Martin's Press, 1982.

Hilton, Boyd. *The age of atonement: The influence of Evangelicalism on social and economic thought, 1785–1865.* Oxford: Clarendon, 1988.

―――. "Whiggery, religion, and social reform: The case of Lord Morpeth." *Historical Journal* 37 (1994): 829–59.

Himmelfarb, Gertrude. *Victorian mind.* New York: Knopf, 1968.

Hole, Robert. *Pulpits, politics, and public order in England, 1760–1832.* Cambridge: Cambridge University Press, 1989.

Holland, Henry Scott, and W. S. Rockstro. *Memoir of Madame Jenny Lind-*

Goldschmidt: Her early art-life and dramatic career, 1820–1851. 2 vols. London: John Murray, 1891.

Houghton, Walter E. *The Victorian frame of mind, 1830–1870.* New Haven: Yale University Press, 1957.

Hubbard, Geoffrey. *Cooke and Wheatstone and the development of the electric telegraph.* London: Routledge, 1965.

Inkster, Ian. "Marginal men: Aspects of the social role of the medical community in Sheffield, 1790–1850." In John Woodward and David Richards, eds., *Health care and popular medicine in nineteenth-century England,* 128–63. New York: Holmes and Meier, 1977.

Jacyna, L. S. "Immanence or transcendance: Theories of life and organisation in Britain, 1790–1835." *Isis* 74 (1983): 311–29.

———. "The physiology of mind, the unity of nature, and the moral order in late Victorian thought." *British Journal for the History of Science* 14 (1981): 109–32.

———. "Principles of general and comparative physiology: The comparative dimension of British neuroscience in the 1830s and 1840s." *Studies in the History of Biology* 7 (1984): 47–92.

———. "Scientific naturalism in Victorian Britain: An essay in the social history of ideas." Ph.D. thesis, University of Edinburgh, 1980.

Jardine, Nicholas. *The scenes of inquiry: On the reality of questions in the sciences.* Oxford: Clarendon, 1991.

Jennings, Humphrey. *Pandaemonium: 1160–1886, the coming of the machine as seen by contemporary observers.* Ed. Mary-Lou Jennings and Charles Madge. London: A. Deutsch, 1985.

Jenson, J. Vernon. "Interrelationships within the Victorian X Club." *Dalhousie Review* 51 (1971–72): 539–52.

Jewson, Nicholas. "The disappearance of the sick man from medical cosmology." *Sociology* 10 (1976): 225–40.

———. "Medical knowledge and the patronage system in eighteenth-century England." *Sociology* 8 (1974): 369–85.

Johnson, James H. *Listening in Paris: A cultural history.* Berkeley: University of California Press, 1995.

Johnson, Richard. "Really useful knowledge." In John Clarke, Chas Crichter, and Richard Johnson, eds., *Working class culture: Studies in history and theory,* 75–102. London: Hutchinson, 1979.

Jordanova, Ludmilla. *Sexual visions: Images of gender in science and medicine between the eighteenth and the twentieth centuries.* Madison: University of Wisconsin Press, 1989.

Jungnickel, Christa, and Russell McCormmach. *Intellectual mastery of nature: Theoretical physics from Ohm to Einstein.* Vol. 1, *The torch of mathematics 1800–1870.* Chicago: University of Chicago Press, 1986.

Kaplan, Fred. *Dickens and mesmerism: The hidden springs of fiction.* Princeton: Princeton University Press, 1975.

————. " 'The mesmeric mania': The early Victorians and animal magnetism." *Journal for the History of Ideas* 35 (1974): 691–702.

Karlin, Daniel. "Browning, Elizabeth Barrett, and mesmerism." *Victorian Poetry* 27 (1989): 65–77.

————. *The courtship of Robert Browning and Elizabeth Barrett.* Oxford: Clarendon, 1985.

Klancher, Jon. *The making of English reading audiences, 1790–1832.* Madison: University of Wisconsin Press, 1987.

Latour, Bruno. *The pasteurisation of France.* Cambridge: Harvard University Press, 1988.

Lawrence, Christopher. "Democratic, divine, and heroic: The history and historiography of surgery." In Christopher Lawrence, ed., *Medical theory, surgical practice: Studies in the history of surgery,* 1–47. London: Routledge, 1992.

————. "Incommunicable knowledge: Science, technology, and the clinical art in Britain, 1850–1914." *Journal of Contemporary History* 20 (1985): 503–20.

————. "The power and the glory: Humphry Davy and romanticism." In Andrew Cunningham and Nicholas Jardine, eds., *Romanticism and the sciences,* 213–17. Cambridge: Cambridge University Press, 1990.

Layton, David. *Science for the people.* London: Allyn and Unwin, 1973.

Leask, Nigel. *British romantic writers and the East: Anxieties of empire.* Cambridge: Cambridge University Press, 1992.

————. "Shelley's magnetic ladies: Romantic mesmerism and the politics of the body." In Stephen Copley and John Whale, eds., *Beyond romanticism: New approaches to texts and contexts, 1780–1832,* 53–78. London: Routledge, 1992.

Leff, A. "Thomas Laycock and the cerebral reflexes: A function arising from and pointing to the unity of nature." *History of Psychiatry* 2 (1991): 385–407.

Leys, Ruth. "Background to the reflex controversy: William Alison and the doctrine of sympathy before Hall." *Studies in History of Biology* 4 (1980): 1–66.

Loudon, Irving. *Medical care and the general practitioner, 1750–1850.* Oxford: Clarendon, 1986.

Mandler, Peter. *Aristocratic government in the age of reform: Whigs and Liberals, 1830–1852.* Oxford: Clarendon, 1990.

Marsh, Peter, ed. *The conscience of the Victorian state.* Syracuse: Syracuse University Press, 1979.

Massey, C. J. "The first public operation carried out under an anaesthetic in Europe." *Anaesthesia* 2 (1946): 51–59.

Masson, J. M. *A dark science: Women, sexuality, and psychiatry in the nineteenth century.* New York: Farrar, Straus and Giroux, 1986.

Masson, Michael. *The making of Victorian sexuality.* Oxford: Oxford University Press, 1995.

Mays, Kelly J. "The disease of reading and Victorian periodicals." In John O. Jordan and Robert L. Patten, eds., *Literature in the marketplace: Nineteenth-century British publishing and reading practices,* 165–94. Cambridge: Cambridge University Press, 1995.

McCalman, I. D. "Popular irreligion in early Victorian England: Infidel preacher and radical theatricality in 1830s London." In R. W. Davis and R. J. Helmstadter, eds., *Religion and irreligion in Victorian society: Essays in honor of R. K. Webb*, 51–67. London: Routledge, 1992.

———. *Radical underworld: Prophets, revolutionaries, and pornographers in London, 1795–1840*. Cambridge: Cambridge University Press, 1988.

Mekeel, Joyce. "Social influence on changing audience behavior in the London theatre, 1830–1880." Ph.D. thesis, Boston University, 1983.

Merrington, W. R. *University College Hospital and its medical school: A history.* London: Heinemann, 1976.

Micale, Mark. *Approaching hysteria: Disease and its interpretations.* Princeton: Princeton University Press, 1995.

Miller, D. A. *The novel and the police.* Berkeley: University of California Press, 1988.

Miller, Jonathan. "Going unconscious." In R. B. Silvers, ed., *Hidden histories of science*, 1–37. New York: New York Review, 1995.

———. "A Gower Street scandal." *Journal of the Royal College of Physicians of London* 17 (1983): 181–91.

Milligan, Barry. *Pleasures and pains: Opium and the Orient in nineteenth-century British culture.* Charlottesville: University Press of Virginia, 1995.

Moore, Doris Langley. *Ada, countess of Lovelace.* London: John Murray, 1977.

Moore, K. "This Whig and Tory ridden town: Popular politics in the Chartist era." In John Belcham, ed., *Popular politics, riot, and labour: Essays in Liverpool history, 1790–1940*, 38–67. Liverpool: Liverpool University Press, 1992.

Morrell, Jack, and Arnold Thackray. *Gentlemen of science: The early years of the British Association for the Advancement of Science.* Oxford: Oxford University Press, 1981.

Morus, I. R. "Correlation and control: William Robert Grove and the construction of a new philosophy of scientific reform." *Studies in the History and Philosophy of Science* 22 (1991): 598–621.

———. "Currents from the underworld: Electricity and the technology of display in early Victorian England." *Isis* 84 (1993): 50–69.

———. "Different experimental lives: Michael Faraday and William Sturgeon." *History of Science* 30 (1992): 1–28.

———. "The electric Ariel: Telegraphy and commercial culture in early Victorian England." *Victorian Studies* 39 (1996): 339–78.

———. *Frankenstein's children: Electricity, exhibition, and experiment in early nineteenth-century London.* Princeton: Princeton University Press, 1998.

———. "Marketing the machine: The construction of electro-therapeutics as viable medicine in early Victorian England." *Medical History* 36 (1992): 34–52.

———. "The politics of power: Reform and regulation in the work of William Robert Grove." Ph.D. thesis, University of Cambridge, 1988.

Morus, I. R., S. J. Schaffer, and J. A. Secord. "Scientific London." In C. Fox, ed., *London: World city, 1800–1840*, 129–42. New Haven: Yale University Press, 1992.

Moscucci, O. *The science of woman: Gynaecology and gender in England, 1800–1929.* Cambridge: Cambridge University Press, 1990.

Nicolson, Malcolm. "The metastatic theory of pathogenesis and the professional interests of the eighteenth-century physician." *Medical History* 32 (1988): 277–300.

Noakes, Richard. "Cranks and visionaries: Science, Spiritualism, and Transgression in Victorian Britain." Ph.D. thesis, University of Cambridge, 1998.

Norman, Edward. *The English Catholic Church in the nineteenth century.* Oxford: Oxford University Press, 1984.

Nuland, S. B. *Origins of anaesthesia.* Birmingham, Ala.: Classics of Medicine Library, 1983.

Olien, D. D. *Morpeth: A Victorian public career.* Washington, D.C.: University Press of America, 1983.

Oppenheim, Janet. *The other world: Spiritualism and psychical research in England, 1850–1914.* Cambridge: Cambridge University Press, 1985.

Owen, Alex. *The darkened room: Women, power, and spiritualism in late nineteenth-century England.* London: Virago, 1989.

Page, Norman, ed. *Wilkie Collins: The critical heritage.* London: Routledge and Kegan Paul, 1974.

Palfreman, Jon. "Mesmerism and the English medical profession: A study of a conflict." *Ethics in Science and Medicine* 4 (1977): 51–66.

Pals, Daniel L. *The Victorian "lives" of Jesus.* San Antonio, Texas: Trinity University Press, 1982.

Parssinen, T. M. "Medical fringe and medical orthodoxy." In R. Wallis, ed., *On the margins of science: The social construction of rejected knowledge,* 103–20. Sociological Review Monograph. Keele, Staffordshire: University of Keele, 1979.

———. "Mesmeric performers." *Victorian Studies* 21 (1977–78): 87–104.

———. *Secret passions, secret remedies: Narcotic drugs in British society, 1820–1930.* Manchester: Manchester University Press, 1983.

Patterson, T. J. S. "Science and medicine in India." In P. Corsi and P. Weindling, eds., *Information sources in the history of science and medicine,* 457–75. London: Butterworth Scientific, 1983.

Pearsall, Ronald. *The table rappers.* New York: St. Martin's Press, 1972.

Peterson, M. J. *The medical profession in the mid–nineteenth century.* Berkeley: University of California Press, 1978.

Picart, Caroline. "Scientific controversy as farce: The Benveniste-Maddox counter trials." *Social Studies of Science* 24 (1994): 7–37.

Pickstone, John. "The biographical and the analytical: Towards a historical model of science and practice in modern medicine." In Ilana Löwy, ed., *Medicine and change: Historical and sociological studies of medical innovation.* Montrouge, France: Institut National de la Santé et de la Recherche Médicale, 1993.

———. "Museological science? The place of the analytical/comparative in nineteenth-century science, technology, and medicine." *History of Science* 32 (1994): 111–38.

Poovey, Mary. *Making a social body: British cultural formation, 1830–1864*. Chicago: University of Chicago Press, 1995.

———. *Uneven developments: The ideological work of gender in mid-Victorian England*. Chicago: University of Chicago Press, 1988.

Pope-Hennessy, James. *Monckton Milnes: The years of promise, 1809–1851*. London: Constable, 1949.

Porter, K. H. *Through a glass darkly: Spiritualism in the Browning circle*. Lawrence: University of Kansas Press, 1958.

Porter, Roy. *Doctor of society: Thomas Beddoes and the sick trade in late-Enlightenment England*. London: Routledge, 1992.

———. *Health for sale: Quackery in England, 1660–1850*. Manchester: Manchester University Press, 1989.

———. "The physical examination." In W. F. Bynum and Roy Porter, eds., *Medicine and the five senses*. New York: Cambridge University Press, 1993.

———. "Under the influence: Mesmerism in England." *History Today* 35 (1985): 30–36.

Porter, Theodore. *The rise of statistical thinking, 1820–1900*. Princeton: Princeton University Press, 1986.

Prakash, Gayan. "Science 'gone native' in colonial India." *Representations* 40 (1992): 153–78.

Pulos, L. "Mesmerism revisited: The effectiveness of Esdaile's techniques in the production of deep hypnosis and total body hypnoanesthesia." *American Journal of Clinical Hypnosis* 22 (1979–80): 206–11.

Quen, Jacques. "Three cases in nineteenth-century rejection: Mesmerism, Perkinism, and acupuncture." *Journal of the History of the Behavioural Sciences* 11 (1975): 149–56.

Raj, Giri, ed. *The social and cultural context of medicine in India*. New Delhi: Vikas, 1981.

Ramasubban, Radhika. *Public health and medical research in India: Their origins under the impact of British colonial policy*. Stockholm: Swedish Agency for Research Cooperation with Developing Countries, 1982.

Ransom, Teresa. *Fanny Trollope: A remarkable life*. London: St. Martin's Press, 1995.

Reed, John R. *Victorian will*. Athens: Ohio University Press, 1989.

Reid, Douglas A. "Interpreting the festival calendar: Wakes and fairs as carnivals." In R. D. Storch, ed., *Popular culture and custom in nineteenth century England*, 125–83. London: Croom Helm, 1982.

Reid, T. W. *The life, letters, and friendships of Richard Monckton Milnes, first Lord Houghton*. 2 vols. London: Cassell, 1890.

Reiser, S. J. *Medicine and the reign of technology*. New York: Cambridge University Press, 1978.

Richards, Graham. *Mental machinery: Part 1, The origins and consequences of psychological ideas from 1600–1850*. London: Athlone Press, 1992.

Richards, R. J. *Darwin and the emergence of evolutionary theories of mind and behavior*. Chicago: University of Chicago Press, 1987.

Richardson, Ruth. *Death, dissection, and the destitute*. London: Routledge, 1987.

Robinson, Kenneth. *Wilkie Collins: A biography*. London: The Bodley Head, 1951.

Roodenburg, Herman, and Jan Bremmer, eds. *A cultural history of gesture from antiquity to the present day*. Ithaca: Cornell University Press, 1992.

Rosselli, John. "The self-image of effeteness: Physical education and nationalism in nineteenth-century Bengal." *Past and Present* 86 (1980): 121–48.

Rothblatt, Sheldon. *The revolution of the dons: Cambridge and society in Victorian England*. New York: Basic Books, [1968].

Rudwick, Martin. *The great Devonian controversy: The shaping of knowledge among gentlemanly specialists*. Chicago: University of Chicago Press, 1985.

Russett, C. E. *Sexual science: The Victorian construction of womanhood*. Cambridge: Harvard University Press, 1989.

Saint Phalle, Thérèse de. *Le métronome*. [Paris]: Gallimard, 1980.

Salberg, D. *Once upon a pantomime*. Luton: Cortney, 1981.

Sanders, Valerie. *Reason over passion: Harriet Martineau and the Victorian novel*. Brighton: Harvester Press, 1986.

Sarbin, T. R. "On self-deception." *Annals of the New York Academy of Sciences* 364 (1981): 220–35.

Schaffer, S. J. "Astronomers mark time: Discipline and the personal equation." *Science in Context* 2 (1988): 115–45.

———. "Babbage's dancer and the impresarios of mechanism." In Francis Spufford and Jenny Uglow, eds., *Cultural Babbage: Technology, time, and invention*, 53–80. London: Faber and Faber, 1996.

———. "History and geography of the intellectual world: William Whewell's politics of language." In Menachem Fisch and S. J. Schaffer, eds., *William Whewell: A composite portrait*, 201–32. Oxford: Clarendon, 1991.

———. "The nebular hypothesis and the science of progress." In J. R. Moore, ed., *History, humanity, and evolution: Essays for John Greene*. Cambridge: Cambridge University Press, 1989.

———. "Self evidence." *Critical Inquiry* 18 (1992): 327–62.

Schiebinger, Londa. *The mind has no sex? Women in the origins of modern science*. Cambridge: Harvard University Press, 1989.

Schott, H., ed. *Franz Anton Mesmer und die Geschichte des Mesmerismus*. Wiesbaden: F. Steiner, 1985.

Schwartz, E. *Thomas Wakley and the "Lancet."* London, 1940.

Scull, Andrew. *The most solitary of afflictions: Madness and society in Britain, 1700–1900*. New Haven: Yale University Press, 1993.

Secord, Anne. "Corresponding interests: Artisans and gentlemen in nineteenth-century natural history." *British Journal for the History of Science* 27 (1994): 383–408.

Secord, J. A. "Behind the veil: William Chambers and *Vestiges*." In J. R. Moore, ed., *History, humanity, and evolution: Essays for John C. Greene*. Cambridge: Cambridge University Press, 1989.

———. *Books of creation: The Victorians read science*. Chicago: University of Chicago Press, forthcoming.

————. "Evolution for the people." Paper presented at annual meeting of the International Society for the History, Philosophy and Social Study of Biology, Northwestern University, July 1991.

————. "Extraordinary experiment: Electricity and the creation of life in early Victorian England." In David Gooding, Trevor Pinch, and Simon Schaffer, eds., *The uses of experiment*, 337–83. Cambridge: Cambridge University Press, 1989.

————. "Speculators in the temple of science: Fieldwork, measurement, and theory in the Glen Roy controversies." Seminar paper, Department of History and Philosophy of Science, Cambridge, Michaelmas term 1991.

Shapin, Steven. "The house of experiment in seventeenth-century England." *Isis* 79 (1988): 373–404.

————. "The politics of observation: Cerebral anatomy and social interests in the Edinburgh phrenology disputes." In R. Wallis, ed., *On the margins of science: The social construction of rejected knowledge*, 139–78. Sociological Review Monograph 27. Keele, Staffordshire: University of Keele, 1979.

————. "Pump and circumstance: Robert Boyle's literary technology." *Social Studies of Science* 14 (1984): 481–520.

————. *The social history of truth.* Chicago: University of Chicago Press, 1994.

Shapin, Steven, and Barry Barnes. "Head and hand: Rhetorical resources in British pedagogical writing." *Oxford Review of Education* 2 (1976): 231–54.

Shapin, Steven, and S. J. Schaffer. *Leviathan and the air pump: Hobbes, Boyle, and the experimental life.* Princeton: Princeton University Press, 1985.

Sharpe, Jim. "History from below." In Peter Burke, ed., *New perspectives on historical writing*, 24–41. Cambridge: Polity Press, 1991.

Shiach, Morag. *Discourse on popular culture: Class, gender, and history in cultural analysis, 1730 to the present.* Cambridge: Cambridge University Press, 1989.

Shiels, W. J., ed. *The church and healing: Papers read at the twentieth summer meeting and the twenty-first winter meeting of the Ecclesiastical History Society.* Oxford: Basil Blackwell, the Ecclesiastical Society, 1982.

Shiman, L. L. *Women and leadership in nineteenth-century England.* Houndmills, Hampshire: Macmillan, 1992.

Shorter, Edward. *Bedside manners: The troubled history of doctors and patients.* New York: Simon and Schuster, 1985.

————. *From paralysis to fatigue: A history of psychosomatic illness in the modern era.* New York: Macmillan, 1992.

Showalter, Elaine. *The female malady: Women, madness, and English culture, 1830–1980.* London: Virago, 1987.

Shuttleworth, Sally. *Charlotte Brontë and Victorian psychology.* Cambridge: Cambridge University Press, 1996.

————. "Female circulation: Medical discourse and popular advertising in the mid-Victorian era." In Mary Jacobus, E. F. Keller, and Sally Shuttleworth, eds., *Body/politics: Women and the discourses of science*, 47–68. New York: Routledge, 1990.

Small, Helen. *Love's madness: Medicine, the novel, and female insanity, 1800–1865.* Oxford: Clarendon, 1996.

―――. "A pulse of 124: Charles Dickens and a pathology of the mid-Victorian reading public." In James Raven, Helen Small, and Naomi Tadmor, eds., *The practice and representation of reading in England*. Cambridge: Cambridge University Press, 1996.

Smith, Crosbie, and M. Norton Wise. *Energy and empire: A biographical study of Lord Kelvin*. Cambridge: Cambridge University Press, 1989.

Smith, R. J. *The Gothic bequest: Medieval institutions in British thought, 1688–1863*. Cambridge: Cambridge University Press, 1987.

Smith, Roger. "The background of physiological psychology in natural philosophy." *History of Science* 11 (1973): 75–123.

―――. *Trial by medicine: The insanity defense in Victorian England*. Edinburgh: Edinburgh University Press, 1981.

Smith, W. D. A. *Under the influence: A history of nitrous oxide and oxygen*. London: Macmillan, 1982.

Smith-Rosenberg, Carol. "Beauty, the beast, and the militant woman." *American Quarterly* 23 (1971): 562–84.

―――. "The hysterical woman." In *Disorderly conduct: Visions of gender in Victorian America*. New York: Knopf, 1985.

Speaight, G. *The history of the English puppet theatre*. London: G. G. Harrap, 1955.

Stamp, Tom, and Cordelia Stamp. *William Scoresby: Arctic scientist*. Whitby: Caedmon Press, 1976.

Stevenson, Lloyd. "Suspended animation and the history of anaesthesia." *Bulletin of the History of Medicine* 49 (1975): 482–511.

Stewart, Garrett. *Dear Reader: The conscripted reader in nineteenth-century British fiction*. Baltimore: Johns Hopkins University Press, 1996.

St. George, Andrew. *The descent of manners: Etiquette, rules, and the Victorians*. London: Chatto and Windus, 1993.

Stocking, George. *Victorian anthropology*. London: Collier Macmillan, 1987.

Sutherland, J. A. Introduction to Wilkie Collins, *The woman in white*. Ed. John Sutherland. Oxford: Oxford University Press, 1996.

―――. *Is Heathcliffe a murderer? Great puzzles of modern fiction*. London: Penguin, 1996.

―――. *Victorian novelists and publishers*. London: Athlone Press, 1976.

Sviedrys, Romualdas. "The rise of physics laboratories in Britain." *Historical Studies in the Physical and Biological Sciences* 7 (1976): 405–36.

Sykes, W. S. *Essays on the first hundred years of anaesthesia*. 3 vols. Edinburgh: Livingstone, 1960–82.

Tatar, Maria. *Spellbound: Studies in mesmerism and literature*. Princeton: Princeton University Press, 1978.

Taylor, Jenny Bourne. *In the secret theatre of home: Wilkie Collins, sensation narrative, and nineteenth-century psychology*. London: Routledge, 1988.

Taylor, R. P. *The death and resurrection show: From shaman to superstar*. London: A. Blond, 1985.

Thatcher, Virginia Sara. *History of anesthesia, with special emphasis on the nurse specialist.* Philadelphia: Lippincott, 1953.

Toole, Betty A. *Ada: The enchantress of numbers.* Mill Valley, Calif.: Strawberry Press, 1992.

Turner, Frank. *Between science and religion.* New Haven: Yale University Press, 1974.

Tyler, G. *Physiognomy and the European novel.* Princeton: Princeton University Press, 1982.

Vandermeersch, P. "The victory of psychiatry over demonology: The origin of the nineteenth-century myth." *History of Psychiatry* 2 (1991): 351–63.

Vicinus, Martha, ed. *A widening sphere: Changing roles of Victorian women.* Bloomington: Indiana University Press, 1977.

Waddington, Ivan. "General practitioners and consultants in early nineteenth-century England: The sociology of an intra-professional conflict." In John Woodward and David Richards, eds., *Health care and popular medicine in nineteenth century England,* 164–68. New York: Holmes and Meier, 1977.

———. *The medical profession in the Industrial Revolution.* Dublin: Gill and Macmillan, 1984.

Warner, J. H. "The idea of science in English medicine: The 'decline of science' and the rhetoric of reform, 1815–1845." In Roger French and Andrew Wear, *British medicine in an age of reform,* 136–64. Cambridge: Cambridge University Press, 1991.

Warwick, Andrew. "Exercising the student body." In Christopher Lawrence and Steven Shapin, eds., *Science incarnate: The physical presentation of intellectual selves.* Chicago: University of Chicago Press, 1998.

Webb, R. K. *The British working-class reader, 1790–1848: Literacy and social tension.* London: Allen and Unwin, [1955].

———. *Harriet Martineau: A radical Victorian.* London: Heinemann, 1960.

Weber, William. *Music and middle-class society.* London: Croom Helm, 1975.

———. "Wagner, Wagnerism and musical idealism." In D. C. Large and W. Weber, eds., *Wagnerism in European culture and politics,* 28–71. Ithaca: Cornell University Press, 1985.

Weiner, M. J. *Reconstructing the criminal: Culture, law, and policy in England, 1830–1914.* Cambridge: Cambridge University Press, 1990.

Weller, E. B., R. A. Weller, and M. A. Fristed. "Use of sodium amytal interviews in prepubertal children: Indications, procedure, and clinical utility." *Journal of the American Academy of Child Psychiatry* 24 (1985): 747–49.

Williams, J. H. H. *Doctors differ: Five studies in contrast: John Elliotson, Hugh Owen Thomas, James Mackenzie, William Macewen, R. W. Philip.* Springfield, Ill.: Thomas, 1952.

Williams, Raymond. *The country and the city.* London: Hogarth, 1985.

———. *Keywords: A vocabulary of culture and society.* New York: Oxford University Press, 1976.

Wilson, J. "British Israelism: The ideological restraints on sect organisation." In B. R.

Wilson, ed., *Patterns of sectarianism: Organisation and ideology in social and religious movements.* London: Heinemann, 1967.

Winter, Alison. "A calculus of suffering: Ada Lovelace and the bodily constraints on women's knowledge in early Victorian England." In Christopher Lawrence and Steven Shapin, eds., *Science incarnate: The physical presentation of intellectual selves,* 202–39. Chicago: University of Chicago Press, 1998.

———. "The construction of orthodoxies and heterodoxies in the early Victorian life sciences." In Bernard Lightman, ed., *Victorian science in context,* 24–50. Chicago: University of Chicago Press, 1997.

———. "Ethereal epidemic: Mesmerism and the introduction of inhalation anaesthesia to early Victorian Britain." *Social History of Medicine* 4 (1991): 1–27.

———. "Harriet Martineau and the reform of the invalid in Victorian Britain." *Historical Journal* 38 (1995): 597–616.

———. "Compasses all awry: The iron ship and the ambiguities of cultural authority in Victorian England." *Victorian Studies* (Autumn 1994): 69–98.

———. "Mesmerism and popular culture in early Victorian Britain." *History of Science* 32 (1994): 317–43.

Woodward, C. Vann. *The strange career of Jim Crow.* New York: Oxford University Press, 1955.

Woodward, John, and David Richards, eds. *Health care and popular medicine in nineteenth century England.* New York: Holmes and Meier, 1977.

Yeo, Richard. "Science and intellectual authority in mid-nineteenth-century Britain: Robert Chambers and *Vestiges of the natural history of creation." Victorian Studies* 28 (1984): 5–31.

Young, G. M. *Victorian England: Portrait of an age.* London: Oxford University Press, 1977.

Youngston, A. J. *The Scientific Revolution in Victorian medicine.* London: Croom Helm, 1979.